THE
NEW
LEFT:
A DOCU-
MENTARY
HISTORY

THE NEW LEFT: A DOCU- MENTARY HISTORY

Edited by
Massimo
Teodori

The Bobbs-Merrill Company
Indianapolis · New York

The Bobbs-Merrill Company, Inc.
A Subsidiary of Howard W. Sams & Co., Inc.
Publishers/Indianapolis—New York—Kansas City

Copyright © 1969 by Massimo Teodori
All rights reserved

First printing 1969
Library of Congress catalogue number 70-81291

Designed by Martin Moskof
Manufactured in the United States of America

for MARCO PANNELLA

brother, friend and comrade

A Note
and Some
Acknowledgments

When I began to work on this anthology on the American New Left, my intention was to collect the material for presentation to an Italian and European audience. In fact, knowledge in Europe of the new radical movements in the United States is very vague and often distorted by the press, even that of the Left.

While at work and with an outline of the material I intended to edit, I had the opportunity of meeting some New Left friends who suggested I publish the anthology also in the United States.

The title of the volume, *The New Left: A Documentary History,* is perhaps too pretentious. The historical and critical notes are not a "history" in any formal sense, but hopefully a contribution from a foreign perspective to the New Left history that has yet to be written. My approach is essentially descriptive and my major insights come not from the use of scholarly tools but from a long participation and experience in the radical and New Left movements in Europe. The goal of the book, therefore, is not academic but to contribute to the international debate on the New Left.

I have debts of gratitude to a number of people who helped me in different ways—with material, with ideas, and with information. In particular,

I want to mention Sam Farber, Joel Geier, Hal Draper, David Rynin, Mario Savio, Wayne Collins, Tom Condit, Mike Parker, Bradley Cleveland, David Horowitz, Steve Weissman, Bob Gottlieb and David Gilbert, Fred Gordon, Todd Gitlin, Carl Oglesby, Hal Haber, Barbara and John Ehrenreich, Norm Fruchter, Carl Davidson, James Weinstein, William Domhoff, Staughton Lynd, Diane Di Prima, Paul Buhle and James O'Brien. Special thanks to Suzanne Pollard for help in working out the details of the manuscript and for the careful translation of the introductory notes. Finally, my gratitude to all the new radicals, activists and spokesmen I have met, discussed with and shared political passions.

I am indebted to them for the valid ideas in the book. The weaknesses of the book are my own responsibility.

M.T.
December 1968

The author is grateful to the following for permission to reprint:

Berkeley Barb [2047 University Avenue, Berkeley, California 94704] for "From the Haight," November 27, 1967.

Julian Bond for "The Future of the Democratic Party" in N.Y. *Free Press*, November 1968.

Gregory Calvert for "In White America: Radical Consciousness and Social Change" in *The National Guardian*, March 1967.

Free Church of Berkeley for "Liberation Litanies."

Bradley Cleveland for excerpts from "A Letter to Undergraduates," 1964.

Rennie G. Davis for "Guerrilla Theater: A Way of Life," 1968.

Diane Di Prima for "Revolutionary Letters," 1968.

William Domhoff for excerpts from "How to Commit Revolution" in *Midpeninsula Observer*, August 1968.

Michael Ferber for "A Time to Say No" in *Resistance*, October 16, 1967.

Todd Gitlin for excerpts from "The Radical Potential of the Poor," in *ISJ*, 1967.

Guardian [197 East 4th Street, New York, New York 10009] for "The Incredible War," April 24, 1965, and for excerpts from "Black United Front" by Eldridge Cleaver, April 13 and 20, 1968, and for "Guardian Viewpoint," November 27, 1968.

Tom Hayden for excerpts from "The Politics of the Movement" in *Dissent*, January/February 1966.

Naomi Jaffe and *Bernardine Dohrn* for "The Look Is You" in *New Left Notes*, April 1968.

Liberation [5 Beekman Street, New York, New York 10038] for excerpts from "A Deeper Disenchantment" by Sol Stern, February 1965, and excerpts from "Coalition Politics or Nonviolent Revolution," June/July 1965, and excerpts from "From Mood to Strategy" by Staughton Lynd, December 1967; for "The Movement to Stop the War in Vietnam" by A. J. Muste, January 1966; for "How to Make a March/Spectacle" by Allen Ginsberg, and for "From Dissent to Parody," by Keith Lampe, November 1966.

Staughton Lynd for excerpts from "The New Radicalism and Participatory Democracy" in *Dissent*, Summer 1965, and excerpts from "The Freedom Schools: Concept and Organization" in *Freedomways*, Spring 1965.

Herbert Marcuse and *Beacon Press* for "On the New Left," a speech given at *The National Guardian* dinner, December 1968.

McGraw Hill, Inc. © for "Some Letters from Mississippi" in *Letters from Mississippi* by Elizabeth Sutherland, 1965.

Monthly Review for excerpts from "The Student Revolt: 1960–1961" by Anne Braden, July-August 1965; and for "From Resistance to Revolution" by John and Barbara Ehrenreich, April 1968.

The Movement [55 Colton Street, San Francisco, California 94103] for excerpts from "The MFDP" by Mike Miller, May 1965, and excerpts from "Interview with

Huey P. Newton," August 1968, and excerpts from "We've Got to Reach Our Own People," November 1967.

Movement for a Democratic Society [225 Lafayette Street, New York, New York] for "Beginning to Begin to Begin" by Bob Gottlieb and Marge Piercy, and "Consumption: Domestic Imperialism" by Bob Gottlieb and Susan Sutheim.

Raymond Mungo for excerpts from "The Movement and Its Media," in *Radicals in the Professions*, January 1968, and "The Road to Liberation," October 1967.

The New Republic © *1966, Harrison-Blaine of New Jersey, Inc.*, for "Power and the Myth of Progress" by Todd Gitlin and "Is the Great Society Just a Barbecue?" by Richard Flacks, published in *Thoughts of the Young Radicals*.

Newsreel for "Some Newsreel Documents," 1968.

North American Congress on Latin America [P.O. Box 57, Cathedral Station, New York, New York 10025] for excerpts from "Who Rules Columbia?" 1968.

Carl Oglesby for "Trapped in a System," 1965, and excerpts from "Dear McCarthy Supporters," 1968.

Ramparts for "Two, Three, Many Columbias" by Tom Hayden, June 15, 1968.

Radio Free People for "Documents."

John and Margaret Rowntree for excerpts from "Youth as a Class," in *Midpeninsula Observer*, August 12–26, 1968.

San Francisco Express Times [15 Lafayette Street, San Francisco, California 94103] for excerpts from "A Declaration of War" by Stokely Carmichael, February 22, 1968, and "The Movement: It's Theory Time" by Marvin Garson, June/July 1968.

Mario Savio for "An End to History," 1964.

Robert Scheer for excerpts from "Scheer Speaks for Himself" in "The Scheer Campaign" by Serge Lang, 1967.

Gary Snyder for "Buddhism and the Coming Revolution," 1968.

Students for a Democratic Society for excerpts from "The Port Huron Statement"; excerpts from Irrelevance" and "Reply," Spring 1965; "Mississippi: Notes on SNCC" Left and the Democratic Left" by Alan Haber; excerpts from "Students and Economic Action" by Carl Wittman, 1964; excerpts from "The New Radicals in the Multiversity" by Carl Davidson, 1968; "High School Reform: Toward a Student Movement" by Mark Kleiman.

Studies on the Left for "On the Ideology of the Campus Revolution" by Dale Johnson, 1961; "Atlanta: The Bond Campaign" by Charles Cobb, Spring 1965; "Up from Irrelevance" and "Reply," Spring 1965; "Mississippi: Notes on SNCC" by Norm Fruchter, Winter 1965; "The Teach-In: Project or Cooptation?" by James Gieber; "The Future of Nonviolence" by Dave Dellinger, Winter 1965.

Steve Weissman and John Gerassi for excerpts from "The Vietnamization of Latin America," published by North American Congress for Latin America, 1968.

Contents

First Part
Massimo Teodori: Historical and Critical Notes

Second Part
Documents

First Part

Massimo Teodori: Historical and Critical Notes

One:
The Beginning
of the
Movement

The fact that a New Left exists in the United States today, in 1968, is the proof of a reality which manifests itself both in society at large and in the political arena. What this New Left is is more difficult to say, because there is very little unity between the various organizations, programs and ideological statements which form the phenomenon usually referred to as "the Movement." Since the New Left is still very much an open subject, the following commentary, which comprises the first part of the volume, does not claim to be definitive. It treats, on the one hand, the development of the Movement which has been taking place for nearly a decade and, on the other, the debate which has grown within and around the New Left. We must explain at the outset that when we speak of the New Left in the United States today, we mean simply the Left, because there exists no traditional left playing an important role on the national scene.

The collection of documents included in the second part of the volume is centered around "young white radicals." This commentary traces the historical and conceptual development of the material contained in these documents. No attempt has been made here to give the black liberation movement, or the liberation movements of the other nonwhite minorities, as careful an analysis as they deserve. There are two reasons for limiting the scope of this study: first, up to the present time, the black liberation movement has been theoretically and practically autonomous; secondly, in its social, cultural and political characteristics, the New Left is a phenomenon which originated and has developed prevalently among young whites. However, although it is necessary to recognize the respective autonomy of the two movements—the one which has witnessed the development of a new radicalism in the 1960s, and the other, the movement for black liberation—the connections and reciprocal influences between them should not be overlooked.

In the second part of the volume, two sections of documents are included which deal respectively with civil rights and Black Power. The documents have been chosen with the double purpose of providing basic source material on these subjects and of putting into focus the relations between the black and white radical movements. It should be noted, however, that the two different phases of the recent history of the black liberation movement are qualitatively different. During the civil-rights campaign, particularly in the period from 1960 to 1965, there was almost total identification between a certain segment of the young white radical group and its counterpart in the black liberation movement. However, beginning with the development of Black Power in 1966, the two movements separated, even though they later began to develop along notably parallel lines. The documents and analysis dealing with Black Power are therefore viewed mainly from the perspective of its relation to the New Left or to parts of the Movement.

The procedure we have followed, both for the introductory commentary and in collecting the documents, has been to concentrate on the development of the different movements and their common features, and not on the history of the organizations. A partial correspondence does exist between *movements* and *organizations*, but it seemed methodologically more correct and closer to the nature of the material under discussion to follow the political track rather than the organizational one.

Finally, an explanation is in order on the use of various terms in this first part of the volume: from time to time the expressions "New Left," "Movement," "movement for," "new radicals," and "new radicalism" appear. In American writings these terms are often used interchangeably; here we will attempt to clarify their use by defining each of them separately. The following glossary will serve as a list of definitions for these expressions:

a. *Movement* (singular, with a capital M)[1] signifies the complex of positions, actions and attitudes which have developed over the last ten years, including not only political and social aspects, but psychological and cultural ones as well.

b. *movement* (either singular or plural, with a small m) designates a particular sector of the Movement which has developed around a specific theme or a particular period. For example, "civil-rights movement," "free speech movements," "antiwar movement," "women's liberation movement," etc.

c. *New Left* (with first letters capitalized)[2] designates a comprehensive position including analyses and propositions derived from or inspiring the various movements and bearing specific reference to political problems.

1. This is the term most widely used among young radicals to indicate their belonging to the same political, cultural and social world. For example, a San Francisco newspaper is called *Movement*, and until a short time ago it bore the note "affiliated with SNCC and SDS," i.e., with the two major organizations of the New Left.

2. This expression is usually used in specifically political language. The SDS weekly bulletin is called *New Left Notes*, and the objective of building a New Left has been stated ever since the drafting of the SDS founding statement (Port Huron Statement) in 1962.

d.   *new radicalism* (with a small r)[3] designates the rebirth of leftist positions during the 1960s. This expression indicates all the leftist positions—New Left and fringe groups of the traditional left—regardless of
their different political and ideological origins.

e.   *new radicals*[4] designates the political actors of the new radicalism.

3. "New Radicalism" is, for example, the title of a debate which took place in the pages of
Partisan Review during 1965 and 1966, in which numerous intellectuals of various tendencies
participated. We should make it clear that the term "radical" in the United States serves to
designate any leftist position; it is not specifically tied to any political or intellectual tradition,
as is the case in Europe. In general, it indicates a position of opposition to the system, in contrast to the term "liberal," which designates the moderate attitude taken by someone who
wishes to reform and correct the system, while accepting its values and basic structures. "Radicals" are radicals in the Italian sense of the word, but they are also socialists of all tendencies,
communists, pacifists, nonviolent revolutionaries, Marxists and libertarians. A social democrat
such as Irving Howe (editor of the review *Dissent*) calls himself a radical, as do the Trotskyists
of the Socialist Workers' party and the Maoists of the Progressive Labor party. With the addition of new elements, the term "radicalism," while remaining generic, has recently taken on a
more precise meaning, indicating those tendencies which have been developing among young
people over the past ten years.

4. *The New Radicals* is the title of a documentary report prepared by Paul Jacobs and Saul
Landau for the Center for the Study of Democratic Institutions (Paul Jacobs and Saul Landau, *The
New Radicals* [New York: Vintage Books, 1966]), and it is also the title of an article by the long
time socialist Hal Draper. Other expressions which appear, although less frequently, are *The
New Student Left*, which has been adopted as the title of a volume edited by Mitchell Cohen
and Dennis Hale, and *The Young Radicals*, used in the title of a collection of essays published
by *The New Republic* and reprinted in 1966 (*Thoughts of the Young Radicals*). More recently,
particularly in relation to the development of Black Power, the expression "white mother-country
radicals" has come to be used by blacks as a designation for white radicals. The black leader
Huey Newton uses it, for example, in the interview which is included in the section of this
anthology devoted to Black Power.

1

A Decade of
Eclipse for the Left

1.1. At the end of the 1950s, a decade of political eclipse for the left in the United States came to a close. Not only was there an absence of relevant organized political forces during that decade, but intellectual activity itself and the search for radical forms of social theories barely managed to stay alive at the margins of a society which was politically dull and lacking in open manifestations of internal conflict. There was a literal disintegration of radical political forces, which had still been active during the 1930s and had vigorously expressed the contradictions of the Depression, capitalistic expansion and the New Deal at that time. The Communist party, which still had over 60,000 members at the end of the war, had broken up in 1954 as a result of internal weakness and outside attacks. Internally, Trotskyism, the Russo-German pact, Stalinism and the inability of the party to bring itself up to date in the face of changed conditions in American society weakened its appeal to intellectuals and its capacity to adopt militant positions. Externally, the witch hunts culminating with the famous inquests carried out by the Senate Permanent Committee on Investigations under the chairmanship of Senator Joseph McCarthy in 1952–1955 paralyzed the activity of the party through the systematic persecution of its members and sympathizers, and many others. The Socialist party, reduced to an empty shell, aligned itself with anticommunist and cold-war positions. The intellectuals who tended toward social-democratic and "democratic left" positions were in reality the very people who most vigorously attacked not only the communists, but independent radical positions as well. With the division of the world into two antagonistic blocs in 1948, identification with the "free world" came to mean, for the "democratic left," the acceptance of capitalism, repression of national liberation movements, and, in general, all the conservative and reactionary merchandise smuggled in along with the safeguarding of Western liberties. With few exceptions, socialists and former Marxists, anticommunist radicals and liberals alike upheld the global picture of the American system, with all that this entailed. They usually ended by identifying themselves with the liberal wing of the Democratic party, i.e., with the system's strongest political force, whether located inside the government, as under Truman, or whether it controlled a wide portion of power in society at large, as during the Eisenhower administration.[5]

> In the name of humanism, socialists in the United States gradually but firmly aligned themselves with the American cause in the deepest political and cultural sense—Castro, the Vietminh and the victims of the postwar world crisis became first as guilty as their potential executioners, as culpable morally and then deserted in a manner that increasingly absolved the executioners. The impact of the Western resistance against revolutionary movements, especially in Eastern Europe and China, was rarely considered in evaluating the social systems that emerged. Again victims were condemned for their responses to the crimes of their executioners, as if the Cubans, Vietnamese and Chinese had chosen with deliberate malice to violate a humanist tradition they too evoked and claimed to act upon. . . . Economic development as a justification was dismissed as worth nothing. The losses involved in such a process were carefully examined, but never weighed and balanced against the gains,

---

5. For an excellent essay on the nature and politics of the Democratic party, see I. F. Stone, "Who Are the Democrats?" *New York Review of Books*, August 22, 1968.

particularly in those areas that had precious little intellectual freedom or political democracy to lose.[6]

The unions which combined in 1956 to form the American Federation of Labor–Congress of Industrial Organizations joined together in defense of capitalist economic structures. They set forth demands which centered essentially on "bread and butter" issues, even when these increased the production of "guns." It was also precisely during the 1950s that the unions were systematically purged of their radical leaders, while simultaneously a breakdown in union solidarity on the international level was actively promoted and decisive financial support was given to anticommunist trade unions abroad.

1.2. Within universities and intellectual circles, no new critical analyses of American society developed which might have nourished perspectives for radical alternatives to the status quo in the area of political debate. Besides, whoever failed to side with "America" was considered, not a spokesman for different perspectives, but an ally of the national enemy—world communism and the Soviet Union. In this desert, where truly dialectical positions posing real alternatives had little chance of survival, Marxist scholars such as Paul Baran and Paul Sweezy, leftist historians such as William A. Williams and independent radicals such as C. Wright Mills occupied marginal positions in the country and were not connected to any political or intellectual movement capable of fusing thought and action. The opposition of independent radicals took on an individualistic quality in the absence of a movement which could incorporate intellectual ferment. In 1952, the young writer Norman Mailer cried, "I can't choose!" (between the East and the West) and accompanied the statement with an existential refutation of the "totalitarian fabric of American society," whose authoritarian symptoms he perceived in all aspects of political, social and cultural life, as well as in taste and morals. Dwight MacDonald, a respectable intellectual who had consecutively abandoned communism, Trotskyism and Marxism, made his own choice of the "West" coincide with his withdrawal from political activity and with the assumption of a negative attitude toward American society, its political machinery, and its intrinsically totalitarian structures.[7]

The channels for political debate on the left—the press and other media—also just barely managed to survive. *Partisan Review*, an important radical publication during the 1930s, was reduced to a colorless arena wherein all the political positions could represent themselves, and nothing else. *The National Guardian*, formerly a spokesman for the Progressive party during the presidential campaign of Henry Wallace in 1948, managed to keep going only with great difficulty as a front for the remaining communists and "fellow

---

6. Gabriel Kolko, "The Decline of American Radicalism in the Twentieth Century," *Studies on the Left*, September/October 1966, p. 24.

7. On the relationship between intellectuals and radicalism, see Christopher Lasch, *The New Radicalism in America* (New York: Vintage Books, 1968); particularly the chapter entitled "The Anti-Intellectualism of the Intellectuals," in which the author examines the positions held by Norman Mailer and Dwight MacDonald during the 1950s. It is interesting to note that intellectuals like Mailer and MacDonald, who were reduced to isolation and to an existential distrust of the possibilities of political action during the 1950s, are today among the most enthusiastic supporters of the "new radicals." The recent episodes of the March on Washington (October 1967), in which these two intellectuals participated in direct action at the Pentagon, and the occupation of Columbia University (May 1968), for which MacDonald organized a campaign of support, give an idea of the extent to which the atmosphere changed in one decade.

travelers."[8] (In 1967–1968, the paper underwent wide editorial changes, becoming a journal of the New Left, and becoming, simply, *The Guardian*.) The *Monthly Review* of Sweezy and Huberman, which came out in the early 1950s, was read only by a few scholars interested in Marxist studies. *Dissent* was begun in 1956 by anticommunist social-democrats; it represented the viewpoint of the group leaning toward Fabian socialism, which gathered around The League for Industrial Democracy and whose activity was restricted to the New York City area.

There were three publications having different characteristics which represented an exception to the general picture of the 1950s, although they were still tied to the isolated initiative of their editors rather than to movements. Starting in 1954, I. F. Stone began publishing a four-page, small-format weekly, *I. F. Stone's Weekly*, which gave evidence of a rare quality of independent journalism, genuinely liberal in tone and scrupulously attentive to factual truth. Anne and Carl Braden, with the *Southern Patriot*, kept alive the progressive and integrationist battle which revolved around the Southern Conference Educational Fund in the deep South. A. J. Muste, at the age of seventy, gathered nonviolent pacifists, humanitarian socialists, anarchical-leaning libertarians, antimilitarists and humanists around the monthly *Liberation*. The magazine promoted and analyzed peace campaigns, nuclear disarmament, civil disobedience and racial integration, developing a "third camp" position which refuted an alignment with either of the cold-war blocs.

1.3. With the exhaustion of typically American movements such as Henry Wallace's election-based progressive reformism, and anticentralist populism, whose last spokesman, Estes Kefauver, had lost in 1952 the Democratic presidential nomination to the liberal Adlai Stevenson; as the communist and Trotskyist groups of various tendencies had been reduced to small cliques and the socialists had aligned themselves with reform democrats, the left continued to survive only on the archeological interest of its past ideological debates, unable to confront the present. There was room only for those forces which tried to "liberalize" the system and expressed themselves through the Americans for Democratic Action (ADA), or through groups and individuals dedicated primarily to the struggle for civil liberties, such as the American Civil Liberties Union. Even the voices of William Meyer and Byron Johnson, which were raised in Congress to propose moderate peace initiatives, remained isolated and unheeded. In 1960, after only one term, these two congressmen were not reelected.

On the whole, the 1950s present a picture of America united behind the rhetoric of affluence of liberty backed by military and economic security. Even the new generations were silent: only small groups attempted to resist conformity by remaining outside of the homogeneous social fabric, and expressed their dissent in individualistic ways.

---

8. On the evolution of positions held by *The National Guardian*, seen as a reflection of the very spirit of the American left, see Michael Munk, "The Guardian from Old to New Left," in *Radical America*, March/April 1968.

2
Mass Conformity and
Individual Revolt

2.1. "Apathetic, silent, indifferent, confused"—these are some of the adjectives used to describe the generation of students which passed through American universities during the 1950s.[9] Looking back over a decade to that period, it seems that youth contributed very little to political and cultural unrest; so little, in fact, that a direct witness of the events of those years[10] speaks in terms of a "non-generation," and the philosopher Walter Kaufmann refers to it as "the uninvolved generation." In the universities, young people seemed mainly "serious" about climbing the ladder of their academic careers and preparing to successfully overcome the obstacles of professional life. This was a trend which involved the mass of new students having access to higher education, which was coming to be looked upon more and more as an instrument for achieving social integration and economic success. The educational institutions themselves were transformed: the traditional temples of learning which had educated the ruling class for centuries—such as the seven Ivy League universities and exclusive women's colleges like the "seven sisters"—were joined by new colleges and universities, mainly through the initiative of individual states favored by a federal program of subsidies to public universities. This quantitative transformation was accompanied by a qualitative one which deeply affected the academic programs themselves: a romantic bourgeois education, prevalently humanistic and liberal in nature, gave way to an education capable of preparing students to fill necessary positions in industry, government, and scientific research. These were the years during which the country became deeply engaged in productive and scientific competition with the Soviet Union following the launching of the first *sputnik;* this competition produced an ever-growing need for personnel capable of operating and developing the civil and military technological apparatus. The universities multiplied, becoming increasingly swollen and bureaucratized, and their academic programs allowed less and less room for so-called extracurricular activities. They assumed to an ever greater extent the form of modern, efficient mechanisms at the service of society, for its particular given purposes. It is this conception of the university as "knowledge factory" which would contribute to the outbreak of the Berkeley revolt of 1964.

Even if there had been a desire for political activity, there was no room for it in the rhythm of studies and other socially respectable activities organized around fraternities and sororities, in which students of the same social class, religious denomination and financial level grouped together. Besides, there could be no great enthusiasm for political activity or for civic responsibility in the absence of new ideas and perspectives. Left-wing activists were few and far between; it seems that during the second half of the 1950s there were not even a hundred of them on all the campuses. Political organizations languished in universities as much as they did among older people: the communist Labor Youth League (LYL) dissolved in 1957; the YPSL (Young People's Socialist League) had practically ceased to exist; and no more than a handful of members remained in the Student League for Industrial Democracy (SLID); while the moderate liberals belonging to Campus Americans for Democratic Action (CADA), although more numerous, gave no sign of any political impetus.

---

9. "Tension Beneath Apathy," *The Nation,* May 16, 1959.

10. Jack Newfield, *A Prophetic Minority* (New York: Signet, 1966), Chapter 2.

2.2.   In revolt against campus routine as
well as suburban affluence, against sexual puritanism as well as bureaucratic
careerism, from the vast middle class—but also from poor and rich segments
of the great urban population—arose the rebels of the beat generation.

> No wonder then that these have been the years of conformity and
> depression. A stench of fear has come out of every pore of American life,
> and we suffer from a collective failure of nerve. The only courage, with
> rare exceptions, that we have been witness to, has been the isolated cour-
> age of isolated people.[11]

Their appearance in Greenwich Village, San Francisco's North Beach,
New Orleans, Chicago and Los Angeles is decisive to the search for the main
thread of the Movement's development in the 1960s. For many of the causes
promulgated by small groups of hipsters and beatniks—rejection of industrial
society and its many aberrations; irrational response to the congenital irra-
tionalism of that society; individualism and communal living; liberation of
sexual energies, with a natural acceptance of homosexual and bisexual as well
as heterosexual behavior; desecration of the traditional values of family, work,
flag, religion and uprightness; negro jazz and folk music; marijuana; freedom
in dress and general appearance—were not only to be shared by an ever-
growing number of young people within a few years' time, but were to transform concretely a great segment of American life with the formation of a
new subculture. Norman Mailer—being an existentialist himself—was able
to provide the best interpretation of the phenomenon, and speaks of the hipster
as a "white negro." The white rebel borrows the risky life of the negro, always
living in the present and refusing the security of those institutions which are
part of white society, security which the negro has never had. His search is
directed entirely toward the pleasures his body can enjoy "here and now,"
since he cannot count on any of the structures which serve to guarantee and
prolong the satisfactions provided by a sophisticated, inhibited civilization.
The hipster, therefore, is violent and sensual, but also apolitical, estranged
from any form of moral judgment that extends above and beyond his own
actions. The other aspect of the beat generation was represented by the
beatniks: more intellectual than the hipsters, they wanted to make of their
existence a living condemnation of materialist, conformist and totalitarian
society.

> The beatnik—often Jewish—comes from the middle class, and twenty-
> five years ago would have joined the YCL. Today, he chooses not to work
> as a sentence against the conformity of his parents. Therefore he can feel
> moral value in his goodbye to society. . . . The beatnik, gentle, disem-
> bodied from the race, is often a radical pacifist. He has taken the vow
> of non-violence—in fact, his violence is sealed within him, and he has
> no way of using it. His act of violence is to commit suicide, even as the
> hipster's is to commit murder, but in his absent-minded way, the beatnik
> is the torch-bearer of those nearly lost values of freedom, self-expression,
> and equality which first turned him against the hypocrisies and barren
> culturelessness of the middle class.[12]

Both groups—hipsters and beatniks, worldly or mystical, violent or nonviolent, searching for pleasure or for intellectual challenge—represent the

---

11. Norman Mailer, "The White Negro," in *Advertisements for Myself* (New York: G. P. Putnam's,
1959), p. 312.

12. "Hipster and Beatnik, a Footnote to 'The White Negro,' " in N. Mailer, *op. cit.*, p. 343.

small but significant movement at the forefront of the mass rebellion in which young Americans would become involved a decade later. All the different means of self-expression employed by this small colony of expatriates from society contained the seeds of the Movement which grew during the 1960s, a movement inspired simultaneously by the desperate revolt of poor and forsaken negroes, by moral repulsion toward well-off whites, by aversion to the irrationality of the violence inherent in military force and technological power and by aversion to the rational violence of social conformity.

3

With the Struggle for Civil Rights, a Movement for Freedom and Democracy is Reborn

3.1. The civil-rights movement, which began to develop in 1960, was the first movement to signal a new struggle for liberty and democracy in the United States, and it contained many of the characteristics which, in a more highly developed form, would become part of the New Left in the course of a few years. Integration was not the only objective at the center of the civil-rights struggle; a new style of action, a new idealism, and a new interest in politics were fundamental characteristics of the movement as well. During the preceding decades there had been isolated groups fighting for integration, and the Supreme Court decision of May 1954 requiring school desegregation could be considered in itself a result of the pressure exercised by these liberal groups, as well as the beginning of a slow movement, through legal action, toward the acquisition of a formally equal legal status for blacks. The new movement was new not so much in its objectives as in the methods it employed, the energy it mobilized, the strong feelings it aroused, and the interest it awoke throughout the country—especially among young people—after a decade of apathy. Its novelty lay precisely in the development of a "movement" which embodied both ideals and action at the same time. It aroused debate, but also deeply involved people's lives, progressively transforming mental attitudes, material habits and perspectives for the tens or hundreds of activists at the center of the movement as well as for those millions of people whose lives were affected by it. What occurred at the beginning of 1960 was a revival of politics itself, both in terms of participation by people in the decisions affecting their own lives and in the rebirth of a radical movement which, in the course of a few years, would come to involve an ever-growing number of young people.

3.2. On January 1, 1960, four black students from a college in Greensboro, North Carolina sat down at the counter of a department-store cafeteria reserved exclusively for whites. The four students were not young revolutionaries—they were not even active in any political organization. When they went to sit down at the lunch counter—an action guided only by personal conviction—they took along as reading matter the Bible and a few philosophy textbooks. They were certainly not conscious of the revolutionary significance of their act, which proved to be the stone that started the avalanche.

In a matter of days, the idea leaped to other cities in North Carolina. During the next two weeks, sit-ins spread to fifteen cities in five Southern states. Within the following year, over 50,000 people—most were Negroes, some were whites—had participated in one kind of demonstration or another in a hundred cities, and over 3,600 demonstrators spent time in jail. But there were results to show: by the end of 1961, several hundred lunch counters had been desegregated in scores of cities—in Texas, Oklahoma, the border states of the South, and even as far as Atlanta, Georgia. A wall of resistance, however, apparently impenetrable, faced the students in the rest of Georgia, South Carolina, Alabama, Mississippi, Louisiana—the hard core of the Deep South.[13]

Sit-ins, pickets, marches, and all kinds of demonstrations took place in the South in 1960 and 1961, without much coordination, through the initiative of groups of student volunteers driven by individual conviction and by their reaction to the living conditions of blacks [**Braden, 1.1.**].* The students responded with growing activism to the brutal reaction of white racists, the intimidations of local authorities—sheriffs, police captains, mayors, governors, political bosses, members of the legislatures—and to the indifference and inertia of the federal government. They chose to serve their sentences in jail rather than pay the fines—"jail, no bail"—imposed by the racist "legitimate" authorities. The new line was direct action, in contrast to integration from above, which had been the strategy of most of the earlier civil-rights groups. Young people were rediscovering in individual terms and developing as a new mass group those methods which had been used by a few minority groups of the political and union left during the 1930s and by pacifists during the First World War, and which had previously been adopted by Martin Luther King in the long Montgomery bus boycott in 1955–1956 and by Bayard Rustin in the high school students' marches on Washington during the academic year 1958–1959. But this time the moral authority of leaders such as King and Rustin was not involved; there were no organizations ready to intervene on behalf of direct action; there was none of the political tension and mass militancy which had characterized the struggles of the 1930s to support the young activists.

The "freedom rides" of buses carrying white and black travelers seated side by side, which covered the entire South from Washington to New Orleans during the spring and summer of 1961, provided another example of the creative development of the direct-action concept, according to which the struggle was carried right to the place where the evil existed, making it immediately visible and tangible. The integrated bus rides, which caused agitation in hundreds óf cities and provoked violent reactions and bloody beatings of activists, were at first promoted by the leaders of CORE,[14] but they continued largely through the efforts of those same activists who had already participated in the sit-ins and who were beginning to form the nucleus of SNCC.[15] In all public or private facilities throughout the South, physical separation marked the inequality of blacks; in all these locations the activists, by their presence, exposed and dramatized the external, material signs of a racist society and tried to combat it "then and there," avoiding extraneous legal processes. In this case, the initiative was no longer in the hands of the "politicians," but rested potentially with the common people, who had been kept out of the decision-making process for so long and who could only realize their hopes by themselves. The development of tension and movement began precisely with a decentralized spontaneous activity; and coordination and strategy took shape slowly and in a disorderly manner, without rigidifying the initial impetus. This aspect of the civil-rights struggle stood out immediately as a new way of engaging in political activity, a novelty similarly present in most of the other movements which subsequently contributed to the development of a New Left position. It is always the movement which

---

* Bracketed references are to writings found in the Second Part of this volume.

13. Howard Zinn, *SNCC, The New Abolitionists* (New York: Alfred Knopf, Inc., 1965), pp. 16–17.

14. Congress of Racial Equality, an organization to promote integration, founded in 1942 and active mainly in the North.

15. Student Nonviolent Coordinating Committee. SNCC is pronounced "snick."

precedes the organization and the political strategy which follows, or which takes shape at the same time as the involvement in the action. There is no separation between masses and intellectuals, movement and party, those who theorize and those who act; between "leaders" and "followers." Direct action is symbolically demonstrative, and at the same time it is capable of solving specific problems; it stimulates the intellectual effort to devise appropriate revolutionary strategies and serves as a means of confronting directly those who hold power and the institutions which represent the status quo. One could almost say that the recently proposed theory concerning the unity between the ideological and practical moments and the coincidence in the development of the two phases of guerrilla warfare,[16] found its embodiment in an altogether different context, precisely in the nonviolent strategy of direct action for civil rights during the five-year period from 1960–1965.

3.3.   SNCC, organized in April 1960, was conceived as an instrument for coordinating the different groups that had participated in the sit-ins during the first three months of 1960 and as an informal source of aid for autonomous direct-action groups in the various Southern states. Originally it received assistance from the SCLC,[17] but as it developed, the two organizations became increasingly different. Although SCLC had an exclusively black base and had utilized direct action in the South, it still acted in the role of a leader for Southern blacks of the *petite-bourgeoisie* rather than as a movement for self-organization at the lower levels of the social and economic scale. For several years SCLC and SNCC worked side by side. SNCC became more and more the nucleus around which the younger activists gravitated and the gathering place for those who were attempting to try out, by direct involvement, a militancy to the left of the other integrationist organizations—such as SCLC, which was backed up by the Southern black church, CORE, supported by the black bourgeoisie in the North, and the NAACP,[18] whose activities mainly took the form of legal action and whose membership was composed of a mixture of black and white liberals. The novelty in SNCC lay in the completely open and flexible nature of its organization, in its lack of a fixed bureaucracy, in the democratic participation in both decision-making process and action on the part of its organizer-members, and in its refusal to operate as a bearer of ideology for the people toward whom its activities were directed. Its fragile structure was continuously changing in relation to the different projects undertaken, and the number of staff members varied greatly between 1960, when there were two people, and 1964, the period of the organization's greatest success, when there were 150. These characteristics create the impression of an institutionalized service organization at the disposition of all those activists who wanted to take initiative in the struggle for the integrationist objectives of justice and liberty.

Although there were few preestablished fixed ideas, a common philosophy developed within the organization, and it marked an entire generation. At the constitutional convention held in Raleigh in April 1960, a declaration of nonviolent principles was adopted [**SNCC, 1.2.**] which constituted a fixed guide to the method of action SNCC was to follow for five years. Nevertheless, the philosophical and religious ideal of nonviolence, which had grown out of the Judeo-Christian tradition, lent itself to different interpretations

---

16. Régis Debray, *Revolution in the Revolution* (New York: Monthly Review Press, 1968).

17. Southern Christian Leadership Conference.

18. National Association for the Advancement of Colored People.

depending on the context in which it was applied. The method of nonviolence is strictly connected with trial and experimentation, which can suggest the type of action to use in different circumstances. In the case of SNCC, as in other episodes in the history of nonviolence, the confrontation with the violence of constituted authority and with the brutal reactions of those in positions of power led young activists to invent new solutions and to reflect somewhat aggressively on the wide spectrum of possibilities which lay between a pure position of "love thine enemy" and violent response. Certainly, SNCC's tactics were always nonviolent, even though, to be historically correct, one must include among them the creation of situations which shattered rigid economic and social structures and disrupted the basic mechanisms of public life.

Apart from nonviolence, the only preestablished ideological vision of the SNCC philosophy was that of common idealism and a widespread faith in the possibilities of effecting immediate radical change.

> The young people in the SNCC have not become followers of any dogma, have not pledged themselves to any rigid ideological system. Unswerving as they are in moving towards certain basic goals, they wheel freely in their thinking about society and how it needs to be changed. . . . They are radical, but not dogmatic; thoughtful, but not ideological. Their thinking is undisciplined: it is fresh, and it is new. . . . The word "revolution" occurs again and again in their speech. Yet they have no party, no ideology, no creed. They have no clear idea of a blueprint for a future society. But they do know clearly that the values of present American society—and this goes beyond racism to class distinction, to commercialism, to profit-seeking, to the setting of religious or national barriers against human contact—are not for them.[19]

3.4.   The two lines of action which came together in SNCC after 1962 were the development of direct action and involvement in a campaign for legal rights, i.e., the registration of great numbers of black voters theretofore excluded from all electoral participation. The decision to conduct a voter-registration campaign was opposed by some activists, for whom the drive for the vote represented a recourse to old-fashioned and discredited methods. Nevertheless, the registration drive was held, first in Mississippi, then in southwest Georgia, Alabama, and the other states of the deep South. In the rural areas, dominated by solitude, poverty and terror, as well as in the cities, rigidly segregated and violently controlled by whites, the voter-registration campaign served essentially as an instrument for organizing the black communities around specific objectives and for bringing activists into contact with the local population.

Far above and beyond the mere acquisition of the vote for large numbers of blacks, the central objectives and most significant results of the campaign were that it educated citizens about their rights, catalyzed energy at the base of the most deprived levels of society and encouraged potential local leaders to adopt participatory methods. But the Kennedy administration was mainly interested in the issue of the vote, and it encouraged the registration drive—without, however, protecting the activists from violence or taking any action to apply federal laws against the local authorities. The Kennedys and other Washington Democrats saw the acquisition of the vote as part of their "liberal" strategy and looked mainly toward the potential this new electorate would provide for the expansion of their own electoral base and national influence.

---

19. Zinn, *op. cit.,* pp. 7 and 13.

To the eyes and minds of the activists, life among the oppressed people of the South, direct experience of hunger, poverty and unemployment, the prison experience, and contact with the inertia of the federal government revealed with ever-increasing clarity the insufficiency and emptiness of the gradualist positions of Northern Democrats, who maintained many stable, concrete connections with the power structure in the racist South. "Which side is the government on?" asked SNCC chairman John Lewis in a speech given at the end of the gigantic march on Washington in August 1963, in which all the civil-rights groups converged [Lewis, 1.3.]. In contrast to the hopeful tone of Martin Luther King's speech, "I have a dream that one day all Americans will be equal," Lewis explicitly presented the critical views of those who were actually carrying out the revolution in the South and who were becoming increasingly aware of the ambiguity of the federal administration, of the insufficiency of merely winning the vote in the face of profound economic inequality, and the need for a radical revolution which would start with direct action in the streets.

> We cannot support the administration's civil rights bill, for it is too little, and too late. . . . We are now involved in a serious revolution. This nation is still a place of cheap political leaders who build their careers on immoral compromises and ally themselves with open forms of political, economic and social exploitation. . . . The party of Kennedy is also the party of Eastland.[20] [Lewis, 1.3.]

From that time on, a political strategy could be seen which was not based on a mere conquest of civil rights or on the enlightened benevolence of reform-Democratic leaders: at the center stood SNCC and the Southern freedom campaigns, which, however, many people have repudiated in recent years as moderate, because they were nonviolent, contrasting to them the revolutionary slogan of Black Power.[21]

In reality, the radical evolution of the civil-rights struggle toward the position of Black Power did not take the form of a qualitative leap; it derived not from a different approach or from different objectives, but rather from a progressive understanding of the structure of American society and from the need to add new victories to those already achieved in the domain of equality, liberty and democracy.

> We all recognize the fact that if any radical social, political and economic changes are to take place in our society, the people, the masses, must bring them about. In the struggle we must seek more than mere civil rights; we must work for the community of love, peace, and true brotherhood.

This is still John Lewis speaking in Washington in 1963. The alternative was not between violence and nonviolence, but between activists who carried on a concrete struggle of direct action and those who wanted to subordinate street battles, direct action, community organization, and militancy of young blacks and whites to strategies which were external to the movement, i.e., inspired by the political and legislative interests of Northern "liberals." It was the contrast between *those who were part of the movement* and made it autonomous, and *those who wanted to use the movement;* between those

---

20.   Senator James Eastland of Mississippi, known for his reactionary positions.

21.   On the themes of continuity between civil rights and Black Power, see, for example, Anne Braden's editorial in *The Southern Patriot,* Vol. 24: No. 5 (May 1966).

involved in its internal dynamics and those who debated its power strategies in magazine columns.[22]

3.5.   From the end of 1962 the voter registration and organizing campaigns were coordinated by the Council of Federated Organizations (COFO), which included, in addition to SNCC (which provided the majority of the activists), other civil-rights organizations such as SCLC, CORE, and NAACP. The success of Bob Moses's position favoring autonomy, according to which it was necessary to develop the freedom movement in the South through the creation of structures and institutions parallel to those officially in power, was evident with the free elections, or Freedom Ballot, held in the autumn of 1963. The elections were free because the local population was called upon to express its own preferences; it voted for a black governor and a white lieutenant-governor of Mississippi, on a ballot which had nothing to do with the official ones and which had been organized by COFO and students from Yale and Stanford. The 80,000 votes (four times more votes than the number of officially registered blacks) which the two candidates obtained was, as Moses declared, proof that great numbers of blacks would have voted if they had not been materially impeded from doing so. The success of the elections also seemed to indicate to the local activists the concrete possibility of reconstructing a different society, starting with free institutions formed by and for the people, without their delegating power to outside authorities and institutions. In 1964 the process which had begun with the Freedom Ballot developed into Mississippi Summer 1964. Its objective was to mobilize wide areas of the South, the majority of which were black but which included poor whites as well, by means of educational projects, organizing drives and direct action. Over 800 students from campuses all over the country went down South to place their energies and technical resources at the disposal of the local communities. Freedom schools were set up [**Lynd, 1.4.**] under the most discouraging conditions; theatrical troupes were formed to develop creative new techniques of education and communication; freedom houses were opened; mass voter-registration drives were held, even in areas which no activists had penetrated before; a bond of solidarity began to develop within the local communities themselves, composed of the most depressed strata of the black and white population; people began directing new energy toward organizing their own communities. The mass campaign of the summer of 1964 was important for a number of reasons, both within and outside of the civil-rights movement. On the local level, the grass-roots organizational work revealed a new method of political activity which contrasted with the manipulation normally found in traditional party politics; a method which had not been taken into consideration even by those progressive union leaders, like Walter Reuther, who had been speaking for some time—although without having fulfilled the promise—about the necessity of organizing those strata of the population marginal to the economic and social life of the country. Furthermore, the method of democratic participation fundamental to the humanistic aims of the SNCC activists was tested creatively, if not in an orderly fashion. Within the organization, people were urged to express themselves, to organize, and to make their own decisions at every level and in all circumstances. On the outside, the experience was just as enlightening for the young people working in the South that summer as it was for the local residents, if not more so. They became acquainted with an America whose existence they had never suspected and began to understand the nature of the country's structures; look-

---

22. See Bayard Rustin, "From Protest to Politics," *Dissent*, January/February 1965.

ing at the South, but quick to apply their observations to the North,[23] they regained the strong emotions they had lost in the sterile atmosphere of the campuses. From that moment, eight hundred potential activists were ready to engage in new radical campaigns, ready to change the very course of their lives and even to die, as some already had during that violent summer [**Letters, 1.5.**].

3.6   A natural outcome of four years of organizing in the South was the formation of an independent political organization—the Mississippi Freedom Democratic party (MFDP). Composed mainly, although not entirely, of blacks, it was a genuine expression of the local communities, free from the control of political bosses. This fact made it a revolutionary phenomenon for the South, and perhaps for the entire nation. Even though blacks constituted a large minority, and in some areas the majority of the population, they had never before organized and expressed themselves politically in the South. In general, experience had shown how difficult it was in America for political organizations independent of the traditional two-party system to survive pressures and power tactics. While the birth of a new party intimately connected with the civil-rights movement and with the method of grass-roots organizing was an indication of the enormous development the young activists had managed to give their movement in only four years, the first confrontation between this movement and national politics meant a loss of all confidence in the country's "liberal" forces. When the MFDP appeared at the national Democratic party convention in Atlantic City in the autumn of 1964 [**Miller, 1.6.**], it challenged the legality of the racist delegation and demanded to be accredited as the representative organization of the Mississippi Freedom Democratic party, because of its democratic structure and its objective of integration. The delegation was not accredited; the racists were recognized as the Democratic party representatives, and the Mississippi Freedom Democratic party was offered two symbolic seats without the right to represent Mississippi. Atlantic City provided a litmus test for the entire American political situation. On the one side, there was the Democratic party machine, in which Southern racists, so-called establishment liberals, and bosses of big-city electoral machines coexisted and supported one another. Hubert Humphrey, who was about to become Lyndon Johnson's running mate, went to considerable lengths to obtain the humiliating concession of the two seats in a manner which would not alienate the Dixiecrat delegations. The liberals exerted pressure for the MFDP to stay within the orbit of the Democratic party structure, at any price. Martin Luther King and Bayard Rustin, who had, after all, distinguished themselves greatly in the civil-rights campaign, supported the compromise in view of a possible alliance on the national level with liberal and union leaders capable of bringing about improvements in the conditions of blacks and the poor. The young SNCC activists who had helped to build the MFDP, together with its local representatives, judged the compromise unacceptable and left the convention more convinced than ever of the great distance that separated the intrigue of traditional political mechanisms from the freshness of their recent experience of direct democracy.

With the episode of the MFDP—whose challenge of the election of two states' representatives to Congress was finally rejected by Congress itself— the possibility ended for the civil-rights movement to reconcile the central aspect of the movement, represented by SNCC's grass-roots organizing work, with the hoped-for national alliance among integrationist, liberal and pro-

---

23. All the leaders of the 1964 Free Speech Movement in Berkeley had been involved in some way in civil-rights experiences.

gressive labor forces. Not that the local-level organizations of blacks and poor whites dissolved, or that their long, difficult struggle to gain their rights stopped: the election of Julian Bond, a local secretary of SNCC [**Cobb, 1.8.**], to the Georgia Legislature, and the failure of the attempt to prevent him from being seated because of his opposition to the Vietnam war, represent the development of those campaigns.

What emerged more clearly was the conflict between the two aspects of the civil-rights movement: the internal one, symbolized by SNCC's activity, and the external one which liberal public opinion attributed to it. SNCC—and we are referring here both to its activists and to the local population they helped organize—was from the very beginning a force which operated with methods altogether different from those of the traditional American political system. Its radicalism consisted in its adherence to participatory democracy and human values above all. On the other hand, the civil-rights movement was viewed from the outside mainly as a realignment of a few sick parts of society with the healthy, democratic body of the nation. This view was false, because both terms of the proposition were inexact: in the first place, the movement was not working for a realignment, but for basic change; and secondly, the nation was being revealed more and more fundamentally sick, even though the germs were different and the symptoms harder to detect than those which were so visible in the South.

4

Against the Totalitarianism of the Cold War: Civil Liberties at Home and Peace in the World

4.1. As was the case in the South, the causes which determined the birth of dissent and protest in the rest of the country were, at the beginning of the 1960s, limited in nature and strictly related to issues of individual liberties or to specific policies of the administration. Students began to stir on campuses and in the streets, not in the name of an alternative political vision or a revolutionary strategy, but for essentially liberal and humanistic motives. Their political involvement moved from the particular to the general, from moral concern to an analysis of structures. Here, as in the civil-rights struggle, the process of radicalization and the growth of a more general opposition to American society and institutions was slow and gradual, and was due more to the kind of response the movement elicited from the liberal wing of traditional political forces than to the intentions of its participants.

Even though cold-war ideology did not assume the paranoiac aspects of the McCarthy years, it still openly and subtly permeated both a foreign policy based on power, with the division of the world into spheres of influence, and the processes of political decision-making domestically. Any evaluation of the rebirth of dissent in America must consider the background of a society which left no room for the development of views different from those considered right for "democracy" and for the "free world." Between 1960 and 1963, the crucial issues around which protest catalyzed and movements organized represented a direct reaction against the systematic cold-war view and concerned two main areas: civil liberties and peace. The 1950s had been particularly conservative with respect to both subjects, and this heredity of conservatism, carried into the next decade, aroused violent opposition.

4.2. In May 1960, eight thousand students from the University of California at Berkeley and other Bay Area colleges, together with habitués of certain cafés in San Francisco's North Beach, frequented by the rebels and artists of the beat generation, held a demonstration in front of the San Francisco City Hall, where the House Un-American Activities Committee (HUAC) was meeting to investigate real or supposed communist activity. The HUAC investigations were imbued with that typical spirit of domestic totalitarianism which caused political dissenters to be treated as criminals. The function of HUAC (which had been founded in 1938) was "to make from time to time investigations of (1) the extent, character and objects of un-American propaganda activities in the U.S., (2) the diffusion within the U.S. of subversive and un-American propaganda that is instigated from foreign countries or of a domestic origin and attacks the principle of the form of government as guaranteed by our Constitution, and (3) all other questions in relation thereto that would aid Congress in any necessary remedial legislation.[24] Not only subversive activity, therefore, but even propaganda was subject to investigation. What the protestors had to deal with was a violation of those very civil liberties that should have been the most precious political inheritance of the Western world.

---

24. David Horowitz, *Student* (New York: Ballentine Books, 1962), pp. 45–46.

The militant methods of the anti-HUAC demonstration were to serve as an affirmation of simple liberal objectives, namely, that a committee which had been established in the prewar period be abolished and that citizens not be persecuted for their political opinions. The students, who had been raised to believe the myth of the great American democracy, found here—no less than in other aspects of their life—a contradiction between fact and principle, between values their upbringing had taught them to cherish and the exercise of authoritarian power by individuals who professed those same values. Beyond the specific episode, that unexpected explosion of physical protest reflected a much more general state of malaise originating in a conflict between ideals and reality.

> We came out to demonstrate against the House Committee on Un-American Activities, not merely as a defense of our right to freedom of thought, but as an affirmation of our duty to think, to think socially and independently, to take part as students in the community and to take responsibility as students for its direction. . . . That morning when we went out to demonstrate against the House Committee, we had other things in our mind as well: capital punishment, integration, peace, and all the issues in which our lives were involved and which we had begun, as students, to think about again.[25]

The spirit of the San Francisco demonstrators was similar to that which, a few months earlier, had motivated Fred Moore, an eighteen-year-old student, to hold a solitary vigil on the Berkeley campus in protest against compulsory military training at a state university [**Moore, 2.1.**]. It was similar to the spirit which had provoked a march against capital punishment and against the execution of Caryl Chessman in February of that same year. When society acts with physical and moral violence—persecution of political adversaries, compulsory military indoctrination, and disdain for human life —the first instinct is a moral reaction; deepening the analysis and transforming it into conscious political opposition follows. This developed during the months following the anti-HUAC demonstration, when an attempt was made, by means of a widespread propaganda apparatus, to gain support for the notion that the disorder had been organized by communists. J. Edgar Hoover, head of the FBI, testified that there had been a prearranged plot whose objective was violence. The film *Operation Abolition,* which was to have supported this idea by showing the confrontations between students and police in San Francisco, produced the very opposite effect in the course of a year: it convinced the majority of those students who had borne the brunt of the unwarranted police violence to continue the debate on civil liberties in the universities. Around this theme, committees for the abolition of HUAC were formed according to a method of political organization which became typical of the new movements, i.e., gathering groups of students and nonstudents around single issues, bypassing already existing organizations.

4.3.   Events in Cuba played an important role in the growth of dissent within the United States. The Cuban revolution, culminating with Castro's seizure of power in January 1959, threatened the division of the world. Just as political dissenters within the United States became national enemies, so in the entire Western world nations and peoples who chose independence from the U.S. could not be tolerated. The principle of self-determination became a value subordinated to power and could in no way be allowed to threaten the established system. President Kennedy

---

25. *Ibid.,* pp. 16–17.

would certainly have preferred a "democratic" regime to Batista's allied with the United States, but when faced with the autonomous development of the Cuban revolution, it became legitimate to bring the *heterodox* phenomenon under control.

We do not intend here to discuss the transformation of the Cuban revolution from libertarian and nationalist to communist, nor to discuss the level of political democracy in the present regime. The fact remains that the United States—first through political and economic pressure, followed by the breaking off of diplomatic relations, and then with the organization of the Bay of Pigs invasion in April 1961—followed a policy of maintaining military and economic supremacy and playing the role of international police.

In order to clarify the relationship between the new movement of dissent and traditional liberalism, it is well to remember that it was John F. Kennedy who enacted a policy toward Cuba which one would have thought characteristic of a much more conservative leader, and that it was the men of the New Frontier who first lied about the role played by the CIA and then justified their own lies in the name of *raison d'état*.[26] Among students, reaction to America's conduct in Cuba once more took on a liberal tone: they formed the Fair Play for Cuba Committee, demanding that the administration take a proper attitude toward the small country and its new regime. The fascination the Cuban revolution held for young people lay precisely in its romantic and humanist character. It seemed to represent the restoration of human action as protagonist of the historical process, in spite of the repressive military and economic apparatus it had to combat, as well as the inflexible international order and the desperate objective conditions of the country.

> Both Cuban and Campus rebels are *strong* dissenters, firm in their convictions and willing to speak out and act militantly in spite of the mighty coercive powers of the American state. . . . Both Cuban and Campus revolutions are inexperienced, groping movements sometimes stumbling, sometimes making mistakes of a tactical nature—with either too much anti-Americanism or too much fear of offending or alienating "public opinion." Most important, their motivating ideologies are neither socialism—Marxian or otherwise—nor liberalism, although they combine elements of both. . . . A refreshing combination of humanism and rationalism. [**Johnson, 2.3.**]

Support for the revolution grew in direct proportion to the increase of American pressure; visits to Cuba became more frequent as people desired to learn firsthand the facts which authorities attempted to hide by various means, including ban on travel; the violence of the revolution gradually came to be understood and justified, even by pacifists, who judged the guerrillas' action in the contexts of international violence and the perpetuation of poverty in Latin America.[27]

---

26. Noam Chomsky, "The Responsibility of Intellectuals," *New York Review of Books,* February 23, 1967.

27. During the course of 1960–1961, the events in Cuba inspired a debate among the editors of *Liberation,* a monthly which gathered nonviolent radical pacifists strongly dedicated to revolutionary change in the United States and the world, into a "third camp" position. A. J. Muste, along with most of the editorial staff of the magazine, took a position in favor of the Cuban revolution. This brought about the resignation of Roy Finch, who saw in the Castro regime dictatorial tendencies contrary to the principles upheld by the magazine. In his response to Finch, Muste declared: "When one advocates the overthrow of something, he must ask what would replace it. After recent events it seems clear to me that:

"(1) There is no *united* alternative agency now which is devoted both to political democracy and to maintaining the social gains of the revolution.

"(2) There is no alternative agency dedicated to nonviolence; and continuation of efforts to overthrow the present régime would almost certainly lead to terrible bloodshed.

4.4. The expropriation of resources by the war industry; the maintenance of a permanent state of preparation for all-out war; the atomic testing carried out by both the United States and the Soviet Union—these are the reasons that the youthful protest movement found peace to be one of the most important objectives of the moment.

We have mentioned that the rebellious instinct always springs from moral considerations, particularly in places like the United States, where there were no forces capable of setting off campaigns more fundamentally political in nature. This was also true for the peace movement, which, in its first mass meetings, concentrated on denouncing the horror of atomic warfare, proclaiming the right to live, appealing to governments to stop nuclear testing, and circulating petitions in favor of controlled disarmament. The San Francisco peace march of 1960 was organized as a means of giving the people a voice in the debate on disarmament. Similarly, the petitions presented to Kennedy and Khrushchev a few months later during the summit conference implied a faith in appealing to heads of state and reminding them of their responsibilities. The peace movement was based on the moral principle of the right to life. The National Committee for a Sane Nuclear Policy (SANE), around which the movement revolved at first, was guided by a hope of stopping the drift toward war through the banning of atomic weapons, and its propaganda did not extend much beyond appeals for survival and warnings on the danger of an accidental outbreak of nuclear war. The most heterogeneous elements were to be found around the peace movement: liberals willing to participate in single-issue movements; communists who saw in the front ranks of the movement possibilities for action which were otherwise precluded; moral and radical pacifists, religious groups, and democratic socialists. However, it was not these kinds of affiliations which caused the peace movement to grow. It became capable of mobilizing on a wider and more active basis only when the initiative passed into the hands of nonaffiliated students, and the issue of peace held for them the same moral imperatives to action as the civil-rights movement in the South.

Two years after its formation in Chicago in 1959, the Student Peace Union (SPU) became the largest student organization in the country, with over 3,500 members by the beginning of 1962. Together with other groups, the SPU promoted educational campaigns on nuclear testing, demonstrations in the form of civil disobedience against bomb shelters and civil defense programs and a picket of 5,000 students in front of the White House and the Soviet embassy in February 1962. Dissociating itself from the generic antinuclear-weapons policy of SANE and from the humanitarian call for peace, the Student Peace Union developed a "third camp" position among the students and proposed a form of political action independent from that of governments.

> After years of bad faith shown by both East and West in disarmament negotiations, the Student Peace Union believes that to be effective, any peace movement must act independently of the existing power blocs and must seek new and creative means of achieving a free and peaceful society. [Student Peace Union, 2.4.]

"(3) It does not seem to be in the cards that an alternative régime should be established in Cuba which would not be the creature of U. S. military and political pressure and compelled to operate in the U. S. power orbit. I cannot in any way favor such a régime. For in the power struggle over Cuba and Latin America being waged between the U. S. and the U. S. S. R. I do not think pacifists should support the U. S. against the U. S. S. R. any more than they should support the U. S. S. R. against the U. S."

We have detailed the position of radical pacifists because we feel that the pragmatism which inspires it—quite distinct from pacifism of a mystical or religious origin—has been an important thread in the development of the New Left and still inspires a wide segment of the new radicals.

While still limited by its single-issue orientation, the SPU (unlike the student wing of SANE, which itself had broken off from the parent organization in 1961 because of SANE's policy of ideological discrimination) represented the first ripening of a position in which moral attitudes became political vision. Along with the SPU members who were recruited on university campuses for the cause of peace, there circulated among the activists and leaders of the organization a small group of young socialists, heretics with respect to the pro-Western line of the Socialist party. It was they who bridged the gap between the remains of the nearly extinct socialist tradition and the new ferment.

The SPU dissolved in 1964, breaking up into different groups and movements. Its end came mainly as a consequence of the signing of the Nuclear Test Ban Treaty in August 1963. In that period it continued to function, however, supporting independent peace candidates in the 1962 election and organizing demonstrations against Madame Nhu in 1963. These can be seen almost as a forewarning of the new problems which were shortly to arise to confront the anti-war movement.

Thus, the Student Peace Union followed the pattern of the other young organizations of the new era: it was a temporary structure whose own organizational success was bound to the very life of the movement and whose action was carried out at the service of the movement.

5
An Attempt to Tackle
Social Problems
of the Country

5.1. Venturing outside of the campus and placing community organization at the center of its activity, Students for a Democratic Society (SDS) began in 1963 to explore the potential for creating a movement whose goal was social transformation. It resolved to penetrate that part of the society where, in the light of the most recent analyses, American democracy seemed to have failed miserably. Michael Harrington's book *The Other America: Poverty in the United States,* which appeared at the beginning of 1963, demonstrated that behind the facade of well-being and affluence were tens of millions of poor people who— according to the given definition of poverty—represented from 16 to 36 percent of the entire population.[28] Not only did many areas of the nation exist in poverty and unemployment, along with millions of citizens who remained outside the system, but some economists and social scientists predicted that the situation would deteriorate, given prospects of a worsening economic situation and increasing use of automation.[29] A group of liberal and radical intellectuals[30]—among whom were some of the founders of SDS, later to become the organizers of the largest community organizing projects, those of Chicago and Newark—had published a manifesto entitled *The Triple Revolution: Cybernation—Weaponry—Human Rights.* The manifesto contained the affirmation that "[C]ybernation is manifesting the characteristics of a revolution in production. These include the development of radically different techniques and the subsequent appearance of novel principles of the organization of production," and that "present [1963] excessive levels of unemployment would be multiplied several times if military and space expenditures did not continue to absorb ten percent of the gross national product." At that moment, it seemed to those young people with the best cultural preparation and the most active political experience that it was necessary to promote, in the large urban centers of the North, a movement which would correspond to the civil-rights movement in the South. In the South there was racial discrimination; in the cities, a clear division existed between the well-being of the first-class citizens and the poverty of those who occupied a marginal position in the economic and social process. The movement in the South served as the point of reference for this new plan of community organizing, and, for some, it was a direct experience which had to be transferred right into the Northern ghettos only a short distance from the campuses where middle-class students received their educations.

The impulse to leave the campuses and go to live and organize among poor whites and blacks arose not only from their analyses of the nature of American society, but also from their having studied those elements of the

---

28. Michael Harrington, *The Other America,* Appendix (New York: Macmillan, 1963).

29. At the beginning of 1963, through the efforts of a young union organizer, Stanley Aronowitz, a conference was held on poverty and other economic problems in Nyack, New York. Many young radical activists attended. At the end of the conference, a National Committee on Full Employment was formed to begin organizing the unemployed and those who would shortly become unemployed because of automation and the reduction in military expenditures. During the conference, the economist Ray Brown had upheld the thesis that "even if new job opportunities were increased at twice the 1963 rate, by 1970 unemployment would be about 13%—and astronomically higher for the young and non-white." Richard Rothstein, "ERAP, Evolution of Organizers," *Radical America,* March/April 1968.

30. Among the signers of the manifesto *The Triple Revolution* were Michael Harrington, historian H. Stuart Hughes, pacifist A. J. Muste, economist Gunnar Myrdal, scientist Linus Pauling, black integrationist leader Bayard Rustin, and the founders of SDS, Todd Gitlin and Tom Hayden.

society which should have been most interested in changing the status quo. The working class had become politically submissive and solidly committed to the defense of its own economic interests, which coincided with those of the large corporations. The middle class, too, seemed interested only in raising its material standard of living. University studies seemed either abstractly isolated from the crucial problems of the moment or directed toward the training of experts who could operate the existing mechanisms. The search for new social groups necessarily included the outcastes of the various underclasses, who were materially, culturally and socially outside of the "American way of life." The hopes invested in the poor derived also from a strong element of populism, which maintained that popular culture and life-style itself could provide alternatives to the materialistic and production-oriented values of American society. It denounced the cult of technical skill, economic expansion as a good in itself, organizations which, because of their increasing complexity, had to be placed in the hands of impersonal bureaucracies—preached the preservation of basic humanistic attitudes toward life, the natural virtue of the "common people," and forms of social intercourse which, being simple, were not manipulative. Populism was combined with the search for a theory of society. The activists made the personal choice of living a more genuine sort of existence than had been afforded by the middle class they came from, and, starting with grass-roots organizing, they attempted to become catalysts for the construction of a radical movement.

5.2.   In August 1963, shortly before the March on Washington for Jobs and Freedom, SDS began to promote the Economic Research and Action Project (ERAP), whose purpose was to study and promote organizing activity in poor black and white communities of Northern cities. Al Haber, the former president of SDS, was placed in charge of the project, an indication of the importance given to the undertaking by SDS, which until then had carried on its activities mainly in the universities. The first trial experiment was the work of Swarthmore College students who entered the black community of Chester, Pennsylvania, in an attempt to organize its residents around issues which had emerged from an earlier socioeconomic study. The first result of the Chester project was to activate a large number of students who on other occasions had been very difficult to mobilize around political issues. This first success led the participants in the SDS National Convention of December 1963 to confirm the line which had been chosen and to dedicate all available energy to organizing rather than to research. By summer 1964, the number of working projects had grown to ten: in Chicago, Cleveland and Appalachia, activists were organizing poor white communities; in Newark, New Haven, Chester, Baltimore, Oakland, Boston, and Cairo, Illinois, they were working in black ghettos. The method generally followed involved moving the SDS people into the heart of the chosen community, setting up a community center which served simultaneously as residence for the activists, meeting place, office, and place of referral for all the projects which the residents of the community were encouraged to take up. The organizers hoped to realize a vast range of goals, sometimes vague but always containing many different themes [**Gitlin, 3.3.**]. During its first year, the ERAP projects emphasized those objectives which seemed most urgent, given the economic forecasts of the moment: the name of the Chicago project itself, Jobs Or Income Now (JOIN), underlined the two most important ones. However, despite the goodwill of the activists, it became increasingly clear as the experiments continued that the struggle for full employment could not be won on the local level. For this reason, the projects' focus shifted in 1964 to more specific problems. The concrete signs of poverty showed themselves in the very places where people lived, and therefore it was necessary to organize the poor around the more material problems arising from a deteriorated environment and from the welfare agencies which represented their only relationship to public administration and the economic power structure. The ERAP national headquarters, whose sole function had been to serve as a channel of communication for the various projects and to allocate funds collected on a nationwide basis, gradually lost its *raison d'être* as the projects came to concentrate increasingly on particular local issues, and it was finally dissolved in spring 1965. Many members of the organization had hoped to form a national union of local communities which would bring the participants in the various local programs into a kind of superorganization of poor people. This never materialized, and, of the early projects so strongly supported by SDS activists, the only ones still remaining are those which gained a local organizing base or which—like that organized in Chicago among poor white migrants from Appalachia—sprang from particular sociocultural roots.

5.3.   Organizational flexibility and experimentation in the nature and forms of action were the two main characteristics of the work carried on in local communities. Without a precise program, but following the method of attacking the problems of poverty and local control where they existed, local organizations became involved in a series of actions aimed at bringing about immediate reforms in specific structures or institutions. They denounced violations of the building inspection code, organized rent strikes, demonstrated in front of the suburban homes of slum landlords, called for the intervention of the Human Rights Commission, staged a sit-in in the mayor's office to protest the conduct of the police and courts, testified at the local War on Poverty headquarters, demanded information from public officials, attacked abuses in the administration of welfare, and carried out studies on home ownership, traffic, and land use.[31] In all these activities, their general approach was to proceed from the particular to the general, from the specific living conditions of the neighborhood poor to profiteering by private capital or to the administration of welfare by the local government. Such an approach implied, implicitly or explicitly, the twofold idea of carrying out immediate reforms and attacking capitalist structures from points other than that of production, where systematic rationalization and economic well-being had made it impossible for the organized working class to fulfill a radical function.

> The crucial point is that the project is committed to two kinds of change at once: the specific remedying of individual, aggravating grievances, and basic structural changes which would replace present systems of production, authority, administration and control with far more egalitarian and participatory institutions. The first kind of change requires the most dogged protest and pressure. . . . The other dimensions of its activity and its existence as "the movement" cannot be judged by the standards relevant to either the neighborhood grievance clinic or the local insurgent political club. . . . Each project in its dimension as "the movement" offers and actualizes, in embryo, the national movement of poor people which constitutes both utopian vision and transcendent possibility.[32]

31. N. Fruchter and Robert Kramer, "An Approach to Community Organizing Projects," *Studies on the Left*, March/April 1966, p. 45.

32. *Ibid.*, pp. 37, 38.

In these experiments, too, the old dilemma of the left appeared: confronting the contradiction between the need for specific reforms within the system, and the prospects for a struggle to overturn the system completely. In America, there is no longer an organized left-wing working class, and the challenge to the legitimacy of the present economic and political order has come, not in the name of the supremacy of public over private property, but from those sectors of the Movement which began to try out local forms of organization based on direct control. The solutions proposed by many European socialist organizations, whether social-democratic or communist, have always been based on change "by decree," or on the priority of "planning" over market. Two elements seem to emerge from the limited experiments in community organizing, still in embryonic form and limited to the most elementary levels of social organization. On the one hand is the strategy of generating tension within all institutions between administrators and "administrated" in the name of direct control; on the other, a participatory method which involves a rejection of predetermined systems deduced from ideological positions.

5.4.   The organizing experience of the local groups developed by the ERAP projects was based on the geographical concept of the neighborhood and on the individuation of subcommunities and interest groups within metropolitan areas. This experience suggests three partial conclusions, to be verified in the dynamic of the next few years: the first is of a political character, the second is pragmatic, and the third, theoretical.

First: even this type of project sprang from the assumption that in American society it was possible to effect change within the system, and that it was necessary, beginning at the bottom and concentrating on the burning issues of the day, to stimulate the liberal and progressive forces represented by certain unions [33] and reform Democrats, with the goal of constructing a welfare state capable of solving the problems of poverty through an interracial movement.[34] This was the reformist aspect of the projects, which coexisted with their populism and participatory democracy, and with their determination to intervene in the place where the economic crisis was felt most heavily.

The relationship with liberal forces and institutions proved to be disastrous **[Hayden and Wittman, 3.2.].** First, the methods of participatory organization and direct action conflicted with the traditional strategy of pressure from liberal groups in a pluralistic society quick to absorb and make bargains with the demands of class and interest groups. Secondly, and more important, one of the fundamental themes which the New Left was developing was the opposition to and rejection of that very welfare state within the capitalist system which was supposed to guarantee full employment and—through various programs, such as the War on Poverty—the concession of marginal improvements to classes lying outside of the process of production. Politically there emerged, through local community work, the contradiction between the strategy of *alliances,* which often ended in co-optation and only marginal improvements, and the strategy of *power,* i.e., beginning to build a movement capable of remaining autonomous, both in its demands and in its control over the institutions in which it participated.

The second conclusion, on the pragmatic level, underlines the unpromis-

---

33. It is significant that the first funding of the ERAP projects came from a $5,000.00 contribution from the union of Automobile Workers (UAW), whose president was the progressive labor leader Walter Reuther, and that in Chicago a consulting committee was formed for JOIN, composed of left-wing union representatives. The committee dissolved after one year.

34. R. Rothstein, *op. cit.*

ing outlook for organizing the poor mainly along geographical lines, as well as the marginal results of the ERAP projects when one compares them, for example, with the birth of the labor movement at the beginning of the century. A national poor peoples' movement did not develop; at least not the kind the plans had indicated. Furthermore, most of the projects could not hold up under the wear and tear of activism and under the difficulty of coupling a disorderly but genuinely democratic and participatory method with the building of effective structures. Still, the seed of the flexible kind of organization which took shape around specific problems was carried outside the ERAP structure, both through the activists themselves and by means of the thousand channels of communication offered by urban life. A great many local programs sprang up—neighborhood political groups, local radio stations, bulletins, cooperatives, tenants' associations, police control committees—some owing their inspiration directly to the propositions and examples the local organizing projects provided. These experiments all attempted to build concrete structures through which the slogans connected with the strategy of power—Black, People, Student, etc.—could be turned into reality and made to function as ideals around which grassroots organizations could be mobilized.

Finally, the theoretical reflection concerns the means by which the idea of gaining power in contemporary society while still living outside it can be formulated in political terms. The formation of countercommunities, toward which certain local organizing projects were aiming, today represents the desire to build values, structures, life-styles and actions which should prefigure the society of tomorrow. But the conflict between that part which wants to be separate (countercommunity) and everything which tends toward integration (society) persists, especially in highly organized and complex societies. One of the possible solutions to the conflict which American radicals could adopt, probably lies "in its attempt first to create, then enlarge, a space in which the possible alternatives can be developed and the possible challenge to the status quo kept alive. The kind of community organizations we have defined are rallying points."[35]

35. N. Fruchter and R. Kramer, *op. cit.*, p. 61.

6
The "Movement" Rebounds on Campus: The Revolt Against Liberal Bureaucracy

6.1. The Berkeley revolt which broke out at the end of 1964 was not a product of the New Left or the result of a preestablished revolutionary strategy; it represented, instead, the outlet for many of the issues, tensions and battles which the Movement had been engaged in for five years, both *within the university* and *directed toward the university*. It was one of those moments in the development of the opposition in which individual feelings and malaise, joined with political events and personal revolt, linked themselves with the action of organized groups. The ideals governing the search for a new life-style which sprang from the campaign for civil rights in the North and South, the defense of civil liberties, which had been a constant factor in the mobilization of the Movement, and finally the rejection of "the American way of life" of smooth efficiency and affluence, rebounded *within the university*. This rebellion was a means of expressing opposition to a university conceived as a "knowledge factory"[36] which avoided the most crucial issues of the moment; it meant also the rejection of its bureaucratic structures, which were so similar to those of other alienating social institutions.

The University of California at Berkeley had a "modern" structure quite different from that of the feudal institutions which still dominate much of Academia in Europe. Its atmosphere was "liberal," and its machinery efficient and well-organized. But it was this very "liberal" and apparently open character, as President Clark Kerr's theory had conceived it, which aroused opposition and revealed the actual substance of certain kinds of liberalism. The multiversity had become a service open to government, industry, finance, labor, and national defense, with expanded facilities dedicated to the preparation and training of personnel qualified to ensure the smooth functioning of a society increasingly subservient to science and technology. On the inside, the mechanism of the university was supposed to be administered in a managerial spirit like that of other units of production, with administrator-entrepreneurs capable of continuously making the programs of study and scientific research meet the demands of outside customers. It seemed that there could be no place for the needs and desires of students or for the autonomy required by professors. Above all, there was no place for critical, as opposed to specialized, training, or for self-government of the institution. The multiversity was "a mechanism held together by administrative rules and fed by money."[37] Just like other organizations of American economic and social life, the model university which was taking shape was that of an organization at the service of goals established by the ruling forces of the society in which all the constituent working parts had to be subordinated to the general pattern. It is within this framework that one must consider the contradiction between the apparent freedom which permitted the consideration of differing viewpoints within a university meant to function as a service for the outside, and the actual limits imposed on its academic programs and educational methods by the general dominant ideology, as well as by economic resources and research contracts. The

---

36. Clark Kerr, *The Uses of the University*, 1963.

37. *Ibid.*, p. 20.

question of *manipulation,* which is often raised by the new radicals, does not refer to a lack of flexibility in programs or to a lack of formal liberty for the expression of different points of view; it considers educational and research facilities in terms of their function with respect to the external situation. When the student and the professor are not in the classroom, sharing fixed objective data, they have no right to take part in the defining of values which education and teaching must cultivate; they can only move within a framework that has already been determined by others. The students' malaise arose precisely from their lack of power to choose in actual practice: the means of controlling the structure they were part of lay beyond them.

> The students' basic demand is a demand to be heard, to be considered, to be taken into account when decisions concerning their education and their life in the university community are being made. When one reviews the history of the Free Speech Movement, one discovers that each new wave of student response to the movement followed directly on some action by the administration which neglected to take the students, as human beings, into account, and which openly reflected an attitude that the student body was a thing to be dealt with, to be manipulated.[38]

In its academic aspect, the revolt against the liberal bureaucracy, as the Berkeley revolt has been defined, represented the contradiction between the two terms which characterized the university administration: the right of a bureaucracy as such to administer a given institution and the prerogative of a ruling class which permits liberty, but only to the threshold of conflict with established goals and values, to call itself *liberal.*

6.2.   In September 1964, all political activity concerned with noncampus issues was prohibited, both by regulation and in practice. The Constitutional guarantees of freedom of speech and assembly were suspended, and the university, with its laws, became a separate world in which the internal rules of the game had to be respected. But outside their academic lives, the students also had the mature interests of citizens; many of them were active in the civil-rights struggle and enthusiastically participated in other political and social activities of a much wider range than mere campus politics. In September 1964, when confronted with the rules prohibiting the holding of meetings on campus, soliciting funds, making speeches, distributing leaflets or setting up tables with political material, the students created a united front of all political organizations,[39] and demanded free speech.[40] At the same time, campus demonstrations were organized, and a thousand people joined them. On October 1, 1964, as part of the action taken to introduce political activity on campus, a few political tables were set up in the central plaza of the university in defiance of the

---

38. Jack Weinberg, "The Free Speech Movement and Civil Rights," in Hal Draper, *The New Student Revolt* (New York: Grove Press, 1965), p. 186.

39. The united front of off-campus political groups which was formed on September 17, 1964, consisted of approximately 20 organizations of various tendencies, such as civil-rights groups, radical and socialist clubs, religious and peace organizations, and Young Democrats. There were also Young Republicans and other conservative groups represented. See Hal Draper, *op. cit.,* pp. 31–32.

40. We are using the term "free speech" in the same manner as it was used during the Berkeley movement, i.e., "free speech is used as a shorthand term for the range of students' demands of freedom of political activity and social action, as well as free speech in the narrow sense." *Ibid.,* p. 23.

administration's ruling. The administration ordered the tables removed from university property, and the activists refused. The police then arrested Jack Weinberg, who was manning the CORE table. At that point, the unexpected occurred: within a few minutes, hundreds of students had surrounded the police car in which Weinberg had been placed and physically, although nonviolently, prevented its being moved. Thirty-two hours passed before the car could be moved. This act of mass civil disobedience, in which several thousand students were personally involved for two days, had obviously not been brought about by activists attempting to encourage political involvement. It indicated the support and solidarity of a large mass of students who, in that specific episode, were expressing a feeling of dissent which arose from many different causes. On October 10, after the administration had reluctantly granted a few partial concessions, the Free Speech Movement was formed. What was the FSM? An "organized-disorganized-unorganized" structure[41] which served the needs of a movement-in-action, representing the interests and desires of its constituents and governed internally by participatory democracy without predetermined leadership. Its steering committee, on which all the groups supporting the goal of "free speech" were represented, had a shifting membership, and it operated through "work centrals." But the outstanding characteristic of the movement's internal structure was the dissolving of organized politico-ideological boundaries during the meetings, where, in the course of long discussions, political goals were formulated and decisions made. The nonideological character of the FSM was also reflected in the type of leaders who emerged in the course of its various actions. Mario Savio, who had appeared from the outset as one of the students' most articulate and popular representatives, was not an ideological leader, but only the genuine spokesman of a movement-in-action. The collective, unified nature of the FSM was confirmed in the series of direct actions of November and December aimed at overcoming the resistance of the administration and culminating in the occupation of the administration building on December 4, at which 700 students were arrested. The Sproul Hall sit-in was a further example of collective participation in the process of self-government. During the occupation of the building, the hundreds of students inside it attempted to form a rudimentary free university, with courses and discussions, and to organize cultural and recreational activities; they all participated in making decisions and, at the end, chose to be arrested, facing collectively the danger of expulsion which had been used earlier to threaten Savio and other spokesmen.

In the end, the FSM was successful, both generally and in its specific objectives. From that moment on, the right to freedom of speech was assured on the Berkeley campus. On January 4, 1965, the first legal rally was held in the plaza. It was the beginning of a long series of student activities aimed toward linking academic life with democratic rights. From a wider perspective, the mobilization of large numbers of students, the support of part of the faculty, and the resignation of the chancellor signified a first attack against the administration's right to control the institution in the name of outside forces and interests. For the students, it seemed clear that collective action linking personal discontentment and political goals could have a shattering effect, even on institutions as apparently strong and solid as the University of California. A few years later, the test experiment would be repeated, with even greater success, at Columbia University in New York.

6.3.   It was not by accident that the massive Berkeley revolt occurred in a university and in the autumn of 1964 [**Savio,**

---

41. *Ibid.,* p. 62.

4.3.]. That fall, Lyndon Johnson was the liberal choice for the voters who would have to elect a new President in November; on the other side was the danger of Senator Barry Goldwater. How could the activists—who had given a new breath of life to American politics with their direct involvement in the South and in poverty areas of the North—not feel alienated from traditional political institutions? The Kennedy myth had vanished with the President's death, and only a few young people still continued to deceive themselves that initiatives like the Peace Corps could satisfy their need to participate directly in building a community where social values would be primary. It was appearing with increasing clarity that the errors of the racist South and the poverty of urban ghettos were not isolated elements. Alongside these glaring manifestations of injustice and oppression was the generalized contrast between affluence and poverty; between the power of the few and the impotence of the masses; between the logic of production and economic development and the lack of community in which human values were maintained. Moreover the university had played a central role in the development of American society; its mass character, its efficiency, the clear distinction which existed within it between administrators and "administrated" were all characteristics reflecting the features of the larger society. In American universities in general, and in the University of California in particular—with its high concentration of students chosen according to the highly selective criteria of the institution—young people of the middle class were in the most opportune position, intellectually and socially, to observe the continuity between the vaunted liberalism of that part of the ruling class found in the university, and the technocratic-capitalistic structure of American society which that ruling class upheld. Behind the issue of "free speech," a more basic confrontation was taking place between those who wanted to use the university as a mechanism for maintaining and rationalizing the status quo, and those who wanted to begin realizing the hope for a different America right there. The conflict between these two positions which exploded in Berkeley revealed for the first time that the university was one of those vital nerves of American society in which basic conflicts manifest themselves, and that it contained seeds of radicalization which sprang from its very nature as a mass institution and from its unique function in modern society.

Two:
The Emergence
of the New Left

7

Five Theses for the
Development of a
New Left Position

7.1. At the beginning of the 1960s, a few isolated acts of protest had broken the crust of consensus and apathy surrounding American society. We have seen how different movements developed within a period of five years: the civil-rights movement in the South, the peace movement in the North, community organizing in metropolitan ghettos, student protest on campus. The various movements did not arise from a single political or ideological source, but rather from a sentiment of difference and detachment from the political and social system and cultural climate of American society. For many, direct action had been both a tactic and a policy, an instrument of action and a verification of judgments and analyses of the social context within which it was operating. Taking into consideration the period of time which separates the isolated protest of young Fred Moore in Berkeley in 1959 and the April 1965 SDS march against the war in Vietnam, with over 20,000 people, it is possible to demonstrate the tremendous development of the opposition within five years and the simultaneous quantitative and qualitative transformation of the Movement. It is difficult to estimate the actual number of followers in the different movements because of the fluctuating and flexible character of the organizations and the episodic nature of the demonstrations. Nevertheless, some facts can be employed as points of reference, considering that the protests and direct actions usually developed into something like a pattern of concentric circles around a central core of activists, according to the tension or drama of each particular situation. It has been estimated that, in 1965, the number of young people belonging to both New Left and traditional left organizations did not exceed 12,000;[42] but the most significant fact, which must be used as term of comparison in the case of the United States, is not the number of people belonging to organizations, but the number of activists in the various movements. In the South, during the period of greatest expansion, there were 150 full-time activists working with SNCC,[43] and about 800 volunteers during the summer of 1964; in 1963, there were probably no more than 100 activists in the peace movement on the various campuses and the same number of SDS organizers in the 12 ERAP projects; in Berkeley, the only certain figure to which one can refer, besides the number of members of various clubs, is the 800 people arrested in the December 1964 sit-in. Around this central nucleus of activists, there were those who participated sporadically or dedicated only part of their time to political activity. In 1965, Professor Amitai Etzioni estimated that approximately four percent of all college students—i.e., 200,000—were committed in various degrees to the new radicalism.[44] In their documentary report on the new radicals, Paul Jacobs and Saul Landau grasp the nature of the new movement well when they note:

> It is possible to count those who are members of the organizations within the Movement, but that would be to misunderstand one of the basic facts of its nature: the Movement is organizations plus unaffiliated supporters, who outnumber by the thousands, and perhaps even hundreds of thousands, those committed to specific groups. The Movement's basic strength rests on those unaffiliated reserves, who are just as much a part of it as the organization youth.[45]

The most indicative figures on the breadth and mobilizing capacity of the different movements are those deduced from the participation in various demonstrations, whose size varied according to their theme, their more or less radical character, the effort put into organizing them, and the situation of the moment. In May 1960, 8,000 people picketed against HUAC in San Francisco; 5,000 demonstrated against nuclear testing in Washington in February 1962; 200,000 participated in the civil-rights march on Washington of April 1963; 80,000 blacks voted on the Mississippi Freedom Ballot in 1963; over 6,000 students were involved in some way in the Berkeley Free Speech Movement of 1964; 25,000 people answered the SDS call and went to Washington to protest against the Vietnam War in April 1965.

7.2.   The most important qualitative leap taken by the Movement, however, lies in the fact that in only a few years

42. Michael Munk, *The New Left*, a *National Guardian* pamphlet, 1965.

43. Zinn, *op. cit.*, p. 3.

44. Munk, *op. cit.*, p. 4.

45. Paul Jacobs and Saul Landau, *The New Radicals* (New York: Vintage, 1966), p.4.

it had broken the climate of consensus in which the country had been resting during the 1950s and had brought to the surface the contradictions in the political system and the profound injustices present in the social fabric. McCarthyism had helped reduce the organized left to impotence; the "end of ideology" theory proposed by those Mills called "NATO-intellectuals"[46] seemed to be conceptualizing the end of structural class and group conflicts, and even of conflicts between ideals and political practice. The Movement, whose actions were often confused and which could certainly not return to the theoretical schemes of the traditional left—not to speak of those of the ruling class—presented the nation with a left which was no longer defensive and defeatist, but which attacked on various fronts and, what is more important, demonstrated the inconsistencies in the theory, proposed by the "end of ideology" model, that conflict in industrially advanced societies had come to an end. New conflicts were arising in new areas (civil rights and civil liberties, universities, foreign policy), in forms (direct action) that were different from those traditionally acceptable and on the part of social groups (the middle class) which were presumed to be solidly rooted to the consensus built around the "American way of life."

What we are interested in analyzing here is whether, out of the different movements, a political position developed, even if a new ideology did not. Our conclusion is affirmative, and it is precisely this political position which we call the "New Left." The adjective "new" is first, but not principally, used to designate the contrast between the political phenomenon that developed during the 1960s and the political movements of the 1930s (which continued until 1948, the symbolic date of the traditional left's collapse) whose forms were communist, socialist of various kinds and, to a lesser extent, anarcho-syndicalist and whose organized expression took place essentially through the labor movement. But what the adjective "new" designates above all is not a temporal or generational fact so much as a political content which has only marginal elements of continuity with the radical tradition of the past. The emergence of a New Left position (not yet a force or an organized movement) relates to the development—more in praxis than in theory—of a series of original themes, varying in quality, which cross the boundaries between specific projects and constitute a common nucleus of experiences between the different movements. In the following five theses we present the characteristics which, in our opinion, constitute the core of the New Left (qualifying both the terms "new" and "left") as it has been maturing since the middle 1960s.

I. Individual *moral revolt* and a desire for nonconformity in all aspects of existence which relate to life-style, come to assume the significance of freedom and of human (and therefore political) liberation themselves, in a context in which both the economic system and social institutions gradually tend, explicitly or implicitly, to invade and define every aspect of citizens' lives, restricting the fundamental rights of self-realization, self-expression and control over one's own life.

II. Analyses of and within the Movement, which, during its early period, concentrated on isolated issues such as civil rights, peace, and poverty, gradually tend to consider the various aspects of American society as a *system,* whose parts are interdependent and closely connected. Following this analysis of the total (or "integral," to borrow an expression generally used to refer to philosophical or religious systems) nature of the technocratic system of corporate liberalism, the new opposition changes from being essentially reformist to being essentially *radical.* The demands for specific changes

---

46. C. Wright Mills, "On the New Left," *Studies on the Left,* 1961.

in sectors of national life give way to a struggle for redistribution of power at all levels and to a different conception of the way in which society should be organized.

III. The earlier faith in the application of pressure to the liberal groups of the nation is replaced by direct action as the essential means of struggle and as the democratic mode of political expression in the specific context of postindustrial society. The strategy of coalition with liberal and labor forces gradually gives way to autonomous grass-roots organization of the new, potentially radical social forces.

IV. Although nonideological at the outset, the different movements develop a conceptual approach which can be summed up in the slogan "participatory democracy," a formula which—although the meaning of the systematic ideological concept cannot be attributed to it—must certainly be considered as a method capable of guiding and inspiring political action.

V. Organizing themselves along lines different from such structures of the traditional left as the "avant-garde party," the "ideological party" and the "disciplined group of revolutionary cadres," the movements suggest a political-organizational praxis which is based on the following criteria: (a) decentralization and multiplicity of structures and actions which serve the movements, and not vice versa; (b) direct method of self-government at all levels, rather than delegated authority and responsibility; (c) abolition of institutionalized political bureaucracies and of the division of political labor between leaders and those who carry out the leadership's policy; (d) nonexclusionism.

We shall now examine whether and in what way these theses can be confirmed, beginning with the movements we have been discussing.

8

When Moral Revolt
Takes on a Political
Significance
8.1. Irving Howe, a severe critic of the New Left, makes two observations about the new radicals which are quite correct:

> What is most impressive about the "new radicalism" is that it springs from a genuine moral feeling, a release of outrage in regard to social wrongs that warrant outrage. . . . Often their rebellion must take the form of seeking modes of personal differentiation rather than strategies for political action.[47]

But the two characteristics he emphasizes, morality and individualism, constitute a source of strength within the New Left, and not, as Howe concludes, a weakness and limitation.

The young people who first sat down at the segregated lunch counter of Greensboro in February 1960 carried the Bible with them; Bob Moses, the leader of SNCC, found a greater source of inspiration in Camus' "Neither Victims nor Executioners"; before the demonstration against the House Un-American Activities Committee in San Francisco, there had been a march to save Caryl Chessman from capital punishment. The volunteers who chose to abandon suburban affluence to live among the destitute people of Mississippi or the derelicts of urban ghettoes followed a moral impulse more than the dictates of political or organizational strategy; the choice of being arrested and going to jail, in Berkeley as in the South, placed individual participation above all else: in general, all the direct action in which the various movements became involved required strong individual conscience and decided moral conviction.

But who were the people who in the first place reacted on a moral level against the injustices of the society? The sons and daughters of the middle class, often of the higher strata of the middle class whose economic problems had been resolved. They had university educations which could have guaranteed them solid careers in the numerous branches of professional life requiring advanced training. We might add that often, as the historian Genovese has pointed out,[48] they are of Anglo-Saxon descent, whereas during the 1930s the left was mainly composed of Jews, Irish, and Italians, i.e., of poor and recently arrived immigrants.

8.2. The moral and individual factors of the rebellion, then, must be considered within the specific context of the social and economic conditions which formed the background from which the young people started; in particular, it was the capitalist system as it had developed in the United States which constituted the determining factor of this wider context. The system had certainly succeeded in resolving the economic problems of two-thirds of the society, producing a great quantity of goods accessible to wide segments of the population. Economic worries are unknown to the young people of the middle class, and even the search for jobs is no longer a problem for those who have achieved a certain level of training. There is no doubt about the particular rationality of capitalism proclaimed by new and old theorists of the market economy; but it is a ra-

---

47. Irving Howe, "The New Radicalism," *Partisan Review*, Summer 1965.

48. Eugene G. Genovese, "American Left—New and Old," *National Guardian*, February 19, 1966.

tionality that is related to a particular set of values. In this case, the value according to which an action is deemed rational or not is the realization of profit (or, in more current terminology, the preponderance of benefits over costs), a concept which not only holds sway over individual economic choices in the United States, but which has been extended from the domain of economics to that of the functional logic of institutions and organizations of all kinds. Surely, according to this philosophy, American society is not only rational but is becoming ever more so, to the extent that every aspect of individual and social life is being increasingly subjected to planning with respect to standards of efficiency, productive expansion, and economic profitability.

> The waste economy, in order to expand and perpetuate itself, extends and intensifies exploitation backwards to the worker in the corporation and forwards to the consumer, and in the process it increasingly invades every area and moment of the individual's life—through advertising, pressures to buy and consumer credit. . . . More and more, the individual, in obediently supporting his economy, surrenders areas of autonomy. The system's demands on him, the stereotyped and standardized forms of amusement, leisure activity and pleasure, block out any possibility for the development of individual interests, needs and desires. In short, the economy has had to extend itself deeply into the individual.[49]

If the word "system," in its most literal sense, ever had a meaning—that is, of closely connected parts within a single homogeneous organism, governed by the laws of functionalism and hierarchical organization—this meaning must be applied to the structures that make up the "American way of life." Social engineering, along with business management and public relations, are the major instruments for resolving conflicts within the system; operational research and systems analysis are becoming superdisciplines increasingly relied upon to provide answers and solutions to problems arising in various areas of social organization. Within this framework, the individual has few possibilities for expanding outside of the preestablished channels. It is difficult for him, in practical and ideal terms, to lead a life different from the kind which conforms to the rules of the game. What the society requires is standardization of personality, conscience and actions; even in terms of "life-style," the adoption of conformist modes of dress and behavior appear as necessary prerequisites for participation in the social mechanism, and therefore for success.

8.3.   In feudal society, the revolt of the poor and hungry expressed itself in the revolts against nobility and in assaults on the public granary; in industrial society, the worker goes on strike against the boss, who represents the incarnation of power and the economic structure on which the worker depends. Against whom and what can the citizen rebel in postindustrial society, where the forces his life depends on do not take the form of simple economic structures but are joined in a complex, diffuse system which imbues every facet of social life and organization? The first stage in the struggle for liberty in advanced modern society is neither economic nor political but concerns the very preservation of the man's humanity and individuality in the face of the invisible, omnipresent dictatorship of forces which tend to integrate and assimilate all elements (including the human one) into the system. Thus, to transcend the established order means, on

---

49. Ronald Aronson and John C. Cowley, "The New Left in the United States," in *The Socialist Register* (London: Merlin Press, 1967), p. 67.

the most basic level, to reject the structures of antifreedom. To react in moral terms means to set a mechanism in motion in the area where the citizen is most strongly repressed: his morality itself. To adopt a pattern of behavior and a life-style which do not conform to those of the majority means demonstrating externally the reconquest of one's individual autonomy. To feel allied with and perhaps to work among the forgotten, the poor, the outcasts of society means to place one's own moral disaffiliation on the same plane as those alienations which the society produces materially as by-products of affluence and profit. In short, the dropout from the university, the office, the academic career or the suburbs performs an act which is equivalent, in the present context, to that of the poor hungry man who attacks the granary or the worker who goes on strike. In this sense, his moral and individual acts are political to the extent to which he concretely singles out what lies at the core of his battle for freedom.

8.4. The official position as well as the praxis of many of the organizations and movements arising from the protest and opposition of the 1960s has been to incorporate the ideals and restore the values of individual liberty; this is manifested in the social sphere by the new generations of students, particularly those of radical tendency. We can say that this attribute is among those which best describe the development of the New Left position, which grew up around "values" much more than "programs." It is not by accident that the Port Huron statement of 1962—the manifesto not only of SDS, but of an entire generation of radicals —begins with a chapter dedicated to values:

> Our own social values involve conceptions of human beings, human relationships, and social systems. We regard *men* as infinitely precious and possessed of unfulfilled capacities for reason, freedom, and love. . . . We oppose the depersonalization that reduces human beings to the status of things. . . . We oppose, too, the doctrine of human incompetence because it rests essentially on the modern fact that men have been "competently" manipulated into incompetence. . . . Men have unrealized potential for self-cultivation, self-direction, self-understanding, and creativity. It is this potential that we regard as crucial and to which we appeal, not to the human potentiality for violence, unreason, and submission to authority. [**SDS, 5.1.**]

A year later, the resolution of the second SDS national convention opened with these words: "Our hope is human freedom. We care that men everywhere be able to understand, express and determine their lives in fraternity with one another" [**SDS, 5.2.**]. In the New Left, the stress thus placed on the humanistic and libertarian aspects of the struggle (man as the center of concern; individual liberty as more important than political or economic structures) seems to constitute—beyond an objective need felt by the new generations—a necessary and determining factor in the development of the left, i.e., that of a force which starts out from the concrete historical situation and carries forward the values of freedom and liberation.

9

The Name of the System Is "Corporate Liberalism," and Its Opposition Is Radical

9.1. The South seemed to the first civil-rights activists like the festering sore of the nation. In foreign policy, before the dramatization of the war in Vietnam, the interventions of the Marines here and there, and the presence of "military advisers" all over the world seemed at worst to be merely episodes brought about by the group of "hawks" in the Pentagon. It semed possible to overcome even poverty, underdevelopment and unemployment through New Frontier–style programs, i.e., greater amounts of federal spending. In short, the first analyses of power made by people who were to form the New Left concentrated mainly on specific areas of national life rather than on the whole picture. Even the Port Huron Statement, which was extremely clear and explicitly radical in the section dedicated to values, semed inspired more by social-democratic than by radical tradition in its analytical part and in its proposals. It is true that the war economy and the military-industrial complex were seen as the greatest disorders of the economic system, but these were opposed by a strengthened public sector which created a solid welfare system for the country. Some specific areas of national life were considered to be malfunctioning: the enormous military expenditures and permanent arms race; the centralization of the huge financial and industrial corporations; the social backwardness of the South; the islands of urban and rural poverty; the excessive errors in foreign policy. These different areas were seen—at least by the majority of activists and by that part of public opinion which was beginning to express opposition—as isolated and isolatable disorders, each of which could be overcome within its own specific limits.

9.2. Then, along with the intensification of the political struggles and social rebellions, the New Left began to draw connections between the various aberrations in economic and social life, and understand the nature of the liberal forces, which should have been allies of the new dissenters but which in reality took action only to defend their own interests. The activists began to discover that many of the important economic structures of the South were in some way connected to and controlled by those of the North; that the programs for huge military expenditures which supported the most highly developed national industries could be approved only thanks to deals made by Southern representatives in exchange for the installation of military bases in their states; that the welfare programs of preceding decades, just like the civil-rights and poverty programs, had not in fact improved the lives of the people toward whom they had been directed, but had only favored the expansion of a powerful bureaucracy [**Hayden, 6.2.**]; that the reason there would be no mass unemployment and economic crisis, as had been predicted, was that the war economy continued to expand. Outside the United States, not only had the conservative Eisenhower permitted the CIA to overthrow Mossadegh in Iran in 1953 and president Arbenz of Guatemala in 1954, but the same policies had been developed under Kennedy and Johnson; in 1960, the attempted invasion of Cuba carried out by men of the New Frontier; political strikes organized in British Guiana in 1963 were financed by leaders from the AFL-CIO; Goulart was overthrown in Brazil in 1964, and President Johnson subsequently congratulated the reactionary Mazzilli; 1965 saw the invasion of the Dominican Republic, when interests of American sugar corporations were endangered—corporations whose boards of directors included Johnson's friend, Justice Abe Fortas; Kennedy's friend, Adolf Berle, a theoretician of liberalism; and the peace negotiator, Ambassador Ellsworth Bunker. 1965 also witnessed the escalated bombing of Vietnam [**Oglesby, 5.3.**]. Behind the CIA, the Green Berets, and the Marines lay the interests of the huge corporations, the connections between the different sectors of economic and political power—those who actually ruled America.[50] The system on which all these various phenomena were based and which provided its ideology, was called "corporate liberalism."[51] One of the instruments through which this system operated to preserve, by means of a flexible program, the political and economic order, was the *welfare-warfare state*.

9.3.   The meaning of corporate liberalism is summed up by a spokesman of the New Left in these terms:

> In both its rhetoric and its practice, liberal corporatism implies a political structure in which principal policy issues are worked out at the federal level, formulated with the active participation of experts, and ratified—not in the legislative arena—but through a process of consultation among a national elite representing those interests and institutions which now recognize each other as legitimate. Such a conception of government is "corporatist" in at least two ways: first, it involves the major corporations and other interest groups actively and directly in the governmental process; second, it models government structure and administrative style in the manner of modern corporation management. It is "liberal" in the sense that it includes the active participation of representatives of groups traditionally favoring liberal reform and democracy—particularly, for example, the unions. Liberal corporatism tends toward the *co-optation* of dissent and reform rather than their suppression. [**Flacks, 5.5.**]

Corporate liberalism promotes internal economic planning, together with increased consumption and planned obsolescence, aims toward the control of distribution and advertising and toward a monopoly over mass communications, finances scientific research applied to the development of technology and social control, requires a liberal policy of coexistence abroad to permit the expansion of markets, supports higher education for the training of

---

50. William Domhoff, *Who Rules America?* (Englewood Cliffs, N.J.: Prentice Hall, 1967).

51. The term "corporate liberalism" was coined, as far as I know, by the American New Left to designate the present American politicoeconomic system. If the typical characteristics of this system are, as Richard Flacks [5.5] points out, (a) direct participation of the largest economic interest groups in the governmental process, (b) administration of the state through technocratic methods, and (c) assimilation of the contradictory demands of the several classes into the orbit of reform programs, we might draw an interesting analogy. At the base of the social and economic doctrines of Italian Fascism, German Nazism, and the nationalist groups of the French Action Française lay corporatism, according to which national political representatives were chosen on a vertical basis through the various groups which shared the productive function. Thus, the national parliaments consisted of representatives—from industry, agriculture, labor, the liberal professions, and so on—chosen from the top on an authoritarian basis. The state's function was to coordinate the various interests, resolving conflicts at the top and seeking the solutions most rational for the system.
   The analogy beween present-day corporate liberalism and the corporatism of the Fascist and Nazi regimes requires greater study than the New Left itself has dedicated to the subject thus far. This technocratic-fascist tendency of the American ruling classes (in corporations, unions and government) was pointed out by the Historian William A. Williams in *The Contours of American History* (1961), Part III, Section 2, when he deals with the first 30 years of twentieth-century American history and with the development of the ideas of such men as Bernard Baruch, Owen D. Young and Swope, not to mention those of Presidents Herbert Hoover and Theodore Roosevelt, the theories of theologian Reinhold Niebuhr, and the practices of the New Deal.

experts and consultants, subsidizes rich foundations which patronize cultural and intellectual developments, and is interested in state promotion of public well-being through welfare programs. In other words, it is a system based on power in the hands of an oligarchy which penetrates and controls— directly through ownership, or indirectly through pressure and influence —the life of the entire nation.[52] As reflected in the political sphere, it was President Kennedy's policies at first, and particularly the "Great Society" of Johnson later, which represented the interests and multiple demands of corporate liberalism at the federal level. With the great coalition of 1964, giant corporations and unions, managers and intellectuals, civil-rights moderates and big-city bosses gathered together in a single front around the Democratic party and its presidential candidate. Consensus was based on a program which supposedly incorporated all the interest groups, but in fact did nothing but protect the status quo: economic expansion, so precious to industrialists and workers alike, had to be accompanied by military expansion; state intervention, through subsidies, in antipoverty campaigns and urban renewal, had to include the participation of private enterprise; coexistence went hand in hand with the defense of America's sphere of economic and commercial influence on Third World markets.

9.4. After 1963 and the publication of the SDS document *America and New Era,* the conviction grew among the new opponents of the system that a reformist position, calling for reliance on the liberal forces within the ruling class, did not conform to the more genuinely democratic and egalitarian ideals that inspired the Movement. At the time the SDS was founded, the adversary to overcome was still the coalition between the racist Southern Democrats and the Republicans who represented the business world, and the hope for a new policy rested on a "realignment" of the Democratic party. The 1963 document, on the other hand, singled out the political forces upholding the corporate-liberal system and stated that these forces comprised the real and powerful enemy:

> American leaders are presently engaged in a politics of adjustment, affecting the conduct of government, industry, the military and all other social institutions. Thus politics represents an attempt to manage social conflict and adjust in minimal ways to the forces loose in the world. But for those who seek new models of life based on commitments to human dignity, democracy and peace, these attempts to stabilize existing power arrangements and traditional institutions present grim images of the future. [SDS, 5.2.]

In analysis and political struggle, the focus of interest shifted from the aberrant manifestations of the system to the very center of the system; from a traditional to a modern left. With the passage from a reformist to a radical position also arose the discovery that wherever there was repression it stemmed first and foremost from those forces at the center of power. It was McNamara —certainly not a reactionary militarist—who devised the formula of escalation; within the Democratic party, the racists were preferred to the forces of change; in the large cities, the exploitation of the ghettoes and the local control of welfare were realized through the efforts of Northern Democrats; in Berkeley the connection between modern science and economic structures was theorized by progressives like Clark Kerr. On the subject of the ruling circles, Carl Oglesby, president of SDS, declared in a speech in Wash-

---

52. The thesis of oligarchical control over the major national policy decisions of the U.S.A. is upheld by Professor W. Domhoff in the previously cited *Who Rules America?*

ington in November 1965; "These are not moral monsters. They are honorable men. They are all liberals"; and on the subject of corporate liberalism, whose ideology and interests were expressed on the political level by that ruling class: "It performs for the corporate state a function quite like what the Church once performed for the feudal state. It seeks to justify its burdens and protect it from change" [**Oglesby, 5.3.**]. The centering of attention on this fundamental framework of American life, over and above its reactionary outcroppings, constituted for the New Left a first step toward an analysis and understanding of the new forms capitalism was assuming in an advanced society, and consequently toward the development of a radical position in the face of the apparently liberal image of the most important sector of the American ruling class.

10

How the Movement Evolved from Pressure Group to Independent Force

10.1. The history of protest movements in the Western world has certain characteristics which repeat themselves periodically: at a certain point in the growth of dissent, the forces which nourish it—whether social, cultural, or political—are either co-opted and integrated into the system they oppose, or organize to express themselves directly in civil society and the political process, refusing to be mediated and expressed by the already existent political structures and the established ruling classes. When, in the process of the development of dissent, a movement is formed with the will and the strength to put forward its objectives directly, then one can say that a left exists, which, if not yet at the level of presenting political alternatives to the established structure, is at least able to propose new values.

The distinction between the strategy of placing pressure on the most open elements of the system and the strategy of independent political organization against the system represents one of the major differences which divide liberals from radicals in the Anglo-Saxon world, and which more generally separates progressives from revolutionaries. In the strategy based principally on placing pressure on particular groups within the ruling class, there is an implicit élitist notion which considers balances in power to be relatively stable and the political structures through which the various groups, interests, classes or social strata express themselves to be decidedly neutral. On the contrary, insofar as "left" also means the anticipation of future utopias "here and now," its development calls for actual struggles for new social structures, new instruments of expression and political participation, and the replacement, or perhaps total elimination, of the ruling class, together with a redistribution of decision-making power. This qualitative distinction between pressure groups and left-wing forces is fundamental, particularly in the United States, where one of the causes of the periodic failure of left-wing movements has been their choice of pressure tactics instead of their presenting themselves as alternatives that could directly represent leftist interests and objectives. In recent history, the ruling class—whose political expression takes the form of the two-party oligarchy—has therefore been able to assimilate all those forces which could represent a subversive element to the economic and political system, whether these were the Populist and Progressive movements, the ethnic minorities that formed the poorest classes of the population, the labor movement, or the Communist and Socialist parties. The New Deal of the 1930s and the postwar Democratic administrations, which represented the direct continuation of that policy, were able to incorporate within the same coalition different and mutually opposed economic groups—workers, farmers and corporations—together with other, frequently conflicting political and intellectual groups.[53] In this way, the various forces which arose on the left paid the price of their pressure tactics and their assimilation into the system by having to renounce long-term radical alternatives. In particular, the policy of infiltration and coalition practiced recurrently by the Communist party contributed to its dissolution; reform-Democratic "realism" exhausted all the vital energy of the Socialist party; Henry Wallace's progressivism did

---

53. For a historical evaluation of recent American history, and particularly of the relationship between the labor movement and the ruling class, see William A. Williams, *The Contours of American History* (Chicago: Quadrangle Books, 1961), Part III.

not sink roots into the country, deriving its strength from a coalition of electoral pressure groups that had grown within the Democratic party rather than from an autonomous base; the labor movement during the last twenty years has expressed nothing but the will of its oligarchy, which represents onè of the pillars of the present regime; the various liberal organizations have produced only groups of academicians, intellectuals, technocrats, and experts seeking power within reformed and modernized capitalism, without developing any serious alternatives. In short, the short-range successes and marginal modifications of the system carried out by different left-wing bodies acting as pressure groups, provided the logical premises for the eclipse of radical movements during the 1950s.

10.2.   The new movements in the 1960s, as in the preceding decade, apparently began as a series of pressure tactics applied to the liberal elements of the ruling class. In the South, the activists who demanded civil rights for blacks turned to the followers of Kennedy in Washington; in the North, they searched for those Democratic congressional candidates who would support peace initiatives; even the first of the new student organizations, SDS, arose under the auspices of the social democrats in the League for Industrial Democracy who believed in exercising pressure on the Democratic party. In the Port Huron Statement of 1962, the whole section devoted to building an alternative did nothing but declare the necessity of an alliance among blacks, peace groups, liberal organizations such as Americans for Democratic Action (ADA), publications like *The New Republic*, and the new student groups, with the intention of bringing about a progressive "realignment" of the Democratic party. Such forces for change could express themselves only through the existing structure, whose nonprogressive policies, they believed, were due only to a deviation from a presumably "liberal" historical tradition; the dispossessed groups "could only *ask* for a Democratic party which would take responsibility for their interests," once it had been freed from its racist and conservative elements (emphasis added). The two-party structure, as the principle vehicle for participation in the political process, seemed at the time not only a historical reality, but also a mental habit which set limits even for the new modes of thinking. But the very logic of direct action and nonelectoral organization of the new grass-roots organizations, as well as the contact with the nation's social and economic realities and power structures, helped evolve the new activists' attitudes toward the ruling class. In 1963, the new SDS statement *America and New Era* criticized the liberal groups, pointing to the organization of the "new insurgents" as the main task of the protest movement. In this document, the two lines of action continue to coexist: pressure to effect change in the composition of Congress and the need to rely on the new constituencies. In 1963, out of this same dialectic, the ERAP community-organization projects arose, and the civil-rights movement developed, within which—although not to the same degree—both coalitionist and autonomist trends coexisted. Even in SNCC president John Lewis's defiant speech of that same year **[Lewis, 1.3.]**, one finds the ambivalence between the Southern blacks' firm determination to go off on their own and the need to turn to Northern liberals. It is true that Lewis accused the administration of not living up to its promises and called for a nonviolent revolution which would place power in the hands of the people rather than in the hands of the President, the Justice Department and Congress. But in fact, dialogue still had to be maintained with the interlocutor, upon whom many activists hoped to exercise the greatest possible pressure.

10.3. It was only in the course of 1965 that the autonomist and anticoalitionist position gained the upper hand. In the 1964 presidential elections, Lyndon B. Johnson had succeeded in catalyzing around the Democratic party the widest coalition of groups, interests and forces that had ever been assembled in recent American history. Faced with the danger of the right wing and Senator Barry Goldwater, the consensus surrounding the Democratic center extended from Wall Street to Harvard, from Martin Luther King to Senator Eastland, from social-democrats to their longtime communist opponents (whose ambiguous watchword was "Beat Goldwater"), from the ADA to a section of SDS (whose slogan was "Part of the Way with LBJ"). The politics of national consensus seemed triumphant, and, for the coalitionists of the Movement, real participation in power seemed to have begun with the isolation of the right. After Johnson's victory, Bayard Rustin presented the coalitionist strategy in a manifesto entitled "From Protest to Politics: The Future of the Civil Rights Movement,"* which marked the definitive separation between the two wings of the Movement:

> Neither that movement nor the country's twenty million black people can win political power alone. We need allies. The future of the Negro struggle depends on whether the contradictions of this society can be resolved by a coalition of progressive forces which becomes the *effective* political majority in the United States. I speak of the coalition which staged the March on Washington, passed the Civil Rights Act, and laid the basis for the Johnson landslide—Negroes, trade unionists, liberals, and religious groups.

A partial suspension of protest in the form of demonstrations and direct action was achieved during the electoral campaign, but it was the subsequent political conduct of the Democratic and liberal ruling class which led to the radicalization of the Movement.

The Democratic Convention, August 1964: the MFDP was not accredited; the racists were. Berkeley, Autumn 1964: the entire liberal ruling class of the university, including President Kerr and Professors Lipset, Glazer, and Feuer, was one of the strongest forces of resistance against which the Free Speech Movement had to struggle. Washington, January 1965: the systematic bombardments of North Vietnam were begun. Santo Domingo, March 1965: the Marines invaded the small republic to "prevent a Communist takeover." Staughton Lynd answered Bayard Rustin's appeal with a phrase that scandalized all the moderates of the Movement: "The coalition he advocates turns out to mean implicit acceptance of Administration foreign policy, to be *coalition with the Marines*" (emphasis added).

An alternative to coalition—whether with the liberals or the Marines— was an *independent power base* resting on the mass of "unqualified" people excluded from the decision-making process. The community-organization projects evolved in this direction toward more autonomous grass-roots actions; the first attempts were made, in Berkeley and New York, to organize "free universities"; independent structures like the Child Development Group of Mississippi (CDGM), promoted by people close to SNCC, were set up in contrast to the official welfare programs. The strategy of autonomous organization from below accentuated the impulse toward building a counter-society which, starting from individual projects, would grow large and strong enough to hold "a Continental Congress called by all the people who feel excluded from the higher circles of decision-making in the country.

Commentary, New York, February 1965.

This Congress might even become a kind of second government, receiving taxes from its supporters, establishing contact with other nations, holding debates on American foreign and domestic policy, dramatizing the plight of all groups that suffer from the American system" [**Hayden, 6.2.**].

10.4.   Proposals such as that of Hayden for a "Continental Congress," and initiatives like the "Congress of Unrepresented People" held in Washington in August 1965, represented the climax of the direct-action strategy which had inspired a large part of the Movement's policy during its early years. For the new radicals, "independent politics" combined with direct action, which rested in the hands of anyone wanting to use it as a means of political participation and intervention in social and economic life. Because of the dispersion of power among complicated institutions and the ever-growing complexity of the organization of post-industrial society, direct action was a form of challenge which could attack the system anywhere. Direct action was a method which returned the initiative to the base and escaped the trap of those ideological disputations over "the necessity of deciding everything in advance" which had paralyzed the traditional left. The method proved successful in at least two respects: it mobilized an ever-growing number of citizens who discovered the possibilities for expression as well as the permanently revolutionary nature of direct action and its possible use as an alternative to both "the bloody futility of civil war and the ineptitude of parliamentary procedure."[54]

---

54. Howard Zinn, *op. cit.*, p. 220.

11
Participatory Democracy as Means and as End

11.1. Many different commentators have seen the new American radical movements as nonideological. The statement is true only to the extent that it describes their process of birth and not their development, and only if one means by "ideology" a static, comprehensive theoretical formulation which a political movement refers to in order to derive an answer to all problems. The statement is schematic if one considers the connection between theory and practice, between political actions and the motives that have inspired them; that is, if one looks at the dynamic interrelation between an idealistic inheritance and its incarnation.

In the first development of the new movements there was no common ideological mark. They lacked the two ingredients which constitute an ideological system, i.e., a theory of society, history, and the structural processes which link them, and a theory of the social forces which can serve as protagonists of change in society. The new radical movements were born without any such theories; their action was based on regional analyses and on the need for confronting immediately the serious individual problems which existed in the racial, economic, and civil situation of the country. Dissent and revolt sprang from individual and social malaise; that is, out of a kind of individual and social alienation from prevalent institutions, values and behavior. The spring which set the action in motion (in ways that can be judged as more or less political, according to one's standard) was the need to reaffirm lost values in the name of ideal objectives and moral standards—freedom, community feeling, right to participate, control of one's own life—rather than a positive vision of society and its structures. The Port Huron Statement declares: "We have no sure formulas, no closed theories—but that does not mean values are beyond discussion and tentative determination." In fact, the values referred to are precisely those which motivated the new politics and attempted to restore to them the significance of worldwide human activity. At this point, then, one wonders whether the people who became involved in social and community activities with the intention of determining their direction, did not implicitly fill their own actions with ideological meaning, i.e., with a desire to realize in the present values, institutions, and forms of behavior which were not to be found in reality. It goes without saying that there are various levels of theoretical knowledge and understanding involved in the effort to fuse reality and utopia, i.e., in the proposal of a different vision of life and the world. The main characteristic of the new radicalism lies in the fact that theoretical reflection is nourished mainly by the experience of reality and does not come from a specific intellectual tradition. Action, not elaboration, defines the crucial moment in the development of attitudes. It might then seem that there is a similarity between the anti-ideological character of liberal-technocratic culture and the culture of the new radicals, but this similarity exists in appearance only. Both are based on experience: the theoreticians of "the end of ideology" maintain that ideologies have been surpassed, because they believe there is no longer a need for total reevaluations of reality; that the present politico-economic order is the historical point of arrival for free societies and that, therefore, the only changes that are necessary are those deriving from technological progress. For the new radicals, the "end of ideology" means the rejection of old ideologies which have proved incapable of sustaining radical movements in the country and which have become only excuses for carrying on empty diatribes aimed at covering up their inability to embody the struggle for a different society into the dynamic of history. For this reason they do not believe in theories which may, perhaps, satisfy a facile speculative inclination, but they consider indispensable the faith in one's own direct experience in the process of understanding reality: "If we are correct in believing that the present social order is systematically—not just occasionally—unjust, then we should be able to illustrate our belief by simply *pointing* to the *facts of* American life. If these facts do not support our theories, so much the worse for the theories."[55]

11.2.   There is, nevertheless, a common de-nominator at the basis of the Movement's action; it appears at the moment when values are translated into political actions. The slogan "participatory democracy," which from the beginning has been the inspiring principle of the politico-organizational proposals of the activists, serves at least to illus-trate the common features of the different projects:

> As a *social system* we seek the establishment of a democracy of in-dividual participation, governed by two central aims: that the individual share in those social decisions determining the quality and direction of his life; that society be organized to encourage independence in men and provide the media for their common participation. [**SDS, 5.1.**]

A few answers can be derived from the movement-in-action. It means making it possible at all levels to divide the power to make decisions for and have control over social, economic, and political institutions, among the people who participate in them. Thus, the poor themselves must admin-ister the welfare system; the giant corporations must be responsible to workers and consumers; the mass media must serve all those who want to use them; political candidates must get their financial support from the public; blacks must have access to the means for self-government; students and professors must have the right to determine academic programs; in a word, the citizen must be able to act as the subject of the social contract which binds him to society, and man must have the power to realize fully his own potential. Participatory democracy then seems, in its application, to correspond to the old concept of self-government, enlarged to take in every expression of communal life, in all its organized moments. The prin-ciple seems more like a political philosophy than an ideology, more like a method for inspiring political action in an experimental way than a sys-tematic plan for the society of the future. In practice, the new radicals' attempt has been to realize in the present those social relationships and values of participation which they uphold as parameters for the organiza-tion of tomorrow's society; countercommunities, parallel institutions, and alternative structures to capitalism and bureaucracy represent their effort to bring about through action a synthesis between utopia and the existing reality.

11.3.   The idea of participatory democracy is not new: many people have noted its affinity with "workers' councils," "soviets," and "dual power"—ideas behind which were considerably more sophisticated ideas than those of the new radicals. What seems to be a special feature of the New Left is its emphasis on open methodology applied to different experiments in different contexts instead of its indicating a

---

55. Mario Savio, participating in the debate which Hal Draper opened with the article "In Defense of the 'New Radicals,' " in *New Politics*, Autumn 1965.

preferential and definitive order of socialist society. The participatory method is not a model, but—to use a term that has become widespread in Europe during the past year—it stands for the possibility of *challenging* all the authoritarian knots which develop in any political and economic system. In this sense, the experimental inheritance deriving from the struggles of the American new radicals contributes to the formation of a New Left position, i.e., a historical response to the structures and forces of antifreedom and oppression in the present society.

The failure to realize democracy, under capitalist no less than under communist regimes, has shown itself precisely in the increasing and generalized domination of institutions over the men for whose service they were supposed to have been organized. In the East as in the West, state, economy, parties, mass media and education are increasingly bureaucratized and centralized; they are organized according to principles which uphold the authoritarian and exclude the masses of workers, citizens, militants, and consumers—individuals, in short—from any control. Particularly in the United States, out of liberal ideology and its nonnecessary corollary, capitalism, have grown the worst illiberal structures; from representative democracy, the most flagrant forms of antidemocratic manipulation of the masses; and from affluence have emerged the most powerful bureaucracies and the most subtly oppressive forms of paternalism.

The radical-participatory response to this kind of modern totalitarian structure seems to contain two apparently opposing tendencies, the *libertarian* and the *communitarian-populist.* The participatory method indicates neither the *model* of future society nor the socialist *solution:* its only objective is the historical one of gaining for individuals the possibility of determining their own future. According to this libertarian approach, man must prevail over institutions, and participation is more important than the need for social organization. On the other hand, there can be no participatory democracy without an effective solution to the problem of how communities should be organized; that is, the question of developing common cultural and political experience on different levels of social participation. *Community* conflicts with the concept of *organization,* through which internal cohesion is effected for the purpose of achieving specific objectives with the most efficient division of labor. Here, the principle of the participatory method— the communitarian principle—gives way to the *populist* one, i.e., trust in the innate virtue of the "common people," of those without "qualification," in whose hands—and not those of the "experts"—the destiny of society must be placed.

11.4. "Participatory democracy," without a doubt, has served as a working guide for the new radicals in a situation where it seemed impossible to mobilize creatively and to politicize masses of indifferent, alienated citizens. The method has inspired numerous political actions; it has enriched the internal experience of radical movements by posing problems related to the search for democracy and offering ideas for the development of decision-making processes and the attainment of consensus. The ideal significance of the participatory method lies in its having reminded a society dominated by the "organization man" of the hierarchy of values between "being" and "doing" and between man and the organized mechanisms which he himself constructs. Much remains to be done, in the United States and elsewhere, along this line of political investigation: the problem of liberating man from the slavery of labor and finding means to realize his potential still remains unresolved. Nevertheless, at the same time that political theory and praxis of the left begin again to deal, through the participatory method, with problems already abandoned by the reform-socialism of affluence and forced planning, democratic centralism, and state powers which control from above, the radical movements also have the task of offering historical solutions to new conflicts, such as the growing need for organization with separate functions *vs.* the participatory method; scientific specialization *vs.* humanistic integration; the necessity for making long-range collective decisions *vs.* the necessity for continually challenging those decisions which become hardened into power structures; the responsibilities of self-government *vs.* the kind of community which takes the form of a huge "love-in."

12
Decentralization and Experimentalism for the New

Organizations   **12.1.** In spring 1965, the editors of
Studies on the Left held a debate on the necessity of building a "radical
center." This debate represented the point of arrival for many political and
organizational problems of the new radical movements. On one hand were
the Movement activists who maintained the necessity for developing action
at the grass-roots level, without worrying about joining the new forces into
a national structure—however flexible; on the other hand was the group,
inspired by socialist tradition, which maintained the necessity for proceeding to a phase of unifying and coordinating the various movements which
had arisen from classes or social groups, with those formed around specific
problems and objectives. Both contingents rejected the Leninist structures
of the avant-garde party and democratic centralism; but while the "socialists" felt the time was ripe for a new party which could unify the different
groups around a theory of social change, the "activists" remained interested mainly in liberating energy at the social and individual level: political
energy, which provided the only possible means for challenging the "from
the top down" style of organization characteristic of American society.

The activists' position merely reflects the nature of the Movement itself
and the kind of organizational characteristics which came to be generally
followed within it. SNCC had an extremely flexible structure, composed
basically of two elements: the activists forming both leadership and base,
spokesmen and militants, inspirers and work cadres; and the groups toward
which these activists' work was directed. SNCC fulfilled in the South the
very function of a "radical center" which the editors of *Studies on the Left*
would have wished to create nationally, but SNCC had a special quality: it
lacked an internal political bureaucracy and a separation between "ideologues"
and "militants," and it identified itself, on the outside, with the civil-rights
movement, whose objectives it had been formed to realize. SDS, which from
1965 became the most representative organization of the Movement, possessed the same characteristics. On the campuses, its influence extended far
beyond its membership rolls. Outside the campuses, SDS dedicated itself
to its projects and, through these, enlarged its own radius of action. In
the Movement's other forms—the Berkeley Free Speech Movement, the Fair
Play for Cuba Committee, the Committee to Abolish HUAC, the Vietnam
Day Committee, the Mississippi Summer Project—the pattern was always
that of "nonorganizations" which served at particular moments in the radical
struggles and dissolved as soon as these battles were won. Even the Student
Peace Union, which, among all the organizations formed during the first
years of the 1960s had the most marked political position, dissolved when
the issues of its campaign were no longer central to the radical movement.

The experience of SNCC, SDS, and the SPU, as well as of the FSM
May 2nd Movement, ERAP, the Mississippi Summer Project and the VDC,
contains some politico-organizational characteristics which can be schematized
and summed up in a series of propositions:

The organization did not have a center and a boundary (SDS,
SNCC), but the initiative rested in the hands of local groups; the national structures, if anything, existed simply to facilitate coordination,
communication and exchange of ideas.
At the local level, the organizations did not develop permanent

leaders, stable bureaucracies or hierarchical relationships between leaders and militants.

The work of the activists (SNCC, ERAP) served to build movements which were then to develop their own cadres independent from those of the organizers.

The area of influence of the different groups (SDS, SNCC, SPU) extended beyond the people who were formally considered members. Membership in an organization meant, in practice, being actively present and working during a certain period of time, and not formal affiliation.

The use of *ad hoc* committees to confront specific events or particular issues (FSM, Cuba, HUAC, VDC and M-2-M, with its accentuated ideological characteristics) served to overcome the divisions between different political groups. In forming the *ad hoc* committees, the members of these groups dispersed themselves into specific movements, which then took on an autonomous existence separate from that of the ideologically oriented groups themselves.

Within the permanent organizations (SNCC, SDS) and *ad hoc* movements (FSM, VDC, and, in part, M-2-M), direct democracy was practiced rather than delegated authority; meetings and work groups (called "centrals" in Berkeley) which fulfilled specific functions, were widely used.

Finally, the organizations and committees followed the principle of nonexclusionism, according to which it was not preconstituted ideological affinities that determined membership in organizations, but the specific nature of the organizations' political activity.

12.2.   The policy of exclusionism has been the Achilles' heel of the left. In Europe and the United States, socialists have split up into an indeterminable number of groups and sects because of their ideological disputes, having reduced themselves in numerous and desperate cases to basing their own *raison d'être* on their struggle against the other groups. The communists have always vacillated between Stalinism on the inside and forming front groups on the outside. For this reason, ideological deviations are condemned as heretical, while tactical alliances with groups as far right as possible represent political victory. In addition to its other features, the cold war has been the supreme force for exclusionism, the necessity for belonging, totally and unconditionally, in one camp or another. What characterizes the placement of many of the new radical movements within the New Left is precisely their rejection of ideological Manichaeism and political schematism, i.e., their practice of nonexclusionism. This means that there is no *a priori* formula determining who may or may not belong to the radical movement, and that the agreement between members' political activity and their organizations, and between activists and their movements, depends on how they behave in certain specific situations.

The positive value of this method of organization seems to be confirmed by the fact that many militants of traditional left organizations, who should have "taken over" or "ideologically converted" those of the New Left, have in fact been converted *to* the New Left. The open method of organization, which refuses to renounce discussion when faced with different positions, has shown a vitality which the politico-organizational methods of the traditional left did not achieve.

Three: The Radicalization of the Movement

13

A Mass Movement
Against the War

13.1. On February 7, 1965, the "peace president," Lyndon B. Johnson, began the escalation of the war, opening the way for bombardment of the Democratic Republic of Vietnam. Until then, Southeast Asia was only one among many places in which the United States had taken it upon itself to "contain communist expansion." A few thousand American soldiers and "military advisers" at the side of the South Vietnamese army was just another of the several military contingents scattered around various parts of the globe: a bastion of defense for the free world. Suddenly, the bombardments and continual increase in the numbers of American soldiers sent to Vietnam—from 25,000 in January 1965 to 200,000 in November 1965—aroused a protest movement which may be considered the most important political phenomenon of opposition that developed in the United States after World War II.

Prior to the beginning of the bombardments, there had been no organized opposition, except for a few strongly ideological groups such as the Maoist May 2nd Movement (M-2-M), which took its name from the date of the first demonstration against the war in the spring of 1964. Vietnam had until then not provided a theme for mobilization even among the new radicals involved in the civil-rights campaigns and organization of the poor. When, at the end of 1964, the national council of Students for a Democratic Society decided to sponsor a nationwide demonstration against the Vietnam war to be held the following spring, the initiative seemed destined to involve only small groups of students. Instead, the protest grew quickly after February 1965, and the new radicals found themselves at the center of activities which incorporated increasingly wide sectors of the population.

The antiwar movement presented new characteristics on three different levels: first, its intensity and mobilizing capability grew progressively from 1965 to 1968, expanding far beyond the activist groups themselves; second, its components represented different forces and positions, which were sometimes conflicting; finally, its action had deep and radical repercussions both within the New Left and in national politics.

13.2.   The first teach-in, held at the University of Michigan on March 24, 1965, had the same symbolic significance for the antiwar movement that the Greensboro sit-in of February 1960 had had for the civil-rights movement. Students and professors felt it necessary to bring discussion and protest against the war inside the walls of the academy, since it appeared obvious that there was no other way for them to make their voice heard and no organized political force that could represent an alternative within the traditional channels of the political process.

The Michigan teach-in, in terms of participation, interest, and repercussions, was a success. Within a few weeks and in the course of several months, teach-ins occurred in hundreds of universities, reaching tens, and perhaps hundreds of thousands of students and nonstudents, faculty members and nonacademic people. The May 22 teach-in at the University of California at Berkeley was a high point in the movement. It lasted 36 hours, 35,000 people attended, and the speakers represented the entire spectrum of opposition, from Senator Gruening to a representative of the Maoist Progressive Labor Party (PLP), and included I. F. Stone, Isaac Deutscher, Staughton Lynd, Benjamin Spock, Mario Savio, and Norman Mailer. The teach-ins met with differing reactions: the radicals wanted them to be instruments of protest and, perhaps, civil disobedience through direct action in the universities, whereas the moderates and "neutral" academicians attempted to transform this new form of pressure from below into a "useful tool" of discussion and into a "forum for national debate," in the words of James Reston of *The New York Times.*[56]

By April, the SDS March on Washington indicated the extent to which the protest movement had grown: in addition to SDS and SNCC, the demonstration was joined by both pacifist organizations, such as the Committee for Non-Violent Action (CNVA) and the War Resisters' League (WRL), and groups representing the traditional left, such as the W. E. B. DuBois Club and the May 2nd Movement. Still, the general tone was given by SDS, which refused to practice exclusionism against the communists (as the representatives of the "Democratic left" had demanded) and succeeded, for the first time since the McCarthy era, in assembling 25,000 people at a militant and openly left-wing demonstration [**Potter, 8.2.**]. In August, through the initiative of Robert Parris (Moses), Staughton Lynd, and Dave Dellinger, the Assembly of Unrepresented People was held in Washington for the purpose of declaring peace with the people of Vietnam; that is,

---

56. James Reston, "The Teach-in Could Be a Useful Tool," *The New York Times,* May 17, 1968.

expressing the split between the official government and popular sentiment. From that assembly arose the National Coordinating Committee to End the War in Vietnam, whose purpose was to unite the various antiwar projects and, more specifically, to organize, together with SDS and other local groups, the International Days of Protest which were held in about 100 cities in the following October.

The teach-ins, marches, demonstrations, acts of civil disobedience, and even the self-immolation of the Catholic Roger La Porte and the Quaker Norman Morrison (whose sacrifices, it should be noted, had a great emotional impact on the Buddhists, the Vietcong and the North Vietnamese, although not on American public opinion) succeeded, during the course of 1965, in dramatizing the character of the war. This became *the* national problem for the press and the public, while the number of Movement activists was growing larger day by day. The SDS, which had numbered 30 local groups and 2,000 members before the April march, increased to 125 and doubled the number of its members after the summer. In June it elected to the presidency a *homo novus,* Carl Oglesby, the first national leader who had not been a part of the organization's founding group and who had become politically active only with the antiwar movement. In November, during a march on Washington organized by SANE, in which SDS participated as an independent organization, Oglesby delivered a speech harshly condemning the liberal ruling class and emphasizing its constant element of imperialism [**Oglesby, 5.3.**]. At the end of the year, the first American delegation, composed of the communist historian Herbert Aptheker and the "New Leftists" Staughton Lynd and Tom Hayden, visited the Democratic Republic of Vietnam at the invitation of the local "Peace Committee." In January 1966, SNCC passed a resolution condemning the war and encouraging resistance to military service [**SNCC, 8.4.**].

During the following year there were actions and demonstrations only at the local level, partly as a result of SDS's decision not to adopt a promotional and leadership role in national antiwar activity, but to leave the widest initiative to the local chapters, especially in the field of grass-roots organizing. Between 1966 and 1967, the escalation increased, despite popular pressure, as did the presence of American troops in Vietnam, which doubled in the course of two years (exceeding 400,000 in 1967). The various actions on the city, campus, and local group level converged in April 1967 into two huge national demonstrations organized by the Spring Mobilization Committee in New York and San Francisco. Approximately 250,000 persons participated in the New York demonstration and 70,000 in San Francisco. The speakers included Martin Luther King and Stokely Carmichael — an indication that even the different militant sections of the black liberation movement came together in the protest. During the summer of 1967, the Vietnam Summer project (which seems to have been financed by the group surrounding the Kennedy family) mobilized over 20,000 people who dedicated themselves more to educational work than to protest, in spite of the participation of some radical groups. The following October, all the groups active within the antiwar movement converged on Washington once again. The majority of the participants (several hundred thousand) marched as usual. But the nonviolent pacifists carried out acts of civil disobedience; the militant radical group attempted to invade the seat of military power itself with new tactics inspired both by guerrilla warfare and by aggressive nonviolence.

With the new year and the presidential election campaign, the antiwar movement, while intensifying, converged and mingled with the other movements of opposition. The war itself was being considered less and less as an isolated phenomenon: imperialism, racism and militarism became evident as motifs common to the various institutions and structures of the country during the Columbia University confrontations in April and again during the August convention of the Democratic party in Chicago, where by this time two opposed and irreconcilable positions found themselves face to face.

13.3. The antiwar movement was and still is a composite of distinct groups and elements working together. We have seen how, in the demonstrations, different components were at work and how these components often came into conflict. Thus, in the SDS march in April 1965, the opposition was between exclusionists (who wanted to keep out the communists) and nonexclusionists; in the demonstration in November of the same year, it was between the moderates of SANE and the anti-imperialists gathered around SDS; in the huge New York march of April 1967, a "revolutionary contingent" appeared in opposition to the "official movement" (against the war) and declared their explicit support of liberation movements throughout the world and of the NLF in Vietnam. In 1965, I. F. Stone singled out three main groups from among the principal components of the protest: the *democratic forces,* who wished to win public support for putting an end to the war; the *religious forces* (though many among them were not religious in the conventional sense of the term), who wanted to give witness to their moral disapproval, even by sometimes committing illegal acts; and the *revolutionary forces,* who expressed their solidarity with the Vietcong and believed the only way to achieve peace was by getting rid of the capitalist order.[57] In reality, as the movement evolved, the principal oppositions resulted from a divergence of analyses and proposals, rather than from disagreements about methods of action. On the one hand were those who judged the war as one among many errors, or simply as a degeneration of American foreign policy, and believed that the possibility to end it existed within the framework of the given (although modified) political and military system; on the other hand were those who emphasized that the institutionalized use of force was nothing but an extension of the logic of American expansionism and imperialism. As consequences of these different evaluations, two conflicting proposals were put forward: negotiated settlement of the war, with American participation, or immediate withdrawal of troops in the name of self-determination. However, the more radical position has been growing steadily, not only through the action of the new radicals but also as a reaction to the failure of the policies of the ruling class, which has left increasingly restricted margins for corrections within the "American position."

13.4. The war introduced into American domestic policy elements of crisis and change in the political framework which perhaps no "ordinary" event could have provoked. In 1964, the New Left groups were weak, isolated, and issue-oriented, with an approach that still left room for agreement with liberal forces. By 1968, even though without definite orientation, internal cohesion, and strategic unity, the radical movement had characteristics of a mass movement; having definitively separated itself from reformist forces, it defined itself as anti-imperialist, and its active cadres increased considerably. The peace theme has been substituted with the anti-imperialist and antimilitarist struggle; considerations centered exclusively on Vietnam have begun to yield to analysis and critique of American foreign policy as a whole, and have led, for example, to the recent

---

57. I. F. Stone, *In a Time of Torment* (New York: Vintage, 1968), p. 78.

formation of groups concentrating on Latin America; the North American
Congress on Latin America (NACLA) and Avoid Vietnams in Latin America
(AVILA) are a first indication of concrete work in this direction. Connections are becoming apparent between the counterrevolutionary strategy which
lay behind the intervention in Vietnam and the invasion of Santo Domingo,
between the dispatching of Green Berets to Latin America and the station-
ing of a hundred thousand soldiers in Laos and Thailand, between American
support of the Greek fascist junta through NATO and the assassination
of Ché Guevara. The war, and the domestic crisis it has brought about, has
produced a progressive radicalization of liberal sectors of the society and
has drawn masses of young people—students and nonstudents—to participate
in that political life which seemed, not so long ago, to be the prerogative of a
professional élite or a purely routine exercise of power. Radical change is
no longer a prohibited subject for discussion, and the word "revolution" (for
the time being still only a word) is increasingly invoked by the new activists. The successes, first of Castro and then of the Vietcong, have contributed
to the growth of the idea that the American colossus is vulnerable, even
though neither a prerevolutionary situation nor any prospect for the development of such a situation in the near future exists in the United States.
But the American new radicals feel themselves part of the same front which is
growing in the Third World. It is significant that the SDS—the largest
organization of the New Left—expresses this idea in its introductory pamphlet:

> SDS completely opposes the US Government's immoral, illegal, and
> genocidal war against the people of Vietnam. We insist on the immediate
> withdrawal of all US personnel from that country. Moreover, we see
> the US policy in Vietnam as part of a global strategy for containing revolu-
> tionary change in the "Third World" nations of Asia, Africa, and Latin
> America. Rather than the result of an essentially good government's mis-
> taken decisions, we see the world-wide exploitation and oppression of
> those insurgent peoples as the logical conclusion of the giant US corpora-
> tions' expanding and necessary search for higher profits and strategic
> resources. That system is most properly named imperialism, and we stand
> by and support all those who struggle against its onslaught. They are our
> brothers and sisters, not our enemies.

The repercussions of the war have been evident, beyond the radical
groups, in the national political process. For years political forces in and
around the two parties could not succeed in expressing an organized opposition within the established mechanisms. The "doves" never caused the President significant trouble, while liberals like Robert Kennedy either remained
silent or acompanied their verbal expressions of dissent with declarations
of solidarity with the administration. Nevertheless, after three years of
immobility, something has happened at the top levels of American politics.
Among the events of 1968, it is difficult to assess the influence of the pressure by the new radicals and by those segments of public opinion that have
found autonomous means of political expression. But it is certain that the
candidacy, first of Eugene McCarthy and then of Robert Kennedy, Johnson's
withdrawal from the presidential race and the defeat of the Democratic
party itself must be evaluated in connection with the radical protest, the
antiwar movement, and the other movements outside the official political
system.

14
Black Power Breaks
Off from the
Movement

14.1. In August 1965, the Voting Rights Bill passed, guaranteeing electoral rights to all citizens. Thereafter, the civil-rights movement, whose purpose it had been to attain legal equality for blacks, weakened perceptibly. The other movement, the one led by SNCC, pledged to achieving effective participation in political life for blacks and poor whites through independent organization, evolved toward more radical objectives.

In fact, the advances in civil rights had not touched the masses in the North who were already formally integrated but in actual fact were more segregated than ever. Even the activists' efforts, which had set in motion a process of grass-roots organizing in the South, had not been extended to the Northern black communities, which were economically desperate, socially fragmented, and geographically imprisoned in the urban ghettoes. Racism was not a moral failing of Southern racists, but rather a characteristic of the economic and social structure of the nation, bound to its history and to the development of its prosperity.

> When a racial group is consistently denied its share of available resources and services, a society can be considered racist. Racism refers to the subordinate position one racial group has relative to another. Attitudes and laws often have little to do with whether or not a nation is racist. In a society where racial groups are systematically denied access to social goods, it matters little if people are not "prejudiced" or if laws exist against discrimination. Where racism exists, groups are poor because some people in the society benefit from the poverty of others—not because of prejudiced feelings or unconstitutional actions.[58]

Thus, confronted with a situation in which the legal conquest of civil rights played only a small part in the more general struggle for equality and in which the South occupied only a marginal position with respect to the country as a whole, the Movement organizations—and SNCC above all—had to reconsider the significance of their own activity and find new paths. 1964 had witnessed the betrayal of the Mississippi Freedom Democratic party and then the failure of the Georgia House to validate Julian Bond's election. Thus, even if the blacks were now able to vote in the South, the party structures remained essentially nondemocratic. Therefore, at the beginning of 1966, SNCC began organizing an independent party in a county of Alabama, the Lowndes County Freedom Organization (LCFO), which took as its symbol a black panther and whose object was to attain local power for the blacks who constituted 80 percent of the population of that area.

> We recognize that people aren't impressed by demonstrations: they're impressed by political power . . . so what we're doing is something even Malcolm X was talking about. Political power has to lie within the community. And that's all: North, South, rural, industrial.[59]

---

58. Terence Cannon and David Wellman, "No Hiding Place: White Radicals and the Civil Rights Movement," unpublished manuscript, 1967.

59. Interview with Stokely Carmichael, *The Movement*, San Francisco, February and March 1966.

Predicting the development of an independent political movement, Carmichael was elected president of SNCC in the following April, succeeding John Lewis, who had approved of SNCC's participation in the White House Conference on Civil Rights. Then, in June, during a march across Mississippi to support an independent initiative by James Meredith (who was shot on the second day of his march), the contrast deepened between the Carmichael view, which focused on winning independent power, and the integrationist view taken by civil-rights leaders such as Martin Luther King. The march became a real "walking seminar" on Black Power—the slogan which had been officially adopted by SNCC and which found its first realization in the experiment of the "black panther" party. Following Meredith's march, the significance of Black Power and the aims Carmichael hoped to achieve through the new strategy were gradually clarified.[60] The new direction may be summed up briefly in the following points: (a) the necessity for a political organization which speaks directly for blacks and represents their needs and interests; (b) recognition of the fact that the only effective instrument for participating in the decision-making process is the exercise of power, and not moral arguments; (c) the right of self-defense, due to the ineffectiveness of nonviolence in situations where blacks are threatened and attacked; (d) the need to build a movement based solely on blacks before any coalition can be formed with whites, so as not to run the risk of being absorbed and betrayed; (e) the need for whites to work in their own communities, in order to free themselves from the racism which exists there; and, finally, (f) reconstruction of the black community and its identity, with the rediscovery of its values and the creation of independent political, social, economic, and cultural institutions.

14.2. After expressing the idea of Black Power, SNCC, which had been an important part of the Movement and, together with other racially mixed organizations, laid the foundations for a New Left position, tried to develop an autonomous organization for blacks. At this point, the black liberation movement and the white radical movement separated, developing along autonomous although notably parallel lines. SNCC's autonomy and its search for an independent political strategy merely reflected a basic principle which guided and inspired much of the New Left, i.e., that groups, classes, and individuals must control directly the institutions which affect their lives and which represent vehicles for social change. Thus, after the summer of 1966, SNCC was composed of blacks only and functioned mainly as a platform for Black Power, gradually losing its grass-roots character, while SDS and the other New Left organizations accepted and supported its new direction.

We are not going to give a detailed account of the development of Black Power here, because it is part of the story of the black liberation movement rather than that of the New Left. In addition, it would be extremely difficult to attempt to evaluate it, even briefly, in so limited a space because now, more than two years after its formulation, it appears clear that "Black Power" (in the words of Robert L. Allen, "more than a slogan but less than a coherent ideology") includes different and conflicting ideas. Perhaps it is not too daring to affirm that "Black Power" represented only

---

60. Among the many articles and documents dealing with the initial development of Black Power, in addition to the interview in *The Movement* which we have already mentioned, see in particular: Lerone Bennett, Jr., "Stokely Carmichael, Architect of Black Power," *Ebony*, July 1966; Anne Braden, "The SNCC Trends: Challenge to White America," *The Southern Patriot*, May 1966; Interview with Stokely Carmichael, *The National Guardian*, June 4, 1966; S. Carmichael, "What We Want," *New York Review of Books*, September 22, 1966.

a point of departure for a new movement which only now (1968) seems to be evolving toward more concrete forms of organization at the base of the social structure. Under the umbrella of the slogan many different plants have bloomed, even though almost all of them have the common features of searching for a new sense of identity for the black communities and attempting to build political, economic, and social structures that will help bring about self-determination. There are many points on which different groups are not in agreement; among these is the question of the relationship to whites, which we would like to examine in particular.

14.3.   Certain groups and leaders seem to embrace the strategy of "black united fronts," either from an estimation of how to gain power at the local level or from analyses which view the future of the United States and the world in terms of an inevitable conflict between oppressed colored peoples and oppressor white peoples [**Carmichael, 9.2.**]. These strategies seem to lead logically to separatism, even though it appears under different forms from the separatism traditionally based on geographical concepts. Others [**Newton, 9.5.**] distinguish between revolutionaries and reactionaries within the black nationalist movement and see the possibility for an alliance with whites, once the black community has become united and after the white radicals have actually closed ranks in the struggle on the side of the oppressed. This latter position, held by the Black Panther party (BPP) of California, permitted the formation of an alliance between that party and the Peace and Freedom party (PFP), composed mainly of whites, during the 1968 elections. This was the first coalition of its kind, which—although it failed on the electoral level—seems to indicate when and how it is possible to undertake this type of collaboration in the future. In the first place, the BPP of California is probably the first Black Power organization to have taken root in the social soil of the ghetto (Oakland). Secondly, the PFP, during its one year of existence, has also come to represent a grass-roots force capable of mobilizing large groups of radicals around concrete struggles, including those against racism in local institutions. Finally, the coalition was realized on the basis of each group's respect for the organizational autonomy of the other and on each group's defining the boundaries of the political initiatives it was capable of undertaking. Therefore, this first attempt at cooperation has been energetic and effective, insofar as it has been based on political action aimed at the outside rather than on futile discussions, such as those carried on at the National Conference on New Politics in Chicago in September 1967 and at the Freedom and Peace Party convention in New York, on the question of whether to grant 50 percent of the vote at these meetings to each racial group.

It is impossible to predict what developments will occur in the alliances between the only two groups presently challenging the "American system." In actions such as those which took place at Columbia University, the activists of Students for a Democratic Society and Students for an Afro-American Society found themselves side by side (although each group used independent tactics) in an attack on imperialist and racist institutions. In Chicago, the demonstrations against the Democratic Convention involved whites only. It is certain that a crisis, which may well be growing, is investing both the black liberation movement and the New Left. Repression is no longer being leveled only against the ghettoes in revolt, but also against the rebels of the middle class; the attempt by the ruling class to control or co-opt with increasingly sophisticated methods at its disposal is being leveled against ghettoes, universities, and militant organizations of every kind. On the other hand, disillusionment brought about by the failure to effect change and fulfill short-range objectives is growing steadily, and it is possible that a gradual process of alienation will occur among masses of young whites and blacks, who may give up the long, hard, and constant work of political organizing which the situation requires. If the possibility of radical change in the "American system" does exist, however, it can only come about through the collaboration of these two groups.

15

Draft Resistance: Individual Action or Mass Political Strategy?

15.1. The movement to resist the draft, distinct from the antiwar movement but related to it, developed in 1967 and 1968. The bombardments and other atrocities committed in Vietnam had the effect of awakening the American middle class, forcing it to search for the connections between the war's immorality and its political causes. At the same time, the radical minorities had developed new analyses which clarified the militarist, imperialist nature of American domestic and foreign policy and the close relationship between this policy and the academic institutions. But the point at which the war directly touched young men of every condition was military service, through which the war machine came into contact with the lives of hundreds of thousands of individuals directly or indirectly affected by the new developments in Vietnam.

There had always been resistance against conscription carried on by individuals with certain religious backgrounds or inspired by strong moral feelings, such as the Quakers and pacifists who had supported conscientious objection. In addition, during World War II and the Korean War there had been a resistance which went beyond religious and moral boundaries, but it had not assumed the proportions or characteristics of the new movement which broke out in 1967. This new movement depended on the active involvement of masses of young people and represented at the same time a means both for individuals to challenge the authoritarianism of existing institutions and for the radical movement to confront the forces of the status quo.

15.2. Although in 1964, 1965, and 1966 opposition and resistance to the draft had been nourished by the war, the resistance was still carried out on an individual, nonorganized, and relatively small-scale basis. The first serious move to refuse national military service was probably in the We Won't Go group, a pledge which became the motto of the resistance. It was coined at the beginning of 1964 by the May 2nd Movement, which was motivated by explicit opposition to the war and by the call to support the Vietnamese peoples' struggle for independence, although M-2-M reaffirmed the obligation to defend the country [**We Won't Go, 10.1.**]. In spring 1965, there were a few calls to refuse induction, such as the petition, signed by the leaders of the peace movement, which appeared in *Liberation*. These met with little success, while the symbolic burning of a few draft cards immediately led to the passage of a law making the act punishable as a crime. The case of David Mitchell—who for some time had been dedicated to antimilitary organizing with a group called End the Draft (ETD) and to the publication of the newsletter *Downdraft* and who burned his draft card during the Fifth Avenue Parade in New York—was particularly significant in that, as part of his defense for refusing military induction, he invoked the principle of the Nuremberg Trials. In June 1966, three soldiers stationed at Fort Hood—D. Mora, J. Johnson and D. Samas, thereafter known in the movement as the Fort Hood Three—challenged orders they had received, on the basis of the illegality of the war in Vietnam. But it was only during the second half of 1966, with the increase of individual cases of draft refusal, that people began discussing the necessity for organizing a resistance movement which would have political significance and be able to play a part in ending the war. In August, at DeMoines, Iowa, prior to a meeting of the SDS national council, two proposals were put forward: mass demonstrations supporting noncooperation, with between 100 and 500 young men burning their draft cards, and the organization of unions and communities of draft resisters formed on the local level around the idea of refusing military service and encouraging others to do the same. In December, the SDS national council approved the second proposal, declaring its own opposition to any form of conscription because of its coercive and antidemocratic character.

The first manifestation of open and collective violation of the law took place in New York's Central Park, before the April 1967 march organized by the Spring Mobilization Committee; 175 young men publicly burned their draft cards in response to the appeal launched by a draft-resistance group, among whom were some SDS members, thus partially fulfilling the plan for a collective action which was to have involved 500 young men. In spring 1967, independent from SDS and the attempts made by local SDS chapters to build a grass-roots movement around the draft issue, autonomous groups of resisters arose which emphasized noncooperation and open confrontation with government and military institutions, inviting the resisters to form a movement of mutual solidarity [**Resistance, 10.2.**]. The various organizations which comprised it were merely furthering a trend that had considerable following among young people, both students and nonstudents, and offering a point of reference for those who opposed conscription and desired at the same time to give a radical and collective meaning to their action. The Resistance was organized in the Bay Area in February 1967, and its appeal took the form of an explicit invitation to oppose not only the war in Vietnam, but also all wars and military adventures, with direct action against the government—action not limited merely to protest, but which would build a real, meaningful resistance movement. At the same time the Resistance was formed in San Francisco, other groups arose: New England Resist in Boston, Cadre in Chicago, Draft Denial in New York, and other affiliated or supporting groups such as Support in Action, The Committee for Draft Resistance, the Boston Draft Resistance Group, and the Wisconsin Draft Resistance Union, some of which joined nationally in May during the Student Mobilization Conference in Chicago. The result of this new independent movement appeared on a large scale the following October with the first Stop the Draft Week, during which 1,400 draft cards were collected in 18 cities and returned to the local and national officials of the Selective Service System.

The thought behind "resistance" and confrontation with government and military institutions has manifested itself in different ways. In Oakland, California, the week of demonstrations in front of the induction center ended with a confrontation between police and demonstrators who applied actual tactics of urban guerrilla warfare. Hundreds of people were arrested and seven of the organizers were indicted for conspiracy—the first time this law was applied to antiwar demonstrations. In December, at a sit-in in front of the New York induction center, 70 more individuals were arrested, including Dr. Benjamin Spock. Together with four other men—Yale Chaplain William Sloan Coffin, the Institute for Policy Studies Co-chairman Marcus Raskin, organizer Michael Ferber and writer Mitchell Goodman—Dr. Spock was indicted for counseling young men to evade military service and interfering with the administration of the Selective Service System. It was a perfect example of a trial for crimes of opinion, and its intent was clearly repressive. The gathering of 600 draft cards in over 30 cities in December was followed by different episodes of resistance—burn-in, turn-in, refusal to be inducted, complicity statements and more—which demonstrated the growing tendency toward mass resistance. This culminated in the antidraft weeks of April and November 1968, during which more than 2,000 cards were collectively sent in to the Selective Service office.

Even inside the armed forces themselves an organized resistance arose; the sporadic episodes which have been made public are very revealing. In the second half of 1968, the movement's attention turned to the soldiers and their condition as individuals subjected to an authoritarian structure. There was a GI march in San Francisco in November 1968, a GI week, and special newspapers were distributed among servicemen.

15.3. How large the draft-resistance movement is and how many people are in some way active in it is a question that cannot be answered precisely, because the resistance takes many different forms. A first group consists of traditional conscientious objectors with religious or moral motivations, those who ask to do alternative service and those who struggle to find legal solutions. A second group consists of real resisters who have taken or are taking action to oppose the law at various stages in the process of conscription; it includes draft-card burners, young men who send their cards in to the federal offices, those who refuse to register with the Selective Service or to appear for induction, and those who have chosen to go into hiding. The third group comprises men already in the armed forces who resist by deserting, going AWOL, etc. Finally, there are the draft resisters who have emigrated to Canada and the small groups which have formed in Europe. If it were possible to sum up the different categories, the result would be an impressive figure of hundreds of thousands of young men involved in the resistance. Among these, of course, there are many who take action out of pure self-interest, but the active nucleus is composed of people who are developing an independent movement, starting from different positions. There are pacifists moved by the moral need to dissociate themselves from any responsibility for the criminal acts of the government, who are led to practice individual witness and nonviolent civil disobedience. There are the political activists who conceive of the resistance essentially as a strategy for combating the existing order and its institutions, including the military structures. Finally, there are the organizers who are attempting to build, around this issue of national importance, a radical movement founded on those groups affected directly or indirectly by the draft.

Politically, the movement represents a potential more than an organized force. Its future is tied both to the developments of the war and to the application of the new laws, which are aimed at students and deprive them of the privileged position they have enjoyed up until 1968. The most important effects of the resistance do not act on a collective but an individual basis and affect the lives of a certain number of young men who have passed from "normal" situations to illegal ones, perhaps even gone to jail. For them, as in general for all moderates particularly sensitive to moral arguments, the resistance is a radicalizing experience which is certain to have repercussions in the future. In fact, one of the most important discoveries which the antidraft movement has publicized is the true nature of the Selective Service System (SSS) whose permanent task is to recruit and control manpower for an economy organized to fulfill military objectives. The SSS's main function is to maintain a card file on several tens of millions of citizens not directly subject to military service, classifying their attitudes, occupations and all other information necessary for maintaining an efficient instrument of social control in the hands of a ruling élite.

In all technologically developed nations, the state is taking on new authoritarian forms which are more sophisticated but are not necessarily less oppressive than those of the old-style fascism. If, in the United States, the antidraft movement could succeed in dismantling the SSS, it would contribute to the defense of the individual against authoritarian structures.

16
Student Power
Arrives

16.1. Berkeley had been the scene of the first mass release of the tension present in American universities. This revolt was the result of the convergence of the civil-rights campaigns outside the campus and opposition to the liberal bureaucracy on the inside; its slogan, "Free Speech," had established a connection between the academic world and the external world. After Berkeley, a myriad of other events repeated the great revolt in rhythm with national events and the actions of the Movement; the issues were the war, poverty, Black Power, resistance to the draft, anti-imperialism. The students who participated in and organized these campaigns worked principally as organizers of other social groups or as activists in struggles of a general character which were not necessarily connected to their status as students. Nevertheless, with the expansion of the radical movement and the increase of issues around which political work was relevant, students began to discover that the university was a microcosmic reproduction of all the characteristics of the society and its power structures, which, whether it was a question of war or racism, of the capitalist system or the controlling apparatus, always had their counterparts within the university. This is why, even when the challenge was directed toward general issues, it came naturally to concentrate on the university.

The radical group which seized upon this tendency to act upon the direct interest naturally present among the students was the one which had gravitated toward the SDS since 1966 and attempted to formulate a theoretical interpretation of the phenomenon. In his pamphlet, "Toward A Student Syndicalism," SDS national vice-president Carl Davidson stated the need to build a student movement to control universities, applying fully the concept of participatory democracy and taking as his model the syndicalism of the IWW ("Wobblies"), which in the past had fought for "workers' control." Then a group of SDS "neo-Marxists" produced a document on "the new working class,"[61] in which they offered an analysis of the American system and the role played in it by university-trained workers. Gregory Calvert, SDS president, gave a talk at Princeton in February 1967 in which he outlined further the need to organize students "as a group" according to a radical and revolutionary strategy:

> Students are the "trainees" for the next working class and the factory-like multiversities are the institutions which prepare them for their slots in the bureaucratic machinery of corporate capitalism. We must stop apologizing for being students or for organizing students. Students are in fact a key group in the creation of the productive forces of this super-technological capitalism. . . . No individual, no group, no class is genuinely engaged in a revolutionary movement unless their struggle is a struggle for their own liberation. [**Calvert, 16.1.**]

Thus students were urged to re-evaluate the university as a mechanism necessary to the productive system of the nation, subjected as such to a process of capitalist socialization whose control has been extended to cover other areas besides that of production. Therefore, it became the task of the Movement to attack the system within the university itself and to develop

---

61. The document, about 60 typewritten pages, has not been published in full (a portion was published in 1967 in *New Left Notes*). It is entitled "Towards a Theory of Social Change in America," signed by David Gilbert, Robert Gottlieb, and Gerry Tenney, and dated January 23, 1967; it is also known among new radicals as the "Port Authority Statement," a parody of the title of the first SDS manifesto.

a class consciousness among those students who comprised the "working class" of the new economic structure.

16.2.   In April 1968, a new student revolt broke out at Columbia University. Tension had been building at Columbia prior to the revolt. In November 1966, a local chapter of SDS had been organized on the campus by students who saw the university as a place conducive to carrying on political work. The SDS chapter incorporated the themes around which the various single-issue organizations had been active (CORE for civil rights, the Independent Committee against the War, and ACTION for university matters) into a unifying framework. In the past there had been demonstrations, petitions, sit-ins, and other forms of student action against recruitment by the CIA and the Marines on campus, the university's submitting students' grades to the draft boards for classification purposes, the construction of a gymnasium on land traditionally used by the black community of Harlem, and, finally, the university's connections with the Institute for Defense Analysis (IDA)—action for which six SDS and Resistance leaders had been prosecuted.

In each of these actions, the customary bureaucratic channels set up to give students a chance to make their voices heard had failed to work. The administration had simply ignored the students' demands and had frustrated all their attempts to widen the decision-making process in university affairs. The revolt which began on April 23 was, therefore, the logical culmination of the action of preceding months and years. The demands were simple: (1) End all university ties with the IDA; (2) stop the construction of the gymnasium on Harlem land; and (3) hold open hearings with full rights of due process for the six students incriminated for their role in the protests against the IDA. The administration's response to these demands was to take refuge behind a facade of formalities; its decisions boiled down to the banning of demonstrations on campus. At this point, the students' exasperation and sense of the impotence of peaceful demonstrations threw them into a new form of direct action. The demonstrators occupied one building, tore down the fence surrounding the construction site of the gymnasium, and then seized the president's and other offices. The group leading the occupation of the offices consisted of only a few hundred activists at first, but several thousand students eventually participated. An emergency committee was set up on the completely paralyzed campus: one building was completely taken over by blacks of Students for an Afro-American Society, acting in the name of Harlem; in other buildings, communes were formed which functioned simultaneously as self-governing bodies and experiments in communal living. A strike committee was formed to coordinate activities and supervise negotiations between the different groups; at first, it was made up of representatives from the groups occupying the university buildings and then of delegates chosen by all groups of over 70 people who took action to support the strike.

Faced with wide participation in an unexpected action, the administration used force to regain control of the campus. The president called in the police, who cleared out the occupied buildings and turned viciously on students and spectators alike. Hundreds of persons were injured and 720 were arrested. A general strike followed, and students organized "liberated classes" outside university property. In collaboration with residents of the adjoining neighborhood, students occupied university-owned buildings destined for demolition to make room for new buildings that Columbia was constructing as speculative ventures.

Two months of strikes, occupations, and battles resulted in the administration's complete discrediting. In concrete terms, the events at Columbia ended with the prosecution of 1,100 individuals, suspension and warning of several hundred students, a divided faculty partly aligned against the administration, and the dismissal of classes before the end of the academic year.

16.3. The issues of the Columbia revolt were the racism, imperialism, militarism, and manipulation present within the university.[62] Racism, because the construction of the gymnasium on Harlem land is only one among many instances of the university's expansion into the surrounding neighborhood and of its policy of real-estate speculation carried out to the injury of the poor nonwhites living there. Imperialism, because of the way the international-studies programs are conceived and of the close relationship between national intelligence agencies and the university's personnel and institutes. Militarism, because of the direct services rendered by the university to research and development for the military complex (the extent of these services is shown by the university's budget, 40 percent of which comes from government projects; half these projects are of a secret nature). Manipulation, because all the effective power of the university's administration rests in the hands of the trustees—a ruling élite extraneous to the academic world and its interests.

These structural characteristics of Columbia are no different from those of the new American university in general. Revolt broke out there as the result of a series of concomitant circumstances (the nearness of Harlem, the urban character of the campus, the political climate of New York, and the work of an able and well-prepared SDS chapter); but it could have occurred at any of the other great educational and research complexes, public or private. It is true that the new American university functions as a service in the "public interest," but this service benefits a system whose values are not to be questioned. Within the compass of the new American university, the true significance of "academic freedom" (a term often invoked to condemn the actions of the new radicals) is freedom to organize a small area of teaching or research within a system whose general directives and goals are taken for granted. It is for this reason that teaching and studies are becoming increasingly specialized, fragmented and departmentalized, following criteria for the division of labor similar to those dictated by the economic laws of industrial and postindustrial society. And since the social and economic structure of American society is increasingly governed, in its broadest outlines, by military interests and those connected to the expansion of the capitalist system, centered on specialized needs of modern corporations for scientific research and rational planning, it is not surprising that the universities also follow and reflect every aspect of this tendency.

At this point, we must ask ourselves whether any effect can be made on the society by grass-roots action by students and teachers who are demanding real "academic freedom"—the chance to form academic institutions which conform to their interests and objectives. The slogan "Student Power" represents an attempt to answer this question. The action at Columbia was only the most clamorous episode in a long series of attempts to gain "student power," starting with the fight against the presence of representatives of the Dow Chemical Company on university campuses, to the Berkeley

---

62. The documentation of these characteristics of Columbia is collected in a pamphlet entitled "Who Rules Columbia?" edited by NACLA; a few selections from the pamphlet are included among the documents in the following section of the book. It should be kept in mind that much of the information contained in the pamphlet derives from official documents of the university president, examined during the occupation.

strike of December 1966 against military recruiting, to the Harvard antiwar teach-in in which McNamara was forced to participate, to the occupation of San Francisco State College in November 1968, which demanded a real self-determination for black and Third World students in the college programs, departments, and structures.

Thus, for universities as well as for other institutions, the questions of what revolution is and whether it is possible to effect radical changes in a single thread of the social fabric poses itself at two levels. On one hand, we must recognize the strict relationship between the structures of a single institution and the general structures of the society. Specific structures can change their nature only to the extent that the general ones can be made to do the same. On the other hand, we must admit that the quality of truly radical change depends on the way various social institutions are used, and the way in which individuals, groups, and classes succeed in playing an active part in their control. The two processes of transformation—the one coming from the top (or, as it is more commonly expressed, the seizure of power) and the one starting at the bottom (changing social relationships) —dynamically intersect in all revolutionary processes.

It appears that "student power," because of the educational role it plays and its strategy of attack against particular problems in the university, responds mainly to the second process necessary for the development of radical action. At the same time, it is a means of liberation for students, in the sense that it is redefining the concepts by which educational structures should be guided and is beginning the task of gaining control from below— an attempt to make partial self-government a concrete reality.

Four:
Beyond Politics—Social
Revolution?

17
Something Is
Happening

17.1. Although the various movements of the past three years must be considered individually, they are all expressions of a common context: the formation of a new culture and politics opposed to the existing order in the United States. If we wish to go beyond the mere succession of events and the phenomenology of the antiwar, antidraft, Black Power, and student power movements, we must ask a number of questions about how and why dissent, protest, resistance, and a new "life-style" are developing.

What actually is this Movement of which an entire segment of America's younger generation feels itself a part? Is it an abstract and metaphysical phenomenon for those in search of an identity, or can it also be considered the expression of new historical forces capable of bringing about profound changes in the society and its institutions? How widespread is the Movement, and how many people are involved in it? What kinds of individuals, which groups and classes participate in this new dimension of culture and politics? What is the importance of the Movement as a whole; what repercussions does it have on the political structures and social and economic order of American life? What do the new radicals want? What is the New Left? Is a revolution in the process of developing? Although our approach is essentially political, we should, in order to answer these questions, consider three different levels of analysis and evaluation:

1. *Psychological:* concerning transformation occurring in the realms of "life-style," morality, and culture within a few groups in the society, and the consequent repercussions on the manner of looking at the social order in general.

2. *Social:* concerning the formation of new social institutions in opposition or as alternatives to those of the existing order.

3. *Political:* regarding the development of analyses and strategies about the entire societal order and the organization of forces capable of bringing about changes in the structures of power.

The phenomena of each of these three levels are not really separate and distinct. In the Movement they exist side by side, interact, and sometimes come into conflict with one another. The reasons for the development of certain actions are sometimes psychological, at other times social or political, but most often all three levels are involved, because protest and the search for alternative values spring from a "one-dimensional" society in which not only have all the organized left-wing forces been rendered impotent in the past, but also where attempts have been made to make values, instincts, and behavior conform to accepted patterns, as we have already pointed out. The process of individual liberation from the oppression of uniformity and conformity often leads to the formation of new social structures in which different relationships between individuals are made possible, and to organized political action for the purpose of transforming power structures. The very dynamic of the Movement and the development of the New Left indicate the simultaneous presence and evolution of all three elements—psychological, social, and political—during the period from the beginning of the 1960s until today. Political action during this period moved through a cycle: originally it was principally motivated by moral considerations and a sense of individual commitment (civil rights, peace, and free speech); then it became collective and community-oriented (participatory democracy), and finally it took on a more specifically political character in the classical sense, with the establishment of a struggle for power at different levels. Nevertheless, the three levels of transformation still remain tightly connected and often complement one another. The Movement must be seen precisely as this open process which affects public and private, psychological and political life. The New Left, with its strong leaning toward experiment, attempts to express all of this in a political praxis which is meant to give direction to the ongoing process of change.

17.2. We must look briefly at the composition of the Movement if we are to understand its social roots.

The first group of insurgents is made up of college and university students, who no longer represent an élite coming from restricted groups, but constitute in themselves an entire segment of the social structure. Before the war, there were no more than a million and a half college and university students in the United States; by the mid-1950s, the number had grown to about 2.7 million, and in 1968 there were over seven million, i.e., nearly three percent of the whole population. Campus life makes them a mass of individuals virtually separate from the rest of the population, with their own cultural needs which relate both to their situation as young people and to the nature and level of the education they receive. Their concentration within certain limited areas creates a completely special situation in which they develop interpersonal relationships particularly intense in degree of change and growth, and collective activities that express ideas, values, and general interests which the very process of "studying" and "learning" makes them respond to more deeply than would occur elsewhere.

The second group of protestors is that of the "dropouts." We use this term here to indicate the wide spectrum of all those who, out of either desire or necessity, are outside of those educational, productive, or social processes considered "normal." It includes those young people—about one-third of the total number—who leave school before they are eighteen years old, one-quarter of nonwhite and one-sixth of white youths who, at the beginning of the normal working age (eighteen and nineteen years), are unemployed and in danger of remaining chronically out of work; the one-third or more of students who drop out of colleges or universities because they feel their education is irrelevant and finally all those who deliberately choose not to become involved in permanent productive activity and get along in one way or another, through temporary or part-time marginal jobs.

This wide and heterogeneous category also includes the hippies. The period when they attracted the greatest publicity, the summer of 1967 (when several hundred thousand dropouts converged on the psychedelic meccas of Haight-Ashbury in San Francisco and New York's East Village) is now past, and the "flower children" are dispersing into small groups scattered over different areas of the country. But in spite of the numerical smallness of this nonmovement, the phenomenon has a strong emblematic importance. The New Bohemia, above and beyond its leaders, is the visible reflection of a state of mind which exists on a more or less conscious level in groups larger than that of the hippies and signifies a psychological break with "one-dimensional" society.

Finally, the third social source of the Movement is the group of adults inside the middle-class melting pot, who are engaged in more or less skilled and well-paying productive activities but do not actively participate in decision-making processes because of their subordinate positions and the centralized structure of the institutions in which they work. Among these we can include teachers, scientific workers at the intermediate level, technicians, and small professionals. The members of this social group, unlike the dropouts, feel the need to have a place in the productive process and to put their intellectual and technical abilities to creative use; they constitute that "new working class" which is numerically expanding in modern society and is finding increasing moral dissatisfaction and decreasing power to control its own activity.

17.3.   Although their sociological conditions, relationships to the economic structure, and ideal objectives are very different, the protestors who come from these different categories—students, dropouts, and the "new working class"—have nevertheless a common characteristic which draws them to protest against and reject the existing order. This characteristic is the rejection, on an individual level, of the American way of life in general and of all the by-products generated by the "system": affluence (enjoyed at the expense of a poor minority) carried to preposterous lengths by the vicious cycle of consumption; education, with its effects of mass stultification and its efforts to make individuals conform to stereotyped models; the undifferentiated use of erotic messages, accompanied by sexual repression and double moral standards; the cult of ownership and the accompanying loss of strong emotional ties with people.

This unity of negation which characterizes the new protest does not go against the democratic values proclaimed by American rhetoric, but against what Paul Goodman calls the "Empty Society," i.e., the incapability of a society at the height of its collective wealth and technological development to bring about conditions of greater material and spiritual freedom.

The unity on positive issues is more vague, although certain major goals are shared widely throughout the Movement. One of these is the rediscovery of the "worldly" value of life, which some have referred to as a "new hedonism," but which can be summed up more accurately as realization "here and now" of all possible conditions of happiness and freedom in a world liberated from the former slavery of labor and struggle against nature. There is also the need for total participation in the life of a community where education, work, and intelligence can be utilized for other than purely materialistic ends. There is the search for new relationships of individuals to one another and of individuals to institutions, relationships not dictated by purely functional needs but by more truly human values.

On the other hand, there are many basic disagreements. If it is possible to proceed to a generalization in a field where there is a great variety of positions and goals, we can use two conceptual categories as means of interpretation. On one hand, there are those who believe that the revolution needed today is a psychological one, and that the movement it is necessary to build must have an exclusively spiritual character. On the other hand, there are those involved in organizing political forces and changing the power relationships in the society, and their goal is the transformation of institutions.

Those who make up the first group, best exemplified by the psychedelic movement, although they represent an attitude that is also widespread elsewhere, reject politics, which is "used to gain power," and seek a "deeper vision of themselves and society." Although it is not accepted by all of them, their general philosophy may be summed up in the slogan "Turn On, Tune in, Drop Out," a process which is to be followed up by the building of a new society through nonpolitical means. "What we need to realize is that there can be, shall we say, a movement . . . a stirring among people . . . which can be *organically* designed instead of *politically* designed. It has no boss. Yet all the parts recognize each other in the same way as the cells of the body all cooperate together."[63]

The members of the second group, the "political" people, are those who developed all the organized movements we have discussed in the preceding chapters.

17.4.   If we leave aside the various phenomena which become fashionable for a brief period only and those aspects of the Movement which are quickly incorporated into the advertising arsenal of consumer industry and the "swinging" style of public relations of Madison Avenue, a "life-style" can be seen to emerge from a significant portion of the new generation which, on the individual level, expresses itself in the search for a new morality and, on the collective level, in the form of a youth subculture or even a real counterculture.

In all the different components of the Movement, it seems that barriers between private and public life are being broken down, i.e., that the continuity between the psychological and social (or political) moments of existence is being affirmed. It is no accident that for many new radicals the choice of political involvement has coincided with the abandonment of fixed professional careers and "traditional" family groups and with the acceptance of prospectives which, not rarely, lead to prison sentences. Double standards,

63. Alan Watts, "Changes," *San Francisco Oracle*, February 1967. The conversation among Allen Ginsberg, Timothy Leary, Gary Snyder, and Alan Watts, published in the *Oracle*, is the most important document on the coexistence of completely different goals and tendencies within the psychedelic movement itself.

which in so many respects are an accepted condition of "normal" life, are rejected on every level. In this sense, the experimentation in the realms of sex and drugs, and particularly the open affirmation of their morality, are part of the necessary psychological break from prevalent modes of behavior, even though new values have not yet completely replaced the old ones. A tradition consistently based on the rejection of sex and pleasure, which were seen as negative things, is being replaced by the notion of the body itself as an integral element of the human patrimony. The widespread practice of cohabitation among young people seems to recall—on the level of custom rather than of ideological awareness—the old practice of the anarchists and socialists of the last century, who proved by their own way of living that they assumed individual responsibilities outside and beyond the institutions of the bourgeoisie. Experience with drugs, in itself, is really nothing but a means of accelerating the process of breaking with the past and searching for a genuine "inwardness" which social pressure constantly rejects in favor of a series of models for behavior. Marijuana has been the sign of rebellion, first of all, against the ethic of work and success which require control, outside discipline, and double standards. "Anything that can be done chemically can be done in other ways. You don't need drugs to get high, but drugs do serve as a useful shortcut at certain stages of the training."[64] And this is precisely what the new generations are doing: looking for a shortcut to the transformation of personality structure and the building of a "new man."

Part of this new morality also consists of a wide search for specific qualities and values typical of different human conditions—sex, age, race— and for a reevaluation of them in the kind of society where there can be no dominant groups and modes of behavior. It is within this framework that one must consider the demands of young people and women for a role in society not defined in relation to the prevalent adult and male culture. Young people are making demands in the realms of economic opportunities, political rights, and social participation. The Women Liberation Movement **[Jaffe and Dohrn, 12.3.]** is, in turn, organized around all those aspects of life in which women in today's society are exploited, treated like consumer items and thrown back on activities considered "proper." Here also, as in other aspects of the Movement, psychology and politics are fused and the struggle for individual liberation coincides with a more general singling-out of the oppressive structures of the productive system.

The youth subculture or counterculture expresses all these attempts and experiments at the collective level. This culture has not yet taken a precise form, and for this reason passing fads and lasting values exist side by side: pop music, with its existential rhythms and its participatory potential, together with forms of dress and appearance which call attention to regained individuality; the tendency toward mysticism and Oriental cults which place their emphasis not on good and evil but on the discovery of a deeper self, together with rejection of material consumption and opposition to all technological development. These are all signs of a search taking place at the cultural level, a symptom more than a statement of opposition to the system of ethics some have identified with the "Western Judeo-Christian tradition, including Marxism, which has led to moral bankruptcy" **[Snyder, 1968, 13.3]**.

More generally, we may say that what is taking place is a process of redefinition of behavior, instincts, values, attitudes and mores, i.e., a collective process of building a new identity.

---

64. William Burroughs, "Academy 23: A Deconditioning," *Village Voice*, July 6, 1967.

18
Toward a
Parallel Society
18.1. A strong tendency to work outside of and in opposition to existing institutions pervades the Movement. This tendency manifests itself in diverse actions which have varying purposes; sometimes these begin before politics itself has been formed, creating the premises for its development. At other times, the actions are undertaken to complement political actions of a general nature, in an attempt to transform institutions and create new ones which can embody "here and now" that ideal of new values and new life-style which we have discussed before. At other times, finally, creating *ex novo* communities or institutions is the very means of rejecting not only the existing society but also any attempt to become involved in changing it.

We have already noted that, from the time of the first appearances of the new movements, "freedom schools" were begun in the South [**Lynd, 1.4.**]; in the North there were attempts at community organizing, and after the Berkeley revolt a free university was organized which soon became the model for other projects of the same type. These examples, in addition to being specifically alternative in content, were also concrete applications of the "participatory democracy" which at the time provided the methodological reference for the new radicals.

With the development of the new movements and the formation of more specific social groups than those the early "populist" phase of the New Left had concerned itself with, the idea of parallel or alternative structures also evolved.

In their own way, even the hippies are creating their own counter-communities: groups gathered in small rural or urban communes. They are attempting to overcome the usual "bourgeois" style of living in organized family groups and emphasize such psychological elements as communion of feelings, experiences, and the joy of living among similar closely knit groups. Their objectives lie within the group rather than with institutional demands on the society at large.

At the other extreme are plans for the creation of alternative institutions which function not as symbolic elements but on the complex levels within society. The attempt is to relate technical instrumentalities to the political movement in a mutual enrichment of radical ideological experiences. The plan of the Movement for a Democratic Society [**Gottlieb and Piercy, 15.8.**] to organize professional people and technicians to challenge existing organizations and/or to create counterinstitutions exemplifies the way some radical groups are trying to provide a theoretical framework and a political outlet for a tendency already manifesting itself spontaneously.

In both of these cases, as in the whole range of attempts to build the foundations of a new structure with which to oppose and substitute for the old one, the phenomenon no longer touches only isolated exceptions, but a significant minority of people in the new generations.

18.2. The mirror of the growth of this parallel society is the "underground" press—itself an alternative structure, the most highly developed and successful one so far. It began in 1965 with the birth of the first two newspapers of this new type, the *Los Angeles Free Press* and the *Berkeley Barb*. The underground, or free, press, as it is sometimes called, burst forth during the years 1967 and 1968, when hundreds of new papers appeared not only in the large metropolitan areas where there is an avant-garde audience, but also in smaller communities, sometimes associated with colleges and universities. It is impossible to calculate the number of new publications or their circulation, because the underground press is a continually changing, decentralized and diversified phenomenon. The Liberation News Service (LNS) in September 1968, for example, listed about 400 papers, of which 111 were called "underground" and 44, "movement." Whatever the exact number of publications and the general breadth of circulation (330,000, according to *The Wall Street Journal* of April 1968; 4.6 million, according to Marshall Bloom of LNS; and 5 million, according to the *Underground Press Directory* published in autumn 1968), this journalistic network certainly represents an alternative structure on a nationwide scale.

In the underground press, as in the Movement as a whole, important distinctions in a political evaluation are necessary. There is the part of the press which performs a service for all the groups in the subculture of protestors and dropouts in a certain geographical area (a typical example is the *Berkeley Barb*); there is the kind which is clearly psychedelically oriented (the *San Francisco Oracle* and the *East Village Other* of New York); and finally there is the political type (*San Francisco Express Times; Rat* of New York) which are involved in formulating and informing radically oriented public opinion. Still, there are certain characteristics common to many of these publications. For the first time in the United States, a press which expresses a culture of opposition (with its undeniable political-radical character and its by-products of conformism "anti") is reaching a mass audience, certainly a few million individuals, who have never before been exposed to left-wing publications. It represents an independent economic structure which cannot be subjugated by pressures from the usual economic or financial channels or forced to alter the manner in which its production, distribution, and publicity are organized. Finally, this means of regulating a mass-communications medium is also significant from the aspect of internal democracy: very often the editors of an underground paper are also its owners and participate in determining the line the paper is to take without there being any separation or subordination between managers and managed.

18.3. The underground press is the example of how new alternative structures can begin to vie with existing ones, replacing them not only in the technical sense but also in the quality of their direction. The tendency toward decentralized programs run by the resources and creativeness of particular groups is itself an indication of the kind of strictly anticentralized and libertarian work carried on by the Movement and the New Left: there is no Watchword handed down from Washington or New York, no Correct Analysis, but a common policy which develops from below on the basis of original, independent experiences.

The press is not the only existing parallel structure working along these lines, although it is the most successful one so far. There are press services operating on a national basis, such as Liberation News Service (LNS) and the Underground Press Syndicated (UPS), which, with their information services and mutual exchange of material, fulfill and increase the possibilities for independent journalism. Other means of expression and mass communication are flourishing as well; there is cinema (Newsreel), theater (Guerrilla Theatre), radio and television (Radio Free People), etc.; attempts are even being made to apply computer technology in a radical context (Meta Information Applications).

The development of autonomous structures is a sign that the transformations taking place in American society do not concern only life-style and the psychological needs of a certain number of individuals or an attempt by a small group of radical activists to "gain power." It is rather an indication of the vitality of the Movement, to the extent that its membership and bases are numerous, varied, and active, each component maintaining its own autonomy and independence. The ongoing tendency is, in a certain sense, utopian, because the intention is to build a new society in the lap of the old. At the moment, there are only a few threads with which to create this new fabric; some are rapidly expanding, such as the communications media; others, like those based on the alternative uses of technical, scientific and professional personnel, are just beginning. On the whole, there is no doubt that a basic movement does exist, and the new fabric is getting larger.

In all cases where two societies—old and new—coexist, the tendency of the established and consolidated institutions is either to incorporate the new ones by assimilation or to crush them by force. Today, in the United States, both tendencies are present. When mutual incompatibility intensifies the conflict, both the method of control and that of repression will probably be perfected and brought fully to bear. Therefore, the contest is open: the creation of structures from below is a guarantee of the strength of the new forces, in the numbers of people involved, the energies which have been mobilized, the value of the patterns and examples provided by the new experiments. However, these are not enough. Dual powers, counterinstitutions, parallel structures are the necessary but not sufficient conditions for the construction of a new society, particularly where power, such as military and industrial power, is concentrated. It is also necessary to build a movement which will work toward the transformation of the central powers of the state and be able to offer tentative solutions to the immense organizational problems which a complex, supertechnological society presents. The response to systematic rationalization and concentration of power can only be anti-authoritarian and decentralized, as is the response being developed by New Lefts everywhere. The response to the failure of the "systems" which have proposed the Final Solution can only be antisystematic and antitotalist, as is the response which emerges in some of the alternative structures of the New Left in the United States. But it is also necessary to resolve the problem of the general strategy the new forces are to follow. It is not a minor problem, and the American New Left has not yet solved it.

19
In Search of Analysis
and Theory
19.1. There is no doubt that a movement whose ambition is to transform society needs a theoretical elaboration. Every political and cultural movement which has influenced the course of history was always conscious of the values it carried forward, i.e., it possessed a theoretical framework which enabled it to form analyses, perspectives, and strategy.

The distinctive trait of the American New Left is that, until now, its theoretical ideas have come more from the experience of political struggle than from conscious intellectual effort. Neither Marx nor Marxism provides the basis of the New Left, and not even writers such as Marcuse, who can be considered the theoretical interpreter of some of the values exemplified by the ongoing Movement, can be said to have led or inspired it. Even in its theoretical aspect, the New Left is a collective phenomenon, and as such it is nourished by the contributions of many different ideals and by intellectual concepts from widely varied traditions and origins.

This is also the reason that there is no one document or Sacred Text to refer to when we want to examine the "theory" behind the New Left. If we hope to find a theory, it must be deduced from the struggles and ideals, from the moral and political issues, which have set the Movement's forces in motion on different occasions. Since the Port Huron Statement (1962), which was mainly a manifesto of values and political proposals, nothing else has been written along those lines, either by SDS or by any other group. In retrospect, if we search for formulas which can provide theoretical examples, it is possible to pick out a few characteristics which are widely present in the most politicized sectors of the Movement, i.e., the part we have more properly referred to as the New Left. In praxis, a strong anti-authoritarian and libertarian tendency is evident, and more recently a strong anticapitalist and anti-imperialist sentiment has developed. If such a term still has any meaning, the New Left tends potentially toward socialism—of a type, however, in which the values of human liberty prevail over the economic aspects, too often associated and identified with the theory and experience of socialist countries and parties.

A new theoretical synthesis, which would include an analysis of the structures of American society, a vision of future society, and the ways and means for bringing about the transformation which will lead from one to the other, does not exist. Experimentation and openness (not absence) of ideology are the real factors which distinguish the American New Left, and which therefore endow it as a movement in the formative process with a high degree of vitality and with utopianism. The New Left is not, in fact, lacking in ideals, partial analyses, and proposals for a method of political action, rather a unifying frame of reference, the priorities for the various points of struggle, and the internal consciousness of building a political force as an alternative to the existing order. Many attempts have been made to fulfill this need for theoretical reflection on the direction the political struggle must take, but so far none of them is comprehensive enough to be considered *the* theory of the New Left. The process of building a theory is historical, taking as its point of departure the failure of those ideologies that have promised a definitive answer to the problem of freedom. It will probably be a long process, requiring the contribution of at least one generation, and strictly bound to the praxis of the struggles that take place now and in the future. A few signs, although they are still very weak, can already be seen.

19.2. Many people agree that the capitalistic society of present-day America is quite different from the classical model with its recurrent economic crises. William Domhoff, for example, underlines four major characteristics of the new, corporation-dominated capitalism: (1) It is flexible and has far more room for reforms to the extent to which it can continue to corporatize the "underdeveloped" world and displace small businessmen and realtors in the cities; (2) it is very much dependent on overseas sales and investments, and therefore affects the political, economic, and military behavior of the ruling class; (3) it has at its command unprecedented, almost unbelievable, firepower and snooping power; and (4) it is opposed to small business, small government, competition, and the marketplace [**Domhoff, 18.1.**]. The structural base of this new capitalism are the giant corporations in whose hands an ever-growing amount of wealth and power is being concentrated. "These supercorporations control a productive capacity that not only makes America the richest nation in the world, but also provides the foundations upon which the allocation of resources, jobs, wealth and income are based."[65] In turn, the structure for control of state power has changed as well. C. Wright Mills, one of the first scholars to inquire into the nature of the American ruling class, maintained that it is made up of a "power élite" into which are gathered the groups and individuals who wield the greatest decision-making power, even though they come from different classes. More recently, Herbert Marcuse has added an examination of the totalitarian characteristics of the system and their expansion into individual psychology, underlining the connection between technological development and systems of social control.

The New Left therefore finds itself operating within a structural context different from the one for which the Marxist left in the past had developed its own analyses and proposals for specific revolutionary strategies. All the developed capitalist nations, and particularly the United States, present new aspects whose internal mechanisms still remain to be discovered. The structures of capitalism and of employer-worker relationships no longer follow the nineteenth-century patterns, and the forms of oppression extend beyond economic exploitation in relation to production. The framework of the democratic system itself seems to be becoming a formal disguise which does not even meet those standards which, in theory, made the system capable of permitting social mobility and economic opportunity. Class structure has changed in relation to a changed productive structure. The concentration of power in the hands of a small group belies the assumption of pluralism upon which American democracy has always pretended to rest. Technological development is accompanied by complex forms of organization, with widespread bureaucratization and hierarchical ordering at every level of social life.

If all this is true, it means also that the forces capable of undertaking revolutionary change can no longer be the same as those conceived by Marxist theory with respect to ninteenth-century capitalism. In this respect, too, the New Left must face a new situation both in terms of theoretical reconsideration and in terms of the empirical evidence provided by the experience of these years.

The social groups opposing the system have been students, or young people in general, a few small segments of the "new middle class," the poor and the nonwhite ethnic minorities. The traditional working class, the one composed of "industrial workers" which Marxism depicts as the agent of social transformation, is for the most part integrated into the economic pattern of capitalism. Or rather, the unions, which are its organized expression

---

65. Ronald Aronson and John C. Cowley, "The New Left in the United States," *The Socialist Register* (London: 1967).

and therefore its political representatives, form one of the mass props of the system.

Ten years ago, C. Wright Mills argued for the necessity of reconsidering the question of the "agency of change":

> What I do not quite understand about some British new left writers is why they cling so mightily to "the working class" of the advanced capitalist societies as *the* historic agent, or even as the most important agency in the face of the really impressive historical evidence that now stands against this expectation. . . . Where labor exists as an agency, of course we must work with it, but we must treat it as the Necessary Lever, as nice old Labour Gentlemen in Britain and elsewhere tend to do.[66]

At that time the New Left had not yet been born in America: ten years of history have shown that in every spontaneous or organized demonstration of political and social struggle, the protagonists have been social groups other than "industrial workers."

Today, on the basis of experience, many attempts at analysis are being made. A few tend to formulate new working hypotheses about "young people as a class" [**Rowntrees, 16.2.**], not only on the basis of ten years of revolt led predominantly by young people, but demonstrating how these individuals constitute the social group that is economically exploited and psychologically oppressed within the new structures of capitalism. The Rowntrees maintain that the American economy is increasingly dominated by two industries which are widespread, public and rapidly expanding, i.e., defense and education; it is these two which absorb the manual-labor surplus, particularly the youth. Others analyze the different class stratifications in the United States in quantitative terms and in reference to production. Greg Calvert and Carol Nieman, tracking down the so-called new working class, point out that "the most rapidly growing job category in the economy during the 1960s has been that of professional and technical workers, with an increase of at least 40 percent by 1970 over that of 1960,"[67] and that the term "middle class," as used by Marx in the nineteenth century, no longer describes in any sense the new working classes of American neo-capitalism. Still others, finally, maintain that the only possible revolution is one which will be triggered by the organization of all the categories of "outsiders" in the society of affluence and manipulation, i.e., the nonclasses of the chronically unemployed, nonwhite ethnic minorities, and dropouts from the white middle class.

All these attempts at analysis and the search for a theory of the Movement's dynamic are going on today and are beginning to outline strategies for the New Left. We still doubt that there can be *a* New Left theory or *a* model for action. Part of the revolutionary character of the New Left consists in its being an open process capable of modifying, in the course of struggles having strategic character and radical objectives, the very assumptions from which it began.

19.3.   If we can, in a single phrase, define the New Left as the continuing struggle for freedom, which concentrates on those crucial points where antifreedom is most clearly visible in America today, it is obvious that such a struggle cannot be guided by a definitive vision of future society, i.e., a program for that hypothetical future time

---

66.   C. Wright Mills, "Letter to the British New Left," in *New Left Review*, Number 5, 1959.

67.   Greg Calvert and Carol Nieman, "Internationalism, New Left Style," *Guardian*, June 15, 1965.

when it will take power. The objection to the New Left's lack of a concrete alternative program, held by those who support the system but at the same time would like to change some aspects of it, is actually quite naïve. A movement must be judged according to the way it carries on its political struggles, in other words, by what it is able to accomplish historically, and not by what it professes. In this sense, the New Left is full of suggestive possibilities, even though, as we have already pointed out, these exist more as potential than as consciously held goals.

The New Left has supplanted the Marxist models of dictatorship of the proletariat and supremacy of a single class in governing the state by the widely shared goal of decentralization of administrative and economic bodies and social institutions. The concept of ownership of the means of production is giving way to an emphasis on participation in decision-making processes which affect the lives of individuals in the various institutions of society, and therefore on the realization, not so much of a "socialist state," as of a society which all citizens can take part in running. The importance of economic structures in the struggle for freedom is taking on a new dimension. The emphasis is on making available effective instruments with which people can control their own lives; in other words, a psychological rather than a purely political or economic dimension. The society dominated by the work ethic is being replaced by one in which creativity and imagination can play an important role in the realization of human potentialities. Faced with the fetishes of economic and technological development as absolute goods, people are seeking new productive arrangements which will permit the creation of a postscarcity economy in which "human activity can be defined by man's own consciously determined needs, and not by needs determined from the outside," and connected with the myth of expansion. In rejecting the concept of rationality that has grown out of the gradual identification of *homo humanus* with *homo economicus,* whose basic law is material incentive and competition, this Movement with its imprecise boundaries is striving toward a society in which behavior and instinct will be inspired by love, brotherhood, and freedom. So the New Left, like every left-wing movement worthy of the name, is introducing a necessary utopian dimension into the society of today.

20

A New Left Force: Between Past and Future

20.1. Until now, opposition in the United States has been characterized by a spontaneous and growing explosion of social forces and by a series of political battles fought around specific issues. The Movement is a vague formula standing for the psychological, social, and political levels that we have been discussing. The New Left consists of a general position based on the lowest political common denominator of the analyses, tactics, and strategies of the different movements. Neither the Movement nor its political expression—the New Left—is or has been an organized political force unifying the many means by which the new radicals' opposition expresses itself.

The editors of *Studies on the Left* in 1966 proposed that: The focus should remain on the exploration of dilemmas instead of proposing organizational formulas [**Editors of** *Studies on the Left*, **6.3.**]. Only a few years have passed since then, but in political terms it has been a long period of maturation and growth for the radical movement. The Movement has moved beyond the debate of whether or not to keep one foot inside the Democratic party and one outside; its content has changed and taken a radical direction, with socialist and revolutionary veins running through it—whatever these two adjectives may still mean in a period of verbal inflation. In newspaper articles, radical meetings, and among Movement spokesmen the question of a national New Left common organization is periodically raised, an organization which could be capable of maintaining its decentralized character and at the same time integrating its projects into a unified strategy and perspective. Furthermore, it has been pointed out that it is necessary to coordinate the different parts of the Movement and, more specifically, to enable the radical student experiences to be followed up within a framework capable of accepting the political work of adults in the New Left as well.

In 1966 and 1967 the attempt to form the national effort was the "new politics." This term, like all those which grow out of the Movement, was vague and held different meanings for different groups. The only unifying themes were those inspired by a negative attitude—anti-Johnson, antiwar— in the absence of a positive vision.

The organizational instrument of these attempts at unification was the National Conference for New Politics (NCNP), formed in November 1965 through the efforts of Arthur Waskow and others. All elements of the opposition were represented on its national executive board: from left-wing Democrats to black civil-rights (as well as Black Power) leaders; from former officers of SDS to representatives of the antiwar movement; from New Left activists involved in community organizing projects to liberal and radical intellectuals. During its two years of existence, the NCNP tried to establish a national network of groups for "new politics," now and then supporting Democratic "peace candidates," electoral campaigns in the Democratic party with radical platforms, such as that of Robert Scheer in California in 1966 [**Scheer, 17.1.**], or independent organizations like the MFDP, the Lowndes County Freedom Organization, and the Connecticut American Independent Movement. The focal point of the different programs was to have been the 1968 presidential elections, with the presentation of an alternative candidate to those of the two major parties. It was with this objective, not explicitly announced however, that the national convention of the NCNP met in September 1967.

All the components of the left were present at the Chicago convention: liberal and radical, New and traditional, white and black. In spite of this, all the plans for starting a third party on the left or launching an independent presidential ticket (whose candidate was to have been Martin Luther King) or for drawing up a unifying program for political work were totally unsuccessful. Each group left the convention without having changed its convictions; each would continue to carry on its own particular political activity, without national involvements.

The convention was on the whole a most accurate reflection of the organizational state of the opposition in the United States and also gave proof of the impossibility of finding unity on the left. The meeting marked the transition between two different periods. On one hand, it demonstrated that for the first time in 20 years 5,000 oppositional cadres could gather to discuss a possible common program, although they could not reach agreement on old arguments and were destined to fail. On the other hand, there was concrete evidence of the presence of new forces in the country (gathered mainly into the Radical Caucus during the convention), whose unifying themes lay in the kind of work they were doing at the base rather than in formal agreements of the electoral type.

20.2. The Peace and Freedom party (PFP) started in California, the only state where it achieved an effective grass-roots mobilization. It stemmed from the NCNP and was the first experiment with a cohesive organizational structure in the New Left. The first impetus for forming this new movement came immediately after the NCNP convention, when it appeared necessary to initiate a peace campaign opposing the stranglehold of the two-party system. The groups which involved themselves in the registration campaign to place the party on the ballot in the primary elections represented both the Community for New Politics groups that had formed around the Scheer campaign of 1966 and other left-wing groups, including the Independent Socialist Club.

In its early stage, then, the PFP was therefore mainly based on electoral goals and principles. On the other hand, the membership and character of the PFP distinguished it from the traditional progressive electoral front. Its activists, and the base which was mobilized in the beginning stages, came from the rank and file of the student and antiwar movements; the majority was composed of New Left radicals. The goals of the party leaders, expressed time and again, were to use the electoral campaign as a means of reaching potential grass-roots groups and organizing them along independent lines, outside the Democratic party.

The PFP's existence was brief and was related to a period of extraordinary events. By January 1968, the party had collected more than the 66,000 registrations required to place its candidates on the California primary ballot. The founding convention was held in March, at the height of the movement's mobilization, with a thousand activists from all over the state attending. In the meantime, Senator McCarthy had won the earliest state primaries, and in California itself there was a strange flow of activists toward the McCarthy campaign. In April, Martin Luther King was assassinated; Eldridge Cleaver was proposed as presidential candidate of the PFP and was nominated in August at the California and national conventions. In November—in an atmosphere of complete demobilization—the PFP election results in California (1.5 percent of the vote going to the senatorial candidate, Paul Jacobs), New York and a few other states confirmed the electoral failure of this first national attempt.

In California the party was not an artificial creation, but arose almost spontaneously as a continuation and complement of the Free Speech Movement, Scheer campaign, Vietnam Day Committee, and grass-roots political work carried on by the various groups. California, and Berkeley in particular, anticipated the need for establishing a left-wing organization of non- and ex-students, capable of functioning on a mass basis as well. Internally, however, the PFP was the scene of conflict between verbose revolutionary, extremist tendency and a group which favored a wide-based radical movement capable also of attracting disillusioned liberals willing to become active in independent politics. The tone of the document which was approved at the founding convention [**PFP, 1968, 17.2.**], with its appeal to "all powerless people," was an indication of movement in the latter direction. The prevalence of the extremist tendency impeded the movement from effectively challenging the surge of the base toward the McCarthy campaign, while it contributed very little to the building of a radical and revolutionary group without sectarian characteristics. The alliance with the Black Panther party of Oakland was also an important and ambivalent factor. It was, in fact, the first time a political movement of white and Black Power radicals entered into a coalition, with each group respecting the other's autonomy. One of the necessary conditions for the success of the alliance was missing, however—an independent movement with substantial roots in the white community. The coalition depended too much on Black Panther issues (of limited political significance for the long run, even though, like the "Free Huey" campaign, they were important), and it seemed that the Cleaver campaign, which evolved into something largely based on personality, no longer responded to the initial objective of seizing an electoral occasion for organizing social groups with radical potential.

On a national scale, the PFP had very little relevance because (with the possible exception of New York) it was mainly a product exported from California, lacking deep local roots. Its campaign was totally unsuccessful in mobilizing New Left groups, even though these groups exist on and off college campuses everywhere.

20.3.   That the New Left is in fact a potential political force, rather than a vague movement, is demonstrated by the number of individuals now dedicating themselves continuously (perhaps permanently) to political work and organizing. This fact is necessary in order to place in proper perspective the problem of creating a New Left organization. Counting the number of activists working throughout the country, we see that we are no longer dealing with a few pioneers, as at the beginning of the 1960s, nor with a definite but restricted group, as at the beginning of 1965 before the second wave of political opposition, which has grown considerably in the last three years. There are few precise points of reference, but those we have permit us to reconstruct approximately the active force of the New Left at the end of 1968. SDS, which is still the main New Left organization and which is composed almost entirely of students, has about 7,000 national members—a figure which may be taken as a meaningful reference point for the number of cadres and activists at the student level. An activist well acquainted with the national situation of SDS[68] estimates that there are about 100,000 local members—people who gravitate toward the organization and its activities on a local level. These are activists of the second category, people who are not so deeply involved as the cadres. And the accuracy of this figure is confirmed by a recent study of the university

---

68. Carl Davidson, *Guardian*, November 16, 1968.

left,[69] which reveals that two percent of all American students (i.e., 135,000 out of 6.7 million) are members of some left-wing movement and that an additional eight to ten percent (700,000 to 750,000) are considered strongly sympathetic to the "movement for social change" and are "capable of being temporarily mobilized around specific issues." After SDS, the largest group is the one which comprises the peace movement. Among the antimilitary, antiwar, and draft resistance groups, there are about a thousand more activists working full-time. The most accurate demonstration of this is provided by the 3,000 to 4,000 draft cards which have been sent in to government offices since October 1967, and which indicate a group of young people strongly determined on a personal level to support the opposition. Then there was the mobilization of the Peace and Freedom party, which numbered 1,000 activists in California alone. Admitting that California groups alone constituted half of all the radical electoral movements that developed in 1968, the number of activists involved in this kind of work—generally distinct from those of SDS, whose organizational position on electoral politics is quite different—amounts to about 2,000. Additionally, there are the organizers of particular projects of local character, for which not even approximate statistical data are available; the technicans and professional people who are affiliated with alternative structures or strongly involved in radical caucuses within various institutions, together with the journalists and radical mass-media organizers, number at least 1,000, judging from the number of projects now going on in this area. Finally, we must include the people belonging to traditional left groups such as the Progressive Labor party (whose members also form part of SDS), Young Socialist Alliance (involved mainly in anti-imperialist and antiwar activities like the National Mobilization Committee), Independent Socialist Club (activists and organizers of the Peace and Freedom party) and the Communists. In all these organizations are another 1,000 activists whose political lines, while different from those considered strictly speaking New Left (some, like the Communists, are actually quite distant; others, such as the members of the ISC, are very close), develop within the more general movement of opposition and often have a dialectically symbiotic relationship with the New Left line.

In all, we estimate that there are today 10,000 to 20,000 activists who not only lead and organize the political battles of the movement, but also make up its solid, continuous network. The hypothesis may also be exposed to nonanalytical data, such as, for example, the circulation of publications like *New Left Notes* (8,000), the *Guardian* (25,000), *Liberation* (10,000), and *Monthly Review* (12,000), which, although they differ considerably, are all read by New Left cadres. These cadres have a notable capacity for political leadership and organization, which, however, is not always fully realized. The potential for a politically radical leading group exists, but the tools remain, at least in part, to be forged.

20.4. Since 1968, the problem of coordination for the New Left has arisen again in both politico-organizational and politico-strategic terms. The growth of struggles concentrated on single problems and the development of a wide group of cadres provide the objective conditions.

The fact that this need is widely felt is reflected in the debate which

---

69. The Study was conducted by the Educational Testing Service of Princeton, N.J., a nonprofit, nongovernmental research foundation. The synthesis of the results was published in *The New York Times* of November 10, 1968.

developed during 1968 and grew sharper toward the end of the year. Well-known New Left spokesmen such as Tom Hayden, who were formerly strongly opposed to any national organization, are now stating that it is necessary "to be decisive and conscious about the kind of left force you want to create so you can shape these natural forces."[70] Others, starting out from completely opposite points of view and from a traditional socialist position, are launching an appeal for a "socialist" and "revolutionary" party;[71] still others declare themselves in favor of a "radical popular party" with an anticapitalist and antisocialist orientation which might become "a means of educating and organizing among radicals and left-wing liberals toward a socialist perspective," and which "need not be monolithic in the Stalinist sense."[72] Even the weekly *Guardian*, now the national organ of expression for various New Left groups, which during the elections declared itself opposed to any electoral involvement, published an editorial on November 23, 1968, that may be taken as representing the most recent tendency of the New Left:

> We think conditions are ripe for a beginning. Clearly the missing ingredient is a broad radical organization which would include many thousands of individuals and some organizations of the left who are isolated or so fractured as to have no impact. The organization we have in mind would provide independent radicals with a base to work from, a grouping within which to find revolutionary relevance. [**Guardian, 18.3.**]

The political formation which seems imminent and which the various New Left groups seem to be referring to when they express ideas like those in the *Guardian* article, is not an ideological party built on the theories of a few intellectuals, but something which includes and starts out from the numerous decentralized experiences that have provided the background for activists in various movements of the past years. The SDS, in its own way, is an organizational model, although its characteristics of a student organization limit its scope. Staughton Lynd has written recently that "as a national network emerges from local resistance politics, it may not take the form of a political party. It may resemble the old I.W.W. rather than the old Socialist Party."[73] The experience of the small closed and sectarian groups such as the Maoist PLP and the Trotskyist SWP, and the character of motionless liberalism such as that of the Communist party, searching for alliances on its right, represent errors which the new radicals certainly cannot repeat. The base of the new party itself must be something which anticipates different forms of affiliation, and a structuring of working groups like that which the Movement for a Democratic Society is developing. The model for the new formation, if such a thing comes about, is yet to be discovered. In a recent interview, Herbert Marcuse stated:

> I don't think I can talk here about forms of organization because these must be developed and concretized in the course of political action. . . . [I]t seems to me that traditional centralized forms of organization have

---

70. Tom Hayden, interview, *New Left Notes*, November 1968.

71. This is the position taken by Christopher Lasch, repeatedly expressed in the columns of the *New York Review of Books* during 1968, and also by a group of socialist intellectuals who gathered at the Socialist Scholars Conference.

72. Stanley Aronowitz, "Task for the New Left: Get Yourselves Together," *Guardian*, November 23, 1968.

73. Staughton Lynd, editorial, *Liberation*, November 1968.

become obsolete. . . . [A] trend toward decentralized forms of organizations corresponds to the real development of advanced capitalist society. . . . I add, however, that mere spontaneity will never suffice. . . . [T]he two extremes must be combined in one way or another, and I like to call that, not entirely flippantly, something like organized spontaneity or spontaneous organization.[74]

It is probable that some kind of flexible national structure will arise in the course of future struggles: certainly it will not be triggered automatically as the result of continuing motionlessness or inability to effect change, but will be the necessary tool that the new radicals must invent if the movement for the transformation of society is not to fall back upon itself.

For the New Left 1968 seemed a crucial year: since the single battles which began with the attack against the Vietnam war in 1965 have largely spent themselves, and the Movement has grown to the point of arousing strong reactions from the forces interested in maintaining the status quo, the most vital forces of the Movement are running the risk of substituting for the long, necessary work of sinking roots into the social reality of the country and of developing a revolutionary praxis starting with action, action in and for itself. Above and beyond the necessary struggle against the "direct action" of the police, there must be something more clearly articulated and directed toward other institutions whose power, even though less visible, is no less oppressive. Only if the analyses, tactics, organizations and actions are spread out along a line of spontaneous unity will the New Left be able to overcome the impasse that now threatens to halt its growth.

---

74. Interview with Herbert Marcuse, *Guardian*, November 23, 1968.

21

Some Final

Considerations

In spite of the limited consciousness the Movement has of itself, the American New Left is perhaps the first, embryonic expression of a new force which confronts the problems of postindustrial society. Its peculiar quality is that it developed out of a search for new values to substitute for old ones, more than from political visions or ideological theories. In spite of itself, the New Left prefigures a movement which is growing throughout the developed capitalist world (and, we hope, the socialist one as well). The value of the American Movement does not lie in its political maturity, but in its message of a search for a different style of life and in the way in which this message is exemplified by a considerable number of young people. It is a utopian message, yet it is restoring to politics its idealistic dimension and its function as a continual struggle for social systems in which the individual can find an ever greater degree of freedom.

The United States has reached a level of development which perhaps marks the end of an era based on economic relations and the beginning of a new society in which structures different from those of production will be at the center of social conflicts. Furthermore, the New Left is the only left, i.e., the only dimension for a possible transformation of society. Europe, unlike America, does not yet have an advanced level of technological development or an ideological one-dimensionality. The labor movement, despite part of its leadership, still represents a mass social force potentially capable of carrying on radical struggles. Moreover, in some countries, such as France and Italy, the Communist party is the political expression of a large part of the labor movement.

In America, thanks to the uniqueness of conditions resulting both from the degree of development of the society and from the nature of the left-wing forces, there are possibilities for experimentation which do not exist in Europe, where the conditions are not yet sufficiently ripe. The American left has the advantage (and disadvantage) of not having any great communist or social-democratic movements like those of European countries. In the Old World, the organized labor movement, under the leadership of more or less orthodox and more or less moderate Marxists, acts as a guarantee in the defense of freedom and at the same time as a curb on political creativity. In the United States the possibility exists to try out new forms of social organization whose structures would be impossible to imagine if it were not for the utopian notions expressed by the Movement.

The experimental patrimony of psychological, social, and political liberation which enriches the American New Left is only the vanguard of the base from which the forces of freedom will grow in the coming decades. These forces won't automatically evolve into new forms of civilization and democracy. In history, nothing is ever automatic. But it is probable that out of the very machinery of the most monstrous power of modern times will emerge the counterforce that will gradually undermine its worst features. It is a problem of struggle. As always, the solution lies in the hands of men.

Second Part

Documents

One:
The Beginning
of the
Movement

I
Civil Rights

1.1. *ANNE BRADEN:* **The Southern Freedom Movement, The Student Revolt: 1960–61**

[At the beginning of 1960, the young black activists of the civil-rights movement in the South moved in a new direction toward direct action. Before this, the civil-rights struggle had been waged primarily through legal action, by traditional organizations (such as CORE and the NAACP) directed by adults. The revolt of the black students, which began with the sit-ins of February 1960, opened the way for a new era, not only for the freedom movement for black people, but for the formation of the New Left as well. In the following article taken from *Monthly Review,* July/August 1965, Anne Braden, who has been involved for a long time in the freedom campaigns in the Deep South with the Southern Conference Educational Fund, describes the first two years of struggle by students and young people.]

It was the Negro student revolt of 1960 that turned the Southern civil rights movement into a Southwide mass movement.

The incident that triggered it was the now famous action of February 1, 1960, when four Negro college students in Greensboro, North Carolina, walked into a dime store, sat at a lunch counter, ordered coffee, were refused service—and continued to sit. From there the idea swept the South; by May there had been student demonstrations in at least 89 cities, including some in every Southern and border state. Hundreds sat at lunch counters; thousands marched in street demonstrations; hundreds went to jail. The Negro South was electrified, the white South was shocked—and the nation as a whole, still trapped in the silence, fear, and apathy of the 1950's, rubbed its eyes and realized that the democratic processes of protest, although rusty from disuse, were still available to those with the courage to use them.

Just as it is impossible to explain why the Montgomery bus protest started when and where it did, so there is no clearcut explanation for the timing and development of what became known as the sit-in movement. The sit-in technique was not new. It had been used since the early 1940's by the Congress of Racial Equality (CORE) in Northern cities. In the late '50's there were a few small CORE groups staging sit-ins around the edges of the South, in such border cities as Baltimore and St. Louis. In Oklahoma City in 1958, an NAACP youth group conducted a mass sit-in campaign that opened lunch counters there; this was widely publicized, but it did not spread.

Many people refused to believe that the sit-in movement growing from Greensboro was spontaneous, but it was, and nobody active in the civil rights movement would have predicted it. In fact, the constant lament among adult activists in that period was, "Where is the younger generation?"

The only explanation is that this generation, unbeknownst to its elders, had simply—individually and collectively—had enough, and when somebody struck the right match at the right moment the social bomb went off. Some sociologists have theorized that it happened to this particular generation because they were just old enough to be aware of what the Supreme Court decision of 1954 should mean to them, and when after six years it had not meant anything, their frustrations broke into action. . . .

When the students finally merged into a Southwide movement, they had no definite goals beyond the lunch counter, but everyone knew that this was only a symbol and the real objective was much larger. . . .

It was partly because the breadth of their vision often seemed too big to put into words that this movement turned so much to song. Music became the movement's most effective means of communication; students learned old songs from the church and the labor movement, added their own words, and made up new songs. Each jail cell produced its own verses. No other movement in our history, not even the early labor movement, has been such a singing movement as this one became. . . .

The defenders of the Old South were still at work in those early 1960's. Police were using tear gas to break up demonstrations. At some state colleges, teachers were fired and student demonstrators were expelled. Libel suits were filed against civil rights leaders (and against *The New York Times*) in Alabama. Many individuals were hurt by these attacks. Some became martyrs—like Clyde Kennard who was sent to jail for seven years on a trumped-up charge after he applied to enter a white college in Mississippi and later died of cancer when early symptoms were neglected in prison. But the movement as a whole pushed forward; in contrast to the 1950's when the segregationists held the initiative, it was now the civil rights forces that were on the offensive and it was a time of victories.

Within six months after the sit-ins started, 28 cities had integrated their lunch counters; by the fall of 1960 the number had risen to almost 100, with protest movements active in at least 60 more. There were kneel-ins to integrate white churches, wade-ins at the swimming pools and beaches. By the spring of 1961, the sit-in movement finally reached Jackson, Mississippi—the first place where police dogs were used against demonstrators. More than 3,500 walked in a silent march to Nashville to protest the bombing of a civil rights attorney's home and forced a statement from the mayor on the City Hall steps supporting equal rights for all. Eight thousand gathered in mass meetings in Atlanta, and 2,000 students marched in the streets. . . .

Permanent organizations coalesced around the student movements in some communities. One of the most remarkable was in Nashville, Tennessee, where entire student bodies participated, and where the first breakthrough on citywide integration of lunch counters occurred in May, 1960. The Nashville students developed a system of "group leadership" under the guidance of a young Negro minister, the Rev. James Lawson. Often they would meet all night until in the dawn hours they could reach unanimous "sense of the meeting" decisions. Because they were ready to go to jail and stay if necessary, they won the trust of the other students, so that when the time came for mass action the masses were there. Out of this Nashville group came many of the students who emerged as Southwide leaders later: the Rev. James Bevel, Diane Nash (later Mrs. James Bevel), Bernard Lafayette, John Lewis, Marion Barry, Lester McKinnie, and others—and also the young ministers, G.T. Vivian and Kelly Miller Smith, who rose to leadership in the Southern Christian Leadership Conference.

Regionally, the lasting organization that came out of the sit-in movement, which probably changed the course of history in the South, was the Student Nonviolent Coordinating Committee (SNCC—pronounced SNICK). This organization was set up at the 1960 Easter conference in Raleigh, to which students from the various sit-in movements came. The Raleigh conference was called by SCLC when it became obvious that some sort of coordination of the sit-in movement was indicated. There were 142 Southern students present, with every Southern state and about 40 campuses represented. SCLC provided some speakers and workshop leaders; and the woman who was to become a kind of godmother, adviser, helper, and patron saint to SNCC, Miss Ella Baker, organized the conference as an SCLC staff member. But when the students gathered, they grabbed the reins for themselves, and it became apparent that they wanted their own independent organization. This became a position that they maintained with dogged determination, and under great counterpressures.

Thus, with the development of mass movements around the sit-ins, the South now had four major civil rights organizations working to organize Southern Negroes: the NAACP, SCLC, CORE, and SNCC. These were in addition to the Southern Conference Educational Fund (SCEF) which had been working for many years to involve white people in the movement for equality.

The NAACP was the pioneer. Theoretically, the NAACP was a mass organization, with its basic support supposedly the $2-a-year membership. In practice it never really became that, and its work was usually carried on in each community by a select few. In the South, these few were an elite only in terms of courage, and they struggled against great odds to involve more people. But the principal thrusts of the organization were through the test cases in the courts, the demand for justice for an individual under attack, the fruitless but persistent push for national legislation, and the steady if largely unsuccessful effort to get Negroes registered to vote.

When direct action broke into the streets in 1960 and afterward, these methods looked very conservative to many people; and the NAACP, although still a devil in the eyes of segregationists, developed the reputation of being the most conservative of the civil rights groups.

. . . .

SCLC, as previously noted, was formed in 1957 under the leadership of Martin Luther King, Jr., and other Negro ministers. Its objective was to develop mass movements in Southern communities and make use of direct action; its channel of work was primarily the Negro church where much of the ferment of the period was brewing. It was not very successful at first in creating mass movements, but its ideas were circulating. One of the healthiest developments of the period was the seemingly spontaneous development of grass-roots social action organizations in Negro communities across the South. Many of these associated themselves with SCLC and some coordination developed.

SCLC's greatest weapon was King himself, for he had captured the imaginations of Negroes and could go into any Southern community, draw a crowd, and electrify it. The organization had no staff initially and depended on communication among the various militant minister-leaders. Then organizational foundations were laid by Dr. John Tilley and Miss Ella Baker, a former director of branches of the NAACP who had pioneered in organizing in the South. Later the Rev. Wyatt Tee Walker, a young Negro minister who had risen to leadership in the Virginia sit-in movement, came and applied both Madison Avenue techniques and a good bit of hard work to welding SCLC together. As civil rights action increased, the organization became more prominent and built a full-time staff. Later it branched from direct action into voter registration, leadership training, and legislative action. But its main thrust remained mass direct action, and its greatest successes were mobilizations of entire communities in a way that attracted national attention.

CORE, like NAACP, was an old organization, but before 1960 a tiny one, concentrated almost entirely in the North. . . .

. . . .

Another organization which is often mentioned nationally as a "major" civil rights group is the Urban League. Chapters of the Urban League have long existed in the South. When the segregationists were on the offensive in the 1950's the Urban League came under vicious attack along with all other groups identified with the Negro cause. However, among people in the movement, the Urban League was not thought of as a real civil rights organization.

. . . .

If there was any one single factor that shaped Southern history in the early 1960's, it was the unexpected turn that SNCC took. For SNCC attracted the young, the unencumbered, the daring, the image-breakers and the pioneers; and they became the catalysts as only the young can be. The important turning point came when SNCC looked away from the campus and into the community.

For its first year and a half, SNCC was exactly what its name implied —a coordinating committee. After the Raleigh conference it set up a tiny cubbyhole office on Auburn Avenue in Atlanta and had one full-time, although rarely paid, employee. The center of SNCC was an actual coordinating committee with representatives from each Southern state, who met approximately once a month between April, 1960, and the summer of 1961.

By the spring of 1961, most Negro campuses were quiet. In some places, lunch counter victories had been won. In others, movements had been crushed by expulsions of students and firings of sympathetic faculty. Everywhere there was a realization that those who continued in the movement would have to take on bigger issues than lunch counters and that the next stages of struggle would be harder. "The glamorous stage is over," said one student at the SNCC conference in late 1960. "From now on, the need is for people willing to suffer."

The Rev. James Lawson was a main speaker and a key influence at that conference. Lawson was a pacifist who had been to India and studied Gandhi's methods. During the 1950's he worked in the South for the Fellowship of Reconciliation and traveled about the region seeking to bring small groups of whites and Negroes together to act. Later he decided that this kind of activity was not the key to social change, and turned instead to the organization of Negro mass movements for direct action—in which his efforts coincided with the rise of the student sit-in movement.

Lawson constantly urged the students to define deeper issues and long-range goals beyond the lunch counter; he advocated what he called "nonviolent revolution" to revamp the entire society. One tactic he advocated was filling the jails and refusing to make bond.

. . . .

In the late winter of the school year 1960–1961, there were some efforts at a jail-instead-of-bail movement on Southern campuses, and at one point there were in various towns as many as 100 students serving sentences instead of appealing. But the student movement, as a campus uprising, had by then passed its peak, and still in the spring of 1965 no campus-based movement comparable to 1960 has yet appeared again in the South.

What happened by the spring of 1961 was that a group of students connected with SNCC emerged from the sit-in movement with the realization that efforts to change the South must, for them, be a serious adult commitment. There were only a handful of them, but within four years they were to become the core of a new army of young people who would not only invade the Deep South but the ghettos of the North and the poverty-stricken areas of Appalachia. By 1965 this army had grown to such proportions that the federal government devised a domestic peace corps (VISTA) and developed semi-official governmental groups such as the Appalachian Volunteers in obvious efforts to absorb the energies of youth looking for something meaningful to do with their lives. People in control of society would prefer that youthful energies go into efforts more easily controlled by the power structure and therefore not likely to challenge the present control.

It was February, 1961, when the first group of SNCC pioneers experimented with the concept of going beyond their own community to challenge segregation. Students were arrested at Rock Hill, South Carolina, for attempting to integrate lunch counters. They chose jail instead of bail and served out 30-day sentences. Meantime, four SNCC leaders from elsewhere went to Rock Hill, demonstrated, were arrested and joined the local students in jail, and then sent out a call to other students across the South to join them there. The four were part of the vanguard who would become full-time crusaders later—Charles Jones of Charlotte, North Carolina, Charles Sherrod of Richmond, Virginia, Diane Nash of Nashville, and Ruby Doris Smith of Atlanta. Their call for other students failed, but the idea of the traveling challenger of segregation and the technique of concentrating many people from many places at one point of challenge was to become important in the Southern movement later.

Meantime, in May, CORE launched its Freedom Ride—a pilgrimage of whites and Negroes riding Southward from Washington, D.C., bound for New Orleans, planning to integrate bus station facilities all along the way. The ride was relatively uneventful until it reached Alabama. Then a bus was burned in Anniston and the riders were attacked by mobs there and in Birmingham; and yet another phase of the Southern struggle was underway.

The original riders, many beaten and bloody, abandoned the ride at Birmingham, but the Nashville student group picked it up, rode a bus on to Montgomery where they were beaten by a mob; from there riders proceeded on to Jackson, Mississippi, where they were quietly and efficiently arrested. Throughout that summer Freedom Riders continued to roll South —all of them destined for the jails of Jackson and Mississippi's Parchman State Prison. By the end of August, more than 300 had come, three-fourths from the North, about half students, and over half of them white. Most got sentences that would amount to six months if fines were not paid, and most stayed in jail for 40 days, the deadline to appeal convictions.

The Freedom Rides were a good illustration of the symbolic nature of the Southern struggle. This was pointed up by a Southern journalist who commented on the difficulties he and other newspapermen had in trying to explain the Freedom Rides on a program recorded for overseas broadcast by the Voice of America. "We had to try to explain, among other things," he said, "how some of those white people who joined the mob that beat the Freedom Riders at the Montgomery Greyhound station rode on integrated city buses to get there. We were not at our most lucid best."

Other newspapermen pointed out in their reports that the Greyhound station in Montgomery had actually been integrated quietly several weeks before the Freedom Riders arrived—by a small group of Negroes who came without fanfare from another Alabama city.

Some Southern white liberals wrung their hands and wondered wistfully why the Freedom Riders had to be so flamboyant in their assault on the segregated waiting rooms.

"I'm no gradualist," one said. "I know somebody has to challenge these things. I don't say there shouldn't be an organized campaign to integrate the bus stations. But why all the advance publicity? That's what stirs people up. Most of the terminals in the South could be integrated if it were just done quietly."

He was probably right. Those white men the journalist found it hard to explain to people abroad—the ones who rode the integrated Montgomery buses to get to the Greyhound station and beat the Freedom Riders—very likely did not consider it a life-and-death matter whether Negroes sat in the "white" waiting room of that station. But they had been aroused to rage by the advance newspaper stories saying the Freedom Riders were coming and their rage resulted from an instinctive knowledge that much more was at stake than seats in a bus station.

The Freedom Riders knew it too, and that, rather than any desire for publicity for its own sake, is why they had to do what they did with flamboyance and publicity and would not, if they could, settle for the quiet one-by-one integration of the South's bus stations. The bus station was the symbol, and the real stakes were much higher: equality, human dignity, a place in the sun. The mobs knew it, and the police in Jackson knew it, and the Freedom Riders knew it. And that is why they all responded as they did—those who felt threatened by the drive for equality reacting in fear and hatred, those identifying with the movement for freedom reacting with a willingness to risk their lives for seats in Southern bus stations.

Finally in the fall, the Interstate Commerce Commission ruled that all bus and train stations must integrate. Thus, although compliance was not immediately complete, the Freedom Riders won their specific objective.

In their broader symbolic significance, they did a good many other things too. They widened the Southern struggle into the national arena, for the first time giving Northerners something direct they could do in the South. They also brought encouragement to thousands of Southern Negroes, and the term Freedom Rider became legendary; even today many a Negro sharecropper in remote areas of the South refers to all civil rights workers as Freedom Riders. The rides also introduced and popularized a new concept which became proverbial in the movement: "Put your body into the struggle." That concept was one factor that helped propel those searching SNCC students from the campus into the community.

They were further propelled, although indirectly, by forces in the national power structure which the Freedom Riders unintentionally set in motion.

1.2.   SNCC Founding Statement

[In April 1960, the Student Nonviolent Coordinating Committee (SNCC) was founded as a flexible organizational structure for coordinating the students involved in direct action. The following statement approved at a meeting in October 1960, represented the Committee's position on the method of nonviolent action: although it was interpreted in different ways, it was a fixed point of reference for SNCC until the development of Black Power in 1966.]

We affirm the philosophical or religious ideal of nonviolence as the foundation of our purpose, the presupposition of our belief, and the manner of our action.

Nonviolence, as it grows from the Judeo-Christian tradition, seeks a social order of justice permeated by love. Integration of human endeavor represents the crucial first step towards such a society.

Through nonviolence, courage displaces fear. Love transcends hate.

Acceptance dissipates prejudice; hope ends despair. Faith reconciles doubt. Peace dominates war. Mutual regards cancel enmity. Justice for all overthrows injustice. The redemptive community supersedes immoral social systems.

By appealing to conscience and standing on the moral nature of human existence, nonviolence nurtures the atmosphere in which reconciliation and justice become actual possibilities.

Although each local group in this movement must diligently work out the clear meaning of this statement of purpose, each act or phase of our corporate effort must reflect a genuine spirit of love and good-will.

1.3.   *JOHN LEWIS:* **A Serious Revolution**

> [In August 1963 there was a march in Washington supported by all the civil-rights groups—Urban League, NAACP, CORE, SCLC and SNCC—which marked the arrival point of the Southern struggles and at the same time the administration for the new bill. Over 200,000 people took part in the march; besides the spokesmen for traditional civil-rights groups, John Lewis, president of SNCC, expressed the radical opinion of the young activists who were concretely bringing about a social revolution in the South. Here is the complete text of Lewis's speech; a few parts—those dealing with the Kennedy administration—were censored during the public speech.]

We march today for jobs and freedom, but we have nothing to be proud of. For hundreds and thousands of our brothers are not here. They have no money for their transportation, for they are now receiving starvation wages . . . or no wages, at all.

In good conscience, we cannot support the administration's civil rights bill, for it is too little, and too late. There's not one thing in the bill that will protect our people from police brutality. (We favorably call attention to the Kastenmeier Bill—H.R. 7702.)

This bill will not protect young children and old women from police dogs and fire hoses, for engaging in peaceful demonstrations. This bill will not protect the citizens of Danville, Virginia, who must live in constant fear in a police state. This bill will not protect the hundreds of people who have been arrested on trumped-up charges. What about the three young men— S N C C field secretaries—in Americus, Georgia, who face the death penalty for engaging in peaceful protest?

The voting section of this bill will not help thousands of black citizens who want to vote. It will not help the citizens of Mississippi, of Alabama, and Georgia, who are qualified to vote, but lack a 6th grade education. "One man, one vote," is the African cry. It is ours, too. (It must be ours.)

People have been forced to leave their homes because they dared to exercise their right to register to vote. What is in the bill that will protect the homeless and starving people of this nation? What is there in this bill to insure the equality of a maid who earns $5 a week in the home of a family whose income is $100,000 a year?

For the first time in 100 years this nation is being awakened to the fact that segregation is evil and that it must be destroyed in all forms. *Your presence today proves* that you have been aroused to the point of action.

We are now involved in a serious revolution. This nation is still a place of cheap political leaders who build their careers on immoral compromises and ally themselves with open forms of political, economic and social exploitation. What political leader here can stand up and say, "My party is the party of principles"? The party of Kennedy is also the party of Eastland. The party of Javits is also the party of Goldwater. Where is *our* party?

In some parts of the South we work in the fields from sunup to sundown for $12 a week. In Albany, Georgia, nine of our leaders have been indicted not by Dixiecrats but by the Federal Government for peaceful protest. But what did the Federal Government do when Albany's Deputy Sheriff beat Attorney C. B. King and left him half-dead? What did the Federal Government do when local police officials kicked and assaulted the pregnant wife of Slater King, and she lost her baby?

It seems to me that the Albany indictment is part of a conspiracy on the part of the Federal Government and local politicians in the interest of political expediency.

Moreover, we have learned—and you should know—since we are here for Jobs and Freedom—that within the past ten days a spokesman for the administration appeared in secret session before the committee that's writing the civil rights bill and opposed and almost killed a provision that would have guaranteed in voting suits for the first time fair federal district judges. And, I might add, this Administration's bill, or any other civil rights bill— such as the 1960 civil rights act—will be totally worthless when administered by racist judges, many of whom have been consistently appointed by President Kennedy.

I want to know, which side is the Federal Government on?

The revolution is at hand, and we must free ourselves of the chains of political and economic slavery. The nonviolent revolution is saying, "We will not wait for the courts to act, for we have been waiting for hundreds of years. We will not wait for the President, the Justice Department, nor Congress, but we will take matters into our own hands and create a source of power, outside of any national structure that could and would assure us a victory." To those who have said, "Be Patient and Wait," we must say that, "Patience is a dirty and nasty word." We cannot be patient, we do not want to be free gradually, we want our freedom, and we want it now. We cannot depend on any political party, for both the Democrats and the Republicans have betrayed the basic principles of the Declaration of Independence.

We all recognize the fact that if any social, political and economic changes are to take place in our society, the people, the masses, must bring them about. In the struggle we must seek more than mere civil rights; we must work for the community of love, peace and true brotherhood. Our minds, souls, and hearts cannot rest until freedom and justice exist for *all the people*.

The revolution is a serious one. Mr. Kennedy is trying to take the revolution out of the street and put it in the courts. Listen, Mr. Kennedy, listen Mr. Congressman, listen fellow citizens, the black masses are on the march for jobs and freedom, and we must say to the politicians that there won't be a "cooling-off" period.

All of us must get in the revolution. Get in and stay in the streets of every city, every village and every hamlet of this nation, until true Freedom comes, until the revolution is complete. In the Delta of Mississippi, in South-west Georgia, in Alabama, Harlem, Chicago, Detroit, Philadelphia and all over this nation—the black masses are on the march!

We won't stop now. All of the forces of Eastland, Barnett, Wallace, and Thurmond won't stop this revolution. The time will come when we will not confine our marching to Washington. We will march through the South, through the Heart of Dixie, the way Sherman did. We shall pursue our own "scorched earth" policy and burn Jim Crow to the ground—nonviolently. We shall crack the South into a thousand pieces and put them back together in the image of democracy. We will make the action of the past few months look petty. And I say to you, WAKE UP AMERICA!!

1.4.   *STAUGHTON LYND:* **The Freedom Schools: Concept and Organization**

> [In the summer of 1964 the Southern movement reached its moment of greatest intensity: over 800 students from Northern universities went south to work in the voter-registration campaign, local community orga-nizing, and in the creation of free structures and parallel institutions. Among them the freedom schools represented one of the most important and stimulating activities. Staughton Lynd had the responsibility of coordinating the freedom-school project. The following article was pub-lished in *Freedomways* in April 1965.]

People sometimes ask me how to start a Freedom School. This question seems almost funny. Few of us who planned the curriculum and administra-tive structure of the Mississippi Freedom Schools had any experience in Northern Freedom Schools. And in any case, our approach to curriculum was to have no curriculum and our approach to administrative structure was not to have any (I will explain this in a moment). So my answer to the question: "How do you start a Freedom School?" is, "I don't know." And if people ask, "What were the Freedom Schools like?" again I have to answer, "I don't know." I was an itinerant bureaucrat. I saw a play in Holly Springs, an adult class in Indianola, a preschool mass meeting in McComb, which were exciting. But who can presume to enclose in a few words what happened last summer when 2,500 youngsters from Mississippi and 250 youngsters from the North encountered each other, but not as students and teachers, in a learning experience that was not a school?

There was one educational experience for which I did most of the initial planning and which I took part in personally: the Freedom School Convention at Meridian on the week-end of August 7–9. Perhaps because this was the one "class" which I "taught," the Convention has loomed larger and larger in my mind as I have reflected on the summer. If I were to start a Freedom School now (and we are about to start one in New Haven), I would suggest: Begin with a Freedom School Convention and let that provide your curriculum.

The Freedom School Convention went a step beyond the thinking which took place before the summer in its implications for the administra-tion and curriculum of a school "stayed on freedom." Originally we planned to have two residential schools for high school students who in the judg-ment of COFO staff had most leadership potential, with a network of twenty day schools feeding into them. Sometime in April it became apparent that sites for residential schools would not be forthcoming, and if they did, there would be no money to rent them. And we realized, after a few painful days, that this was a good thing. It meant that teachers would live within Negro communities rather than on sequestered campuses. It meant that we would have to ask ministers for the use of church basements as schools. In short, it meant we would run a school system without buildings, equipment or money (which we did: less than $2,000 passed through my office in Jackson in the course of the summer, about half of it for film rental).

It meant, too, that each school would be on its own, succeeding or failing by improvisation without much help from a central point. In my own mind the image which kept recurring was that of the guerrilla army which "swims in the sea" of the people among whom it lives. Clearly, whether we swam or drowned depended on the naked reaction of Negro children and their parents. No apparatus of compulsion or material things could shield us from their verdict. At the Oxford orientation, I kept repeating that when the Freedom School teachers got off the bus and found no place to sleep, despite previous assurances, and no place to teach, because the minister had gotten scared; when they were referred to an old lady of the local church for help in finding lodging, and to a youngster hanging around the COFO office for help in finding students—as they did these things, they would be building their school, their teaching would have begun. After about a week we knew that somehow, some way it was working. We had expected 1,000 students at the most; I can remember the night when I wrote on a blackboard in the Jackson COFO office: "1,500 students in Freedom School. *Yippee!*"

The Freedom School Convention went a step beyond this. For once the Freedom School coordinators (our word for "principals") approved the idea of a young peoples' mock convention, coinciding with the statewide convention of the Mississippi Freedom Democratic Party, the young people took over. *They became the administrators.* About a dozen students from all over the state met in Jackson to plan the convention (out of this group, incidentally, came a new impetus for the Mississippi Student Union). The Meridian Freedom School agreed to play host to the Convention, partly because Michael Schwerner, James Chaney and Andrew Goodman had been killed attempting to start a Freedom School near Meridian, partly because Meridian possessed the palace of the Freedom School circuit, a three-story Baptist seminary which could easily house 100 delegates. Meridian young people, therefore, took on the complicated task of finding lodging and arranging transportation. The planning committee worked out a program. Essentially it was workshops each morning, plenary session each afternoon, and a Freedom School play Saturday night. Joyce Brown of McComb and Roscoe Jones of Meridian were chosen as the Convention's principal officers.

And not only did the youngsters plan the Convention. At the Convention, there was a noticeable change in tone between the first and second days. By Sunday, these teenagers were rejecting the advice of adults whether in workshops or plenary sessions, for they had discovered they could do it themselves. Beyond the Convention one could discern still one more stage in the development of academic self-government. A resolution of the Convention pledged the support of all the schools to a Freedom School in the

Delta, planning to boycott the public school there. Here was a program not only executed by the youngsters, but initiated by them. The curriculum of next summer's Freedom Schools, it has been suggested, may be built around preparation for a statewide boycott.

Indeed the Freedom School Convention's implications for curriculum were more revolutionary than its implications for administration. The curriculum presented to the teachers at Oxford had been drafted by Noel Day. Essentially it was a series of questions, beginning with the students' most immediate experience of housing, employment and education, and working out to such questions as: What is it like for Negroes who go North? What are the myths of our society about the Negro's past? What in Mississippi keeps us from getting the things we want? Beyond this, teachers were given some fragmentary written material on Negro history, and the advice to emphasize oral rather than written instruction. We were afraid that as a predominantly white group of teachers we would be rejected. The fear was unnecessary; but it helped us to break away from the conventional paraphernalia of education, to remember that education is above all a meeting between people. We said at Oxford: If you want to begin the summer by burning the curriculum we have given you, go ahead! We realized that our own education had been dry and irrelevant all too often, and we determined to teach as we ourselves wished we had been taught.

But ideas can run only a certain distance beyond experience; as in administration, so in curriculum, we had a lot to learn. We learned that *students can and should make their own curriculum.* How? Simple. Already in March at a curriculum planning conference in New York City it was my belief that the curriculum should be built around the political platform of COFO's Congressional candidates. Mississippi suggested something more. *Curriculum should be built around the political platform the students themselves create.* For this was what the Freedom School Convention was. Our emphasis at this convention was not (like that of the FDP) on people, but on program. We sought to provide a model for how people can democratically put together a political platform. The students of each Freedom School asked: If we could elect a mayor (or a state legislator, or a senator) what laws would we ask him to pass? Having drawn up a program in this way, each school sent delegates to Meridian, where in eight workshops—on public accommodations, on housing, on education, etc.—they put together the twenty-odd platforms of the different schools, and reported the results to the plenary session.

I think now it would have been better if the schools had begun with such a convention, and if the statewide program brought back to each school by its delegates had then become the curriculum for the summer.

. . . .

Saturday morning the Convention began. Over the front of the room was a large handpainted sign: "Freedom Is A Struggle." At one side was another neatly-lettered sign with the times and places of workshops and plenary sessions. At lunch we gathered around Roscoe Jones and sang and sang. That evening the Holly Springs Freedom School presented "Seeds of Freedom," a play based on the life of Medgar Evers. At the end, the girl playing Mrs. Evers said she would carry on her husband's struggle, and each member of the cast ("students" and "teachers") told why they had come to Freedom School. Then the Free Southern Theater, a group of professional quality, organized by SNCC's John O'Neal and Gilbert Moses (no relation to Bob), presented Martin Duberman's *In White America*. It too had an interpolated ending. Susan Wahman, wife of Tom Wahman who helped me with Freedom School administration, spoke the words which Rita Schwerner had said to President Johnson: "I want my husband."

Half a program had been adopted Saturday afternoon, the rest Sunday afternoon, after a second round of morning workshops. A. Philip Randolph addressed the youngsters on the need for economic as well as political programs, something their program showed that they already knew. Jim Forman, SNCC's Executive Secretary, talked about the students of Africa who went on to higher education but came back to their people to put this education to work. Bob Moses, characteristically, asked the Convention questions. Did they want to carry on Freedom Schools in this winter? Why? Did they want Freedom School *after* public school, or *instead* of public school? Why? What about the problem of graduating from an unaccredited school? Most of the delegates favored returning to public school and attempting to improve them (here was the seed of the idea of boycott).

At the end of Sunday afternoon all were exhausted, as always at conventions. We struggled on to the end of the program. With a joyful shout, the program was declared adopted. Then one young man asked for the floor. "Wait," he said, "I move that copies of this program be sent to every member of the Mississippi legislature, to President Johnson, and to the Secretary General of the United Nations [tumultuous applause], and—wait, wait— a copy to the Library of Congress for its permanent records [pandemonium]."

He was asking that the program of the Mississippi Freedom School Convention be taken seriously. I think it should be. The Civil Rights Movement has been strangely neglectful of program. Who remembers the specific demands of the March on Washington, for instance? What planks were advocated by the Mississippi Freedom Democratic Party? It is true enough that the central demand was in the one case for a civil rights bill, and in the other for seating at the Democratic Convention; and this was as it should have been. But in the not very distant future candidates running for Congressional office will be real, not mock, candidates, and will have to declare themselves intelligently on a variety of issues. These candidates may come out of Freedom Schools. If we do not take their program seriously, it means not taking their ideas seriously. If we do not take their ideas seriously, we should ask ourselves what the Schools are for.

Meridian, Miss.
Aug. 8–9, 1964

1.5.   **Some Letters from Mississippi**

[The human and political experience of the young people who participated in the activities in the South during the summer of 1964 was no less important for the Movement than the actual results. We reprint here several letters from the volume *Letters from Mississippi,* edited by Elizabeth Sutherland (1966).]

Tchula, August 30

There is some strong ambivalence which goes with this work. I sometimes fear that I am only helping to integrate some beautiful people into modern white society with all of its depersonalization (I suppose that has something to do with its industrial nature). It isn't 19th century pastoral romanticism which I feel, but a genuine respect and admiration for a culture which, for all the trouble, still isn't as commercialized and depersonalized as is our Northern mass culture. It is somewhat annoying to see a grubby little Negro cafe with a four foot by six foot tall full color picture of a young handsome Negro in a white dinner jacket next to his beautiful young Negro wife in a $200 cocktail dress in the backyard of their $40,000 brick home standing in front of a massive barbecue with prime ribs of beef and tender young duckling in beautiful glistening copperware serving Pabst Blue Ribbon Beer. A typical American Negro couple on a typical Sunday afternoon. Let's all escape and be like the white man. . . .

Gulfport, July 8

Canvassing, the main technique in voter registration, is an art, and like an art, it is not a scheduled thing. You don't work from 9 to 5. There is no such thing as a completed job until *everyone* is registered. When you cheat and take a lunch hour (and it feels like cheating) you suddenly find yourself reviewing a failure or a success to discover the whys: maybe I should have bullied him slightly, or maybe I should have talked less—and relied on silences. Did I rush him? Should I never have mentioned registering at all, and just tried to make friends and set him at ease? It goes on and on. . . .

Techniques and approaches vary. Mine is often like this:

Hi. My name is Steve M. (shake hands, having gotten name, address, from a mailbox). I'm with COFO. There are a lot of us working in this area, going from house to house trying to encourage people to go down and register to vote. (Pause.) Are you a registered voter? (This is the direct technique. Often people, being afraid, will lie and say yes, but you can usually tell, because they will be very proud.) Are you planning on going down soon? (This makes them declare themselves. Usually they say "yes" or "I hadn't thought about it much." The other answer is "No, I ain't going down at all.") "Well, I have a sample of the registration form." (Take it out and hand it to them.) "You know, some people are a little afraid to go down because they don't quite know what they're getting into. It's something new and different, and they're not sure about it."

Then I go on, "You know, it is so important that everyone get the vote. As it stands now, that man downtown in charge of roads doesn't have to listen to the Negroes. They can't put him out of office. He should be working *for* you." (Much gossip, chatter, mutual questions through all this).

Then pull out the Freedom Democratic Party application.

"This is a protest party. Anyone can join to protest the laws about voter registration and the way elections are carried out."

Moss Point, July 9

On Monday night we had a mass meeting, and the fifth district director, Lawrence Guyot, gave a terrific speech. The gist of his speech was that people say Moss Point is an easy area, "we have nice white folks here," that everyone has what they want already. But we don't have such nice white folks here, he said, and even if we did it shouldn't make us apathetic, it should make us want to take advantage of that extra little space. . . . He kept saying, "What will it take to make you people move? A rape? A shooting? A murder? What will it take?"

At the very end of the meeting we were singing the last verse of "We Shall Overcome," 300 people in a huge circle. Suddenly there were gunshots, and all these people including me, hit the floor in a wave. . . . A few seconds later we all got up trembling. A car of whites had gone by on the road outside and fired three shots through the open door. One Negro girl was hit in the side. She is in the hospital and is going to be all right, but nobody knew that at the time. The whole thing was additionally frightening because during the confusion when everybody was taking cover under tables, etc., a piece of wire or something got caught in an electric fan and made a noise like a machine gun.

All during the meeting, the deputy sheriff was sitting there and the police patrol outside. The sheriff left shortly before the meeting was over and with him the police protection. At the time of the shooting there were no police anywhere around. Instead, they came fifteen minutes later, long after the whites had gotten away. . . .

Meridian, August 4

Last night Pete Seeger was giving a concert in Meridian. We sang a lot of freedom songs, and every time a verse like "No more lynchings" was sung, or "before I'd be a slave I'd be buried in my grave," I had the flash of understanding that sometimes comes when you suddenly think about the meaning of a familiar song. . . . I wanted to stand up and shout to them, "Think about what you are singing—people really have died to keep us all from being slaves." Most of the people there still did not know that the bodies had been found. Finally just before the singing of "We Shall Overcome," Pete Seeger made the announcement. "We must sing 'We Shall Overcome' now," said Seeger. "The three boys would not have wanted us to weep now, but to sing and understand this song." That seems to me the best way to explain the greatness of this project—that death can have this meaning. Dying is not an ever-present possibility in Meridian, the way some reports may suggest. Nor do any of us want to die. Yet in a moment like last night, we can feel that anyone who did die for the Project would wish to be remembered not by tributes or grief but by understanding and continuation of what he was doing. . . .

As we left the church, we heard on the radio the end of President Johnson's speech announcing the air attacks on Vietnam. . . . I could only think, "This must not be the beginning of a war. There is still a freedom fight, and we are winning. We must have time to live and help Mississippi to be alive." Half an hour before, I had understood death in a new way. Now I realize that Mississippi, in spite of itself, has given real meaning to life. In Mississippi you never ask, "What is the meaning of life?" or "Is there any point to it all?" but only that we may have enough life to do all that there is to be done. . . .

Dear Mother and Father: Gulfport, August 12

I have learned more about politics here from running my own precinct meetings than I could have from any Government professor. . . . For the first time in my life, I am seeing what it is like to be poor, oppressed, and hated. And what I see here does not apply only to Gulfport or to Mississippi or even to the South. . . . The people we're killing in Viet Nam are the same people whom we've been killing for years in Mississippi. True, we didn't tie the knot in Mississippi and we didn't pull the trigger in Viet Nam—that is, we personally—but we've been standing behind the knot-tiers and the trigger-pullers too long.

This summer is only the briefest beginning of this experience, both for myself and for the Negroes of Mississippi.

Your daughter,
Ellen

Dear Mom and Dad,   Philadelphia, October 4

As I write this letter I am on the roof of our headquarters observing a sunset I cannot even begin to describe. The hills of red dirt, the pine woods, the mountains and shacks silhouetted against the blood-red sun and clouds, all this and the rest of it takes my breath away. Now and at all such times I find myself possessed by a deep melancholy, a heart-rending feeling for the black and white toilers of this state; both victims of a system that they neither created nor flourish under.

There have been incidents of violence and intimidation but they hardly seem worth noting at a time like this. I only know that I must carry on this struggle that other people have died in, and that some day that system will be changed. . . .

Love,
Tommy

1.6.   *MIKE MILLER:* **The Mississippi Free-dom Democratic Party**

[One outcome of the civil-rights campaign in the South was the creation in 1964 of the Mississippi Freedom Democratic party. The crucial moment for the new political organization came at the national convention of the Democratic party, when the regular racist-dominated delegation from that state was seated in preference to the MFDP. The clash between the new grass-roots movement and the national "liberal" groups on that occasion led directly to a change in the relationship between the two forces and to the civil-rights movement's evolution in a radical direction.]

The Mississippi Freedom Democratic Party was a logical extension of the concept of freedom votes and freedom candidates. That the new Party be a Democratic Party was a matter of some discussion in the State. Following the November, 1963 freedom election success, another state-wide meeting of civil rights activists in Mississippi, held April 26, 1964, discussed the future. Their decision was to create a parallel Democratic Party—one that would, in every respect, comply with the rules and regulations set down by the Mississippi State Constitution for the conduct of political parties, and that would be Democratic because it was in the Democratic Party that significant decisions about the lives of the people in the State were made. However, the MFDP was independent in the sense that it owed no patronage or appointments to the National or State Party. This double character of the Freedom Democratic Party, at once inside and outside the system, is a major source of its national strength and the fear that it later caused the "pros" of the National Democratic Party.

Underlying the Atlantic City Convention challenge were three basic considerations. A special MFDP report named them as "(1) the long history of systematic and studied exclusion of Negro citizens from equal participation in the political processes of the state. . . . ; (2) the conclusive demonstration by the Mississippi Democratic Party of its lack of loyalty to the National Democratic Party in the past . . . ; (3) the intransigent and fanatical determination of the State's political power structure to maintain the status-quo. . . ." At its founding meeting, the MFDP stated, "We are not allowed to function effectively in Mississippi's traditional Democratic Party; therefore, we must find another way to align ourselves with the National Democratic Party." So that such an alignment could be established, the MFDP began organizing meetings throughout the State to send delegates to the Atlantic City Democratic Convention.

Beginning at the precinct level, moving then to county meetings and Congressional District caucuses, and ending with a State Convention on August 9, 1964 in Jackson, Mississippi, the Freedom Democrats went to work. The meetings were conducted under the leadership of a temporary State MFDP Executive Committee which had been chosen on April 26th. Out of the meetings came a full delegation, ready to go to Atlantic City claiming the right to sit as the Democrats of Mississippi.

At the same time as work was being done in the State, representatives of the MFDP were traveling across the country seeking support from Democratic Party delegations for the Challenge. As Convention opening drew near, the following States were among those whose State Democratic Executive Committees or State Conventions had passed resolutions (some of them not binding) supporting the MFDP's Challenge: New York, Massachusetts, District of Columbia, Minnesota, Wisconsin, Michigan, Oregon, California, and Colorado. A SNCC worker who travelled across the Country seeking support for the MFDP later described the Convention experience. Writing in the October, 1964 *Liberator* (an independent Negro monthly), Frank Smith said,

". . . By the time the Convention started, there were eight state delegations which had passed resolutions supporting the seating of the Mississippi Freedom Democratic Party, but word had come down from Washington that President Johnson wanted the Regulars seated and the FDP ousted. The word from the President came as an unexpected shock to the FDP, because their basic strategy had been built around the idea that the President would either be on their side or be neutral. There were, however, political considerations involved, and there is an old political adage that says 'whenever there is cake to be cut, never fail to get your two cents' worth.' With this in mind, it now seems foolish that the FDP could have ever expected the President to be either on their side or neutral."

. . . .

Smith notes that FDP delegates learned a great deal at the Convention. It was clear, he said, that at the Convention "the delegates did not vote on anything. . . . It seems, however, that the delegates were satisfied to have their right to vote as urged, and the decision handed down to them." He points to the contradiction between this and the FDP position. "The FDP philosophy was one-man, one-vote, a philosophy born of the democratic process, and fostered in the faith that if the people are allowed to decide they will make the right and just decisions."

The credentials committee, reflecting the Johnson Administration, offered a series of compromises. The "best" compromise they offered was to give Aaron Henry and Rev. Ed King votes as Delegates-at-Large, to require the Regular Democratic Party of Mississippi to pledge support for the national Democratic ticket and to establish a committee to work on requirements for ending racial discrimination in the Party by the 1968 Convention. Liberal spokesmen across the country could not understand why the FDP refused to accept the compromise. Among other things, they called the decision "apolitical." The FDP answered its critics—though the press never saw fit to carry the answer. In its reply to critics, the FDP said,

> . . . In analyzing why the FDP did not accept this compromise, it is important to understand first what the FDP delegation represented and what it accomplished at the convention. The FDP delegation was not simply an "alternative" delegation chosen by Negro instead of white Mississippians. The FDP is not a Negro party, but an integrated party, open to all whites. It grows directly out of the civil rights movement in Mississippi. It came to Atlantic City demanding, not simply that Negroes be represented, but that racism be ended—in Mississippi and in the Democratic Party.
>
> Moreover, the conditions under which the FDP delegation was chosen were certainly unique. Though the FDP delegation was chosen according to the laws of Mississippi, its role was only partially political. This is so because simply to take part in political processes of the state makes the Negro in Mississippi automatically a rebel against the segregated society. This means that he is in immediate and grave danger of losing his job, his home, and possibly his life. Many of those who represented the FDP at Atlantic City have suffered the most brutal and continual reprisals ever since they began working for their political rights. This lends a peculiar and unique air to their efforts to attend the Convention, and means that they were literally gambling their lives against the right of being seated in Atlantic City.
>
> The third thing that must be understood is that the FDP had the support it needed to win the fight at Atlantic City. Within the Credentials committee there was sufficient support to get the FDP's demands on the floor, there was sufficient support to force a roll call vote. Once a roll call was allowed, most observers agreed that the FDP would have been seated. What prevented this was the massive pressure from the White House, through the mediation of Hubert Humphrey. The FDP delegation was aware of all of this, and it therefore knew that the leadership of the Party and the Convention was denying it what in fact it had the popular support to win. This kind of dictation is what Negroes in Mississippi face and have always faced, and it is precisely this that they are learning to stand up against.

. . . .

The basic tool of political education and decision-making in the FDP at the local level is the workshop. Workshops are designed to do two things: (1) to share information; (2) to open discussion and begin to break through the feeling of being unqualified that still exists among many Negroes in the State. In most places, workshops are now led by members of the MFDP. Only in new, unorganized areas do staff members organize initial workshops and these are soon led by people from the local community. Workshops deal with real problems confronting the FDP, like organizing in the next community or county, or developing a program for coming county elections, or circulating Freedom Registration forms, or selecting local Freedom candidates to run for council, sheriff and other local posts.

Atlantic City represented a major new stage in the development of the FDP. Conservative civil rights spokesmen joined with conservative—and some liberal—Democrats in questioning this new maverick party. Since Atlantic City, FDP leaders have been warned against starting a Third Party. They are told to be "realistic." They are urged not to move too fast. These warnings are reflected by the behavior of the NAACP National Staff person in Mississippi, Charles Evers. The NAACP said it was pulling out of COFO (though the National was never really in) and Evers became the spokesman within the State of this position. Despite Evers' position, branches of the NAACP in Mississippi remained active in the FDP, some of them providing the Party with active members. In other places, local people had their first real internal political fights. It is interesting to note that recently national columnists, like Evans and Novak, have sought to use these internal debates as a lever to split the FDP and to weaken its Northern support. In their nationally syndicated column, Evans and Novak spoke of three known Communists in the FDP delegation. Mrs. Fanny Lou Hamer, former sharecropper and now a major spokesman for the FDP, whose testimony before the Atlantic City Credentials Committee stirred the Nation, was recently called "demagogic." More interesting and important than the attacks has been their apparent lack of success in changing the minds of either Negroes in Mississippi or people across the country who are tired of the Eastlands, and Whittens who have for so long represented the Magnolia State in Congress.

With Atlantic City behind them, the Freedom Democrats went back to Mississippi to begin work on two new endeavors. First, and by this time almost a routine, was a freedom election, with freedom candidates from the FDP running for office and supporting the national Democratic ticket. Second, and now the major national effort of the FDP, was the Congressional Challenge.

. . . .

1.7.   *NORM   FRUCHTER:* **Mississippi:**
                                                           Notes on SNCC

[After the episode of the MFDP, the conflict between the method and objectives of the organization promoted by SNCC in the South and the "liberal" policy of the administration in Washington became increasingly clear. In the following article, Norm Fruchter, a New Left activist involved in community organizing in the North and editor of *Studies on the Left,* gives his impressions. From *Studies on the Left,* Winter 1965.]

1

It takes less than the crammed week I spent in Mississippi to explode the myth that a Federal "presence" is required to enforce a minimum respect for legality and constitutional guarantees, and to eventually integrate the Negro into Mississippi society. Federal presence has been comfortably established in Mississippi for half a century, and is now integrated into a rigid system of discrimination. The host of Federal agents, from income tax collectors to Department of Agriculture employees, who supervise and administer the Federal offices and services which Mississippi utilizes as a sovereign state of the union, violate constitutional guarantees of equality, and departmental regulations concerning equality, as a normal part of their working day. The entire machinery of Federal power and function, which citizens of non-racist states usually take for granted, collaborates with, submits to, and props up institutionalized racism in Mississippi. The spectacle and the experience of illegality is overwhelming to a northerner who had allowed himself to believe, sloppily, that only native white Mississippians were committed to racism and segregation; the reality in Mississippi is that the enormous and supposedly neutral power and function of the Federal government has been traduced to reinforce *apartheid.* To Negroes in Mississippi, Federal presence is a reality; thus far they perceive its use as part of the machinery of white oppression.

The ironies here are enormous. Consider that just last summer, when the hundreds of northern students flooding into Mississippi were threatened with brutality and murder (threats quickly carried out), Robert Kennedy, then Attorney General, plaintively explained to the nation that he had no power or authority to dispatch any Federal presence to Mississippi to protect the young civil rights volunteers. Kennedy's rigidly minimal interpretation of both the situation in Mississippi and the limitations on the exercise of Federal power was disputed by a host of constitutionalists, legal experts, and liberals and radicals more interested in the realities of combatting the violence and illegality of racism in Mississippi than in the political tightrope on which Robert Kennedy was balancing. But what nobody realized (except SNCC) was that the already *existing* Federal machinery in Mississippi could reassert the rule of law and the *formal* equality most states of the union take for granted, if that Federal machinery followed its own rules and guarantees instead of accommodating to the *mores* and customs of segregation. Liberals may have hailed the passage of the 1964 Civil Rights Act as a triumph and a major step toward integration, but SNCC understands, through its experience in Mississippi, that new legislative codes and Federal guarantees of equality may well prove as irrelevant as the already numerous guarantees of equal treatment violated daily *by Federal officers and employees in Mississippi.* Enforcement is the key, and the chances are dim that the new provisions of the 1964 Civil Rights Act will be enforced so radically that they actually disrupt the intricately constructed monolith of segregation which has condemned Mississippi Negroes to a serf-like existence for fifty years. Interviews with leading Mississippi financiers and industrialists indicate that they expect both business as usual and society as usual to result from the passage of the 1964 Civil Right Act. Though the Klans, in rural counties, may be spurred to violence and murder by the work of SNCC organizers with Negro farmers, and though the White Citizens Councils will continue to direct intimidation, violence, and economic reprisal against the burgeoning COFO organizations in the towns, the centers of white power in Mississippi seem undisturbed by both national activity and local organization aimed at breaching the structures of racism. Those centers of white power understand the flexibility and permanence of the monolith they have created; the final irony is that only they, and SNCC, understand how deeply Federal power is implicated in the operation of that monolith, and how totally Federal power and policy is committed to its perpetuation.

2

A short week in Mississippi encourages the perception of countless scalding ironies. Consider that it took the spectacle of almost saintly bravery by the sit-inners, Freedom Riders, and the early SNCC organizers who infiltrated the deep south in the early 1960's, to convince the liberal elements in the nation that some sort of national focus and effort was necessary to begin to integrate the Negro into Mississippi society. The various martyrdoms of some of the most courageous of our youth were required, to dramatize the extent of racism in Mississippi. Now we, as a nation, have progressed to the point where some notions of the spread, and incalculable damage, of racism in Mississippi (but not in the other states of the deep south, where conditions are similar) are generally accepted, and the debate, in liberal quarters, concerns the minimum of Federal involvement necessary to integrate the Mississippi Negro. But SNCC (and by SNCC I mean the movement, and its evolving local organizations, both SNCC organizers, and the local people who sustain them and act with them) seems to have abandoned the goal of eventual integration into *existing* Mississippi society as both unrealistic and undesirable. Instead, SNCC seems to be working to develop alternative organizations and institutions which are responsive to what local Negroes need and want, existing *outside* the majority society. The notion of a counter-community, which builds institutions and relationships based on assumptions about identity, personality, work, meaning, and aspirations *not accepted* in the majority society, is elaborated both in discussions within SNCC and within the new institutions the movement is evolving. There is much sterile debate, outside SNCC, about how revolutionary the Mississippi Freedom Democratic Party is; within SNCC, the debate concerns how the MFDP will be used. Its future, and its ultimate goals, are open, but most people in SNCC understand that the MFDP is not a reform caucus operating within the Democratic Party, pledged to the creation of LBJ's "Great Society."

3

Primarily a movement, SNCC is only incidentally an organization. As a movement, it is committed to certain assumptions which approximate ideals, rather than to a series of specific goals achieved through defined programs. SNCC's cardinal assumption is that an individual is free only when he can effectively control, and carry out, all the decisions affecting the way he lives his life. SNCC's subsidiary assumption, more a statement of faith defining how it must operate than a statement of its orienting ideal, is that the rural southern Negro has been so systematically excluded from and oppressed by the majority society that his clear desire is for his freedom, and that he does not define that freedom according to the values and aspirations accepted in the majority society. From these two assumptions, one about the meaning of human freedom, the other concerning the consciousness of the rural southern Negro, all the paradoxes of SNCC's style follow. For what many northerners, especially northerners with organizational experience, perceive as a fuzziness in SNCC's ideology, a failure to formulate programs and goals, and a paralyzing confusion about direction, all stem from SNCC's conscious choice to leave all those questions open. More than that; since SNCC assumes that the demand for freedom, on the part of local Negroes, will remain constant, and that the only meaningful freedom is a situation where a man controls his own life, they accept the inevitable conclusion that SNCC ought not to *lead* local people, or impose leadership, solutions, programs on them, but should become the tool by which local people can begin to transform, and control, the organizations and institutions which presently dominate their lives. SNCC accepts what seems to be organizational confusion stemming from a refusal to utilize bureaucracies, hierarchies of responsibility and all the mechanisms of rationalized decision-making, and an inefficiency which seems nightmare, because it is concentrating all its energies on *reducing* the gap between organizers and local people, and attempting to translate its own embryonic organizational structures into institutions which evolve out of local communities and meet local needs. Out of this refusal to organize, to lead, to bureaucratize, and to specialize functions, come real failures; judged by the standards of a normal centralized organization, SNCC *is* hopelessly inefficient. There are hundreds of services it cannot provide, and thousands of tasks it can only lamely accomplish. But one of SNCC's purposes is to raise the question of just how well all the organizations operating on bureaucratic assumptions within the majority society have served human freedom; what SNCC assumes is that eventually organizations will be established to meet the needs of the southern Negro which are currently denied, and that these organizations will be as irrelevant and damaging as the Federal structures operating in the South today. SNCC tries to take its definition of human freedom, and the operating imperatives which follow from it, as absolutes; it is prepared to accept all its supposed failures, and to judge what it is doing not by standards of efficiency or progress toward a solution, but by the numbers of local people it has involved, the qualities of relationships within the local organizations, and the new forms and institutions local people evolve to meet their own needs. Prediction in this fluid situation is hazardous, but given current examples like the MFDP, the cooperatives evolving in some rural areas, and the hope that the embryonic Freedom Schools develop into an alternative educational system, organized on different assumptions from kindergarten to college, it is not too difficult to perceive the possibility that the movement may evolve an alternate set of institutions, developed and run by local Negroes, across the entire Black Belt.

4

Orthodox left-wingers sometimes find SNCC disconcerting because it meets none of their criteria for radical organizations, and shares none of their totemic demands (planning for public rather than private ends, extension of public ownership and control, a national health service, massive public housing programs, an equally massive public works program). But consider the relevance of any of those incantations to SNCC's ideal of human freedom. From the standpoint of whether a man is actually controlling the decisions that shape his life, or whether those decisions are being made for him, planning for public ends rather than for private accumulation is certainly more beneficent but hardly more relevant. What is crucial is the *mechanism* of planning, for if the decisions which affect countless lives are still so centralized and concentrated that the person affected is rendered impotent, a radical planner is little better than an entrepreneurial planner, or than decisions which result from controlled market competition. A similar argument holds for all the totems of realignment; the necessity to reshuffle our national parties into a liberal-conservative confrontation. Until the entire *mechanism* of our political life is transformed, and the basis of our representation and its power to make decisions altered, national politics will continue its rehearsals of current myths and banalities, and the basic gap between the real issues facing people's lives and the unreality of our political processes will remain. SNCC's ideal is a basic change in the experienced quality of life, rather than new opportunities within hitherto closed institutions. The genuine "movement" characteristics are evident in the basic assumptions SNCC people constantly challenge. Left-wingers whose original generating ideals have atrophied or petrified into slogans or programmatic solutions find themselves as alienated from SNCC as from all the "quality of life" responses to the decay of the majority society which have been variously labelled Bohemian, Beat, Hip, or simply non-political. The difference is that SNCC is political, is clearly acting in political and historical space, and in three short years, has become the most significant radical organization in America.

5

There are a series of labels for the assumptions about human freedom to which SNCC is committed, and similar labels for SNCC's operating faith in local people's ability to sustain their movement and develop their own institutions. More important than the labels is the conventional judgment that no group committed to similar assumptions has ever endured, let alone approached realizing their ideals. (It is also possible to reverse the argument, and declare that no organization committed to *any* ideals has ever succeeded by accepting and practicing manipulation; the damage to personality evident within so many left-wing groups in America testifies to the incalculable danger in choosing ends over means.) What is so exciting about SNCC is that many of its staff are aware of the problematic, hazardous, even utopian nature of their ideals while at the same time remaining passionately committed to them and to the movement. The consciousness of the enormous odds against what SNCC is attempting, and all the historical, social, and personality factors which indicate its failure, become part of the consciousness which the movement carries. But for all the portents of failure, there are arguments for SNCC's continued development which transcend the omnipotent fact that it *is* developing. Given the Negro majority in the Black Belt, the certainty that the white racist society within that Black Belt will never open to permit even the formal accommodations which characterize the North, and the continuation of national attention, so that open repression and genocide remain an uneasy option even for fanatic racists, SNCC has the time, the room, and (perhaps) the resources to evolve across the entire Black Belt.

The question of resources seems problematic; it may not be. Right now SNCC depends on the continuation of a certain small amount of Federal cooperation, because some of the institutions SNCC evolves take shape within Federal jurisdictions and services. SNCC also depends on private financial support to meet the growing cost of all its operations. There are indications that the Johnson administration may attempt to detach SNCC from the umbrella of civil rights organizations by Red-baiting SNCC; the NAACP, when it withdrew from COFO, indulged in what seemed preliminary Red-baiting. If SNCC were to be seriously Red-baited and isolated, both government cooperation and private financing might dry up. Would community resources prove sufficient, and allow SNCC to continue as a movement while fading into local communities? Even if SNCC is not deliberately isolated by the government, will its own evolution isolate it, and alienate its support and financing? And finally, if SNCC sustains its movement, and spreads across the Black Belt, what will it do about the southern cities, where the bulk of the southern Negroes will live in ten years' time? And what about the northern cities, where the majority of northern Negroes live now? What implications does SNCC's work have for the young community organizers in the northern ghettos, and for the embryonic work with the unemployed throughout this country's metropolitan areas? Is it significant that some of the leaders of the Berkeley Free Speech Movement have worked with SNCC in Mississippi? What are the possibilities of coalition, and of the shape of a new politics, inherent in the movement? To all these questions, SNCC people's response is characteristic. "We don't know. But we have to find out."

1.8.   *CHARLES COBB:* **Atlanta: The Bond Campaign**

[In the summer of 1965, Julian Bond, secretary of a local chapter of SNCC, attempted to use the electoral process to challenge the power of the racist structures in the South. He ran for the Georgia legislative assembly, defeating a Negro minister in the primaries, and was subsequently elected to the state assembly. Twice, however, he was denied his seat because of his expressed opposition to the war in Vietnam. Now a recognized member, he was among those who supported the nomination of Eugene McCarthy in 1968 as Democratic party presidential candidate. The following report is a direct account of his first electoral campaign, written by another SNCC field secretary, Charles Cobb. From *Studies on the Left,* Spring 1965.]

I approached the campaign with some misgivings based on a serious question I had about anyone being able to function effectively in the state legislature without the support of the "establishment." I will confess that I was also worried about the corrupting influence of politics in general. I felt, and I still feel, the threat of American "politics" has on people who "play the game"—you know, like touch (politics) and be tainted.

On the other hand, I felt that Julian on the floor of the Georgia State Legislature would, by virture of the fact that he was a young, black SNCC worker, inherently focus attention on the politics that he articulated. In Julian's politics, I have faith, so in the end I based my decision to work on knowing Julian.

Most people on staff say the cities are hardest to organize. They say the people there tend to be "too apathetic." We don't know yet what can tap and sustain the energies of the people locked up in the city ghettoes. What is clearest to me in the cities is that the politics that runs things is out of the hands of the people who need to use it most. (People can enter into politics, e.g., registration and voting, but they can't control it.) Julian's campaign, then, was a chance for me to explore the possibilities of people being able to use the politics that exist. Within the confines of today's "political realities," I don't think that SNCC ever had such a *real* opportunity before.

. . . .

State legislatures are a mystery. What we know about them, generally, is that a group of people sit up there and do something or other—that is called politics. Which is, in reality, outside of the day-to-day concerns of the majority of people since they don't understand it. It is important to understand that during the campaign Julian was *seen* and *known*. End then the mysterious political aura around at least one state legislator-to-be. People voted for someone they knew and felt comfortable with. Very important; a *politician* who took the time to walk streets, knock on doors and know people, a politician who was not threatened by a constituency that was organized around issues and not the politician. An operating philosophy of ours was that if hard work can win a campaign then we sure as hell intended to win it.

I think that literally 100 per cent of the people I canvassed had *never* had anyone come to their house, sit down and seriously talk to them about their community. Certainly not a political campaign worker or candidate, suggesting that a community had to act as a community if they wanted to talk about and make relevant politics. Imagine a politician suggesting that he wasn't the most relevant thing in politics! Imagine that politician winning! Think if that can be sustained and extended.

. . . .

We were taken very seriously. First in the neighborhoods, where, as in the rural areas, people judged us by what they saw us doing in relation to what we said we hoped to do and see happen. We were honest and consistent. We got support from the neighborhoods. House meetings were held.

We did not need the Negro democratic machine in terms of the politics we were organizing, which was politics that did not belong to politicians. We were taken seriously by this machine because, if we won we couldn't be controlled by them, which seriously threatens the operation of this machine. Especially, if what we do catches on and extends itself. Leroy Johnson (Negro State Senator) wants "politicians" he can control and use for his political ends.

Negro politics in Georgia, not to mention other Deep South states, is still *new* enough and open enough for Negroes to force a whole new concept of what politics is.

Immediately after it became clear that Julian had won, I thought that SNCC could have pulled off the same thing in all of the Districts where Negroes had won. There were districts in Georgia where *nobody* even bothered to qualify. I guess these seats are still open. What that could mean is that the issues and questions that are raised in communities as a result of our work could be amplified on the floor of the Georgia House, hooking communities together on common issues. Imagine, ten SNCC guys in the Georgia House committed to organizing their districts to using the seats in the House to meet community needs defined by the community.

I think we will increasingly find, especially in the urban South, chances to explore American politics and the ways it can be shaped (if it can at all) to meet our needs. This can mesh and hook up with the radical forms of our own (like FDP) that we are developing.

Admittedly, there are dangers inherent in this exploration, (e.g., pressure of traditional politics, isolation, the fact that some people will be corrupted). However, I am fascinated by the idea of communities moving in and out of traditional American political forms. It implies a creation of instability of these political forms, created by people whose needs are not being and probably will not be met by the forms anyway. I think it is to our advantage to have oppressive government unstable. They have to release some of their control to steady themselves, or they try and steady themselves by increasing control, which heightens the potential for rebellion.

It is a fact now that Julian is the Democratic nominee for the Georgia House from the 136th District. More than likely he will be elected on June 16. I think that SNCC needs to commit itself to an all-out effort to get an *overwhelming* turnout for this election. For one thing that characterizes all comment on this election is the expected poor turnout and interest.

We need to disprove "voter apathy" which really is *election irrelevancy*. The concept we need to focus attention on is that of people's right to shape and use politics. If that can happen in any *one* district in Georgia (or anywhere) it poses a threat to current politics all over. In effect, it means that our political campaign *does not end* on June 16.

One more note: Julian's opponent was a minister. I think this was the first time I've been in the South that I've seen a large reaction against the ambitions of a minister. Apparently people just draw the line at having a minister *overtly* involved in *political decision-making*. "I ain't havin' no damn preacher up there." Maybe it hints at a general awareness of their exploitation by ministers. Anyway, I think it helped us that Bill Creacy was a preacher.

What I learned mostly from the campaign was, that in the final analysis, organizing the urban is the same. What people need—all over!—is something they can grab hold of, or build, that is their own. Even if it's just their individual life. So Mrs. Williams now wants a Freedom School and Mrs. Bolden wants action. The Board Umbrella was Julian's campaign which was our (SNCC's) idea but there is no reason why it can't be taken over by the community that makes up the 136th House District to be shaped and reshaped by them and made theirs by them and what they do.

I found that my own fears about controlling people or manipulating them blurred in the give and take dialogue (which implies give and take of decision-making and ideas) with the community; within the context of Julian's campaign, at least, I was part of that community.

FURTHER READINGS

Altbach, Philip. "The Quiet Campus." *New Leader,* August 5, 1963.
Apple, R. W. "Ivy-League Integrationists." *The Reporter,* February 14, 1963.
Braden, Anne. "The Southern Freedom Movement in Perspective." *Monthly Review,* July/August 1965.
_____. "The Students: A New Look." *The Southern Patriot,* May 1963.
Cannon, Terence, and Wellman, David. *No Hiding Place: White Radicals and the Civil Rights Movement.* Unpublished manuscript, 1967.
"Civil Rights and the Birth of Community." *Studies on the Left,* p. 5, Spring 1964.
Fruchter, Norm, and Rabinowitz, Victor. "An Exchange on SNCC." *Studies on the Left,* Spring 1965.
Hayden, Tom. "SNCC, The Qualities of Protest." *Studies on the Left,* Winter 1965.
_____. *Revolution in Mississippi.* SDS pamphlet, 1964.
Jones, Charles. "SNCC: Nonviolence and Revolution." *New University Thought,* September/October 1963.
Kempton, Murray. "Conscience of the Convention. "*New Republic,* September 5, 1964.
King, Martin Luther. *Where Do We Go From Here: Chaos or Community?* New York: Harper and Row, 1967.
Kopkind, Andrew. "Bureaucracy's Long Arm: Too Heady a Start in Mississippi?" *The New Republic,* August 21, 1965.
_____. "Seat Belts for Mississippi's Five." *The New Republic,* July 24, 1965.
_____. "The New Radicals in Dixie." *New Republic,* April 10, 1965.
"MFDP Runs Candidates in Local Elections." *The Movement,* May 1965.
Payne, Bruce. "SNCC: An Overview Two Years Later." *The Activist,* November 1965.
Rosenfield, Gerard. "What Happened to the Trials of CDGM?" *The Movement,* March, April and June 1966.
Rustin, Bayard. "From Protest to Politics: The Future of the Civil Rights Movement." *Commentary,* February 1965.
Shapiro, Herbert. "Julian Bond: Georgia's Uppity Legislator." *The Nation,* February 7, 1966.
Southern Regional Council. *The Student Protest Movement: A Recapitulation.* September 1961.
Sutherland, Elizabeth. "Mississippi: Summer of . . . Discontent." *The Nation,* October 11, 1965.
_____(ed.). *Letters from Mississippi.* New York: Signet Books, 1966.
Trillin, Calvin. "Letter from Jackson." *The New Yorker,* August 29, 1964.
Walzer, Michael. "A Cup of Coffee and a Seat." *Dissent,* Spring 1960.
Watters, Pat. "Encounter with the Future." *New South,* May 1965.
Zinn, Howard. *Albany: A Study in National Responsibility.* Southern Regional Council, 1962.
_____. "The Double Job in Civil Rights." *New Politics,* III: 1 Winter 1964.
_____. *SNCC: The New Abolitionists.* Boston: Beacon Press, 1965.

2
Peace, Protest and Civil Liberties

2.1. *FREDERICK MOORE:* **Statement About ROTC**

[In October 1959, the isolated gesture of the eighteen-year-old student Frederick Moore, who conducted a one-man vigil on the Berkeley campus against compulsory military training through the university's ROTC (Reserve Officer Training Corps) program, represented the first sign of the future peace and antimilitary protests. The following text is part of a two-page document explaining the reasons for the protest.]

I refuse to take ROTC. I filed an exemption form asking to be excused from the military training requirements. I gave as my reason: I am a conscientious objector. . . . I object to killing and any action aiding war or purpose of war due to my religious and conscientious beliefs. It was rejected.

I talked to students and some instructors about my problem with ROTC. Although some were sympathetic, they agreed nothing could be done. I went to the Dean of Students Office and explained my reasons for not wanting to take ROTC. They showed me a list stating the exemptions. My case did not fall under any of the exemptions (exemptions were: physical disability, previous military training or service, or foreign citizenship). I was advised to take ROTC if I wanted to attend the University of California. I left the office wondering why the University did not respect conscience.

Many times I was advised to give up my beliefs, take military training and "get it over with." I could not bring myself to agree with them.

He (the Dean of Students) made it quite clear that I either sign up and take ROTC or withdraw from the University.

Through fasting for seven days I hope to help bring about action which will result in a provision making ROTC voluntary or exempting students who cannot participate in military training due to their religious and conscientious beliefs.

This fast is undertaken to show my earnestness concerning this problem. I seek to get the Regents to agree with me not by force or coercion but by appealing to their better judgment and understanding.

I will neither participate in nor support any action whose purpose is killing. The purpose of military training is to train men for war—train men to kill. I therefore cannot comply with the ROTC requirement.

2.2. **SLATE Peace Committee: Statement**

[The theme of peace was of fundamental importance in the new student protest at the beginning of the 1960s. In 1960, at a national meeting of Students for a Sane Nuclear Policy, it was proposed that SANE promote student peace marches during the Easter vacation. The president of a Berkeley student group, the SLATE Peace Committee, supported the motion with the following statement.]

If there is one question that touches us closely, it is the question of peace in the world. That is natural because we are young, because we have much that is still before us, much that is still to be done. Because we are young, we live in the shadow of tomorrow; our hope is towards the days to come, towards all that they hold open to us, towards the future and all within it that we were born to fulfill. Because we are young, life, itself, is cherished by us; we wait for the flood of its fullness, its grief and its joy, to nourish us; we wait for its touch to complete us.

But because we live in these times of nuclear arms, we live in the shadow of death. We live under the threat of a doom that menaces not one but all of us, not merely ourselves, but our children, and their children as well. The weight that has been placed upon us is a weight that no other generation in the history of man has had to bear—it is the weight of the future itself, for we, here, and every day of our lives, stand responsible for the future, stand responsible for its being and for its birth.

Because we are young, and because we come to the scene of human history in the hour of its crisis, we face the prospect of war between nations with special feelings, we face the idea of such war with a special reserve and fear.

Our fathers came to manhood when, in Europe, men were dying brutally by the tens of thousands in the war "to end all wars." And when we were born, the war which was to win for us "one world," was already there or on the way.

Seventy million people were killed in that war, seventy million in our first few years of life, and the hope that they died for and that they cherished was lost. For they fought not only to stop the threat of Nazism, but to give birth to a world community in which people might seek out decency and richness in their lives without peril and without fear.

But the work of creation is a long and arduous way, the skill by which it is won is difficult and hard to secure. That is why the whole concept of war between nations is a difficult concept for us in this war-born generation to conceive, the whole concept of realizing positive ends by such war, impossible for us to understand.

We remember our older brothers, some of us, and the "big kids" on the block who went away ten years ago to Korea; we remember them and we look in dismay at the Spring papers which tell of the revolt of the Korean students, a revolt to throw out the very dictator for whom our brothers died. Is this what they died for? We remember that Chiang Kai-shek is a dictator too. . . .

Most of all, we think of Japan, of Hiroshima. We think of the 100,000 lives snuffed out, judged in a matter of moments, without appeal; we consider the women and children, consumed, where they stood, in a fire without pity.

We think of the children born now in Japan, those who are born deformed as the result of a blast of fifteen years ago, in whose history they had no part. What can one tell a child, doomed to die of leukemia before he is twenty, because, two decades before he was born, members of his grandparents' generation bombed Pearl Harbor?

What kind of justice is it that punishes the future?

What kind of justice can there be in a war in which mankind, itself, may die?

We cannot envision war between nations as anything but self-destruction and world disaster in these terms. Democracy cannot be imposed by ballistic missiles. We have found it difficult enough to nourish the democratic ideal in our country in which it was born. How then are we to force democracy on nations that have no democratic traditions? How will mass annihilation further our ends?

It is clear that the power of democracy is a living idea. Freedom of speech, equality, self-determination of peoples, are the most powerful political ideas in the world. To believe in democracy is to believe in this fact and to know, that given peace and stability, and freedom from hunger, these ideas will inevitably come to prevail.

That is why we, as students, see the struggle for peace as the major struggle of our times, and by peace we mean a non-partisan peace, an unequivocal peace. Peace itself is a victory for us and for what we stand for; it is the victory that we have to win. For only through peace can mankind be won to the democratic way and the democratic ideal; only through peace can we enter the fields of tomorrow and seed them for the generations to come.

2.3.   *DALE L. JOHNSON:* **On the Ideology of the Campus Revolution**

[In addition to peace, the demand for civil liberties within the country and the protest against the government's attitude toward Cuba were the central themes of student protest during the period 1960–1962. The following article was written for *Studies on the Left* by Dale L. Johnson, a graduate student in sociology at Stanford and a leader of the committee against American intervention in Cuba. From *Studies on the Left,* II: 1.]

It used to be that the wise and benevolent elder generation bemoaned the apathy and lack of direction of their off-spring. They wondered at the lack of response in the college atmosphere of ideas, they were amused at the prevalence of Spring water fights and panty raids, and raised their eyebrows at those who withdrew to North Beach. In recent months it seems to many that a revolution has taken place on Campus. Disturbed by recent student political activities, California legislators have questioned the wisdom of granting salary increases to a Berkeley faculty and administration which allowed its students to flaunt, unpunished, the "law and order" represented by the HUAC. Furthermore, U. of C. faculty members have been attacked as willing agents of the conspiracy to corrupt the pliable minds of youth.

Although many campuses are experiencing this upheaval, the center of activities seems to reside in the San Francisco Bay Area, particularly at the University of California. Space does not permit a complete analysis of the campus revolution's development, but it is possible to note briefly something of the nature of the movement.

U. of C. students, by and large inactive since the 1930's, took the first step several years ago by organizing SLATE, a "liberal" campus political party. Since the inception of SLATE, which managed to stimulate, organize, and direct student protest toward the world of politics, a multitude of single-purpose groups, permanent and *ad hoc*, have sprung up. Last year the Chessman case brought on a tremendous student drive for an end to the death penalty; there have been dramatic protests against compulsory ROTC; students have worked to end discrimination in housing; Woolworths has been picketed almost daily; demonstrations against missile bases have been conducted by students with strong pacifist convictions. By far the most effective in stirring protest, however, have been the sit-ins and the demonstrations against the HUAC in San Francisco. The effective use of direct action techniques in the sit-ins and the highly dramatic nature of the anti-HUAC campaign brought nationwide attention. As a result of these instances, several thousand students of this area and throughout the country have become aware that they can express their discontent effectively by joining others of like mind on the picket-line.

Since the May anti-HUAC "riots," new organizations and spontaneous protest movements have grown up; the socialist groups of the area have reported a high degree of interest in their programs (the Young Peoples Socialist League and the Socialist Party—Social Democratic Federation of Berkeley, blessed with highly skilled leadership, have been particularly successful of late). The American Legion Convention in San Francisco last summer invited a demonstration by manhandling a few students who had the audacity to carry signs questioning the wisdom of Legion resolutions. Several hundred from this area called for civil rights and "freedom now" in front of the Democratic Convention in Los Angeles. The audience for Nixon's San Francisco speech was shocked to see students raise placards calling for "No More U-2's." There was some talk, but not much action, for a "Vote No For President" campaign. Finally, and I think this may prove to be the most important of all, there has been the impact of the Cuban Revolution.

To a remarkable degree there are ideological similarities between the Cuban and Campus revolutions. Both Cuban and Campus rebels are *strong* dissenters, firm in their convictions and willing to speak out and act militantly in spite of the mighty coercive powers of the American state. Both are pragmatic, always putting first things first, with rarely an eye to ultimate ends. In Cuba this takes the form of "the year of agrarian reform," the "year of education," the "year of industrialization." . . . Here at home the pragmatic outlook is manifested in the multitude of single-issue groups devoted simply to getting things done in the most effective manner possible. Organizations form almost overnight to work on specific questions—civil liberties, academic freedom, ROTC, the death penalty, civil rights. Both Cuban and Campus revolutions are inexperienced, groping movements sometimes stumbling, sometimes making mistakes of a tactical nature—with either too much anti-Americanism or too much fear of offending or alienating "public opinion." Most important, their motivating ideologies are neither socialism—Marxian or otherwise—nor liberalism, although they combine elements of both. Rather, the ideology of both the *Barbudos* of Cuba and the campus revolutionaries is a refreshing combination of humanism and rationalism. The Fidelista *knows* the meaning of misery and exploitation, of disease and illiteracy, of unemployment and squalor in the midst of plenty, of graft and corruption—he has lived it; the campus rebel, lacking the Cuban experience, nonetheless *feels* it—it violates his sense of values. The Fidelista understands the ailments of Cuba—and of Guatemala, Haiti, the Dominican Republic, and all the remaining "hungry nations"—and he intends to translate this knowledge into action. In at least one sense the Fidelista is very fortunate. He is confronted with the opportunity to steer Cuba's, and perhaps Latin America's, destiny upon the path which he chooses. So he sets about, rationally, to build a new society. Many students at U. of C., Stanford, San Francisco and San Jose State Colleges, at Wisconsin, and Chicago and NYU grasp and appreciate this attempt to direct human history, to take hold of one's environment and shape it, to institutionalize the better human values. These students also recognize the dangers involved, both for themselves and the Cubans. They would oppose both American intervention and totalitarianism in the name of Cuban nationalism or socialism, but they are not without understanding for revolutionary excesses.

There are also, of course, important differences between the Cuban and Campus rebels. The former are united, sure of themselves and where they are going. The latter, though often united on specific issues, are divided over basic questions, hesitant, and with no permanent goals or direction.

No all-inclusive term adequately characterizes the range of ideologies which influence the campus rebels. While such a characterization might fairly represent the convictions of one subgroup, it would radically conflict with those of another. The link which binds the various tendencies within the student movement is a firm belief in the value and necessity of *active dissent*. In the course of its short existence, the campus revolution has forged an ideology of dissent which sustains its adherents during the thick of political action and in some sense represents a compromise between the opposing trends of individualism and mass action.

Most of us radicals of the 1960's would agree with Daniel Bell that the post war years have witnessed the "end of ideology." This we lament rather than applaud. We take violent exception to his statement that the "tendency to convert concrete issues into ideological problems, to invest them with moral color . . . is to invite conflicts which can only damage a society." This is the voice of a disillusioned man whose ideology is anti-ideology. It is a conservative message and it is nonsense.

The old-left is dead; and many of the reasons offered in Bell's book seem valid. Contemporary "liberalism" is impotent; and no longer even *is* liberalism in our sense. We are tired of the stereotyped responses of the Marxist, and disgusted with the liberal's rhetoric, agnosticism, and incapacity for political action. We are radical, but disregard the orthodoxy of Marxism. We are liberal, but not tied to the status quo. In a sense we are eclectic, willing to accept the best of both philosophies. The books of C. Wright Mills are well thumbed by us, and it is his sort of radicalism with which many of us identify. Yet Mills is not our intellectual leader, nor are we blind to his faults. We criticize him for his elitism and a certain callousness toward fact. These criticisms reflect what we have learned from the writings of Lenin and others about mass movements and from the neo-positivists about science.

In a sense we are lost, for we do drift about in rough and uncharted seas. We are fearful that if we do establish a steady course, it may take us somewhere we do not want to go. We also know that the huge waves tossed up from the depths of conservative tradition and state authority may weaken, or even destroy us.

Perhaps this is why we have only a dissenting ideology. We unhesitantly express what we are against, but are less sure of what we are for. Because of this, we are rather more reformist than revolutionary. We tend to believe in non-violence not only because it is effective, but also because it is inherently good.

To be sure, most of us are uncommitted—except to humanism, rationality, and an action program. However, we do number among our supporters some who are, but even their commitment may be of a transient nature. Some are "Stevensonians," others are social democrats, a few fall in with the Socialist Workers Party. The techniques of non-violent action are appealing, especially to those among us of pacifist inclination. There are even a few among us who sympathize with the goals and means of the Communist Party. Communism is, of course, an issue that splits us. It is a thing pushed upon us by old loyalties and politics of the past. Fortunately, the freedom and tolerance that we preach and the tendency to issue-orientation minimize the potential disruptive aspects of the situation.

In short, our humanism and acceptance of democratic principles sensitize us to problems, our rational faculty reveals solutions consistent with our values, and both propel us to action. The future is replete with issues. Let us unite in optimism and action.

POSTSCRIPT: The American intervention in Cuba, undertaken after this communication was in print, has had a tremendous impact on both the size of the student movement and its ideology, at least in the Bay Area. Many student "hangers-on" and potential rebels have been activated by the gross nature of the irrationality in high places. Most important, however, is the fact that U.S. imperialistic ventures have served to *radicalize* the dissenters. For example: (*a*) the concept of demonstration has been altered to include "dramatic non-violent acts of civil disobedience"; (*b*) new and truly radical students have gained leadership positions and the old activists have moved to the left along with their student base of support.

2.4.   **Student Peace Union: Documents**

> [The Student Peace Union was the first nationwide political association of a student character. Formed in Chicago in 1959, it adopted in 1961 a "third camp" position, particularly through the influence of the young socialists who occupied a heretical position with respect to the pro-Western line taken by the Socialist party. The following documents are the SPU statement of purpose and the text of a leaflet distributed in November 1962.]

Statement of Purpose

The Student Peace Union is an organization of young people who believe that neither war nor the threat of war can any longer be successfully used to settle international disputes and that neither human freedom nor the human race can long survive in a world committed to militarism.

Without committing any member to a precise statement of policy, the SPU draws together young people for a study of alternatives to war and engages in education and action to end the present Arms Race. The SPU works toward a society which will ensure both peace and freedom and which will suffer no individual or group to be exploited by another. Because both East and West have pursued foreign policies which are not in the interests of their own people or the people of the world and because both bear major responsibility for the Cold War, the Student Peace Union believes that the peace movement must act independently of both East and West, must apply the same standard of criticism to both, and must seek new and creative means of achieving a free and peaceful society.

Students Speak for Peace

November 11 was originally set aside for the celebration of the armistice ending World War I, and today is used to honor all veterans, living and dead, who fought for the peace and freedom of this country. We honor these men; and we ask, "Wouldn't they, who fought for peace and freedom, be best honored by our seeking peace, with freedom, today?"

No one can deny the horrors of nuclear war. Against the monstrous weapons of push-button warfare, there can be little defense. Few, if any, missiles can be stopped. Cities, when attacked, will become seas of fire sucking the oxygen out of the air and suffocating those left unburned. Fallout shelters cannot provide the protection needed for the very long period of time after an attack during which return to the face of the earth would be fatal.

Yet both major powers are engaged in a headlong arms race to prepare for war. Tensions increase constantly, while communications between the power blocs are frustrated by mutual fear and hostility. The influence of the military is rising throughout the world. Nuclear weapons will be acquired by many more nations. The danger of accidental war becomes greater. An error of human judgment could produce a catastrophe. These factors make the arms race more suicidal daily.

Freedom is not being preserved. The military approach to the solution of basic conflicts between the U.S. and the U.S.S.R. leads to restriction of freedom and negation of basic human dignity and human rights within both blocs. Former President Eisenhower, on Jan. 17, 1961, and again on Oct. 12, warned the American people that "we must guard against the acquisition of unwarranted influence by the military-industrial complex." This growing power "is a very serious matter . . . a very difficult thing to get out of after you've once got into it—no matter how intelligently you went in." In the Soviet Union, likewise, there are suppressions in the name of defense against "western imperialism."

Both sides are contributing to the arms race. Neither is actively seeking a way out of this spiral of terror. Both are more concerned with maintaining their military power than with the welfare of the world's peoples. WHAT ALTERNATIVES ARE THERE?

All over the country today students are acting, each group in its own way, in search of alternatives. We seek consideration of the points listed below, believing that only by adopting such policies can the U.S. obtain a lasting peace, with the courage to take steps which will free the world from the sword hanging over its head, the courage to accept one's responsibilities in a complex and changing world. These steps would constitute a turn towards peace and away from war. We urge:

—that America not heed the hysterical cry of those who would duplicate the criminal act of the Soviet Union by testing in the atmosphere;
—immediate cessation of all testing, followed by further American initiatives towards peace;
—settlement of the Berlin crisis by the creation of a nuclear-free and disarmed zone in Central Europe—both Germanies must be taken out of the Cold War;
—investigation of alternative use of the huge sums spent for ineffective "defense" measures, in order to cut the tie of our economy to the Cold War;
—massive aid to the economically underdeveloped countries;
—the building of a strong U.N., with increased responsibilities in the field of arbitration of crisis situations.

FURTHER READINGS

Bluestone, Donald M. "Unity in the Peace Movement." *Sanity,* Spring 1962.
Brickman, Allan. *The Campus Movement Against R.O.T.C.* SPU pamphlet.
Deming, Barbara. "The Ordeal of SANE." *The Nation,* March 11, 1961.
Horowitz, David. *Student.* New York: Ballantine Books, 1962.
Hughes, H. Stuart. "No War of Liberation." Speech. *Liberation,* December 1962.
Mitford, Jessica. "The Indignant Generation." *The Nation,* May 27, 1961.
Oppenheimer, Martin. *Students and the Peace Movement: Problems and Perspectives.* Mimeograph, 1961.
Roberts, Steven V. "Something Had To Be Done." *The Nation,* March 3, 1962.
Werthman, Carl. "The Student Organization of Protest." *New University Thought,* Fall 1960.

3

Community
Organization

[In summer 1963 Students for a Democratic Society (SDS) became involved in a program of research and action on problems of poverty (ERAP), which led to community organizing projects. Carl Wittman, one of the SDS activists most involved in those projects, had been president of the Swarthmore Political Action Committee and had worked in Cambridge, Maryland and Chester, Pennsylvania. The following piece was one of the first documents to explain the reasons for student involvement in social problems at the local level. SDS pamphlet, April 1964.]

It is important that campus political activists take stock of the new opportunities which are increasingly evident for campus programs which engage large numbers of students in constructive action, and still permit those participants and others on the campus to relate to the major issues of our society.

Four years ago, this was not possible. There were those activities which a small number of activists with enough initiative and foresight could do. There were also a number of mass activities, e.g. peace marches, resolution adopting, etc., in which many students could participate. There were grave limitations to that approach, however; most of the very active participants were motivated by ideas which they received otherwhere than the campus (and indeed, who except second generation radicals could be expected to be active, after 15 years of red-baiting), and as a result the base of any activities was limited except the most superficial of activities. Large numbers of students could be brought only to the point of protesting violations of civil liberties, and making "good-willish" manifestations of their desire for peace and security. And even though our southern counterparts were beginning the Negro revolution, the most we could do would be to perform the "cheerleading" role: fund raising, moral support, and perhaps congressional pressure. This does not deny, of course, that a few individuals carried on meaningful (both in terms of results and in terms of education) political activities: some went south, some probed into the depths of research in vital areas, some became leaders of organizations.

In the last exciting nine months, however, things have changed radically. Two major changes have come about in the nation. The first is that *the Negro movement is no longer a southern movement,* for it is beginning to realize that access to "civil rights" gets the Negro in the south no more than a Harlem. It is therefore possible for students on northern campuses to participate in the Negro movement without migrating south. Most of the east coast colleges and many of the midwestern and western colleges are located in urban or suburban areas near Negro ghettoes, which are increasingly becoming the home of the Negro movement.

The reason for this transfer of the focus of attention of the movement from south to north is complex, but two concepts are of major significance for the northern student: 1) that the problems of the American Negro are not essentially racial, but are problems of poverty focused on a racial minority; 2) and that the problem of poverty is the result of an unhealthy economy. The northern movement, then, is really a movement of poor people, the Negro being the sole major element at this time, with assistance from intellectuals who see the need for economic change, and from humanitarians, who refuse to concede the necessity of poverty in twentieth century America.

These ideas would probably have become clear in a southern movement frustrated by its failure and by an already-tense situation in the northern ghettoes. But the situation has been greatly exacerbated by a second major change in the nation: *the economy is stagnating and automation is increasing unemployment.* Related to the activities of the Negro movement is this secular decline in the economy. Again, the reasons for this change are beyond the scope of the problem. Although it is increasingly hopeless to look to the gradational American method of integrating a poverty-stricken minority into the mainstream (i.e., equality of opportunity, education and high motivation), it also raises the chances for the Negro minority to find allies in the society. For although the Negro still shoulders a good part of unemployment, cybernation and automation are color blind and a ten-percent minority can only absorb a limited amount of unemployment.

The possibility of allies in white America broadens the already expanded field of action for the student: labor unions seem to be responding to some degree to the threat of automation, and for some time a number of predominately white areas have already been struck by unemployment, most conspicuously the large Appalachian area.

Before beginning a discussion of how campus programming is to fit into this new situation, I think there are a number of reasons, other than geographical proximity, which make it easier for students to participate. Until now, race has been a major drawback for college participation in the movement—most students are white, and have felt that they are in some way intruding, or at least tagging along, on what has been a Negro movement. But the shift of the movement away from an explicitly racial basis enhances the possibilities for the white student. The possibility of working in areas of high white unemployment makes the white student not secondary or supportive, but the catalyst of the movement.

Secondly, the realization of the basic economic inadequacies of the American system increases the importance of the scholar-activist. In the movement for civil rights, the students have been important and whites were able to lend their assistance in a number of ways. The fact that these whites were college students was of minimal importance: they could, perhaps, add administrative and tutorial talents to the Negro movement, and that aid is still needed.

However with the new character of the movement, there is a desperate need for analysis; the scholarship of poverty in America has been neglected, and only through a few occasional efforts (Harrington, Boggs) and the work of groups like SDS has any literature appeared on the subject. Both on the informational level (who, in a given community, are subject to automation? are steadily employed? are unskilled? are a potential political force? are concerned about various issues?), and on a theoretic level (can public works remove unemployment? is a 30-hour week the answer? what will be the net effect of an economic movement on the political scene? how will such groups as trade unions, the Muslims, and southern Negro leadership, react to automation, and to any movement which challenges increasing unemployment?) there is a crying need for research, which students active in the movement *can* do. We cannot rely completely on the spontaneity of the movement to show itself what it is up against, and to respond in a constructive manner. Our description and analysis is needed.

A successful beginning has been made at Swarthmore in adjusting to the changes in the movement. In September, two of us were driving through Chester, Pennsylvania, on the way home from an SDS convention, and after the summer in Cambridge we looked upon the situation somewhat differently than we had previously. If all the 20- and 30- year- old Negroes move away from the Eastern Shore, and presumably from the whole south, where but here must they have gone? Aren't these really the same people we were working with this summer? Why, then, shouldn't we shift our activities here, only 2 miles from Swarthmore?

We faced, I guess, the problem which faces most northern campus activists: how to get into the community. We had had a number of contacts with the Negro community. One was an employee at the college cafeteria who quit because of degrading working conditions, and subsequently became head of the Youth Chapter of the NAACP in Chester. For three years we had been attending its sporadic meetings, and mourning the middle-class and non-action orientation. A year ago we launched a 100-student tutorial in coordination with them, which is still going strong, but didn't lead to anything further.

But the summer's experience in Cambridge made us more confident in "invading" a community, and we immediately decided that in lieu of more provocative projects, we would begin a survey similar to the one which we did in Cambridge (which ultimately led to a 70-page report on the political, social, and economic conditions, in addition to a chronology of the movement there). After getting the nominal support of the Chester NAACP, we initiated such a survey to canvass the southern end of the town, visiting every fourth house, asking questions about occupational status, income, housing, schooling, politics, religion, and attitudes toward the movement. The major value of this program was to gain a certain familiarity with the problems of Chester, and to make ourselves known in the community.

The real turning point came a month later, however, when a group of students visited the NAACP executive secretary, with whom we had worked in Cambridge. From that meeting followed the Franklin school boycott, the subsequent demonstrations, and the arrest of 200 Chester Negroes and 50 Swarthmore students, the formation of the executive committee of the local movement by 15 adults of Chester, and the drafting of the 37-demand platform (which included demands for fair and full employment, new housing, new schools, adequate medical treatment, and fair police practices).

The most significant event, one which would not have been possible without the demonstrations, etc., is the formation of the neighborhood organizations. Over Thanksgiving three neighborhoods of approximately 400 families were pamphleted on our initiative, and groups of 10–20 in each neighborhood met to launch block organizations. Since then attendance has gone up to as high as 40 at the weekly meetings, and they are planning to combat housing conditions. They have begun to draw up lists of housing complaints, and are contacting the housing authorities and slumlords. More radical action is being considered, including a city-wide rent strike. We assume that the Negro movement in Chester, although most concerned about employment, will be most active in those areas where local changes can bring about improvement, i.e., public services, housing, and schools. The above activities, whether in Chester or in any northern ghetto, have certain short and medium range benfits which alone are enough to make such a project worthwhile as the major activity of a local SDS chapter. These benefits might be divided into two categories: the chapter and the community.

For the chapter, the benefits are obvious. The interdependence of issues about which we speak so much is amply demonstrated, and the large number of students who are attracted to the project for the first time are forced to face up to the realities of the problems facing America. The same students who came skeptically to the weekly seminars which discussed the Negro and the economy became less skeptical and more committed. The intellectual process of radicalization was speeded-up for a large number of students. On an emotional level, too, the jail experience, the visiting of tenements, and long discussions at neighborhood meetings made students more concerned with social issues.

The SPAC seminars, which had been running since the beginning of the semester, stopped meeting regularly because of commitments in Chester and to academics, but the substitute was the accumulation of hours of serious discussion, which is now a matter of course at the dinner table, late at night, and at social gatherings, for an increasingly large number of students.

The Chester project, especially the organization of neighborhoods, has opened extraordinary opportunities for leadership training and has given enthusiastic newcomers room for expanding their potential. Two freshmen are now the chief organizers in two of the neighborhoods; they perform and organize whatever is necessary from the campus and to keep the neighborhood organizations active; they perform administrative duties until local people are able to take them over; they provide an intellectual perspective in the meetings themselves; help in mediation of disputes in nascent and competing leaders. Each of the neighborhoods has one student organizer, and this person has begun to train other students and Chester adults to take over future neighborhoods. The effect on these students has been electric: they have learned in a few weeks administrative and leadership techniques for radical activity. And they have begun to face, alone, but with the consultation and advice of the rest of the chapter, the realities of machine politics, slum conditions, democracy, (or lack of same), and what will and won't work in facing these problems. The opportunities of expanding this experience are limited only to the number of neighborhoods.

The necessity of other information, e.g., housing codes, urban redevelopment plans and models, legal details, information on schools, has become most pressing. The SPAC Chester Political Research subcommittee had been organized last year, and since September it has been active, but when a neighborhood needed to know the legality of such and such an act, CPRC became active as never before. A number of other jobs have been created by necessity: someone to write press releases and phone them in; someone to organize and advertise mass meetings; someone to prepare a voter registration campaign. The responsibilities which the project is forcing students to accept has created an esprit de corps within the chapter. If socialism is necessary, Negroes must first see that traditional solutions of American problems are inadequate. Only then will it be possible for them to consider such an alternative.

I do not believe, however, that this kind of change in belief, this kind of positive evaluation from failure, is a natural spontaneous chain of events. I think it is necessary for leadership to point out conclusions: the community is not used to dealing in abstract terms, and is more willing to say, "It was Wilbur's fault that we didn't win that employment demand," than to say, "Maybe full employment isn't possible on the local level." The role of students in pointing out these abstract conclusions is most important: the perspective we have in combining direct action with seminars to produce long-run answers is one of the contributions we can make.

The most natural result of failure on either the direct action level or on the political level is to look around for allies. These allies are in Chester: poor whites, perhaps 10–20% of the total population (Negroes are 40%). It is in this group that there is already great hostility toward Negroes, and if the movement were to press *fair* employment demands very far, there would be actual fighting in the streets between black and white workers over the few jobs there are, hardly a thing to look forward to. The realization that this group will have to be won over must be made by both students and Negroes, students so that they will begin to go into the white lower class neighborhoods to organize there, Negroes so that they can begin to adjust to a class, rather than race, approach to their problems. This is the major failure of the project: the neglect of whites in Chester. There is a natural antipathy toward whites among those of us who have spent time in the Negro movement, and a disinclination to work with this group. They are most open in their racist feelings, most likely to beat one up in a demonstration. And it takes a good deal of courage and initiative to launch into this area which none of us has experience or confidence in.

A major problem faces us in Chester, and will face all areas which begin similar movements in the north: if one puts all one's hopes in a national solution and therefore a national movement, how will Chester hook up with this national movement, and what form will such a movement take? This has been in the backs of our minds, and for this precise reason we have made efforts to circulate our lists of total demands throughout the north, in hopes that other movements would adopt them, providing some uniformity of program. This, however, is not enough. Chester will soon reach the end of the number of projects which can achieve some success on the local level, and if leadership is good enough, Chester will soon face squarely the fact that national unemployment is the key issue, that working on other issues is dilatory. When Chester comes to that point, as indeed Cambridge did, must it stagnate, die, or wait for the rest of the north to catch up so that it can proceed along with the rest?

This, of course, is somewhat far from the subject of campus programming. I think there are sufficient reasons for campuses to engage in such programming: one must make the jump of faith and believe that some national solution is possible, and that any job of radicalizing students, and making a local movement more sophisticated and realistic is a positive contribution toward that solution.

It is, however, the responsibility of the more farseeing of us to project the movement on a national scale. Whether it is through SDS, SNCC-SDS-NSM union, or some other vehicle, this must be done and it must be done soon, or much of the work which is being done in communities like Chester will be lost. It is this tie between the local movement and the national movement, paralleling the local chapter and the national organization of SDS, which provides the rationale for a national organization at all: not only to cross-pollinate local groups, and permit our experiences to be of some assistance elsewhere, but to take the lead in the formation of and execution of plans for a national movement and national solution which local movements, partially the product of campus programming, can relate to.

3.2.

> TOM HAYDEN and CARL WITT-MAN: **Summer Report, Newark Community Union**

> [The Newark Community Union project (NCUP) was one of the most important ERAP projects of the SDS activists. After the first months of activity, Tom Hayden and Carl Wittman, two of the initiators of the Newark project, prepared the following report.]

The Newark Project came into Clinton Hill, Newark, on the inaccurate assumption that both poor Negroes and whites lived there. As it turned out, only the eastern, or lower, half of the area could in any sense be called poor—the rest was working- and middle-class, mostly Negro also. In a city where over half the population is Negro or Puerto Rican, there are only three areas where white unemployment is significant, only one of them of any size.

Despite the racial imbalance of the SDS group (all but one were white, and all three of the present staff are white) there was practically no overt opposition within the project area to the staff. Instead, both old members of the Neighborhood Council (our host group) and the newly organized block members accepted us with remarkable alacrity and warmth. And by the time the projects came under major attack, from a group whose spokesmen included Negro liberals, neighborhood people defended the white staff instead of capitulating to the race-baiting of our antagonists. It would be highly desirable to have Negro organizers on the staff, but at this point that is not mandatory. . . .

One important fact is the substantial integration of big business with the city government and the Urban League, NAACP and CORE. City officials themselves testify to this fact as a reason for the absence of summer riots, and they depend on it for continued social peace, urban renewal and the local war on poverty.

This unity is not unbreakable—CORE, for instance, has picketed both City Hall and certain business establishments; and the Essex County Democrats contain a faction opposed to the city administration. But there is a widely held consensus on "acceptable" program, and a high degree of coordination among elite groups compared to other cities. The consensus on program is that society should adjust to the Negro only in terms of racial attitudes, not in terms of national economic change; that the Negro should adjust to society through greater basic education and improvement of skills. This outlook characterizes the leading civil rights groups, the business leaders committed to civil rights, and the Newark war on poverty planners. This is not just an individually held consensus, but one that is generated in common because of the high rate of overlap and intermingling among groups.

This is the overt civil rights program of a sophisticated corporate-liberal establishment. The covert program is urban renewal, which removes Negroes from choice business sites and relocates them, at "best," in hideous high-rise ghettos. Newark is one of America's "pilot cities" in this field having spent as many urban renewal dollars in the postwar period as any other city of comparable size. Built into the dynamics of "successful" urban renewal are the preconditions of an urban ruling elite: durable organization, comprehensive program, immunity from democratic review. The local Housing Authority elite with a virtual empire of faithful staff and patronage, has lasted relatively intact through the last three city administrations. Besides its durability, the Housing Authority is comprehensive in the scope of operation —at this point all of Newark has succeeded in falling under the "blight" category in the federal housing codes. The Housing Authority becomes the institutional channel through which the city's economic and racial development proceeds. This process is simplified for the authorities by the undemocratic nature of the program. All research and decision-making is done privately among businessmen, federal agents, and the Housing Authority, then presented as fiat to the City Council. Urban renewal, then, is the basic response by this Northern liberal city to the problems of Negro poverty. Urban renewal has been nicknamed by its integrationist critics, "Negro removal." This is true only in part, for the real motivation would seem to be as much economic as racial. It is a major domestic means of government subsidy to private commercial growth; as such, it runs against the interests of all the poor, Negro as well as white.

Given this sophisticated elite operation, it is surprising that the project has been the object of so much alarm and hostility from "downtown" elements. Part of this can be explained by the temporary but profound fear of a summer race riot. The civil rights-city-business "coalition" had concurred in the so-called moratorium on demonstrations, so there was a somewhat undue amount of fear of the SDS "outsiders" when we scheduled the first of five demonstrations. But this fear of a riot does not explain the repeated attacks by our local councilman, comments from neighborhood people of city-owned reports and pictures of us participating in nearby riots and other subversive activity, scurrilous anti-project leaflets in the area, reliable rumors that one or more FBI personnel are assigned to the project, vehement attacks on block organizations by the local urban renewal representative, and threats from the councilman's local strongman. The causes of this tension seem to be: first, the general fear that the existing Negro majority will express itself militantly in city affairs; second, the specific fear of any new groups "outside" of the existing civil rights consensus; third, the fear that stable elite control of urban renewal will be upset by insurgent demands, leaving the city in a weakened competitive position in relation to other Northern areas. Whatever the reasons, the fact is that we can expect major attention from the city as our activity progresses, especially since our leaflets identify it with the slumlords and other moneymakers.

More surprising than the negative response from the city is the unwillingness of the small liberal circle in the city to accept the project and its implications. Since they had invited us to Newark, one would expect that the liberal community (the ADA, CORE, the activist wing of the NAACP, some labor unions, community improvement groups) would be a major ally. But major reconsideration of this assumption has been forced by the course of events. It has turned out that practically every one of the groups has come to see the project as a problem if not a danger, and the only significant support for the project is within the project area. This phenomenon should be dealt with on both the organizational and programatic plane.

Much of the difficulty and friction between the project and the liberal groupings is related to problems in the structure of the project. Originally it was to be directed by a group called the Newark Committee on Full Employment, which consisted of representatives from the various liberal groups. The organization through which policy would be implemented was also a leading force within the Committee: the Clinton Hill Neighborhood Council. The Council is a nine-year-old neighborhood improvement association, formed as the neighborhood began to turn from Jewish middle class to Negro middle and lower class. Its major accomplishment has been the litigation holding up the urban renewal in the lower or eastern half of the Hill (where we work). It consisted of several hundred members, once active and now mostly on paper. Its leadership was mostly white, its constituency mostly colored. It once was an all-homeowner group; it never contained many tenants.

The obvious problem is whether and how to build coalition with other "liberal forces" in the area. Our initial experience has been with extremely self-serving people who have wide community contact but no active and radical membership base. Their aspirations are for political self-aggrandizement and orthodox liberal reforms. The problem in any coalition with them is they will work with nearly anyone to upset the city administration and send in a new set of officials; or, in general, their program would do very little to change the real lives of the poor. This means we are viewed by them as cogs and not as people whose need for democratic participation and basic change must be served. We cannot enter into this kind of political bartering without violating the basic trust we have with the neighborhood people. Our place is at the bottom. . . .

The problem of leadership was only in part identified by neighborhood people as racial: "This is 1964 and things is changin' all over" is the way one put it. However, the SDS staff was white also, a fact which neighborhood people defended when the local Negro CORE chairman used race-baiting arguments against SDS. The deeper way in which the problem was identified was, very simply, *democratic control*. The sharpest attacks were against domination of the people by a manipulative clique, and against anyone displaying marks of snobbishness or privilege. The neighborhood people readily identified themselves as "the little people," and they regarded SDS staff as "ordinary people" who were with them.

The positive manifestation of this democratic feeling was the form of the new organization which emerged: the program committee. This was a committee which was formed of representatives from all blocks, the staff, and *anyone who could attend the meetings*—one man, one vote. The committee would meet weekly and make all policy decisions, decide its own organizational form, and be chaired by an elected president rotating once a month. Although many of these suggestions were made by us, they were readily agreed upon and defended when questioned.

One of the larger questions throughout the summer was how a mostly white staff would relate to a Negro constituency. The subject is often discussed, and especially when broached by us, in a frank manner. For obvious reasons, there is no consciousness of poor whites being their allies, as none have come to them as allies. But partly because of the economic orientation of our program, partly because of our occasionally pushing the idea, and partly out of a flexibility in their outlook as to who allies are, the possibility of hooking up with white groups does not seem at all difficult.

In contrast to an apparent informality in race consciousness, the attitudes toward class are somewhat tighter. There is a strong strain of being of a deprived class, resenting and ridiculing privilege; picketing a slumlord at his suburban residence inspired glee as well as fear; the "lower" hill consciousness is strong, as is "the little people" concept. The corresponding attitude toward "the other America" is to lump all those with power and privilege into one group; little which the mass media, or the statements of the liberal protest groups say has any effect on our constituency.

However, there is a strange mix of attitudes toward those immediately above and below them on the economic ladder. Probably a minority of the group has no antagonistic or snobbish feelings about anyone in the neighborhood: they are either the very "nitty" tenants in the worse slums, or people in leadership who are comfortably situated. But in contrast to this, there is a strong feeling among many that much of the problem is the people's fault, and that they must be educated to be responsible; the reason things are so bad is that people are lazy, stupid, and apathetic. This is not only a homeowner attitude; anyone who is already in the movement has certain initiative, and they often resent or scorn those who do not have this initiative or ability to stay above water.

One function of this attitude is a belief in individualism rather than group action, and further, that change comes about through argument and instruction rather than through power. On the other hand, the rent strikes function completely on a collective basis, premised on the concept of power and conflict. . . .

On the other hand, the world of local politics seems quite real. They comprehend how local politics works, and realize they are of interest to local politicos. It is perfectly possible for the movement to turn to politics as an arena, and even now our telephone squads invite politicians to demonstrations, in order to line them up with or against us.

3.3.   *TODD GITLIN:* **The Radical Potential**
                                  of the Poor

[Community organizing was the main focus of SDS activity in 1964 and 1965. This experience was and remains a source of reflection and discussion within the Movement. Todd Gitlin, president of SDS in 1963–1964 and initiator of the Chicago JOIN project, draws in the following article what may be considered a conclusive picture of the poverty organizing experience. Excerpts from *International Socialist Journal,* XXIV: 24.]

The radical experience in organizing the poor has been as misunderstood as it has been brief. Often organizers have not spoken clearly to criticisms from within as well as without, though for good reason—the premium has been on organizing the poor, testing some principles, not embroidering a theory somebody else might someday apply. As a result the theory of this new work—implicit and explicit—has been written mostly by those who would caricature it to suit their own political slants, sympathetic or not. And as some of the early projects collapsed, there has also been something of a crisis in confidence among radical organizers grappling for ways to make sense of a complex and exhausting experience. Clarity about what has and has not been done has become not just a matter of courtesy to critics, but of balance and survival for present and prospective organizers.

Why organize? At first, as SDS people and others moved into poor communities in 1964, the main ideas were there: In a system that satisfies many needs for most Americans, the poor are still demonstrably in need—and know it. They are also less tied to the dominant values, just as—and partly because—they are less central to the economy that creates and expresses those values. They have a certain permanence necessary for a sustained movement. Though a minority they are a substantial minority. The exhibit a potential for movement—for understanding their situation, breaking loose, and committing themselves to a radical alternative.

Those beliefs are basic, and basically valid. But at this juncture the purposes of radical organizing projects can be listed more precisely, even at the risk of drawing artificial distinctions:

First, to enable the most powerless people to get a handle on the decisions and non-decisions, now made *for* them, that debase and deform their lives. Second, to help the poor get more of the material goods and services prerequisite to a decent life. Third, to undergird serious proposals for the humane extension of the welfare state, and keep them responsive to the needs of those "for whom" they are proposed and granted. Fourth, to help maintain momentum for a Negro movement in need of reliable allies.

Fifth, to raise, insistently, in poor communities and at every level outside, these issues, among many: who runs the society, and in whose interest? Who is competent to make which decisions for the poor, or for anyone? Who is "for" the poor? what do the poor "need"? how tolerant is America? how in America do people get what they want? how do they want what they "want"? what happens when people govern themselves? what institutional changes would make a difference? Sixth, to strengthen the poor as a source and reservoir of opposition to the final rationalization of the American system: to keep the country open to authentically different values and styles.

Seventh, to galvanize students, professionals, and others into durable confrontations with the ethos and structure of the society; and to lend urgency and values to parallel movements. Eighth, to amass pressure for public, domestic spending, and thus, in political effect, against an aggressive foreign policy.

And ninth, to plant seeds that might grow into the core of a mass radical movement sufficiently large and serious and conscious and strategically placed to transform American institutions.

How are these objectives practical, and how are they compatible? Provisional answers might be found in the experience of two "community unions" seeded by SDS-JOIN in a mostly Southern-white neighborhood of Chicago, and the Newark Community Union Project (NCUP) in a black ghetto.

Issue-organizing

The underclass has its most abrasive contacts with the ruling elites less at the point of production than outside it. Bad housing, meager and degrading "welfare," destructive urban renewal, vicious police, hostile and irrelevant schools, inadequate community facilities (hospitals, nurseries, traffic lights, parks, etc.) are the general rule and are felt as a pattern of victimization above and beyond each of these separate issues. The job of the organizer is to find those people most aroused by felt grievances; to organize, with them, action on those issues; to amplify the feeling that these are common, *caused* problems, not individual faults, accidents or exceptions; to build through tangibly successful action a confidence in the weight of collective action, and to discover and teach through failures the limits of present capabilities and the work that lies ahead. The more engaged and mature the organization, the more "success" or "failure" becomes the subtle estimate of organizer and organized as they begin to see "the problem" as larger, more complex than before. In this new context, gradually, success comes to mean both the achievement of specific change (getting a landlord to make repairs, winning a welfare right, etc.) and the commitment of a resident to participate in the project's work. Organization on any single issue may span only a few individuals (welfare rights) or a block (traffic light) or the entire neighborhood or city (police, urban renewal). The smaller the unit, the easier a visible victory.

As the action on one issue runs its course—through meetings, pickets, confrontations with city officials, etc.—many of the people involved drop away; most to become passive supporters, some to become critics. Some get more involved and decide to stick with it. They generate, discover, happen upon, are asked to consider further issues—thus, more actions, further discoveries, new people, and so on. The model is an amoeba. The nuclei are a hard-core of people attracted by one campaign, or by the notion of fundamental change in the neighborhood or city or country, or by the novelty and spirit of the project; slowly and with difficulty they carve out a place in the proto-organization. Its motion is compounded of *purpose* (to attain what seems central in most people's lives, or to draw in new groups of people—"building the organization"—or to achieve visible change, or to generate issues of control and social structure, or to maintain the community itself against outside pressures), *circumvention* (what cannot be tackled at *this* level of organization), and *randomness* (who shows up, wanting what done).

Long dead is any speculation that any one issue will be the key to unlock the local structure of power, let alone the national one. When SDS first sent students into poor communities in 1963–64 there was a strong feeling that the issue of jobs or income might be a single decisive lever of change, a feeling based on some naïve expectations about the pace and effect of automation. JOIN, the first organizing venture, stood for "Jobs or Income Now." During the course of the summer of 1964, some organizers argued that white unemployment was far too little and diffused (in Chicago, at any rate) to be the basis for organization; moreover, that jobs or income were too remote as early demands. They proposed instead an emphasis on smaller, neighborhood demands more easily won. The debate was jocularly summarized as one between "JOIN" and "GROIN" ("Garbage Removal or Income Now"). GROIN prevailed (NCUP had been GROIN from the start), and the JOIN office was relocated that fall in the uptown neighborhood, the largest concentration of poor whites in the city, as JOIN Community Union.

Issues are connected through argument as well as experience so that the common elements of powerlessness and exploitation take on a new concreteness. As a prerequisite, the organization must concern itself with a span of issues (the jargon is "multi-issue"), not confine itself to one or two alone. In this way it reaches a greater variety of people, generates a feel for the relatedness of issues, binds different types of people together, and lessens the chance that success or failure on any one issue will determine the fate of the budding movement. This openness toward issues leaves the organization free to take advantage of new situations, new grievances, new moods as they arise. But the danger of a multi-issue organization is that as it grows, it might spin off so many issues, each with its own work-force and constituency, that "the center cannot hold." The centrifugal force swells (paradoxically) as the organization becomes more solid—as community people become more confident, gain organizational skills, take on pieces of work genuinely their own. At such peaks, many of the pent-up envies, aggressions, and cupidities this society bestows on its victims are likely to burst out. Cohesion, the stuff of permanence, then depends in part on a rhythm of activities, in part on the level of good feeling, and on the ideological and symbolic identity built up over a period of time. (Ideally there should probably be cycles of activity, periods of disparate projects alternating with times when a single activity will involve the entire organization.)

The special quality of *radical* issue-organizing is the intertwining of two different kinds of demands: demands for tangible concessions, which can be granted by existing institutions, and demands for control and substantial restructuring of those institutions. It is too early to say when the first kind of demands will be met; results have something to do with the elite embarrassment that would be caused otherwise, the legitimacy of the demand as measured by prevailing standards (e.g., pressure for a welfare right provided in law), the economic power that can be massed (e.g., rent strikes), the institution's best judgment of how to thwart the movement's growth ("unearned" concessions). The second kind can be thought of as transcendent, "utopian" demands, not capable of being met on the neighborhood or even the city level. These are demands that touch on the structure of authority, the question of legitimate power. They are tinged—locally and nationally—with a certain absurd pathos; the bravado of the powerless telling the powerful to disband because they are illegitimate, because they have no right to decide, because they have botched the job and must move aside. At that extreme, the placing of demands blurs into "challenge and disruption," because an institution will not agree to its wholesale destruction, and the movement lacks the strength to force it. But the radical insistence does not degenerate into "speaking truth to power" when it keeps the powerful on the defensive, extorts more and more concessions while diluting the agencies' legitimacy in the community—all of which are possible as the organization grows and community people become more comfortable making demands that will not be granted tomorrow.

In fact limitations of experience may lead us to overestimate the concrete futility of both material and structural demands on the local level. Certain of the structural demands could only be met through national and state legislation (e.g., that welfare recipients administer the welfare program), but others, in theory at any rate, could be won locally if pressure is "strong enough." (Organizers learn to guess at the chances for victory, but revise their guesses in the process of working toward a goal.) Those demands could be achieved without a massive shuffling of resources; their common motif is *autonomy;* they should be thought of as middle-range possibilities, lodged between the demands of the moment and a thoroughgoing reconstruction. For example, there seems to be no intrinsic reason why the New York City Board of Education could not grant the right of parents to control Intermediate School 201; it would threaten their legitimacy to be sure, but might be the easiest way out if the parents' movement were deep and relentless enough. Likewise, the demand that the people affected by urban renewal dominate planning for their community, and be granted the resources (information, planners, money) to do so, does indeed require "a whole revision of the operation, a revision unimaginable without structural changes in the urban renewal agencies, and finally, subordination of the land-use cycle, and of contractual developers, to local initiative and control." What is *not* yet clear is that this goal, even when seen in its radical light, is impractical. There have been some few occasions when community organizations (not community unions) have turned urban renewal to their own uses, a result tantamount to curbing the violence of the land-use cycle. A victory is *conceivable* if not imminent, and might spread to other neighborhoods and critics. Similarly, groups may decide that the police cannot be pressured politely through civilian review boards, but must be contained and rendered illegitimate if brutality is to stop. The objective would not be to change police policy at the top, but to watch and challenge the occupiers so closely that they decide finally to let the community govern itself. Difficult as this would prove, it still seems more practical than the centralist approach, and could not be less effective in curbing terror than the showpiece review boards. Victories of the sort—"a whole lot of lettin' alone," as one JOIN member put it—would also illustrate and refine certain tensions in the concept of participatory democracy. Control over a local institution in a vacuum may inspire opposed groups to control *theirs* (though rightwing and other middle-class groups are likely to have that control already); it may also detract from efforts to change the larger structures and win new resources. Parents' control over I.S. 201 alone would leave the rest of New York's educational machine untouched, and so on for each of the other victories. The gamble of a community union, then, is that its local successes and strategies can be communicated as models for other groups and organizers to copy, and that its own people are firm enough in their direction to use the victory for momentum, not coasting or cooptation. This implacability may be as much a matter of education and consciousness of "objective conditions."

Not so ironically, the strength of national and local systems of authority has been in their flexibility with regard to all aspects but the most central: private property is still sacrosanct but local control is a prevailing rhetoric whose limits are yet to be tested and extended. A victory on the city-wide level for the right of welfare recipients to organize "at the point of distribution" (the welfare office), conceivable in a city like Chicago in the foreseeable future, would not provide control over a central social structure, but would open up space for contact, organizing, and influence. Thus even at the level of the city, structural goals are not entirely utopian, and material goals are unevenly possible; the upshot might be a basis for natural expansion in the neighborhood and city; not fundamental change in structure or resources, but preconditions for and intimations of both. Material and structural victories even at the national level—abolition of stringent welfare regulations, guaranteed income, democratization of urban renewal—

become at least imaginable as community unions sink roots and demonstrate, level by level, what can be done. But each step is agony.

Democracy and Durability

The community union seeks to become permanent without freezing. There is a long beginning stretch when residents are reached, temporarily involved, and then fade back into their personal lives and a passive sort of support. As some fall away there is renewed pressure to find others. If the organizer wades through the early frustrations, he is likely to find people who will stick. As they show interest, pieces of manageable work can be divided between the ex-students and the recruits. Something like a formal division of labor develops, through which people usually considered incompetent and inept find their own capabilities and make new ones. In both Newark and Chicago, community people have been taken on staff and play crucial roles. "Roles" are rather loosely defined to permit choice, but structured sufficiently to achieve specific aims (an issue-project, reaching new people, managing the office, research, fund-raising, etc.). Roles are also set up to reflect varying levels of commitment: in JOIN there are full-time staff and a network of "stewards"—part-time contacts and organizers who relay problems to the central office, distribute newsletters, suggest and join in activities, and provide feedback; and then the wider span of members. Every so often all the levels come together for mass meetings, large actions, movies, skits, parties. The organization then has roots as well as a conscious thrust.

The mood of informality appeals to some community people, but confuses and alienates others; for most, at the beginning, a meeting means a time to dress up and listen quietly, though new people discover that it is easy to get up and talk. Community unions have moved from the dogmatic anarchism which some critics observed to be the pathology of the middle-class organizer. In JOIN at least there are formal leaders elected by an organizing committee (the staff and the most active people) and the membership as a whole. Offices rotate every month so that the skills and experience that come with nominal authority and the spokesman role can be spread, and power kept close to its source. (Among chairmen of the JOIN organizing committee have been day-laborers, an ex-hairdresser, a junkie ex-con, a fired building manager, a preacher without pulpit, a go-go dancer, a teen-age "tough," and welfare recipients.) Meetings are freewheeling, sometimes baroque, but capable of making decisions. What emerges through those formal functions as well as through discussions, actions, and symbols is an identity that bears some relation to the community style. (What is hard is blending that style with the demands of decision-making; results are uneven.) Thus there is a hillbilly cast to JOIN songs—mostly adapted from Baptist hymns, some from civil rights anthems—reflecting the dominant population and culture, though most of the active hillbillies in JOIN do not exert formal policy influence in meetings. But then policy emerges mostly from an interplay among organizers' ideology, people's readiness to move, and mutual perceptions of the situation; it only surfaces at official meetings.

. . . .

The experience in JOIN is that a working mesh of formal democracy and decentralized work is possible, but that it takes the most excruciating patience. Trust is established slowly and delicately, as organizers prove that action can get results, and make explicit their commitment to stay until, by general consent, it is time to get to work elsewhere. Organizers must ride what seems to be a recurrent cycle of turnover and crisis. After several waves of turnover, as the organization seems more stable, emphasis shifts to equipping the people who have committed themselves. Organizers perceive crisis: they have made now organizers, stabilized the organization, but have stopped reaching the unreached. They resolve, after much talk, to plunge outward again. Then relative stability tests the ability of organizers to make room for new people, and repeat the process. It is a tension built into the organizing approach. Understood that way, it can be the project's greatest strength, its propulsion. Misperceived as failure, it becomes a self-fulfilling gloom.

What I mean to say is that as it grows the project aims, in a complicated way, to embody and symbolize and prove the possibility of a democratic society. It is somewhat like, but more complex than, the "live-in" conceived by Staughton Lynd:

> The spirit of a community, as opposed to an organization, is not, We are together to accomplish this or that end, but, We are together to face together whatever life brings. . . . The spiritual unity of the group is more important than any external accomplishment . . . the building of a brotherly way of life even in the jaws of Leviathan.

For as the project forges the idea of shared decision-making in a political community, it is also constantly pushing outward, its fraternity testing the outside world, challenging and disrupting it, creating and seeking openings, looking to replicate itself; and it is also prepared to risk its satisfaction for the rude receptions it is likely to get when it ventures outside. There is *restless community*, "something of our own" that dares its own exclusiveness, that thrives insofar as it sets itself problematic goals, that foregoes certainties as it constantly probes for a momentum of changes. By taking risks it avoids stasis and cynicism, the final victories of a society closing in. To the degree that Fruchter and Kramer are right about the closure and containment of tangible radical possibilities—and I am not yet judging the likelihood—their conclusions hold up:

> In an environment where the possibilities for fundamental change are obscure, where even the desire for change based upon assumptions different from those of the society presents itself as either irrational or pathological, there is a continuous pressure toward finding ways to "separate" from the society. The negation of the status quo in theory, language, acts, lacking any focus that would make change a real possibility, is always driven to seem partially utopian.

But while such despair is natural, it goes too far to say that "at the present time there is no adequate way of formulating this idea of existing 'outside' that does not over-emphasize utopian tendencies." The problem is rather, having formulated the idea, to make it work.

The project must resist the temptation to cut itself off from the whole society. The dangers are most acutely those of sectarian politics, apolitical posturing and the cultivation of relations with middle-class groups and the powers that be at the expense of roots in the community. The project must continue to find in the culture of poverty at least a culture of resistance, and remain engaged with the sources of that resistance. It must replenish those sources and embody them in a *political* resistance, facing outward from the project. It must challenge the dominant trends and oppressive structures while challenging itself to refuse to take the future for granted. When the organizer despairs he may find solace in marveling at the community he has helped forge; but that is a fragile and short-lived pleasure. If he is to survive and work, he must again grow restless, and his beloved community must keep itself on the firing line.

The Education of Radicals

The education goal in a radical project is something called "radical consciousness," which incorporates analysis, technique, information, and ideology, and is more than the sum of them. The means are "experience" and "teaching."

The organizing process itself is rich with usable experience. As people are brought into the project, their pre-existing populism is nurtured and made explicit. The organizer is constantly trying, as directly as possible, to dramatize the basic validity of that populism, clarifying its images of targets and allies, while challenging its destructive stereotypes (like white supremacy). Experience can provoke two sorts of lessons: discoveries about the common situation of separate groups of poor people (blocks, neighborhoods, races, regions, countries), and deepening senses of the structure of the society. People are not babied by being fed through different learning situations in measured stages; rather there is a dynamic which teaches from the experience at hand. Almost any grievance or the most casual political remark can be lent a radical meaning. Given a certain forward motion either "success" or "failure" can teach; in the early stages especially, a certain proportion of "successes" is crucial.

. . . .

It is true enough, as some Marxists point out, that poor people's experience with the political-corporate system is located mostly at the level of neighborhood issues, not directly with capitalists. The too-quick conclusion is that poor people—more than workers—are prevented from understanding capitalism. But, as Fruchter and Kramer insist, it stretches the point to pose an iron law of consciousness,

> positing a traditional form of exploitation as the only experience which yields an accurate analysis of capitalist structure, as if similar analysis was not possible from the starting-point of slum-ownership or the administration of welfare. . . . It may be that there is no hierarchy of necessary experience which yields selectively different levels of structural perception; in this tightly knit political economy, the analysis of any specific dehumanizing process, whether primary (class exploitation) or secondary (authority and control, resource distribution) contradictions, may lead one to an adequate structural perception of imperialist monopoly capitalism.

Propped by a unifying ideology of free enterprise, nationalism, and law and order, the class-consciousness of the well-fed worker, blue- or white-collar, is limited by his relative prosperity: that of the slum-dweller, by his contacts with city bureaucracies and the shifting middle class. But the poor are probably still better equipped to understand—and find *new* ways of understanding—the class structure of American society than are most organized workers. The poor, benefiting less from America's world position, are more open to radical views of foreign policy. They may have more trouble discriminating between a political machine and its corporate backers, between a public bureaucracy and the economic system; but the experience of fighting urban renewal tends to draw the lines vividly—for "students" as well. Anyway, while the phrase "imperialist monopoly capitalism" is rich with meaning, a grasp of its lines of authority and its operations simply does not flow directly out of *anyone's* experience. One cannot demand of poor people what one would want of no one else—the abandonment of debate over the makeup and dynamic of the American system; not at this early stage. The risks of intellectual flexibility, given some elementary components of a radical view, seem to me less than the power of sharp, visible intellectual conflict. It makes for radical thinkers, not quoters of political theology.

But the organizer needs no excuses for using ideology to clarify targets, to enrich and sharpen experience and supplement it as well. Ideology is not flaunted as a text but elaborated as organizers work with residents: it flows through ordinary conversation—the daily business of the staff—and through more self-conscious structures. As the community union becomes more solid, the formal methods of education become more feasible. Thus, after two years of painfully slow organizing, JOIN started a school for committed community people, where questions of class, power, social structure, American history and foreign policy are raised through specially prepared pamphlets, films, discussion, and role-playing. Far from resenting such mind work, these people are wildly enthusiastic; having become organizers through the issue-movement process, they want bearings in the world they hope to change.

Though the ability to communicate radical views of the world is no substitute for movement and drive, it should not be underestimated. OEO community action people, by contrast, cannot fail to notice that the Vietnam war erodes the resources of the "war on poverty," but the insight stops there. They demand, then, simply that the foreign war not be allowed to hinder the "war" at home. But in a community union people can and do demand of officials that they must end the war in order to make concessions, as well as for its own sake. The radical demand also renders the moderate one less risky, and is no more ineffectual; equally important, it tells the truth, moving past the idea that the President has just made a "mistake." On its face the radical demand cannot be met—not on the local level anyhow—but raising it is key to the radical approach. In the same way, while the draft looms large in the lives of young men who are poor, to confront it immediately might be suicidal. Yet JOIN organizers have been able to broach the issue, gradually, with young Southern men who were first drawn into a movement against police brutality—not side-tracking their primary concern with police, but working from it to more general ideas about authority and violence. Consequently, a slowly widening circle of people think it legitimate to talk about proscribed issues. As the limits of permissible debate are extended, some people fall away, but the losses are tolerable. And those who agree to learn and argue seem to become more serious, rather than discouraged, as they appreciate the dimensions of tolerable controversy.

Radical education does not justify itself solely in its intrinsic worth. In the end, built on and reinforcing an open, democratic, and aggressive movement, the values and ideas crystallized by radical organizers are also the best protections against cooptation into liberal structures and ordinary reforms. Not that radical consciousness, God knows, will always suffice; as liberal mechanisms bloom and become more sophisticated, the temptations will grow to rest satisfied, to drown in neo-colonial projects because they are "real," to decide that structure demands are after all peripheral, to sacrifice the "dogma" that ordinary people must participate in the major decisions. Right now, between the political price T.W.O. paid for minimal urban renewal concessions and the refusal of JOIN to pay that price (even for more substantial concessions, short of community say-so) there is much more than a marginal difference. To sustain that sort of difference if the stakes pile up, *without growing indifferent to needs,* will be a delicate and agonizing job. Radical organizers have yet to face the dramatic and decisive test of building a radical, catalytic movement of poor people while a triumphant coalition of modernizers and liberals is setting to work. While that event seems remote right now, it could develop in five or ten years on the backs of poor people's movements. How radicals would fare then—to the extent our planning matters—is more a function of how we organize than after it; how we exist "outside" while making raids on the "inside"; how we learn to "keep our eyes on the prize." So far, people in JOIN and NCUP have usually been able to resist the varied blandishments—substantive and stylistic—of modernizing elites without sacrificing access to visible accomplishments, and have been able to move into potentially "effective" but spongy structures without foundering. The risk is probably not so much that leaders will be brainwashed and bought by liberal structures as that they will be more gently tamed, "socialized," convinced that bureaucratic rationality is basically healthy and radical challenges and new styles "childish"—until finally the disruptive ideas and associations become uncomfortable, and victories become defeats. As this happens, organizers will have to learn to see a few people go, and return to work finding new people to keep up pressure on the liberal structures from the bottom. Against the authority of approved ways of doing things there are no guarantees in anyone's strategy; but there are safeguards available that have so far stood the test, and kept radical alternatives alive and on the offensive.

Counter-institutions and Catalysis

In the here and now there are a range of needs which orthodox political organizing cannot fulfill. For these purposes "counter-institutions" of different sorts have been conceived, and some set in motion. What they share in common is the attempt to "initiate the unorganized into the experience of self-government," to gain the justified allegiance of the community, and to extend the model of a democratic and accessible movement farther into the world of concrete needs. All the different types of counter-structures depend on a pre-existing level of organization and a shared sense of their intermediate positions—less than revolutionary, more than therapeutic. To propel and not stall the movement that gives rise to them, they must represent "something of our own" in tension with what is not, but should be. Erected prematurely they will devolve into bureaucracy, not self-government, and as centrifugal features drain energy from the rock-bottom work of organizing. It is a subtle business to judge when to start.

At one level are *economic counter-institutions* that meet urgent material needs for the community and, within it, for the movement, when the larger society cannot be forced to yield. Credit unions and job consumer cooperatives can make some jobs for organizers while filling wider needs. But even these efforts, small as they seem when set against the size of those needs, usually require more than the project's own resources. Southern "tent cities" organized by local SNCC groups to house displaced sharecroppers encounter the same trouble. Once there is a roof over people's heads there remains the need to raise thousands of dollars to capitalize a brick factory—to build homes while providing jobs. When public funds are precluded, these sorts of counter-institutions are forced to depend at first on fund-raising from liberal foundations and individuals. With rare exceptions, even if those sources do not want to impose conditions, their rules and values may require a timetable (like amortization within a very short time) or a certain accounting procedure that badly strains the possibility of structural innovation, the training and participation of local people. The project, organizers and residents together, must judge whether it can meet the conditions implied without sacrificing its identity; and then balance the sacrifice against the need. (It would be mistaken to judge in advance that residents will always be more malleable than "students," though that will usually and naturally be the case.) Then, once conditions can be accepted, the larger pressures of the society begin to operate: a monopolistic market squeezing producers' coops, various economic and political arrangements (bank-induced legislation, licensing, etc.) militating against credit unions and consumers' coops. Some job coops in the Southern movement have survived by carving out markets among sympathetic Northerners and—more important for the spread of the movement—among local people. But the movement had to be solid enough first to make a market for "movement producers" among "movement people." Tom Hayden proposed a few years back that Southern farm coops might be linked to Northern poor people's at some take-off stage of organization which would allow Northern and Southern groups to conceive the need, meet and discuss the possibilities. While all such schemes should be explored, and their limits are nowhere near reached, most radical organizers see them as stop-gaps and tools of organization, not ends in themselves.

Yet there are times when to sustain momentum and self-determination a community union will try to set up something itself rather than demand it of authorities. There are no set rules; rather there is a rhythm of approaches which can only be judged by the standards of a particular project at a particular time. The issue then is not whether the government *ought* to force companies to pay day-laborers the union scale rather than $1.25 an hour (of course it ought to). The question becomes: *At this point in time* should JOIN invest energy in lobbying for minimum wage extension and state-run employment offices, or should it try to get money to set up its own non-profit day-labor agency? Should JOIN bargain with the alderman to turn a parking lot into a playground, or try to set up the playground itself? In the first case JOIN tried—unsuccessfully—to get OEO money for its own agency, discouraging some members who had worked hard on the proposal and wanted to run the agency. (Thus the risk of aiming for the counter-institution without the power to produce it.) In the second, JOIN organized a mock election of kids in favor of the playground and recruited middle-class help in convincing the owner to turn over his land; it turned out JOIN was too weak to find people to build and maintain the playground; but more than a year after the "election," when OEO workers built a playground on another lot on the block, residents promptly dubbed it "the JOIN playground." (Even a premature "success" can force a small change and spread a reputation for effectiveness.) At most, counter-institutional tactics may bring a spiral of results; strength for the organization, pressure for top-down change, and popular participation in both means and goal. Ordinarily, though, success will mean parks and stop signs, not new housing.

At a second level are *counter-institutions of culture and information.* JOIN's newspaper, *The Firing Line,* circulates 4,000 copies a week in the neighborhood and is eagerly written for, edited, and read by community people. Its theater, weekly topical skits put together by organizers and community people, has a smaller but even more dedicated following. Both are expanding as the level of organization permits. NCUP's neighborhood radio station, transmitting through power lines, is imminent. JOIN also shows movies on organizing and issues, with great effect. These projects have an intrinsic validity—telling the truth. They are easier to set up than economic counter-institutions; and the mainstream proposes a less compelling alternative. . . .

Finally there are *political counter-institutions,* aiming to effect a transfer of legitimacy in more strategic zones. Some, like the Mississippi Freedom Democratic Party, arise because there is simply no other way to accomplish a goal (register voters); they can offer alternatives but cannot take power. Others, like the Lowndes County Freedom Party, reject the available alternative of party politics in favor of independent structure. . . .

Some critics, holding fast to the vanishing myth of Southern exceptionalism, would validate such political innovations only for the Black Belt. But in cities where important material needs cannot be achieved for a long time, political counter-institutions might also become serious intermediate objectives. When the good citizens of Los Angeles refuse to pass a bond issue for a hospital in Watts, it makes sense to think about the secession of Watts from Los Angeles. Watts lacks the resources to build a hospital, Los Angeles has them but will not release them. A movement in Watts would have to do some hard thinking to balance the risks of secession against the gains of substantive legitimacy, freedom from the L.A. cops, pressure on would-be allies. Nominal secessions of that sort might light more fires under liberals, churches, and unions than all the more orthodox appeals put together—and make "something of our own" more resistant to melting into other people's crucibles. Yet the movement must continue to see these moves as precedents for deeper changes, not ends in themselves.

Frontal assertions of newly-made legitimacy are probably best adapted to situations of overt, intolerable terror and police tyranny. In cities like Chicago, traditional protest movements—including JOIN's—against police brutality have accomplished no more than the transfer of some of the worst sadists to other ghettoes in the city. Riots may temper brutality for a while, get Negroes on the police force, coax liberals to set up *papier-mâché* review boards, but tend to let the cops clamp down all the harder (either directly, as in Watts, or through electoral backlash, as in New York). In the long run the only serious change would have police forces directly accountable to residents, under the law of a community that controls its own resources; but in the present oppressive context this is utopian. To build for that possibility, though, a movement can invent other ways to contain the police, to deprive them of their legitimacy, to erase fear—in the ghetto, and in the city at large. Following the example of a Watts group, JOIN has experimented with a radio-car patrol, run by young neighborhood men, to keep an eye on police behavior. The danger that the counter-structure might become simply a branch of the central structure—local people taking on exactly the old functions—is lessened by self-awareness and constant re-examination. The evidence compiled by the patrol helps undercut the abusive authority of police in the neighborhood—if people can withstand (as often they have not) the new terrorism. At the same time the patrol would tie in with a developing network of lawyers, clergymen, doctors, and liberal people—*itself induced by the publicity of local organizing*—to begin filing damage suits, inhibit some excesses, record some successes, and finally develop a network of informal neighborhood review boards to publicize atrocities and catalyze some political pressures for substantial reforms. Aside from weakening the moral basis of oppressive "law and order," this support promises to open more space (through needed protection) for grass-roots organizing; local people remain in charge but fashion an honest, functional relationship with middle-class allies.

Counter-institutional forms may in fact be the best means to attract middle-class allies for specific purposes, and link them to the ongoing movement. Sometimes direct action itself can spur the initial contacts: Southern demonstrations catalyzed a national grouping of doctors and nurses that has grown into the Medical Committee on Human Rights, which is now committed to more than first-aid; urgent legal needs led to national committees of lawyers and law students with durable ties to local movements. But in both cases it has been the more or less permanently rooted counter-institutional structures that have coaxed *ad hoc* professional actions into more lasting, committed, potentially radical groupings—as allies and direct supports for poor people's groups, and as radical caucuses within the professions. The 1964 Mississippi Freedom Schools probably meant less in the lives of Mississippi children than in their impact on the Northern teachers.

Once these allies are drawn to the movement, they can become functioning radicals with a fresh orientation toward the society as well as toward the meanings and potentials of their professions. Contact with a poor people's movement, more than a merely theoretical grasp of the need to change the relation of professionals to "clients," can prove decisive. First, the professionals can get to know the poor as people, people rooted in a *milieu,* as political actors, not clients; and to fathom, concretely, the consequences of this society for the people at its bottom. Second, they can learn to make their skills accountable to constituencies with collective needs—a new departure for professions that flaunt expertise (e.g., social work) or the law of the marketplace (medicine) where they need not. Third, radical organizers gain access to raise questions about the structure of the profession and its radical requirements. Fourth, as allies are exposed to blatant attempts to repress the movement, they become more open to radical interpretations of the political process. Fifth, they can develop methods of work, within the movement and on its borders, which sustain their political radicalism and give it roots. The more compelling these learning experiences—and the evidence is that they happen, though unevenly—the more likely are professionals to serve as serious defenders of the gains and potentials of grass-roots movements and as self-motivating radicals in their own rights. Against local repressions they can provide "cover"; against national mechanisms of cooptation they can be buffers, helping to protect the integrity of substantive local participation and radical ideas against the onslaughts of centralism and resources. Otherwise, without serious contact, angry "clients" and organized professionals—the two greatest forces for a potent radicalism—are likely to end up racing off as antagonists, hopelessly divided over questions of control and priorities. Much of the burden is on the professionals, to transcend their narrow self-interest and re-discover the professions' essences in an ethic of responsiveness to human need; but community unions should also be looking for ways to encourage the process.

. . . .

FURTHER READINGS

Allen, Jessie. "Newark Community Union." *Studies on the Left,* Winter 1965.

Aronowitz, Stanley. "New York City: After the Rent Strike." *Studies on the Left,* Winter 1965.

Brown, Connie. "Cleveland: Conference on the Poor." *Studies on the Left,* Spring 1965.

Cloward, Richard A. and Piven, Francis F. "The Weight of the Poor: A Strategy to End Poverty." *The Nation,* May 2, 1966.

Fruchter, Norm, and Kramer, Robert. "An Approach to Community Organizing." *Studies on the Left,* March/April 1966.

Gitlin, Todd. "Organizing the Poor." In *Beyond Dissent: Papers from the New Left.* New York: Doubleday, 1967.

Hayden, Tom. "Community Organizing and the War on Poverty." *Liberation,* November 1965.

————. *Student Social Action: From Liberation to Community.* SDS pamphlet, 1962.

———— and Carl Wittman. *An Interracial Movement of the Poor?* SDS pamphlet, Winter 1963.

"Interview with Some Organizers of the Chicago JOIN Project," by Fruchter, Norm and Aronowitz, Stanley. *Studies on the Left,* V: 3 Summer 1965.

Kopkind, Andrew. "Of, By and For the Poor: The New Generation of Student Organizers." *New Republic,* June 19, 1965.

Miller, Mike. "San Francisco: Freedom House." *Studies on the Left,* V: 1, Winter 1965.

Miller, William G. "New Brunswick: Community Action Project." *Studies on the Left,* V: 2, Spring 1962.

O'Connor, James. "Toward a Theory of Community Union." *Studies on the Left,* Spring/Summer 1964.

Rothstein, Richard. "E.R.A.P.: Evolution of the Organizer." *Radical America,* March/April 1968.

————. "E.R.A.P. and How it Grew." In *Don't Mourn—Organize!* The Movement Press, May 1968.

Schechter, Dan. "Reveille for Reformers." *Studies on the Left,* VI: 1, Fall 1965; January/February 1966.

Sinclair, Hamish. "Hazard, Ky.: Committee for Miners." *Studies on the Left,* Summer 1965.

Where It's At—A Research Guide for Community Organizing. 1967.

Williams, James H. "On Community Unions." *Studies on the Left,* IV: 3, Spring 1964.

Films. Fruchter, Norm and Mackover, Robert. *Had Us a Time* (Cleveland Conference of the Poor), *We Gotta Live Here,* and *The Troublemakers* (Newark Community Union Project).

4

"Free Speech"

4.1. BRADLEY CLEVELAND: A Letter to Undergraduates

[In addition to political reasons extraneous to the university itself, the origins of the Berkeley revolt of 1964 included widespread discontent caused by the educational system of the university itself. A few days before the outbreak of the revolt, Brad Cleveland, a former graduate student who called himself a student-agitator, published a letter to undergraduates in which he described and criticized the institution. Eight thousand copies of the letter, published as part of The SLATE supplement, were sold in a few days; it was subsequently cited as proof of a revolutionary plot. The following are some excerpts from it.]

In this multiversity, you will not learn so much as a cursory meaning of what a world-in-revolution means to you. You will not learn the utterly profound fact of what a revolution is:

That a revolution comes about when enormous numbers of fellow human beings are oppressed to points far beyond what we blandly label an "intolerable set of conditions."

Nor will you learn that to be a counter-revolutionary is to go about the business of slaughtering enormous numbers of human beings whose inflamed spirits and starved stomachs force them to cry out for the freedoms which you spit upon in your apathy.

And you will learn most of all not to entertain so much as the possibility that American foreign policy in Korea and South Viet Nam are precisely counter-revolutionary . . . that the American nation is involved in destroying popular national revolutions, and appears to be getting itself locked more and more in that suicidal and inhumane policy.

Are you aware that the most salient characteristic of the "multiversity" is massive production of specialized excellence? *Specialized Excellence.* It will be some time before machines will displace the super-trades; thus massive training centers are necessary. But why do we insist upon calling them educational centers rather than training centers?

The multiversity is not an educational center, but a highly efficient industry: it produces bombs, other war machines, a few token "peaceful" machines, and enormous numbers of safe, highly skilled, and respectable automations to meet the immediate needs of business and government.

. . . In the sciences and technical fields your courses are bluntly and destructively rigorous. . . . You become impatient with "that social sciences and humanities crap." How did you get to be such puppets? You *perform.* But when you do think? Dutifully and obediently you follow, as a herd of grade-worshiping sheep. If you are strong at all, you do this with some sense of shame, or if you are weak, you do it with a studied cynicism . . . as jaded youth with parched imaginations that go no further than oak-paneled rooms at the end of the line . . . *But whether you are strong or weak you perform like trained seals, and like sheep you follow . . . with the thoroughbred . . . sheep leading you!!* up the golden stairway . . . to the Happy Consciousness, to success and a very parochial mind. This is the core of your dutiful daily lives, and your homage to respectability. Reluctantly or otherwise, you permit it to be applied by administrators who use computers on you as much because they are afraid of personal contact with you as for the reason that they wish to keep the assembly line moving efficiently. You permit professors to extract your performance by . . . coercion. . . . Why do you permit this apostasy of learning . . . a process which prevents you from extending your thought beyond a shallow dilettantism?

. . . .

. . . You are blinded to the fact that you are really getting something of terrible importance while you are here:

Training in the capacity for unquestioning obedience to a complex flood of trivial bureaucratic rules. In the name of human learning you acquire the capacity to be docile in the face of rules. While you are training, the rules which tell you how to go about your training are displacing your freedom to think . . . skill and obedience are what you acquire.

Aren't you the least bit aware that such a capacity is not only necessary for life in America's giant public and private corporations, but that it is also a first-class ticket to a traditional form of statehood under the designation of tyranny?

. . . .

. . . There is only one proper response to Berkeley from undergraduates: that you *organize and split this campus wide open!*

From this point on, do not misunderstand me, my intention is to convince you that you do nothing less than begin an open, fierce, and thoroughgoing rebellion on this campus.

. . . .

And if you get this far you will . . . have witnessed nationwide publicity which will have exposed Berkeley for the undergraduate sham that it is. Not to say that the public in general will feel that way, what with the press "redbaiting" you, but that students all over the country will read between the lines. By this time you may also be able to call for a mass student strike . . . something which seems unthinkable at present. If a miracle occurs, or two, you might even get to say that you were the seeds of an educational revolution unlike anything which has ever occurred. Remember one thing:

"The task of genius, and man is nothing if not genius, is to keep the miracle alive, to live always in the miracle, to make the miracle more and more miraculous, to swear allegiance to nothing, but live only miraculously, think miraculously, to die miraculously."

Henry Miller

4.2.   *SOL STERN:* **A Deeper Disenchantment**

[Sol Stern, author of the following article, was a witness of the events at Berkeley. He was a graduate student there and editor of the magazine *Root and Branch*. Selections from *Liberation,* February 1965.]

The University of California is probably the most impressive and prestigious state university in the country. It boasts a world-famous faculty that includes a half dozen Nobel Prize winners and its many departments are all considered "first rate." It is the "compleat" university. . . .

Despite all the academic glitter and the bountiful social life Berkeley offers, there is deep and bitter resentment among many students about their life at the university. It is a resentment that starts from the contradiction between the public image and reputation of the university and their actual day-to-day experiences as students. For these students recognize that all that is exciting and stimulating about Berkeley comes from the frills and extras of university life; the formal university-learning experience is generally a deadening one.

The new undergraduate learns quickly that of all the functions of the Great University his own education is perhaps the least important. He has almost no contact with the famous professors he has heard about. They, for their part, seek ways to escape the "burden" of teaching to be able to devote full time to the pursuit of their professions (which are not defined to include teaching). Graduate teaching assistants do most of whatever face-to-face teaching the undergraduate encounters. For the most part, however, the undergraduate learns that his success at school depends on his ability to master a four-year system of lectures, reading lists and examinations that have little to do with genuine learning. A student organization, SLATE, publishes a *Supplement to The General Catalogue,* every semester, which advises the undergraduate on ways to beat the "system" and get a reasonable education in spite of it. Whether the undergraduate is morally revolted by the system, or whether he shrugs it off as merely another facet of the lifesmanship he must master, it is as a "system" that his education is commonly perceived and becomes a central part of the undergraduate folklore.

Many graduate students share a more special malaise. They have already made something of a commitment to academic and university life, but it is a commitment beclouded with ambiguities and doubts. The graduate students, in their closer proximity to the professors and the specialized disciplines, have also become privy to the intellectual dishonesties and political scheming that go on at the upper levels of Academia. There is a widespread sense that they are prisoners in a system of professional rewards and penalties, determined by those very professors whose manipulations they observe at first hand. It is a system they have no power to change and leaves them only the option of playing the academic game according to the rules or getting out.

This alienation in the midst of the apparent good life finds symbolic expression at a campus gathering place known as "The Terrace"—an outdoor pavillion of the Student Union cafeteria, where one can bask in sunshine most of the year and enjoy a majestic view of San Francisco Bay. Many of the more active and concerned students gather here for the usual rounds of student gossip and political banter. Their range of political opinion and affiliation is extremely wide; they include every variety of revolutionary and reformist socialist, radicals and liberal democrats, civil-rights activists, anarchists, pacifists and even an occasional Goldwaterite. When the talk is of national and international politics the arguments are heated, but when the talk turns to what can only be described as "university politics" there is a sudden change of perspective. A common note of cynicism enters the dialogue. Common enemies are easily identifiable: they are the university bureaucracy, the graduate school system, the political schemers among the faculty. Most often and most pointedly the enemy is the president of the university, Clark Kerr.

It tells us much about the mood of these students that the man who is most clearly viewed as the enemy carries all the traditional credentials of the modern political liberal. In his speeches and writings, Clark Kerr is indeed always on the side of the angels: for academic freedom, for free speech, for freedom of inquiry. He has received the highest award of the American Association of University Professors for his efforts on behalf of academic freedom. Yet if Kerr is a bonafide card-carrying liberal he also typifies much of what the students consider the failure of American liberalism during the Cold War era. Official establishment liberalism offers nothing to these students because it has lost its passion and crusading spirit. It has become manipulative, crafty and cautious. In domestic and international politics it has become identified with *realpolitik* and opportunism.

. . . .

But more than matters of personality and style mark Kerr as an appropriate symbol for the bureaucratic "system." Kerr has also become the foremost spokesman and ideologist for the new bureaucratic style in American higher education. In his Godkin Lectures, at Harvard in 1963, he first coined the term "multiversity" to describe the model American university of the future. This "multiversity" is no longer primarily a citadel for learning. It becomes a service center for society. The "multiversity" will increasingly service the established institutions of business, government, labor and the national defense effort. In Kerr's own words, "the university is being called upon . . . to respond to the expanding claims of national service; to merge its activity with industry as never before."

Now all of this is not so terribly new or provocative. Many educators have commented upon and lamented this trend. But it is different with Kerr: he cheerfully accepts the trend as the inexorable path of development and draws the appropriate conclusions. For if the "multiversity" is to become more and more attuned to the needs of industry and national defense, then the requirements of tough-minded bureaucracy and management must have first claims on those who lead the "multiversity." The "Managerial Revolution" has come to the campus; now the most important stratum of the university is not the faculty, nor the students, nor any single educational Idea, but rather the manager and administrator. The "multiversity" is a "mechanism held together by administrative rules and powered by money." To guide this mechanism through its many complex functions, the university president must be guided primarily by the tools and arts of manipulation and mediation.

At the University of California Clark Kerr has indeed appeared as that model administrator-manager. As both the author of this scenario of the future and the leading player in it, Kerr has made himself the perfect target for all the resentment that the development of the "multiversity" arouses. That is why the students regard Kerr's liberalism as irrelevant. It is also why "multiversity" takes on, in conversations on the terrace, all of the emotional connotations of the term "1984."

Perhaps what has been most infuriating to the students on the terrace is the fact that all the physical evidence about them seemed to point inescapably to the power of Clark Kerr's vision of the future. The University of California was becoming more and more like the model "multiversity." Moreover, the average student, despite his private anxieties and resentments, did not appear to be in the mood for any rebellion against the role assigned to him by the "multiversity." Nor did the faculty appear terribly upset about the consequences of the "multiversity"; they seemed rather to be enjoying the increased emoluments it was bringing them in the form of grants, consultation fees, and most important of all, freedom from teaching.

During the course of the free-speech struggle last fall, the students at the terrace learned that they did have resources available to fight back against the "multiversity." They were not yet reduced altogether to private and impotent grumblings. They learned how they could stake out an area of autonomy and take some of the initiative out of the hands of the administrators and managers.

When the issue of free speech was first raised, it did not seem that all the above sentiments would be brought to bear. It was after all a move not uncharacteristic of the old-fashioned university that precipitated the free-speech struggle. At the beginning of the fall semester the administration enforced an old but never used rule which had the effect of prohibiting the use of the campus by students for soliciting of funds and recruiting for political activities. Representatives of nineteen student political organizations then formed themselves as an *ad hoc* group to press for a removal of these restrictions. So far there was nothing in this that suggested the beginning of a student rebellion. Student protest is accounted for by the theorist of the "multiversity." Indeed it is one of the characteristic talents of the new administrator-manager of the "multiversity" that he is able to contain and divert student protests so that they do not interfere with the efficient functioning of the university machine.

What did give a clue that this was more than the ordinary student protest was the refusal of the students to play their roles entirely according to those "administrative rules" which keep the university bureaucracy functioning smoothly. From the beginning the students showed a unique and surprising determination to assert their autonomy. Whenever the university administration attempted to use the "normal" channels as a means of diverting them, the students were ready to take the dispute outside those channels for a more direct confrontation with the administration. A unique quality of audacity marked this protest. *Life* magazine was forced to recognize it, with a slight tinge of awe, as a "Tough Campus Revolt."

This toughness showed itself almost immediately. The students' first response to the new administrative regulations was direct and simple. They ignored them. Taking the position that the restrictions were a violation of their constitutional rights, they left it to the administration to try to enforce them. They set up their tables on the campus and continued to recruit and collect money. When the administration tried to bring disciplinary action against five of the students who had been manning the tables, six hundred students signed statements saying that they, too, had been guilty of violating the rules. When the Dean summoned the five students to his office, three hundred showed up and demanded to be seen too.

Finally the Dean announced that eight students had been suspended for various activities in protesting the new rules. The students again had a ready response. They set up their tables directly in front of the administration building. The administration replied by having one of those manning a table arrested and placed in a campus police car (he had gone limp and a car had to be summoned to take him away). At this point a group of students spontaneously threw themselves in front of the car and blocked its path. Soon they were joined by hundreds of others and within an hour the police car was surrounded by a solid phalanx of one thousand bodies.

This spontaneous demonstration developed rapidly into a massive sit-in and rally around the police car that lasted thirty-two hours. As it grew and grew, student speakers mounted the embattled police car, using it as a podium from which to address the throng and state the demands the administration must meet to end the demonstration. At the end of the second day, five hundred helmeted police stood by with their nightsticks, ready to wade in and disperse the students. Serious violence was averted only at the last minute as a settlement was reached between the student leaders and Clark Kerr. The crowd heard and approved the terms of the agreement and then dispersed voluntarily. Audacity had won the students a number of points. The suspensions of the eight leaders would be reviewed by a faculty committee, the university agreed not to press charges against the arrested student, and the rules of political activity would be submitted to a study committee on which students would be represented.

Much was learned during this first skirmish with the administration: the students realized that audacity and directness could move the bureaucracy where normal channels failed. Now the students turned to organizing themselves more effectively. The *ad hoc* group of the political organizations was turned officially into the Free Speech Movement, and an executive committee of fifty and a steering committee of twelve were set up. Intensive organizing among the student body was conducted to gather more support, and new groups were urged to send representatives to the movement (or F.S.M., as it was now generally called). An F.S.M. Newsletter was published and leaflets by the score were put out to explain F.S.M.'s position and the latest developments to the student body. A massive and well documented report was put together by graduate students, tracing the history of past administration attempts to limit student political rights.

After six weeks of student petitions, testimony at committees, and more rallies and demonstrations, the administration bent a little more. . . .

. . . .

At this point, however, the F.S.M. was split on tactics for the first time. Many were for resuming the dramatic direct-action methods used earlier in the term. Others felt that the issues were not clear-cut enough to demand such a course. As the F.S.M. floundered, the administration gave it back its *raison d' être*. The administration now decided that it was going to bring disciplinary action against four of the student leaders for their actions during the demonstrations around the police car some two months before. This was seen by the students as nothing less than an attempt to break the movement by cutting off its head.

Thus on December 2nd, over one thousand students marched into the administration building, taking over all four of its floors. They announced that they were prepared to sit there until the administration had called off its action against their leaders. In the meantime, the powerful organization of graduate students, which had been formed during the free-speech struggle, announced its intention to call a university-wide strike in a few days in support of the F.S.M. demands.

· ·

On leading the students into the administration building the day before, Mario Savio, the leader of F.S.M., had uttered the classic words of the movement:

> There is a time when the operation of the machine becomes so odious, makes you so sick at heart that you can't take part; you can't even tacitly take part, and you've got to put your bodies upon the levers, upon all the apparatus and you've got to make it stop. And you've got to indicate to the people who run it, to the people who own it, that unless you're free the machine will be prevented from working at all.

This was a sentiment that now seemed to be shared by a majority of the student body, to whom the operation of the machine was now revealed as extremely odious. No longer was it merely a question of certain administrative rules that were at issue, but the whole stumbling and faceless bureaucracy that had stood by as political pressures forced a virtual police occupation of the campus.

So the students did indeed bring the machine to a grinding halt. A strike plan went into effect immediately and scores of picket lines were thrown around the classroom buildings. Many faculty members now supported the strike. A philosophy professor announced to the students gathered at a rally that he was calling off all his classes, as he could not in conscience conduct classes while the campus was under police occupation.

Most of the education that took place in the next few days came outside the classrooms, in the innumerable knots and crowds of students and faculty that sprang up everywhere on the campus. They argued and discussed the nature of democracy, the rule of law, and civil disobedience. The F.S.M. organized classes off the campus at their "Free University of California." It was truly an amazing scene. Nothing less than a revolution, though a gentle one, seemed to be taking place.

· ·

Whatever the final outcome, it is clear that the meaning of these events lies deeper than the use of the Berkeley campus for political activity. The students themselves, slightly amazed at the proportions of the movement they had touched off, also looked about for meanings.

It was widely understood that some deeper disenchantment lay behind the free-speech fight. A campus minister had written to the school newspaper that he saw behind the student rebellion a reaction to "the modern isolation and alienation of the spirit" and that the students were trying to restore a lost sense of "community." "Alienation" and "community": these words were much heard from the students during their rallies and demonstrations. The computer, too, somehow became a symbol of the "system" that the students were objecting to. "Are you a student or an I.B.M. card?" Thus read one of the F.S.M. leaflets urging students to support the strike.

Yet this revolt was not just a blind lashing out at the machine—a modern Luddite rebellion. The I.B.M. card and "the bureaucracy" were symbols, but behind the symbols stood men. And among the students there was a widespread feeling that the men who ran the system here at Berkeley, those who rationalized it and those who spoke for it, had betrayed them. That these men spoke with the rhetoric of sophisticated liberalism was only more appalling. Here on the campus, Clark Kerr and others like him were bowing to and abetting all the forces of mindless bureaucracy and alienation. One must admit that even Clark Kerr had known and spoken of the alienation of students. In his Godkin Lectures he had recognized that the student was often confused and lonely and without purpose, in the "Knowledge Factory." But for Kerr, the source of this alienation lay not with any policies of men, nor with any institution. Like the "multiversity" itself, alienation was an immutable, inevitable consequence of the growing complexity of modern society.

Thus Kerr and many other observers could not fully understand the nature of this revolt against the university administration and against Kerr himself. Were not all the rallies and demonstrations and sit-ins slightly irrational, like tilting against history itself? Sometimes, to Kerr and others, these events, being irrational and inexplicable, had to have some sinister force behind them. Thus Kerr at one point spoke of outside agitators, Maoists, Castroites and other such devils stirring up the students. A professor at the university, Lewis Feuer, in an article* which otherwise showed under-standing of the terrible effects of the "multiversity" also had to explain much of the student revolt as being instigated by a collection of Maoist-beatnik-sexual libertine pseudo-students who were all looking for some syn-thetic revolution to make up for the emptiness which they felt in their lives. Finally, everyone spoke of the unreasonableness of the students. They were rejecting all the "normal channels" for settling disputes; they showed a contempt for Law and Order. They were, according to Clark Kerr, attempt-ing to disrupt the orderly processes of the university and impose anarchy on the campus.

To the students however all the talk about "reasonableness," "orderly processes" and "normal channels" seemed but a facade behind which a "higher irrationality" was being practiced by the administrators, the bureau-crats and the politicians. These men defined "orderly processes" and "rea-sonableness" as all that was consistent with the on-going system. To Clark Kerr, for example, it was presumably "reasonable" that the university engage in contracted research for the Defense Department, "reasonable" for the university to allow its facilities to be used by the Marine Corps to recruit students, but it was "unreasonable" for the students to recruit civil-rights workers to disrupt the flow of commerce in the outside community.

Behind all the talk of "orderly processes" was a demand that the stu-dents accommodate themselves to a style of protest that would have frozen them to the very administrative apparatus that they were trying to change. It was this administrative style that was as much a source of the students' alienation as "the complexity of modern society." Correspondingly, it was the style of the student protest that most upset so many of the important people of the state and the university. The students had set up their own

---

*"Rebellion at Berkeley," The New Leader, December 21, 1964. Other articles dealing with these events include "Paul Goodman on the Berkeley Riots," New York Review of Books, January 14, 1965; and "The Student Riots at Berkeley: Dissent in the Multiversity," by Joseph Paff et al., The Activist, January 1965.

counter-community, independent of the university system. Their own standards of justification prevailed and they kept their own counsel, not paying too much attention to the pleas for "realistic" approaches that came from their elders, many of whom were jaded ex-radicals.

In acting as they did the students achieved some unique results. They took the first genuine steps toward that sense of community everybody was always vainly searching for. It was widely remarked that there was more face-to-face communication among the faculty and between faculty and students during the days of the strike than there had ever been before. The classroom had been replaced by the open and unstructured forum. In those innumerable spontaneous sessions between professors and students, important educational experiences unfolded. There was a give and take and an openness that could not have occurred in the classroom. The professors faced the students without their academic regalia, without their grade books, without the prospects of giving or withholding a recommendation. There was much talk during those days of a "Free University of California." Unlike Clark Kerr's "multiversity" it was an idea and a model of a future university that *the students* would have liked to create and participate in—one that would more often act in opposition to the powers-that-be in the society outside.

In all this a new mood seemed to grip the students. The "multiversity," with all its horrendous consequences, was not historically inevitable as the technological determinists were continuously announcing, but would come because men with power abetted it. The new technology should have brought with it greater opportunities for community and more meaningful purposes in life. The problem was how to make those in power and in the entrenched bureaucracy use those opportunities for decent purposes. To bring such pressure, it became necessary to shake up the bureaucrats and dramatize the gap between them and the students by creating new and audacious styles of protest.

One does not wish to exaggerate or romanticize what the students at Berkeley did. The "multiversity" is still omnipresent and students must go back and play by its rules. Yet it must not be forgotten that behind the facade of orderly and pleasant campuses there are deep currents of unrest and dissatisfaction. White, middle-class students in the North also need a liberation movement, for they have no community in which they exercise citizenship. They feel imprisoned and oppressed by a smiling and genial bureaucracy.

The issues at Berkeley are deeper than civil rights and civil liberties. These issues merely provided the form of this first serious revolt against modern liberal bureaucracy. When and if the "pocket" problems of civil rights and poverty are solved, this society will still have to deal with a crisis that is more basic to the lives of most of its citizens. It is this that concerns the students at Berkeley, and in response to that crisis they created an important little wedge against the creeping totalitarianism that threatens all of us.

4.3.   *MARIO SAVIO:* **An End to History**

[Mario Savio was the major spokesman of the Berkeley Free Speech Movement. The following article was originally published in the December

1964 issue of *Humanity;* it is the text of a speech he delivered during a sit-in of the same month.]

Last summer I went to Mississippi to join the struggle there for civil rights. This fall I am engaged in another phase of the same struggle, this time in Berkeley. The two battlefields may seem quite different to some observers, but this is not the case. The same rights are at stake in both places—the right to participate as citizens in democratic society and the right to due process of law. Further, it is a struggle against the same enemy. In Mississippi an autocratic and powerful minority rules, through organized violence, to suppress the vast, virtually powerless majority. In California, the privileged minority manipulates the university bureaucracy to suppress the students' political expression. That "respectable" bureaucracy masks the financial plutocrats; that impersonal bureaucracy is the efficient enemy in a "Brave New World."

In our free-speech fight at the University of California, we have come up against what may emerge as the greatest problem of our nation—depersonalized, unresponsive bureaucracy. We have encountered the organized status quo in Mississippi, but it is the same in Berkeley. Here we find it impossible usually to meet with anyone but secretaries. Beyond that, we find functionaries who cannot make policy but can only hide behind the rules. We have discovered total lack of response on the part of the policy makers. To grasp a situation which is truly Kafkaesque, it is necessary to understand the bureaucratic mentality. And we have learned quite a bit about it this fall, more outside the classroom than in.

As bureaucrat, an administrator believes that nothing new happens. He occupies an a-historical point of view. In September, to get the attention of this bureaucracy which had issued arbitrary edicts suppressing student political expression and refused to discuss its action, we held a sit-in on the campus. We sat around a police car and kept it immobilized for over thirty-two hours. At last, the administrative bureaucracy agreed to negotiate. But instead, on the following Monday, we discovered that a committee had been appointed, in accordance with usual regulations, to resolve the dispute. Our attempt to convince any of the administrators that an event had occurred, that something new had happened, failed. They saw this simply as something to be handled by normal university procedures.

The same is true of all bureaucracies. They begin as tools, means to certain legitimate goals, and they end up feeding their own existence. The conception that bureaucrats have is that history has in fact come to an end. No events can occur now that the Second World War is over which can change American society substantially. We proceed by standard procedures as we are.

The most crucial problems facing the United States today are the problem of automation and the problem of racial injustice. Most people who will be put out of jobs by machines will not accept an end to events, this historical plateau, as the point beyond which no change occurs. Negroes will not accept an end to history here. All of us must refuse to accept history's final judgment that in America there is no place in society for people whose skins are dark. On campus students are not about to accept it as fact that the university has ceased evolving and is in its final state of perfection, that students and faculty are respectively raw material and employees, or that the university is to be automatically run by unresponsive bureaucrats.

Here is the real contradition: the bureaucrats hold history as ended. As a result significant parts of the population both on campus and off are dispossessed, and these dispossessed are not about to accept this a-historical point of view. It is out of this that the conflict has occurred with the university bureaucracy and will continue to occur until that bureaucracy becomes responsive or until it is clear the university cannot function.

The things we are asking for in our civil rights protests have a deceptively quaint ring. We are asking for the due process of law. We are asking for our actions to be judged by committees of our peers. We are asking that regulations ought to be considered as arrived at legitimately only from the consensus of the governed. These phrases are all pretty old, but they are not being taken seriously in America today, nor are they being taken seriously on the Berkeley campus.

I have just come from a meeting with the Dean of Students. She notified us that she was aware of certain violations of university regulations by certain organizations. University friends of SNCC, which I represent, was one of these. We tried to draw from her some statement on these great principles: consent of the governed, jury of one's peers, due process. The best she could do was to evade or to present the administration party line. It is very hard to make any contact with the human being who is behind these organizations.

The university is the place where people begin seriously to question the conditions of their existence and raise the issue of whether they can be committed to the society they have been born into. After a long period of apathy during the fifties, students have begun not only to question but, having arrived at answers, to act on those answers. This is part of a growing understanding among many people in America that history has not ended, that a better society is possible, and that it is worth dying for.

This free speech fight points up a fascinating aspect of contemporary campus life. Students are permitted to talk all they want so long as their speech has no consequences.

One conception of the university, suggested by a classical Christian formulation, is that it be in the world but not of the world. The conception of Clark Kerr, by contrast, is that the university is part and parcel of this particular stage in the history of American society; it stands to serve the need of American industry; it is a factory that turns out a certain product needed by industry or government. Because speech does often have consequences which might alter this perversion of higher education, the university must put itself in a position of censorship. It can permit two kinds of speech: speech which encourages continuation of the status quo, and speech which advocates changes in it so radical as to be irrelevant in the foreseeable future. Someone may advocate radical change in all aspects of American society, and this I am sure he can do with impunity. But if someone advocates sit-ins to bring about changes in discriminatory hiring practices, this can not be permitted because it goes against the status quo of which the university is a part. And that is how the fight began here.

The administration of the Berkeley campus has admitted that external, extra-legal groups have pressured the university not to permit students on campus to organize picket lines, not to permit students on campus to organize picket lines, not to permit on campus any speech with consequences. And the bureaucracy went along. Speech with consequences, speech in the area of civil rights, speech which some might regard as illegal, must stop.

Many students here at the university, many people in society, are wandering aimlessly about. Strangers in their own lives, there is no place for them. They are people who have not learned to compromise, who for example have come to the university to learn to question, to grow, to learn—all the standard things that sound like clichés because no one takes them seriously. And they find at one point or other that for them to become part of society, to become lawyers, ministers, businessmen, people in government, that very often they must compromise those principles which were most dear to them. They must suppress the most creative impulses that they have; this is a prior condition for being part of the system. The university is well structured, well tooled, to turn out people with all the sharp edges worn off, the well-rounded person. The university is well equipped to produce that sort of person, and this means that the best among the people who enter must for four years wander aimlessly much of the time questioning why they are on campus at all, doubting whether there is any point in what they are doing, and looking toward a very bleak existence afterward in a game in which all of the rules have been made up, which one cannot really amend.

It is a bleak scene, but it is all a lot of us have to look forward to. Society provides no challenge. American society in the standard conception it has of itself is simply no longer exciting. The most exciting things going on in America today are movements to change America. America is becoming ever more the utopia of sterilized, automated contentment. The "futures" and "careers" for which American students now prepare are for the most part intellectual and moral wastelands. This chrome-plated consumers' paradise would have us grow up to be well-behaved children. But an important minority of men and women coming to the front today have shown that they will die rather than be standardized, replaceable and irrelevant.

FURTHER READINGS

Draper, Hal. *Berkeley: The New Student Revolt.* New York: Evergreen Books, Grove Press, 1965.

Glazer, Nathan, and Draper, Hal. "Debate on FSM." *New Politics,* IV: 1.

Kerr, Clark. *The Use of the University.* Cambridge: Harvard University Press, 1962.

Lipset, Seymour M., and Wolin, Sheldon S. *The Berkeley Student Revolt.* New York: Doubleday Anchor Books, 1965.

Miller, Michael V., and Gilmore, Susan. *Revolution at Berkeley.* New York: Dell, 1965.

Nagler, Michael. "Berkeley: The Demonstrations." *Studies on the Left,* V: 1, Winter1965.

"New Voices on Campus." Originally published in *Mademoiselle* and reprinted as SDS pamphlet, August 1965.

"The Position of the Free Speech Movement on Speech and Political Activity." FSM pamphlet, 1964.

Rosenfield, Gerald. "Generational Revolt and the FSM." *Liberation,* December and January 1965.

Rossman, Michael. "Barefoot in a Marshmallow World." *Ramparts,* January 1966.

Spence, Larry. "Berkeley: What it Demonstrates." *Studies on the Left,* V: 1, Winter 1965.

Warshaw, Steven. *The Trouble at Berkeley* (photographic documents). Berkeley: Diablo Press, 1965.

Two:
The Emergence of
a New Left Position

5

Analyses and
Proposals for
American Society

5.1. SDS: Port Huron Statement

[The 1962 convention of Students for a Democratic Society (SDS) was held at Port Huron, Michigan, in a United Auto Workers center. The document approved by the convention derived from an outline prepared by Tom Hayden according to the decision of an earlier preparatory meeting held in 1961. At the time the text was published, the Convention declared that the Port Huron Statement was a "living document open to change with our times and experiences." Although many of its conclusions are no longer shared by a large part of the New Left, as a whole the document may be considered the first manifesto of the New Left. Over 100,000 copies of the 60-page pamphlet have been distributed in five years. Only a small selection of the complete version printed by SDS is reprinted here.]

Introduction: Agenda for a Generation

We are people of this generation, bred in at least modest comfort, housed now in universities, looking uncomfortably to the world we inherit.

When we were kids the United States was the wealthiest and strongest country in the world; the only one with the atom bomb, the least scarred by modern war, an initiator of the United Nations that we thought would distribute Western influence throughout the world. Freedom and equality for each individual, government of, by, and for the people—these American values we found good, principles by which we could live as men. Many of us began maturing in complacency.

As we grew, however, our comfort was penetrated by events too troubling to dismiss. First, the permeating and victimizing fact of human degradation, symbolized by the Southern struggle against racial bigotry, compelled most of us from silence to activism. Second, the enclosing fact of the Cold War, symbolized by the presence of the Bomb, brought awareness that we ourselves, and our friends, and millions of abstract "others" we knew more directly because of our common peril, might die at any time. We might deliberately ignore, or avoid, or fail to feel all other human problems, but not these two, for these were too immediate and crushing in their impact, too challenging in the demand that we as individuals take the responsibility for encounter and resolution.

While these and other problems either directly oppressed us or rankled our consciences and became our own subjective concerns, we began to see complicated and disturbing paradoxes in our surrounding America. The declaration "all men are created equal . . ." rang hollow before the facts of Negro life in the South and the big cities of the North. The proclaimed peaceful intentions of the United States contradicted its economic and military investments in the Cold War status quo.

We witnessed, and continue to witness, other paradoxes. With nuclear energy whole cities can easily be powered, yet the dominant nation-states seem more likely to unleash destruction greater than that incurred in all wars of human history. Although our own technology is destroying old and creating new forms of social organization, men still tolerate meaningless work and idleness. While two-thirds of mankind suffers undernourishment, our own upper classes revel amidst superfluous abundance. Although world population is expected to double in forty years, the nations still tolerate anarchy as a major principle of international conduct and uncontrolled exploitation governs the sapping of the earth's physical resources. Although mankind desperately needs revolutionary leadership, America rests in national stalemate, its goals ambiguous and tradition-bound instead of informed and clear, its democratic system apathetic and manipulated rather than "of, by, and for the people."

Not only did tarnish appear on our image of American virtue, not only did disillusion occur when the hypocrisy of American ideals was discovered, but we began to sense that what we had originally seen as the American Golden Age was actually the decline of an era. The worldwide outbreak of revolution against colonialism and imperialism, the entrenchment of totalitarian states, the menace of war, overpopulation, international disorder, supertechnology —these trends were testing the tenacity of our own commitment to democracy and freedom and our abilities to visualize their application to a world in upheaval.

Our work is guided by the sense that we may be the last generation in the experiment with living. But we are a minority—the vast majority of our people regard the temporary equilibriums of our society and world as eternally-functional parts. In this is perhaps the outstanding paradox: we ourselves are imbued with urgency, yet the message of our society is that there is no viable alternative to the present. Beneath the reassuring tones of the politicians, beneath the common opinion that America will "muddle through," beneath the stagnation of those who have closed their minds to the future, is the pervading feeling that there simply are no alternatives, that our times have witnessed the exhaustion not only of Utopias, but of any new departures as well. Feeling the press of complexity upon the empti- ness of life, people are fearful of the thought that at any moment things might be thrust out of control. They fear change itself, since change might smash whatever invisible framework seems to hold back chaos for them now. For most Americans, all crusades are suspect, threatening. The fact that each individual sees apathy in his fellows perpetuates the common re- luctance to organize for change. The dominant institutions are complex enough to blunt the minds of their potential critics, and entrenched enough to swiftly dissipate or entirely repel the energies of protest and reform, thus limiting human expectancies. Then, too, we are a materially improved society, and by our own improvements we seem to have weakened the case for further change.

Some would have us believe that Americans feel contentment amidst prosperity—but might it not better be called a glaze above deeply-felt anxieties about their role in the new world? And if these anxieties produce a developed indifference to human affairs, do they not as well produce a yearning to believe there *is* an alternative to the present, that something *can* be done to change circumstances in the school, the workplaces, the bureaucracies, the government? It is to this latter yearning, at once the spark and engine of change, that we direct our present appeal. The search for truly democratic alternatives to the present, and a commitment to social experimentation with them, is a worthy and fulfilling human enterprise, one which moves us and, we hope, others today. On such a basis do we offer this document of our convictions and analysis: as an effort in under- standing and changing the conditions of humanity in the late twentieth cen- tury, an effort rooted in the ancient, still unfulfilled conception of man attaining determining influence over his circumstances of life.

Values

Making values explicit—an initial task in establishing alternatives— is an activity that has been devalued and corrupted. The conventional moral terms of the age, the politician moralities—"free world," "people's democ- racies"—reflect realities poorly, if at all, and seem to function more as ruling myths than as descriptive principles. But neither has our experience in the universities brought us moral enlightenment. Our professors and adminis- trators sacrifice controversy to public relations; their curriculums change more slowly than the living events of the world; their skills and silence are purchased by investors in the arms race; passion is called unscholastic. The questions we might want raised—what is really important? can we live in a different and better way? if we wanted to change society, how would we do it?—are not thought to be questions of a "fruitful, empirical nature," and thus are brushed aside.

Unlike youth in other countries we are used to moral leadership being exercised and moral dimensions being clarified by our elders. But today, for us, not even the liberal and socialist preachments of the past seem adequate to the forms of the present. Consider the old slogans: Capitalism Cannot Reform Itself, United Front Against Fascism, General Strike, All Out on May Day. Or, more recently, No Cooperation with Commies and Fellow Travellers, Ideologies Are Exhausted, Bipartisanship, No Utopias. These are incomplete, and there are few new prophets. It has been said that our liberal and socialist predecessors were plagued by vision without program, while our own generation is plagued by program without vision. All around us there is astute grasp of method, technique—the committee, the *ad hoc* group, the lobbyist, the hard and soft sell, the make, the projected image—but, if pressed critically, such expertise is incompetent to explain its implicit ideals. It is highly fashionable to identify oneself by old categories, or by naming a respected political figure, or by explaining "how we would vote" on various issues.

Theoretic chaos has replaced the idealistic thinking of old—and, unable to reconstitute theoretic order, men have condemned idealism itself. Doubt has replaced hopefulness—and men act out a defeatism that is labelled realistic. The decline of utopia and hope is in fact one of the defining features of social life today. The reasons are various: the dreams of the older left were perverted by Stalinism and never recreated; the congressional stalemate makes men narrow their view of the possible; the specialization of human activity leaves little room for sweeping thought; the horrors of the twentieth century, symbolized in the gas-ovens and concentration camps and atom bombs, have blasted hopefulness. To be idealistic is to be considered apocalyptic, deluded. To have no serious aspirations, on the contrary, is to be "toughminded."

In suggesting social goals and values, therefore, we are aware of entering a sphere of some disrepute. Perhaps matured by the past, we have no sure formulas, no closed theories—but that does not mean values are beyond discussion and tentative determination. A first task of any social movement is to convince people that the search for orienting theories and the creation of human values is complex but worthwhile. We are aware that to avoid platitudes we must analyze the concrete conditions of social order. But to direct such an analysis we must use the guideposts of basic principles. Our own social values involve conceptions of human beings, human relationships, and social systems.

We regard *men* as infinitely precious and possessed of unfulfilled capacities for reason, freedom, and love. In affirming these principles we are aware of countering perhaps the dominant conceptions of man in the twentieth century: that he is a thing to be manipulated, and that he is inherently incapable of directing his own affairs. We oppose the depersonalization that reduces human beings to the status of things—if anything, the brutalities of the twentieth century teach that means and ends are intimately related, that vague appeals to "posterity" cannot justify the mutilations of the present. We oppose, too, the doctrine of human incompetence because it rests essentially on the modern fact that men have been "competently" manipulated into incompetence—we see little reason why men cannot meet with increasing skill the complexities and responsibilities of their situation, if society is organized not for minority, but for majority, participation in decision-making.

Men have unrealized potential for self-cultivation, self-direction, self-understanding, and creativity. It is this potential that we regard as crucial and to which we appeal, not to the human potentiality for violence, unreason, and submission to authority. The goal of man and society should be human independence: a concern not with image of popularity but with finding a meaning in life that is personally authentic; a quality of mind not compulsively driven by a sense of powerlessness, nor one which unthinkingly adopts status values, nor one which represses all threats to its habits, but one which has full, spontaneous access to present and past experiences, one which easily unites the fragmented parts of personal history, one which openly faces problems which are troubling and unresolved; one with an intuitive awareness of possibilities, an active sense of curiosity, an ability and willingness to learn.

This kind of independence does not mean egotistic individualism—the object is not to have one's way so much as it is to have a way that is one's own. Nor do we deify man—we merely have faith in his potential.

Human relationships should involve fraternity and honesty. Human interdependence is contemporary fact; human brotherhood must be willed, however, as a condition of future survival and as the most appropriate form of social relations. Personal links between man and man are needed, especially to go beyond the partial and fragmentary bonds of function that bind men only as worker to worker, employer to employee, teacher to student, American to Russian.

Loneliness, estrangement, isolation describe the vast distance between man and man today. These dominant tendencies cannot be overcome by better personnel management, nor by improved gadgets, but only when a love of man overcomes the idolotrous worship of things by man. As the individualism we affirm is not egoism, the selflessness we affirm is not self-elimination. On the contrary, we believe in generosity of a kind that imprints one's unique individual qualities in the relation to other men, and to all human activity. Further, to dislike isolation is not to favor the abolition of privacy; the latter differs from isolation in that it occurs or is abolished according to individual will.

We would replace power rooted in possession, privileged, or circumstance by power and uniqueness rooted in love, reflectiveness, reason, and creativity. As a *social system* we seek the establishment of a democracy of individual participation, governed by two central aims: that the individual share in those social decisions determining the quality and direction of his life; that society be organized to encourage independence in men and provide the media for their common participation.

In a participatory democracy, the political life would be based in several root principles:

that decision-making of basic social consequence be carried on by public groupings;

that politics be seen positively, as the art of collectively creating an acceptable pattern of social relations;

that politics has the function of bringing people out of isolation and into community, thus being a necessary, though not sufficient, means of finding meaning in personal life;

that the political order should serve to clarify problems in a way instrumental to their solution; it should provide outlets for the expression of personal grievance and aspiration; opposing views should be organized so as to illuminate choices and facilitate the attainment of goals; channels should be commonly available to relate men to knowledge and to power so that private problems—from bad recreation facilities to personal alienation—are formulated as general issues.

The economic sphere would have as its basis the principles:

that work should involve incentives worthier than money or survival. It should be educative, not stultifying; creative, not mechanical; self-directed, not manipulated, encouraging independence, a respect for others, a sense of dignity and a willingness to accept social responsibility, since it is this experience that has crucial influence on habits, perceptions and individual ethics;

that the economic experience is so personally decisive that the individual must share in its full determination;

that the economy itself is of such social importance that its major resources and means of production should be open to democratic participation and subject to democratic social regulation.

Like the political and economic ones, major social institutions—cultural, educational, rehabilitative, and others—should be generally organized with the well-being and dignity of man as the essential measure of success.

In social change or interchange, we find violence to be abhorrent because it requires generally the transformation of the target, be it a human being or a community of people, into a depersonalized object of hate. It is imperative that the means of violence be abolished and the institutions—local, national, international—that encourage nonviolence as a condition of conflict be developed.

These are our central values, in skeletal form. It remains vital to understand their denial or attainment in the context of the modern world.

The Students

In the last few years, thousands of American students demonstrated that they at least felt the urgency of the times. They moved actively and directly against racial injustices, the threat of war, violations of individual rights of conscience and, less frequently, against economic manipulation. They succeeded in restoring a small measure of controversy to the campuses after the stillness of the McCarthy period. They succeeded, too, in gaining some concessions from the people and institutions they opposed, especially in the fight against racial bigotry.

The significance of these scattered movements lies not in their success or failure in gaining objectives—at least not yet. Nor does the significance lie in the intellectual "competence" or "maturity" of the students involved —as some pedantic elders allege. The significance is in the fact the students are breaking the crust of apathy and overcoming the inner alienation that remain the defining characteristics of American college life.

If student movements for change are still rarities on the campus scene, what is commonplace there? The real campus, the familiar campus, is a place of private people, engaged in their notorious "inner emigration." It is a place of commitment to business-as-usual, getting ahead, playing it cool. It is a place of mass affirmation of the Twist, but mass reluctance toward the controversial public stance. Rules are accepted as "inevitable," bureaucracy as "just circumstances," irrelevance as "scholarship," selflessness as "martyrdom," politics as "just another way to make people, and an unprofitable one, too."

Almost no students value activity as citizens. Passive in public, they are hardly more idealistic in arranging their private lives: Gallup concludes they will settle for "low success, and won't risk high failure." There is not much willingness to take risks (not even in business), no setting of dangerous goals, no real conception of personal identity except one manufactured in the image of others, no real urge for personal fulfillment except to be almost as successful as the very successful people. Attention is being paid to social status (the quality of shirt collars, meeting people, getting wives or husbands, making solid contacts for later on); much, too, is paid to academic status (grades, honors, the med school rat race). But neglected generally is real intellectual status, the personal cultivation of the mind.

"Students don't even give a damn about the apathy," one has said. Apathy toward apathy begets a privately constructed universe, a place of systematic study schedules, two nights each week for beer, a girl or two, and early marriage; a framework infused with personality, warmth, and under control, no matter how unsatisfying otherwise.

Under these conditions university life loses all relevance to some. Four hundred thousand of our classmates leave college every year.

But apathy is not simply an attitude; it is a product of social institutions, and of the structure and organization of higher education itself.

. . . .

Politics Without Publics

The American political system is not the democratic model of which its glorifiers speak. In actuality it frustrates democracy by confusing the individual citizen, paralyzing policy discussion, and consolidating the irresponsible power of military and business interests.

A crucial feature of the political apparatus in America is that greater differences are harbored within each major party than the differences existing between them. Instead of two parties presenting distinctive and significant differences of approach, what dominates the system is a natural interlocking of Democrats from Southern states with the more conservative elements of the Republican party. This arrangement of forces is blessed by the seniority system of Congress which guarantees congressional committee domination by conservatives—ten of 17 committees in the Senate and 13 of 21 in the House of Representatives are chaired currently by Dixiecrats.

The party overlap, however, is not the only structural antagonist of democracy in politics. First, the localized nature of the party system does not encourage discussion of national and international issues: thus problems are not raised by and for people, and political representatives usually are unfettered from any responsibilities to the general public except those regarding parochial matters. Second, whole constituencies are divested of the full political power they might have: many Negroes in the South are prevented from voting, migrant workers are disenfranchised by various residence requirements, some urban and suburban dwellers are victimized by gerrymandering, and poor people are too often without the power to obtain political representation. Third, the focus of political attention is significantly distorted by the enormous lobby force, composed predominantly of business interests, spending hundreds of millions each year in an attempt to conform facts about productivity, agriculture, defense, and social services, to the wants of private economic groupings.

What emerges from the party contradiction and insulation of privately held power is the organized political stalemate: calcification dominates flexibility as the principle of parliamentary organization, frustration is the expectancy of legislators intending liberal reform, and Congress becomes less and less central to national decision-making, especially in the area of foreign policy. In this context, confusion and blurring is built into the formulation of issues, long-range priorities are not discussed in the rational manner needed for policy-making, the politics of personality and "image" become a more important mechanism than the construction of issues in a way that affords each voter a challenging and real option. The American voter is buffeted from all directions by pseudo-problems, by the structurally-initiated sense that nothing political is subject to human mastery. Worried by his mundane problems which never get solved, but constrained by the common belief that politics is an agonizingly slow accommodation of views, he quits all pretense of bothering.

A most alarming fact is that few, if any, politicians are calling for changes in these conditions. Only a handful even are calling on the President to "live up to" platform pledges; no one is demanding structural changes, such as the shuttling of Southern Democrats out of the Democratic Party. Rather than protesting the state of politics, most politicians are reinforcing and aggravating that state. While in practice they rig public opinion to suit their own interests, in word and ritual they enshrine "the sovereign public" and call for more and more letters. Their speeches and campaign actions are banal, based on a degrading conception of what people want to hear. They respond not to dialogue, but to pressure: and knowing this, the ordinary citizen sees even greater inclination to shun the political sphere. The politician is usually a trumpeter to "citizenship" and "service to the nation," but since he is unwilling to seriously rearrange power relationships, his trumpetings only increase apathy by creating no outlets. Much of the time the call to "service" is justified not in idealistic terms, but in the crasser terms of "defending the free world from communism"—thus making future idealistic impulses harder to justify in anything but Cold War terms.

In such a setting of status quo politics, where most if not all government activity is rationalized in Cold War anti-communist terms, it is somewhat natural that discontented, super-patriotic groups would emerge through political channels and explain their ultra-conservatism as the best means of Victory over Communism. They have become a politically influential force within the Republican Party, at a national level through Senator Goldwater, and at a local level through their important social and economic roles. Their political views are defined generally as the opposite of the supposed views of communists: complete individual freedom in the economic sphere, non-participation by the government in the machinery of production. But actually "anti-communism" becomes an umbrella by which to protest liberalism, internationalism, welfareism, the active civil rights and labor movements. It is to the disgrace of the United States that such a movement should become a prominent kind of public participation in the modern world—but, ironically, it is somewhat to the interests of the United States that such a movement should be a public constituency pointed toward realignment of the political parties, demanding a conservative Republican Party in the South and an exclusion of the "leftist" elements of the national GOP.

. . . .

The University and Social Change

There is perhaps little reason to be optimistic about the above analysis. True, the Dixiecrat-GOP coalition is the weakest point in the dominating complex of corporate, military and political power. But the civil rights, peace, and student movements are too poor and socially slighted, and the labor movement too quiescent, to be counted with enthusiasm. From where else can power and vision be summoned? We believe that the universities are an overlooked seat of influence.

First, the university is located in a permanent position of social influence. Its educational function makes it indispensable and automatically makes it a crucial institution in the formation of social attitudes. Second, in an unbelievably complicated world, it is the central institution for organizing, evaluating, and transmitting knowledge. Third, the extent to which academic resources presently are used to buttress immoral social practice is revealed first, by the extent to which defense contracts make the universities engineers of the arms race. Too, the use of modern social science as a manipulative tool reveals itself in the "human relations" consultants to the modern corporations, who introduce trivial sops to give laborers feelings of "participation" or "belonging," while actually deluding them in order to further exploit their labor. And, of course, the use of motivational research is already infamous as a manipulative aspect of American politics. But these social uses of the universities' resources also demonstrate the unchangeable reliance by men of power on the men and storehouses of knowledge: this makes the university functionally tied to society in new ways, revealing new potentialities, new levers for change. Fourth, the university is the only mainstream institution that is open to participation by individuals of nearly any viewpoint.

These, at least, are facts, no matter how dull the teaching, how paternalistic the rules, how irrelevant the research that goes on. Social relevance, the accessibility to knowledge, and internal openness—these together make the university a potential base and agency in a movement of social change.

1. Any new left in America must be, in large measure, a left with real intellectual skills, committed to deliberativeness, honesty, reflection as working tools. The university permits the political life to be an adjunct to the academic one, and action to be informed by reason.

2. A new left must be distributed in significant social roles throughout the country. The universities are distributed in such a manner.

3. A new left must consist of younger people who matured in the postwar world, and partially be directed to the recruitment of younger people. The university is an obvious beginning point.

4. A new left must include liberals and socialists, the former for their relevance, the latter for their sense of thoroughgoing reforms in the system. The university is a more sensible place than a political party for these two traditions to begin to discuss their differences and look for political synthesis.

5. A new left must start controversy across the land, if national policies and national apathy are to be reversed. The ideal university is a community of controversy, within itself and in its effects on communities beyond.

6. A new left must transform modern complexity into issues that can be understood and felt close-up by every human being. It must give form to the feelings of helplessness and indifference, so that people may see the political, social, and economic sources of their private troubles and organize to change society. In a time of supposed prosperity, moral complacency, and political manipulation, a new left cannot rely on only aching stomachs to be the engine force of social reform. The case for change, for alternatives that will involve uncomfortable personal efforts, must be argued as never before. The university is a relevant place for all of these activities.

But we need not indulge in illusions: the university system cannot complete a movement of ordinary people making demands for a better life. From its schools and colleges across the nation, a militant left might awaken its allies, and by beginning the process towards peace, civil rights, and labor struggles, reinsert theory and idealism where too often reign confusion and political barter. The power of students and faculty united is not only potential; it has shown its actuality in the South, and in the reform movements of the North.

The bridge to political power, though, will be built through genuine cooperation, locally, nationally, and internationally, between a new left of young people, and an awakening community of allies. In each community we must look within the university and act with confidence that we can be powerful, but we must look outwards to the less exotic but more lasting struggles for justice.

To turn these possibilities into realities will involve national efforts at university reform by an alliance of students and faculty. They must wrest control of the educational process from the administrative bureaucracy. They must make fraternal and functional contact with allies in labor, civil rights, and other liberal forces outside the campus. They must import major public issues into the curriculum—research and teaching on problems of war and peace is an outstanding example. They must make debate and controversy, not dull pedantic cant, the common style for educational life. They must consciously build a base for their assault upon the loci of power.

As students for a democratic society, we are committed to stimulating this kind of social movement, this kind of vision and program in campus and community across the country. If we appear to seek the unattainable, as it has been said, then let it be known that we do so to avoid the unimaginable.

5.2.   SDS: America and New Era

[The SDS convention of June 1963 approved the document *America and New Era,* which reiterated the principles of the Port Huron Statement but drew political conclusions from them which were much more radical, particularly with respect to collaboration with the liberal establishment.]

Introduction

Our hope is human freedom. We care that men everywhere be able to understand, express and determine their lives in fraternity with one another.

We seek to participate in the construction of a society in which men have, at least, the chance to make the decisions which shape their lives. Our quest is for a political and economic order in which power is used for the widest social benefit and a community in which men can come to know each other and themselves as human beings in the fullest sense.

Instead, the legacy of our generation has been the Cold War. Our lives have been shaped by the increasing tempo of militarization. Our hopes for the future have been corroded by the Bomb. Our reason has been blunted by Official ideologies which served to increase consensus and inspire passive acquiescence rather than an active quest for freedom and fraternity.

. . . .

The Era of the Cold War

From the end of World War II until the close of the Eisenhower Administration, the conception of an American Century seemed to be supported by reality. Enormous pent-up demands for consumer goods, a huge reserve of capital savings, and the added stimulation of defense expenditures resulted in an unprecedented expansion of the American economy. Immensely and increasingly rich, and faced with a world in chaos, it is not surprising that America moved quickly to assert its power and influence in every area. American power was able to dominate in Western Europe, to control events in the Middle East and Latin America, to stabilize politics in many parts of Asia.

For a generation, the single great challenge to American influence remained the Soviet Union and the closed, seemingly irreconcilable conflict between the two blocs created a world in which virtually every human value was distorted, all moral standards seemed weirdly irrelevant, all hopes and aspirations appeared utopian. For the Cold War resulted in an arms race in which enormous resources and human energy were squandered and preparation for the murder of innocent millions became basic policy, while the elemental needs of these millions remained unsatisfied. It produced societies in which the requirements of huge military, industrial and political bureaucracies took precedence over all other social or individual priorities. It poisoned and corroded all aspects of intellectual activity. To it were sacrificed the essential ingredients of democratic process—free debate, the right to dissent, political engagement and controversy. And its final outcome was a balance of terror so precarious and so infinitely dangerous that, in the end, all interests and all security were in jeopardy.

It is now clear that in the midst of the Cold War forces were being generated which were incompatible with the international system just described. Now, in 1963, these forces are verging and bringing into being a new world, whose shape and structure is suprisingly different from the one in which we have grown up.

. . . .

America and the New Era

Just as technological and social revolution have shattered the international system developed during the Cold War era, so, too, have these forces undermined America's post-war economic prosperity and are beginning to disrupt the political and social arrangements which accompanied that prosperity.

The technological revolution occurring in the post-war period created a new type of automated production, one critical economic result of which is the shrinkage of the industrial labor force. Automation has sharply reduced the demand for employment, mass production industries, agriculture and many trade and service enterprises. During the fifties, for example, manufacturers were able to increase productive output by seventy per cent, with no increase whatever in the number of manufacturing workers.

Just when the need for workers was being reduced, a radical increase in the number of people needing jobs was taking place, due to the coming of age of millions of young people born during the war-time baby boom.

Thus advancing technology and an exploding population create an enormous employment problem. One measure of the problem is the fact that just to keep employment at its present rate, the Federal Government estimates, 75,000 new jobs must be created *each week* in order to absorb those who are in search of employment. The present rate of new job openings is 6,000 per week.

But it has now become evident that certain central features of our economy operate directly to exacerbate the growing problems of stagnation and unemployment:

1. *Poverty and the maldistribution of income:* Despite the post-war boom, the impoverished fifth of the population still find themselves trapped in the same relative income position they held before World War II. One out of nine Americans is presently living below the level of subsistence as defined by the Department of Labor—that is, they are members of families with income below $50 a week. More broadly, 70 million Americans are living below officially defined minimum standards of decency—with incomes of less than $100 a week for families of four. These figures signify, in human terms, the fact that a vast portion of our population continues to exist in conditions of misery and hopelessness.

2. *The arms race and the maldistribution of resources:* The defense establishment has been celebrated as a major stimulant to the economy. It is now apparent, however, that the $60 billion military budget, and the "permanent war economy" it represents, accelerates and makes more acute the worst trends in our economic system.

. . . .

3. *Oligopoly and the maldistribution of power:* The post-war period has seen a major increase in the tendency for American economic power to be concentrated in a number of giant corporations. Oligopolistic control of major American industries is both a cause and a consequence of technological advance. It is, however, generally unrecognized that this increasing concentration of power has also contributed greatly to the crisis of the economy.

. . . .

American Responses to the New Era

We have described a variety of trends, long accumulating in effects which have now converged—each interacting with the others—their combined impact has been the shattering of established systems and power structures, of people's expectations, of the plans and designs of leaders, and of the hopes and aspirations of ordinary men and women.

It is now necessary to examine the responses which are being made to this emerging new era by various groups within our society. In this way we hope to achieve a clearer definition of the present political scene, so that guidelines for a democratic political strategy can be proposed.

The American political spectrum includes five main groupings: The "traditionalist Right," the "Establishment," "the labor movement and organized liberalism," "Negroes and the civil rights movement," and "the new insurgents." These groupings do not fit conventional categories based on party, but they do seem to reflect divergent bases of power, styles of political action, political ideology and political program:

The Response to the Establishment

By the "Establishment" we mean those men who have direct influence over the formulation of national domestic and foreign policies. These include the President and his advisors, and major officials of the executive branch of the government, but the Establishment extends into private centers of power as well—many corporate leaders, foundation officials, some labor leaders, and some leaders of the Republican Party are decisive figures in the formulation of one or another aspect of policy. It is the function of any Establishment to formulate policy in such a way that the going system can be preserved and existing power arrangements can be maintained. As the Eisenhower Administration drew to a close, it became evident that these responsibilities were not being effectively met. That Administration, responding primarily to particular corporate and military interests, was plainly failing to cope with the colonial revolution, with the New Europe, and domestic economic and social need.

The Response to the New Frontier

The Kennedy Administration, with its campaign rhetoric of "getting the country moving again," and its style of a "New Frontier," explicitly recognizes the need for an Establishment capable of responding actively to the crises of the new era. The Administration has reasserted an active and managerial role for government, after the Eisenhower years of government subservience to narrow military-industrial interests. The emergence of an activist political elite is a reflection of the inability of major social economic and military institutions to agree on the means of pursuing the American mission. For example, businessmen generally have taken little interest in the inequalities and deprivation which have brought on the crisis in the economy, while leaders of organized labor are acutely aware that their position is being weakened by the interacting pressure of business, conservative politicians and automation. Deep conflicts exist within the armed forces over issues of strategy and emphasis. These and other conflicts within American centers of leadership have created a need for an active, technically skilled government elite—a need which is strongly reinforced by the rapid tempo of international events which demand quick administrative action. Thus the first characteristic of the New Frontier is that it is the central agency for strategy and decision-making for the American Establishment. Because its principal function is a mediating, rationalizing, and managerial one, the Kennedy Administration views its problems as technical and administrative, rather than in ideological or moral terms. For example, the President has repeatedly emphasized that the anti-business image of the Democratic Party is a myth based on irrelevant ideologies of the past, and that our economic problems are entirely technical. Basic social issues are thus reduced to problems requiring administrative manipulation; they are never seen as a reflection of the clash of opposing interests.

This distinctive style of the New Frontier is manifested in the major policies of the Administration. Everywhere policies are pursued that are aimed at adjusting to the revolutions of the new era in order that the old order of private corporate enterprise shall be preserved and rationalized.

The New Frontier Abroad. From the commitment to a corporate America follows a foreign policy aimed at creating and preserving general economic compatibilities and political influence in a world no longer subject to blunt American direction:

1. The New Frontier, while regarding the Soviet Union as its chief short-run problem, now believes that political stabilization with the Russians is a distinct possibility on such matters as preventing thermonuclear war, controlling the arms race, and influencing the direction of social revolution in underdeveloped areas. . . .

2. The New Frontier increasingly regards China as the primary state threatening American interests. . . .

3. The anti-colonial revolution is accepted as legitimate, as is the policy of non-alignment. . . .

4. A deep desire to avoid general nuclear war is fundamental to the Administration's "rational military policies." . . .

Finally, the Administration recognizes that some forms of agreement with the Soviet Union are necessary if nuclear war is to be prevented. Thus, it has accepted a test ban, and some measures to prevent the spread of nuclear weapons and other first-step efforts at curtailing the arms race. What is not on the agenda is general disarmament—a state of affairs which, it is thought, would reduce the United States to impotence in the face of revolution, ideological and economic competition.

5. The Grand Design of The New Frontier involves at its bases an interdependent European-American community which would serve as the bastion of Western power and a renovating mechanism for the sluggish United States economy. America, in the Grand Design, is to determine Western political-military strategy, while economic ties with Europe would both stimulate and prevent excessive competition with the stagnating United States economy.

The New Frontier at Home. Internally, the New Frontier is moving toward the image of the "corporate state," following such countries as France and West Germany, in which government and business recognize that national planning by central bodies and strong programs of social welfare are necessary if social conflict which threatens the corporation economy flows from this conception:

1. The economic overflow of the Kennedy Administration is a mix of

Keynesian advocacy of government intervention (including military spending as a major pump-primer) with faith in the essential genius of the American corporate system. . . .

2. The New Frontier is engaged in systematic and unprecedented intervention in labor-management disputes, as a representative of the "national interest," to attempt to set guidelines for settlement of labor problems. The thrust of this policy has been in the direction of tax and other incentives and concessions to business and strongly against the use of the strike by the labor movement.

3. The administration interprets the rise of unemployment as a "cost of increased productivity" and apparently feels that only conventional programs are needed to solve the problems. . . .

4. The Administration has no program for the alleviation of poverty. The Medicare program, skimpy compared to Truman's National Health Insurance bill, represents the only major Administration commitment to help America's dispossessed. . . .

5. While being attacked by some business interests as "unfavorable" to business, the general trend of the New Frontier is toward the strengthening of large corporation power (while continuing to extol the free market system), and the courting of the business elite. . . .

6. As the Administration came to power, civil rights was regarded as a problem requiring a gradual yet necessary solution. The primary means of diminishing the problem was thought to be the process of voter registration in the South—which the Kennedys supported financially and legally, as well as conceptually. . . .

7. It is crucial that the rationalizing, managerial and adjustive politics of the New Frontier does not have unanimous support within the Establishment, and that the Administration is vehemently opposed by the traditionalists of the Right. . . .

. . . .

This, then, is the essential shape of the Establishment as it strives to respond to the new era—it intends to be rational, active and adaptive, but its policies and style flow from its necessary commitment to the preservation of the going system.

For those who are, instead, committed to democracy and human dignity, two things need to be strongly emphasized.

First: In a world where countless forces work to create feelings of powerlessness in ordinary men, an attempt by political leaders to manipulate and control conflict destroys the conditions of a democratic policy and robs men of their initiative and autonomy. The New Frontier is engineering a society where debate is diminishing and the opportunities to express opposition and create ferment are declining. When consensus is manipulated, when reforms emanate from the top while active movements for change are described, then the process of democratic participation has been defeated. In the short run, efforts to dampen social conflict and prevent popular upsurge limit drastically the possibilities for real reform and innovation in the society. In the long run, the encroachment of the engineered consensus will permanently frustrate the long human struggle to establish a genuinely democratic community.

Second: The policies of this Administration can be characterized as "aggressive tokenism." And tokenism, no matter how forthrightly it is proposed, is in its essence no more than measured adjustments by a faltering social system to radical demands from all sides. It is clear that, in the present situation, the New Frontier cannot solve the three most pressing needs of our time: disarmament, abundance with social justice, and complete racial equality.

Alternatives to the New Frontier

A peace-making foreign policy in which disarmament is the central goal is the first need. The program of the Administration is a dangerous attempt to make the world safe for limited and irregular warfare conducted under the stalemate of nuclear deterrence. Certainly all sane men will support the Administration's apparently determined effort to achieve detente with the Soviets. But they must face the fact that the resulting world is likely to be one of continued brutality and bloodshed. For the Administration has not yet abandoned its resolve to meet revolution with force if necessary, and this means the sure devastation of country after country in the Third World, as Vietnam, for instance, is now being destroyed. It means a continuing danger of escalation to full-scale war. This turn of events is not caused simply by communist aggression, but by the basic inability of the U.S. government to offer political and economic alternatives to people in revolutionary upsurge—alternatives which can meet their needs for radical economic development under planning. The present "modernization" program of the New Frontier, which results in either fully fraudulent or seriously inadequate redistribution of land and power and which has not even been applied seriously in many parts of the world, cannot meet the need.

The tokenism of the Administration with respect to unemployment, automation, poverty, and social stagnation is clear. No program has been offered which can begin to cope with these problems. The New Frontier has failed to experiment in government programming to meet the radical changes in the condition of production and consumption in America. Corporate power and its "ethic" have therefore grown, while the counter-vailing and creative possibilities of independent public intervention and development have been completely ignored. It is clear that old institutions and assumptions are not adequate to the technological revolution, and that central control, planning and integration of the economy will have to occur. Insofar as the Administration has moved in this area, it has been the direction of supporting elitist, private industry-wide "planning" with the government ratifying these plans as part of the corporate "team." There is a different road—toward bold new advances in democratic and responsible planning which makes production available to all the world and equally to all Americans. It is this road which the New Frontier seeks to close off.

Tokenism cannot bring racial equality to a society which is racially segregated, nor can it meet the increasing demands of the Negro freedom movement. Many Kennedy policies in civil rights need support if they are to be implemented, but it should be recognized that the essential demands for job equality, housing, and school integration and voting rights are hardly coped with by the Administration's program. It is also crucial to note that present policies make no provision for meeting, even minimally, the Negro demand for jobs and relief from economic distress.

The Civil Rights Movement

The most direct, visible and powerful challenge to the status quo and established power in America now comes from the upsurge of Negroes. The general setting of this upsurge is the frustration of economic opportunity for both middle and working class Negroes—for the former, the professional opportunities which exist are few and low paying; for the latter unemployment has reached unprecedented proportions. A further enabling condition of the Negro movement has been the migration of Negroes into cities North and South, either to escape the terror and isolation of rural living, or because of the relative availability of work in the cities as compared with the rapid decline in agricultural employment. Inspired by the colonial revolution, and frustrated by the hypocrisy and tokenism of established political leadership, a sense of initiative and an impulse to direct action became widespread in the late fifties, climaxing in the student sit-in movement.

The student movement in the South has become more radical and impatient through its experience. From a direct action attack on segregated lunch counters, the goals of the student movement have grown to include economic equality and a more direct assault on the white power structure of southern communities. Moreover, the Southern movement now involves increased participation by Negro masses, including lower-class, unemployed and unskilled workers. In the six weeks between the Birmingham events and this writing the intensity, scope and breadth of the movement have grown enormously. In these weeks, for example, 10,000 people have been arrested in the South for participation in demonstrations and the direct action movement has sprung up in at least 100 Southern communities.

The inspiring and increasingly successful Southern revolution has converged with the increasing frustration and despair of Northern Negroes, to produce a vast upsurge of action in Northern cities. In the North, Negroes are confronted not with a system of legal segregation, but rather with a surface promise of equality which masks unemployment, squalid ghettos, "urban renewal," *de facto* school segregation, police brutality and a thousand other indignities. These conditions belie the liberal sentiments expressed by Northern politicians, and the outcome of a long history of patience, trust and hope has been a steady worsening of the lot of the Northern Negro.

. . . .

The Dilemma of Labor and Liberal Forces

While the Negro population stirs itself, the traditional sources of power for movements for social justice find themselves on the defensive. The labor movement, and the institutions of liberalism have been caught in two eviscerating pincer movements: the automated economy—the jobs it kills and the labor relations problems it raises—strikes at the heart of labor's power in the heavy production industries. And the capture of liberal rhetoric and the liberal political base by the corporate liberalism of the New Frontiersmen means that the reformers and the democratically oriented liberals are trapped by the limitations of the Democratic Party, but afraid of irrelevancy outside it.

The effects of technological and industrial changes, so strikingly expressed in the shifting composition of the labor force, presents organized labor with one of its greatest immediate problems, and perhaps its greatest single threat over the course of the next twenty years. In the late fifties for the first time, white collar jobs exceeded in absolute numbers blue collar industrial jobs. The traditional base of labor's power and social influence—the production line worker—is vanishing. Labor, however, has failed to achieve the kind of organizing successes with white collar workers that it did with industrial workers. Combined with imminent as well as actual automation of these job categories, the percent of unionized workers in the work force is decreasing.

. . . .

The Decay of Liberal Militancy. In power for a generation, Liberalism has adopted a neutral managerial role. Unable to disassociate itself from the errors or the immoralities of Democratic officeholders, the major liberal organizations—and even more so, their public spokesmen—have abandoned the populist and progressive strands of their tradition; strands which dictated a positive, change-oriented political role with militant rhetoric. In its actions Liberalism no longer identifies as the critical targets of protest, the social conditions which it attacked during the "New Deal revolution." During the fifties Liberal social critics talked of problems of leisure, mass society and abundance. But all the while poverty and racial oppression, and public squalor and selfish interests continued to exist, neglected and unsolved by liberal organizations.

At present, the major liberal organizations devote their political energies to various kinds of lobbying operations, usually in support of policies emanating from the administration. Proposals are offered to the President or to Congress, with only rare efforts to organize popular support of them; blame for the failure of liberal programs is usually accorded to the Congress or occasionally to the Administration.

Organized liberalism, however, must take at least part of the credit for America's political stalemate. A style of politics which emphasizes cocktail parties and seminars rather than protest marches, local reform movements, and independent bases of power, cannot achieve leverage with respect to an establishment-oriented administration and a fundamentally reactionary Congressional oligarchy.

. . . .

The New Insurgency

In a growing number of localities a new discontent, a new anger is groping towards a politics of insurgent protest.

At present, the major resource for these efforts is a number of individuals who are thinking and acting in radical ways as a result of a variety of recent political events and experiences.

Chief among these are the activists in the civil rights movement. Discovering that mass protest is more effective than patient suffering, the Negro community finds that its efforts to achieve equality are bound in complex ways to more general economic problems of employment and economic growth. Behind local segregation there lies a far more pervasive pattern of national political, economic, and social oppression; slowly, the civil rights movement is learning that the demand for freedom is a demand for a new society.

Activists in the peace movement have learned that concentration of international power often is less important to American foreign and military policy than considerations of domestic power. Their demands increasingly take the tone of economic reform, and a redress of power abused in this society.

Students in the great centers of higher learning have learned, though still in inchoate ways, that higher learning divorced from high purpose reflects a society in which initiative is seen as an administrative problem: and as the universities begin to approach the model of other institutions of the society—in their organization as well as their tasks—the problem of university reform takes on many of the same burdens as more general social reform.

Intellectuals, in and out of universities, have found that too often their skills are merely used, not cherished, their rewards are merely sops, not signs of esteem, their work is merely apology, not expression of an inner human reality.

Many liberals and radicals have discovered that the complacency, the cynicism, and the loss of political will which permeated the traditional liberal, reform, and radical movements and organizations are neither the price of victory nor the symptom of the end of ideology, but rather are the effects of bureaucratic perspectives and Cold War approaches to politics. Consequently it is becoming evident that the hope for real reform lies not in alliances with established power, but with the re-creation of a popular left opposition—an opposition that expresses anger when it is called for, not mild disagreement.

Some trade unionists have found that union reform depends on having an economic program which meets the demands of union membership. Thus, political pressures within unions impel many of them to positions far more forthright than was ordinary in the fifties.

Thus, there seems to be emerging a collection of people who in thought and action are increasingly being radicalized as they experience the events of the new era. Moreover, the radical consciousness of these individuals is certainly representative of wider currents of urgency and disaffection which exist in the communities from which they come. The militant resolve of Negroes North and South, the urgency and dedication of middle class peace advocates, the deepening anxiety of industrial workers, the spreading alienation of college students—this kind of motion and discontent in the population has given new stimulation to the development of radical thought, and is leading to a search for new forms of insurgent politics.

The new insurgents are active generators of a wide variety of political activities in the neighborhoods and communities where they are located. Local insurgent actions include: mass direct action and voter registration campaigns among Negroes, political reform movements directed against entrenched Democratic machines, political action for peace, tutorials and other community-based attempts to reach underprivileged youth, discussion groups, periodicals and research aimed at analysis and exposure of local political and economic conditions. Barely begun are efforts to initiate organized protest in depressed areas and urban slums, to organize nonunion workers, to focus reform political clubs and candidacies on issues and programs directly relevant to the urban poor, and to involve slum-dwellers directly in political efforts.

The outcome of these efforts at creating insurgent politics could be the organization of constituencies expressing, for the first time in this generation, the needs of ordinary men for a decent life. Many signs point to a vastly increased potential for this kind of popular upsurge—and as Lippman suggests, the most crucial of these is the "exploding nucleus" of Negro protest. But the effort will be a long and difficult one. For one thing, the militancy of summer, 1963, among Negroes is sure to ebb and flow—as with all popular movements. Second, the new insurgents need to learn ways of gathering the physical and financial resources to support their activities. Finally, and most important, an adequate analysis of the American scene, and a political program consistent with it, have yet to be devised. Such analysis and such program are needed if there is to be relevant local and national political action which can effectively create the impetus for a democratic society and genuinely meet the needs of the new era.

. . . .

5.3.   *CARL   OGLESBY:* **Trapped in a System**

> [The speech delivered by Carl Oglesby, then president of SDS, at the October 27, 1965, antiwar march in Washington, has become a classic in the New Left because of its open indictment of corporate liberalism. In its various reprintings, the speech has been entitled either "Trapped in a System" or "Let Us Shape the Future."]

Seven months ago at the April March on Washington, Paul Potter, then President of Students for a Democratic Society, stood in approximately this spot and said that we must name the system that creates and sustains the war in Vietnam—name it, describe it, analyze it, understand it, and change it.

Today I will try to name it—to suggest an analysis which, to be quite frank, may disturb some of you—and to suggest what changing it may require of us.

We are here again to protest again a growing war. Since it is a very bad war, we acquire the habit of thinking that it must be caused by very bad men. But we only conceal reality, I think, by denouncing on such grounds the menacing coalition of industrial and military power, or the brutality of the blitzkrieg we are waging against Vietnam, or the ominous signs around us that heresy may soon no longer be permitted. We must simply observe, and quite plainly say that this coalition, this blitzkrieg, and this demand for acquiescence are creatures, all of them, of a Government that since 1932 has considered itself to be fundamentally *liberal*.

The original commitment in Vietnam was made by President Truman, a mainstream liberal. It was seconded by President Eisenhower, a moderate liberal. It was intensified by the late President Kennedy, a flaming liberal. Think of the men who now engineer that war—those who study the maps, give the commands, push the buttons, and tally the dead: Bundy, McNamara, Rusk, Lodge, Goldberg, the President himself.

They are not moral monsters.

They are all honorable men.

They are all liberals.

But so, I'm sure, are many of us who are here today in protest. To understand the war, then, it seems necessary to take a closer look at this American liberalism. Maybe we are in for some surprises. Maybe we have here two quite different liberalisms: one authentically humanist; the other not so human at all.

Not long ago, I considered myself a liberal. And if someone had asked me what I meant by that, I'd perhaps have quoted Thomas Jefferson or Thomas Paine, who first made plain our nation's unprovisional commitment to human rights. But what do you think would happen if these two heroes could sit down now for a chat with President Johnson and McGeorge Bundy?

They would surely talk of the Vietnam war. Our dead revolutionaries would soon wonder why their country was fighting against what appeared to be a revolution. The living liberals would hotly deny that it is one: there are troops coming in from outside, the rebels get arms from other countries, most of the people are not on their side, and they practice terror against their own. Therefore, *not* a revolution.

What would our dead revolutionaries answer? They might say: "What fools and bandits, sirs, you make then of us. Outside help? Do you remember Lafayette? Or the 3,000 British freighters the French navy sunk for our side? Or the arms and men we got from France and Spain? And what's this about terror? Did you never hear what we did to our own loyalists? Or about the thousands of rich American Tories who fled for their lives to Canada? And as for popular support, do you not know that we had less than one-third of our people with us? That, in fact, the colony of New York recruited more troops for the British than for the revolution? Should we give it all back?"

Revolutions do not take place in velvet boxes. They never have. It is only the poets who make them lovely. What the National Liberation Front is fighting in Vietnam is a complex and vicious war. This war is also a revolution, as honest a revolution as you can find anywhere in history. And this is a fact which all our intricate official denials will never change.

But it doesn't make any difference to our leaders anyway. Their aim in Vietnam is really much simpler than this implies. It is to safeguard what they take to be American interests around the world against revolution or revolutionary change, which they always call Communism—as if that were that. In the case of Vietnam, this interest is, first, the principle that revolution shall not be tolerated anywhere, and second, that South Vietnam shall never sell its rice to China—or even to North Vietnam.

There is simply no such thing now, for us, as a just revolution—never mind that for two-thirds of the world's people the 20th Century might as well be the Stone Age; never mind the melting poverty and hopelessness that are the basic facts of life for most modern men; and never mind that for these millions there is now an increasingly perceptible relationship between their sorrow and our contentment.

Can we understand why the Negroes of Watts rebelled? Then why do we need a devil theory to explain the rebellion of the South Vietnamese? Can we understand the oppression in Mississippi, or the anguish that our Northern ghettos make epidemic? Then why can't we see that our proper human struggle is not with Communism or revolutionaries, but with the social desperation that drives good men to violence, both here and abroad?

To be sure, we have been most generous with our aid, and in Western Europe, a mature industrial society, that aid worked. But there are always political and financial strings. And we have never shown ourselves capable of allowing others to make those traumatic institutional changes that are often the prerequisites of progress in colonial societies. For all our official feeling for the millions who are enslaved to what we so self-righteously call the yoke of Communist tyranny, we make no real effort at all to crack through the much more vicious right-wing tyrannies that our businessmen traffic with and our nation profits from every day. And for all our cries about the international Red conspiracy to take over the world, we take only pride in the fact of our 6,000 military bases on foreign soil.

We gave Rhodesia a grave look just now—but we keep on buying her chromium, which is cheap because black slave labor mines it.

We deplore the racism of Verwoerd's fascist South Africa—but our banks make big loans to that country and our private technology makes it a nuclear power.

We are saddened and puzzled by random back-page stories of revolt in this or that Latin American state—but are convinced by a few pretty photos in the Sunday supplement that things are getting better, that the world is coming our way, that change from disorder can be orderly, that our benevolence will pacify the distressed, that our might will intimidate the angry.

Optimists, may I suggest that these are quite unlikely fantasies. They are fantasies because we have lost that mysterious social desire for human equity that from time to time has given us genuine moral drive. We have become a nation of young, bright-eyed, hard-hearted, slim-waisted, bullet-headed make-out artists. A nation—may I say it?—of beardless liberals.

You say I am being hard? Only think.

This country, with its thirty-some years of liberalism, can send 200,000 young men to Vietnam to kill and die in the most dubious of wars, but it cannot get 100 voter registrars to go into Mississippi.

What do you make of it?

The financial burden of the war obliges us to cut millions from an already pathetic War on Poverty budget. But in almost the same breath, Congress appropriates $140 million for the Lockheed and Boeing companies to compete with each other on the supersonic transport project—that Disneyland creation that will cost us all about $2 billion before it's done.

What do you make of it?

Many of us have been earnestly resisting for some years now the idea of putting atomic weapons into West German hands, an action that would perpetuate the division of Europe and thus the Cold War. Now just this week we find out that, with the meagerest of security systems, West Germany has had nuclear weapons in her hands for the past six years.

What do you make of it?

Some will make of it that I overdraw the matter. Many will ask: What about the other side? To be sure, there is the bitter ugliness of Czechoslovakia, Poland, those infamous Russian tanks in the streets of Budapest. But my anger only rises to hear some say that sorrow cancels sorrow, or that *this* one's shame deposits in *that one's* account the right to shamefulness.

And others will make of it that I sound mighty anti-American. To these, I say: Don't blame *me* for *that!* Blame those who mouthed my liberal values and broke my American heart.

Just who might they be, by the way? Let's take a brief factual inventory of the latter-day Cold War.

In 1953 our Central Intelligence Agency managed to overthrow Mossadegh in Iran, the complaint being his neutralism in the Cold War and his plans to nationalize the country's oil resources to improve his people's lives.

Most evil aims, most evil man. In his place we put in General Zahedi, a World War II Nazi collaborator. New arrangements on Iran's oil gave 25-year leases on 40% of it to three U.S. firms, one of which was Gulf Oil. The CIA's leader for this coup was Kermit Roosevelt. In 1960 Kermit Roosevelt became a vice president of Gulf Oil.

In 1954, the democratically elected Arbenz of Guatemala wanted to nationalize a portion of United Fruit Company's plantations in his country, land he needed badly for a modest program of agrarian reform. His government was overthrown in a CIA-supported right-wing coup. The following year, Gen. Walter Bedell Smith, director of the CIA when the Guatemala venture was being planned, joined the board of directors of the United Fruit Company.

Comes 1960 and Castro cries we are about to invade Cuba. The Administration sneers, "poppycock," and we Americans believe it. Comes 1961 and the invasion. Comes with it the awful realization that the United States Government had lied.

Comes 1962 and the missile crisis, and our Administration stands prepared to fight global atomic war on the curious principle that another state does not have the right to its own foreign policy.

Comes 1963 and British Guiana, where Cheddi Jagan wants independence from England and a labor law modelled on the Wagner Act. And Jay Lovestone, the AFL-CIO foreign policy chief, acting, as always, quite independently of labor's rank and file, arranges with our Government to finance an eleven-week dock strike that brings Jagan down, ensuring that the state will remain *British* Guiana, and that any workingman who wants a wage better than 50¢ a day is a dupe of Communism.

Comes 1964. Two weeks after Under Secretary Thomas Mann announces that we have abandoned the *Alianza's* principle of no aid to tyrants, Brazil's Goulart is overthrown by the vicious right-winger, Ademar Barros, supported by a show of American gunboats at Rio de Janeiro. Within 24 hours, the new head of state, Mazzilli, receives a congratulatory wire from our President.

Comes 1965. The Dominican Republic. Rebellion in the streets. We scurry to the spot with 20,000 neutral Marines and our neutral peacemakers —like Ellsworth Bunker, Jr., Ambassador to the Organization of American States. Most of us know that our neutral Marines fought openly on the side of the junta, a fact that the Administration still denies. But how many also know that what was at stake was our new Caribbean Sugar Bowl? That this same neutral peacemaking Bunker is a board member and stock owner of the National Sugar Refining Company, a firm his father founded in the good old days, and one which has a major interest in maintaining the status quo in the Dominican Republic? Or that the President's close personal friend and advisor, our new Supreme Court Justice Abe Fortas, has sat for the past 19 years on the board of the Sucrest Company, which imports black-strap molasses from the Dominican Republic? Or that the rhetorician of corporate liberalism and the late President Kennedy's close friend Adolf Berle, was chairman of that same board? Or that our roving ambassador Averell Harriman's brother Roland is on the board of National Sugar? Or that our former ambassador to the Dominican Republic, Joseph Farland is a board member of the South Puerto Rico Sugar Co., which owns 275,000 acres of rich land in the Dominican Republic and is the largest employer on the island—at about one dollar a day?

Neutralists! God save the hungry people of the world from such neutralists!

We do not say these men are evil. We say rather, that good men can be divided from their compassion by the institutional system that inherits us all. Generation in and out, we are put to use. People become instruments. Generals do not hear the screams of the bombed; sugar executives do not see the misery of the cane cutters—for to do so is to be that much *less* the general, that much *less* the executive.

The foregoing facts of recent history describe one main aspect of the estate of Western liberalism. Where is our American humanism here? What went wrong?

Let's stare our situation coldly in the face. All of us are born to the colossus of history, our American corporate system—in many ways, an awesome organism. There is one fact that describes it: With about 5% of the world's people, we consume about half the world's goods. We take a richness that is in good part not our own, and we put it in our pockets, our garages, our split-levels, our bellies, and our futures.

On the *face* of it, it is a crime that so few should have so much at the expense of so many. Where is the moral imagination so abused as to call this just? Perhaps many of us feel a bit uneasy in our sleep. We are not, after all, a cruel people. And perhaps we don't really need this super-dominance that deforms others. But what can we do? The investments are made. The financial ties are established. The plants abroad are built. Our system *exists*. One is swept up into it. How intolerable—to be born moral, but addicted to a stolen and maybe surplus luxury. Our goodness threatens to become counterfeit before our eyes—unless we change. But change threatens us with uncertainty—at least.

Our problem, then, is to justify this system and give its theft another name—to make kind and moral what is neither, to perform some alchemy with language that will make this injustice seem to be a most magnanimous gift.

A hard problem. But the Western democracies, in the heyday of their colonial expansionism, produced a hero worthy of the task.

Its name was free enterprise, and its partner was an *illiberal liberalism* that said to the poor and the dispossessed: What we acquire of your resources we repay in civilization. The white man's burden. But this was too poetic. So a much more hard-headed theory was produced. This theory said that colonial status is in fact a *boon* to the colonized. We give them technology and bring them into modern times.

But this deceived no one but ourselves. We were delighted with this new theory. The poor saw in it merely an admission that their claims were irrefutable. They stood up to us, without gratitude. We were shocked— but also confused, for the poor seemed again to be right. How long is it going to be the case, we wondered, that the poor will be right and the rich will be wrong?

Liberalism faced a crisis. In the face of the collapse of the European empires, how could it continue to hold together our twin need for richness and righteousness? How can we continue to sack the ports of Asia and still dream of Jesus?

The challenge was met with a most ingenious solution: the ideology of anti-Communism. This was the bind: we cannot call revolution bad, because we started that way ourselves, and because it is all too easy to see why the dispossessed should rebel. So we will call revolution *Communism*. And we will reserve for ourselves the right to say what Communism means. We take note of revolution's enormities, wrenching them where necessary from their historical context and often exaggerating them, and say: Behold, Communism is a bloodbath. We take note of those reactionaries who stole the revolution, and say: Behold, Communism is a betrayal of the people. We take note of the revolution's need to consolidate itself, and say: Behold, Communism is a tyranny.

It has been all these things, and it will be these things again, and we will never be at a loss for those tales of atrocity that comfort us so in our self-righteousness. Nuns will be raped and bureaucrats will be disembowelled. Indeed, revolution is a fury. For it is a letting loose of outrages pent up sometimes over centuries. But the more brutal and longer-lasting the suppression of this energy, all the more ferocious will be its explosive release.

Far from helping Americans deal with this truth, the anti-Communist ideology merely tries to disguise it so that things may stay the way they are. Thus, it depicts our presence in other lands not as a coercion, but a protection. It allows us even to say that the napalm in Vietnam is only another aspect of our humanitarian love—like those exorcisms in the Middle Ages that so often killed the patient. So we say to the Vietnamese peasant, the Cuban intellectual, the Peruvian worker: "You are better dead than Red. If it hurts or if you don't understand why—sorry about that."

This is the action of *corporate liberalism*. It performs for the corporate state a function quite like what the Church once performed for the feudal state. It seeks to justify its burdens and protect it from change. As the Church exaggerated this office in the Inquisition, so with liberalism in the McCarthy time—which, if it was a reactionary phenomenon, was still made possible by our anti-Communist corporate liberalism.

Let me then speak directly to humanist liberals. If my facts are wrong, I will soon be corrected. But if they are right, then you may face a crisis of conscience. Corporatism or humanism: which? For it has come to that. Will you let your dreams be used? Will you be a grudging apologist for the corporate state? Or will you help try to change it—not in the name of this or that blueprint or "ism," but in the name of simple human decency and democracy and the vision that wise and brave men saw in the time of our own Revolution?

And if your commitment to human value is unconditional, then disabuse yourselves of the notion that statements will bring change, if only the right statements can be written, or that interviews with the mighty will bring change if only the mighty can be reached, or that marches will bring change if only we can make them massive enough, or that policy proposals will bring change if only we can make them responsible enough.

We are dealing now with a colossus that does not want to be changed. It will not change itself. It will not cooperate with those who want to change it. Those allies of ours in the Government—are they really our allies? If they *are,* then they don't need advice, they need *constituencies;* they don't need study groups, they need a *movement.* And if they are *not,* then all the more reason for building that movement with a most relentless conviction.

There are people in this country today who are trying to build that movement, who aim at nothing less than a humanist reformation. And the humanist liberals must understand that it is this movement with which their own

best hopes are most in tune. We radicals know the same history that you
liberals know, and we can understand your occasional cynicism, exasperation,
and even distrust. But we ask you to put these aside and help us risk a leap.
Help us find enough time for the enormous work that needs doing here. Help
us build. Help us shake the future in the name of plain human hope.

5.4.   *TODD GITLIN:* **Power and the Myth
                                                     of Progress**

> [The following article by Todd Gitlin is part of a collection of state-
> ments by young radicals which were originally published in the weekly
> magazine *The New Republic* in 1966. The editors had asked several
> spokesmen of the radical movement their opinions on the connection be-
> tween consensus and social progress, the errors of American society, and
> the possibilities for changing them. From the collection *Thoughts of the
> Young Radicals, New Republic,* 1966.]

What irritated liberals about Eisenhower's '50's was the slick assumption
that the essential problems had been solved. That delusion was crippled by
John F. Kennedy's rallying cry to "get the country moving again," and buried
by Lyndon Johnson's mighty sermons on the Great Society. The upshot is a
new orthodoxy: There are problems, but solutions are on their way. If the
dissidents would only shoulder their load, we could get there a lot faster and
with less aggravation all around.

But who are "we" and where is "there" and what is the route?

"We" are said to be classless, pluralistic, happy in our wealth or, if poor,
not for long.

"There" is a bigger and better welfare state.

The route is legislation in the New Deal style.

But the consensus is hollow. Its analysis is a fantasy, its objective defies
democracy, and its strategy is aspirin for a cancer. Let me indicate what I
mean.

The basic liberal misapprehension about America is that power is dispersed among competing institutions which balance each other. The national
interest, or the "best for all concerned," is supposed to emerge from the orderly conflict among government, business, unions, interest groups, on down
to the PTA. Individual liberty is supposed to be guaranteed because there is
always room for one more interest.

But the brute reality is that for most Americans the reins of power—
control over elemental life decisions—are remote. Most of us are reduced to
apathy, sensing that the world is indifferent to us.

Political free enterprise is as illusory as the economic, largely *because* the
economic model is a fraud. The dual engines of industrialization and war
have created a tightly planned corporate complex that dominates the economy. Its power extends over work, information and policy, colossal in degree
and unchallenged in kind. The New Deal institutions intended to circum-
scribe that power do so marginally if at all. The unions, remote from their
members, remain largely unable or unwilling to do much more than bargain
for incremental dollars and cents. The regulatory commissions putter harm-
lessly. Progressive taxation is eaten away by regressive exceptions. After each
price showdown, government quietly yields another prerogative to the offend-

ing companies—and uses its tough-on-business image to clamp down all the harder on wages. Capital export restraints are not allowed to interfere with the business of exploitative investment abroad.

Much of the sham of pluralism stems from the unchallenged domination of the values of the marketplace, the fact that profit still motivates production, communication, education. If the sheer bulk of goods is all-important, who needs democracy? How can the New Deal prevail against the Fast Deal?

Yet it would be a mistake to cast government in the role of hapless bystander, for it too is a mechanism of irresponsible power, almost as free of democratic control as are the corporations, and as comfortably respectful of business as business is of it. Cementing the alliance at the top is the postwar marriage of the defense plants and the Pentagon, necessary to each for its own reasons. Comsat and the supersonic transport and commodity subsidies are not isolated boondoggles, but part of a pattern of industry-government symbiosis.

Locally, take urban renewal: a revealing example, because mass powerlessness grips the poor most of all, and the quality of a society must be measured by the way it treats its outcasts. Urban renewal is overwhelmingly a matter of negotiation (tacit or explicit) among federal bureaucrats, local business aggregations, and city governments for whom "renovation" and "modernization" have a very special meaning. "Public" power does not countervail against "private" power—instead, the two combine to exclude from their plans the people most abruptly affected by their decisions. In the white ghetto of Chicago's Uptown, where I live and work, private developers plan to convert the neighborhood into still another stretch of luxury apartment buildings. Neither City Hall nor Washington will interfere: renewal would be good for the city tax base, good for the burgeoning middle class. But who asked the welfare recipients, the migrant Southerners, the day-labor hirelings who live here? (What do *they* know about the intricacies of urban planning? Who do *they* know?) Of course, if they wait long enough, they may be admitted into public housing—where they will be treated like caged animals.

The special powerlessness of the poor derives from the same welfare state that was intended to remedy the excesses of unbridled capitalism. While the poor have been kept alive, they have been subjected to a new set of institutions that extort elementary freedoms as the price of sustenance. This all-or-nothing humanitarianism pays a husbandless mother not quite enough to live decently, never enough to dress the kids so they won't be laughed at in school. To stay on welfare she must submit to a battery of regulations, not of her own making, which keep her on welfare. In the meantime, she has almost no say over how she budgets, where she can live, whether investigators will intrude looking for unauthorized men, whether her son will be beaten by the cops.

Her dependency derives from class structure, not personal fault. In a supposedly fluid America, it is class that apportions a man's share of justice, health, culture, education, ordinary respect—as any visit to a jail, an emergency room, a theatre, a college or a municipal bureau will illustrate. And class perpetuates itself. Material poverty generates inequalities that income alone will not alter, at least at first.

Still, material equality would be one valid criterion of progress. But the liberal assumption of upward mobility conceals the fact that the poor *as a class* are going nowhere. Of course, if you draw an arbitrary income line (even allowing for inflation) and count the number of families subsisting below it, the measure declines over the years. But if equality is your standard, the more relevant index is the distance between the actual and the fair. Thirty years ago the poorest fifth of the population earned 4.1 percent of national income. Last year the poorest fifth earned 4.6 percent. At that rate, equality is nearly a literal millennium away.

The war on poverty, while acknowledging the fact of class stratification, is irrelevant at best and inimical at worst to the standard of democracy. "Maximum feasible participation of the poor" is most honored in the breach. The rationalization of top-down social agencies is no help. The Head Start educational blitz might have meaning—if the schools the kids went back to didn't beat them down all the harder. And militarized drill teams and business-operated training centers offer only caricatures of dignity. After all, the new consensus is that the poor must be changed because they have been "left behind." The assumption is that the rest of us are OK, so we know what the poor need: they need what we have. The arrogance may be wrapped in good intentions, but it is there nonetheless.

But just where is the middle class going? Its schools tend to be training programs in obedience: they break the spirit and condition the reflexes. Its universities? Clark Kerr's smoothly humming knowledge factory may be an exaggerated bad dream, but the reality like the nightmare serves state and business more than education. Despite the teach-ins, faculties are generally encapsulated, like the disciplines they expound. For students, the doctrine of *in loco parentis* still holds sway, accepted as the price of a degree when educational community is missing. It is all good preparation for the life beyond commencement: for meaningless work, for engineering and being engineered, for empty politics and spectator culture—and a smugness that sustains the fragile sense of worth. So this divorce-ridden society clucks over Daniel Moynihan's discovery that the urban Negro family is a wreck. Expense-account executives wonder why the poor are so dirty. Supporters of a $50 billion military budget deplore "crime in the streets." And the terrified occupants of organizational slots believe that revolutions are exported like Coca-Cola or Aston-Martins.

So deep lie the distempers of the society that they are barely scratched by the traditional liberal instruments of change: gradual legislation and the ballot-box. The liberal faith in additive progress mistakes quantity for quality, or, where it hazards innovation (as in the civil rights bills and the war on poverty), fails to come to grips with powerlessness, inequality, human waste.

It is not simply that choices turn out to be echoes, though this is certainly true. Worse, elections have been irrelevant because the public issues of control—foreign policy, militarism, economic power, decentralization—have been defined *out* of politics by an elite's appeals to free enterprise and exclusive expertise. Then too, the personalized consequences of mass impotence—boredom, conformity, inconsequentiality, violence, indifference—are mostly immune to changes in nominal power.

The same blindness arises as liberalism addresses the hungry majority of the world. To the anger of the peasant it offers only the chimera of "orderly change"—and, that failing, napalm. Legitimately horrified at the price some revolutionaries are willing to pay for economic development, it brands them indistinguishable, treating the name "Communist" as the end rather than the beginning of political discourse. Vietnam is thus no tragic mistake: it is the logic of American "law and order."

The New Left is said to be longer on critique than on prescription. The charge is rather accurate on its face, but we have had good reason to be tentative and skeptical about blueprints. For one thing, we have learned that blueprints tend to freeze. But rigid agnosticism too can be and is being transcended. Values and experience generate certain guidelines.

1. *Power must be shared among those affected, and resources guaranteed to make this possible.* This formula is quite precise. It means, for example, that slums should be rebuilt according to plans adopted by the residents, with capital provided from public funds and labor from the neighborhood. Welfare programs should be supervised by the recipients, until welfare becomes superfluous because a decent income is guaranteed for all who will not or cannot work. The mass media should be opened up to all comers, with no restrictions except a bias toward dissent. Political candidates should be publicly subsidized. The university's curricular and extracurricular decisions should be up to students and faculty alone. The great corporations should, somehow, be made responsible to workers and consumers. (Here we are in special need of fresh thinking and honest experimentation.) New political institutions are needed to localize and distribute as much power as possible: police forces elected by residents; neighborhood courts with authority over the quality of goods, the availability of loans, the behavior of municipal, state and federal agencies, etc.; computerized referenda on national issues like war and compulsory health insurance; and so on.

2. *The institutional props of racism must be extirpated.* This would entail not just the vigorous enforcement of existing laws and the Constitution but the guarantee of income, the razing of the ghetto by its unemployed and the founding of new, integrated communities, the provision of land and crop allotments for sharecroppers and small farmers, the extension of a serious federal presence in the vigilante South, fair jury legislation, and more along these lines.

3. *America must put down the big stick and take self-determination seriously.* Revolution must at least be tolerated if not embraced—then we may earn the right to be critical. Foreign investments must be withdrawn unless invited by governments committed to their people. Disarmament is imperative, and this means rapprochement with China. Overall, whatever progress the comfortable make must not be at the expense of the miserable.

But a great deal depends on how change takes place. The top-down facsimiles of these proposals would amount to little, if anything. Far more than any particular program, America needs a movement dedicated to remaking America at the roots. The solid and decisive changes must be the burden of people who see the need and organize, wherever they are, to demand and create a society that would honor men. *Only* the experience of movement confronting institutional power can generate the issues now submerged in rhetoric and helplessness.

There are stirrings of this new politics:

• In a civil rights movement beginning to grapple with the hard issues of sustenance (the Mississippi Poor People's Corporation) and dignity (organizing work among gang kids on the West Side of Chicago) and power (the Mississippi Freedom Democratic Party);

- in the SDS-catalyzed "community unions" of poor whites and Negroes in the North, concerned with welfare, housing, the police, cooperatives and a political voice for the poor;
- in university reform movements and teach-ins and a scattering of independent Free Universities (*à la* Paul Goodman) where student-faculty community emerges;
- in outbreaks of low-level union agitation over working conditions and shop control, and migrant worker strikes;
- with artists and writers who are not only seeking truth and spirit but are finding and fashioning audiences who care about truth and spirit;
- with doctors who not only support Medicare but are organizing to plan the institutions of equal medicine; lawyers and law students who enlist with those most in need of justice; clergymen taking the social gospel seriously; scientists who resist the militarization of their skills;
- and with the many who refuse to countenance the war in Vietnam, and try to stop it.

If the whole seems puny when matched against the requirements of its vision, that is simply a measure of how powerful the powerful are, and how beaten—or comfortable—the powerless. Yet in this movement's variousness and its growing coherence there is a strength that will not be easily drowned, or purchased, or sloughed off. There *is* a chance. Let democrats and humanists seize it while we can.

5.5.   *RICHARD FLACKS:* **Is the Great Society Just a Barbecue?**

[The following article is part of a collection of essays from *The New Republic,* published as *Thoughts of the Young Radicals* (Washington, D.C.: The New Republic, 1966). Richard Flacks, who teaches sociology at the University of Chicago, has been one of the initiators of the *New University Conference,* an organization of radical teachers and graduate students.]

Traditionally, we have understood politics to mean the clash of men independently organized with respect to their interests and ideologies; we have expected that policy would emerge out of public debate; we have believed that men in power require viable opposition; we have favored a system with dispersed centers of power. Instead, the Johnson consensus establishes the Democratic Party as *the* national party of the center—we no longer have a two-party system on the national level. This situation is facilitated by the inclusion of a large proportion of the business community in the Democratic Party coalition. This is where Mr. Johnson has particularly succeeded and where other Democratic Presidents failed—on the one hand, he has won full-fledged corporation participation in welfare-state policies; on the other hand, he has won wholehearted labor, liberal and ethnic group support for what is, in fact, a center-conservative government. Thus, "consensus" is a conveniently bland term which covers a new politics in America—the politics of what might be called "liberal corporatism."

In both its rhetoric and its practice, liberal corporatism implies a political structure in which principal policy issues are worked out at the federal level, formulated with the active participation of experts, and ratified—not in the legislative arena—but through a process of consultation among a national elite representing those interests and institutions which now recognize each other as legitimate. Such a conception of government is "corporatist" in at least two ways: first, it involves the major corporations and other interest groups actively and directly in the governmental process; second, it models government structure and administrative style in the manner of modern corporation management. It is "liberal" in the sense that it includes the active participation of representatives of groups traditionally favoring liberal reform and democracy—particularly, for example, the unions. Liberal corporatism tends toward the *co-optation* of dissent and reform rather than their suppression.

It seems to me that the basic issue for the present national leadership is the preservation of a corporation economy while coping with the disastrous potentialities of a free competitive national and international system. Among such potentialities, of course, are economic slumps, intense labor-management conflict, internal political unrest and major war. Thus, the Johnson consensus seems to include a fundamental commitment by government to avoid such threats to the viability of the going system. The main way to do this, apparently, is to harness an extensive social welfare system to a centrally coordinated but privately controlled economy. So the Great Society program includes a commitment to the need for federal action to avoid economic recession and maintain adequate growth rates; for active government intervention in collective bargaining and the regulation of wages and prices; for large-scale public action to reduce the likelihood of unrest and violence in the slums and ghettoes of the cities; for welfare benefits which can maintain and expand popular support for the Democratic Party locally and nationally.

As Oscar Gass has recently suggested, however, this full-scale, if belated and diluted, implementation of the New Deal promise does not necessarily imply that the Great Society will be a place of greater social justice and equality. For the current program is thoroughly circumscribed—it cannot seriously encroach on substantial corporate interests. Such interests include the maintenance of less than full employment, a decidedly impoverished public sector, a very strong emphasis on private consumption, and the use of public funds to subsidize private interests. Moreover, a more equitable distribution of wealth is unlikely because the Great Society consensus does not grant legitimate political voice to substantial sectors of the population. It took a century of bitter struggle for organized labor to win legitimacy; still millions of workers remain unorganized and voiceless. The voting rights law appears to guarantee, finally, the right of Southern Negroes to gain political voice; still, it will take further violent struggle before full enfranchisement is reached—and, still, it is not evident that the society is prepared to accept the right of Negroes to organize and exercise power in their own interest. The absence of the poor from the Great Society Barbecue keeps the consensus stable—and explains why it neglects egalitarian goals.

I do not know if liberal corporatism can indefinitely continue to maintain private control of the economy while preventing slump and dampening discontent. But it is a source of wonderment that so many who profess commitment to liberal and democratic traditions seem so complacently at home within the Johnsonian consensus. For the centralization of power, its grossly unequal distribution among interest groups and constituencies, and the techniques of control now available to authority present a situation which ought to be inherently antithetical to the committed Democrat. But the consequences of liberal corporatism for America are as appalling as its intrinsically undemocratic structure.

First, the centralization of power, information and interests is taking place in the most powerful nation-state in human history.

This state has the technological capacity to destroy civilization; hence it appears to have the military power to impose its will on all small, weak countries, and, within the limits of its rationality, on strong nations as well. The most immediately frightening thing about the Johnson consensus is that it is eroding any effective internal check on the use of that power; it is permitting the aquiescence of the public to any use of American power which the predominant interests deem desirable. And it is creating a situation in which the *capability* to use this power is becoming synonymous with the *desirability* of using it. When attempts by a government to justify its overseas adventures are no longer in moral terms—then it seems to me we have clear evidence that the popular will is no longer relevant. If the American elite has a commanding sense of its power to preserve its international interests intact, and no longer feels particularly responsible even to its own people—then I think humanity has a right to shudder.

Second, the predominance of corporate interests and the underrepresentation of the poor, the black, the old, the young, etc. lead to a glaringly inhumane allocation of resources and priorities in the society. It means, for instance, the continued allocation of public funds and technical manpower toward military and space technology—not simply because of Cold War necessity, but because the vast aerospace corporations cannot be sustained in any other way. Or, for another instance, it means the huge outlay of public funds for interstate highway construction (without public debate) and the consequent impoverishment of public transportation—not because this is the most efficient, safest, most comfortable way to travel, but because of the power of the auto lobby. And, for a final instance, it means that our cities are sinking into ungovernable chaos—not simply because their problems are so complex, but because no one is willing to govern them in behalf of the human beings who inhabit them. As long as corporate interests dominate, as long as power is badly skewed, every public venture becomes a subsidy for special interests, every regulatory agency becomes a lobby for the industry it regulates, every social reform is twisted and diluted to avoid jeopardizing private greeds, and so even the very air and water and land are made spoiled and dangerous for human use.

A final consequence of liberal corporatism is that it *requires* mass apathy. Since decisions are made centrally and at an elite level, policy formulation can only work when constituencies are immobilized. For if institutional leaders and organizational spokesmen were responsible and responsive to actively involved publics, then the bargaining away of popular rights and interests and the ritual devotion to public welfare which is the very substance of consensus politics would no longer be possible. Further, the preferred technique of social control—namely the exchange of benefits for acquiescence —instructs the people well as to the virtues of elite management and personal withdrawal from citizenly activity. Such management and such withdrawal occur not only in the sphere of national politics, but also in the arenas of decision-making to which people are more routinely related—in the cities and towns, the neighborhoods, the voluntary associations, the school systems, etc. It is my view that the system now emerging requires the end of citizenship as we have understood and hoped for; therefore, it signifies an abortion of the possibilities for authentic community and meaningful individuality in American life.

Having said all this, I should stress that I do not think an American version of *1984* is inevitable, but I think it can be averted only through a radical reconstruction of the way we live and act now. What our country needs first of all is a restoration of democratic consciousness and democratic action.

Such a restoration can only come in the process of building a large-scale grass-roots movement for a democratic society. Such a movement would have on its agenda the following:

• It would insist on first-class citizenship for every person in the society. This means, for example, that it would actively engage in the task of organizing the politically disenfranchised and voiceless so that they can independently and effectively pursue their interests and rights in the political arena. It means, too, the development of a concept of citizenship which extends beyond the conventional political sphere to all the institutions of the society— the workplace, the school, the corporation, the neighborhoods, the welfare bureaucracies. The idea that men are citizens with respect to all exercise of authority, that each man has responsibility for the actions of the institution in which he is imbedded, that all authority should be responsible to those "under" it, that men ought not to be infantalized in their relations with each other, that they should have a voice in decisions which determine their fate— this view of man would be a core operating value of the movement for a democratic society.

• It would actively challenge the legitimacy of antidemocratic authority, laws and institutions in the society. The civil rights movement challenges the legitimacy of racist politicians, racist laws and racist practices. Similarly, I think we may be seeing the emergence of an antiwar movement which has begun to challenge the scope of military authority and influence in the society. A movement for a democratic society would extend these challenges to all instances of bureaucratic encroachment, special privilege and elite domination, in a permanent revolution against overweening power.

Each effort to achieve first-class citizenship and to undermine undemocratic authority represents an effort to redistribute power, a step away from overcentralization, and a challenge to corporatist ideology and practice. But it is clear that the organization of such activity is not sufficient; in addition, people need a vision of the possibilties for citizenship, democracy and community which would represent a concrete alternative to the present. Consequently, a third item on the agenda of the developing movement would be the expansion of democratic consciousness through the formulation of substantial models of a democratic future. I do not know what such models might look like. I am sure, however, that they will contain at their center such ideas as the decentralizing of decision-making, the development of diverse loci of power, the breaking up of gargantuan organizations, the use of technology to eliminate demeaning labor, the development of new definitions of work and status based on humanistic criteria. The need for serious intellectual work on the problem of democracy and culture in a society of our sort is extremely urgent.

My point then is this: liberals and radicals have spent their greatest energy in arduous campaigns for social reform and against reaction; they have succeeded in helping to construct a version of the welfare state. The task for authentic democrats now, however, is not to continue to "modernize"

American politics so as to make the state more efficient or correct the flaws in the present system. Instead, we must restore democracy—and to do that we must find and build constituencies at the grass roots, we must challenge the encroachments of anti-democratic authority and ideology, we must announce a democratic vision which is concretely relevant to the technology of the future and the troubles and discontents of the people.

There is, I think, hope that this can be done. For a new generation is here, unburdened by the irrelevancies of the past, and imbued with a quest for idealism and a disdain for authority and status by their experience of growing up in liberal and affluent homes. Already, in their efforts to organize the poor and dispossessed, in their growing campaign to democratize the universities, in their intensifying campaign against militarism and cold-war ideology, and in their posture of plain honesty, they are providing the framework for the democratic revival.

Two years ago, the main issues were between a President perceived as "left" and his right-wing opposition. Today, increasingly, the terms of debate are shifting—the President is becoming defined as a conservative and is having to cope with opposition to his left. Well, the President *is* a conservative, the nation *needs* a left opposition, the issues coming into focus through the action of the new generation are the real ones for 1966 and beyond. The time for democrats to choose between sustaining their own values and supporting a conservative Administration is coming upon us. Do we dare hope that liberals will strike out on their own?

FURTHER READINGS

Ad Hoc Committee on the Triple Revolution. "The Triple Revolution: Cybernation-Weaponry-Human Rights." *Liberation,* April 1964.

Ferman, Louis, Kornbluh, Joice, and Haber, Alan (eds.). *Poverty in America.* Ann Arbor, Mich.: University of Michigan Press, 1965.

Gitlin, Todd. Review of *The Rich and the Super-Rich. Guardian,* August 17, 1968.

———. "Triple Revolution: Some Questions and Notes." *Monthly Review,* XVI: December 8, 1964.

Glick, Brian and Ruth. *The Rich Get Richer and the Poor Get Pushed Around.* Unpublished document.

JOIN Movement. "Take a Step into America." *The Movement,* December 1967.

Harrington, Michael. *The Other America.* Baltimore: Penguin Books, 1963.

Hayden, Tom. *A View of the Poverty Program: "When It's Dry You Can't Crack it with a Pick."* Center for the Study of Unemployed Youth, Graduate School of Social Work, New York University.

Kolko, Gabriel. *Wealth and Power in America.* New York: Praeger, 1964.

Lasch, Christopher. "The Banality of Liberalism." *New York Review,* December 1965.

Oglesby, Carl, and Shaull, Richard. *Containment and Change.* New York: Macmillan, 1967.

Ross, Bob. "Notes on the Welfare State." SDS pamphlet, June 1966.

Thoughts of the Young Radicals. A New Republic Book, Harrison-Blaine, 1966.

Williams, William A. Speech published in *The National Guardian,* November 27, 1964.

6

The Politics of the Movement: Coalition, Autonomy and Organizational Structures

6.1 *STAUGHTON LYND:* **Coalition Politics Or Nonviolent Revolution?**

[This article is Staughton Lynd's response to Bayard Rustin, supporter of the liberal-labor-progressive coalition within the Democratic party. Lynd, who has been a professor of history at Yale and the University of Chicago, recently abandoned his academic career in order to dedicate himself completely to the Movement. Author of several books on history and politics, Lynd may be considered one of the most important spokesmen of the New Left. His position is intransigently radical, nonviolent and libertarian-socialist. From *Liberation,* June/July 1965.]

Bayard Rustin's "From Protest to Politics: The Future of the Civil Rights Movement," an article which appeared in *Commentary* magazine for February 1965, has been widely criticized in radical publications. Ronald Radosh wrote an effective response in *Freedom North,** and Stanley Aronowitz will comment in a forthcoming issue of *Studies on the Left.*

The gist of the radical critique of Rustin might be summarized as follows:

1. Rustin writes that "the objective fact is that Eastland and Goldwater are the main enemies." In so doing he exaggerates the liberalism of the Johnson coalition, even asserting that Big Business, forced into the Democratic Party by Goldwater, "does not belong there."

2. Not only does Rustin urge that direct action be abandoned for politics, he argues also that independent political action is only rarely appropriate. The accurate perception that Negroes need white allies leads him to the conclusion that one must choose between existing aggregations of political forces: "The issue is which coalition to join and how to make it responsive to your program."

3. Thus, by exaggerating the Johnson coalition's capacity to solve fundamental social problems and by underestimating the need for independent action by Negroes, Rustin arrives at a stance which (in Radosh's words) "leads to a dissolution of the old Rights movement, as well as assuring that any new Movement will not develop in a more radical fashion." The effect of his advice would be to assimilate Negro protest to the Establishment just as labor protest was coopted at the end of the 1930's, in each case leaving the poorest, least organized parts of the population out in the cold.

I agree with Radosh's analysis, but I think it is not sufficiently fundamental. Fully to appraise Rustin's *Commentary* article, one must see it as the second in a series of three Rustin actions during the past year. First was his attempt to get the credentials committee offer of token seating accepted by the Mississippi Freedom Democratic Party delegates at Atlantic City (August 1964). Second was the article (February 1965). Third was the effort to un-

---

*Published by the Northern Student Movement, 514 West 126 Street, New York 27, N. Y.

dermine and stop the March on Washington against the war in Vietnam (March–April 1965). In this perspective, the most basic criticisms of his article should be these: 1. The coalition he advocates turns out to mean implicit acceptance of Administration foreign policy, to be coalition with the marines; 2. the style of politics he advocates turn out to mean a kind of élitism which Bayard has been fighting all his life, in which rank-and-file persons would cease to act on their own behalf and be (in the words of "From Protest to Politics") "merely represented."

In opposing the March on Washington against the war in Vietnam Bayard Rustin has permitted himself to drift into that posture which once evoked epithets such as "labor lieutenant of capitalism." Exaggerated as such labels may have been, they designated something real. There were in Europe and there are now in America pacifists and socialists who always support their own government in its international confrontations when push comes to shove. Such Americans insist on condemning Washington and Moscow "equally," but end up supporting the U.S. government which "after all" and "on the whole" stands on the side of "freedom." They specialize in advising revolutionary movements overseas to be nonviolent, forgetting that American arms and aggression play a major role (as in Vietnam) in driving peaceful protest toward insurrection. They cultivate the concept that the President is a man of peace misled by his advisors, who if only one could reach him, would surely turn on the military-industrial complex and overcome. Theirs is the *stance* of telling Washington what *they* would do were *they* in power. If there is to be protest, so they say, let it be decorous protest which (as Norman Thomas said in his April 22nd letter to the *Times*) "goes off well," i.e., poses no serious embarrassment to the good man in the White House.

The basic error in this analysis seems to me the assumption that there now exists what Michael Harrington calls "*de facto* coexistence" between the United States and world revolution. Rustin and Harrington confine their analysis to domestic problems, as if believing that foreign affairs are frozen and can be forgotten. But as Harrington conceded in *Partisan Review:* " 'escalation' of the Vietnamese—or any other—crisis would . . . end talk of the War on Poverty, and of the Great Society." That escalation has occurred.

Coalitionism, then, is pro-Americanism. It is what Sidney Lens has called "two-and-a-half campism." It is a posture which subordinates foreign to domestic politics, which mutes criticism of American imperialism so as to keep open its channels to the White House, which tacitly assumes that no major war will occur. But war is occurring in Vietnam, major enough for the innocent people which it has killed. How can one reconcile virtual silence on Vietnam with the screams of Vietnamese women and children?

Coalitionism is also élitism. Its assumption is that major political decisions are made by deals between the representatives of the interests included in the coalition. Negro protest, according to the Rustin formula, should now take on the role of such an interest. And men like Rustin will become the national spokesmen who sell the line agreed-on behind doors to the faithful followers waiting in the street.

This was the meaning of Atlantic City. What was at stake, as it seemed to the S.N.C.C. people there, was not so much the question, Should the compromise be accepted? as the question, Are plain people from Mississippi competent to decide? Rustin, Martin Luther King and Roy Wilkins answered the latter question: No. The decision, they insisted, involved "national considerations." In some sense the destiny of America rested in the hands of those who made this decision. Hence it should be made wisely, by the leaders, and put over to the delegates from Mississippi.

But what those delegates and their S.N.C.C. associates learned at Atlantic City was simply no longer to trust these "national civil-rights leaders." They learned, as Mrs. Hamer put it on her return, that hypocrisy exists all over America. They learned, so Robert Parris told the *National Guardian* dinner in November, that the destiny of America was *not* in their hands, that they should seek their own objectives, "let the chips fall where they may."

So as some sunk deeper into the coils of coalitionism, S.N.C.C. people have joined with Students for a Democratic Society this winter in laying a new emphasis on "participatory democracy." Democracy, they say, means ordinary people making decisions for themselves. It means the staff of an organization making decisions rather than an executive committee, it means the organization itself working itself out of a job so that new popular organizations take over Freedom parties, Freedom schools.

All this Bayard Rustin used to believe. Direct action is inseparable from the idea that everyone involved in a movement has some ultimate responsibility and initiative. Decentralization was the hallmark of the early LIBERATION, which Bayard helped to found. Participatory democrats, as they move from direct action into politics, insist that direct action must continue along with politics, that there come into being a new politics which forces the representative back to his people, and politics back to life.

There is very little point in criticizing the coalition strategy suggested by Rustin unless one has an alternative to offer.

I think the time has come to begin to think of "nonviolent revolution" as the only long-run alternative to coalition with the marines. The civil-rights movement, so often called a revolution, is thus far no more a revolution than the trade-union movement of the 1930's. Presumably the definition of a revolution is that the direction of society's affairs shifts from one group to another, and that the economic foundation of political power is transformed so as to make this shift permanent. A revolution in this sense—and not merely public works planning by an Administration whose power rests on private ownership and lack of planning—seems to me required both to prevent war and to satisfy the needs of the other America. But is talk of revolution merely what Rustin calls moral gesturing?

So long as revolution is pictured as a violent insurrection it seems to me both distasteful and unreal. The traditional alternative, the Social Democratic vision of electing more and more radical legislators until power passes peacefully to the Left, seems equally illusory. However, the events of the past year —the creation of the Mississippi Freedom Democratic Party and the protest against the war in Vietnam—suggest a third strategy. One can now begin to envision a series of nonviolent protests which would from the beginning question the legitimacy of the Administration's authority where it has gone beyond constitutional and moral limits, and might, if its insane foreign policy continues, culminate in the decision of hundreds of thousands of people to recognize the authority of alternative institutions of their own making.

Robert Parris has sketched out such a scenario as a possibility in Mississippi. What, he has asked, if Mississippi Freedom Democratic Party voters elected not only legislators but public officials as well? What if the Negroes of Neshoba County, Mississippi began to obey the instructions of the Freedom Sheriff rather than Sheriff Rainey? What if the Freedom Sheriff impanneled a Freedom Grand Jury which indicted Sheriff Rainey for murder?

The value of these imaginings is that they break up the concept of "revolution" as a monolithic, unitary event, and remind us that revolution begins as the decision of individuals to say, No, and take a first step. Even the most violent revolutions involved a larger component of nonviolent civil disobedience than is often recognized. Masses of poor men who defy constituted authority typically lack weapons, and succeed only when they convince the government's soldiers not to fire on them but to join them. Thus Trotsky presents the crux of the Russian Revolution as an encounter between mounted Cossacks and unarmed poor people rioting for bread; when the soldiers decided to join the rioters, the revolution was essentially won. St. Exupery, writing of the Spanish Civil War, describes two peasants, one in the Nationalist army and one in the Republican, whose units were stationed on opposite slopes of a valley and who as night fell hurled to each other across the great distance single words which sought to persuade: "Liberty," "Brotherhood." This is how real revolutions, as distinct from plots and insurrections, succeed or fail. Camus was wrong in presenting revolution and rebellion as mutually exclusive: no popular revolution is possible which is not composed of hundreds of smaller rebellions. Thus the American Civil War, our closest approach to revolution, began with solitary decisions to defy Congress and the Supreme Court and to succor fugitive slaves.

Needless to say all this makes sense only if our situation is desperate. I think it is desperate. If it was desperate in Mississippi when perhaps two dozen people were murdered over a period of five years, what is it in Vietnam where a hundred thousand lives have needlessly been thrown away since 1954? If there are, in Camus' phrase, "limits" inherent in human nature to permissible government policy, what more can we do after what we have done in Vietnam? If Vietnam is permissible, can anything be forbidden? And how many more secret undebated Presidential decisions will it take to convince us that a constitutional crisis exists in America, that we have moved into a twilight zone between democratically delegated authority and something accurately called "fascism"? When the President sent troops into the Dominican Republic he called in Congressmen to tell them, he explained, before they read about it in the newspapers. As *The New York Times* has pointed out, government management of the news, characteristic of previous temporary crises such as the U-2 and Bay of Pigs affairs, has in connection with Vietnam become settled public policy over a period of months and years. I believe we should have seen that America could not endlessly practice Seven Days in May in underdeveloped countries all over the world, making and unmaking governments at the behest of generals and C.I.A. agents, without these habits crossing the Rubicon between foreign and domestic politics to become our political style at home as well. I think the situation is desperate.

Yet nonviolence offers rational hope which can forestall desperation issuing in apathy or senseless violence. The situation of the Administration is more desperate than ours, and its present policy is the blind lashing-out of the cornered and frustrated, who see no orderly method to achieve their goals. On the other hand, few as we are our aspirations run along the grain of the hopes and strivings of the majority of mankind. International public opinion constitutes some check even on an Administration which has determined to go it alone without friends. When suffragettes were over and over again imprisoned and mishandled on the streets of Washington during World War I, public opinion was aroused, some high government officials resigned, and women's suffrage was enacted into law. If students chained themselves to the Capitol this summer in wave after wave of massive civil disobedience, even the Johnson Administration would be constrained in its choice of means.

What then is to be done? Let me offer an imagined scenario, comparable to Parris' for Mississippi, which without presuming to define a "position" or lay down a "line" which may help our thinking converge toward common action.

Suppose (I take this idea from Tom Hayden) there were convened in Washington this summer a new continental congress. The congresses of 1774 and 1775 came about on the initiative of committees of correspondence of the individual colonies. The continental congress of 1965 might stem from the initiative of the community union in a Northern ghetto, or the Freedom Party of a Southern state. Suppose, at any rate, that such a call goes out, saying in effect: This is a desperate situation; our government no longer represents us; let us come together at Washington to consult on what needs to be done.

Already there are in Washington Freedom Democratic Congresswomen who are, in a sense, tribunes of all the unrepresented people in America. As the actions of the Administration systematically exclude Congress from effective decision-making, the category of the unrepresented comes to include not only those (like 95 percent of adult Mississippi Negroes) who cannot vote, but the rest of the American people who no longer have decision-makers that represent them. Although Mrs. Hamer and Mrs. Gray have held no "freedom legislative hearings" and introduced no "freedom bills," their presence is a symbol of the determination of the American excluded to have some say in what their government does.

The continental congress goes one step further. The act of convening it would stem from a conviction that even the victory of Mrs. Hamer and her colleagues would have little significance if the Congress which they joined no longer had effective power. The continental congress would be the coming-together of project and community union representatives who, were they one day to be elected to Congress, might refuse to go on the ground that Congress has given up its power.

Just as the American colonists organized Provincial Conventions and a Continental Congress to take the place of the colonial legislatures and the British Parliament, so the continental congress of 1965 would seriously and responsibly begin to debate the policies of the United States. The discussions which have failed to take place in the Senate about Vietnam, would take place here. Resolutions would be adopted and the form of treaties ratified; emissaries of the congress could seek to make direct contact with the people of other countries. In effect the continental congress would begin to govern.

The transfer of allegiance would apply, to begin with, only to specific acts. Those refusing to pay taxes might pay them to the continental congress. Those refusing to serve in the army might volunteer their labor to community projects under congress sponsorship. Some, with or without the explicit authorization of a congress majority, might initiate systematic civil disobedience in their own communities or in Washington (just so in 1774 Massachusetts moved out ahead of the Continental Congress and began to organize its own government and to prepare for war). Professors might organize a committee to hold foreign policy hearings, since the Senate Committee on Foreign Relations has failed to do so. Men of spiritual authority from all over the world might be convened as a parallel Supreme Court, to assess guilt and responsibility for the horror of Vietnam.

The pressures on American policy-makers suggest an iron drift toward more and more blatant repression at home and abroad. Yet even if this is so, all is not lost. Six months ago the air-conditioned nightmare seemed secure and invulnerable. Liberals congratulated themselves that America had turned its last corner, integrating the Negro into the happy permanent societal consensus. This was an illusion. America's situation was less secure, Johnson was less rational, the American people were less brainwashed, than they seemed six months ago. Now we know: whom the gods would destroy they first make mad; but also: we can overcome.

At the April 17th march in Washington it was unbearably moving to watch the sea of banners and signs move out from the Sylvan Theater toward the Capitol as Joan Baez, Judy Collins and others sang "We Shall Overcome." Still more poignant was the perception—and I checked my reaction with many many others who felt as I did—that as the crowd moved down the Mall toward the seat of government, its path delimited on each side by rows of chartered buses so that there was nowhere to go but forward, toward the waiting policemen, it seemed that the great mass of people would simply flow on through and over the marble buildings, that our forward movement was irresistibly strong, and that even had some been shot or arrested nothing could have stopped that crowd from taking possession of its government. Perhaps next time we should keep going, occupying for a time the rooms from which orders issue and sending to the people of Vietnam and the Dominican Republic the profound apologies which are due; or quietly waiting on the Capitol steps until those who make policy for us, and who like ourselves are trapped by fear and pride, consent to enter into dialogue with us and with mankind.

6.2.   *TOM HAYDEN:* **The Politics of the Movement**

[Tom Hayden is one of the founders of SDS, organizer of the Newark Community Union Project in 1964, member of an American delegation invited to North Vietnam in 1965, and coordinator of the National Mobilization Committee against the war in Vietnam in 1968. In this article, he explains the autonomous political line of the Movement and its rejection of coalitionist strategies. Excerpts from *Dissent,* January/February 1966.]

. . . .

III

Why have liberal strategies failed to secure substantial reforms over the last three decades? The answer can only be grasped by looking at the general organizing concepts of American liberal and labor leaders. These begin with the view that the American masses are "apathetic" and can only be roused because of simple material needs or during short periods of great enthusiasm. The masses most likely to move, it is said, are those who have gained something already: the unionized workers, registered voters, property owners. Those less likely to move are the people on the absolute bottom with nothing to lose, for they are too damaged to be the real motor of change.

From this rough description of the masses, liberals go on to argue the need for certain sorts of organizations. The masses need skilled and responsible leaders, they insist. It is best if these leaders have rank-and-file experience and operate within a formally democratic system. But this grass-roots flavor must not obscure the necessity for leaders to lead, that is, put forward a program, a set of answers that guides the movement. And because they monopolize leadership experience, it soon appears to these leaders that they alone are qualified to maintain the organization.

The perilous position of the movement, due to attacks from centralized business and political forces, adds a further incentive for a top-down system of command. The need for alliances with other groups, created in large part through the trust which sets of leaders develop for each other, also intensifies the trend toward vertical organization. Finally, the leaders see a need to screen out anyone with "Communist-oriented" views, since such individuals are presumably too skilled to be allowed to operate freely within the movement. Slowly an elite is formed, calling itself the liberal-labor community. It treats the rank and file as a mass to be molded; sometimes thrust forward into action, sometimes held back. A self-fulfilling pattern emerges: because the nature of the organization is elitist, many people react to it with disinterest or suspicion, giving the leadership the evidence it needs to call the masses apathetic.

The pressures which influence these leaders come, not primarily from below, but from the top, from the most powerful men in the country. Sometimes bluntly and sometimes subtly, the real elite grooms responsible trade union and civil rights leaders. The leaders' existence comes to depend upon the possibility of receiving attention from the President or some top aide, and they judge organizational issues with an eye on this possibility. There is usually no question about the leaders' primary loyalty to the "national interest" as defined by the Administration, even though they always believe their judgments are independently made. Thus most of the civil rights leadership in 1964, fearing the Goldwater movement and hoping for civil rights legislation from a victorious Johnson Administration, called for a "moratorium" on mass demonstrations. The labor leadership performed the same function for the same reasons during World War II; the irony is that their critics in that period included A. Philip Randolph and Bayard Rustin, two Negroes who pushed for the 1964 moratorium.

A recent incident clarified the political role of this leadership and pointed towards the possibility of an alternative strategy. This was the challenge posed by the Mississippi Freedom Democratic party and the Student Nonviolent Coordinating Committee at the 1964 Democratic National Convention.

Members of the FDP trooped into Atlantic City to argue for their rightful control of the Mississippi Democratic seats. They found substantial support from rank-and-file members of Northern delegations who favored their modest demand for at least equal treatment with the racist party at the convention. Here was a chance, it was thought, to end Southern obstruction of the Johnson Administration's program. But then the Democratic leadership let its position be known: the FDP was morally sound, but "illegal" and "not qualified." Support within the delegations wavered. The FDP's last chance for success depended on rallying national liberal-labor leaders to support its demand for a floor debate, in front of the television cameras. But some Negro leaders worked against the Mississippi party, others took a vacillating position and no one would stand firmly with them. To do so, the leaders claimed, would jeopardize Humphrey's chance at the vice-presidency, strengthen Goldwater's hand and split the FDP from its "allies" in the liberal-labor world. The FDP members decided that the fate of Humphrey and Goldwater depended in fact upon the same power structure that was determining their own fate. Not wanting the kind of "allies" and "victories" being offered, they went home. Their real allies were the poor people waiting in the Delta; and their real victory was in being able to maintain fidelity to those allies. This was a victory because it kept the movement alive and gave its members some real understanding of what was needed to change the national situation.

IV

The Mississippi Convention challenge points towards a new kind of politics and a new kind of organizing, which has at least an outside chance of truly changing American society. This stirring we call the Movement.

The Movement tries to oppose American barbarism with new structures and opposing identities. These are created by people whose need to understand their society and govern their own existence has somehow not been cancelled out by the psychological damage they have received. For different reasons such needs survive among the poor, among students and other young people, and finally among millions of other Americans not easily grouped except by their modest individual resistance to the system's inhumanity. It is from these ranks that the Movement is being created. What kind of people, more exactly, are they, and what kind of organizational strategy might they develop?

1. An Interracial Movement of the Poor

The Mississippi sharecroppers are most visible and inspiring representations of an awakening that is taking place among the poor in America. Their perspective centers on Negro freedom, of course, but they are committed deeply to the idea of a movement of all the powerless and exploited. In certain ways theirs is a radicalism unique because of Black Belt conditions. Their strength comes from a stable system of family life and work. Politics is new and fresh for them; they have not experienced the hollow promises of an opportunistic liberal-Negro machine. Their opposition's naked brutality keeps them constantly in a crisis framework. The broadening of their movement into Arkansas, Alabama, Louisiana, Georgia, the Carolinas and Virginia, already underway, can be expected to challenge fundamentally the national coalition directing the Democratic party. Already the Democrats are trying to groom moderate and liberal politicians to provide an "alternative" to the segregationists and the independent FDP. Probably this effort will succeed, in the sense that political moderates will begin to compete for electoral power and leadership of the civil rights forces, mostly basing their strength in the cities, among privileged Negroes. The FDP, as a structure, may be absorbed into the national party, if only because it has no other, more effective place to go. But since the new Southern power structure will not solve the problems of poverty and race which have plagued the North for generations, there is very little chance that this movement of poor people will be entirely coopted or crushed.

In the black ghettos of the North, the Movement faces heavier obstacles. There work is often deadening, family life distorted: "proper" political channels are sewers; people are used to, and tired of, party organizers exploiting them. The civil rights movement does not touch these hundreds of ghettoes in any significant way because of the middle-class nature of its program and leadership. However, the Harlem rent strikes and the activities of Malcolm X are clear evidence that there are in the ghettoes people prepared to take action. Some of them are of Southern background; some are housewives with wasted talents; some are youth with no future for their energy; some are junkies and numbers men with little loyalty to their particular game. Different as the forms of their discontent may be, the discontent itself is general to the ghetto and can be the spring for action. Under present conditions political movements among these people are likely to be based on a race consciousness which is genuine and militant—and which is also vital because of the failure of whites to act in favor of equal rights. The ghetto race consciousness, however, is intertwined with the consciousness of being both poor and powerless. Almost of necessity, the demands that the ghetto poor put forward are also in the interest of the white poor, as well as of middle class professionals who depend on the expansion of the public sectors of the economy.

But will white working class and poor people take up these issues, which the "Negro problem" by its nature tends to raise? The negative evidence is plentiful. Poor whites, such as those in parts of the South who are truly irrelevant to the modern economy, tend to see their plight (sometimes with accuracy) as personal rather than social: a function of sickness, bad luck, or psychological disorder. Poverty is not seen clearly as the fate of a whole interracial class, but only as the fate of individuals, each shamed into self-blame by their Protestant ideology. Working-class whites, on the other hand, are more likely to be conscious of their problems as a group, but they tend to defend their scarce privileges—jobs, wages, education for their children—against what they see as the onslaught of Negro competition. While "backlash" did not split the alliance of white working people with the Democratic party in 1964, it does serve as a barrier to an alliance with the Negro poor. But it is foolish to be rigid about these notions. Whites *are* being organized, on a mass basis, in areas of Appalachia where there exists a common culture and an industrial union tradition, and where the blame for misery can be laid to the coal operators, the conservative United Mine Workers, and the government. They also have been organized in Cleveland, where they face the "welfare situation" together.

But these organizing efforts were led by local people or independent organizers outside the structure of the labor movement. Today there are millions of workers trapped by the organizational framework of the AFL-CIO. Their unrest at times moves the international unions slightly, but the internationals are more dependent on government and business than on their own members, and, in addition, they seem to possess effective techniques for curbing shop revolts. It is not simply the "better objective conditions" which split the white from the Negro poor, but the existence of trade unions which actively distort the better aspirations of their workers. Economic and social conditions, of course, are not improving and workers' discontent is evidenced by the recent wave of rank-and-file revolts. But whether this discontent spurs a coalition of poor whites with Negroes depends, most of all, on whether a way can be found to organize workers independent of AFL-CIO routines. Concretely, that means democratic control by the workers of their union locals, and the entry of those locals into political activities and coalitions on the community level. It also means community action and organization among the millions of low-paid workers presently outside the labor movement.

The crucial importance of community work can only be grasped if one understands the sorts of ideas the American poor have about themselves. They operate with a kind of split consciousness. On the one hand, poor people know they are victimized from every direction. The facts of life aways break through to expose the distance between American ideals and personal realities. This kind of knowledge, however, is kept undeveloped and unused because of another knowledge imposed on the poor, a keen sense of dependence on the oppressor. This is the source of that universal fear which leads poor people to act and even to think subserviently. Seeing themselves to blame for their situation, they rule out the possibility that they might be qualified to govern themselves and their own organizations. Besides fear, it is their sense of in- adequacy and embarrassment which destroys the possibility of revolt. At the same time, this set of contradictory feelings results in indirect forms of protest all the time: styles of dress and language, withdrawal from political life, de- fiance of the boss's or the welfare worker's rules and regulations.

There can be no poor people's movement in any form unless the poor can overcome their fear and embarrassment. I think the release comes from a cer- tain kind of organizing which tries to make people understand their own worth and dignity. This work depends on the existence of "material issues" as a talk- ing organizing point—high rents, voting rights, unpaved roads, and so on—but it moves from there into the ways such issues are related to personal life. The organizer spends hours and hours in the community, listening to people, draw- ing out their own ideas, rejecting their tendency to depend on him for solutions. Meetings are organized at which people with no "connections" can be given a chance to talk and work out problems together—usually for the first time. All this means fostering in everyone that sense of decision-making power which American society works to destroy. Only in this way can a movement be built which the Establishment can neither buy off nor manage, a movement too vital ever to become a small clique of spokesmen.

An organizational form that suggests the style of such a movement is the "community union," involving working-class and poor people in local in- surgency. Open and democratic, the community union offers a real alternative to the kind of participation permitted in civil rights groups, trade unions and Democratic party machines. It might take a variety of forms: block clubs, housing committees, youth groups, etc. The union's insistence on the relevance of "little people," as well as it position outside and against the normal chan- nels, would create a rooted sense of independence among the members.

The problem of politics among the poor is severe. In the first place, their potential electoral power is low because of their location in gerrymandered political districts, their rapid movement from house to house, and the com- plicated and discriminatory electoral procedures in many cities. Beyond these problems lies the obvious and well-grounded cynicism of the poor about elec- tions. Given all these conditions, it is barely conceivable that a poor person could be elected to an important political office. Even were this possible, it would be on a token basis, and the elected official would be under strong pres- sure to conform to the rules of the game. Thus, the orthodox idea of politics is contradictory to building a movement. The movement needs to discover a politics of its own. This might be done by electing people who will see their office as a community organizing tool, letting community people participate directly in decisions about how the office should be used. This experiment is being made in Atlanta where a SNCC field secretary, Julian Bond, was elected in June 1965 to the State Legislature. Or what might be done is to contest the basic class and racial injustices of American politics, demanding that poverty areas be granted political representation, or running freedom elections to dramatize the lack of representation for the boxed-in poor. This sort of thing would probably mobilize more poor people than orthodox electoral activity. The mobilization would be "practical" from the standpoint of getting modest reforms; more important, it would point toward the need to rearrange American political institutions to fit the needs of excluded people.

2. A Student Movement

If poor people are in the movement because they have nothing to gain in the status system, students are in it because, in a sense, they have gained too much. Most of the active student radicals today come from middle to upper-middle class professional homes. They were born with status and affluence as facts of life, not goals to be striven for. In their upbringing, their parents stressed the right of children to question and make judgments, producing perhaps the first generation of young people both affluent and independent of mind. And then these students so often encountered social institutions that denied them their independence and betrayed the democratic ideals they were taught. They saw that men of learning were careerists; that school administrators and ministers almost never discussed the realities the students lived with; that even their parents were not true to the ideals they taught the young.

It was against this background that young people became concerned about war, racism and inequality in the early sixties. By now, the empty nature of existing vocational alternatives has pushed several hundreds of these students into community organizing. Working in poor communities is a concrete task in which the split between job and values can be healed. It is also a position from which to expose the whole structure of pretense, status and glitter that masks the country's real human problems. And, finally, it is a way to find people who want to change the country, and possibly can do so.

When a student comes into a community, there are countless obstacles in his way. He is an outsider, he is over-educated, he has nothing concrete to offer people, and often, he is white in a Negro ghetto. At the same time, however, he brings something with him: the very presence of students suggests to the poor that their more activist notions may be right after all. The student alone can say, "Look, I come from the world that says you are not qualified, and I know that is a lie. I come to you because you can teach me as much as I can teach you." Students can also make the poverty problem visible and threatening because they create resources previously unimaginable. Parents and universities become energized; money can be raised; contacts can be set up with other people's organizations around the country. Finally, students and poor people make each other feel real. What has flowed from this connection is most of the vitality of the civil rights and anti-poverty movements over the past five years.

Now it appears that students are finding ways to organize effectively around other problems too: university reform and peace. The Berkeley "uprising" and the April march of 20,000 against the war in Vietnam were major departures from the inconsequential student politics of the old days. On many campuses students are beginning to form unions of their own, as well as independent seminars pointed toward the eventual organization of a "free university." In addition, they are beginning to mobilize community action against the Vietnamese war—thereby encountering their friends already at work among the poor. These efforts may thread the several protest movements in the country into a grass-roots coalition.

3. Middle-class insurgents

A centralized and commercial society wastes the talents and energies of millions of individuals. Some of these are women who are excluded from male-dominated vocations. Some are people with human values who cannot assert them effectively within organizations attached to the cold war consensus. Some were politically active in the thirties, but faded away when popular movements declined. Some are part of the postwar generation which missed the experience of a radical movement altogether, and who are lodged uncomfortably in publishing houses, universities, and labor bureaucracies.

The new movements are opening great possibilities for participation by such middle-class people. Their activity often includes vital financial support, but it can and does go farther. Insurgency within American institutions is spreading: professors fighting their administration, lawyers against the bar association, welfare workers against the political machine, muckrakers against the press establishments. This insurgency is bound to increase as the new generation of student activists graduates into the professions. And it is an insurgency which needs a movement of poor people, insistently demanding new social purposes from the professionals.

To summarize: the Movement is a community of insurgents sharing the same radical values and identity, seeking an independent base of power wherever they are. It aims at a transformation of society led by the most excluded and "unqualified" people. Primarily, this means building institutions outside the established order which seek to become the genuine institutions of the total society. Community unions, freedom schools, experimental universities, community-formed police review boards, people's own anti-poverty organizations fighting for federal money, independent union locals—all can be "practical" pressure points from which to launch reform in the conventional institutions while at the same time maintaining a separate base and pointing towards a new system. Ultimately, this movement might lead to a Continental Congress called by all the people who feel excluded from the higher circles of decision-making in the country. This Congress might even become a kind of second government, receiving taxes from its supporters, establishing contact with other nations, holding debates on American foreign and domestic policy, dramatizing the plight of all groups that suffer from the American system.

If it is hard to imagine this kind of revolutionary process in the United States, it might be because no previous model of revolution seems appropriate to this most bloated and flexible of the advanced societies. There may be no way to change this country. At least there is no way we can bank on. Both technological change and social reform seem to rationalize the power of the system to drain the heart of protest. The Movement at least suggests that we bank on our own consciousness, what there is of our own humanity, and begin to work.

6.3.   *Editors of Studies on the Left:* **Up From Irrelevance**

> [The problem of how to organize the New Left opposition in the United States has been and still remains one of the major issues of debate within the Movement. In spring of 1965, *Studies on the Left,* the theoretical review closest to the positions of the New Left, published a debate between the two groups which constituted the editorial staff on the theme of the organization of a "radical center." One side was taken by Tom Hayden and the younger Movement activists; the other by James Weinstein and the group of intellectuals connected to the socialist tradition. From *Studies on the Left,* Spring 1965.]

In the past *Studies* concentrated on the broad contours of American social structure and history; now it focuses on specific problems of social revolution is this country. This makes the magazine identify with "insurgent forces": people in the civil rights movement, community unions, trade unions, student organizations, radical intellectuals and artists. Our last editorial, "After the Elections," tried to analyze the few possibilities for change open to these new insurgents. Our editorial board agreed on a description of this society as "the most flexible of totalitarianisms," in which nearly all human activity is paralyzed in dependence on welfare-capitalism and the Cold War. There was disagreement among the editors, however, when we faced the question of finding a way to effectively confront this society and to change it.

Since this problem, which has split radicals in the past, still causes bafflement and conflict, it seemed to me that the editors should focus on exploring dilemmas instead of proposing organizational formulas. However, most members of the *Studies* board favored an organizational call of some sort: a unification of the new movements; a coalition of the old and new left; a new Socialist Party; or at least a common and guiding radical ideology. The editorial concluded by calling ambiguously for a "radical center" that could serve as a communications and coordinating agency linking the new insurgents with the traditional left. While this new center should be built around the insights and needs of the new radicals, the editorial argued, it should make a basic place for the older radicals who now are lodged in single-issue groups (traditional civil rights, educational reform, peace activity) where their radicalism is subdued and isolated from the new movements.

This seemed to me an artificial attempt to order the chaos of the contemporary Left; as such, it short-circuits an important discussion that began in *Studies* with last summer's focus on the issues of community organizing.

Proposing a "radical center" assumes there is a sufficiently large radical movement in need of coordination; or, at least it assumes that "radical center" could forge existing materials into such a movement. But, as *Studies* also pointed out, the new movements are in their infancy. From Washington, it may look as though the Freedom Democratic Party is organized; from McComb, it is clear that only the beginnings have been made. The movement is even less developed in other reaches of the Black Belt, and no movement at all is current in the major Southern and Northern cities. Work among poor whites is negligible. New organizing campaigns among youth and industrial workers are just being conceived. Only this year are students becoming a legitimate and profound force, both in community organizing and on campuses; but again, the student movement is just beginning to become massive. Assuming these movements must and will expand, as I think events indicate, it seems rather early to pull them into a national center. The critical work still remains at the base, and only an overemphasis on the *image* of a national movement can make one believe it exists. We ought not to fall into the trap of confusing widespread outbursts with a solid movement. Behind the sit-ins, teach-ins, freedom votes, wildcat strikes and other protests which are beginning to shake society; behind the "new unrest" reported everywhere from *Life* to the *National Guardian,* is the presistent reality of human inertia which still is stronger than the few energies now being released.

Moreover, I think the development of a radical movement depends on what force can be freed by the current civil rights movement. The civil rights issue is pivotal because it is exposing the limits of American economics and politics; it is beginning to arouse the interest of poor people; it is forcing a realignment of people within labor, liberal, religious and left groups; it is the problem which moves and educates the effective students. But I doubt that these tendencies can change into the strands of a wider movement, a movement with a total program for change, in the near future. This is partly because the first task for most organizations will be to clear up whatever racial problems can be cleared up without taking on the whole country. The more important point, in explaining why an independent radicalism is stymied, is that the radical and moderate wings of the civil rights movement are mutually dependent. Martin Luther King needs SNCC to do basic organizing; SNCC needs King to support the FDP; both need the NAACP to support national legislation. Thus, while people in SNCC, SDS, FDP, and even CORE and SCLC form a loose "left" in the movement, with their emphasis on poverty and community organization, this "left" is partially dependent on the more conservative establishment that reaches all the way into the national government. Certainly it is desirable to loosen this conservative grip. But for this to take place, there must be something to break *towards:* other people in the society who together can make up an alternative community to the establishment. But such people are not available at the present time in sufficient numbers and strength and unless they are, it is hollow to call for a "radical center."

If this is true, it is irrelevant also to "choose" between the political alternatives which usually are presented to radicals: working within the Democratic Party for realignment versus independent political action. The new movements which give us hope *are* realigning the Democratic Party even though they often work outside the Party and their values go far beyond those of the Democratic leadership. The new movements are neither fully dependent nor independent; at present, they are creating tensions in both directions. The FDP is the most obvious case in point. At Atlantic City it sought entry into the national Democratic Party, not because the Freedom Democrats believed in political realignment, but because the current situation permitted no more radical stance. This situation, which is subject to change, is made up of: 1) the political weight of the radical-democratic sharecroppers in the FDP against the more conservative "teachers and preachers" who are allied with the national NAACP and the Johnson Administration; 2) how effectively FDP organizers can expand the Party's base in the rural areas; 3) whether there are similar power groups, North or South, which the FDP can connect with instead of the national Democratic Party; 4) the ability and desire of the Administration to meet the needs of the FDP.

How much can a single movement in one state liberate itself from the national power centers which can guarantee its survival and short-term gains? This depends on whether the support for the FDP comes from Democratic machines and liberal reformers in the North, or whether the sharecroppers can expect to join up with other people around the country who have the same needs. If the FDP cannot depend on strength from local people's movements elsewhere, then its most democratic qualities will be held back as the price of acceptance within a "realigned" Democratic Party—a Party, however, which will be committed still to elite domination of politics, industry and war.

This means that, instead of assuming that a viable radicalism is present, an assumption which leads to the idea that a "radical center" is needed, we instead ought to focus on the obstacles to a radical movement in the first place. To an overwhelming degree American society has controlled its internal class, radical and psychological strains. With social controls ranging from terrorism to welfare, the country has moved far in the direction of the "one-dimensional society" Herbert Marcuse describes. Almost everyone develops a vested interest of some kind in the American system as a whole, and within the system there are virtually no legitimate places from which to launch a total opposition movement. Politically, any group looking for a radical alternative to liberal-left politics seems to be either isolated and destroyed, or swallowed into an uncomfortable coalition with the leadership of labor, civil rights and religious organizations.

Some radicals now accept this situation by claiming it is impossible to go "outside" the system. Bayard Rustin, for example, argues that poor people are incapable of leading a revolutionary movement. ("Rousseau was not a cotton-picker," he told an Antioch audience recently.) From this, he goes on to embrace the idea that a coalition of organizational leaders, pressured by the discontent of their rank-and-file, is needed to carry through a program of new liberal social legislation. *Studies,* along with the new movements, suspects the wisdom of this approach. Our suspicion begins with the belief that welfare-state reforms, conducted within the private, selfish control of the economy, are ineffective because they are not conceived by the poor people they are designed for. Instead, they mangle and manipulate the poor while relaxing most of the middle-class into the comfortable sense that everything is being managed well. But this criticism itself indicates why there is no present radical alternative: the welfare state effectively satisfies or contains its subject population. Rustin can invent a clear strategy because he chooses to move with, and in fact rationalize, the main trends in this society: he even argues that ending poverty would be good for big business. But anyone wishing to counter these dominant trends, as the new left is trying to do, is facing a mystery when they look for a workable strategy. What we seek to make viable, against the grain of an affluent and coercive society, is a thoroughly democratic revolution, in which the most oppressed aspire to govern and decide, begin to practice their aspiration, and finally carry it to fulfillment by transforming decision-making everywhere. The emphasis in the movement on "letting the people decide," on decentralized decision-making, on refusing alliances with top leaders, stems from the need to create a personal and group identity that can survive both the temptations and the crippling effects of this society. Power in America is abdicated by individuals to top-down organizational units, and it is in the recovery of this power that the movement becomes distinct from the rest of the country, and a new kind of man emerges.

This kind of man cannot be purchased because his needs cannot be translated into cash; he cannot be manipulated because it is precisely against manipulation that he has defined his rebellion. Should it be possible to create this new identity on a large scale, then the movement can avoid two key dangers. The first of these is dependency on fixed leaders, who inevitably develop interests in maintaining the organization (or themselves) and lose touch with the immediate aspirations of the rank and file. The second danger is that the rank and file will not understand or commit themselves to the long-range goals of the movement. What results from these tendencies is the present structure of all liberal and left organizations: they are shells.

What we should try to do, on the contrary, is assume that we have failed so far to discover the relationships and the forms that will free individuals to think and work as radicals, and build a movement where "everybody is a leader." Not until then will a "center" reflect anything radical and deep in society.

In the course of discussing new movements, much is being said in criticism and defense of the "traditional left." The *Studies* editorial called for the inclusion of the older radicals in a coalition with the new movements. My own feeling is that too many traditional leftists are still engulfed by the communist-anti-communist debate; adhere to overly bureaucratic conceptions of organizing; or are limited fundamentally by their job and family situations, to be considered mainstays of a new movement. The many people who are exceptions to this general picture should concentrate on organizing the millions of people who never experienced the history of the American left, instead of attempting to reconstruct their old-left colleagues.

Perhaps these comments are too harsh; most of the *Studies* editors are probably more sympathetic to these views than I have been able to convey. Nevertheless, there are differences. A "radical center" is an overly administrative concept, a false way of making the insubstantial substantial. It is a way of sliding over the frightening possibility that American radicalism may be baseless and doomed, that the imperial arrogance of this country will be safely rooted until a thermonuclear war destroys it. It is also a way of sliding over the richest possibility we have, that of beginning to slowly organize people. In the effort to open up this possibility for a new identity and a new movement, we are going to drift and experiment for sometime to come.   **Tom Hayden,**
Norm Fruchter, Alan Cheuse

REPLY:

We agree with Tom Hayden that the problem of finding an effective way to "confront this society and change it" has split radicals and continues to baffle them. But while we attempt to confront this problem, Hayden skips over it and focuses on the problems of organizing the poor. Our proposal was not to solve the problem with new "organizational formulas," but to begin the search for effective strategies to challenge and change this society. Our goals are the same as Hayden's. We agree on the need to build a movement that is fully conscious of the need to transcend the values and priority systems of America's present rulers. We disagree on the need for radicals to discuss and work out the necessary theories and strategy of social change.

Underlying this disagreement is a difference over the nature of potential radical constituencies, and a confusion between the problem of organizing the poor and that of working toward a coalition of radical constituencies capable of becoming an effective political force on the left. Hayden's concern is with the former; ours is with the latter. We focus on different problems, but there is nothing inherently contradictory or mutually exclusive in our two approaches. Stated simply (hopefully not oversimply), Hayden's theory has two parts: 1) the poor, both in the rural South and the Northern ghettoes, are the only potentially radical mass constituencies (because they are most cheated by this society and least corrupted by involvement in its institutions); 2) the poor cannot be organized along traditional liberal or old left lines (because these are bureaucratic, exclusive, and hierarchical and only serve to further alienate the already most alienated people in our society). Hayden spends a great deal of time on the second question, but he simply assumes the first. Our argument with him is over this assumption. We agree with much of what he says about organizing the poor.

There are several aspects of Hayden's position that do not seem to us to hold up under examination. He assumes that work among the urban poor and Southern rural Negroes is politically relevant, but he sets up a model which can only lead to defeat or insignificance. Assuming that the poor can be fully organized and will become fully conscious of the need for radical politics, by themselves they must remain impotent. There are not enough of them, nor do they command sufficient resources to constitute a political force that can win power. Hayden concedes that students are also a potential radical base, but his view of the radical student is essentially as an organizer of the poor. He presents no prospective for organizing a mass radical student movement, and explicitly denies or ignores the existence of other possible components of a radical coalition. Yet if a significant movement is to be built it must be around a coalition large enough, at least in theory, to contest for political power. Every group of potential allies should be explored. Programs of action should be developed to facilitate connections between the various components—including the poor—when they become sufficiently conscious to engage in explicitly political action. Such a coalition needs a common view of the existing society, common programmatic demands (or at least complementary ones), a common vision of a new form of social organization designed to satisfy human needs. We feel it is necessary to begin the theoretical work on which such a movement can be based.

Of course it may be that other groups or classes cannot develop mass radical consciousness (it may also be impossible to build this among the poor). If that is so then a meaningful radical politics will be impossible, and radicals will be well advised to retire from politics or join the mainstream as the loyal opposition to our liberal totalitarianism. But before this is done we believe radicals have the responsibility to explore the possibilities for the development of mass radical consciousness and to attempt its organization among several other groups in the society.

We see two general types of potential constituencies that should be analyzed and explored as potential components in a new radical coalition, or ideological center. First are class or social groupings: students, industrial workers, urban poor whites and working poor, the aged. Recent protests and demonstrations about the purposes and organization of universities and the surge of activity against further American intervention in Vietnam have made clear the possibility of a mass radical movement among students. The great increase in the student population that will continue to take place in the immediate future suggests an increasing potential for such radical activity. Among industrial workers, despite ever higher wages, questions of job control and job security have led to wildcat strikes, as in the automobile industry last fall, and to the displacement of entrenched leaders in two basic old CIO unions, the Steelworkers and the International Union of Electrical Workers. The obstacles to radical organization among these workers are immense, given the tight structure and control that exists in most union locals in the basic industries; but discontent is widespread, the conditions of work continue to worsen and security will diminish steadily with the continued spread of automation. Urban poor whites and working poor, unlike the organized industrial workers, have been excluded from even the monetary benefits of the warfare state. The conditions under which they work are worse, and politically they are even more powerless. The aged are another surplus, and therefore excluded, group in the Great Society. As living costs, particularly medical care, go up, their real income goes down. One of the responses to automation is earlier retirement, but the retired are neither financially or socially prepared for their lives of leisure. We do not know that all, or any, of these groups will be sources of radical consciousness. Certainly they will not be if left to chance. But we believe the conditions under which each group works and lives require radical changes if the individuals involved are to fulfill themselves as human beings. None of these social groups have control over their own lives. Even where, as in the trade unions, the leadership of a group is included in the consensus, the rank and file are almost as powerless as the poor. Although most receive more money, all are excluded from decision-making, are manipulated by elites they are unable to defeat. Hayden argues that these groups are not potentially radical because they share in the material rewards of this society. But they do not differ substantially from the poor in the degree to which they control their own destinies. Hayden is right to argue that they *are* less alienated and are psychologically incorporated into the dominant society by a rising standard of living. But if the poor are capable of organizing politically and developing their own pressures and leadership, there is no reason to assume that they, too, cannot be granted material rewards. Certainly our society is wealthy enough to be able to make such concessions if threatened. Hayden's defense against this is to organize around the concept of participatory democracy; if this works for the poor, however, there is no reason why it should not work for other social groups. Before such groups are abandoned to continued manipulation and use as producers or consumers in our welfare state, we should at least examine the possibilities for organizing them and developing a radical consciousness among them.

The second type of constituencies are those built around issues or areas of social concern: the peace movement, housing and urban renewal movements, school and parent associations. These movements cut across class lines to some extent. They have at least a theoretical possibility for radicalization in that the solution of most of the problems they confront will require deepgoing changes in the nature and priorities of existing American society. This will also require a change in the nature of these movements, or , at least, in the strategy of radicals within them. If the peace movement, for example, is to develop a radical consciousness of its own, and to serve to radicalize others, it must be reoriented around a root opposition to the imperial role of the United States in world affairs and an explicit rejection of the underlying assumptions of our intervention against all popular revolutions. Radicals cannot be concerned with arguments about the most effective way to defeat communism, or agree that intervention is necessary (no matter how painful) if the absence of it might lead to a new communist government. In the other movements radicals should examine the kinds of changes that will be needed to solve the problems of housing, schools, etc., and seek to develop programs and activity that increase people's awareness of the relatedness of each issue to an over-all reorganization of society. Again, this may not be fully possible. As sufficient pressures around issues develop the "great society" may solve particular problems. But this has always happened to some extent; the value of such activity beyond the immediate victories is in the degree it serves to build a vision of a better society and an understanding that change can be achieved by concerted social action.

When we spoke of the need for a new radical center we did not have in mind an organizational short circuit of the new experiments with community organization. Our use of the term was ideological, not organizational; what we sought was discussion, analysis, examination of all these social movements with a view to finding common programs, a common attitude toward existing American social organization, a common vision of a new society, and a long range strategy for putting together a coalition that might have some political relevance. We do not believe this can be done by limiting ourselves to the problems of organizing or working within communities of Northern poor and Southern rural Negroes, even if that work is now the most advanced and has the greatest potential for rapid development. If it develops fully in the absence of other movements it will lead nowhere.

Beyond that, there are other movements developing and they already suffer from the lack of such a strategy. In the absence of a new radical ideology and center the student and peace movements remain unable to free themselves of the ideological and organizational influences of the old left, with its archaic concerns about Stalinism and anti-Stalinism. Or, worse, they remain under the influence of the liberal ideologies of the Johnson Administration.

As Hayden points out, the radical and moderate civil rights organizations are mutually dependent, and within the over-all picture King sometimes aligns with the left forces. But King (not to mention the NAACP) does not share SNCC's perspective on the Freedom Democratic Party and the development of a radical independent political movement in the South. King is committed to the Administration and to the integration of Negroes into the existing Democratic party structures in the South. King's strategy is carefully worked out in consultation with high Administration liberals, and it is King who becomes the publicly acknowledged leader when he moves into situations created by SNCC. He gives the political content to SNCC's groundwork, whatever SNCC's intention, although there is often compromise and operational unity. Yet Northern whites, both liberal and radical, are unaware of the differences and support both thinking they are supporting the same thing. Because there are no independent radical connections in the North, SNCC has no way of making public its differences and attempting to rally independent support, both financial and political, for its position. In a way this experience is analogous to the role of the left in organizing the CIO in the 1930's. Then, too, the left were the militant organizers; then, too, the ideological content was provided by leaders with connections in the Administration (John L. Lewis and Sidney Hillman). The difference is that the left in the 1930's had no strategy of opposition to absorption in the liberal consensus, whereas some in SNCC do. But while SNCC's rivals receive vast political and organizational support, SNCC, because of the absence of a general consciousness of the content of the struggle, can rely only on general appeals to sentiment, or on private appeals based on strategic considerations. Unlike King, they are part of no ideological community from which they can get support and with which they can work out and coordinate strategy.

The discussion in our editorial about unaffiliated radicals also relates to the point, and was not understood by Hayden. Many former old leftists reject the approaches, and especially the bureaucratic forms of organization and the sterile debates over Stalinism versus social democracy, of such old left sects as the Socialist Party, the Communist Party and the Socialist Workers Party. To some extent, of course, these people still think and act in the old ways, even though they reject the organizations of the old left and the context of old left politics. This is precisely why they share, in common with the new movements, a need for a new radical center. Such people are now either without direction, except that which they give themselves, or follow vaguely the old styles and tactics. They often serve as the militant organizers of activity in the peace movement, in the reform movements within the Democratic party, in PTA's, in tenants organizations, in trade union locals, but almost invariably the ideological content and political impact of such activity is determined by others—by the "big names" who are pushed into action by these radicals, or by the liberal leadership of the organizations in which they are active.

The new left's diversity and decentralization is one of its greatest strengths and should be supported and aided in every way. Those who, consciously or not, adopt a "Leninist" concept of political organization offer structural or administrative solutions for political and ideological problems. Such an approach, however necessary or appropriate under the conditions that existed in Czarist Russia or Kuomintang China, can only inhibit the search for new political forms, can only stifle the kind of initiative and experimentation in the development of radical consciousness and program which is the strength of SNCC in Mississippi and some of the ghetto projects in the North. We do not propose "democratic centralism" or highly disciplined structures when we assert the need for a radical center. In this sense, the experience of radical organizations in the United States since the early 1920's is useless. Organizationally one must go back to the old Socialist party of Debs to find any meaningful precedents. The great success of pre-1919 Socialism depended on its democratic and decentralized character. Local Socialist organizations then had their own press, developed their own programs, adopted different tactics. This often led to serious debates and to factional antagonisms, but these remained within the confines of the Party because of general agreement on the nature of American capitalism and on the desirability of basic social reorganization, so that workers and farmers might control the conditions under which they worked and lived. This changed and ended after 1919 when the "Leninist" concept of party organization began to stifle the kind of free development and local participation that Hayden defends. In defending something that we also appreciate, he misconstrues our proposal.   **James Weinstein, Stanley Aronowitz, Lee Baxandall, Eugene D. Genovese, Helen Kramer**

FURTHER READINGS

"After the Election." Editoral. *Studies on the Left*, V: 1, Winter 1965.

Gans, Herbert. "The New Radicalism: Sect or Action Movement?" *Studies on the Left*, V: 3, Summer 1965.

Haber, Al. "Students and Labor." SDS pamphlet, 1962.

Hayden, Tom. "Student Social Action." SDS pamphlet, 1964.

Kopkind, Andrew. "The Liberal-Labor Coalition and the CDGM." In *Beyond Dissent: Papers from the New Left*. New York: Doubleday, 1967.

Lens, Sidney. "The New Left and the Establishment." *Liberation*, September 1965.

Mills, Herb. "In Defense of the Student Movement." *New University Thought*, II: 1, Fall 1961.

Radosh, Ronald. Reply to Bayard Rustin's article. From "Protest to Politics." Mimeograph, 1965.

Raskin, Marcus. "Issues *vs*. Institutions." *New University Thought*, I: 2, Fall 1960.

7

New Left Methodology: Nonexclusionism, Participatory Democracy, and Direct Action

7.1. *ALAN HABER:* **Nonexclusionism: The New Left and the Democratic Left**

[The practice of ideological "nonexclusionism" has consistently been one of the characteristics which differentiate the New Left from the traditional left, of which the "Democratic left" represents a part. Alan Haber was president of SDS in 1962, director of the Economic Research Action Project (ERAP) in 1963, director of the Radical Education Project in 1966, researcher at the Institute of Labor Industrial Relations in Ann Arbor, Michigan, and at the Institute of Policy Studies in Washington. From a mimeographed SDS pamphlet of 1965.]

As a principle and as a policy for democratic radicals, I believe that "nonexclusionism" is both a moral and a pragmatic necessity. It is not an easy approach to politics, but neither is democracy. Nonexclusionism is not a negative principle. Like nonviolence, it requires an affirmation. If the movement is to be open, and yet its fundamental values and its relation with the wider public preserved, its program and entire styles must be positive. There must be: a conscious preoccupation with root values and long-term goals, internal discussion of the varied potentialities of a complex political reality, a constant striving for clear statement of how values conjoined with facts lead to specific programs of institutional and policy change, and an attempt to formulate, however tentatively, programmatic "solutions" for the short run and long run that make democratic values manifest and on which action can be based.

. . . .

The Need for Openness

The chief premise of my argument is that the left must have complete openness to all issues of controversy relevant to its basic values. This does not mean that we should be without convictions, or that some ideas and realities are not more distasteful than others or that the ongoingness of debate should deter us from action on tentative conclusions. But the debate must be ongoing.

Why? *First,* because the power of the left is largely its ability to persuade. With no immodesty, we must have more answers to more questions, more and better ideas and proposals, and more facts than anyone else around. Only as we pursue debate do we develop the ability to see and lead others to see beyond the slogans by which the truth is obscured and controversy converted to concensus. *Second,* because many of the issues are important, not only for the public, but for the program and strategy of radical democrats seeking to influence the public.

What are some of these issues? I will name several which now torment

SDS and which seem central to the lines of disagreement between the "new left" and the "democratic left": the responsibility of the United States in the Cold War; the reformability of American society and the processes through which significant social change is possible and the "agents" of change; the strategy of radical organization and the relation radicals should have to "mainstream liberalism" (for example, the Democratic Party, the organized civil rights movement, the churches and the labor movement); the role of and alternatives to violent revolutions in the "third world," with its attendant suppression of democratic rights; and the internal dynamics of communist and centralized socialist regimes, particularly in terms of their potential for democratic reform, their motivations in world politics and the institutional models they can provide for democrats. A general issue in these disagreements concerns moral absolutism and relativism. Does democratic absolutism for America imply a similar absolutism in underdeveloped countries? What is the relation between the humanist ideal of improving the lot of men and the democratic ideal of insuring individual freedom and grass-roots determination of resource allocation? What are the conditions under which the only response to a nondemocratic society is condemnation, and those where one should temper criticism in order to support or work for the good or progressive aspects of the society? Does revolutionary centralism lead *inevitably* to bureaucratization and then totalitarianism, and if not, in what ways can democrats in the West play a role in directing the process of development toward democratic forms?

I submit there are legitimate questions and issues of disagreement, even among radicals whose commitment to the broad ideals of democracy is uncompromising. They are by no means resolved (nor, I fear, adequately debated) in the "new left." On them turns not only the strategy for democratic social change in America, but also an understanding of how to end the Cold War and extend democracy abroad. If they are closed questions for the "democratic left," that closure, I believe, is premature. It can lead only to an intellectual and political myopia. The issues are too complex and too important for intellectual and political myopia. The issues are too complex and too important for anyone to claim that the truth is in hand, that the time for debate and new learning is past, that people should declare their colors and take their stand. In effect, closure means that discussion within the "democratic left" shifts from analysis and basic issues to tactics, and that communication with radicals outside the "consensus" becomes stilted and antagonistic, if there is communication at all. This is the context, an intellectual openness, in which the "new left" poses (or should pose) the nonexclusionist issue, in particular, and its attitude toward anti-communism, in general.

Nonexclusionism

The position of nonexclusionism, as I think most in SDS would express it, has two facets. Both of them relate to a rejection of anti-communism as the primary principle of democratic radicalism.

(1) There shall be no *a priori* ideological formula of who shall be in and who out of the democratic radical movement. Whatever a person might think of communism, the National Liberation Front, *New America,* guided democracy, social democracy, capitalism or Lyndon Johnson, the movement is open to him. It is his decision to join—or to leave.

(2) People shall be judged by their behavior in the movement. Behavior is

the evidence of intention. If they support and participate in the actions which radicals of democratic commitment support and democratically determine, they shall be considered "friends"—no further questions asked. If privately they smoke pot (or don't) or belong to YSA or the SP or the CP or DP or YAF or SDS or the Chamber of Commerce (or don't) that's their affair—with which others may agree or disagree, privately. When their public actions weaken the movement, or when they refuse to discuss and argue their beliefs with their colleagues, then they lose their right to speak in the movement or for it.

Thus, there *is* internal "ideological control." But it operates individually through continual debate and examination of action. It assumes that people in the organization are essentially honest and themselves open to persuasion. And if there must be "exclusion" the process is the traditional one of grass-roots democracy: their colleagues stop listening to them and grant them no responsibility and support in the organization.

Exclusionism

The position of exclusionism is different. It begins with a principled anti-communism. This is seen as the most relevant implication and test of commitment to democratic values. Communists, or leftists who support, identify with or apologize for authoritarian regimes are not wanted in the movement. You may tolerate them; certainly you defend their civil liberty to organize their own groups and demonstrations and to speak in their own behalf. But you seek to make clear to the public that their voice, as part of your movement, is "illegitimate." Organizationally, the means to this is some kind of formal "exclusionist clause" and a minimal statement of belief in the organization's constitution. Programmatically, it involves, particularly on international issues:

(1) some kind of statement, slogan or formula laying at least equal blame on "the other side";

(2) great care in the statement of proposals and programs to insure that they would give no advantage to "the other side" or its supporters;

(3) noncooperation with other groups which do not have a similar exclusionist position.

This position is grounded in principle, pragmatism and analysis.

Principle: If we are anti-communist, we should "take the cotton out of our mouths" and say so, in the most direct way possible.

Pragmatism: If there is any question that our program would give aid and comfort to the enemy, it will be rejected on its face by the American people. Furthermore, the presence of their like in any part of our movement will be used to discredit us and our position on every issue on which we might work.

Analysis: Communist countries are basically unscrupulous in their domestic and international affairs, cannot be trusted and will take advantage of any "fuzzyness" in the West to extend and/or consolidate their own repressive forms of government and social organization. And, "nondemocrats" in America will act in much the same way; if they get access to the movement they will seek to misuse and control it for their own purposes.

Problems of Left Anti-Communism

SDS would, I think, take issue with various aspects of each of these propositions.

Without at this point exploring the particulars of disagreement, it can be said that SDS rejects the formulation of anti-communism implicit (and explicit) in the exclusionist position. This rejection should not, however, be confused with an acceptance or tolerance of authoritarian or totalitarian values. For instance, while there has been much controversy generated by the elimination of the "exclusion clause" from the SDS constitution, that constitution does say:

> SDS is an organization of and for democrats. It is civil libertarian in its treatment of those with whom it disagrees, but clear in its opposition to any anti-democratic principle as a basis for governmental, social or political organization.

There are complex psychological roots in the "new left" to anti-anti-communism. These undoubtably involve elements of pugnacious defiance, generational rebellion, limited historical experience, repugnance of loyalty oaths and their association with McCarthyism and profound estrangement from mainstream America. Basically the "new left" represents a desperate search for new ways in the face of the failure of the old. They are repelled by the history of left sectarianism (though without knowing the history). They seek a style of politics which is direct, which speaks to the immediate issues and which deals with people as individuals, assuming their good intentions or basic morality. They believe that ideology evolves from action, and that any imposition of predetermined standards or categories or analysis narrows the creative potential of the movement. It may be easy to point to the deep contradictions in these "gut feelings" and to their violation in practice. But their potency must be acknowledged. They reflect the combination of mysticism, humanism, innocent idealism and moral urgency which is perhaps the chief motive force to the resurgence of protest politics in the '60's. They certainly reflect the apolitical roots of the "movement." Without exploring these roots, there are several strong, and I think valid, political underlying anti-anti-communism and nonexclusionism.

Another point is important here. The rationale for debate on anti-communism, *per se,* is that only thereby can the left sectarians, the youthful adherents to Marxism-Leninism, be identified and isolated. The experience, however, has been the opposite. This level of debate welds such people into a self-conscious faction, one that can be "expelled" only at the risk of destroying the organization. SDS does not have such destructive, sectarian factions, and the reason is clear: Because with an atmosphere of openness, people operate as individuals, and as individuals they open themselves to persuasion. This should not be hard to understand. When the political survival of a group of individuals is threatened, as for instance by exclusion from the organization in which they work and seek to express themselves, then communication with one another is increased and intensified. They are *forced* to develop a strategy of self-preservation. This involves a highlighting of common minority beliefs and mutual reinforcement of the conviction that these beliefs are essential to preserve in the organization, whatever the consequences for others in the organization. On the other hand, without this pressure, their communication patterns are much more "random." And, even if they have *leadership* positions, their interdependence is more with people of different beliefs, which makes personal dogmatism personally dysfunctional.

One more point should be made here. The "democratic left" can certainly point to its historical experience with the Communist movement in America and with cadres of infiltration within the movements of democratic radicalism. And the "new left" should learn that history and be sensitive to its lessons. But the "new left" now has its *own* history. And built on that history, its own successes. This is the reality check against which the lessons of the past are tested. And if their experience does not check with that of their elders, it is understandable, at least, that their choice should be with the present. And it is even understandable that they might be a touch haughty in suggesting that the "democratic left" restudy its history, to see if it has drawn the right lessons, to see if there were not mistakes for which it bears responsibility, and to see if those lessons, in any case, are relevant to the present.

Let it not be said that I am merely flailing a straw man, that no one in the "democratic left" advocates a loyalty oath or the physical expulsion of non-democrats from our organizations and demonstrations. All exclusionism demands is that we insure that our movement is consistent in its support of democracy and individual freedom, and not for the victory of one oppressor over another. And all we ask is that the individual play by the rules. Of course he can march, but under our slogans, and if he is not happy with those slogans, he is free to march elsewhere.

First, the straw man has some flesh and bones. There are many in the democratic left who take the "hard line" and many even a harder line of declaring public anathema on any organization which would tolerate such elements. But my argument is really pointed to the more moderate position that the anti-communist issue has a prime relevance and must be debated. The problems are these: (1) that debate is often posed as interrogation, provisional suspension of moral recognition and legitimacy until the "new left" gives an "acceptable" accounting of itself, (2) that the debate does not allow for irresolution or its own continuity. It demands agreement, it cannot tolerate the idea that people could have differences on this issue and still be democrats. And (3) that the debate is framed in categories that are abstract and perceived as irrelevant to the immediate concerns of the movement. It should be evident that on these bases there is hardly debate in any normal sense of the word. And it is precisely these terms of "debate" which produce the destructive consequences of exclusionism.

The third basis for anti-anti-communism is a political response to the nature of anti-communism in America. Anti-communism has become the chief ideological weapon of defenders of the status quo, by which they not only justify political imperialism abroad, but also by which they outlaw the expression of radical vision and dialog at home. This ideology provides a view of reality which is static, internally consistent and self-justifying. Communism, however defined, is the central category dividing good and evil. On this basis, the ideology of anti-communism is able to mobilize energy in the irrational defense of the established system—at least, is "our" system the lesser evil. Left anti-communism may have a different motivation, formulation and intent—it certainly derives from a clearer understanding of the realities and complexities of the "communist world." But as it *functions* and is heard by the American public, these subtleties are lost; its absolutism is translated into just one more prop supporting all-American consensus anti-communism.

Reflect: democratic planning, control of corporate power, public ownership or control of natural and major economic resources, public guarantee of basic standards of income, health, education and welfare: these "old-fashioned" ideas of radical democracy are now undiscussable, to say nothing of "workers' control" or the support of "third world" revolutions against America. Has the "democratic left" dropped these ideas from our demonstrations and pronouncements because, in our 1960's wisdom of prosperity capitalism, we judge them irrelevant, as public issues even for discussion? That, in part, may be where the "end of ideologists" and the trumpeters of the American celebration have brought us. But more I think it is because these ideas are tainted. They can too easily be associated with "communism" and thence dismissed, indeed pilloried, along with their advocates. We learn from this political reality to be relevant, it is safer to stick, at least in our public face, with the liberal issues and the campaigns for marginal reform. The basic structure of the institutions which dominate men's lives and processes of power and decision making: these are best left untouched, since they are untouchable.

The "new left" takes a different lesson from this reality. It argues that if we wish to be relevant, as radicals, we must attack, in our words and practice, the basic categories of thought, the false consciousness, if you will, which otherwise guarantees our irrelevance. As long as the rhetoric of anti-communism, and the view of reality which it enshrines, remain unchallenged in the American public, the left will always be marginal. However neatly we dress or sweetly we talk, we will have to operate under other guises, on issues not of our choosing and with our vision kept to ourselves. We will have to operate as liberals, restricted to the crisis issues which periodically mobilize American liberalism. We may be successful in forming coalitions, rather than its educator or a radicalizing initiator. And a coalition formed on this basis, cannot easily be transformed. As with exclusionism on the left, so in a liberal coalition, a deviant view will be labeled and excluded before it is heard or has its chance to persuade. As long as we offer no challenge to anti-communism as the public's political frame of reference, our program, no matter how democratic, will gain no hearing or debate in that public—that is if our program would touch the cherished institutions of free corporate enterprise, private property, and the almighty market. These are, after all, the institutions by which anti-communists distinguish American freedom from communist tyranny.

The "new left" refuses quietly to submit to such a future for itself and for democratic radicalism. If the creation of a democratic left and especially a left which can speak to "the people" and develop, in its own name, a mass base requires that we oppose and defeat the rhetoric of anti-communism, then that shall be one of our tasks. Communists *symbolize* in America the threat to the basic institutions and economic forms of "our way of life." But do not we, as radicals, threaten and threaten even more deeply many of those same elements of the status quo—albeit with different ends? In this regard, we are called communists. Their exclusion, in other contexts, will be our exclusion. And it is not enough to say we will defend their civil liberties. We must defend their right to participate, to express with us their views and to be heard on the merits of their views. For we demand nothing less than that for ourselves. We must create and make legitimate a style of politics in which radically divergent views can operate openly and engage one another.

This does not mean that we embrace "communism" or espouse its values, but we should be under no misapprehension that this may not put us in "working alliance" with people whose values we oppose—just as we work with people to our "right." There are other ways, more positive than "exclusionism," to deal with such consequences as may follow from this problem. The overriding consideration is that we cannot practice internally that which isolates and destroys us externally. People may disagree with this sketchy analysis. But it is not sufficient to deny its relevance, and the rejection of anti-communism and exclusionism which follow from it, simply on the basis of moral absolutism or even a pragmatism that sees no further than the immediate crisis. The argument requires elaboration, and if counter argument and analysis is persuasive, then modification. The entire left, and such public as we have, could profit from debate on this level. I do not believe the "new left" is so dogmatic or its position so psychologically determined, that it would not enter rational discussion. But attack which sidesteps or dismisses the issues people in the "new left" see as important, which fails to distinguish between relevance as liberals and relevance as radicals, and which appears more concerned with its appeal to the public than to themselves: such attack is hardly the basis for such discussion.

Problems of Nonexclusionism

To accept the principle is not to celebrate the practice. Nonexclusionism poses certain inherent organizational problems and it requires a tremendous commitment to discussion and internal democracy. SDS and the "new left" generally have not adequately confronted these problems or manifested in practical organizational terms, that commitment. I should say here that much of their failure is the result of the position taken by the "democratic left." Their posture has been, too often, one of attack or passive agnosticism, rather than initiative in promoting and sustaining debate on the substantive issues of radical politics in process. The energy and intellect and resources of the "democratic left" have been largely devoted to abstract argument about the appropriate style of politics, or they have been withheld altogether. And even then, the concerns have been articulated not in the newsletters, conferences, chapter meetings and homes of the movement, but in publications either directed to the general public or in left publications which (perhaps unfortunately) are not widely read in the new left.

This itself illustrates a consequence of exclusionism. The forum is open, the channels of communication exist, desire for a deeper understanding of American and world problems is widespread. It should be clear that many of the problems that exist now could be avoided if the movements critics had spent as much time over the last five years participating in its activities and internal dialog as they spent in trying to reform the terms of the dialog.

To identify the problems of nonexclusionism requires that we identify first what those problems are not. They are not, as Carl Oglesby, SDS president, has rightly said, that converse with nondemocrats will convert or corrupt us, or that alien elements will "take over" control of our organizations. To the first pseudo-problem, we answer that in free debate we have confidence in our conviction and our power to persuade. Indeed, if reason might lead us to other views (such as socialist centralism) it is well that we subject ourselves to the agony of that confrontation. To the second, we can point variously to our democratic organizational structure and the absence of centralized levers of organizational power, to the relative absence in the organization of those hard-minded, cynical, doctrinaire manipulators so much feared, and to our daily experience, that in relying on the good sense and decency of the people attracted to us, ordinary persuasion and honest discussion have been fairly successful.

But if these are pseudo-problems, there are real problems that must be faced. The first is that sincere people have an honest suspicion of the non-exclusionist position. They say: if you refuse to ask at the outset the values of people with whom you work and exchange trust, when common sense and historical experience make clear that there are some people holding anti-thetical values who would misuse your trust, then it is legitimate to question either your maturity or your understanding and commitment to those values. This suspicion is, itself, largely a product of left anti-communism, but none-theless, it requires precise response.

There are three answers given by the "new left." *First,* trust is essential to radical democratic politics; we must risk its misuse—as indeed democracy itself is risky and mistakes will be made by dealing with people as individuals rather than by objectifying them with predetermined categories. *Second,* people come to the radical movement from many motivations, many backgrounds of experience and with a wide range of knowledge and historical understanding. There is no unambiguous formula or formulation of belief that would dif-ferentiate those who are "really" sincere in their commitment to democracy from those who only profess sincerity. As with all "loyalty criteria, however complex, the people excluded or who exclude themselves are often those most reflective and sensitive in their adherence to democratic values. Unless there are strong sanctions and provision for investigation and judicial proceedings, and even then, the "nondemocrats" can easily "slip by" and it goes all the harder for you if they are later discovered and exposed by your opponents. *Third,* the only way to determine who your friends are is to work with them and to gain an understanding of their ideas and ultimate goals through con-tinual discussion on the specifics of social progress that follow from those ideas. This, too, is the only way to change people's ideas and to carry on the process of radical education, particularly essential in a youth movement.

Implicit in this response is an important clarification of the "behavioral standard" in nonexclusionism. Behavior is not simply, as in the civil rights movement, a willingness to "put your body on the line." Behavior is also speech, a willingness to talk and argue. For radicals, where our prime power is the power to persuade, speech is crucial. In a movement of wordless activism or moral witness (all too prevalent in the "new left") where you put your body is all that counts. In a radical movement, though, intellectual action is of equal, if not greater importance. And the refusal to talk, to formulate in specifics the political meaning of broad values, that too is action—action in disservice to the movement.

Well enough, but that raises the *major problem of nonexclusionism.* The effect of allowing an ideological diversity within an action movement can be to suppress both internal debate and external statement of social program in order to maintain solidarity for action. There are two sides of this issue. First is a *leadership* problem: in a movement which recruits and expresses itself through action, the organizational leadership has dual and conflicting responsibilities. They may be good democrats all, yet the structure of the situation can make them hesitant to promote internal ideological discussion. For, if ideological diversity exists, discussion is sure to produce conflict, and internal conflict weakens the action potential of the organization. The fear of this can have multiple and interacting consequences: analysis, reflection and argument may be replaced by an embracing rhetoric, a minimally explicit ideology, under which consensus is preserved and all elements can operate comfortably. The educational functions of the organization may be neglected, since with the absence of a manifest value on internal debate, the organization must increasingly justify itself by external action. The formal channels of internal democracy can become sterile, because the "hard issues" underlying strategic decisions are obscured by the rhetoric and suppressed by those concerned primarily with action goals or maintaining group cohesion. The intellectual and programmatic initiative (i.e., organizational power) may increasingly devolve to an informal, fluid leadership group which is able to generate the rhetoric and maintain the illusion that action is following from analysis. The political activities of the organization, its program, can become faddish, as one rhetorical construct is exhausted (or stymied) in its action potential and is replaced by another and that again by another, all with no underlying, continuing analysis of political objectives. Then the organization becomes uninteresting or frustrating, or both, to many serious radicals and intellectuals who desire to go beyond rhetoric and witness in their attempt to translate values into political action. And finally, the movement can lose its ability to speak to the public, as it specializes its language, ignores its facts and education, and becomes unreflective on the issues to which it wishes to speak. In sum: the movement can develop its own false consciousness. It can deprive itself of vital resources and sources of creativity. It becomes a home for the disaffected, but a dead-end for those who seek effectiveness. By the failure of its leadership to recognize and deal with the problems of non-exclusionism, it excludes itself.

The second consequence of ideological diversity is a *membership problem*. Those in the organization who are activists only, or those who, for whatever reason, want to keep their beliefs to themselves, have leverage beyond their numbers to influence the style of the organization. They can speak for and take initiative in promoting *ad hoc* actions which require little internal debate or education. They can create and magnify the illusion that severe internal disruption would follow from discussion of "touchy" issues. And they can turn the nonexclusionist rhetoric of the organization against those in the leadership who attempt to be "too specific" about program or raise issues which make some people uncomfortable. The organization is not taken over in any traditional sense since varied political and apolitical viewpoints produce the effect, without any explicit cooperation or even intent. It is simply diverted from its very hard educational and intellectual tasks to simpler, less threatening (but also and necessarily less radical) action concerns. The only conspiracy is one of objective cross pressures and limited resources.

This situation is, of course, self-perpetuating. The more the organization is identified with action alone, the more it will recruit people whose only concern is action and the larger will be the body of membership who have no interest in and do not understand the importance of debate. The larger this body of "passive" membership, the harder is the job of radical leadership and the greater the leverage of those who would avoid debate.

This picture, while drawn in the abstract and in the extreme, roughly approximates the current organizational crisis in SDS. The chief qualitative difference is that a wide segment of the leadership and members are concerned with these problems and actively seeking to cope with them. Simply put, the problem is this: education is harder than action. With limited resources, the desirable principle of an open radical movement can be distorted to the practice of an activist movement without perspective on its radicalism.

The critics of nonexclusionism will be quick to point to these problems as the product of a nondemocratic minority self-consciously manipulating the situation in order to protect their freedom of operation. There may be an element of this, but, if so, it is a minority of the already small nondemocratic minority. The experience in SDS, however, is that most of those who might in some sense be labelled "nondemocrats" are more than willing to talk and debate. Such is the result of "openness."

By far, the major sources of this problem are the "moral activist" and the single-issue "radical-liberal." They avoid and thwart internal education. How? By disinterest and hence nonparticipation, and by the force of their energy and enthusiasm for action which creates an action pace pre-empting organizational resources and allowing no time for educational work. Why? Because self-education is hard; because it is slow; because they are not sure and secure in their beliefs; because the urgency of direct moral expression outweighs for them all other considerations; and because of their experience with learning in the university which makes them doubt the value of education, of sterile lectures and teachers who preach high truths but seem remote from the practice of those truths.

Exclusionism, the elimination of ideological diversity, however, is certainly no way to deal with this problem. On the one hand, to adopt anti-communist formulas and program statements under which "authoritarian elements" cannot feel comfortable would have any justification only if these elements were the chief cause of the problem. They are not. On the other hand, if the problem is a "natural" one, in contrast to an artificial manipulation, there is all the more reason to deal with it "directly."

Those who recognize the problem must initiate, insist on, promote and push the necessary examination of values and program. But it should be clear that the education of the movement cannot operate at a distance. The educators must be participants. Their right to be heard as comrades and friends derives from their willingness to engage in the activities of the movement at the local level—where the movement is—as equals and without preconditions. Their effectiveness derives from their direct contact with other participants in the movement and their willingness to hear and help others to develop their thinking. Their relevance as educators derives from the facts, analysis, perspective, ideas and creativity they bring to the particular issues and problems with which the movement is engaged. If, on the other hand, their only contribution is to insist that the level of debate become more abstract, that the priority of issues be shifted, as for example by insisting that anti-communism and exclusionism be debated rather than the nature of the National Liberation Front and the kind of solution to the Vietnam War that would meet the needs of the Vietnamese people, then they guarantee their own irrelevance and ineffectiveness. Does this require patience? Certainly. Hard work? Of course. A "leap of faith"? Perhaps. But then does not democracy itself require these?

If there is such internal debate, grounded in fact and focused on particulars, ideological diversity ceases to be a problem. This is not just a hopeful hypothesis. It is the experience of SDS, whenever there are the resources for the task. The anti-democrats either have to change (a very likely product of debate, especially among youth) or be organizationally passive or get out. But the process is open and democratic—and it is a continuing one. More important, though, is the benefit for those "activists" who have not sufficiently reflected on the connections between moral belief and programmatic expression.

The conjunction between debate and action does, in fact, radicalize. And if those whose concern is with education would devote their principle energies to the task, then there would be education. The energies now are not sufficient, and this is the hub of the problem. If they can be increased, then perhaps activism might become more than an abortive first step toward radicalism.

. . . .

7.2.   *STAUGHTON LYND:* **The New Radicals and "Participatory Democracy"**

> [The New Left movement did not emerge from an ideological matrix, but from the development of various political actions and projects. The method which has been common to the different movements is "participatory democracy," a concept developed in theory and tried out in political practice in Movement organizations and in the organization of society. The participatory method seems to be the most concrete contribution to emerge from the thought and practice of the American New Left during the first five years of the 1960s. Selections from *Dissent,* Summer 1965.]

For some time after Students for a Democratic Society in 1962 coined the term "participatory democracy," it was received with more humor than respect by civil rights workers in the South. The concept has become important this past winter, for two reasons. First, a number of SDS leaders have left college and are seeking to apply the idea in Northern ghettoes. Second, many members of the staff of the Student Nonviolent Coordinating Committee have begun to look beyond voter registration to what SDS, in its Port Huron Statement, called its

> two central aims: that the individual share in those social decisions determining the quality and direction of his life; that society be organized to encourage independence in men and provide the media for their common participation.

A new style of work, fusing politics and direct action into radical community organization, is emerging in both SDS and SNCC.

. . . .

I

What is the strategy of social change implicit in the concept of participatory democracy? What is its relation to older philosophies of the Left: socialism, nonviolence, anarchism? As one distant from the scene I offer the following observations diffidently, in the hope that they will stimulate comment from "participatory democrats," North and South.

One aspect of participatory democracy is the idea of parallel structures. The FDP is a parallel political party, prompted by the conclusion that registration of Negroes in the regular Democratic party of Mississippi is presently impossible. Freedom Schools were parallel schools, although delegates to the Freedom School Convention decided they would return to the public schools and seek to transform them rather than continue into the winter a parallel school system. In the North, neighborhood unions organized by SDS represent parallel antipoverty agencies, challenging the legitimacy of the top-down middle-class "community organizations" sponsored by urban renewal and antipoverty administrators.

The intent of these structures is still unclear, even to those involved in organizing them. There is a spectrum of possibilities. At one end of the spectrum is the concept of using parallel institutions to transform their Establishment counterparts. Thus it would follow that when Mississippi Negroes *can* register and vote, the FDP would wither away. At the spectrum's other end is the conviction that in an America whose Establishment is inherently and inevitably hostile, existing institutions cannot be transformed, participation will always mean cooptation and merely token successes, hence parallel institutions must survive and grow into an anti-Establishment network, a new society.

For the moment participatory democracy cherishes the practice of parallelism as a way of saying No to organized America, and of initiating the unorganized into the experience of self-government.The SNCC or SDS worker does not build a parallel institution to impose an ideology on it. He views himself as a catalyst, helping to create an environment which will help the local people to decide what they want. Recognizing himself as a part of the society's sickness, the organizer inclines to regard the unorganized poor as purer than himself. There is an unstated assumption that the poor, when they find voice, will produce a truer, sounder radicalism than any which alienated intellectuals might prescribe. In the meatime the very existence of the parallel institution is felt to be a healthier and more genuine experience than any available alternative. It seems better to sit in the back of the room in silent protest against the bureaucrats up front than to seek to elect a man to join the executive committee.

In form, parallelism suggests a kinship between participatory democracy and Trotsky's conception of the Soviets as a "dual power," or Gandhi's concern to preserve the Indian village community. But thus far the new movement does not feel itself a part of either the Marxist or anarcho-pacifist traditions. What is most clear at the moment is the call reminiscent of the Radical Reformation to "come out of Babylon." Let the teacher leave the university and teach in Freedom Schools; let the reporter quit his job on a metropolitan daily and start a community newspaper; generally, let the intellectual make insurgency a full-time rather than a part-time occupation. As the Russian radical movement grew from Tolstoyism and the Narodnik's concern to dress simply, speak truth, and "go to the people," so participatory democracy at this point speaks most clearly to the middle-class man, daring him to forsake powerlessness and act.

I for one believe that participatory democracy, even thus vaguely conceived, offers a growing point far more alive than conventional coalition politics. At the same time, it is incumbent upon new radicals to explain how they propose to answer the problems which conventional politics purports to solve. How will participatory democracy feed and clothe the poor, as well as stimulate and involve them? If voting is a snare and a delusion, what is not? Unless in time these questions can be answered participatory democracy could become a subtle, even if heroic, form of self-indulgence.

Employment appears to be the Achilles heel of parallelism. From time to time SNCC workers have sought to organize producers and consumers cooperatives, and the leather-working business in Haywood and Fayette counties, Tennessee, has had considerable success. The thriving toy business of the Society of Brothers (Bruderhof) proves that even in the age of monopoly a small cooperative enterprise can survive. But one cannot imagine such economic beginnings becoming, like the free cities of the Middle Ages, the "germ of a new society within the womb of the old." In Mississippi the movement has hardly been able to provide for Negroes fired as a result of civil rights activity, let alone address itself to the larger problem of cotton-picking machinery and the displacement of farm labor; and what provision there has been has come, not through the creation of a new economic base, but from charity.

It would seem, therefore, that in the area of economics participatory democracy cannot provide a full alternative to established institutions except by capturing and transforming them. By pressure it can democratize the distribution of income, as SDS does in boring-from-below against antipoverty programs, as SNCC does in demanding the participation of Negroes in local committees sponsored by the Department of Agriculture. Perhaps, like Dolci in Italy, radical community organizers can use symbolic direct action to dramatize the need for that massive public works program which the March on Washington called for (and then forgot). Thus Noel Day proposes using money collected from rent strikes to employ unemployed youngsters at a $2.00 an hour wage to repair substandard housing. But can we not agree that participatory democracy, understood as a movement building new institutions side by side with the old, cannot provide bread and land? Failure to face this problem realistically will result in the poor turning for help to those who can provide it at least in part, and the cooptation of protest movements by the Establishment.

A similar perspective is suggested by turning to the theorists of existential radicalism in other countries. Let us use the term "socialism" to designate the movement for a planned publicly owned economy which, in Europe as America, preceded the newer radicalism of "participatory democracy." If one examines carefully the formulations of the latter tendency in Europe (and I believe much the same thing would appear from a scrutiny of Africa), one finds it articulated as a partner in dialogue with socialism, as a humane affirmation constantly necessary to correct (but not to supplant entirely) bureaucratic institutions and political action. Thus in Silone's *Bread and Wine* the protagonist, like Thoreau, asserts that the social action needed above all is individual lives displaying morality and truth. But Silone adds:

> He had not forgotten that the social question is not a moral one and is not resolved by purely moral means. He knew that in the last resort the relations established among men are dictated by necessity and not by good will or bad. Moral preaching did not suffice to change them. But there came a moment when certain social relations revealed themselves as outworn and harmful. Morality then condemned what had already been condemned by history.

This is a formulation which has not yet created an impassable gulf between itself and Marxism. Silone's statement could be rendered, more woodenly to be sure, as an assertion that when "objective" conditions are "ripe" for change, the "subjective factor" becomes all-important.

To much the same effect, Martin Buber in *Paths in Utopia* takes public ownership as a matter of course, arguing that the critical question is: "What sort of Socialism is it to be?" The relation between centralization and decentralization, between bureaucracy and community is, says Buber,

> a problem which cannot be approached in principle, but, like everything to do with the relationship between idea and reality, only with great spiritual tact, with the constant and tireless weighing and measuring of the right proportion between them.

This is to say of popular participation much what Howard Zinn has insisted regarding nonviolence, that to ignore its limitations invites hypocrisy and, ultimately, a tendency for it to turn into its opposite.

Even Camus—so far as I can judge the strongest intellectual influence on the thinking of Bob Parris—does not quite turn his back on the Marxist "logic of history." Rather, he writes in "Neither Victims Nor Executioners":

> Since these forces are working themselves out and since it is inevitable that they continue to do so, there is no reason why some of us should not take on the job of keeping alive through the apocalyptic historical vista that stretches before us, a modest thoughtfulness which, without pretending to solve everything, will constantly be prepared to give some human meaning to everyday life.

Others of us, then, will continue to address ourselves to structural changes, to socialism. In the words of the Port Huron Statement, "a truly 'public sector' must be established," and the new left should include socialists "for their sense of thoroughgoing reforms in the system."

II

In itself, however, this formulation papers over a difference rather than resolving it. What could be more sterile than a movement with two predefined wings, a left one and a right one (we could argue endlessly about which was which)? If "some of us" were committed to one traditional concept and others of us to another, would it not be another version of coalition politics, frustrating and dead?

Some common ground, some underlying vision needs to be articulated which genuinely unites socialism and "participatory democracy," which challenges each to transcend itself. Here one strikes out into unexplored territory which can only be adequately clarified by experience. A helpful starting point may be the concept of "community." "Politics," affirms the Port Huron Statement, "has the function of brining people out of isolation and into community." And A. J. Muste writes, correctly I think, of the civil rights movement:

> No one can have a fairly close contact with the civil rights movement and the people in it, including the young people, without feeling that, in spite of all contrary appearances and even realities in the movement, deep near its center is this aspiration for a blessed community and the faith that this is what they are working for and already in a sense realizing now.

Community was what one Freedom School teacher meant who wrote to me: "The summer project presented itself to us as a potentially life-endangering situation, and so we all worked our fears out together, which gave coherence to our group. We had temporarily put aside our human fears and were accepting a responsibility which was ours and we were doing it together."

Lest this seem maudlin utopianism, let us begin with the most hard-headed meaning of community to a new radical movement: the political. How can one build a political campaign, or a political party, without sacrificing the shared intimacy experienced in a direct action "project"? If it be true that both peace and civil rights activists must turn toward politics to cope with the economic problems which confront their movements, can it be done without losing the spiritual exaltation of the direct action years?

I think a clue here is to begin to think of politics as administration. Political representation was devised as a mechanism to obtain consent for taxation. It is an institutional process peculiarly appropriate to an economy in which production is in private hands, and the state takes money from the citizen to spend it on a separate category of public activities. In a communal economy— by which I simply mean an economy wherein men share the fruits of their labor in the spirit of a family—many functions, now centralized in private hands, would be centralized in the hands of the government; but also, many functions now locally privatized would at once become neighborly responsibilities. Consider urban renewal. If land were publicly owned and building a public function, slum clearance could really become a process in which the people of a site participated at each stage. Nation- and city-wide considerations would enter in, of course: but much that now happens in public and private offices on upper floors could then be left to the collective discretion of neighborhood meetings.

In centering its attention on grass-roots participation in urban renewal and antipoverty programs, rather than on running candidates, SDS appears instinctively to recognize the communal opportunities of public economic administration. As more and more candidates begin to run for public office on a movement platform, so also new forms of direct action will be improvised to democratize administration; and as regional and national coordination takes form in the one area, so will it in the other, too. Thus entrance into politics need *not* mean an abandonment of direct action demonstration, nor of its spirit.

In conversation after the recent March on Washington, Bob Parris suggested two specific ways in which an elected "freedom candidate" could keep himself from being absorbed by conventional politics. First, if an MFDP candidate were elected to the Mississippi legislature he could act as a representative of *all* the Negroes of Mississippi rather than of a particular locality. Second, an elected candidate could simply decline to "take his seat" in a legislature and remain in his constituency as a symbol of identification with their concerns.

The local project can grow from protest into administration; if necessary it could also be the building block for resistance to more extreme forms of repression, for protest against Fascism. Like a biological cell it can take many forms, responding in a variety of appropriate ways to alternate stimuli from the environment.

But for this to be so it becomes necessary to think of a project from the beginning, not merely as a tool for social change, but as a community. The community is made up both of people from the neighborhood and of staff persons who, on a long-term basis, so far as they can become part of the neighborhood. The spirit of a community, as opposed to an organization, is not, We are together to accomplish this or that end, but, We are together to face together whatever life brings.

The experience of Utopian or "intentional" communities suggests certain ground rules which all groups seeking to live as brothers should consider. One is: It is important to be honest with each other, to carry grievances directly to those concerned rather than to third parties. Another is: The spiritual unity of the group is more important than any external accomplishment, and time must be taken to discover and restore that unity even at the cost of short-run tangible failures.

If indeed, as Marxism affirms, mankind will one day enter a realm of freedom that will permit men to guide their behavior by more humane and immediate criteria than the minimum and maximum demands of political programs, the work of transition can begin now. The need for structural change (socialism) should neither be ignored nor overemphasized. Provided we do not deceive ourselves as to the bleakness of our society's prospects for hopeful change or the catastrophic dangers of nuclear war and domestic totalitarianism, perhaps it is not unreasonable to look for a more firm and definite strategy to develop as the collective experience of the movement unfolds.

Peculiarly difficult, I think, will be the coming-together of "staff" and "neighborhood" persons on questions of foreign policy. This was a problem which confronted the Freedom Democratic Party, obliged by its strategy to support a President just then escalating the war in Vietnam. Tentatively it would seem that staff must be honest about such questions; and surely the ideological framework of brotherhood and community should make it easier to be so than one simply oriented to pragmatic goals.

In sum, then, participatory democracy seems to be driving toward the "live-in," the building of a brotherly way of life even in the jaws of Leviathan. It is conscientious objection not just to war, but to the whole fabric of a dehumanized society. It is civil disobedience not just by individuals, but, hopefully, by broad masses of alienated Americans. Like the conscientious objector, however, the participatory democrat has unfinished business with the question: Is what's intended a moral gesture only, or a determined attempt to transform the American power structure?

7.3.   *DAVE DELLINGER:* **The Future of**
                                        Nonviolence

[Nonviolent direct action has been often misunderstood as a moderate and mainly moral method of political action. The following article is a clear statement of the revolutionary value of nonviolence as practiced by radical pacifists. Dave Dellinger, a lifelong activist and spokesman for this group, is editor of *Liberation* and co-chairman of the National Mobilization Committee to End the War in Vietnam. *Studies on the Left,* Winter 1965.]

The theory and practice of active nonviolence are roughly at the stage of development today as those of electricity in the early days of Marconi and Edison. A new source of power has been discovered and crudely utilized in certain specialized situations, but our experience is so limited and our knowledge so primitive that there is legitimate dispute about its applicability to a wide range of complicated and critical tasks. One often hears it said that non-violent resistance was powerful enough to drive the British out of India but would have been suicidal against the Nazis. Or that Negroes can desegregate a restaurant or bus by nonviolence but can hardly solve the problem of jobs or getting rid of the Northern ghettos, since both of these attempts require major assaults on the very structure of society and run head on into the opposition of entrenched interests in the fiields of business, finance, and public information. Finally, most of those who urge nonviolent methods on the Negro hesitate to claim that the United States should do away with its entire military force and prepare to defend itself in the jungle of international politics by nonviolent methods.

I

There is no doubt in my mind that nonviolence is currently incapable of resolving some of the problems that must be solved if the human race is to survive—let alone create a society in which all persons have a realistic op-portunity to achieve material fulfillment and personal dignity. Those who are convinced that nonviolence can be used in *all* conflict situations have a re-sponsibility to devise concrete methods by which it can be made effective. For example, can we urge the Negroes of Harlem or the *obreros* and *campesinos* (workers and peasants) of Latin America to refrain from violence if we offer them no positive method of breaking out of the slums, poverty, and cultural privation that blight their lives and condemn their children to a similar fate? It is contrary to the best tradition of nonviolence to do so. Gandhi often made the point that it is better to resist injustice by violent methods than not to resist at all. He staked his own life on his theory that nonviolent resistance was the superior method, but he never counselled appeasement or passive nonresistance.

The major advances in nonviolence have not come from people who have approached nonviolence as an end in itself, but from persons who were passionately striving to free themselves from social injustice. Gandhi discovered the method almost by accident when he went to South Africa as a young, British-trained lawyer in search of a career, but was "sidetracked" by the shock of experiencing galling racial segregation. Back in India, the humiliations of foreign rule turned him again to nonviolence, not as an act of religious with-drawal and personal perfectionism, but in line with his South African ex-perience, as the most practical method Indians could use in fighting for their independence. During World War I, not yet convinced that the method of nonviolence could be used successfully in such a large-scale international conflict, he actually helped recruit Indians for the British Army. By contrast, during World War II, after twenty more years of experimentation with non-violence, he counselled nonviolent resistance to the Nazis and actually evolved a plan for nonviolent opposition to the Japanese should they invade and occupy India.

In 1958 the Negroes of Montgomery, Alabama, catapulted nonviolence into the limelight in the United States, not out of conversion to pacifism or love for their oppressors, but because they had reached a point where they could no longer tolerate certain racial injustices. Martin Luther King, who later be-came a pacifist, employed an armed defense guard to protect his home and family during one stage of the Montgomery conflict. In 1963, one of the leaders of the mass demonstrations in Birmingham said to me: "You might as well say that we never heard of Gandhi or nonviolence, but we were determined to get our freedom, and in the course of struggling for it we came upon nonviolence like gold in the ground."

There is not much point in preaching the virtues of nonviolence to a Negro in Harlem or Mississippi except as a method for winning his freedom. For one thing, the built-in institutional violence imposed on him every day of his life looms too large. He can rightly say that he wants no part of a nonviolence that condemns his spasmodic rock-throwing or desperate and often knowingly unrealistic talk of armed self-defense, but mounts no alternative campaign. It is all too easy for those with jobs, adequate educational opportunities, and decent housing to insist that Negroes remain nonviolent—to rally to the defense of "law and order." "Law and order is the Negro's best friend," Mayor Robert Wagner announced in the midst of the 1964 riots in Harlem. But nonviolence and a repressive law and order have nothing in common. The most destructive violence in Harlem is not the bottle-throwing, looting, or muggings of frustrated and demoralized Negroes. Nor is it the frequent shootings of juvenile delinquents and suspected criminals by white policemen, who often reflect both the racial prejudices of society and the personal propensity to violence that led them to choose a job whose tools are the club and the revolver. The basic violence in Harlem is the vast, impersonal violation of bodies and souls by an unemployment rate four times that of white New Yorkers, a median family income between half and two thirds that of white families, an infant mortality rate of 45.3 per thousand compared to 26.3 for New York as a whole, and inhuman crowding into subhuman housing. (It has been estimated that if the entire population of the United States were forced to live in equally congested conditions, it would fit into three of New York City's five boroughs.) Many white Americans are thrilled by the emotional catharsis of a law-abiding March on Washington (or even a fling at civil disobedience), in which they work off their guilt feelings, conscious and unconscious, by "identifying" for a day with the black victims of society. But when the project is over the whites do not return home anxious to know whether any of their children have been bitten by a rat, shot by a cop, or victimized by a pimp or dope peddler.

Commitment to nonviolence must not be based on patient acquiescence in intolerable conditions. Rather, it stems from a deeper knowledge of the self-defeating, self-corrupting effect of lapses into violence. On the one hand, Gandhi did not ally himself with those who profit from injustice and conveniently condemn others who violently fight oppression. On the other hand, he temporarily suspended several of his own nonviolent campaigns because some of his followers had succumbed to the temptations of violent reprisal. In perfecting methods of nonviolence, he gradually crystallized certain attitudes toward the nature of man (even oppressive, exploitative, foreign-invader man), which he formulated in the terminology of his native religion and which he considered indispensable for true nonviolence. Just as his basic insights have been translated by religious Western pacifists (including Martin Luther King) from their original language to that of Christianity, so they can be clothed without loss in the secular humanist terminology which is more natural to large numbers of Northern Negroes and white civil rights activists.

The key attitudes stem from a feeling for the solidarity of all human beings, even those who find themselves in deep conflict. George Meredith once said that a truly cultivated man is one who realizes that the things which seem to separate him from his fellows are as nothing compared with those which unite him with all humanity. Nonviolence may start, as it did with the young Gandhi and has with many an American Negro, as a technique for wresting gains from an unloved and unlovely oppressor. But somewhere along the line, if a nonviolent movement is to cope with deep-seated fears and privileges, its strategy must flow from a sense of the underlying unity of all human beings. So must the crucial, semi-spontaneous, inventive actions that emerge (for good or ill) in the midst of crisis.

This does not mean that Negroes, for example, must "love" in a sentimental or emotional way those who are imprisoning, shooting, beating, or impoverishing them. Nor need they feel personal affection for complacent white liberals. But it is not enough to abandon the use of fists, clubs, Molotov cocktails, and guns. Real nonviolence requires an awareness that white oppressors and black victims are mutually entrapped in a set of relationships that violate the submerged better instincts of everyone. A way has to be found to release the trap and free both sets of victims. Appeals to reason or decency have little effect (except in isolated instances) unless they are accompanied by tangible pressures—on the pocketbook, for example—or the inconveniences associated with sit-ins, move-ins, strikes, boycotts or nonviolent obstructionism. But for any lasting gain to take place the struggle must appeal to the whole man, including his encrusted sense of decency and solidarity, his yearnings to recapture the lost innocence when human beings were persons to be loved, not objects to rule, obey, or exploit.

This reaching out to the oppressor has nothing to do with tokenism, which tends to creep into any movement, including a nonviolent one. In fact, tokenism is a double violation of the attitude of solidarity, because it permits the oppressor to make, and the oppressed to accept, a gesture which leaves intact the institutional barriers that separate them. One can gain a token victory or make a political deal without needing to have any invigorating personal contact with the "enemy," certainly without bothering to imagine oneself in his place so as to understand his needs, fears and aspirations. But the more revolutionary a movement's demands, the more imperative it is to understand what is necessary for the legitimate fulfillment of the persons who make up the opposition.

"We're going to win our freedom," a Negro leader said at a mass meeting in Birmingham last year, "and as we do it we're going to set our white brothers free." A short while later, when the Negroes faced a barricade of police dogs, clubs and fire hoses, they "became spiritually intoxicated," as another leader described it. "This was sensed by the police and firemen and it began to have an effect on them . . . I don't know what happened to me. I got up from my knees and said to the cops: 'We're not turning back. We haven't done anything wrong. All we want is our freedom. How do you feel doing these things?' " The Negroes started advancing and Bull Connor shouted: "Turn on the water!" But the firemen did not respond. Again he gave the order and nothing happened. Some observers claim they saw firemen crying. Whatever happened, the Negroes went through the lines. The next day, Bull Connor was reported by the press to have said: "I didn't want to mess their Sunday clothes, all those people from church." Until now this mood of outgoing empathetic nonviolence has been rarely achieved in this country. It was only part of the story in Birmingham, where in the end a more cautious tokenism gripped the top leaders. But it is the clue to the potential power of nonviolence.

Vinoba Bhave indicates something of the same sort on the level of international conflict when he says: "Russia says America has dangerous ideas so she has to increase her armaments. America says exactly the same thing about Russia. . . . The image in the mirror is your own image; the sword in its hand is your own sword. And when we grasp our own sword in fear of what we see, the image in the mirror does the same. What we see in front of us is nothing but a reflection of ourselves. If India could find courage to reduce her army to the minimum, it would demonstrate to the world her moral strength. But we are cowards and cowards have no imagination."

II

The potential uses of nonviolent power are tremendous and as yet virtually unrealized. But it is important to understand that nonviolence can never be "developed" in such a way as to carry out some of the tasks assigned to it by its more naive converts—any more than God (or the greatest scientist) could draw a square circle. It would be impossible, for instance, to defend the United States of America, as we know it, nonviolently. This is not because of any inherent defect in the nonviolent method but because of a very important strength: nonviolence cannot be used successfully to protect special privileges that have been won by violence. The British could not have continued to rule India by taking a leaf out of Gandhi's book and becoming "nonviolent." Nor would the United States be able to maintain its dominant position in Latin America if it got rid of its armies, navies, "special forces," C.I.A.-guerrillas, etc. Does anyone think that a majority of the natives work for a few cents a day, live in rural or urban slums, and allow forty-four per cent of their children to die before the age of five because they love us? Or that they are content to have American business drain away five hundred million dollars a year in interest and dividends, on the theory that the shareholders of United Fruit Company or the Chase Manhattan Bank are more needy or deserving than themselves?

It follows that advocates of nonviolence are overly optimistic when they argue from the unthinkability of nuclear war and the partially proven power of nonviolence (in India and the civil rights struggle) to the position that simple common sense will lead the United States (the richest, most powerful nation in the world, on whose business investments and armed forces the sun never sets) to substitute nonviolent for violent national defense. In recent years a number of well-intentioned peace groups have tried to convince the government and members of the power elite that the Pentagon should sponsor studies with this end in view. But nonviolent defense requires not only willingness to risk one's life (as any good soldier, rich or poor, will do). It requires renunciation of all claims to special privileges and power at the expense of other people. In our society most people find it more difficult to face economic loss while alive than death itself. Surrender of special privilege is certainly foreign to the psychology of those who supply, command, and rely on the military. Nonviolence is supremely the weapon of the dispossessed, the underprivileged, and the egalitarian, not of those who still addicted to private profit, commercial values, and great wealth.

Nonviolence simply cannot defend property rights over human rights. The primacy of human rights would have to be established within the United States and in all of its dealings with other peoples before nonviolence could defend this country successfully. Nonviolence could defend what is worth defending in the United States, but a badly needed social revolution would have to take place in the process. Guerrilla warfare cannot be carried on successfully without the active support and cooperation of the surrounding population, which must identify justice (or at least its own welfare) with the triumph of the guerrillas. Nonviolence must rely even more more heavily than guerrilla warfare on the justice of its cause. It has no chance of succeeding unless it can win supporters from previously hostile or neutral sections of the populace. It must do this by the fairness of its goals. Its objectives and methods are intimately interrelated and must be equally nonviolent.

The followers of Gandhi were imprisoned, beaten, and, on more than one occasion, shot by the British during the Indian independence campaign. Today, some Americans consider the death of a nonviolent campaigner as conclusive evidence that "nonviolence won't work" and call for substitution of a violent campaign—in which people will also be killed and the original aims tend to be lost in an orgy of violence. But instead of allowing the British in effect to arm them, thereby giving the British the choice of weapons, the Gandhians kept right on fighting nonviolently and in the end succeeded in "disarming" the British. A number of times the first row of advancing Indians was shot, but a second and a third row kept on moving forward until the British soldiers became psychologically incapable of killing any more, even risking death at the hands of their superiors by disobeying orders to keep on firing. Eventually it became politically impossible for the commanders and the Prime Ministers to issue such orders. Need I add that if the Indians had been shot while trying to invade England and carry off its wealth, it would not have mattered how courageously nonviolent they had been; they could not have aroused this response.

If a Medgar Evers or a Goodman, Schwerner, or Chaney is killed fighting for a cause that is considered unjust, he is quickly dismissed as a fanatic. Indeed, at this stage of the struggle that is exactly what many white Southerners have done. But if the nonviolent warriors freely risk death in devotion to a cause that people recognize, even against their wills, as legitimate, the act has a tremendous effect. Willingness to sacrifice by undergoing imprisonment, physical punishment or, if need be, death itself, without retaliation, will not always dislodge deeply engrained prejudice or fear, but its general effect is always to work in that direction. By contrast, infliction of such penalties at best intimidates the opposition and at worst strengthens resistance, but in any case does not encourage psychological openness to a creative resolution of the underlying conflict of views or values.

Perhaps we can paraphrase Von Clausewitz's well-known observation that war is but the continuation of the politics of peace by other means, and say that the social attitudes of nonviolent defense must be a continuation of the social attitudes of the society it is defending. A little thought should convince us of the impossibility of keeping Negroes and colonial peoples in their present positions of inferiority once privileged white America is unable to rely on overt or covert violence. Secondly, it is ludicrous to expect such persons to join their oppressors in the uncoerced defense of the society that has treated them so poorly. (Even with the power of the draft at its disposal—backed by the threat of imprisonment and ultimately the firing squad—the United States found it necessary to make unprecedented concessions and promises to Negroes during World War II in order to keep up black morale.) Finally, there is the crucial question of how we can expect to treat our enemies nonviolently if we do not treat our friends and allies so.

On the crudest level, as long as we are willing to condemn two out of five children in Latin America to early death, in order to increase our material comforts and prosperity, by what newly found awareness of human brotherhood will we be able to resist the temptation to wipe out two out of five, three out of five, or even five out of five of the children of China in overt warfare if it is dinned into us that this is necessary to preserve our freedom, or the lives of ourselves and our own children? If we cannot respect our neighbors more than to keep large numbers of them penned up in rat-infested slum ghettos, how will we develop the sense of human solidarity with our opponents, without which nonviolence becomes an empty technicality and loses its power to undermine and sap enemy hostility and aggressiveness? How will we reach across the propaganda-induced barriers of hate, fear, and self-righteousness (belief in the superiority of one's country, race or system) to disarm ourselves and our enemies?

FURTHER READINGS

Aronson, Ronald. "The Movement and its Critics." *Studies on the Left,* January/February 1966.
Buckley, Neil. "Participatory Democratic Centralism, or . . ." *The Movement,* May 1968.
Calvert, Greg. "Participatory Democracy, Collective Leadership and Political Responsibility." *New Left Notes,* December 18, 1967.
Flacks, Richard. "Freedom as a Constant Struggle: Some Political Implications of Participatory Democracy." Unpublished mimeograph, 1967.
Haber, Al. "The End of Ideology as Ideology." *Our Generation,* Vol. 4: No. 3.
Oppenheimer, Martin. *The Sociology of Participatory Democracy.* Revised from a paper read at Pennsylvania Sociological Society, October 29, 1965.
Radosh, Ronald. "American Radicalism: Liberal or Socialist?" *Monthly Review,* February 10, 1963.

Three:
The
Radicalization
of the
Movement

8

Antiwar Protest

8.1. *JAMES GILBERT:* **The Teach-in: Protest or Co-optation?**

[One of the centers of action in the mass protest movement against the war which developed after the beginning of the bombardments of North Vietnam in February 1965, was the universities, where the teach-ins were born and developed. James Gilbert was a graduate student in the department of history at the University of Wisconsin. From *Studies on the Left,* Summer 1965.]

The Johnson Administration's policy in Vietnam and its cavalier dismissal of criticism has generated a strong current of opposition on university campuses throughout the country. A series of "teach-ins" (lectures and discussions by faculty and students) have proven to be valuable vehicles for articulating this growing opposition. Although the national "teach-in" which finally emerged before television and radio on May 15th in Washington earned the praise of respectable elements of the press, the movement as a whole is subversive to the prevailing idea that the student is a second-class citizen and the university his ghetto. It is defiant of the belief that criticism is somehow treasonable, a notion which has buttressed an unreal and often unsuccessful foreign policy. Admittedly, it is difficult to characterize the whole movement, for there is no movement as such, but a conglomeration of undirected and frequently contradictory protests against a specific policy. This fact was painfully apparent in Washington, and perhaps one source of the national "teach-in's" respectability. The "teach-in" at the University of Wisconsin and the events which followed it (particularly the rough treatment given to a State Department "truth squad") indicate that more is at stake than a gentlemanly disagreement among experts about the strategy of foreign policy. A comparison of the two "teach-ins" at Washington and Wisconsin indicates the diversity within the movement and the different levels of protest against post-war foreign policy.

The idea of the "teach-in" emerged from the efforts at the University of Michigan to hold a meeting to protest the Vietnam war. State officials refused to allow the use of classrooms during regular hours, but the students refused to be diverted and held a meeting, after hours, on March 24. Other universities responded quickly with a rapid succession of "teach-ins" across the country, uncovering a strong but undirected undercurrent of criticism among students and faculty.

The "teach-in" at the University of Wisconsin took on its particular tone for a number of reasons. First the long-term liberal tradition in the administration, faculty, and student body, has enabled the left to initiate and set the tone for campus political discussions. Unlike events at Berkeley which were caused in part by the repressive nature of that school's administration, what happened at Wisconsin was influenced by the fact that university officials supported the right of the group to hold a "teach-in" and cooperated as much as they would with any campus group. This stand brought sharp criticism from some within the university (i.e., those who supported United States policy) and from conservatives in the state. This point leads to the second background factor, the activity of the right wing, led by a reactionary Madison radio commentator and allied to elements within the business community and the state legislature. This attack did not begin with the "teach-in" but rather with the Goldwater campaign and an attempt to smear opponents of the conservative messiah. The DuBois Club on campus and the student newspaper were the major targets of the campaign which culminated in an unsuccessful drive to pass legislation banning Communist speakers from campus. The impact of these activities in the short run was to give criticism of the "teach-ins" reactionary overtones which led many to dismiss all supporters of government policy as right-wingers and made discussion between people who genuinely disagreed over policy difficult.

A third, and perhaps the most important element was the enthusiasm with which a significant part of the faculty greeted the opportunity to speak out on Vietnam and related subjects, and the degree to which an ongoing partnership between faculty and students was established in the joint "Faculty-Student Committee to End the War in Viet Nam." Underlying this seems to be an uneasy but persistent soul-searching about the meaning of education and the role of the university, thoughts triggered by the rise of the mass university and the race to publish. Often this introspection has included a flat rejection of the Cold War mentality which has garroted criticism and meaningful discussion for so long. Instrumental to the rise of this attitude has been the struggle against poverty and segregation which has ruffled the placid surface of American society and challenged the passive ideology which supports it. It would not be inaccurate to say that without the sit-ins, the marches, and the struggle for Negro rights, the "teach-in" would not have occurred.

The Wisconsin "teach-in" was organized by separate groups of faculty and students under the aegis of a joint committee. The principal aim was to merge education with protest, to challenge the detachment of the university from the political community and assert the elementary connection between thought and action. Yet it is this latter notion which raised the greatest furor from critics. Charges of emotionalism and lack of objectivity typified the anti-intellectual snipping of the opposition. To protest and force the university community's attention on Vietnam, the committee organized rallies, pickets, leaflet distribution, newspaper and radio coverage. Everything done led up to the "teach-in."

This included lectures and discussions by 26 professors—few of them experts on South East Asia, a fact that outraged the self-appointed custodians of truth in the political science department. Nor were the lectures all devoted to Vietnam; in fact, the most important was probably a speech on the meaning of commitment by Germaine Brée, formerly an associate of Albert Camus and a member of the French Resistance during World War II. The most interesting fact is that five of the lecturers spoke explicitly to the problem of the function of the university in society, and rejected the concept that students and faculty should accept the emasculated role of the non-political intellectual which society has designated for them. Five others helped dissect the intellectual premises behind foreign policy, the style of thinking which has dominated foreign policy since the end of World War II. Only four or five lectures were directly concerned with Vietnam as such (which critics were delighted to point to). But this, it seems to me, hints at the central meaning of the "teach-ins"; that the Vietnam war has implications for every aspect of life; that it actually means something to the university itself; and that ultimately it forces the question of one's role as a student, professor, and citizen. In other words, it rightly raised an alternative to the whole numbing range of presuppositions which have supported the Cold War and separated the intellectual from the implications of his own thought. Vietnam was for some, then, a symbol for the deeper ills of American society. The "teach-in" was not so much radical in its attack on Vietnam policy, as it was in an educational sense. And as such, it cut a much deeper mark in campus politics than any other activity perhaps since the 1930's.

Was this a revolution in educational procedures? The "teach-in," in its format, was essentially the same as the classroom; the professor delivered a lecture, students listened, and then, time permitting, asked questions. Yet the emotional content was not at all like that of a traditional lecture. Speakers were applauded during their presentation—and several were given standing ovations. This degree of excitement is simply never generated by the ordinary educational experience.

There was a strong feeling, especially among faculty members, that something strikingly important had occurred. In the first place there was provided a forum for the professors from different specialities to exchange ideas—a very rare occurrence today in the universities which have compartmentalized subjects and invented jargon known to few outside the various departments.

Second, was the belief that the faculty were not speaking as experts, but primarily as members of a university community, as individuals who felt that the university is more than the sum of its courses and the student more than the tally of his grade credits. There was some self-consciousness by those who were not experts and perhaps some doubts. And there is always the possibility that audiences who attended the "teach-ins" were attracted because they felt that the experts in history, philosophy, sociology, and the sciences would point some way out of the Vietnam mess. Finally, the protest and the thought which it engendered cannot help but feed back into the disciplines of the professors who engaged in the "teach-in." One's assessment of American society— whether from the viewpoint of foreign policy, ethics, intellectual history, or sociology—can never be quite the same. Thus the "teach-in" was an ambiguous institution; it had many of the older aspects of education, the lecture form, the professor-student relation, but its spirit was new and challenging. This clash between form and spirit indicates the need to develop new ideas in education—and in political protest.

The response of the university was surprisingly enthusiastic; approximately 5,000 students and faculty members attended the different lectures and symposiums. A sense of the general attitude of the audience was revealed when, at the final session, one of the professors was asked if he had accepted money from Communist sources in return for his remarks. His answer received a standing ovation; this, in itself, was an affirmation that McCarthyism as a criticism of independent thought was totally irrelevant to the audience.

A different sort of response was the organization of a "Committee to Support the People of South Viet Nam," a group tethered to the political science department and straddling the political right and center. The Committee, rejecting "undignified" protests such as placard-carrying wrote a catch-all petition and was able to send 6,000 signatures to Washington.

A second part of the "teach-in" activities was more concerned with direct action. This culminated in a march and an outdoor rally addressed by faculty members and Marcus Raskin, formerly a member of the National Security Council (under Kennedy) and the editor of the *Liberal Papers*. Rallies about one issue or another are a frequent occurrence on campus, although this one was much larger than most. The significance lies, however, in joining the "teach-in," the academic form of the protest, to a form of political action.

Newspaper, radio, and television coverage of the events was thorough and often favorable in Wisconsin. National CBS-TV covered the meetings and took over 5,000 feet of films, none of which was ever broadcast. The "teach-in" itself got almost no notice nationally despite the fact that the story was carried by wire services. This news black-out is not as important by itself as the contrast it provides with the glaring lights turned on the university by television, radio, and such magazines as *Time,* after a visit to the campus of three Johnson Administration officials. Headed by State Department expert Thomas Conlon, the group also included Earl Young, an AID representative who had served in Vietnam, and an army adviser who looked remarkably like Buck Turgidson in *Dr. Strangelove* (and who appropriately commented that the United States faced the "people problem" in South Vietnam). The trio, invited by the pro-Johnson campus committee, was riding the circuit of college campuses where hostility to Vietnam policy had flared up. Their mission was to measure the depths of political heresy and shore up the faithful with readings from Administration testament. This purpose was painfully obvious at an afternoon reception for the three when the State Department's Conlon retorted to the question, "What are the political affiliations of the Viet Cong?" with "The head of the Viet Cong is a Leftist . . . I mean a Crypto-Communist." Most of what followed was on the same level.

It was the evening session, however, which finally brought the University national attention. To protest the war in Vietnam, about 300 supporters of the "Committee to End the War" attended the meeting, wearing black-armbands and stood along the sides of the hall. This left about 50 empty seats since the pro-Johnson people probably numbered only 350. In an effort to finesse the demonstrators and so make it appear to the television cameras present that no one opposed government policy, the chairman of the meeting (and a member of the ubiquitous political science department) ordered the demonstrators to be seated. He was very nearly greeted with a riot. When some of the demonstrators did sit down, the three speakers answered questions from the audience. The press almost unanimously described what happened next as a rude interruption of the speakers with boos and heckling. This did, of course, happen, although not in exactly the above fashion, but only after repeated lies and evasions by the Administration trio. Besides illustrating a case of news distortion, the national attention directed at Wisconsin because of the State Department visit did a number of things. First, it provided ammunition for the right wing which now screamed that the left was destroying academic freedom on the campus. This forced the university again to affirm its support for Student political activities. Further, the visit demonstrated clearly the attitude of Washington; that it was not interested in listening to its critics, but merely in answering them. Finally, it forced faculty and student supporters of the "Committee to End the War in Viet Nam" to rethink their positions on the nature of protest. That a great number of them defended the student demonstrators, indicates a surprisingly firm commitment to political action. It is in the light of these experiences that the ten faculty and student representatives of the "Committee" travelled to Washington to attend the national "teach-in."

It should not be denied that the spectacle of a professor taking a stand on a political issue is encouraging. But what happened in Washington is deceptive, both for the participants who optimistically believed that a dialogue was somehow possible, and for the Administration, which may be led to dismiss future criticism as academic hair-splitting—which, indeed, it seemed to be. But the anti-Vietnam war movement, diverse as it is, is neither a dialogue nor a discussion; it is fundamentally a protest.

One of the basic causes for the weakness of the national "teach-in" was the absence of students in any leadership capacity. It is unreal to imagine that somehow a group of unaffiliated intellectuals can convince a government of the corruption of its foreign policy. If a professor's ideas have any political viability, this rests ultimately upon his student constituency. Only the University of Wisconsin included students on its official delegation to Washington. The point is not that Wisconsin is so advanced in its program of political protest, but that the search for and discovery of experts on South East Asia necessitated making student participation minimal. The context of the debate was defined by the Administration. Yet the March on Washington sponsored by SDS indicates that a great many students do not accept that context. The price of respectability was exacted in the content of the speeches and in the balanced format of the debate. By confusing what occurred at the national "teach-in" with true protest, some interpreters have indicated how far we must yet travel to be rid of the intellectual baggage of the 1950's, and particularly of the idea that to raise a question is to commit an act of political opposition.

The national and local "teach-ins" provide a number of important lessons. What everyone should have known since the State Department "truth squad" made no effort to hide its purpose, and Rusk and Bundy had already scolded the academic community, was that the Administration had no intention of listening to its critics. It is sometimes forgotten that a good deal of critical writing is easily available to the Administration. If genuine debate was impossible, then no purpose was served by balancing the debate other than to cloud the issues. There are now two forms of "teach-ins," one respectable and modeled after the Washington debate, the other a forum for protest. One embraces the concept that we must suspend judgment (perhaps forever) while the experts bicker, the other assumes that faculty and students have the right to commit themselves and act. The existence of the two models has been harmful, for it enabled Professor Scalapino, for example, to denounce the Berkeley "teach-in" (held after the Washington debate) as one-sided and unfair because it was not a balanced program. With the movement split, the Administration will be able to label real protests as extremist and undemocratic. Already the Senate Internal Security Subcommittee has taken testimony from the right-wing Madison commentator in an effort to smear a red hue on the Wisconsin protest.

An assessment of the meaning of the "teach-in" may be suggested by returning to the locus of the movement itself, the campus. Two questions are relevant: Is a permanent change of mind occurring on the campuses? and What are the causes for the increase in radical activity? The answer to both lies, in part, in the validity of what sociologists and psychologists have called alienation. This overworked and overdefined term perhaps at best means a rejection of the conventional role of students and faculty and a rejection of the premises which society uses to define this role. The term designates, in other words, a politically neutral state, but one which, ironically, has radical overtones since that role which "alienated" students and faculty reject for themselves is one of political neutrality and intellectual quiescence. But alienation tells us nothing of the precise content of political commitment. Here, factors such as the intense struggle for Negro rights and the campaign against poverty are crucial, for they have forced the student to face up to some very ugly facts of American society.

There has also been a rapid degeneration of the liberal rhetoric under the Johnson Administration. The President, after all, when he appears on radio and television, speaks with the accent of Bull Conner and Governor Wallace. Moreover, students today in no way relate to the 1930's, and few even to the intensive period of the Cold War with the Soviet Union. Yet these are the sources for liberal rhetoric. The "humming wires of the REA" and the memories of the Berlin Blockade simply are not relevant to this generation of students. The energy generated by the New Deal and the Cold War does not spark the minds of students today. Finally, there are the facts of the case itself—the brutality of the war and the arrogance which defends it.

Has there been created, then, a new radical constituency? It is too early to answer definitively, although it is certain that the function of the university is due for a good amount of questioning, and students, particularly, will not accept old roles and definitions. What would happen if the liberal rhetoric were beefed up by new recruits cannot be predicted. It appears, however, that there is the beginning of a radical movement on the campuses today. How deep it is will be fathomed by the future. The future of the "teach-in" as an institution is also uncertain. As it stands now it is seriously compromised by the national example. Moreover its effectiveness may be destroyed by repetition. Perhaps one indication of the direction of future protests is the projected creation at Wisconsin of a "freedom university" designated to make some aspects of the "teach-in" a permanent feature of the campus. If revolutionary ideas in education are joined with and help sustain student movements, then the "teach-in" is an important first step toward a genuine radicalism on the campus.

8.2.   *PAUL POTTER:* **The Incredible War**

[The Washington march of April 17, 1965, organized by SDS, was the first in a long series of mass demonstrations against the war. Following the "nonexclusionist" line, SDS invited organizations and individuals from the entire range of the left, causing the withdrawal of those spokesmen of the "Democratic left" who did not appreciate the participation of anti-imperialist groups which sided with the Vietcong, such as the May Second Movement. Paul Potter was president of SDS at that time. The following are excerpts taken from the text of his speech, published in the *National Guardian* of April 29, 1965.]

The incredible war in Vietnam has provided the razor, the terrifying sharp cutting edge that has finally severed the last vestiges of illusion that morality and democracy are the guiding principles of American foreign policy. The saccharine, self-righteous moralism that promises the Vietnamese a billion dollars of economic aid at the very moment we are delivering billions for economic and social destruction and political repression is rapidly losing what power it might ever have had to reassure us about the decency of our foreign policy. The further we explore the reality of what this country is doing and planning in Vietnam the more we are driven toward the conclusion of Senator Morse that the U.S. may well be the greatest threat to peace in the world today. . . .

The President says that we are defending freedom in Vietnam. Whose freedom? Not the freedom of the Vietnamese. The first act of the first dictator (Diem) the U.S. installed in Vietnam was to systematically begin the persecution of all political opposition, non-Communist as well as Communist. . . .

The pattern of repression and destruction that we have developed and justified in the war is so thorough that it can only be called "cultural genocide." I am not simply talking about napalm or gas or crop destruction or torture hurled indiscriminantly on women and children, insurgent and neutral, upon the first suspicion of rebel activity. That in itself is horrendous and incredible beyond belief. But it is only part of a large pattern of destruction to the very fabric of the country. We have uprooted the people from the land and imprisoned them in concentration camps called "sunrise villages." Through conscription and direct political intervention and control we have broken or destroyed local customs and traditions, trampled upon those things of value which give dignity and purpose to life. . . .

Not even the President can say that this is war to defend the freedom of the Vietnamese people. Perhaps what the President means when he speaks of freedom is the freedom of the Americans.

What in fact has the war done for freedom in America? It has led to even more vigorous governmental efforts to control information, manipulate the press and pressure and persuade the public through distorted or downright dishonest documents such as the White Paper on Vietnam. . . .

In many ways this is an unusual march, because the large majority of the people here are not involved in a peace movement as their primary basis of concern. What is exciting about the participants in this march is that so many of us view ourselves consciously as participants as well in a movement to build a more decent society. There are students here who have been involved in protest over the quality and kind of education they are receiving in growingly bureaucratized, depersonalized institutions called universities; there are Negroes from Mississippi and Alabama who are struggling against the tyranny and repression of those states; there are poor people here—Negro and white— from Northern urban areas who are attempting to build movements that abolish poverty and secure democracy; there are faculty who are beginning to question the relevance of their institutions to the critical problems facing the society. . . .

The President mocks freedom if he insists that the war in Vietnam is a defense of American freedom. Perhaps the only freedom that this war protects is the freedom of the warhawks in the Pentagon and the State Department to "experiment" with "counter-insurgency" and guerrilla warfare in Vietnam. Vietnam, we may say, is a "laboratory" run by a new breed of gamesmen who approach war as a kind of rational exercise in international power politics. . . .

Thus far the war in Vietnam has only dramatized the demand of ordinary people to have some opportunity to make their own lives, and of their unwillingness, even under incredible odds, to give up the struggle against external domination. We are told however that that struggle can be legitimately suppressed since it might lead to the development of a Communist system—and before that menace, all criticism is supposed to melt.

This is a critical point and there are several things that must be said here— not by way of celebration, but because I think they are the truth. First, if this country were serious about giving the people of Vietnam some alternative to a Communist social revolution, that opportunity was sacrificed in 1954 when we helped to install Diem and his repression of non-Communist movements. There is no indication that we were serious about that goal—that we were ever willing to contemplate the risks of allowing the Vietnamese to choose their own destinies. Second, those people who insist now that Vietnam can be neutralized are for the most part looking for a sugar coating to cover the bitter pill. We must accept the consequences that calling for an end of the war in Vietnam is in fact allowing for the likelihood that a Vietnam without war will be a self-styled Communist Vietnam. Third, this country must come to understand that the creation of a Communist country in the world today is not an ultimate defeat. If people are given the opportunity to choose their own lives it is likely that some of them will choose what we have called "Communist systems." . . . And yet the war that we are creating and escalating in Southeast Asia is rapidly eroding the base of independence of North Vietnam as it is forced to turn to China and the Soviet union.

But the war goes on; the freedom to conduct that war depends on the dehumanization not only of Vietnamese people but of Americans as well; it depends on the construction of a system of premises and thinking that insulates the President and his advisers thoroughly and completely from the human consequences of the decisions they make. I do not believe that the President or Mr. Rusk or Mr. McNamara or even McGeorge Bundy are particularly evil men. If asked to throw napalm on the back of a 10-year-old child they would shrink in horror—but their decisions have led to mutilation and death of thousands and thousands of people.

What kind of system is it that allows "good" men to make those kinds of decisions? What kind of system is it that justifies the U.S. or any country seizing the destinies of the Vietnamese people and using them callously for our own purpose? What kind of system is it that disenfranchises people in the South, leaves millions upon millions of people throughout the country impoverished and excluded from the mainstream and promise of American society, that creates faceless and terrible bureaucracies and makes those the place where people spend their lives and do their work, that consistently puts material values before human values—and still persists in calling itself free and still persists in finding itself fit to police the world? . . .

We must name that system. We must name it, describe it, analyze it, understand it and change it. For it is only when that system is changed and brought under control that there can be any hope for stopping the forces that create a war in Vietnam today or a murder in the South tomorrow. . . .

If the people of this country are to end the war in Vietnam, and to change the institutions which create it, then, the people of this country must create a massive social movement—and if that can be built around the issue of Vietnam, then that is what we must do. . . .

But that means that we build a movement that works not simply in Washington but in communities and with the problems that face people throughout the society. That means that we build a movement that understands Vietnam, in all its horror, as but a symptom of a deeper malaise, that we build a movement that makes possible the implementation of the values that would have prevented Vietnam, a movement based on the integrity of man and a belief in man's capacity to determine his own life; a movement that does not exclude people because they are too poor or have been held down; a movement that has the capacity to tolerate all of the formulations of society that men may choose to strive for; a movenment that will build on the new and creative forms of protest that are beginning to emerge, such as the teach-in, and extend their efforts and intensify them; a movement that will not tolerate the escalation or prolongation of this war but will, if necessary, respond to the Administration war effort with massive civil disobedience all over the country that will wrench the country into a confrontation with the issues of the war; a movement that must of necessity reach out to all those people in Vietnam or elsewhere who are struggling to find decency and control for their lives.

For in a strange way the people of Vietnam and the people on this demonstration are united in much more than a common concern that the war be ended. In both countries there are people struggling to build a movement that has the power to change their condition. The system that frustrates these movements is the same. All our lives, our destinies, our very hopes to live depend on our ability to overcome that system. . . .

8.3.   **Vietnam Day Committee: Attention
                                         All Military Personnel**

[The leaflet reprinted here was originally printed by the Berkeley Vietnam Day Committee in October, 1965; it was distributed in induction centers and on American military bases and sent to soldiers in Vietnam. Its circulation among military personnel provoked a denunciation by civil and military authorities and threats of incrimination for treason.]

You may soon be sent to Vietnam. You have heard about the war in the news; your officers will give you pep talks about it. But you probably feel as confused and uncertain as most Americans do. Many people will tell you to just follow orders and leave the thinking to others. But you have the right to know as much about this war as anyone. After all, it's you—not your congressman—who might get killed.

We are supposed to be fighting to protect democracy in Vietnam, and yet our own government admits that South Vietnam is run by a dictatorship. General Ky, the latest military dictator, is as bad as they come. In a recent interview he said: "People ask me who my heroes are. I have only one—Hitler. I admire Hitler because he pulled his country together when it was in a terrible state." (*London Sunday Mirror,* July 4, 1965).

General Ky doesn't mean much to us; we're not even sure how to pronounce his name, but the South Vietnamese have lived under men like him for years. As far as the Vietnamese are concerned, we are fighting on the side of Hitlerism; and they hope we lose.

U.S. military spokesmen have often said that their greatest problem is finding the enemy. The enemy, they say, is everywhere. The old woman feeding her chicken may have a stock of hand grenades in her hut. The little boy who trails after the American soldiers during the day slips out to give information to the guerrillas at night. The washerwoman at the American air base brings a bomb to work one day. It is impossible, say the military, to tell which are the Viet Cong and which are the civilians.

And so, because the whole Vietnamese people seem to be the enemy, the military is taking no chances. They use tear gas—a weapon designed for use against civilians. They order American troops to fire at women and children—because women and children, after all, are firing at American troops. American fighter planes destroy civilian villages with napalm; American B-52's are flattening whole regions. That is why the war in Vietnam is so often called a "dirty war."

When the South Vietnamese people see you in your foreign uniform, they will think of you as *their* enemy. You are the ones bombing their towns. They don't know whether you're a draftee or a volunteer, whether you're for the war or against it; but they're not taking any chances either.

The Vietnamese would like to *vote* the foreigners out of their country, but they have been denied the chance. According to the Geneva Agreement of 1954, there were supposed to be elections throughout Vietnam in 1956. But the U.S. government was certain that our man in Vietnam, Premier Diem, would lose. So we decided not to allow any election until we were sure we could win. Diem set up a political police force and put all political opposition—Communist and anti-Communist—in jail. By 1959, it was clear there weren't going to be any elections, and the guerrillas known as the Viet Cong began to fight back. By 1963 our government was fed up with Diem, but still wasn't willing to risk elections. Our CIA helped a group of Vietnamese generals to overthrow Diem and kill him. Since then there have been a series of "better" military dictators. General Ky—the man who admires Hitler—is the latest one.

Your job as a soldier is supposed to be "to win the people of South

Vietnam." Win them to what—democracy? No, we keep military dictators in power. What then? The American way of life? But why should they care any more about our way of life than we care about theirs? We can't speak their language or even pronounce their names. We don't know anything about their religion or even what it is. We never even heard of Vietnam until Washington decided to run it.

We are supposed to be fighting "to save the Vietnamese people from Communism." Certainly Communist influence is very strong in the National Liberation Front, the rebel government. Yet most of the people support the NLF. Why? Many of the same people who now lead the NLF led the Vietnamese independence movement against the Japanese during World War II, and then went on to fight against French colonial rule. Most Vietnamese think of the NLF leaders as their country's outstanding patriots. In fact, many anti-Communists have joined the guerrilla forces in the belief that the most important thing is to get rid of foreign domination and military dictators. On the other hand, very few Vietnamese support the official government of General Ky. His army has low morale and a high desertion rate.

The newspapers and television have told us again and again what a tough fighter the Vietnamese guerrilla is. Short of ammunition and without any air cover, he can beat forces that outnumber him five or ten to one. Why do they have such high morale? They are not draftees; no draftees ever fight like that. They are not high-paid, professional soldiers. Most of them are peasants who work their fields; they can't even spare the ammunition for target practice.

Their secret is that they know why they are fighting. They didn't hear about Vietnam in the newspapers; they've lived there all their lives. While we were in high school, they were living under the Diem regime and hating it. Now American planes are bombing their towns and strafing their fields; American troops have occupied their country; and if they complain out loud, an American-supported dictator sentences them to jail or the firing squad. Is it any wonder that they fight so fiercely?

The war in Vietnam is not being fought according to the rules. Prisoners are tortured. Our planes drop incendiary bombs on civilian villages. Our soldiers shoot at women and children. Your officers will tell you that it is all necessary, that we couldn't win the war any other way. *And they are right.* Americans are not more cruel than any other people; American soldiers don't enjoy this kind of war. But if you are going to wage war against an entire people, you have to become cruel.

The ordinary German soldier in occupied Europe wasn't especially cruel, either. But as the resistance movements grew, he *became* cruel. He shot at women and children because they were shooting at him; he never asked himself *why* they were shooting at him. When a certain town became a center of resistance activity, he followed his orders and destroyed the whole town. He knew that SS men were torturing captured resistance fighters, but it wasn't his business to interfere.

As a soldier you have been trained to obey orders, but as a human being you must take responsibility for your own acts. International and American law recognize that an individual soldier, even if acting under orders, must bear final legal and moral responsibility for what he does. This principle became a part of law after World War II, when the Allied nations, meeting in London, decided that German war criminals must be punished even if they committed war crimes under orders. This principle was the basis of the Nuremburg trials. We believe that the entire war in Vietnam is criminal and immoral.

We believe that the atrocities which are necessary to wage this war against the people of Vietnam are inexcusable.

We hope that you too find yourself, as a human being, unable to tolerate this nightmare war, and we hope that you will oppose it. We don't know what kind of risks we are taking in giving you this leaflet; you won't know what risk you will be taking in opposing the war. A growing number of GIs have already refused to fight in Vietnam and have been court-martialed. They have shown great courage. We believe that they, together with other courageous men who will join them, will have influence far out of proportion to their numbers.

There may be many other things you can do; since you are in the service, you know better than civilians what sorts of opposition are possible. But whatever you do, keep your eyes open. Draw your own conclusions from the things you see, read and hear. At orientation sessions, don't be afraid to ask questions, and if you're not satisfied with the answers, keep asking. Take every chance you get to talk to your fellow soldiers about the war.

You may feel the war is wrong, and still decide not to face a court-martial. You may then find yourself in Vietnam under orders. You might be forced to do some fighting—but don't do any more than you have to. Good luck.

8.4.   **SNCC: Statement on Vietnam War**

> [One of the first public acts of the radicalization of SNCC, before the turning point of Black Power, was taking up a position *vis à vis* the Vietnam war. The following statement was approved at a January 6, 1966, SNCC conference at Atlanta.]

The Student Nonviolent Coordinating Committee assumes its right to dissent with United States foreign policy on any issue, and states its opposition to United States involvement in the war in Vietnam on these grounds:

We believe the United States government has been deceptive in claims of concern for the freedom of the Vietnamese people, just as the government has been deceptive in claiming concern for the freedom of the colored people in such other countries as the Dominican Republic, the Congo, South Africa, Rhodesia and the United States itself.

We of the Student Nonviolent Coordinating Committee have been involved in the black people's struggle for liberation and self-determination in this country for the past five years. Our work, particularly in the South, taught us that the United States government has never guaranteed the freedom of oppressed citizens, and is not yet truly determined to end the rule of terror and oppression within its own borders.

We ourselves have often been victims of violence and confinement executed by U.S. government officials. We recall the numerous persons who have been murdered in the South because of their efforts to secure their civil and human rights, and whose murderers have been allowed to escape penalty for their crimes. The murder of Samuel Younge in Tuskegee, Ala., is no different from the murder of people in Vietnam, for both Younge and the Vietnamese sought and are seeking to secure the rights guaranteed them by law. In each case, the U.S. government bears a great part of the responsibility for these deaths.

Samuel Younge was murdered because U.S. law is not being enforced.

Vietnamese are being murdered because the United States is pursuing an aggressive policy in violation of international law. The United States is no respecter of persons or law when such persons or laws run counter to its needs and desires. We recall the indifference, suspicion and outright hostility with which our reports of violence have been met in the past by government officials.

We know for the most part that elections in this country, in the North as well as the South, are not free. We have seen that the 1965 Voting Rights Act and the 1964 Civil Rights Act have not yet been implemented with full federal power and concern. We question the ability and even the desire of the U.S. government to guarantee free elections abroad. We maintain that our country's cry of "preserve freedom in the world" is a hypocritical mask behind which it squashes liberation movements which are not bound and refuse to be bound by expediency of U.S. Cold War policy.

We are in sympathy with and support the men in this country who are unwilling to respond to the military draft which would compel them to contribute their lives to U.S. aggression in the name of the "freedom" we find so false in this country. We recoil with horror at the inconsistency of this supposedly free society where responsibility to freedom is equated with responsibility to lend oneself to military aggression. We take note of the fact that 16 percent of the draftees from this country are Negro, called on to stifle the liberation of Vietnam, to preserve a "democracy" which does not exist for them at home.

We ask: Where is the draft for the freedom fight in the United States?

We therefore encourage those Americans who prefer to use their energy in building democratic forms within the country. We believe that work in the civil-rights movement and other human relations organizations is a valid alternative to the draft. We urge all Americans to seek this alternative, knowing full well that it may cost them their lives, as painfully as in Vietnam.

8.5.   *A. J. MUSTE:* **The Movement to Stop the War in Vietnam**

> [A. J. Muste can be considered the symbol of the antiwar movement in the United States since the beginning of the century. Until his death in 1967, he was active in a number of organizations (Committee for Non-Violent Action), committees (National Mobilization Committee to End the War in Vietnam) and publications (*Liberation*). The following article appeared in *Liberation* in January 1966.]

As the year 1965 draws to a close the Johnson administration is clearly on the point of a further escalation of the Vietnam war on such proportions that the character of the war itself may change from one which can still be regarded as in some sense limited, to one which approaches global proportions and which may well get out of control. At the same time serious dialogue over the Johnson policy continues in this country, and opposition is, in my opinion, still mounting or at least holding its own. "Patriotic" counter-demonstrations and public opinion polls indicate that there is backing for the President but not anything like enthusiasm for the war. In these circumstances reflection on the war itself and the foreign policy of the United States and on how the opposition can be developed effectively is needed. What follows is a contribution to the discussion of these matters.

They were discussed also in an article which appeared in the November 25, 1965, issue of the *New York Review of Books* entitled "The Vietnam Protest" and was signed by Irving Howe, Michael Harrington, Bayard Rustin, Lewis Coser and Penn Kimble. It was a thoughtful contribution to the discussion, free from invective, and seems a convenient starting point from which to state some of my own views.

The signers of the statement declare their belief "that the present United States policy in Vietnam is morally and politically disastrous." Very welcome, also, in view of the contrary opinion frequently expressed, is their categorical rejection of the argument that recent demonstrations against the war may persuade the Chinese and the Vietnamese Communists to prolong the war because they might be misled into supposing that the American people do not support the government's policy: "It is the kind of demagogic appeal characteristically advanced by governments embarked upon adventures in which they do not have full confidence."

It is when the signers undertake to set forth their own proposal and the arguments in support of it and to criticize aspects of the developing protest movement that questions rise.

For example, a "significant protest movement" such as they propose, which would appeal presumably to a broad public, should "clearly indicate that its purpose is to end a cruel and futile war, not to give explicit or covert political support to the Viet Cong." It is argued that "this is both a tactical necessity and a moral obligation, since any ambiguity on this score makes impossible, as well as undeserved, the support of large numbers of American people."

Similar questions are raised by the argument that an effective protest movement cannot be organized around a full-scale historical and political analysis of the Vietnam situation.

The kind of difficulty with which we are faced, in my opinion, is illustrated by the fact that the signers immediately criticize as "vague and unfocused" the slogan employed in the October 16 New York parade: "Stop the War in Vietnam Now." It provided "no guidelines for action." (Spokesmen for various points of view were represented on the platform on that occasion and organizations were free to distribute leaflets of their own which were quite specific.) The program of a protest movement must, then, after all, be somewhat focused, and it has to take considerable account of the historic background and political context, as indeed the signers do in their opening section. The problem then arises of how the movement is to be focused.

To tackle a delicate question: the purpose of the movement is to end a cruel and futile war, "not to give explicit or covert political support to the Viet Cong." Many Americans will hold that for the United States to declare, as the signers propose, its readiness to negotiate with the National Liberation Front, the political arm of the Viet Cong, does give explicit, *de facto* political support to the Viet Cong. The Saigon regime, which recently has explicitly rejected negotiation with "the enemy," will certainly also regard this as giving the latter political "encouragement" if not support.

Similarly, when it is proposed that assignment of historical responsibility is ruled out, does this mean that the National Liberation Front—North Vietnam, on the one hand, and the United States intervention in Vietnam, on the other hand, are placed *politically* on the same basis? The resort to violence and slaughter on either side, as a pacifist I must and do condemn. On the basis of corruption and ultimately self-defeating character of organized violence, I am prepared to appeal to either side to disarm unilaterally. But to leave out of account the political wickedness and stupidity of United States military intervention in Vietnam and the Dominican Republic, either when campaigning for an end to the war or in connection with negotiations, seems to me wrong and impractical, even "utopian" in its way. It seems to me that socialists or progessives have to take account of the problem of United States interference with popular revolts and cannot deal with the problem of stopping the fighting in abstraction from this factor. If, as is true, this will at first call forth opposition or skepticism on the part of many Americans, we have to face it and in any case will not be able to evade it.

The first proposal made in the *New York Review* article as a basis for common action is that "the United States immediately cease bombing of North Vietnam." Presumably the United States is to take this step unilaterally, and adhere to it whether or not this leads to Hanoi withdrawing troops from South Vietnam. As an unrepentant unilateralist, on political as well as moral grounds, I am of course all for this move. But is it going to be argued, explicity or inferentially, that ceasing to bomb North Vietnam does not seriously affect the military position of the United States? If the projected movement does take this stand, it will have to prove its case to the satisfaction of the military and of informed civilians. I doubt that it can. If it fails, then it will have to decide whether to withdraw that proposal because it does not want to be "responsible" for a military defeat of the United States and because Americans generally will not welcome it; or whether it will argue that taking a risk which, from a military standpoint, is inadmissible is still required on political and moral grounds. In the latter case, the whole question of the role of the United States in Southeast Asia and as a power state in the atomic age has to be faced, including the very crucial one of whether the United States has to give up trying to play a traditional big-power role in this era.

A similar dilemma arises in relation to other proposals in the statement under discussion such as that the United States propose to Hanoi and the Viet Cong a cease-fire and urge them to accept that proposal and declare themselves ready for immediate and unconditional negotiations. Up to the President's Johns Hopkins speech in April, the United States would not negotiate. "Negotiation" in the relations between warring nations is something that is based on an estimation of the power relationships of the moment; each government is ready to negotiate when it deems the situation favorable to itself. The Johnson administration is making a good deal of the (alleged)) fact that it is now ready to negotiate but Hanoi and the Viet Cong stand in the way—"It's up to them now." I am sure that the signers of the present statement do not intend to help the Administration to make capital out of the situation, but they will in that case have to devise ways to guard against the Administration's doing just that; and this will hardly be possible without going into the historical background and other delicate matters which they propose to avoid in order to make peace proposals more palatable to Americans.

Assume that Hanoi and the Viet Cong refuse to negotiate, which they well may, perhaps on the ground that the United States has no business in Vietnam. Will the proposed movement to end the war collapse at that point and, in effect, take the position that under such circumstances the United States "has no choice" but to keep on fighting and quite possibly to further escalate the war? Escalating the war *is* what the United States is doing. There are those who regard the idea of whether or not the United States is to proceed to kill more babies, children, old people, and adults generally is subject to "negotiation" as gruesome, inhuman and dishonorable.

One other plank in the platform of the proposed movement is that the United States "recognize the right of the South Vietnamese to determine their own future, whatever it may be, without interference from foreign troops, and possibly under UN supervision."

The tentative tone of that last clause both covers up and hints at a basic problem. The proposal is that the Vienamese be their own masters and free from interference from foreign troops. This suggests, for one thing, that United States troops have no legitimate business there now. Certainly their presence has not in recent years left the Vietnamese people free to determine their own course and it has been the instrument for terrorizing and killing many of them. The argument for withdrawing foreign troops, leaving the Vietnamese free, but maintaining some kind of "presence," possibly UN, is that otherwise there may be a purge—a purge of people whom we have pledged to protect. It hardly can be said that we have afforded them much protection up to now or that if we keep on fighting longer we eventually shall save lives, after having destroyed more in the interim. Again the question arises: do the signers of this statement propose that fighting continue if Hanoi and the Viet Cong do not accept its provisions? It is such considerations which lead to the question of whether the way to begin to end the war is not for the United States to plan for a cease-fire of its own, a cessation of adding to the troops already there, a clear declaration that it will withdraw them—and on that basis proceed to what might prove to be genuine negotiation. This is not to indicate insensitivity to the problem of retaliation which might be resorted to by either side after a bitter civil war, but to insist that if we are fighting for self-determination for the Vietnamese people, we have to start at that point and that an international "presence," whatever form it may take, cannot be imposed on them.

The United States is deriving little, if any, honor from its role in Vietnam now. It is not altogether fantastic to suppose that for the United States to recognize that the day of Western military intervention in Asia is at an end and that to act on that assumption would accrue to its honor, would save lives there and in other parts of the world, and would be a much more efficacious way to stop "Communist or Chinese" expansion than the course we are now pursuing. Both George F. Kennan, the American political analyst, and Enoch Powell, the defense expert of the British Conservative Party, are on record to the effect that the longer Western nations try to maintain their "presence" in Asia, for example, the longer it will be before indigenous resistance to Chinese or Communist expansion develops in those regions. I am not for a moment suggesting that it is a simple matter to carry out the approach I am advocating, any more than is that set forth in the *New York Review* statement under discussion. I am suggesting that it is politically and morally a sounder one, that we may be forced to take it in any case and that it will be to our honor and a boon to mankind if we choose to take it.

In the light of what I have said and of the situation in the country, what the *New York Review* statement has to say about civil disobedience and other aspects of the protest movement seems to me in part beside the point and in part mistaken and unfortunate. For one thing, I could wish that those who are critical of the end-the-war movement, as hitherto conducted, would not only make alternative proposals as to program but would be explicit as to how a more effective movement could and should be built. Do they, for example, expect that the labor movement can be won away from its present position of support for the Johnson program to anything remotely resembling opposition? Since a power factor is involved in actions which influence government policy in an immediate sense, do they anticipate that unions might be called on to refuse to produce or transport war material? Similar questions could be asked about what support of an end-the-war movement might be expected, and how to go about getting that support, from the various sections of the civil rights movement.

As it is, the *New York Review* statement devotes itself largely to criticism of forms of protest and resistance which have hitherto been resorted to. With some of the criticisms I am in agreement, but not with others. Before dealing with some specific instances, there is a general observation. The statement begins with the assertion of the belief that the debate in this country about Vietnam is by no means over, that "the protest movement has an important role to play" and that "there is now a genuine opportunity for the movement that wishes to change United States policy in Vietnam." But, it is contended, this can become true only if the movement adopts some such program and methods as the signers advocate. Otherwise it will not gain the approval of "more than the small band already committed to protest."

I already have said that these proposals should be taken seriously, but it surely should be noted also that we do now have a debate and at least a substantial beginning of a protest movement. Immediately after the October 16 demonstrations there was a series of attacks on them and not a few predictions that the protests had "failed." This clearly has not proved to be the case. Even those who argue that the parades, demonstrations, draft card burnings, and self-immolations did not in any way help the situation, cannot possibly make a case for the proposition that they destroyed a protest and a debate which obviously exist. Admittedly the "patriotic" counter-demonstrations have been poorly attended and have produced no evidence of popular enthusiasm for the war. There is, as a matter of fact, a lot of evidence that the various protests have had an impact on public opinion and in Washington. The Johnson administration has had to take notice of the various forms of criticism and protest during the past year even though, in spite or in defiance of them, it has continued its escalation. It is also significant now that almost universally a distinction is drawn by the press and other mass circulation agencies between pacifists and conscientious objectors on the one hand and other kinds of protesters. I cite this fact merely to meet the criticism made by some that pacifism and nonviolence have been submerged. The fact is that they have never before received so much attention in this country. The evidence seems to me, therefore, all in favor of continuing the forms of pressure which have been used rather than abandoning them—by which I do not mean that all the things that have been done should be continued, or that there is not room for other forms of pressure.

I turn to the deprecation, in the statement, of resort to civil disobedience. Take the reference to recent efforts to stop the operation of troop trains in California. I, too, questioned the wisdom of that action, but not on the grounds that these efforts involved "an action by a small minority to revoke through its own decision the policy of a democratically elected government," etc. This implies a characterization of the war policy in relation to Vietnam as "democratically" arrived at, which Senators Morse and Fulbright—judging by their utterances—would not share. Would it not rule out the men and women who operated the Underground Railway a century or so ago? To get at the question from another angle, do the signers rule out strikes of transport or munitions workers on the ground that they cannot any longer take an active part in what they may come to regard as a "dirty" war? Presumably all of the signers who have a history of support of labor would back up a strike of such workers for higher wages, or of Negroes against discrimination, even if the strike interfered with war production. Or would they rule out strikes in wartime?

I do not mean to suggest that the situation is simple; nor do I approve or condone any and every act of protest however bizarre, or adventurist "revolutionary" actions in what is not, I grant, in the Marxian sense a revolutionary situation. But surely great care must be exercised in statements relating to the "democratic" character of our regime and the role of direct action and civil disobedience. The role of the latter in the civil rights movement has obviously not been eliminated by the gains so far achieved.

Finally, a word about the discussion of conscientious objection. It is true that there is a difference between individual moral objection and a political movement against the draft, but perhaps not so clear and sharp as the signers of the *New York Review* statement seem to think. For example, if there were enough young men who, on essentially religious or moral grounds, could not stomach participation in any war or in a particular war, if the number of such individuals went beyond a certain point—taking into account the inevitable side effects of such escalation among youth—it would become impossible for a government to wage war, especially if the dissenters included—as would almost certainly be the case in such a climate—some scientists and engineers in key positions. Such individual conscientious objection would constitute a political action of profound impact. The government would undoubtedly regard it as political and subversive if it went beyond a certain point. Presumably the signers of the *New York Review* statement would not argue that conscientious objection is permissable only if there are not enough objectors to interfere in any way with the smooth operation of the war, but should be ruled out as being "political," or "action by a minority to revoke through its own decision the policy of a democratically elected government," if the number should pass the critical point. Would they not agree also that unless there are a good many conscientious objectors, a movement to end the war is not likely to get very far?

I agree with the criticism of using the conscientious objector provisions in the Selective Service Act "as a tactic of the protest movement," and of filing as a C O merely in order to delay induction, because I think both individuals and movements are built by openness and not by evasion or what amounts to trickery. There are other tactics which have had some support that I would strongly oppose. It goes without saying—and the signers of the statement need hardly have taken the space to say it—that organizations should scrupulously inform young men of the possible consequences of a course they might take. An immense amount of such counseling is in fact being given these days by organizations such as the War Registers League and the Central Committee for Conscientious Objectors.

But, granted that such conditions must be observed, I cannot understand why an anti-draft movement should not be a legitimate and highly useful part of a movement to end the war. Where else would a young man "vote," i.e., exercise his democratic duty, if not at the point where he is called upon to do what he holds is unwarranted and injurious, not only to himself but to society?

What does the Nuremburg trial mean if not that young men do not obey, but disobey, orders at that point? And what is wrong about acting concertedly in such a movement? (I would agree with those who contend that opposition to the draft board should not be carried on in such a way as to divert attention and energy from opposition to the war itself.)

Lastly, I think it is most unfortunate that the signers of the *New York Review* statement should have made a plea to young men who refuse to serve in a war of which they disapprove to "recognize their responsibilities to authentic conscientious objectors, that is, pacifists who refuse on principle to employ violence under any circumstances." The former are urged not to claim status under the Selective Service Act since "the present status of conscientious objectors, achieved only after long and hard struggles," might be endangered!

In the first place, this is to define "authentic conscientious objection" in a narrow way which would be rejected by great numbers of C Os, and also by many ethical and religious teachers who are not pacifists themselves. If the government is to make provision for C Os, the definition of conscientious objector should by all means be broadened, not kept narrow and in effect discriminatory. A young man may be a sincere and genuine conscientious objector to a *particular* war, though not to every conceivable war. Strictly speaking, a Roman Catholic can be a C O on only one of two grounds: either that he has a special vocation to pacifism, as a monk or nun would have to the monastic life, or that a given war is "unjust." Would anyone argue, to cite another instance, that there were not in Germany, under Hitler, men who were not "authentic pacifists" according to the above definition but unquestionably sincere in their opposition to Hitler and war, perhaps even more so than the "authentic" pacifists?

Above all, any notion that pacifists ought to be protected or given special consideration under the law should be firmly rejected. The law affecting conscientious objectors at present is limited to those who refuse participation in any war on grounds of religious training and belief, and it defines "religious belief" as implying belief in a Supreme Being. The courts have, to all intents and purposes, eliminated the Supreme Being clause, ruling in effect that anyone to whom pacifism is a matter of deep conviction comes under the law. Personally I have always held that when religious C Os were offered special *status*, religious bodies should have refused it and insisted that government agents were not qualified to distinguish between one man's conscience and another's in such a context. Religious believers above all should not seek privileged status.

Furthermore I deny the right of a government, certainly in a military context, to conscript a man for so-called civilian service. The place where he is may be the place where he ought to be, the work he is doing may be what he ought to be doing. It is presumption and an invasion of human dignity for a government, because it happens to be waging war or preparing for it, to order him against his will to drop what he has been doing and do something else which it deems useful and fitting. Some of the proposals which have been made in statements issued for consideration by Students for a Democratic Society have, in my opinion, disregarding this important consideration. Moreover, they have not always made clear that they are not proposing "alternative service," in the context of the Selective Service Act, which seems to me only to make it easier for the government to administer the draft and carry on the war.

In conclusion, we are experiencing an unprecedented development of open opposition to a war in the midst of the war. That this opposition has not been suppressed so far by governmental action; and that, for example, in New York city, Park Department authorities issue a permit for space in which draft card burners may perform a supposedly illegal act; and that the Police Department provides protection for such an assembly is heartening evidence that American society is in some degree democratic.

It is to be expected that in the midst of this upsurge of antiwar sentiment and of a war such as the one in Vietnam, proposals for an "end-the-war movement" should emerge and efforts to build such a movement—*the* movement which would do the job—should be undertaken. It also is inevitable that the question of whether the "end-the-war movement" might not be made the starting point for a new political alignment, a new "revolutionary" line-up, and what have you, should be broached, and that various groups should think they have *the* answer to that broader question and proceed to act upon it. All this is obviously too vast a matter to be discussed in detail here.

I am not at the moment sanguine that *the* "movement" is about to come into existence. But I am convinced that movement, revolt, cannot be suppressed and that this in itself is a "revolutionary" development. If the revolt is to express itself in various ways, and not in a single "movement," then it is my hope that the adherents of each tendency or program will work very hard at their job as they see it and, while not abandoning political dialogue, will not dissipate energy in personal or organizational attacks on each other. The issue will in any event be decided largely by forces and developments over which none of us exercises a substantial measure of control.

8.6.   *STEVE WEISSMAN and JOHN GERASSI:* **The Vietnamization of Latin America**

[For a large sector of the radical movement, the war in Vietnam is not so much an anomalous incident in American foreign policy as one episode in the strategy of the economic expansion and repression of national liberation movements which characterizes the military and economic system of the United States. In Latin America is a situation already similar in many respects to that of Vietnam, even though there is no open, direct military conflict. Steve Weissman has been an analyst and activist in the New Left for many years; John Gerassi is a specialist on radical movements in Latin America and the author of several books, including *The Great Fear in Latin America, North Vietnam: A Documentary,* and *Latin American Radicalism.* Selections from a pamphlet published by the North American Congress on Latin America (NACLA) in 1968.]

By the fall of 1966, there was at least one good reason for the Johnson Administration to ignore the pleas of protestors, dissenters, critics, teach-ins, and cop-outs: The U.S. was winning. Said Johnson, himself, jubilantly, "We're winning militarily in Vietnam" (*Newsweek,* Sept. 26, 1966).

Defense Secretary McNamara thought we were winning in Latin America, too. He took pride in the fact that "U.S.-trained units of [Venezuela's] armed forces and police have spearheaded a government campaign both in the cities and in the countryside. . . . U.S.-trained and supported Peruvian army and air force units have played prominent roles in this counter-guerrilla campaign. In Columbia, U.S. training, support, and equipment, including several medium helicopters, have materially aided the Columbia armed forces to establish government control in the rural insurgent areas." (Feb., 1966, before a joint session of the Senate Armed Services Comm. and the Senate Subcomm. on Dept. of Defense Appro.)

Even Leftist observers were pessimistic. The French Marxist, Henri Edme, wrote in Jean-Paul Sartre's magazine, *Les Temps Modernes* (May, 1966), that "for the moment, imperialism, alas, has gained the initiative and the upper hand. . . in Latin America."

No wonder, then, that Walt W. Rostow, Johnson's assistant for national security affairs, felt confident that the "romantic revolutionaries who have long disturbed world order are passing from the scene." He claimed that they were being overtaken, not only by the U.S. on the ground but also, generally, "by history and by increasingly pervasive attitudes of pragmatism and moderation" (speech at the Univ. of Leeds, Feb. 23, 1967, as reported in *The N.Y. Times* the next day).

To these acute observers, therefore, it seemed obvious that America, the most powerful nation on earth, would keep the world as it wanted for the forseeable future—under Pax Americana.

Yet, this fall, one year after Johnson's gloating remarks, nothing is so obvious. The U.S. is certainly not winning militarily in Vietnam. The Huk guerrillas are fighting again in the Philippines. The national liberation fronts of Africa have become Socialist and anti-American. And in Latin America, all hell has broken loose. Even before the solidarity conference in Havana last August, it was clear that "an epidemic of guerrilla fighting is sweeping over Latin America" (Herbert Matthews, *N.Y. Times,* April 10, 1967), and the U.S. Defense Department was no longer so cock-sure of its program.

General Robert W. Porter, Jr., Commander in Chief of the U.S. Southern [Hemisphere] Command was downright alarmed when he testified before the House Committee on Foreign Affairs on April 25, 1967. He said, "Active insurgency operations continue in Colombia, despite determined government efforts to eliminate the threat. During the past few weeks, Communist guerrillas, who are operating in an area larger than South Vietnam, renewed their attacks and killed over 35 security force personnel in five widespread incidents. . . . The Communist insurgency situation in Guatemala is potentially dangerous. Communists have recently opened a new guerrilla front in Bolivia. . . . There has been an upsurge in guerrilla activities and an increasing capability of the Venezuelan Communists to open a third guerrilla front in the East."

At the Organization of Latin American Solidarity (OLAS) Conference in Havana in August, guerrilla delegates from all over Latin America were convinced that this upsurge would eventually lead to the defeat of Pax Americana. They had no illusions. They knew that it will take a long time and that it will often look hopeless and that it will be very costly. But they were prepared to take such time and endure such despair and pay such cost. Comandante Nestor Valle of the Guatemalan Fuerzas Armadas Revolucionarias (FAR) said that "we have learned from the Vietnamese that to be free not just a few militants but a whole people can be willing to endure an unimaginable amount of suffering." Added Comandante Francisco Prada of the Venezuelan Fuerzas Armadas de Liberacion Nacional (FALN), "Our subjugation under the combination of U.S. imperialism and native oligarchical repressions has taught us the true meaning of life, which in turn has taught us, paradoxically, to accept death. This makes us, eventually, invincible." And, as if answering Rostow, Comandante Fidel Castro said, "A revolutionary is a man who can no longer be enticed to think of his personal future except as part of a collective. To be a revolutionary, a man must first be a romantic" (interviews with John Gerassi, August 9, 11, and 12 respectively).

At OLAS, such romantics responded to U.S. control of the economics and politics of all the countries of the underdeveloped world, and most specifically of Latin America, These romantics spoke of how the U.S. directed the cultures, philosophies, the conceptual frameworks, in sum, the total way of life of their countries. They saw such domination as an attempt to mold them into "pragmatics and moderates," as Rostow would say, into *acomodados* capable and willing to profit as much as possible from U.S. superiority in exchange for upholding the American way of life and profit. To these romantics, therefore, it is both legal and moral for the underdeveloped countries to bind together to combat the U.S. (Yes, romantics inevitably think in moral terms!) They decided to help each other, to coordinate their activities, and gradually to build up a continental army of the peoples of Latin America to destroy the oligarchical elites, the foreign exploiters, and their *acomodado* friends. OLAS gave birth to a new international, an international of the poor and have-nots. It is their response to the international of the rich, which operates pragmatically and moderately to maintain the violence of the status quo.

The new international does not hedge. For example, the Cubans, who have already offered to send troops to Vietnam, now openly admit—indeed are proud of the fact—that they are helping the guerrillas in Latin America. They are sending arms there and Cuban volunteers are filtering into the continent. Latin American guerrillas are being trained in Cuba. Not just to Fidel and the members of the Central Committee of the Cuban Communist Party, but also to most ordinary Cubans, the continental war of liberation already exists.

Cubans consider their own homeland as just the first totally liberated area of the continent. As such, it can be lost—when the U.S. invades it. At that time, every Cuban will fight—as a regular soldier and militiaman at first, as a guerrilla later. Most Cubans expect this will happen soon. They have no illusions about President Kennedy's 1962 promise to Nikita Khrushchev not to assault Cuba; in fact, in August, 1967, the Johnson State Department denied such a promise was ever made bindingly. Such are the risks of war, say the Cubans. A battle can be lost, a free territory enslaved, yet at a cost which shortens the overall struggle. Cubans may have to do the fighting in Cuba, Venezuelans in Venezuela, Bolivians in Bolivia, but each belongs to an overall army, and its ultimate victory is shared by all.

This militancy has long existed in Cuba. The slogan of OLAS—"El deber de todo revolucionario es hacer la revolución," the duty of all revolutionaries is to make the revolution—was not invented in 1967. Fidel shouted it from Revolution Square in 1962, when he proclaimed the Second Declaration of Havana.

It has always been Ché Guevara's motto, too. And it was Ché, not "Carlos Marx" or Lenin, as *Time* magazine falsely reported, who was one of the two heroes of OLAS. The other hero was not even a Marxist—just a revolutionary. But, like Ché, he believed in liberating people irrespective of frontiers; like

Ché, he wandered the continent, fighting the imperialist forces of his day. His name was Simon Bolivar, and he stood side by side with Ché on the walls of Havana in the summer of 1967.

The U.S. and the oligarchies of Latin America are now worried. The U.S.-trained air force generals of Bolivia and the U.S.-financed reformers of Venezuela want to bring Cuba down. The hemisphere's foreign ministers insist that they must "combat and publicize Cuban Communist subversion" (S. F. Chronicle, Sept. 25, 1967). The rich in the U.S. agree, especially since they are convinced that even Detroit and Newark ghettos are in danger of being controlled by Havana (*U.S. News and World Report*). And, in a way, they're correct, since all revolutionaries, whether in the Peruvian Andes or in American slums, jointly share a hatred for that pragmatic democracy which offers them hand-outs and platitudes instead of equality and dignity.

Pragmatic men can be talked to, bribed, bought, cajoled, wooed, scared. They can be "moderated." If they are dissenters, they can be encouraged to channel their protests through official outlets. They can be enticed into becoming loyal opponents. They can be turned into "personalities"——into brave and daring men. In other words, they can be rendered ineffective.

But romantics! They are so unmanageable. They can be mad enough to think that they can start a revolution with seven bodies from atop an isolated mountain or by burning their own homes. They can be crazy enough to think they can defeat napalm and fragmentation bombs with museum-vintage *escopetes*. They can be insane enough to believe openly that social justice is possible, that man can be re-educated to think of his fellow men instead of himself. To the pragmatics, such men are incomprehensible—and, hence, deadly enemies.

Ché Guevara is such a romantic. For a while, he was thought to be dead, and while liberals and conservatives alike debated the causes and meaning of his death, both were profoundly relieved. Why? Because Ché did not believe in playing the game by its established rules; because Ché did not espouse the rule of law set up by Liberals. Pragmatics hated him because Ché made a pragmatic evaluation of conditions in the world around him and came to the conclusion that the rich never give up their money or power or privilege voluntarily, that laws and rules are concocted to defend the status quo, that liberals and do-gooders always fortify imperialism by "trying to moderate it."

But now, it is clear, Ché is alive, and he haunts the wealthy and powerful from Patagonia to Washington. He seems to be everywhere at the same time, fomenting trouble, launching guerrillas, harassing the establishments. Unlike most Marxists, Ché knows that capitalism is not static, but dynamic; that it can create the illusion of progress by generating some genuine mobility. He knows that its "internal contradictions" will never bring it down by itself. He knows that the U.S. can wage war in one country after another for years, decades, perhaps even centuries, without cracking economically. He knows that the U.S. can operate in the underdeveloped world without risk of retaliation from Russia.

Ché also knows that urban proletariats can be brought into the economic structure through minor reforms, turning them into Fabians. They will agitate and settle for bread and butter gains, and in the process, they will forget their fellow poor isolated in the hills, in the jungles, in the mountains. Why have the Communist parties of France, Italy, Belgium, etc., not led revolutions? he asked himself. His answer: Because their rank-and-file members, fairly well-off workers in the cities, are pragmatics. They think of themselves, their families, and their own individual futures. They are not a revolutionary force. In America, most of the urban proletariat profits so much from the increase in economic activity due to such wars as Vietnam, that it tends to be among the wars' strongest supporters. In the underdeveloped world, too, the urban proletariat profits from American expansionism. That is why city workers go to the polls; that is why they like stability; that is why, as Henri Edme reported, imperialism seems to have gained "the upper hand."

But in the countryside, where the majority live outside the money economy, the picture is quite different. As the Columbian Catholic priest and oligarch, Camilo Torres, who died, gun in hand, with the guerrillas, wrote at the end of 1965, "The people don't believe in elections. The people know that legal ways have been exhausted. The people know that there is nothing left but armed struggle. The people are desperate and resolved to risk their lives so that the next generation [shall] not be slaves. So that the children of those who now want to give their lives shall have education, housing, food, clothing, and, above all, DIGNITY. So that future [generations] can have their own nation, independent of Northamerican power." (*Christianismo y Revolución*, Buenos Aires, Sept., 1966.)

While Ché was still in Cuba, other revolutionaries realized that such campesinos were ready to rebel. They began to organize them, and quickly became confident that victory was near. In Peru, for example, such revolutionaries as Luís de la Puente and Guillermo Lobatón had no trouble gathering troops. So, they set up revolutionary "foci" and established liberated areas. They were surrounded, hit by napalm, and destroyed. De la Puente was killed, Lobatón, reportedly killed but probably only wounded and secretly jailed. The guerrilla force was routed.

(The napalm used in Peru on Peruvians was loaded into American planes by Americans in Panama and flown to Peru by the American Air Force. The bombing and military operations were directed by American Special Forces "advisers" [NBS Special, *The Undeclared Wars*, shows in June, 1966]. The information and research on Peruvian peasant habits and activity was culled from reports prepared, innocently enough, by American academicians, specifically by Cornell University's Vico research team. The combination was deadly.)

The guerrillas learned from such mistakes. Today, as Regis Debray reports in *Revolution in the Revolution* (Monthly Review Press), the guerrillas operate in small, mobile bands. They do not try to hold liberated areas. They strike often; then withdraw. They rob banks to pay peasants well above market prices for their food necessities. They respect those peasants who remain neutral.

The repressive forces do not. They must track down the guerrilla bands; hence, they must get information from the peasants who know where they are. The peasants rarely offer such information voluntarily. Thus, counterinsurgency makes enemies for the regime. The guerrillas do not respect frontiers, created by military *caudillos*, not by people. But local military forces must, to a certain extent, keep within their own borders. Only the American advisers are free to operate on all sides. They become the identifiable enemy of the peasantry. The revolutionary struggle becomes literally a war between guerrillas of each nation against one common enemy. In the practice of battle, too, then, the American international confronts the new OLAS international.

But it is not limited to Latin America. Guatemalans have been in Vietnam. Ché has traveled throughout Africa. Cuban volunteer soldiers have saved at least one African president from a military coup. The first Tri-Continental Conference, held in Havana in January, 1966, was mostly organized by Ben Barka, the Moroccan revolutionary. The next Tri-Con is scheduled for January, 1968—in Cairo.

In his Message to the Tri-Continental (*Treason* magazine, summer, 1967), Ché Guevara explained his tactics—to help launch "two, three, many Vietnams." He didn't mean just in Latin America, but throughout the underdeveloped world. In this sense, then, he is fostering a global civil war, as Rostow has said. But it is a civil war between the rich and the poor—a civil war that dates back to Spartacus and to the Canus, to 1848 and to the French Communards, to the Russian and to the Chinese revolutions. But only today does it begin to have world-wide commitment.

In Latin America, of course, the civil war already has a long history. Though it has been an undeclared civil war and though the U.S. has not often been fingered as the true enemy of the Latin Americans since it has kept its activities to behind-the-scenes, few are the American historians who would deny America's imperialist role. However, rare is the American historian who has squarely faced the consistency of that imperialism. Perhaps this is because historians simply don't ask themselves what imperialism really is all about, or if they do, they seem incapable of coming up with the briefest of answers; namely, a policy aimed at material gain. And this in spite of the fact that he knows full well that there has never been a stronger or more consistent justification for intervening in the affairs of other countries than the expectation of material benefit therefrom.

. . . .

The continent as a whole must use from 30 to 40 percent of its foreign earnings to pay off interest and service charges, *not the principal,* on loans to the industrialized world, mostly the United States. The Alliance for Progress claims that it is helping Latin America industrialize on a social progress basis. Now more than six years old, it has chalked up remarkable successes: right-wing coups in Argentina, Brazil, Honduras, Guatemala, Ecuador, the Dominican Republic, and Salvador. In exchange, U.S. businessmen have remitted to the U.S. $5 billion of profits while investing less than $2 billion. And the Alliance itself, which is supposed to lend money for strictly social progress projects, has kept 86 percent of its outlay to credits for U.S. made goods, credits which are guaranteed by Latin American governments and are repayable in dollars.

Interventionist and imperialist policies of the United States in Latin America are now successfully in the third stage. Not only does the United States control Latin America's sources of raw material, not only does it control its markets for American manufactured goods, but it also controls the internal money economy altogether. Karl Marx had once warned that the first revolutionary wave in an imperialized country will come about as the result of frustration by the national bourgeoisie, which will have reached a development stage where it will have accumulated enough capital to want to become competitive to the imperializing corporations. This was not allowed to happen in Latin America.

As American corporations became acutely plagued by surplus goods, they realized that they must expand their markets in underdeveloped countries. To do so, however, they would have to help develop a national bourgeoisie which could purchase these goods. This "national" bourgeoisie, as all such classes in colonialized countries, had to be created by the service industries, yet somehow limited so that it did not become economically independent. The solution was simple. The American corporations, having set up assembly plants in São Paulo or Buenos Aires, which they called Brazilian or Argentinian corporations, decided to actually help create the subsiduary industries—with local money—themselves.

Take GM, for example. First, it brought down its cars in various pieces called parts (thus eliminating import duties). Then it assembled them in São Paulo and called them Brazil-made. Next it shopped around for local entrepreneurs to launch the subsidiary industries—seat covers, spark plugs, etc. Normally, the landed oligarchy and entrepreneurs in the area would do its own investing in those subsidiary industries, and having successfully amassed large amounts of capital, would bind together to create their own car industry. It was this step that had to be avoided. Thus General Motors first offered these local entrepreneurs contracts by which it helped finance the servicing industries. Then it brought the entrepreneurs' capital into huge holding corporations which, in turn, it rigidly controlled. The holding corporations became very successful, making the entrepreneurs happy, and everyone forgot about a local, competitive car industry, making GM happy.

This procedure is best employed by IBEC, Rockefeller's mammoth investing corporation in Latin America. IBEC claims to be locally-owned by Latin Americans since it does not hold controlling interest. But the 25 to 45 percent held by Standard Oil (it varies from Columbia to Venezuela to Peru) is not offset by the thousands of individual Latin investors, who, to set policy, would all have to agree among themselves and then vote in a block. When one corporation owns 45% while thousands of individual investors split the other 55%, the corporation sets policy—in the U.S. as well as abroad. Besides, IBEC is so successful that the local entrepreneurs "think American" even before IBEC does. In any case, the result of these holding corporations is that the national bourgeoisie in Latin America has been eliminated. It is an American bourgeoisie.

IBEC and other holding corporations use their combined local-U.S. capital to invest in all sorts of profitable ventures, from supermarkets to assembly plants. Naturally, these new corporations are set up where they can bring the most return. IBEC is not going to build a supermarket in the Venezuelan province of Falcón, where the population lives outside the money economy altogether and hence could not buy goods at the supermarket anyway. Nor would IBEC build a supermarket in Falcón because there are no roads leading there. The creation of IBEC subsidiaries in no way helps develop the infrastructure of the country.

Since such holding corporations as IBEC have their tentacles in every region of the economy, they control the money market as well (which is why U.S. corporations backed, indeed pushed, the formation of a Latin American common market at the 1967 Punta del Este Conference. Such a common market would eliminate duties on American goods assembled in Latin America and being exported from one Latin-American country to another). Hence no new American investment needs to be brought down even for the 45% of the holding corporations. A new American investment in Latin America today is a paper investment. The new corporation is set up with local funds which only drains the local capital reserves. And the result is an industry benefiting only those sectors which purchase American surplus goods.

Having so tied up the local economic elites, the U.S. rarely needs to intervene with marines to guarantee friendly governments. The local military, bought by the American-national interests, guarantees friendly regimes—with the approval of the local press, the local legal political parties, the local cultural centers, all of which the local money controls. And the local money is now tightly linked to American interests.

Latin-American reformers have finally realized all this. They now know that the only way to break that structure is to *break* it—which means a violent revolution. Hence there are no reformers in Latin America anymore. They have become either pro-Americans, whatever they call themselves, who will do America's bidding, or else they are revolutionaries.

American liberal historians, social scientists, and politicans insist that there is still a third way: a nonviolent revolution which will be basically pro-democracy, i.e., pro-American. They tell us that such a revolutionary process has already started and that it will inevitably lead to equality between America and its Latin neighbors. Liberal politicians also like to tell Americans that they should be on the side of that process, help it along, give it periodic boosts. In May, 1966, Robert Kennedy put it this way in a Senate speech: "A revolution is coming—a revolution which will be peaceful if we are wise enough; compassionate if we care enough; successful if we are fortunate enough—but a revolution which is coming whether we will it or not. We can affect its character, we cannot alter its inevitability."

What Kennedy seems incapable of understanding, however, is that if the revolution is peaceful and compassionate, if Americans *can* affect its character, then, it will be no revolution at all. To try to affect it is to be imperialist, no matter how well-intentioned.

Of course, few Liberals support outright interventions. Most refuse to see themselves as supporters of imperialism. Some, who call themselves the sophisticated ones, accept the inevitability of a global "sphere of influence" dichotomy between the great powers. They refer to this inevitability as "the responsibility of power." But even they are well-intentioned and, like all well-intentioned Americans, claim that some good can come out of the evil imperialism. If only power is used wisely, argue these Liberals and Social Democrats, the poor can still profit from our richness. Thus, they wage campaigns against the shipment of arms to underdeveloped lands, insist that the U.S. instead send social aid. They want to export the New Deal, the welfare state. They are welfare imperialists.

But it is precisely these liberal commitments, precisely this welfare imperialism which creates the setting, sets up the conditions, and generates the attitudes for old-style military and economic imperialism. The best example is Vietnam, where, after the collapse of the French, the U.S. moved in not as a policeman but as a social worker. As John McDermott explained in *The Nation* (July 25, 1966):

> The Americans had influenced the choice of Diem in the first place. They gave technical and dollar support to a revamping of the entire Vietnamese educational system from elementary schools through the university and technical institute level. This included both teacher training and the rewriting of textbooks. They gave technical assistance in revising the bank-

ing and currency system and in framing general economic and monetary policy. The United States Operations Mission (USOM—the AID Mission) undertook planning and dollar support for the reconstruction and development of the entire Vietnamese transportation and communications network—railroads, canals, highways, civil aviation, coastal transport, radio and television, and the telephone system. They assisted in planning and executing the various agricultural programs, including crop diversification, land reclamation, land reform, agricultural extension and mass peasant regroupment, (the Refugee Resettlement, Land Development, Agroville and later Strategic Hamlet Programs). Finally, they exerted extremely strong influence over the nation's two largest economic activities (exclusive of farming)—military operations and the import business.

Half a million U.S. soldiers have caused us to forget this earlier escalation. But military intervention was a natural follow-up. The U.S. aid apparatus had overwhelmed the Vietnamese government and destroyed its independence. American welfare imperialism had disrupted the Vietnamese economy, politics and culture. And the success—not the failure—of the U.S. development program set off such changes in Vietnamese society and institutions that the resulting social and political disorder overcame American efforts to establish stability. There was just no way for the peasantry to fit into the new U.S.-made society in Saigon. Hence from 1954 to 1961, while U.S. aid to Vietnam amounted to $1,544 million, only $42 million (less than 3 percent) went into rural projects (and at that, the figures include education and health from which the peasants did not really benefit).

The Vietnamese peasants, unable to partake in the high-consumption urban economy, became more and more isolated, more and more prone to reject the American way of life, hence more and more repressed. Thus, U.S. social democracy created an enemy out of a people who were generally unpolitical, uncommitted, and unsophisticated. What's more, the process was inevitable for even if America had wanted to help the peasantry, the mechanism for doing so simply didn't exist.

This is even truer in Latin America, where AID officials must work with and through an already established U.S. presence—American corporations, totally and naturally geared to meet the demands of urban consumers. Under such conditions, U.S. aid programs can only increase the gap between the urban consumer (including the so-called rising "middle sectors") and the poor, unintegrated campesinos, who generally make up the majority.

As that gap continues to widen, both American investors and U.S. AID expectantly focus more, for both profits and political showmanship, on visible returns. What has happened to public utilities is indicative. In Latin America, three North American firms—International Telephone and Telegraph, American and Foreign Power, and Brazilian Light, Power and Traction companies—have long exercised a virtual monopoly over all public utilities. In recent years, however, profits have dwindled while political costs have risen. Highly visible, dependent upon politically determined rates, and in direct daily contact with ordinary people, the public utilities became a natural target for nationalists. As a result, the companies felt reluctant to invest money on new equipment and instead began to withdraw.

With the Alliance for Progress, this withdrawal was speeded up. The three companies ended up with over $1 billion of Alliance funds, investing much of it into higher paying sectors of the economy. In Argentina, for example,

AMFORP poured its sell-out wealth into consumer industry, in housing (with the Rockefeller-owned IBEC), and in money-lending (at 18 percent on 90 to 180 day notes.) Meanwhile, their poorly equipped, overpriced, costly-to-operate facilities became the property of the local governments, turning them into symbols of the inefficiency of government involvement in the economy. Whereas, one of the industrial investments, the PASA Petroleum complex, which was made possible only through an Alliance for Progress "extended risk guarantee" loan by the Agency for International Development, became "the largest privately financed project in a developing country. It is important to the future of private enterprise in Argentina, and to the United States, that it not fail." (Hearings on Foreign Assistance, 1964).

It certainly is important to the U.S.—and to private enterprise in Argentina. But it is not important, on the contrary it is another form of subjugation, to the poor of Argentina. That project will increase the poverty of the population of such provinces as Salta and Tucumán. There, where the poor don't have cars or oil heaters or factories to work in, petroleum products are meaningless. The project itself will augment their isolation. Like the peasants of Vietnam, the disenfranchised sugar growers of Salta will learn to view the city, the bureaucrats, and eventually the Americans as their enemy. They will join Ché Guevara in revolution.

They will do so anyway because no social democratic or liberal government, no local oligarchy or local entrepreneur class can cope with the problems of the poor. Their profit-oriented or pay-as-you-go type of structure, no matter how well meaning, does not embody the mechanism capable of dealing with lower classes. Rebellion therefore becomes natural. With the U.S. involved on the side of modernization, i.e., the establishment, the poor's fight necessarily becomes long and costly. Yet it all started with well meaning liberals who wanted to help, who looked upon Food for Peace as altruistic, upon Foundation help as generous, upon church group volunteers as dedicated, upon civic action programs as forward looking, upon academic "objective" research programs as constructive.

In Vietnam it is now too late. If the U.S. aggression there is to end, it will be only because the Vietnamese people will have forced the U.S. to get out. Well-motivated Americans now oppose that aggression. But it started in 1954. Such Americans should have opposed U.S. aid then. Instead, they tried to turn Diem into a nationalist. They campaigned for social measures. They argued for elections. They still argue for free elections. Such is the stuff from which empires are born.

Unlike Vietnam, the initial and overriding U.S. interest in Latin America has been clearly economic: 9 billion dollars of U.S.-owned direct investment plus markets and raw materials have consistently proved persuasive in the formulation of official policy. Nonetheless, the Alliance for Progress has produced a Vietnam-like increase in the day-to-day administrative involvement in Latin America. The Food for Peace program has given the United States control of vast sums of local currencies, and the forthcoming War on Hunger promises a direct involvement in agriculture. AID has brought U.S. government and university personnel into advisory and administrative posts in local housing programs, agricultural programs, labor departments, industrial investment and trade union activities, education, communications, transportation, health and sanitation, community development, social welfare, and police training programs. The Department of Agriculture, the Housing and Home

Financing Agency, the Social Security Administration, the Internal Revenue Service, and literally hundreds of other government agencies engage in training programs for Latin Americans here in the United States and in long- and short-term on-the-spot advisory capacities within the Latin-American bureaucracies. The government also cooperates closely with the work of private agencies such as the National Catholic Welfare Conference, the National Council of Churches (Division of Foreign Missions), the Evangelical Foreign Ministers Association, the National Council of Jewish Women, the Cooperative League of the United States of America, the Carnegie Corporations, the Ford Foundation, and the Rockefeller Foundation.

As in the case of Vietnam, most of these activities are undertaken with an ostensible concern for the political and economic development of Latin America. At their best, however, they bolster North American influence and control over the every-day decision-making of the Latin Republics, render policy-making literally irresponsible to the majority of Latin Americans (even where there are elections), perpetuate a colonial mentality among Latin Americans, and impose North American models of development where they are probably not relevant. At their worst, which is all too often the case, these programs directly serve the priorities of North American corporations and military counter-insurgency programs. And, regardless of their day-to-day impact within Latin America, the public commitment to economic development has rationalized increased economic intervention (e g. the Hicklenlooper Amendment, the Investment Guarantee Treaties, etc.) and increased support for military imposed stability.

From the perspective of Vietnam, this new pattern of "Welfare Imperialism" implies that the escalation of U.S. involvement in Latin America will not always be as sudden and clear as in the Dominican Republic, but rather as a slow series of new programs, often in the name of liberal-supported foreign aid. It is these programs that radicals must oppose.

That is the task of NACLA, The North American Congress on Latin America.

A research, educational and informational organization, NACLA proposes, through intensive documentation, publication and public participation by its members, to:

1. Identify the escalation decisions, alert liberal and radical groups to the implications of various foreign aid programs, and build a movement for withdrawal before the United States becomes clearly and publicly committed to military intervention.

2. Dramatize the presence of the Green Berets in Latin America and mount a movement for immediate withdrawal of the MAAGs and cessation of all military or police training.

3. Join with the radical anti-war movement in raising a more fundamental critique of the Vietnam intervention that will not open the door to "acceptable" interventions in this hemisphere; challenge the sphere of interest notions and the assumptions of hemispheric unity implicit in so much of the academic treatment of Latin America.

4. Work to withdraw support from liberal foreign policy and to demand a rephrasing of the question "What can we do to help develop the countries of Latin America?" to "What can we do to stop the U.S. government agencies

and private corporations from hindering the independent development of Latin America?"

5. Support Latin America's movements of national liberation by publicizing their aims, programs and activities.

And, since we are mostly academicians ourselves, specifically and most intensively:

6. Expose counter-insurgency research activities currently undertaken in American universities.

FURTHER READINGS

Dellinger, Dave. "The March on Washington and Its Critics." *Liberation,* May 1965.

Finn, James. *Protest: Pacifism and Politics.* New York: Vintage Books, 1968.

Gilbert, James. "The Teach-In: Protest or Co-optation?" *Studies on the Left,* V: 3, Summer 1965.

Ginsberg, Allen. "To To Make a March/Spectacle—Berkeley Vietnam Day." *Liberation,* January 1966.

Kopkind, Andrew. "Anti-Vietnam Politics." *The New Republic,* June 4, 1966.
————. "Radicals on the March." *The New Republic,* December 11, 1965.

Levitas, Mitchell. "Vietnam Comes to the University of Oregon." *New York Times Magazine,* May 9, 1965.

Lynd, Staughton. "Call for Nonviolent Revolution." Speech at Vietnam Day Teach-in, May 10, 1965. Published in *We Accuse,* Berkeley: Vietnam Day Committee, 1965.

————. "The Dilemma of Americans." *The National Guardian,* April 24, 1965.

———— and Hayden, Thomas. *The Other Side.* New York: Signet Books, 1967.

Mailer, Norman. "On LBJ." *The Realist,* June 1965.

————. *The Armies of the Night.* New York: New American Library, 1968.

Oglesby, Carl. "The Vietnam War: *World Revolution and American Containment.* SDS pamphlet, April 1965.

"Report from the Editors: The SDS March on Washington." *Studies on the Left,* V: 2, Spring 1965.

Rubin, Jerry. "Alliance for Liberation." Speech at the Fifth Avenue Parade, March 26, 1966. *Liberation,* April 1966.

Scott, Joann Wallach. "The Teach-In: A National Movement or the End of an Affair?" *Studies on the Left,* V: 3, Summer 1965.

"SDS. From Protest to Radicals Politics," presented by Paul Booth and Lee Webb. *Our Generation,* May 1966.

Smith, Jack. "The Demand Is Peace." *The National Guardian,* April 24, 1965.

"Teach-In: New Forum for Reason." *The Nation,* May 31, 1965.

Teach-Ins U.S.A.—Reports, Opinions, Documents, edited by Louis Menashe and Ronald Radosh. New York: Frederick A. Praeger, 1967.

Vietnam Day Committee. *Letter to the Faculty.* Mimeograph document, 1965.

Washington Free Press, special issue on the Pentagon confrontation. December, 1967.

We Accuse, by Vietnam Day Committee of Berkeley, 1965.

Wolfe, Robert. "American Imperialism and the Peace Movement." *Studies on the Left,* VI: 3, May/June 1966.

Zinn, Howard. "Dow Shalt Not Kill." *New Left Notes,* November 20, 1967.

9
Black Power

9.1. *SNCC:* The Basis of Black Power

[In Spring 1966, with the election of Stokely Carmichael as president, the Student Nonviolent Coordinating Committee (SNCC) officially changed its political position—from "Civil Rights" to "Black Power." The following is a position paper prepared by SNCC in Spring 1966 and circulated in order to explain the content of the new position. It was also published in *The New York Times* of August 5, 1966.]

The myth that the Negro is somehow incapable of liberating himself, is lazy, etc., came out of the American experience. In the books that children read, whites are always "good" (good symbols are white), blacks are "evil" or seen as savages in movies, their language is referred to as a "dialect," and black people in this country are supposedly descended from savages.

Any white person who comes into the movement has the concepts in his mind about black people, if only subconsciously. He cannot escape them because the whole society has geared his subconscious in that direction.

Miss America coming from Mississippi has a chance to represent all of America, but a black person from either Mississippi or New York will never represent America. Thus the white people coming into the movement cannot relate to the black experience, cannot relate to the word "black," cannot relate to the "nitty gritty," cannot relate to the experience that brought such a word into existence, cannot relate to chitterlings, hog's head cheese, pig feet, hamhocks, and cannot relate to slavery, because these things are not a part of their experience. They also cannot relate to the black religious experience, nor to the black church, unless, of course, this church has taken on white manifestations.

White Power

Negroes in this country have never been allowed to organize themselves because of white interference. As a result of this, the stereotype has been reinforced that blacks cannot organize themselves. The white psychology that blacks have to be watched, also reinforces this stereotype. Blacks, in fact, feel intimidated by the presence of whites, because of their knowledge of the power that whites have over their lives. One white person can come into a meeting of black people and change the complexion of that meeting, whereas one black person would not change the complexion of that meeting unless he was an obvious Uncle Tom. People would immediately start talking about "brotherhood," "love," etc.; race would not be discussed.

If people must express themselves freely, there has to be a climate in which they can do this. If blacks feel intimidated by whites, then they are not liable to vent the rage that they feel about whites in the presence of whites—especially not the black people whom we are trying to organize, i.e., the broad masses of black people. A climate has to be created whereby blacks can express themselves. The reasons that whites must be exluded is not that one is anti-white, but because the effects that one is trying to achieve cannot succeed because whites have an intimidating effect. Oftimes the intimidating effect is in direct proportion to the amount of degradation that black people have suffered at the hands of white people.

Roles of Whites and Blacks

It must be offered that white people who desire change in this country should go where that problem (racism) is most manifest. The problem is not in the black community. The white people should go into white communities where the whites have created power for the express purpose of denying blacks human dignity and self-determination. Whites who come into the black community with ideas of change seem to want to absolve the power structure of its responsibility for what it is doing, and saying that change can only come through black unity, which is the worst kind of paternalism. This is not to say that whites have not had an important role in the movement. In the case of Mississippi, their role was very key in that they helped give blacks the right to organize, but that role is now over, and it should be.

People now have the right to picket, the right to give out leaflets, the right to vote, the right to demonstrate, the right to print.

These things which revolve around the right to organize have been accomplished mainly because of the entrance of white people into Mississippi, in the summer of 1964. Since these goals have now been accomplished, whites' role in the movement has now ended. What does it mean if black people, once having the right to organize, are not allowed to organize themselves? It means that blacks' ideas about inferiority are being reinforced. Shouldn't people be able to organize themselves? Blacks should be given this right. Further, white participation means in the eyes of the black community that whites are the "brains" behind the movement, and that blacks cannot function without whites. This only serves to perpetuate existing attitudes within the existing society, i.e., blacks are "dumb," "unable to take care of business," etc. Whites are "smart," the "brains" behind the whole thing.

How do blacks relate to other blacks as such? How do we react to Willie Mays as against Mickey Mantle? What is our response to Mays hitting a home run against Mantle performing the same deed? One has to come to the conclusion that it is because of black participation in baseball. Negroes still identify with the Dodgers because of Jackie Robinson's efforts with the Dodgers. Negroes would instinctively champion all-black teams if they opposed all white or predominantly white teams. The same principle operates for the movement as it does for baseball: a mystique must be created whereby Negroes can identify with the movement.

Thus an all-black project is needed in order for the people to free themselves. This has to exist from the beginning. This relates to what can be called "coalition politics." There is no doubt in our minds that some whites are just as disgusted with this system as we are. But it is meaningless to talk about coalition if there is no one to align ourselves with, because of the lack of organization in the white communities. There can be no talk of "hooking up" unless black people organize blacks and white people organize whites. If these conditions are met, then perhaps at some later date—and if we are going in the same direction—talks about exchange of personnel, coalition, and other meaningful alliances can be discussed.

In the beginning of the movement, we had fallen into a trap whereby we thought that our problems revolved around the right to eat at certain lunch counters or the right to vote, or to organize our communities. We have seen, however, that the problem is much deeper. The problem of this country, as we had seen it, concerned all blacks and all whites and therefore if decisions were left to the young people, then solutions would be arrived at. But this negates the history of black people and whites. We have dealt stringently with the problem of "Uncle Tom," but we have not yet gotten around to Simon Legree. We must ask ourselves, who is the real villain—Uncle Tom or Simon Legree? Everybody knows Uncle Tom, but who know Simon Legree? So what we have now in SNCC is a closed society, a clique. Black people cannot relate to SNCC because of its unrealistic, nonracial atmosphere; denying their experiences of America as a racist society. In contrast, the Southern Christian Leadership Conference of Martin Luther King, Jr., has a staff that at least maintains a black facade. The front office is virtually all black, but nobody accuses SCLC of being racist.

If we are to proceed toward true liberation, we must cut ourselves off from white people. We must form our own institutions, credit unions, co-ops, political parties, write our own histories.

To proceed further, let us make some comparisons between the Black Movement of the early 1900s and the movement of the 1960s—i.e., compare the National Association for the Advancement of Colored People with SNCC. Whites subverted the Niagara movement (the forerunner of the NAACP) which, at the outset, was an all-black movement. The name of the new organization was also very revealing, in that it presupposed blacks have to be advanced to the level of whites. We are now aware that the NAACP has grown reactionary, is controlled by the black power structure itself, and stands as one of the main roadblocks to black freedom. SNCC, by allowing the whites to remain in the organization, can have its efforts subverted in the same manner, i.e., through having them play important roles such as community organizers, etc. Indigenous leadership cannot be built with whites in the positions they now hold.

These facts do not mean that whites cannot help. They can participate on a voluntary basis. We can contract work out to them, but in no way can they participate on a policy-making level.

Black Self-Determination

The charge may be made that we are "racists," but whites who are sensitive to our problems will realize that we must determine our own destiny.

In an attempt to find a solution to our dilemma, we propose that our organization (SNCC) should be black-staffed, black-controlled, and black-financed. We do not want to fall into a similar dilemma that other civil rights organizations have fallen into. If we continue to rely upon white financial support we will find ourselves entwined in the tentacles of the white power complex that controls this country. It is also important that a black organization (devoid of cultism) be projected to our people so that it can be demonstrated that such organizations are viable.

More and more we see black people in this country being used as a tool of the white liberal establishment. Liberal whites have not begun to address themselves to the real problem of black people in this country—witness their bewilderment, fear, and anxiety when nationalism is mentioned concerning black people. An analysis of the white liberal's reaction to the word "nationalism" alone reveals a very meaningful attitude of whites of any ideological persuasion toward blacks in this country. It means previous solutions to black problems in this country have been made in the interests of those whites dealing with these problems and not in the best interests of black people in this country. Whites can only subvert our true search and struggle for self-determination, self-identification, and liberation in this country. Reevaluation of the white and black roles must NOW take place so that whites no longer designate roles that black people play but rather black people define white people's roles.

Too long have we allowed white people to interpret the importance and meaning of the cultural aspects of our society. We have allowed them to tell us what was good about our Afro-American music, art, and literature. How many black critics do we have on the "jazz" scene? How can a white person who is not part of the black psyche (except in the oppressor's role) interpret the meaning of the blues to us who are manifestations of the songs themselves?

It must be pointed out that on whatever level of contact blacks and whites come together, that meeting or confrontation is not on the level of the blacks but always on the level of the whites. This only means that our everyday contact with whites is a reinforcement of the myth of white supremacy. Whites are the ones who must try to raise themselves to our humanistic level. We are not, after all, the ones who are responsible for a genocidal war in Vietnam; we are not the ones who are responsible for neocolonialism in Africa and Latin America; we are not the ones who held a people in animalistic bondage over 400 years. We reject the American dream as defined by white people and must work to construct an American reality defined by Afro-Americans.

White Radicals

One of the criticisms of white militants and radicals is that when we view the masses of white people we view the overall reality of America, we view the racism, the bigotry, and the distortion of personality, we view man's inhumanity to man; we view in reality 180 million racists. The sensitive white intellectual and radical who is fighting to bring about change is conscious of this fact, but does not have the courage to admit this. When he admits this reality, then he must also admit his involvement because he is a part of the collective white America. It is only to the extent that he recognizes this that he will be able to change this reality.

Another common concern is, how does the white radical view the black community, and how does he view the poor white community, in terms of organizing? So far, we have found that most white radicals have sought to escape the horrible reality of America by going into the black community and attempting to organize black people while neglecting the organization of their own people's racist communities. How can one clean up someone else's yard when one's own yard is untidy? Again we feel that SNCC and the civil rights movement in general is in many aspects similar to the anticolonial situations in the African and Asian countries. We have the whites in the movement corresponding to the white civil servants and missionaries in the colonial countries who have worked with the colonial people for a long period of time and have developed a paternalistic attitude toward them. The reality of the colonial people taking over their own lives and controlling their own destiny must be faced. Having to move aside and letting the natural process of growth and development take place must be faced.

These views should not be equated with outside influence or outside agitation but should be viewed as the natural process of growth and development within a movement; so that the move by the black militants and SNCC in this direction should be viewed as a turn toward self-determination.

It is very ironic and curious that aware whites in this country can champion anticolonialism in other countries in Africa, Asia, and Latin America, but when black people move toward similar goals of self-determination in this country they are viewed as racists and anti-white by these same progressive whites. In proceeding further, it can be said that this attitude derives from the overall point of view of the white psyche as it concerns the black people. This attitude stems from the era of the slave revolts when every white man was a potential deputy or sheriff or guardian of the state. Because when black people got together among themselves to work out their problems, it becomes a threat to white people, because such meetings were potential slave revolts.

It can be maintained that this attitude or way of thinking has perpetuated itself to this current period and that it is part of the psyche of white people in this country whatever their political persuasion might be. It is part of the white fear-guilt complex resulting from the slave revolts. There have been examples of whites who stated that they can deal with black fellows on an individual basis but become threatened or menaced by the presence of groups of blacks. It can be maintained that this attitude is held by the majority of progressive whites in this country.

Black Identity

A thorough re-examination must be made by black people concerning the contributions that we have made in shaping this country. If this re-examination and re-evaluation is not made, and black people are not given their proper due and respect, then the antagonisms and contradictions are going to become more and more glaring, more and more intense, until a national explosion may result.

When people attempt to move from these conclusions it would be faulty reasoning to say they are ordered by racism, because, in this country and in the West, racism has functioned as a type of white nationalism when dealing with black people. We all know the habit that this has created throughout the world and particularly among nonwhite people in this country.

Therefore any re-evaluation that we must make will, for the most part, deal with identification. Who are black people, what are black people, what is their relationship to America and the world?

It must be repeated that the whole myth of "Negro citizenship," perpetuated by the white elite, has confused the thinking of radical and progressive blacks and whites in this country. The broad masses of black people react to American society in the same manner as colonial peoples react to the West in Africa, and Latin America, and had the same relationship—that of the colonized toward the colonizer.

9.2.   *STOKELY CARMICHAEL:* **A Declaration of War**

> [Between 1966 and 1968, various and conflicting political positions developed around the slogan "Black Power." Carmichael, one of the major figures in the early formulation of the slogan in 1966, seemed at the beginning of 1968 to propose a strategy of "black united fronts." The following is an excerpt from a speech delivered in Oakland, California, in February 1968, which represents the most explicit formulation of that thesis. Taken from the *San Francisco Express Times,* February 22, 1968.]

Tonight we have to talk about several things. We're here to celebrate Brother Huey P. Newton's birthday. We're not here to celebrate it as Huey

Newton the individual, but as Huey Newton part and parcel of black people wherever we are in the world today. And so in talking about Brother Huey Newton tonight we have to talk about the struggle of black people not only in the United States but in the world today and how he becomes part and parcel of that struggle, how we move on so that our people will survive America.

Therefore we are not talking about politics tonight, we're not talking about economics tonight, we are talking about the survival of a race of people. That is all that is at stake. We are talking about the survival of black people—nothing else, nothing else, nothing else. And you must understand that. Now why is it necessary for us to talk about the survival of our people? Many of us feel— many of our generation feel—that they're getting ready to commit genocide against us. Now many people say that's a horrible thing to say about anybody. But if it's a horrible thing to say, then we should do as Brother Malcom said, we should examine history.

The birth of this nation was conceived in the genocide of the red man, genocide of the red man, of the red man. In order for this country to come about, the honky had to completely exterminate the red man, *and he did it.* And he did it. He did it. And he did it where he doesn't even feel sorry but he romanticizes it by putting it on television with cowboys and indians, cowboys and indians.

Then the question we must ask ourselves is if he's capable of doing it to the red man, can he also do it to us?

Let us examine history some more. People say it is a horrible thing to say that white people would think about committing genocide against black people. Let us check our history out. It is a fact that we built this country, nobody else. I'll explain that to you. When this country started, economically it was an agricultural country. The cash crop on the world market was cotton. WE PICKED THE COTTON! We picked the cotton. We did it. So it is *we* who built this country. It is we who have fought in the wars of this country.

This country is becoming more and more technological so that the need for black people is fastly disappearing. When the need for black people disappears, so will we, and he will consciously wipe us out. He will consciously wipe us out.

Let us check World War II. He will not do it unto his own. Notice who he dropped an atomic bomb on, some helpless yellow people in Hiroshima, some *helpless* yellow people in Hiroshima, in Hiroshima. If you do not think he's capable of committing genocide, against us, check out what he's doing to our brothers in Vietnam, *check* out what he's doing in Vietnam. We have to understand that we're talking about our *survival* and nothing else, whether or not this beautiful race of people is gonna survive on the earth. That's what we're talking about, nothing else, nothing else.

If you do not think he's capable of wiping us out, check out the white race. Wherever they have gone they have ruled, conquered, murdered and plagued—whether they are the majority or the minority they *always* rule. They always rule, always rule.

And check out the pattern in which they move. They came to this country—they didn't know a damn thing about this country. The red man showed them how to adapt to this country. He showed them how to grow corn. He showed them how to hunt. And when the Indians finished showing him, *he wiped them out.* He wiped them out, he wiped them out.

As much as he has tried, our people have resisted for 413 years in this wilderness. And they resisted for *this* generation to carry out what must be done. We cannot fail our ancestors, cannot fail our ancestors, cannot fail our ancestors. We resisted in every way you can point to.

Take the English language. There are cats who come here from Italy, from Germany, from Poland, from France—in two generations they speak English perfectly. We have *never* spoken English perfectly, never have we spoken English perfectly, never, never, never. And that is because our people consciously resisted a language that did not belong to us. Never did, never will, anyhow they try to run it down our throat we ain't gonna have it, we ain't gonna have it. You must understand that as a level of resistance. Anybody can speak that simple honky's language correctly. Anybody can do it. We have not done it because we have resisted, resisted.

Check out our way of life. No matter how hard he's tried, we still maintain a communal way of life in our community. We do not send old people to old people's homes—that's junk, that's junk, that's junk, that's junk. We do not call children "illegitimate" in our community, we take care of *any* child in our community, any child in our community.

It is a level of resistance that we must begin to look for among our people. Pick up that thread and do what has to be done so that our people will survive. Three things: First and foremost, he has been able to make us hate each other. He has transplanted the hate and the love for each other for the love of his country—*his* country. We must begin to develop, number one, and this is the most important thing we can do as a people—we must first develop an undying love for our people, our people, our people, our people. We must develop an undying love as is personified in Brother Huey P. Newton. Undying love for our people, undying love. If we do not do that, we will be wiped out. We must develop an undying love for our people. Our slogan will become: First, our people, then and only then me and you as individuals. Our people first, our people first.

Following from that comes secondly the slogan: Every Negro is a potential black man. We *will* not alienate them, we will not alienate them, we will not alienate them. And we must understand the concept of Negro and the concept of black man. We came to this country as black men and as Africans. It took us 400 years to become Negroes. Understand that. That means that the concept of a black man is one who recognizes his cultural, his historical and the roots of his great ancestors who were the greatest warriors on the face of this earth—Africans, Africans, Africans.

Many of our people's minds have been whitewashed. If a Negro comes up to you and you turn your back on him, he's got to run to the honky. We're gonna take time, and patience with our people because they're *ours*. They're *ours*. All of the Uncle Toms, we're gonna sit down and we're gonna talk, and when they flap we're gonna bow, and when they flap we're gonna bow and we're gonna *try* to bring them home, and if they don't come home, we gonna off them, that's all, that's all.

We have to recognize who our major enemy is. The major enemy is not your brother, flesh of your flesh and blood of your blood. The major enemy is the honky and his institutions of racism, *that's* the major enemy, *that* is the major enemy. And whenever anybody prepares for revolutionary warfare, you concentrate on the major enemy. We're not strong enough to fight each other and also fight him. We *will* not fight each other today. There will *be* no fights in the black community among black people. There will just be people who will be offered. There will be no fights, there will be no disruptions. We are going to be united!

Thirdly, and most importantly, we must understand that for black people the question of community is not a question of geography. It is a question of color. It is a question of color. If you live in Watts, if you live in Harlem, South Side Chicago, Detroit, West Philadelphia, Georgia, Mississippi, Alabama, wherever you go, the first place you go is to your people. Not the land, to your *people*. For us the question of community is a question of color and our people—*not* geography, *not* land, not land, not land, not geography.

That is to say that we break down the concept that black people living inside the United States are black Americans. That's nonsense. We got brothers in Africa, we got brothers in Cuba, we got brothers in Brazil, we got brothers in Latin America, we got brothers all over the world, all over the world, all over the world. And once we begin to understand that the concept of community is simply one of our people, it don't make a difference where we are—we are with our people and therefore we are home. Therefore we are home.

Now then, speaking of survival, it is necessary to understand the moves of our enemy. The United States works on what we call the three Ms—the missionaries, the money, and the marines. That's precisely the way it's moved all over the world, it is the way it moves against *us*. They have sent the missionaries in—we sent them out. They have sent the money in, with the poverty program—the Vietnamese and the Koreans are pulling the money out. The next thing comes the marines. Comes the marines. And if we're talking seriously, we get prepared for the marines. Now if some black people do not think that the white man is gonna wipe us out completely, then it won't be no harm being prepared just in case he decides to do it, just in case he decides to do it. So there'll be no harm in us preparing ourselves for the marines.

Now there's a lot of tactics we can learn. The V[iet] C[ong] are showing us the best way to get it done, best way to get it done. And don't be afraid to say, yeah, you want the Vietnamese to defeat 'em 'cause they wrong from the jump. They wrong from the jump. They wrong. Don't get up there and play games with them. You ever see them on TV—"Well actually, we were wrong going into Vietnam but we can't get out unless we save face." To save that honky's face, millions of Vietnamese got to die. That's a lot of junk. If you're wrong, say you're wrong and get out. Get out, get out, get out.

We have to then go down the programs that they run through our throats and see how they relate to us. The first one is the vote. They got a new thing now: "Black power is the vote." The vote in this country is, has been, and always will be irrelevant to the lives of black people, that is a fact. We survived in Mississippi, Alabama, Georgia, Louisiana, Texas, South Carolina, North Carolina, Virginia and Washington, D.C. without the vote. Without the vote. Two years ago when Julian Bond was elected by black people in Georgia, they took him off the seat, there was no representation but black people in Georgia are surviving today. They took Adam Clayton Powell out of office, they had him out of office for a year and a half—black people in Harlem are still surviving. That should teach you the vote ain't nothing but a honky's trick, nothing but a honky's trick.

. . . .

And we must understand our communities. In our communities there are dope addicts, there are pimps, there are prostitutes, there are hustlers, there are teachers, there are maids, there are porters, there are preachers, there are gangsters. If I go to high school I want to learn how to be a good maid, a good porter, a good hustler, a good pimp, a good prostitute, a good preacher, a good teacher, or a good porter.

And education is supposed to prepare you to live in your community. That's what our community is like. If the educational system cannot do that, it must teach us how to change our community, how to change our community. It must do one or the other. The schools that we send our children to do not do one or the other. They do neither, they do something absolutely opposite. And when our youth, who are more intelligent than all those honkies on those boards drop out of that school 'cause they recognize it's not gonna help them, then we turn around and yell at them, dividing our community again, dividing our community again. We have to understand that unless *we* control the education system where it begins to teach us how to change our community where we live like human beings—no need to send anybody to school, that's just a natural fact.

We have no alternative but to fight, whether we like it or not. On every level in this country black people have *got* to fight, *got* to fight, *got* to fight.

Now let us move down and talk about organizing in a concept. We have in our community black people—the masses and the bourgeoisie, that's about the level of breakdown. The bourgeoisie is very, very minute inside our community. We have to bring them home. We have to bring them home for many reasons. We have to bring them home because they have technical skills which must be put to the benefit of their people, not for the benefit of this country which is against their people. We've got to bring them home, we've got to bring them home.

One of the ways of bringing our people home is by using patience, love, brotherhood and unity—not force—love, patience, brotherhood and unity. We try and we try and we try. If they become a threat, we off them. We off them.

But we must begin to understand that in a context of forming inside our community a united front—a *black* united front which engulfs every sector, every facet and every person inside our community working for the benefit of black people, working for the benefit of black people. And that is for each other's survival. A lot of people in the bourgeoisie tell me they don't like Rap Brown when he says, "I'm gonna burn the country down." But every time Rap Brown says, "I'm gonna burn the country down," they get a poverty program. They get a poverty program.

A lot of people say to me, we don't like the Black Panthers for Self-Defense walking around with guns. I tell you now, if the honkies in San Francisco take off the fighters who happen to represent the Black Panthers for Self-Defense (ain't nobody in this community prepared to fight right now), everybody gets offed. Everybody get offed.

We need each other, we have to have each other for our survival. We got to have each other, from the revolutionaries to the conservatives—a *black united front* is what we're about, a black united front is what we're about. Now there's some people may not understand Brother Rap when he talks about whom we ally with. He says we have to ally with Mexican-Americans, Puerto Ricans, and the dispossessed people of the earth. He did not mention poor whites. We must understand that. I will not deny that poor whites in this country are oppressed. But there are two types of oppression. One is exploitation, the other is colonization. And we have to understand the difference between both of them. Exploitation is when you exploit somebody of your own race. Colonization is when you exploit somebody of a different race. *We* are colonized, *they* are exploited. They are exploited.

Now let us explain how the process of exploitation and colonization works. If I am black and I am exploiting you who are also black, we have the same values, the same culture, the same language, the same society, the same institutions, so I do not have to destroy those institutions for you. But if you are of another race, if you have a different culture, different language, different values, I have to destroy all of those who make you bow to me. And that is the difference between poor black and poor white. Poor whites have their culture, have their values, have their institutions, ours have been completely destroyed, completely destroyed, completely destroyed.

So when you talk about alliances you recognize you form alliances with people who are trying to rebuild their culture, trying to rebuild their history, trying to rebuild their dignity, people who are fighting for their humanity. Poor white people are not fighting for their humanity, they're fighting for more money. There are a lot of poor white people in this country, you ain't seen none of them rebel yet, have you? Why is it that black people are rebelling? Do you think it's because it's just poor jobs? Don't believe that junk the honky is running down. It's not poor jobs—it's a question of a people finding their culture, their nature and fighting for their *humanity*, for their humanity, for their humanity, for their humanity.

. . . .

Now then that brings us to the point of this thing about communism and socialism. Let's get to that, once and for all. Communism is not an ideology suited for black people, period. Period. Socialism is not an ideology fitted for black people, period. Period. And I will tell you why. And it must become crystal clear in our minds. Now we don't say that because the honkies call us communist, we don't care what they call us, it don't make a difference, don't make a difference. The ideologies of communism and socialism speak to class structure. They speak to people who oppress people from the top down to the bottom. We are not just facing exploitation. We are facing something much more important, because we are the victims of racism. Communism nor socialism does not speak to the problem of racism. And racism, for black people in this country, is far more important than exploitation. 'Cause no matter how much money you make in the black community, when you go into the white world you are still a nigger, you are still a nigger, you are still a nigger.

So that for us, the question of racism becomes uppermost in our minds. It becomes uppermost in our minds. How do we destroy those institutions that seek to keep us dehumanized? That is all we're talking about. On the question of exploitation, it comes second.

Now for white people who are communists, the question of communism comes first, because they're exploited by other people. If you were exploited by other black people, then it would be a question of how we divide the profits. It is not that for us, it is not that for us. It is a question of how we regain our humanity and begin to live as a people—and we do not do that, because of the effects of racism in this country. We must therefore consciously strive for an ideology which deals with racism first, and, if we do that we recognize the necessity of hooking up with the nine hundred million black people in the world today. That's what we recognize.

And if we recognize that, then it means that our political situation *must* become international. It cannot be national, it cannot be national, it *must* be international, *must* be international. It must be international because if we knew anything, we would recognize that the honkies don't just exploit *us,* they exploit the whole Third World—Asia, Africa, Latin America. They take advantage of Europe, but they don't colonize Europe, they colonize Asia, Africa, and Latin America. Understand *that.*

. . . .

It's not a question of right or left, it's a question of black. You dig where we coming from? We coming from a *black* thing, from a *black* thing, that's where we coming from. Because we can begin to pick up the threads of resistance that our ancestors laid down for us. And unless we begin to understand our people as a people, we will not do that, because they *will* split us and divide us. That means consciously we have to begin to *organize our people!* Organize our people! Organize our people! Organize our people! Organize our people! Nothing else! Organize our people, our people! We have no time for them; all our sweat, all our blood, even our life must go to our people, nothing else.

We have to understand this consciously. Our youth must be organized with a revolutionary perspectus. A revolutionary perspectus says that we're fighting a war of liberation. In order to fight a war of liberation, you need an ideology of nationalism. We do not have this country. The nationalism can be nothing but black nationalism. It is insane to think of anything else. Black nationalism has to begin to be our ideology. While blackness is necessary it is not sufficient, so we must move on, we move on then to consciously organize in our communities. And we recognize today while we're organizing: we do not have the money to feed our people, so there's no use to say "organize, we can get you a job." We can't get 'em, they control 'em, that is a fact. That isn't a reason for you to sit down, it is only more the reason for you to fight, to think that you can't give your people a job. That's more of an inspiration to fight so you *can* give them a job rather than to sit down and say the honkies got us on every end. They are not God, they are not God. We are a beautiful race of people, we can do anything we want to do, all we got to do is get up, get up, get up and do it, get up and do it, get up and do it, get up and do it.

Now then we have to discuss very cold the question of rebellions. It is a fact that they're prepared to meet rebellions anywhere in the cities. Now what's gonna happen if one of our brothers get offed? What happens if they go ahead and off Huey Newton? We must develop tactics where we do the maximum damage to them with minor damage to us. And when we move into that arena, that means that this black community must be organized. So if Huey Newton goes, and ten honky cops goes, won't a black man in this community get up and open his mouth, 'cause if he does, *he* goes too, he goes too, he goes too, he goes too. That means that in organizing for the maximum damage against them and minor damage against us, we must be consciously aware of the fact that there will be people in our community who are going around doing just that. In our community we see nothing, we hear nothing, we know nothing. We see nothing, we hear nothing, we know nothing.

. . . .

We are talking about survival. We are talking about a people whose entire culture, whose entire history, whose entire way of life have been destroyed.

We're talking about a people who have produced in *this* year a generation of warriors who are going to restore to our people the humanity and the love that we have for each other. That's what we're talking about *today*, that's what we're talking about today. We are talking about becoming the executioners of our executioners. For example, you should give a lot of money to that defense fund, because while some of that money gonna go for that court thing, the rest of the money's gonna go for the executioners. So that if they execute Huey, the final execution rests in *our* hands, our hands, in our hands.

. . . .

Our problem is to develop an undying love for our people, an undying love for our people. We must be willing to give our talents, our sweat, our blood, even our life for our people. Nothing else! Not this country—our people!

We must develop the concept that every Negro is a potential black man. You do not alienate your potential allies. Let's bring our people *home*. Let's bring our people *home*.

We must understand the concept that for us the question of community is not geography, it is a question of us—black people—wherever we are, so we have to consciously become a part of the nine hundred million black people that are separated over this world. We were separated by *them*. We are blood of the same blood and flesh of the same flesh. We do not know who is our sister, who is our brother, or where we came from. They took us from Africa and they put thousands of miles of water between us, but they forgot—blood is thicker than water. We coming together, we coming together. Blood is thicker than water, blood is thicker than water.

We are an African people with an African ideology, we are wandering in the United States, we are going to build a concept of peoplehood in this country or there will be no country. Or there will be no country.

As I end, brothers and sisters, Brother Huey P. Newton belongs to us. He is flesh of our flesh, he is blood of our blood. He may be Mrs. Newton's baby, he's our brother. He's our brother. We do not have to talk about what we're going to do if we're consciously preparing and consciously willing to back those who prepare. All we say: Brother Huey will be set free—or else.

9.3.   Black Panther Party: Platform and Program

> [The Black Panther Party of California, formed in 1967 on the basis of nationalist revolutionary principles originally inspired by Malcolm X, has developed two new motifs in the black liberation movement: grass-roots organization in the black community (of Oakland), and the alliance with the Peace and Freedom party, a California organization composed mainly of white radicals.]

The program is usually divided into one section of ten points entitled "What We Want" and then ten paragraphs explaining these points in a section entitled "What We Believe." For the sake of clarity, we have put each one of the ten points in "What We Want" immediately above its corresponding paragraph in "What We Believe."

1. *We want freedom. We want power to determine the destiny of our Black Community.*

We believe that black people will not be free until we are able to determine our destiny.

2. *We want full employment for our people.*

We believe that the federal government is responsible and obligated to give every man employment or a guaranteed income. We believe that if the white American businessmen will not give full employment, then the means of production should be taken from the businessmen and placed in the community so that the people of the community can organize and employ all of its people and give a high standard of living.

3. *We want an end to the robbery by the white man of our Black Community.*

We believe that this racist government has robbed us and now we are demanding the overdue debt of forty acres and two mules. Forty acres and two mules was promised 100 years ago as restitution for slave labor and mass murder of black people. We will accept the payment in currency which will be distributed to our many communities. The Germans are now aiding the Jews in Israel for the genocide of the Jewish people. The Germans murder six million Jews. The American racist has taken part in the slaughter of over forty million black people; therefore, we feel that this is a modest demand that we make.

4. *We want decent housing, fit for shelter of human beings.*

We believe that if the white landlords will not give decent housing to our black community, then the housing and the land should be made into cooperatives so that our community, with government aid, can build and make decent housing for its people.

5. *We want education for our people that exposes the true nature of this decadent American society. We want education that teaches us our true history and our role in the present-day society.*

We believe in an educational system that will give to our people a knowledge of self. If a man does not have knowledge of himself and his position in society and the world, then he has little chance to relate to anything else.

6. *We want all black men to be exempt from military service.*

We believe that Black people should not be forced to fight in the military service to defend a racist government that does not protect us. We will not fight and kill other people of color in the world who, like black people, are being victimized by the white racist government of America. We will protect ourselves from the force and violence of the racist police and the racist military, by whatever means necessary.

7. *We want an immediate end to POLICE BRUTALITY and MURDER of black people.*

We believe we can end police brutality in our black community by organizing black self-defense groups that are dedicated to defending our black community from racist police oppression and brutality. The Second Amendment to the Constitution of the United States gives a right to bear arms. We therefore believe that all black people should arm themselves for self-defense.

8. *We want freedom for all black men held in federal, state, county and city prisons and jails.*

We believe that all black people should be released from the many jails and prisons because they have not received a fair and impartial trial.

9. *We want all black people when brought to trial to be tried in court by*

*a jury of their peer group or people from their black communities, as defined by
the Constitution of the United States.*

We believe that the courts should follow the United States Constitution
so that black people will receive fair trials. The 14th Amendment of the U.S.
Constitution gives a man a right to be tried by his peer group. A peer is a
person from a similar economic, social, religious, geographical, environmental,
historical and racial background. To do this the court will be forced to select a
jury from the black community from which the black defendant came. We have
been, and are being tried by all-white juries that have no understanding of
the "average reasoning man" of the black community.

10. *We want land, bread, housing, education, clothing, justice and peace.
And as our major political objective, a United Nations-supervised plebiscite
to be held throughout the black colony in which only black colonial subjects
will be allowed to participate, for the purpose of determining the will of the
black people as to their national destiny.*

When, in the course of human events, it becomes necessary for one people
to dissolve the political bands which have connected them with another, and
to assume, among the powers of the earth, the separate and equal station to
which the laws of nature and nature's God entitle them, a decent respect to the
opinions of mankind requires that they should declare the causes which impel
them to the separation.

We hold these truths to be self-evident, that all men are created equal;
that they are endowed by their Creator with certain unalienable rights; that
among these are life, liberty, and the pursuit of happiness. *That, to secure these
rights, governments are instituted among men, deriving their just powers
from the consent of the governed; that, whenever any form of government becomes destructive of these ends, it is the right of the people to alter or to
abolish it, and to institute a new government, laying its foundation on such
principles, and organizing its powers in such form, as to them shall seem most
likely to effect their safety and happiness.* Prudence, indeed, will dictate that
governments long established should not be changed for light and transient
causes; and, accordingly, all experience hath shown, that mankind are more
disposed to suffer, while evils are sufferable, than right themselves by abolishing the forms to which they are accustomed. *But, when a long train of abuses
and usurpations, pursuing invariably the same object, evinces a design to reduce them under absolute despotism, it is their right, it is their duty, to throw
off such government, and to provide new guards for their future security.*

9.4.   *ELDRIDGE CLEAVER:* **An Interview**

[Eldridge Cleaver, minister of information of the California Black
Panther party, is the author of the book *Soul on Ice* and was the U.S.
presidential candidate of the Black Panther–Peace and Freedom party
coalition. Selections from the *Guardian,* April 13 and 20, 1968.]

*You just came here directly from the Peace and Freedom (PFP) founding
convention in California. What sort of programs are emerging in the PFP at
this point?*

Well, the PFP has really started its life in an unusual manner, and I think
they did this in order to avoid some of the pitfalls the other political parties in
this country have fallen into. For instance, power in the PFP rests on the local

level. And different position papers, different ideas were presented at the convention, but they originated at the local level and a lot of these were not enacted at the convention but just discussed and sent back to the local level for ratification.

As far as the Black Panther party is concerned, one of the major successes of the convention was that the PFP as a whole took a position on Huey Newton; they took a position that he should be set free and they nominated him to run for the 7th Congressional District office there. And so we feel PFP has taken positions that squarely support the black liberation struggle in this country and we're quite satisfied with that.

I think the thing that attracted a lot of attention there was the question of what was going to be the relationship of black and brown people to the PFP. Everyone was thinking in terms of impending catastrophe. They had memories of Chicago on their minds, and they wanted to know how that would be settled in California. It was fortunate, I think, that a pilot project had already been underway in Alameda County. The Black Panther party had formed a loose coalition with the Alameda County branch of the PFP and we had had about three months of experience in working together, so that we had managed to get rid of a lot of the fears, a lot of the insecurities that black and white people had had in working together.

This experience was taken into the PFP convention and we were able to go into the Black Caucus and discuss our experience with the black and brown delegates from all over the state of California and to explain the mechanism of coalition as we had developed it with the Alameda County branch of the PFP. And we showed to them that it was a workable arrangement and it was accepted by the black and brown caucus. This is what averted any confrontation or any walkout or really any chaos or crisis.

What is the nature of that coalition?

The coalition is based on the recognition of the dual status of so-called minority people in this country. The point is that black people, Mexican-Americans and Puerto Ricans do have this paper status in this country; on paper they're entitled to the vote, on paper they're citizens, etc., but in actual fact they also have a national consciousness that develops out of their oppression so that in the black and Mexican-American communities today, much organizing is going on centered around the national consciousness and a neglected aspect has been this paper status that we have. We felt it would not be inconsistent with our goals if at the same time that we developed our organizations around our national consciousness, we also got whatever mileage could be gotten out of this paper status. All issues relating to the national question we defined as nonnegotiable issues of self-determination. The PFP has to recognize that when it comes to questions and issues that concern the black community solely, over which black people must have final say, this is not a negotiable issue and should not be run through machinery that is meant for negotiations. So that our suggestion was that we work in terms of a coalition on those items.

Machinery was established. We call it the California Coalitions Council. This body is composed of representatives from the PFP and the Black and Brown Caucus and issues of self-determination are brought before that body for discussion and for implementation. It's not to be voted upon and not to be kicked around; just for the purpose of determining ways and means of implementing it. We feel this will give black people the type of security they were seeking in Chicago with that 50%. All other issues of a general nature we felt could be handled through the regular machinery of the PFP. And on all those other issues the black and brown members of the PFP could participate in that manner.

Would your object in engaging in electoral politics be more educational or really aimed at achieving some sort of local power? Local political power?

No. We feel it would be an organizing tool. That's the only valid approach to electoral politics for black people in this country because this whole political system is so rigged, so based on huge amounts of money, that we couldn't really make a major drive for our liberation through that electoral process. We only entered the political arena in order to destroy the status quo. We feel the PFP acts as a vehicle for pulling people out of the Republican party and out of the Democratic party. We recognize there are a lot of black and white people in this country who are dissatisfied with the politics of this country and we feel it is very important that all pressure possible be exerted on the present Democratic and Republican parties. The ideal thing would be to destroy both of these parties.

. . . .

What effect will the recent merger with the Student Nonviolent Coordinating Committee (SNCC) have on the Panthers' relation to the PFP?

We don't think that it will have any effect as such. What it does is bring a lot of new ideas into play. People have to realize that there is an ideological struggle underway in the black community just as in the white community, and this is really an internal affair of the black colony and will be settled by black people and for black people. There are a few differences in the positions and ideas of the various people involved in the Black Panther party and in SNCC, but we don't feel that our merger with SNCC will bring about any earth-shaking change in our overall position.

We feel that we add to each other—this was the whole motivation behind the merger. The Black Panther party manages to reach people in the black community that no other organization in history has managed to reach, not even the Muslims or SNCC, and by getting the last man on the totem pole, which the Black Panther party will do, we are able then to begin uniting the black community from top to bottom. SNCC has great success in getting, say, college students together. Add the college students that SNCC is able to get to the hard brothers on the block that the Black Panther is able to get and you then have a mighty force that could do a helluva job here in Babylon.

What are the characteristics of this ideological struggle that you mention?

There's the whole question of whither black America? Some people feel we must move solely around our national consciousness. And some people feel we must put the major emphasis around our status as so-called American citizens, and this means that we move in terms of a Marxist class analysis; that the economic system is primary and that we must move as, say, the Communists move on the basis of their analysis, or the socialists' analysis. Some people are only able to utilize one or the other of these analyses, while the Black Panther party feels both of these are involved and we must make use of both of them.

We recognize the problem presented to black people by the economic system—the capitalist economic system. We repudiate the capitalist economic system. We recognize the class nature of the capitalist economic system and we recognize the dynamics involved in the capitalist system. At the same time we recognize the national character of our struggle. We recognize the fact that we have been oppressed because we are black people even though we know this oppression was for the purpose of exploitation. We have to deal with both exploitation and racial oppression, and we don't think you can achieve a proper balance by neglecting one or the other. So there are contradictions in the positions of different people. Some people, as I said, base their moves on one to the exclusion of the other. But we feel we have to harness both of these aspects and move on both of them at the same time. We don't have the luxury of just picking or choosing one or the other. We have to deal with the overall situation at one and the same time.

How does the class analysis break down in terms of the black community itself? For example, there is a great move afoot now to use the united front as a tactic in organizing the black community, to unify the whole black community if possible, but you're still going to have to deal with the class question within the community itself. Does this pose a special problem, do you think?

I think that there is a danger involved in the great desire for black unity, which is that some people become so overly optimistic because to them black unity is so desirable they cannot understand how anyone would work against it. But I think we have to realize that in the black community we have people who are just as vicious and degenerate as Chiang Kai-shek or Batista ever were, and that these people would never become part of a united front, and they would only join a united front to subvert it. When you start talking about building a united front and bringing every black man in the black community into this united front, I think you're chasing an illusion. At the same time, this may be the proper posture that one must maintain in order to make manifest the disruptive elements within the community. So that we say okay, let's push the black united front, and we'll go with you all the way, but let's be on our toes and be wary of the enemies within so that when they make themselves manifest we move against them. There are classes within the black community; they're not as elaborate and as stable as the class division within the white community because they don't have as strong an economic base, but they do exist. They have various interests that conflict with the interests of the black masses and they're going to guard these very jealously. We call on the black bourgeoisie to come home, we leave the door open for them to come home, but I think that we have to assume that a lot of them are not going to.

. . . .

There's a great deal of debate going on within the black liberation movement as to what should be its ultimate goals. That is, should there be, for example, total separation, control of the cities, integration, or what have you. You have called for a black plebiscite to deal with this question. Would you comment on that?

Yes. I think that for too long now individuals and splinter organizations have stood up and spoken out as to what they think the dreams and the will and the desire of black people is as to their national destiny. We feel the only way to settle this is to have a plebiscite held throughout the U.S., so that black people can go into a polling booth and state for themselves what they want; that the United Nations should come in and supervise the plebiscite, and that people on both sides of the question can campaign throughout the country and organize throughout the country. This is why we called for a UN-supervised black plebiscite.

What alternatives would be offered in the black plebiscite?
I think that in the black plebiscite the alternatives are clear. Whether or not black people want to be part of America, and to have citizenship in America. Or whether or not they want to be separated into a sovereign nation of their own.

What about the third alternative being suggested by some people which would be control of certain cities?
We don't think this is realistic. As long as you have sovereignty in the hands of a force that you're not able to control you're in trouble. So I say the political structure of this country has to be totally rearranged so that black people can have some control over the implementation of the sovereignty of this country—which means they must have power in their hands.

Do you believe that such a UN-supervised black plebiscite is a realistic objective to work for, or would this again be an organizing tool?
I think it is a realistic objective, but at the same time I think it would be a tremendous organizing tool. I think that what we could do now is to form committees for the black plebiscite throughout Afro-America and start the agitation and the call for the black plebiscite, and inject this now into our politics. It would give the whole black liberation struggle a national focus which is very important, because at this particular time the national focus is lacking.
One other thing, a companion call to the black plebiscite is a call for UN observers to be stationed in the large cities of this country. We feel that unless something like this is done, unless the situation is taken out of the hands of the racist American government, we're going to have a civil war in this country, because black people are not just going to accept the escalation of the power structure against black communities.

It seems that the U.S. government is arming itself for some sort of massive confrontation this summer with the black communities. It has been suggested that black people are not ready, realistically speaking, for such an armed confrontation with the massive repressive forces of the establishment. What posture should black radicals adopt in this impending confrontation and how should they relate this to the black communities?
The posture that we have adopted is to open every avenue of defense that we possibly can, and this explains everything we've done in terms of the political arrangement, the alliance with the white radicals, our call for the black plebiscite, our call for UN observers and also our program of calling upon the black community to arm itself. We feel that in the last analysis black people must rely upon themselves. There's a world of difference between 20,000,000 unarmed black people and 20,000,000 armed black people.

One serious problem that will have to be dealt with, assuming that the black liberation struggle is successful and that the mother country revolution is successful, is that the black colony is dispersed throughout the mother country. Would you see physical separation as being necessary or do you be-

lieve some sort of dual sovereignty arrangement could be worked out on a political basis without necessitating physical separation?

Let me say that you've touched on what I think is the most important problem the black people have had to grapple with historically in this country—the land question. The fact is that black people are dispersed throughout the population of the mother country and that we've been subjected to a form of decentralized colonization. The hang-up I think Marcus Garvey was confronted with was the land question again. He sought to solve the land question by focusing on Africa and attempting to transport black people back to Africa, but he didn't have the wherewithal to do that. The same thing happened in the case of the Black Muslim movement and Elijah Muhammed in calling for several of these states to be set aside, but he was not able to implement this either.

The beauty and the function of the slogan of black power, the reason that it caught on is because it did not reject the land question but it held the land question in abeyance. It was a local application of the dictum of Kwame Nkrumah that stated, "Seek ye first the political kingdom and all things shall be added unto you." We feel that this is the reason the black power concept caught on so much, because at the present time the land question is insoluble. We're not in a position to force any settlement on the land question.

I say that the world is becoming such a small community that the whole question of geographic homelands does seem to dwindle in importance. At the same time a lot of black people do want a geographic homeland of their own. But as far as I'm concerned this whole question can remain up in the air a little while longer. The primary function of black people now is to get this organizational power. Once they get that power they can relate to the third world powers throughout the world, and through this coalition of forces we can force the type of settlement upon the U.S. that we decide we want.

9.5. *HUEY P. NEWTON:* **An Interview**

[Huey P. Newton was one of the initiators and is now the "Minister of Defense" of the Oakland Black Panther party, whose theoretical bases he repeatedly enunciated. The following interview, published in *The Movement,* August 1968, may be considered one of the most articulated documents of Black Power. Huey P. Newton is now in jail, serving a two- to fifteen-year term for shooting and killing a policeman.]

The question of nationalism is a vital one in the black movement today. Some have made a distinction between cultural nationalism and revolutionary nationalism. Would you comment on the differences and give us your views?

There are two kinds of nationalism, revolutionary nationalism and reactionary nationalism. Revolutionary nationalism is first dependent upon a people's revolution with the end goal being the people in power. Therefore to be a revolutionary nationalist you would by necessity have to be a socialist. If you are a reactionary nationalist you are not a socialist and your end goal is the oppression of the people.

Cultural nationalism, or pork chop nationalism, as I sometimes call it, is basically a problem of having the wrong political perspective. It seems to be a reaction instead of responding to political oppression. The cultural nationalists are concerned with returning to the old African culture and thereby regaining their identity and freedom. In other words, they feel that the African culture will automatically bring political freedom. Many times cultural nationalists fall into line as reactionary nationalists.

Papa Doc in Haiti is an excellent example of reactionary nationalism. He oppresses the people but he does promote the African culture. He's against anything other then black, which on the surface seems very good, but for him it is only to mislead the people. He merely kicked out the racists and replaced them with himself as the oppressor. Many of the nationalists in this country seem to desire the same ends.

The Black Panther Party, which is a revolutionary group of black people, realizes that we have to have an identity. We have to realize our black heritage in order to give us strength to move on and progress. But as far as returning to the old African culture, it's unnecessary and it's not advantageous in many respects. We believe that culture itself will not liberate us. We're going to need some stronger stuff.

A good example of a revolutionary nationalism was the revolution in Algeria when Ben Bella took over. The French were kicked out but it was a people's revolution because the people ended up in power. The leaders that took over were not interested in the profit motive where they could exploit the people and keep them in a state of slavery. They nationalized the industry and plowed the would-be profits into the community. That's what socialism is all about in a nutshell. The people's representatives are in office strictly on the leave of the people. The wealth of the country is controlled by the people and they are considered whenever modifications in the industries are made.

The Black Panther Party is a revolutionary Nationalist group and we see a major contradiction between capitalism in this country and our interests. We realize that this country became very rich upon slavery and that slavery is capitalism in the extreme. We have two evils to fight, capitalism and racism. We must destroy both racism and capitalism.

Directly related to the question of nationalism is the question of unity within the black community. There has been some question about this since the Black Panther Party has run candidates against other black candidates in recent California elections. What is your position on this matter?
Well a very peculiar thing has happened. Historically you got what Malcolm X calls the field nigger and the house nigger. The house nigger had some privileges, a little more. He got the worn-out clothes of the master and he didn't have to work as hard as the field black. He came to respect the master to such an extent until he identified with the master because he got a few of the leftovers that the field blacks did not get. And through this identity with him, he saw the slavemaster's interest as being his interest. Sometimes he would even protect the slavemaster more than the slavemaster would protect himself. Malcolm makes the point that if the master's house happened to catch on fire the house Negro will work harder than the master to put the fire out and save the master's house. While the field Negro, the field blacks was praying that the house burned down. The house black identified with the master so much that when the master would get sick the house Negro would say, "Master, we's sick!"

The Black Panther Party are the field blacks, we're hoping the master dies if he gets sick. The Black bourgeoisie seem to be acting in the role of the house Negro. They are pro-administration. They would like a few concessions made, but as far as the overall setup, they have a little more material goods, a little more advantage, a few more privileges than the black have-nots; the lower class. And so they identify with the power structure and they see their interests as the power structure's interest. In fact, it's against their interest.

The Black Panther Party was forced to draw a line of demarcation. We are for all of those who are for the promotion of the interests of the black have-nots, which represents about 98% of blacks here in America. We're not controlled by the white mother country radicals nor are we controlled by the black bourgeoisie. We have a mind of our own and if the black bourgeoisie cannot align itself with our complete program, then the black bourgeoisie sets itself up as our enemy. And they will be attacked and treated as such.

The Black Panther Party has had considerable contact with white radicals since its earliest days. What do you see as the role of these white radicals?

The white mother country radical is the off-spring of the children of the beast that has plundered the world exploiting all people, concentrating on the people of color. These are children of the beast that seek now to be redeemed because they realize that their former heroes, who were slave masters and murderers, put forth ideas that were only facades to hide the treachery they inflicted upon the world. They are turning their backs on their fathers.

The white mother country radical, in resisting the system, becomes somewhat of an abstract thing because he's not oppressed as much as black people are. As a matter of fact his oppression is somewhat abstract simply because he doesn't have to live in a reality of oppression.

Black people in America and colored people throughout the world suffer not only from exploitation, but they suffer from racism. Black people here in America, in the black colony, are oppressed because we're black and we're exploited. The whites are rebels, many of them from the middle class and as far as any overt oppression this is not the case. So therefore I call their rejection of the system somewhat of an abstract thing. They're looking for new heroes. They're looking to wash away the hypocrisy that their fathers have presented to the world. In doing this they see the people who are really fighting for freedom. They see the people who are really standing for justice and equality and peace throughout the world. They are the people of Vietnam, the people of Latin America, the people of Asia, the people of Africa, and the black people in the black colony here in America.

This presents somewhat of a problem in many ways to the black revolutionary, especially to the cultural nationalist. The cultural nationalist doesn't understand the white revolutionaries because he can't see why anyone white would turn on the system. So they think that maybe this is some more hypocrisy being planted by white people.

I personally think that there are many young white revolutionaries who are sincere in attempting to realign themselves with mankind, and to make a reality out of the high moral standards that their fathers and forefathers only expressed. In pressing for new heroes the young white revolutionaries found the heroes in the black colony at home and in the colonies throughout the world.

The young white revolutionaries raised the cry for the troops to withdraw from Vietnam, hands off Latin America, withdraw from the Dominican Republic and also to withdraw from the black community or the black colony.

So you have a situation in which the young white revolutionaries are attempting to identify with the oppressed people of the colonies and against the exploiter.

The problem arises then in what part they can play. How can they aid the colony? How can they aid the Black Panther Party or any other black revolutionary group? They can aid the black revolutionaries first by simply turning away from the establishment, and secondly by choosing their friends. For instance, they have a choice between whether they will be a friend of Lyndon Baines Johnson or a friend of Fidel Castro. A friend of Robert Kennedy or a friend of Ho Chi Minh. And these are direct opposites. A friend of mine or a friend of Johnsons. After they make this choice then the white revolutionaries have a duty and a responsibility to act.

. . . .

As far as our party is concerned, the Black Panther Party is an all black party, because we feel as Malcom X felt that there can be no black-white unity until there first is black unity. We have a problem in the black colony that is particular to the colony, but we're willing to accept aid from the mother country as long as the mother country radicals realize that we have, as Eldridge Cleaver says in *Soul on Ice,* a mind of our own. We've regained our mind that was taken away from us and we will decide the political as well as the practical stand that we'll take. We'll make the theory and we'll carry out the practice. It's the duty of the white revolutionary to aid us in this.

So the role of the mother country radical, and he does have a role, is to first choose his friend and his enemy and after doing this, which it seems he's already done, then to not only articulate his desires to regain his moral standard and align himself with humanity, but also to put this into practice by attacking the protectors of the institutions.

. . . .

Would you like to be more specific on the conditions which must exist before an alliance or coalition can be formed with predominantly white groups? Would you comment specifically on your alliance with the California Peace and Freedom Party?

We have an alliance with the Peace and Freedom Party. The Peace and Freedom Party has supported our program in full and this is the criterion for a coalition with the black revolutionary group. If they had not supported our program in full, then we would not have seen any reason to make an alliance with them, because we are the reality of the oppression. They are not. They are only oppressed in an abstract way; we are oppressed in the real way. We are the real slaves! So it's a problem that we suffer from more than anyone else and it's our problem of liberation. Therefore we should decide what measures and what tools and what programs to use to become liberated. Many of the young white revolutionaries realize this and I see no reason not to have a coalition with them.

Other black groups seem to feel that from past experience it is impossible for them to work with whites and impossible for them to form alliances. What do you see as the reasons for this and do you think that the history of the Black Panther Party makes this less of a problem?

There was somewhat of an unhealthy relationship in the past with the white liberals supporting the black people who were trying to gain their freedom. I think that a good example of this would be the relationship that SNCC had with its white liberals. I call them white liberals because they differ strictly from the white radicals. The relationship was that the whites controlled SNCC for a very long time. From the very start of SNCC until here recently whites were the mind of SNCC. They controlled the program of SNCC with money and they controlled the ideology, or the stands SNCC would take. The blacks in SNCC were completely controlled program-wise; they couldn't do any more than these white liberals wanted them to do, which wasn't very much. So the white liberals were not working for self-determination for the black community. They were interested in a few concessions from the power structure. They undermined SNCC's program.

Stokely Carmichael came along and realizing this started to follow Malcolm X's program of Black Power. This frightened many of the white liberals who were supporting SNCC. Whites were afraid when Stokely came along with Black Power and said that black people have a mind of their own and that SNCC would be an all-black organization and that SNCC would seek self-determination for the black community. The white liberals withdrew their support leaving the organization financially bankrupt. The blacks who were in the organization, Stokely and H. Rap Brown, were left very angry with the white liberals who had been aiding them under the disguise of being sincere. They weren't sincere.

The result was that the leadership of SNCC turned away from the white liberal, which was very good. I don't think they distinguished between the white liberal and the white revolutionary, because the white revolutionary is white also and they are very much afraid to have any contact whatsoever with white people. Even to the point of denying that the white revolutionaries could give support, by supporting the programs of SNCC in the mother country. Not by making any programs, not by being a member of the organization, but simply by resisting. Just as the Vietnamese people realize that they are supported whenever other oppressed people throughout the world resist. Because it helps divide the troops. It drains the country militarily and economically. If the mother country radicals are sincere then this will definitely add to the attack that we are making on the power structure. The Black Panther Party's program is a program where we recognize that the revolution in the mother country will definitely aid us in our freedom and has everything to do with our struggle!

I think that one of SNCC's great problems is that they were controlled by the traditional administrator: the omnipotent administrator, the white person. He was the mind of SNCC. And so SNCC regained its mind, but I believe that it lost its political perspective. I think that this was a reaction rather than a response. The Black Panther Party has NEVER been controlled by white people. The Black Panther Party has always been a black group. We have always had an integration of mind and body. We have never been controlled by whites and therefore we don't fear the white mother country radicals. Our alliance is one of organized black groups with organized white groups. As soon as the organized white groups do not do the things that would benefit us in our struggle for liberation, that will be our departure point. So we don't suffer in the hangup of a skin color. We don't hate white people; we hate the oppressor. And if the oppressor happens to be white then we hate him. When he stops oppressing us then we no longer hate him. And right now in America you have the slave-master being a white group. We are pushing him out of office through revolution in this country. I think the responsibility of the white revolutionary will be to aid us in this. And when we are attacked by the police or by the military then it will be up to the white mother country radicals to attack the murderers and to respond as we respond, to follow our program.

. . . .

You mentioned at another point that the guerrilla was the perfect man and this kind of formulation seems to fit in directly with the guerrilla as a political man. Would you like to comment on this?

Yes. The guerrilla is a very unique man. This is in contrast to Marxist-Leninist orthodox theories where the party controls the military. The guerrilla is not only the warrior, the military fighter; he is also the military commander as well as the political theoretician. Debray says "poor the pen without the guns, poor the gun without the pen." The pen being just an extension of the mind, a tool to write down concepts, ideas. The gun is only an extension of the body, the extension of our fanged teeth that we lost through evolution. It's the weapon, it's the claws that we lost, it's the body. The guerrilla is the military commander and the political theoretician all in one.

In Bolivia Ché said that he got very little help from the Communist Party there. The Communist Party wanted to be the mind, the Communist Party wanted to have full control of the guerrilla activity. But yet weren't taking part in the practical work of the guerrillas. The guerrilla on the other hand is not only united within himself, but he also attempts to spread this to the people by educating the villagers, giving them political perspective, pointing out things, educating them politically, and arming the people. Therefore the guerrilla is giving the peasants and workers a mind. Because they've already got the body you get a unity of the mind and the body. Black people here in America, who have long been the workers, have regained our minds and we have a unity of mind and body.

. . . .

Would you comment further on what you mean by Black Power?

Black Power is really people's power. The Black Panther Program, Panther Power as we call it, will implement this people's power. We have respect for all of humanity and we realize that the people should rule and determine their destiny. Wipe out the controller. To have Black Power doesn't humble or subjugate anyone to slavery or oppression. Black Power is giving power to people who have not had power to determine their destiny. We advocate and we aid any people who are struggling to determine their destiny. This is regardless of color. The Vietnamese say Vietnam should be able to determine its own destiny. Power of the Vietnamese people. We also chant power of the Vietnamese people. The Latins are talking about Latin America for the Latin Americans. Cuba Si and Yanqui, Non. It's not that they don't want the Yankees to have any power they just don't want them to have power over them. They can have power over themselves. We in the black colony in America want to be able to have power over our destiny and that's black power.

. . . .

How would you characterize the mood of black people in America today? Are they disenchanted, wanting a larger slice of the pie, or alienated, not want-

ing to integrate into a burning house, not wanting to integrate into Babylon? What do you think it will take for them to become alienated and revolutionary?

I was going to say disillusioned, but I don't think we were ever under the illusion that we had freedom in this country. This society is definitely a decadent one and we realize it. Black people are realizing it more and more. We cannot gain our freedom under the present system; the system that is carrying out its plans of institutionalized racism. Your question is what will have to be done to stimulate them to revolution. I think it's already being done. It's a matter of time now for us to educate them to a program and show them the way to liberation. The Black Panther Party is the beacon light to show black people the way to liberation.

You notice the insurrections that have been going on throughout the country, in Watts, in Newark, in Detroit. They were all responses of the people demanding that they have freedom to determine their destiny, rejecting exploitation. Now the Black Panther Party does not think that the traditional riots or insurrections that have taken place are the answer. It is true they have been against the Establishment, they have been against authority and oppression within their community, but they have been unorganized. However, black people learned from each of these insurrections.

They learned from Watts. I'm sure the people in Detroit were educated by what happened in Watts. Perhaps this was wrong education. It sort of missed the mark. It wasn't quite the correct activity, but the people were educated through the activity. The people of Detroit followed the example of the people in Watts, only they added a little scrutiny to it. The people in Detroit learned that the way to put a hurt on the administration is to make Molotov cocktails and to go into the street in mass numbers. So this was a matter of learning. The slogan went up "Burn, baby, burn." People were educated through the activity and it spread throughout the country. The people were educated on how to resist, but perhaps incorrectly.

What we have to do as a vanguard of the revolution is to correct this through activity. The large majority of black people are either illiterate or semiliterate. They don't read. They need activity to follow. This is true of any colonized people. The same thing happened in Cuba where it was necessary for twelve men with a leadership of Ché and Fidel to take to the hills and then attack the corrupt administration; to attack the army who were the protectors of the exploiters in Cuba. They could have leafleted the community and they could have written books, but the people would not respond. They had to act and the people could see and hear about it and therefore become educated on how to respond to oppression.

In this country black revolutionaries have to set an example. We can't do the same things that were done in Cuba because Cuba is Cuba and the U.S. is the U.S. Cuba has many terrains to protect the guerrilla. This country is mainly urban. We have to work out new solutions to offset the power of the country's technology and communication; its ability to communicate very rapidly by telephone and teletype and so forth. We do have solutions to these problems and they will be put into effect. I wouldn't want to go into the ways and means of this, but we will educate through action. We have to engage in action to make the people want to read our literature. Because they are not attracted to all the writing in this country; there's too much writing. Many books makes one weary.

FURTHER READINGS

Allen, Robert. "Dialectics of Black Power." *Guardian,* May 25, 1968.
Barbour, Floyd (ed.). *The Black Power Revolt.* Boston: Porter Sargent, 1968.
"Black Power: A Discussion." *Partisan Review,* Spring 1968.
Bennett, Lerone, Jr. "Stokely Carmichael, Architect of Black Power." *Ebony,* July 1966.
Braden, Anne. "The SNCC Trends: Challenge to White America." *The Southern Patriot,* May 5, 1966.
Boggs, James. "The American Revolution—Pages from a Negro Writer's Notebook." *Monthly Review,* XV: July/August 1963.
Brown, Rap. "Racism and Revolution" (interview). *Guardian,* June 15, 1968.
Carmichael, Stokely. "Statement on Black Power." *National Guardian,* June 25, 1966.
————. "What We Want." *New York Review of Books,* August 1966.
———— and Charles V. Hamilton. *Black Power—The Politics of Liberation in America.* New York: Vintage, 1967.
Cleaver, Eldridge. "Requiem for Nonviolence." *Ramparts,* May 1968.
————. *Soul on Ice.* New York: New American Library, A Ramparts Book, 1968.
Edelman, Irwin. "White Radicals and Black Liberation, the Necessity of Coalition." *Liberation,* September 1968.
Fanon, Frantz. *The Wretched of the Earth.* New York: Grove Press, 1963.
Forman, Jim. "1967: High Tide of Black Resistance." Pamphlet, 1967.
Grant, Joanne. *Black Protest.* Fawcett, 1967.
Hayden, Tom. *Rebellion in Newark: Official Violence and Ghetto Response.* New York: Random House, 1967.
Interview with Stokely Carmichael on the Alabama Black Panther Party Organizer, *The Movement,* February and March 1966.
Interview with Rap Brown. *The National Guardian,* July 1967.
Interview with Stokely Carmichael. *The National Guardian,* June 4, 1966.
Jacobs, Harold. "SNCC and Black Power." *International Socialist Journal,* August 1967.
James, Mike, and Lawson, Bob. "Poor White Response to Black Rebellion." *The Movement,* August 1967.
King, Martin Luther, Jr. "It is Not Enough to Condemn Black Power." *The New York Times,* July 26, 1966.
Kopkind, Andrew. "The Future of Black Power." *The New Republic,* January 7, 1967.
Landy, Sy, and Capper, Charles. "In Defense of Black Power." *Independent Socialist Club,* 1967.
Lester, Julius. *Look Out Whitey!* New York: The Dial Press, 1968.
————. "White Radicals and Black Liberation, Coalition with Whom?—A Reply." *Liberation,* October 1968.
Malcolm X. *Autobiography.* New York: Grove Press, 1965.
Malcolm X Speaks. George Breitman, ed. New York: Merit Publishers, 1965.
Meier and Broderick (eds.). *Negro Protest Thought in the 20th Century.* Indianapolis: Bobbs-Merrill, 1966.
Miller, Mike: "Is There a Change in SNCC?" *The Movement,* July 6, 1966.
Rustin, Bayard. "Black Power and Coalition Politics." Reprinted in *Commentary,* September 1966. Philip Randolph Institute, New York.
SDS statement on SNCC. *New Left Notes,* May 27, 1966.
Silberman, Charles. *Crisis in Black and White.* New York: Random House, 1964.
Williams, Robert F. *Negroes with Guns,* Marc Schleiffer, ed. Marzani and Munsell, 1962.

10

Antidraft Resistance   10.1.   "We Won't Go" Statement

[The following is probably the first "We Won't Go" statement circulated by members of the May Second Movement and signed by about 500 people in Spring 1964. The May Second Movement was an anti-imperialist group of pro-Maoist orientation.]

WE THE UNDERSIGNED,

ARE YOUNG AMERICANS OF DRAFT AGE. We understand our obligations to defend our country and to serve in the armed forces but we object to being asked to support the war in South Vietnam.

Believing that United States' participation in that war is for the suppression of the Vietnamese struggle for national independence, we see no justification for our involvement. We agree with Senator Wayne Morse, who said on the floor of the Senate on March 4, 1964, regarding South Vietnam, that "We should never have gone in. We should never have stayed in. We should get out."

BELIEVING THAT WE SHOULD NOT BE ASKED TO FIGHT AGAINST THE PEOPLE OF VIETNAM, WE HEREWITH STATE OUR REFUSAL TO DO SO.

10.2.   **Resistance: "We Refuse to Serve"**

[The movement against military service, which developed in 1967–1968, is distinct from and yet parallel to the movement against the war in Vietnam. Among the various groups, The Resistance arose in the San Francisco Bay area and then joined with similar groups throughout the country. The declaration "We Refuse to Serve" was distributed in April 1967; it states a position of noncooperation, open confrontation with the military authorities, and mutual solidarity among the resisters.]

I. *We Refuse to Serve*

IN THE PAST few months, in many parts of the country, a resistance has been forming . . . a resistance of young men—joined together in their commitment against the war. . . .

We will renounce all deferments and refuse to cooperate with the draft in any manner, at any level. We have taken this stand for varied reasons:

    oposition to conscription

    opposition only to the Vietnam war

    opposition to all wars and to all American military adventures.

We all agree on one point: the war in Vietnam is criminal and we must act together, at great individual risk, to stop it. Those involved must lead the American people, by their example, to understand the enormity of what their government is doing . . . that the government cannot be allowed to continue with its daily crimes. . . .

There are many ways to avoid the draft, to stay clear of this war. Most of us now have deferments . . . but all these individual outs can have no effect on the draft, the war, or the consciousness of this country. To cooperate with conscription is to perpetuate its existence, without which, the government could not wage war. We have chosen to openly defy the draft and confront the government and its war directly.

This is no small decision in a person's life. Each one realizes that refusing to cooperate with Selective Service may mean prison. Again we agree that to do anything but this is to effectively abet the war. The government will not be permitted to use us on its way to greater crimes and destruction. We prefer to resist.

The organization is an action committee, composed of those who make this commitment. We stand all-for-one, one-for-all. We are prepared to act together to support anyone singled out for arrest by every means possible, including civil disobedience and unified, public violations of the Selective Service Act. As the resistance grows, the government will either have to allow the draft noncooperators to go free and thereby swell our ranks, or fill the jails. . . .

II. *The Politics of Resistance*

. . . The government's success in countering the challenge of the anti-war movement is directly related to its ability to co-opt the ideals and strategy of the movement. . . . The challenge presented by the peace movement has become assimilated into the dominant structure of power, and hence transformed into an integral part of that structure. . . . To accept the bounds of the established structure of authority and to define the political action of the movement in terms of that structure, means to accept political emasculation and the inevitable co-optation of the movement's spirit and energies.

The stance of resistance is active, rather than passive, offensive, rather than defensive. The aim of resistance is to provoke continual confrontations with the governmental institutions linked to the war. The resistance confronts the government with an unresolvable dilemma: to prosecute and imprison us, which will generate new waves of protest and dissent, of unsurpassed intensity; or to set us free, which will provide greater impetus for the expansion of the movement. . . .

III. *Going Beyond Prayers to an Unjust King*

. . . It is becoming increasingly clear that peace cannot be attained unless some fundamental change is first effected within American society, that there is something about the functioning of the American "system" that does not permit it to respond other than violently to the yearnings of the people it oppresses. . . . One cannot appeal to a repository of justice that does not exist. The incantation of protest must become resistance if we are to avoid the co-optation, invisibility, and sheer impotence that have, up to now, been our experience with regard to the war and the whole issue of the garrison society in America. There is, however, one potential repository of justice, and that is "the people."

. . . If the normal day to day pattern of American life were sufficiently disrupted, people in large numbers would have to begin thinking about the nature of their lives and the society around them. . . . People and societies have a hard time existing out of equilibrium. If we can succeed in breaking the emptiness of the current equilibrium of American society (and it is already being severely threatened by a monstrously confusing war, and by bewildering revolt in our own cities) a new equilibrium will have to be found. . . .

. . . Noncooperation must be seen in its larger context: a seizing of control of our own lives and a conscious effort to redirect the movement of American society.

. . . If all the issues can be clarified and tied together by competent community organizers, if viable courses of action can then be charted by an organized people, we will again see America moving in the direction of justice and democracy. . . .

IV. *The Resistance*

Since the United States is engaged in criminal activity in Vietnam,

Since the major instrument of that criminal activity is the American military establishment,

Since the machinery of the military cannot effectively function without the acquiescence of the people it is supposed to represent,

Since we are young Americans who still believe in the ideals our country once stood for,

The RESISTANCE has been formed to organize and encourage resistance to, disruption of, and noncooperation with all the war-making machinery of the United States.

The RESISTANCE is a nationwide movement with organizations in New York, Illinois, Massachusetts, Iowa, Ohio, Wisconsin, Michigan, Oregon, and California.

ON OCTOBER 16, 1967, WE WILL PUBLICLY AND COLLECTIVELY RETURN OUR DRAFT CARDS TO THE SELECTIVE SERVICE SYSTEM IN MAJOR CITIES THROUGHOUT THE COUNTRY. We will clearly challenge the government's right to use any young lives for its own nefarious purposes. Our challenge will continue, and we will openly confront the Selective Service System, until the government is forced to deal with our collective action. After October 16, we will organize campuses and communities for similar waves of resistance in December, March, etc. We have gone beyond the "We Won't Go" statements in that we are renouncing all deferments, joining the forces of those who can and those who cannot afford deferments, and forcing an immediate confrontation by practicing total noncooperation with the military establishment. By turning in rather than burning our draft cards, we will be proudly giving our names to the public at large, and to the powers that be. Our hope is that upon our example every young man in America will realize that *he* must decide whether to resist or acquiesce to the draft and the war. We are confident that many will resist. . . . .

Report by Marjorie Swann in *Direct Action*, the newsletter of the New England Committee for Nonviolent Action:

It was a beautiful, sunny day on October 16th on the Boston Common, thousands of miles away from the jungles and paddies of Vietnam, where men and women and children were dying at that very moment. I walked around with a sign, "They Are Our Brothers Whom We Kill," watching between 4,000 and 5,000 people assemble for the ceremonies known as The Resistance. . . . An attractive, blonde woman . . . carried a sign, "LBJ Killed My Son." . . .

Amid some heckling, the speeches got underway, and professors, clergymen, and young resisters gave their reasons for resistance and supporting the resistance. . . . We lined up then, the young men and clergy first, and walked the long way around the Common to Arlington Street Church, which has a history of harboring war resisters. There were so many of us that at least a thousand stayed outside, lined along the sidewalks and filling the corner of the Garden, listening through loudspeakers placed on the spire of the church.

Inside there took place what must have been a most moving service. Perhaps what was the most exciting for some of us was the sense that the church was finally coming into its own—doing what a church and its representatives should be doing in a society wracked by violence and injustice. . . . The Reverend William Sloane Coffin, Chaplain of Yale University, offered on behalf of a number of clergy to provide sanctuary in churches and synagogues to draft resisters. A "breaking bread together" took the place of communion. Then draft age men were invited to come to the altar and turn their draft cards in to representatives of various faiths (including humanist and atheist) or to burn them in the flame of the altar candle. A moment of silence called in memory of all the victims of war even brought silence for at least half a minute, from the right-wing hecklers and the multitudes of police standing out on the street corners with us. Approximately 180 young men turned in their cards, and 80 more burned theirs. A final hymn and carillon chimes ended the service, and the young war resisters filed out of the church to the applause of the outside listeners.

The October 16 Resistance was billed as "a beginning." . . . Maybe this is a beginning of fulfillment of the old adage, "Wars will cease when men refuse to fight."

10.3.   *MICHAEL FERBER:* **A Time to Say No**

[During the first "antidraft" day held on October 16, 1967, 1,158 young men sent their draft cards to the federal authorities in 18 cities. This act of civil disobedience, punishable by a maximum of $10,000 fine and five years in prison, signified the refusal to cooperate in any manner whatever with the Selective Service System. Michael Ferber, a draft resister on the basis of religious conviction, was tried together with Doctor Benjamin Spock and three other men accused of illegally counselling virtually all American draft-age males to refuse military service. The following is the text of a speech given by Michael Ferber in the Arlington Street Church of Boston and published in *Resistance,* June 15, 1968.]

We are gathered in this church today in order to do something very simple: to say No. We have come from many different places and backgrounds and we have many different ideas about ourselves and the world, but we have come here to show that we are united to do one thing: to say No. Each of our acts of returning our draft cards is our personal No; when we put them in a single container or set fire to them from a single candle we express the simple basis of our unity.

But what I wish to speak about now is what goes beyond our saying No, for no matter how loudly we all say it, no matter what ceremony we perform around our saying it, we will not become a community among ourselves nor effective agents for changing our country if a negative is all we share. Albert

Camus said that the rebel, who says no, is also one who says Yes, and that when he draws a line beyond which he will refuse to cooperate he is affirming the values on the other side of that line. For us who come here today, what is it that we affirm, what is it to which we can say Yes?

To be honest we have to admit that we in the Resistance still disagree about a great many things, whether we speak out about them or not. For example, here we all are in a church, and yet for some of us it is the first time we've been inside one for years. Here we are receiving the help of many clergymen, and yet some of us feel nothing but contempt for the organized religions that they represent. Some of us, therefore, feel a certain hypocrisy in being part of this service.

But it would not surprise me if many of the clergymen who are here today feel some of the same contempt for organized religion that our unreligious or anti-religious brothers feel. They know better than we do the long and bloody history of evils committed in the name of religion, the long history of compromise and Erastian subservience to political power, the long history of theological hair-splitting and the burning of heretics, and they feel more deeply than we do the hypocrisy of Sunday (or Saturday) morning. Perhaps the things that made some of us leave the church are the very things that made some of them become ministers, priests, and rabbis, the very things that bring them here today. Many of them will anger their superiors or their congregations by being here but they are here anyway.

There is a great tradition within the church and synagogue which has always struggled against the conservative and worldly forces that have always been in control. It is a radical tradition, a tradition of urgent impulse to go to the root of the religious dimension of human life. This tradition in modern times has tried to recall us to the best ways of living our lives: the way of love and compassion, the way of justice and respect, the way of facing other people as human beings and not as abstract representatives of something alien and evil. It tries to recall us to the reality behind religious ceremony and symbolism, and it will change the ceremony and symbolism when the reality changes.

As a part of this service we will break bread together. We do this, however, not because some churches happen to take Communion; we do this for one of the root reasons for Communion itself: that men around the world and for all time have found it good to eat together when they are sharing in something important.

The radical tradition is still alive: it is present here in this church. Those of us who disregard organized religion, I think, are making a mistake if they also disregard this tradition and its presence today. This tradition is something to which we can say Yes.

There is another disagreement among us, or if not a disagreement then a difference in attitude toward what we are doing today. It is a difference that cuts through the other differences, perhaps because it is a little inside each of us, and it leads to a mistake that we are liable to make no matter how else we agree or differ. In religious terms, it is to dwell too much on the possibility of the Apocalypse; in political terms, it is to dwell too much on the possibility of a Utopian Society. We must not confuse the ceremony and symbolism of today's service with the reality that we are only a few hundred people with very little power. And we must not confuse the change inside each of us, important though that may be, with the change that we have yet to bring about in this country and the world. Neither the Revelation nor the Revolution is at hand, and to base our hopes and plans on them would be a tragic blunder.

Maybe all of us—Leftists or Liberals, Reformers or Revolutionaries, Radical Religionists or Hippies—maybe all of us are apocalyptarians, I don't know. Surely something else besides a cold rational calculation of sociological options has brought us here to this church. And surely we are in this church partly to celebrate the occasion of our noncooperation (and many of us will celebrate in a somewhat different way at parties with friends tonight). But let us not be deceived. The sun will rise tomorrow as it does every day, and when we get out of bed the world will be in pretty much the same mess it is in today. American bombers will continue to drop incendiary bombs on the Vietnamese people and American soldiers will continue to "pacify" their villages. The ghettos will continue to be rotten places to live in. Black and Mexican farm workers will continue to get miserable wages. America's schools will continue to cripple the minds and hearts of its pupils. And the American Selective Service System will continue to send young men out to the slaughter.

Today is not the End. Today is the Beginning.

This is the Beginning because, very simply, we have to dig in for the long haul. It is not going to be easy to change this country. To change it is going to mean struggles and anguish day in and day out for years. It will mean incredible efforts at great human cost to gain a few inches of ground. It will mean people dedicating their lives and possibly losing them for a cause we can only partly define and whose outcome we can only guess at. We must say Yes to the long struggle ahead or this service will be a mockery.

We are brought to a third difference among us. Earlier today Nick Egleson spoke out against the kind of resistance whose primary motivation is moralistic and personal rather than political. He is saying that we must make ourselves relevant to the social and political condition of the world and must not just take a moral posture for our own soul's sake, even though that too is a risk.

To some extent this argument depends on terminology rather than fact. Today we have heard our situation described in religious terms, moral terms, political terms, legal terms, and psychological terms. Very few of us are at home in all these different modes of speech, and each of us habitually uses only one of them to talk and think in. But what is happening today should make it clear that these different modes of speech all overlap one another and they often all say the same essential things. Albert Camus, who struggled in a more serious Resistance than ours, believed that politics is an extension of morality, that the truly moral man is engaged in politics as a natural outcome of his beliefs.

To return to Nick's concern, the real difference is not between the moral man and the political man, but between the man whose moral thinking leads him to political action and the man whose moral thinking leads him no farther than to his own "sinlessness." It is the difference between the man who is willing to dirty himself in the outside world and the man who wishes to stay "clean" and "pure."

Now this kind of "sinlessness" and "purity" is arrogant pride, and I think we must say No to it. The martyr who offers himself meekly as a lamb to the altar is a fool unless he has fully taken into account the consequences of his sacrifice not only to himself but to the rest of the world. We cannot honor him for his stigmata or his purple hearts unless he has helped the rest of us while he got them.

So then what are we to do? We must look at ourselves once more. We all have an impulse to purification and martyrdom and we should not be ashamed of it. But let us be certain that we have thought through the consequences of our action in the outside world, and that these consequences are what we want to bring about. Let us make sure we are ready to work hard and long with each other in the months to come, working to make it difficult and politically dangerous for the government to prosecute us, working to help anyone and everyone to find ways of avoiding the draft, to help disrupt the working of the draft and the armed forces until the war is over. Let us make sure we can form a community. Let us make sure we can let others depend on us.

If we can Yes to these things, and to the religious tradition that stands with us today, and to the fact that today marks not the End but a Beginning, and to the long hard dirty job ahead of us—if we can say Yes to all this, then let us come forward together to say No to the United States government.

Then let our Yes be the loudest No our government ever heard.

10.4.   **The Movement: We've Got to Reach Our Own People**

[For thousands of young men, the refusal of military service has meant also the abandonment of a "normal" life. One tendency in the resistance movement has been to focus grass-roots organizing activity around this specific problem. The following text is the collective product of a group of editors and friends of the San Francisco publication *The Movement,* a radical monthly paper formerly affiliated with SDS and SNCC. From *The Movement,* November 1967.]

There is a movement now in this country that it makes sense to describe as a resistance. What a year ago was merely a slogan has begun to take shape at induction centers, in the corners of small offices, in the character and style of increasing amounts of anti-war work and the consciousness of growing numbers of people that they can create a real opposition to the Johnson Regime. There is still a great deal of confusion and groping. The resistance exists at the fringe—on the edge of the student movement and the university community, at the margin of the poor and decaying communities where the offices and apartments of most of the resistors are to be found.

This article outlines a program of resistance; it seeks to clarify objectives and describe a way in which part of the resistance can root itself in poor white and lower paid working class communities; it attempts to suggest the urgency, need and potential for establishing those roots now.

Much of the anti-war movement, regardless of rhetoric, seems predicated on the assumption that existing power is legitimate and that the regular channels of political opposition are sufficient to end the war. For that reason it has concentrated on proving that there is substantial, growing public sentiment against the war (through large demonstrations, petitions, newspaper ads, referenda, etc.) and it has done this quite effectively. Its method has concentrated on anti-war propaganda and education and symbolic appeals to power. Even the most militant, civil disobedience advocates have generally directed their energy toward a Ghandian confrontation with and appeal to power.

We are convinced that power throughout this society is illegitimate and will continue to be basically unresponsive to public opinion and normal political pressure. That conviction FORCES us to a conception of resistance— an effort to impede and disrupt the functioning of the military/political machinery wherever it is local and vulnerable. We join a resistance movement out of no great optimism about its capacity to end the war; indeed we call this a resistance, not a revolution, because entrenched power is too strong to be broken. At best a resistance can delay and harass, strengthening the internal conflicts that make the war costly, aiding marginally the Vietnamese whose prosecution of the war is the most critical determinant of its outcome; at best a resistance sets seeds throughout the country of a movement aimed directly at imperialism and domestic exploitation.

What we do believe, however, is that the resistance can draw together those people who seek real power to deflect the war. We believe that a resistance can draw together people who are sufficiently detached from the integrative social mechanisms of this country so that they could never participate in a propaganda/symbolic-confrontation-oriented movement. In this sense, we think the resistance can make available to many people who are now denied it, a credible (believeable, possible) form of opposition to the war.

It is here that the war hits hardest. It is young men from these communities who do most of the dying in Vietnam and it was their fathers and brothers who did most of the dying in Korea. It is their union that will be surpressed in the name of the war effort, their wage gains that will be erased by war inflation, their checks that will feel hardest the squeeze of a war tax. And it is also the token programs of relief, job training, school improvement, and rent supplement that will be cut off in their communities because of the war.

But it is here that the anti-war movement has had least experience and least success. Paradoxically, the people most brutalized by material and social exploitation, the people pushed unceasingly through the processing of school, military and job seem unmoved by the anti-war effort. Partly this is explained by the massive, unthinking, unchallenged racism and patriotism (anti-communism) which these communities share with the rest of white America and which must be broken if a movement is to succeed. But more important, we feel that these are exactly the communities that will not be reached by the symbolic, propaganda tactics of the current sense of REAL GAIN, a sense that political activity represents more than the demonstration of disaffection. It is in these communities that a resistance makes most sense.

Because grievances are so deep, so much a part of the marginal economic and social web of people's lives, the movement of opposition, once triggered could be very powerful. We choose to work here because people do have a deep sense of exploitation that can lead them to identify not only with their own struggle, but with oppressed people everywhere. It makes sense to talk in these communities about the need and right of self-defense and self-preservation and to speak of democracy as the unadorned right of people to make the most important decisions about their lives. There is little of the legalism and formalism that can paralyze other sectors of the society, but rather a profound but segmented anger that can be kindled and united by the existence of a credible opposition to the war.

The draft and the war are issues now, everywhere. There is no need to manufacture them or convince people of their importance; the conviction is implanted twenty times a day by television, radio, papers, conversations and the visible signs of war inflation and pressure—not the least of which is the caskets rolling back into the community from Vietnam. Unlike some of the other things community projects have tried to work on, there is no need to produce "consciousness" about this issue.

We want to focus on the draft because it is the MOST IMPORTANT AND MOST TANGIBLE manifestation of the war in most people's lives. Hardly anyone exists in a lower class working community who does not have friends or close relatives who are in the army or threatened by it. Coming into the community with a program that will help people deal with this problem, that will keep themselves or their friends or their children or their loved ones out of the damned war, cuts through to the very heart of the issue. It is a way of fighting back, a method of self-defense, and it makes the opportunity for opposition credible and compelling.

Unlike many issues, the draft is important enough so that the people will take a stand and accept the risks that that implies. It is only when an issue or movement is so important that the good average American will take a stand against his neighbor or his bowling team or the men he drinks with or works next to that you have a chance for a significant social movement. Revolutions always tear communities apart. It is that tearing that represents the splitting of the social fabric which has held people in belligerent allegiance to their country in spite of their disaffection. Very few of the issues we have organized around have been that powerful. This one is.

And although opposition to the war will divide a community in very important ways, it will unite it in others. There are few issues that will unify a marginal community across its fractured status and economic lines. For example, the antagonism between workers and welfare recipients frequently keeps them from working together. But the draft cuts across those lines. It can bring the welfare mother, worker, parent, young person into one cause and into a common sense of themselves and their position as opponents.

The clarity of this issue and its importance can strengthen the opposition to other institutions when they are used to suppress it. When the school expels students for forming a high school draft resistance league, the general anger of the community about the school has a foundation and anchor that the abstractness of the "school problem" may have prevented from forming before.

Finally, however, there is one reason that overrides all others in making us attempt a community-based draft resistance movement. That simply is the preservation of the movement. Because the movement is in danger. The war in Vietnam, despite its gravity is neither the last act or a continuous feature of this society. It will end eventually; and eventually could be soon. If the movement it has generated is to live beyond it, two things must happen. First, large sections of that movement must become rooted deeply, not simply in communities, but in the lives and difficulties of people. Second, it must get far enough beyond the symbolism of protest to convince ITSELF (the people in it) that it can effectively combat and resist power.

We think the effort to make a base for the movement in people's lives and in its capacity to bring tangible, real gain to those people must become the programmatic focus for large numbers of people. We must begin to develop an edge, a sharpness, a clarity about our direction that can combat the current tone of political indecisiveness that is so strong inside the anti-war movement and the overwhelming sense of dissolution that will follow the end of the war.

We do not claim the insight of orthodoxy about this program. We do not feel compelled to urge everyone to drop what they are doing and join our ranks. There is a richness and a life to the anti-war movement that laughs at orthodoxy and that we respect despite disagreement. What we do feel is that a focus is needed that can unify some of the divergent strands of the movement around a political and programmatic perspective and that can place that perspective in communities where it can grow and endure beyond today's horrible, but preliminary skirmish against human suffering.

For that we need many people. Not just people to join this program; but people throughout the movement who will look at their work from this perspective—the simply crying need of the movement to sink roots, to seek real confrontations with power—and to endure—to survive—to live.

Draft resistance is growing. The momentum the peace movement gained this summer has turned more and more towards draft resistance. "It is the one anti-war organization that really pulled together." "It is the one issue around the war that really touches people personally and desperately."

On the other hand, draft resistance groups have very different reasons for existing, and are now moving in several different directions. Some had their start in moral pacifist protest, some in a tendency towards direct violent confrontation with the establishment, some again in a longer-range perspective of building a movement for social change.

But the Vietnamese struggle for liberation continues, and the political repression of some in this country, the economic regimentation of others and the political powerlessness of many also continues. We have choices to make and a responsibility for our political actions.

Neither the skills or techniques of counselling, or the tactics of induction center demonstrations are talked about here. A direction for draft resistance is presented and a discussion of possible techniques is set out.

Draft resistance can grow faster and more strongly in sectors of the population which are already disaffected with the war and with the political machinery local and national. Think of black and ethnic communities, like Puerto Rican, Polish, American Indian, German, Portugese. Think also of lower class white working class communities: less than half of these communities vote because they don't believe political leaders will do anything for them, they are generally against the war, and they are the ones primarily who are getting drafted.

On the other hand, none of these communities are particularly open to ordinary, large organization funded, top down peace propaganda programs. They have to be approached by people who settle into their own communities, are familiar with and militant about their community problems and who gain respect and credentials in their community.

These are the people who are run powerless through this society—through the schools, the army and the jobs—and these are the people who can form a base of power to resist the war machine. Draft resistance is the way to reach them because the draft is touching almost every one of their families. They got a reason to fight the draft. Let's talk about getting them the chance.

Who are you? Some of you have roots in communities where draft resistance centers could be started, but a great many of you are students, or at least without those roots in potentially insurgent communities. Some of you are already involved in draft resistance work in student areas and don't feel you have the time or the manpower to try to reach into the community. Why should you? Haven't you got your own job to do?

Students are most often the troops of the movement, but they are not all the people. A significant resistance to the war and to the unrepresentative political machine which directs it must be based not only among students but among working people. A real resistance must last to fight against the next war like Vietnam which the government involves us in, and to last it must have a base among people who have their own reasons for defending themselves against an oppressive social system. Since students are very often the ones with the time and background development that allows them to develop opposition to and organization against the establishment, they must be the ones to bring agitation and organization to Americans who don't have that time or background.

A lot of us have believed that these poor and working class communities are filled with super-patriots. They ARE filled with people who have fought in Korea, and with families who have lost men in Korea. Some of them support the war, and the government, blindly. But more of them know it is not being fought for them or for freedom or for our national security. They will be quick to learn what the Vietnamese people are really fighting for, and they will be quick to defend themselves and their sons against the draft. They have not been vocal against the war, because they have not had the time. They have not had the time in their whole lives.—They were busy being processed, meeting responsibilities and making a living.

What follows here is a program for setting up community-based draft resistance unions. It is hoped that you will move in that direction. On the other hand, many student-based groups or organizers just do not have the time or in some cases the experience to work in the community full time. In that case it makes sense to talk about a "flying" group that, during the course of its work, tries various ways of reaching out into potentially insurgent communities. In some cases, people can be found to establish community draft unions, and in other cases enough contact can be made, enough information gathered, to follow up when organizers are available.

Pick the neighborhood for some good reason. Maybe you know some good, sympathetic people there who know their way around. Look for areas where a peace referendum was optimistic, where there is a ROOTED neighborhood peace group, where there are welfare rights organizations, where there is a fight with the political machine, where there have been rent strikes, where there may be an urban renewal issue or an issue of control of the schools, the hospitals or the police.

Check on the listings of men who are 1-a in the city. The draft board won't give out their addresses and if you can't trace them down then you can send them a letter through the draft board; they are required by law to forward mail to men with 1-a classifications. If you make contact with one in an insurgent neighborhood and if he wants to refuse induction or refuse to fight in Vietnam, ask him for permission to get his neighborhood out to support him. BUT GET HIM TO DO THE WORK. Start a leaflet campaign and a petition of support for his refusal in the neighborhood.

It is not necessary to get a storefront, if you can't afford one. Even a pair of rooms on the second floor is good enough, if you clean them up and make them look decent. Try to get the neighborhood kids to help you fix up the place. They are your base: tell them what you are there for.

. . . .

Draft Resistance Unions have found it important everywhere to set up support groups among lawyers, doctors, labor union staff people, and other professionals. They can help with property bond, with legal services, with publicity contacts and with money. It has been worthwhile to spend a lot of time with each individual in the support group, explaining your perspective and activities in order to get a stronger commitment from them. A lot of men and women who have drifted away from the old left are anxious to help new left groups. They are part of your security, don't forget them. If it is possible to get someone, a lawyer or the like, to organize that group with you, do it.

Organize adults to keep the young men in the neighborhood from enlisting or acquiescing to the draft. A mothers' group, a group of veterans, a group of workers—any of these will be good at convincing young men not to go, and probably better than someone nearly their own age: they can speak from experience.

Organize young women in a group to keep young men from going and to support those men who refuse. Young women can break through a lot of the "Be a man" propaganda which lures young guys into the army. In organizing this kind of a group you want to find and help develop someone who will see themselves as an organizer, and give him or her as much of the responsibility for the group as possible: Your purpose is to spread INTO the neighborhood.

Middle-class, professional support groups can provide some money, so can peace groups. Fund-raising letters should include newsletters, sample leaflets, etc. Try to get monthly pledges. There are usually organizations around like Vietnam Summer to give a little seed money, but don't count on that. If the Draft Resistance Union is going to have a real base in the community, it must be supported mostly by the community. Don't be afraid to ask poor or working people for money: it's their fight they've got to pay as much as they can. People are more suspicious of organizations that exist with no visible means of local support than of people who ask them for money to keep going. If you do a good job, you'll get supported. But you should also think about trying to support yourself by having some members of the union take jobs and bring home paychecks. Working will also give you both roots and credibility in the community.

Draft resistance groups, especially in the community, should see themselves as trying to get enough community people involved as organizers that some of the original organizers can set up another union in another community. Therefore, it is important that the group be run so that everyone gets experience in running meetings (rotating chairman), making decisions about demonstrations, doing door-to-door work, etc. Leadership always develops, but new people must be constantly trained to take over the duties and roles of leadership.

Since the draft resistance group is an attempt to reach into the community, it must be run so that new community people can have an equal share in making decisions and coming up with ideas. On the other hand, you do have a political point of view and it is important sometimes to just throw some people out of the group. Use your judgment: groups have been nearly destroyed by going too far in either direction.

. . . .

Let's be straight. What's got to be done is to get the people in this country who neither support nor confront the government's misuse of power, MOVING. To do that we've got to find issues on the local level, in the community, around which people can demand control of what the political machine, or a minority of landlords and businessmen now control. If Draft Resistance Unions establish themselves genuinely in the community and find the people there who will confront the government's use of poor and working people in the war, it may be possible to form a community union which will try to take local power.

The war in Vietnam will be over some day. There may be a lapse before the next one the government gets us into. We've got to be building the kind of multi-issue local control unions which will last and grow through that lapse, or the American people will never have a chance to run their own country: or we will have to start from nothing again to build a resistance to the next war.

While the war continues, conditions in poor and working class communities are getting tighter. Groceries for a family are costing $25 a week instead of $19. Credit is getting tighter. Old credit liens still have to be paid, the rent has to be paid and babies are still being born. Wages are not going up but taxes are, to pay for the war. While the war continues less and less money will go into urban programs, or poverty programs and grievances at the local level will grow louder. We've got to organize now while people are feeling the pressure of a useless and tyrannical war and knowing their own anger. We've got to get people in motion. Draft centers, in the community, can provide the beginning focus for that motion.

. . . .

Anybody who has tried to organize in the U.S. knows that anti-communism is the strongest force holding a people alienated from their government in support of that government. We can begin to break through the anti-communism if we begin to talk in our literature about the way people live in Cuba and North Vietnam, in Eastern European countries and in all over the new revolutionary third world countries. We don't have to defend Chinese communism, or any other communism: we simply have to bring people to a consciousness of the particular way people live in the countries Americans have been taught to hate. We have to discuss, say, Cuban institutions for choosing leaders and directing the economy and decide whether that amounts to tyranny. It is a tyranny we are fighting against, and if there turns out not to be a tyranny in Cuba, or China, then we don't have to hate those countries.

But again, education doesn't mean anything if we are not involved in real struggles. The war against the Vietnamese people continues. Our government is using and murdering our own people. WE'VE GOT TO REACH OUR OWN PEOPLE.

10.5.   *STAUGHTON LYND:* **Resistance: From Mood to Strategy**

[With the development of the draft-resistance movement, a debate has arisen on the political strategy which should form the framework for this kind of civil disobedience. In the following article, Staughton Lynd proposes a strategy for the Movement. From *Liberation,* December 1967.]

Since roughly January 1967, the Movement has turned toward what it terms resistance. The new slogans are "from protest to resistance" (title of an article by former S.D.S. national secretary Greg Calvert), "from dissent to resistance" (slogan of the October 21 mobilization in Washington) or just "resist" (S.D.S. button). Resistance is thus far a mood rather than a strategy. Often when a movement is groping toward a new strategy there must be an initial period when individuals take a new kind of action without fully understanding what strategy the action implies. Thus, in the South, the mood exemplified by Rosa Parks' refusal to move to the back of the bus and by the Greensboro sit-inners of 1960 crystallized by late 1961 into the strategy of voter registration in Southwest Georgia and Mississippi.

Similarly, the teach-in with the troops at Washington on October 21-22 profoundly expressed the new mood of direct confrontation with oppressive authority. But it was not yet a strategy. The Washington mobilization, like the Albany, Georgia marches of 1962 or the Birmingham demonstration of May 1963, requires a complementary program of day-to-day activity to keep people at work in the same spirit of militancy between semiannual mass events. In the South the day-to-day activity that tied together mass demonstrations was voter registration. In the North the day-to-day activity that functions as the equivalent of voter registration in the South may be draft resistance.

The activity of draft resistance may express either a mood or a strategy. When young men say "hell no, we won't go," what is uppermost in their minds may be either a personal, conscientious refusal to fight or the hope of producing consequences that will help to stop the war. Naturally, any given man, any particular action, is likely to reflect both of these attitudes in some measure, but as draft resistance moves from a mood toward a strategy the concern to produce consequences will be increasingly important.

This means that the traditional pacifist scenario which leads from dramatic individual witness to the martyrdom of jail will be questioned in terms of its effects. Thus Carl Davidson of S.D.S. inquired last spring whether the onlooker, watching the pacifist dragged off to jail, may find his own will to resistance weakened rather than made stronger. Thus, too, the question has been raised as to whether ways cannot be found such that the draft resister publicly says "No"—for example, at a preliminary court hearing—yet does not permit himself to be jailed and thereby lost to the Movement for the period of his imprisonment. Finally, conceptualization of draft resistance from the standpoint of strategy will mean understanding this act of refusal as a transition to long-term radical activity. In the Movement, saying "No" to the draft at the inception of one's adulthood will become a characteristic rite of initiation—a commencement exercise, so to speak—for the man brave or foolish enough to drop out of preparation for a conventional career and turn his face instead toward the vocation of revolution. And the draft-resistance organizer will seek to create conditions such that as many persons as possible from the groups most exposed to the draft undergo this radicalization in the shortest possible time.

Clearly, draft resistance—thus far the characteristic expression of the new resistance mood—is linked to another widespread concern of the past year: the tendency to visualize radicalism as the work of a lifetime rather than a two-year or three-year "experience," with the attendant need to ask how one can be a radical if he is married and has children, or is involved with a professional career. David Harris, an initiator of The Resistance movement, the members of which returned their draft cards on October 16, explained at a conference this summer that for him going to jail for five years no longer signified compulsory retirement from the Movement, since he expected to work in the Movement all his life. At another summer conference, on "radicals in the professions," teachers, lawyers, city planners, social workers debated whether it is possible to be radical yet make a living as a professional. Three things stand out from this new questioning still very much in process.

• First, the problem to be solved is seen more seriously and somberly than was the case only a few years ago. A liberal ideology was implicit in the pattern of dropping out for a few years and then returning to graduate school, catching up and proceeding to a conventional career. America, basically a good society, was understood to have a problem: "the Negro problem." Just as the problem was small compared to the goodness of the society as a whole, so one devoted only a fraction of a lifetime to its solution. Two or three years was felt to be equivalent to the magnitude of the difficulty.

Now there is a different vision. The civil-rights movement has become a black-liberation movement. The movement against the war in Vietnam has been understood to be necessarily a movement against all the similar wars which will follow the termination of this one. The Movement as a whole—even though operating in separate white and black parts—has redefined itself as a movement against racist capitalist imperialism at home and abroad. The question is no longer that American society *has* a problem. What we think now is that American society *is* a problem. Accordingly, we demand of ourselves a commitment of all our energies to the solution of this pervasive problem. Little as we yet understand what these words mean, awkwardly as we move toward their expression in decisions about job and family, nevertheless we are now clear that nothing less than all our lives will be enough.

• Second, there is new thinking about what it means to be an "organizer" and what constitutes a "project." In the old days an organizer was an unmarried student who lived in a freedom house where, when he was not in jail, he slept on the floor and ate peanut-butter sandwiches. A project was the several students who lived in that freedom house and worked together in the neighborhood. If radicalism is to become a lifetime vocation, these definitions must be expanded. Married couples with children must be able to be part of a project. It follows that members of a project may not all live under one roof. And not all project members will do the same work. What remains of a project? Perhaps the following elements:

1) All members of the project regard the Movement—the task of social change—as their principal work, the axis of their lives, regardless of how each one makes a living.

2) Project members determine together a rough sense of priorities as to what kinds of organizing most need to be done, who should do them, what has to happen to make that possible.

3) Belonging to the project makes it possible for each participant to take greater risks on behalf of their shared task. The teacher risks dismissal with less anxiety because he knows others will help financially should he be temporarily unemployed. The mother joins students in blocking an induction center because she knows that, should she be arrested, others will care for her children.

• Third, it follows from these new understandings of radical vocation that Movement activity becomes simultaneously more demanding and less specified. More demanding, because in a Movement turned toward resistance every member *must* be ready to lose a job, go to jail, perhaps to die. Less specified, because a variety of roles become possible. Consider draft resistance. A given draft-resistance project might involve:

a full-time student organizer, leafleting draft boards and induction centers, visiting men classified 1-A, himself refusing induction and extracting from that circumstance maximum legal and public-relations leverage;

a lawyer specializing in Selective Service law who takes draft cases free of charge;

housewives who man a draft-counseling center in their spare time;

high-school students who stimulate discussion among their schoolmates through all available channels;

a minister who offers his church as a sanctuary for resisters and ceremonially presides at draft-card burnings;

professors who, besides returning their own draft cards, make their time available to speak on the political philosophy of resistance;

other full-time organizers who, while mainly concerned with other community issues, see draft resistance to be connected with their activity; and so on.

No longer is it possible for Dick or Jane to excuse himself from the Movement on grounds of temperamental unfitness for a supposed single task. The task has been diversified at the same time that its risk has been escalated.

Come back now to the question of resistance strategy. On the campus, there has been a transition from publication in the student newspaper of a letter saying "We Won't Go" (a somewhat quixotic gesture since the signers characteristically held II-S deferments) to burning and return of draft cards and, at the same time, campaigns for driving the military from the campus. The latter take the form of exposing war-related research, as at the University of Pennsylvania or, now, the University of Chicago, or obstructing the activity of Dow Chemical or United States Navy recruiters, as at the University of Wisconsin and Oberlin College. What is needed is a similarly explicit strategy for draft resistance off the campus. The community has come to the campus in the form of policemen called in by university authorities. The campus must find means to go to the community. As usual, Berkeley points a direction in its week-long attempt to obstruct the functioning of the Oakland Induction Center. Yet so long as the activists remain students sheltered from the draft the action retains a symbolic character.

A draft-resistance strategy in the community will develop not from abstract speculation but from practical experimentation, much of which is presently afoot in Chicago. Nevertheless I want to conclude by offering a few general observations about the strategy of a resistance movement.

Resistance is negative. It is a movement against something. The rhetoric of a resistance movement—whether in America in 1776, or in France, Italy, China and Vietnam during the 1930's—calls on an entire national community to put aside former differences and unite against a common foe. Student and general, merchant and tenant farmer, join in creating a united front. Communists shelve their ultimate ambitions. S.D.S. and Y.A.F. members find common ground, for example in opposing conscription. Inevitably a resistance movement tends to the restoration of a status quo ante: the British empire as it was governed before the Stamp Act or United States foreign policy in the creative year between the Cuba missile crisis and the Dallas assassination. The gravitation of a resistance movement to a normalcy assumed to have previously existed is suggested by the conclusion of Camus' *The Plague:* the weekend family picnic, the restoration of ordinariness.

This implicit ideology of resistance movement is delusive. Very rarely is the status quo ante recoverable. The causes which led to the crisis have typically changed the entire society so that mere return to the past it not possible. Accordingly, within the resistance coalition some will become frustrated and embittered as the recovery of things past forever eludes them. Others, foreseeing the power vacuum which will ensue from the oppressor's fall, will reach out all too firmly toward a future which may be the vision only of a small minority. There needs to be found a method to work democratically toward the future in the midst of saying "Here I stand," "Don't tread on me," "They shall not pass," "Not with my life you don't." Responsible resistance must be both for and against, positive as well as negative. But this makes extraordinary demands on the resistance fighter, who is constantly in danger, forever hardening his heart to enormities unthinkable in ordinary times, yet is at the same time required to practice the flexibility, the patience, the tolerance and the ability to see things from many standpoints simultaneously which are essential to democracy.

This dilemma it not so abstract as it may seem. It is at the heart of the unresolved tension within the Movement between violence and nonviolence. It accounts for the universal nostalgia for the first years when people held hands in a circle and sang "We Shall Overcome."

This problem, like the problem of inventing a community draft-resistance strategy, will be resolved in practice. Indeed practice holds out a very specific hope. Is it not the case that the objective circumstances of a resistance movement impose many of the same habits previously adhered to for subjective, idealistic reasons? Decentralization, for instance, once espoused because of the presumed ethical superiority of participatory democracy, is an objective requirement of resistance work. Hence those Communist movements which came to power through decentralized guerrilla warfare prove most resistant to bureaucratization and class inequality after the seizure of power. What can be said of the distinction between leaders and followers can also be said of distinctions between manual and intellectual work, or between the work of men and women. The elemental conditions of resistance struggle break down the barriers between persons. An unintended community, a necessitarian brotherhood, comes into being. Just as the early Christian church discovered itself under the heel of Caesars, so twentieth-century revolutionary socialism finds in repression and the need for resistance an opportunity to clarify its positive vision. Chinese and Cuban revolutionaries seek to forestall the development of Soviet revisionism by harking back to "how it was in the mountains" or "how we did it in the jungle" as an experienced spiritual regulator. The American New Left need not fear that its turn toward resistance must destroy the idealism of the early 1960's.

But maturation in such a way as to become more effective without sacrificing humaneness will not happen spontaneously. To move from a resistance mood to a strategy of resistance we need to create the functional equivalent of a revolutionary vanguard party.

This need is felt both by those involved in national mass action, as at the Pentagon, and by those working at a local level. Coordination, discipline, a mechanism for evolving a common perspective of action, training of replacements for leaders who may be arrested, systematizing the recreation of successful organizing initiatives: these tasks are upon us, are required by what we call "being serious." None of us can yet envision how socialism will come to the United States. But it is clear that fundamental change in our society will not occur unless (a) more and more of us determine to make producing that change the main business of our lives and (b) those who have made that commitment find more effective ways to coordinate their work.

In this, too, experimenting is underway in Chicago. The hundred or so white organizers in the city have divided themselves into eight groups. Care has been taken that each group include staff members from each of the city's principal organizing efforts: the JOIN community union among Appalachian poor whites, the 49th Ward Committee for Independent Political Action among middle-class whites, the Chicago Area Draft Resistance, the new attempts at organizing in white working-class communities. For the time being the groups restrict themselves to discussion, with the aim that a Movement perspective for city-wide action emerge from below.

We move now into a year during which all creative work will be distracted by elections. But throughout the Movement, hopefully, another kind of voting and a different sort of party participation will be in process these next twelve months. Hundreds of graduating college seniors will vote their whole selves, in Thoreau's phrase, by choosing the Movement as a vocation. And on the other side of that decision, in the humdrum, frustrating, lonely world of day-to-day organizing, comrades will draw together to transform their Movement from a mood into a weapon.

10.6.   **A Message to GIs and to the Movement**

[In 1968 a new development of the antiwar movement took place among the military. The following leaflet was prepared by the National Mobilization Committee for distribution to both GIs and civilians during the GI Week, November 1968.]

To GI's

You have seen kids against the war, marching around with their signs. The lifers will tell you these kids are your enemy. And the brass will issue you orders that they are your enemy. (The brass would like to issue you everything but brains.) But the truth is the kids against the war are people, most of them your own age, who want to see you come home alive.

Every kind of American is now against the war. You all know someone —a teacher, a preacher, a truck driver—who says we have no business turning over the lives of thousands of Americans to a bunch of crooks running the corrupt government of South Vietnam. You may know that even retired brass like General Shoupe and General Gavin say that American interest in Vietnam is not worth a pile of peanut shells. Probably the Americans most against this war are the men who fought it—the Vietnam veterans.

Each day, more and more Americans stand up against the senseless slaughter of GIs and Vietnamese. These Americans make up the "anti-war movement." You may only know them as the kids with long hair, the ministers of your own religion or the guy beside you in the barracks. They get called peaceniks, Communists, and unAmericans—especially by the people who make a fortune in keeping the war going.

But as a soldier, you know better than anyone what it means to be harassed and humiliated by the lifers and the brass, especially if you open your mouth the wrong way. And everyone in the anti-war movement knows something about harassment too, for opening their mouths for American soldiers' right to return to civilian life.

Probably you resent the fact that peace demonstrations include kids who can wait out the war in college. You have every right to be mad about that. But do you know that the anti-war movement is trying to do away with the draft laws that give special privileges to some? In fact, the anti-war movement is trying to do away with all the laws that force people to fight and die in Vietnam while a few politicians haggle over how to keep the war going forever.

The lifers, the brass and the old people who run this country will stop at nothing to keep the spirit of the anti-war movement locked out of every base. So in case your commanding officer didn't tell you, the kids against the war SUPPORT soldiers. They support the man who says he may be forced to give his body to Uncle Sam but damn if he'll turn over his brain. And they support the idea that when a war cannot be defended, even by a double-talking, money-making politician, GIs have a right to come home—now.

To the Movement

The average GI is under the thumb of the military machine; he is not the operator of it. Either he was drafted, or he volunteered under pressure from a society that won't give a non-college man a job unless he has an honorable discharge—especially if he is black.

His first two months are spent in basic training at a huge post, far from home (by design) and far from any major city. In "basic" he is whipped into good physical shape and taught elementary skills such as rifle-firing. Most important of all, he gets broken down emotionally and intellectually by a process known as HARASSMENT. The trainee is forced to buff floors that don't need buffing, scream instead of talk, run instead of walk, memorize meaningless lists, prepare his belongings for inspections so petty that hygiene is forgotten (you have to have an UNUSED tube of toothpaste in your locker). . . .

After basic comes AIT—"advanced individual training"—or, for the vast majority, advanced infantry training. Men are given specialties: typing, machine-gunning, radio operation, and so on. Then they are assigned duty stations—Vietnam, most likely.

The GI's immediate enemy, from basic on, is the noncommissioned officer, or NCO, also known as the E-5, 6 or 7 (a reference to his pay grade) or "lifer." The lifer is a man who knows that his Army standard of living beats anything he could attain in the civilian world. Most lifers are poor southerners, white and black. They have sold their souls to the military, very much like factory foremen who owe their jobs to devotion to the boss.

The officer corps has its lifers, too, but—especially in Vietnam—it is made up mostly of college graduates. Sometimes generation ties replace caste ties. That is, young second lieutenants, in the field, sometimes join their men in blowing grass while the older officers and EMs drink alcohol. In general, though, the Army is like the rest of America—the well-educated give the orders, the less educated carry them out.

From the barracks to the front-lines, the mood of the American soldier is, today, THOUGHTFUL. A basic trainee, like a college freshman of the same age, is going through a hell of a time deciding what he wants to do with his life and what he wants the world to be like. He knows that the war is costing him and his buddies more—limbs, lives—than it costs the rest of the American people. Given the huge percentage of people who oppose the war, and the fact that young people are significantly more liberal than their parents, ours is certainly one of the most reluctant armies in histories.

Of course, the officers and NCOs pressure GIs constantly to stop thinking, to simply obey. But men have always overcome attempts to bully and blind them, and this is what American soldiers are doing, in rapidly increasing numbers, today.

FURTHER READINGS

Calvert, Gregory. "From Protest to Resistance." *New Left Notes,* January 13, 1967.

Cannon, Terry. "Stop the Draft Week: A Political Analysis." *The Movement,* November 1967.

Chomsky, Noam. "Resistance." *New York Review,* December 7, 1967.

————, Lauter, Paul, and Howe, Florence. "Reflections on a Political Trial," *New York Review,* August 22, 1968.

Cloke, Ken. *A Pocket Manual on Draft Resistance.* A Guardian pamphlet, 1968.

Facing the Draft: Your Rights, Your Alternatives, Your Decision. Campus Draft Opposition, February 1968.

Hamilton, Steve. "October 16 . . . A Moral Witness?" *New Left Notes,* October 2, 1967.

Handbook for Conscientious Objectors. Central Committee for Conscientious Objectors, 1967.

Henig, Peter. "On the Manpower Channelers." *New Left Notes,* January 20, 1967.

Interview with William Sloane Coffin. *Playboy,* July 1968.

Liberation. Special issue on Resistance. November 1967.

Lynd, Staughton. "A Time for Compassionate Solidarity." *National Guardian,* August 6, 1966.

Lynd, Alice (ed.). *We Won't Go, Personal Accounts of War Objectors.* Boston: Beacon Press, 1968.

Lynn, Conrad J. *How to Stay out of the Army: A Guide to Your Rights under the Draft Law.* Monthly Review Press.

McReynolds, David. "The Resistance." *New Politics,* VI: 1, Winter 1967.

"Make Love Not War: The Campaign Against the Draft." *Liberation,* December 1967.

Mayer, Peter (ed.). *The Pacifist Conscience.* New York: Holt, Rinehart and Winston, 1966.

Meacham, Stewart. "Resistance to the Draft." *Liberation,* March 1966.

Miller, James C. III. *Why the Draft: The Case for a Volunteer Army*. Baltimore: Penguin Books, 1967.

The Movement on Stop the Draft Week at Oakland. November 1967.

New Left Notes. Special issue on Draft Resistance. March 27, 1967.

Pearlman, Robert. "Two Worlds of Draft Resistance." *Paper Tiger*, March 1968.

SDS "Our fight Is Here—Essays on Draft Resistance," with articles by C. Davidson, P. Henig, C. Wiekerson and F. Silbar. SDS pamphlet, 1968.

Win. Special issue on "Draft Resisters in Prison," May 1968.

11
Student Power

[In the high schools also, a considerable movement of protest developed during recent years. Mark Kleiman was a student at a Southern California high school when he wrote this paper, which has been reprinted as an SDS pamphlet.]

What I remember most about my school is that there is a 10-foot fence around it. In parts, there are three rows of barbed wire strung along the top. What concerns me most about the fence is not that it keeps me in—but that it keeps the rest of the world out, only admitting those portions of "reality" which the administration deems safe for us to view. Those responsible for our education have done their utmost to create an artificial community on the high school campus; a community which will demonstrate to us that it is better to "adjust" to an unsuitable society than to change the society into something in which we can live with honor and dignity. If we are to lead meaningful lives, and do more than pass on our problems to the next generation, we shall have to break out of that artificial community. It is to that end that this is being written.

There is already a considerable degree of unrest on the high school campus. At Palisades High School (Los Angeles), an "underground" paper has been started. Similar papers have begun at Arcadia and Westchester. At Westchester, 30 students destroyed their Student Activity Cards and "sat in" for the first ten minutes of fifth period in protest of an assembly being called off for the third time. At University High School there has been a storm of protest over the suspension of a student for wearing his hair too long and an administration threat to take away nutrition unless we had a clean campus. Even such seemingly destructive actions as starting trash can fires and pulling fire alarms are actually forms of protest directed at the school as it is now constituted. Not only the defense of hair and clothing styles against administration attack, but the adoption of such styles themselves indicates a general disgust with the values and attitudes that our generation has been force-fed.

These problems, though, and the struggle against the oppressiveness of bureaucratic solutions to them, only serve as rough indicators of the *real* problem confronting us. We can get a clearer picture of the problems confronting high school students by looking at a few more aspects of campus life. Many schools have some form of police-squad with students being recruited for the purpose of guarding entrances of buildings and informing on fellow students.

All schools spend a great deal of money on staffing and supplying an Attendance Office with an elaborate and highly complex system of files, checks, and cross-checks. The very existence of such a system would indicate a belief on the part of the administration that we are unwilling to play by the rules that were made by them, and must be coerced into doing so. It is clear that the motivating factor behind acceptable behavior is not understanding, but force. If so great and complex a structure is needed simply to ensure physical attendance, we may legitimately be concerned about why we are unwilling to even place our bodies in school, let alone pay attention to what happens there. We can only wonder about what would happen if even half the effort spent in *making* us attend school would be expended in an attempt to improve school so that we would want to attend.

There is one primary cause behind why we set trash can fires, why we cannot communicate with one another on campus, and are forced to make use of off-campus publications, and to why they have to build fences around us. *High School is not worth the time we spend there.* This is a truth which every student realizes on at least one level.

The courses which are irrelevant to the point of being ludicrous are forced upon us. Scientific courses are compulsory for those who will have little to do with science. "Health" classes warn us about drugs proven to be physically harmless, and blithely ignore sex education. "Guidance" classes aimed at fitting us neatly into the system and supplying us with a prefabricated moral code are so structured as to prevent any serious discussion of vital matters.

English classes in which we should be learning of the ideas of the great writers are hopelessly bogged down in an attempt to "cover enough ground" and have a "balanced curriculum." Both of which have the effect of stretching the class over so much material in 20 weeks that none of the real value may be gotten from it. Controversial contemporary authors such as Albee, Jones, and Ferlinghetti are not mentioned in class, so as to save our minds from perversion.

History and government classes, which could be relevant to all, are bogged down with irrelevant data to be digested and given back at a later date. We have a history book which tells us: "Though the Indians did help the early settlers, and have made some cultural contributions, on the whole, their effects on this country have been bad because they hindered *our* Western expansion." In Government, the classes are structured like Congress so we can learn How Things Really Work. Would we not learn more about legislative operations if government classes were truly creative, rather than being a mockery of the word, and we could learn by structuring the legislature as we wished? Why is more emphasis placed upon the regurgitation of the various articles of the Constitution, and very little placed upon the motives behind the formation of that Constitution?

In speaking with students, I have heard a nearly unanimous opinion that Current American Problems is one of the worst of the required courses. That such a vital course should be considered drudgery amazes me. How is it that a course with such a dynamic potential could be thought of like this? Obviously, little effort is being spent to tap even part of that potential. On one hand, the course is taken "seriously," as it is required. On the other hand, the teaching of the course is not serious, but superficial. Since we are the objects of that teaching, it would seem as though we are not being taken seriously either.

Most of the people who teach us make sacrifices to do so. They could get much better jobs if they wanted to. They must, at least at the beginning, enjoy their work. We have all seen student teachers who, with but a few notable exceptions, have become tired and passive after a few years on the job. What could have caused this change? Surely, not the students are at fault, or many teachers would have taken up new professions. Since the first schools consisted solely of teachers and students, it is conceivable that the same institution which squeezes the joy of living out of the students also oppresses the teachers.

Let us consider briefly the roles taken by students and teachers in our schools. It is the function of a teacher in our system to feed us material data designed to help us fit into a ready-made life in society. We, as students, undergo this change, and "help" our peers change through social pressure. Who dictates the nature of this change? Who tells teachers what to teach and how to teach it? Who tells students under what conditions they may learn in this Great and Free society? Both student and teacher are tool *and* product of administrative totalitarianism. The student comes out of high school a finished product to be consumed by either the agro-business or the war machine. He is by then also a tool, to be used to make others conform. The teacher, who began as a tool, in an Orwellian nightmare finally believes that he is helping his students to lead useful and moral lives in our society.

What madness is this? The administrator, whose real function is nothing greater than the maintenance of the campus (a task which could be easily performed by a simple-minded computer) has become the lord and master of our schools, commanding unbounded fealty.

The educative process should be a learning experience for both teacher and student. The teacher and his students should sit down and freely discuss the topics of the course and the method of study. This idea is workable. At least it worked for all the great philosophers. We've strayed a long way from that path. It will take great effort on our part to return to it.

Students cannot effectively change things through individual action. What is needed is an organization which will struggle for a free, viable, and realistic education for all students, which will base itself on mass student support. Such an organization will require more than some coalition between "liberal" and "conservative" elements of the student population. If we are to be at all effective, we must be able to talk to students who have not yet reached our level of concern, and are still trying to escape from society, rather than change it.

If we accept the three levels of anti-administration sentiment to be dress regulations, attendance, and finally, the education itself, we may consider these three different strata of understanding. Most students are already hostile to the administration on at least the first level. It is our job, then, through a combination of educational and action projects, to raise the level of understanding of the students, and help them to act upon that new understanding.

Many of us will find it initially difficult to communicate meaningfully with segments of the student population with which we have had little previous contact. Quite a few of these people regard us with a mixture of respect and hostility because we are "intellectuals," "kooks," or just plain "snobs." First of all we must realize that we have earned these titles in one way or another. We have our own cliques, if not as formal as the social ones, and tend to look down our noses at those who do not measure up to our own standards of intelligence, sensitivity, or social concern.

Our first task, then, is to show the students that we *are* on their side, and have many of the same concerns they do. One method is to begin agitation around issues students are already concerned about. We should be in the forefront of any student protest against administrative action. One of the best opportunities to talk to students about things which bother them comes during physical education classes. The unstratified (we all wear the same clothes), nonacademic, and naturally friendly atmosphere is conducive to easy discussion of mutual problems. In "mixed" schools, it is essential that we break down the barriers and establish communications between minority groups. These schools often have exorbitantly high fees for Student Activity Cards, Grad Nite, and Senior dues. These high charges effectively prevent most members of minority groups from participating in student activities. If this discriminatory pattern can be shown to these groups (if they aren't aware of them already) and the ideal of collective action is successfully presented, large numbers of these groups (which are usually closely knit), may be activated. Since these groups are often disproportionately represented on athletic teams, a very strong case may be made to the majority of the student population. With a majority of the students then mobilized, the administration will be forced to lower prices.

In order to show students that we are not similar to student government and that we do more than hold offices and talk, while we are formally organizing and having our first membership drive, we must do something concrete, which can be readily seen as an attempt to help *all* students. On virtually every college campus, there is some sort of "book" on professors and associate professors who teach at that college. Such a "book" is needed on our campuses. The legal problems of distribution should be carefully researched, but a tactful and respectively written handbook on different aspects and quirks of individual teachers and courses would be received very well by the students, and if done properly, unhappily accepted by the administration. A manual should also be prepared for incoming B10s. This should contain practical information about hashlines, shortcuts across campus, ways to see guidance counselors quickly, etc.

There is also the possibility of some organizing being done on junior high school campuses. Many people connected with our movement will have younger brothers and sisters in junior high schools. They should be introduced to our movement *before* they have already entered high school.

One way to get some publicity for community service is a tutorial project. They are easy to organize, open the door to communication with minority groups at different schools, and demonstrate to the community-at-large that we are a positive, rather than a negative force in the community.

We should not look with disdain upon student government. We have much to learn from SLATE, the Berkeley campus political movement. Everyone connected with us should run for student council, Boy's League, or Girl's League, on the issue of Student Government reform. On any campus where we are fairly strong, we should run candidates for Student Body Offices, and try to organize mass active support of our candidates, as opposed to the efforts of 20–30 people. In marginal elections, we can control the swing vote and get concessions from run-off candidates. Where we win control of any offices, we force the administration to either give in on major points, or continually override our actions, which makes the administration look silly to the students, our parents, and our principal's bosses downtown.

"Underground" newspapers have proven to be highly successful at two schools already. The first few issues should be written and produced by four or five people (to distribute reprisals, as well as the work load). These students should continue to take responsibility of the production of the paper, *but most of the material should come from other segments of the student population as soon as possible, so that it is a true reflection of student opinion.* The first issue should be sent to the leadership of as many social cliques as possible (so the paper is IN), and should be MAILED TO THEM. Mailing is emphasized because any attempt to distribute such a paper on campus would result in those responsible for it being crushed by the administration. Special care should be taken to send copies to all the people in Journalism, as many of them will compare the "underground" paper favorably to the school paper, and can then be converted to our movement. Copies should be sent to friendly teachers. Mailing costs may be partially defrayed by contributions, but there should be no charge for subscription.

Efforts as great and broad-based as those outlined here will require a considerable degree of organization on both a school-wide and a city-wide level. Both levels should maintain as flexible a structure as possible. Campus groups should have small functional committees which will be responsible for projects undertaken on a local level. There should be larger meetings so that the rank and file both understand and control all that is happening. New situations may be handled by quick lunchtime meetings. Decisions should be reached by consensus rather than voting whenever possible. This serves the dual purpose of keeping the group dynamic through the synthesis of ideas rather than the total acceptance of one or the other, and keeps hostility down to a minimum. A level of order should be maintained, but parlimentarianism should be avoided as it stifles creative thinking. The leadership of the meetings should be rotated around the group so that an elitist clique doesn't develop and all participating members get valuable experience at chairing meetings.

The city-wide groups should operate along these same general lines. A city-wide coordinating council should be set up as open to all members, but with required attendance for at least one person from every campus. Membership cards should be made available at a nominal cost, to give as many people as possible some tangible connection with the movement. If possible, later on, a small aesthetically-pleasing button bearing the group symbol could be sold as a fund-raiser and to denote membership.

A city-wide newsletter should be started to maintain and strengthen contact with various schools. It should contain organizational news and other things that may be of interest to our membership.

Ours is a *student movement*. It is not a movement of liberals, radicals, or conservatives. If it is to succeed, it must steer clear of political issues such as civil rights and Vietnam, or other tempting topics except where they directly relate to our education. We should remember that the Young Republicans actively participated in the Free Speech Movement at Berkeley. They were able to do so because the FSM limited itself to campus problems.

Once we are organized, we can count on a considerable degree of support from teachers. They already recognize that the administration has come between them and the students, but feel neither strong enough, nor sufficiently moved to do anything about it. I am confident that many would be activated by a student movement. One of the most exciting things they could help with would be the creation of "Freedom Schools," with lunchtime and after-school discussions on topics of interest. One possibility would be the creation of a parallel course in Current American Problems, free of feeble-minded texts and restraining administrators. This would show to the entire community, but especially to the students and their parents, how fresh and exciting a school could be if administrators would leave it alone.

We must also make an attempt to reach all segments of the outside community. Each student should convert his parents and get them to do as much as possible. Religious groups (especially Unitarian Churches and Reform

Temples) should be contacted. Preferably, this should be done by someone whose parents are active in that local church. Individual members of the California Democratic Council could be approached. We should get in touch with the American Federation of Teachers and the American Civil Liberties Union, and request their formal organizational support. We can contact trade unions and ask for help, stressing the many parallels between early union development and what we are doing now. We should get our parents active in PTA *and make a concerted effort to get PTA support.* In all our dealings with these groups, our position should be polite, but firm. We are asking them for support because we feel that in many areas, our interests are mutual, but that this is a *student* movement, and we have no intention whatsoever of giving up any of our power to adults.

What, then, are some of the specific things we are fighting for?

1) The creation of a joint Student-Faculty Council to set up general rules on each individual campus.

2) The right of teachers and students to collectively decide upon their courses and methods of study.

3) Full academic freedom and freedom of advocacy on the high school and junior college campus.

4) No more than 25 people in a class, with a school average of 20, and a maximum of 8 for special groups.

5) An end to unprofessional clerical and policing jobs for teachers.

6) An end to student police squads and oppressive Attendance Officers, replacing them with a voluntary honor system.

7) The right of students to take or not take courses as they see fit.

We should recognize that the nature of a group such as ours and the struggle it will undertake shall have a lasting effect on those who take part in it. It will not be enough for someone to be a "card-carrying member" of our movement, and have no other connection with it. Every member should take an active role in helping us organize. We have large and powerful forces arrayed against us. Anyone who wants to see us win will have to help us win.

We must not lose sight of our central goal. We want to change the educational system because we are disturbed at the type of "individual" that system is turning out. We want a society where all men are free to give the fullest expression to their beliefs and feelings. Where we are all free to communicate with one another on an equal, dignified, and nonviolent plane. This is not the GREAT artificial SOCIETY we are building; merely a decent one.

11.2.   *CARL DAVIDSON:* **The New Radicals and the Multiversity**

> [Carl Davidson sets forth in the document here reprinted (third part of an SDS pamphlet, 1968) a political line for the radicals in the universities that he had already delineated in 1966 with "Towards a Student Syndacalism." Davidson has been interorganizational secretary of SDS (1967–1968) and is now on the staff of the radical newsweekly *Guardian.*]

Perhaps the single most important factor for the student power movement to keep in mind is the fact that the university is intimately bound up with the society in general. Because of this, we should always remember that we cannot liberate the university without radically changing the rest of society. The lesson to be drawn is that any attempt to build a student movement based on "on-campus" issues only is inherently conservative and ultimately reactionary. Every attempt should be made to connect campus issues with off-campus questions. For example, the question of ranking and university complicity with the Selective Service System needs to be tied to a general anti-draft and "No Draft for Vietnam" movement. The question of the presence of the military on the campus in all its forms needs to be tied to the question of what that military is used for—fighting aggressive wars of oppression abroad—and not just to the question of secret research being poor academic policy. Furthermore, the student movement must actively seek to join off-campus struggles in the surrounding community. For example, strikes by local unions should be supported if possible. This kind of communication and understanding with the local working class is essential if we are ever going to have community support for student strikes.

If there is a single over-all purpose for the student power movement, it would be the development of a radical political consciousness among those students who will later hold jobs in strategic sectors of the political economy. This means that we should reach out to engineers and technical students rather than to business administration majors, education majors rather than to art students. From a national perspective, this strategy would also suggest that we should place priorities on organizing in certain *kinds* of universities—the community colleges, junior colleges, state universities, and technical schools, rather than religious colleges or the Ivy League.

One way to mount political action around this notion is to focus on the placement offices—the nexus betwen the university and industry. For example, when Dow Chemcal comes to recruit, our main approach to junior and senior chemical engineering students who are being interviewed should not only be around the issue of the immorality of napalm. Rather, our leaflets should say that one of the main faults of Dow and all other industries as well is that their workers *have no control* over content or purposes of their work. In other words, Dow Chemical is bad, not only because of napalm, but mainly because it renders its workers *powerless,* makes them *unfree.* In short, Dow and all American industry oppresses *its own workers* as well as the people of the Third World. Dow in particular should be run off the campus and students urged not to work for them because of their complicity in war crimes. But when other industries are recruiting, our leaflets should address themselves to the interviewees' instincts of workmanship, his desires to be free and creative, to do humane work, rather than work for profit. We should encourage him, if he takes the job, to see himself in this light—as a skilled worker—and of his self-interest of organizing on his future job with his fellow workers, skilled and unskilled, for control of production and the end to which his work is directed. The need for control, for the power, on and off the job, to affect the decisions shaping one's life in all arenas; developing this kind of consciousness, on and off the campus, is what we should be fundamentally all about.

There are three virtues necessary for successful radical organizing; honesty, patience, and a sense of humor. First of all if the students we are trying to reach can't trust us, who can they trust? Secondly it takes time to build a movement. Sometimes several years of groundwork must be laid before a student power movement has a constituency. It took most of us several years before we had developed a radical perspective. Why should it be any different for the people we are trying to reach? This is not to say that everyone must repeat all the mistakes we have gone through, but there are certain *forms* of involvement and action that many students will have to repeat. Finally, by a sense of humor, I mean we must be life-affirming. Lusty passionate people are the only kind of men who have the enduring strength to motivate enough people to radically transform a life-negating system.

Ché Guevara remarked in *Guerrilla Warfare* that as long as people had faith in certain institutions and forms of political activity, then the organizer must work *with* the people *through* those institutions, even though we might think those forms of action are dead ends.* The point of Ché's remark is that people must learn that those forms are stacked against them through their *own experience* in attempting change. The role of the organizer at this point is crucial. He or she should neither passively go along with the student government "reformer" types nor stand apart from the action denouncing it as "sell-out." Rather, his task is that of *constant criticism* from within the action. When the reformers fail, become bogged down, or are banging their heads against the wall, the organizer should be there as *one who has been with them throughout their struggle* to offer the relevant analysis of *why* their approach has failed and to indicate future strategies and tactics.

However, we also need to be discriminating. There are certain forms of political action, like working within the Democratic Party, that are so obviously bankrupt, that we need not waste our time. In order to discern these limits, an organizer has to develop a sensitivity to understand where people are. Many radical actions have failed on campuses because the activists have failed in laying a base for a particular action. It does no good to sit in against the CIA if a broad educational campaign, petitions, and rallies on the nature of the CIA have not been done for several days before the sit-in. It is not enough that we have a clear understanding of the oppressiveness of institutions like the CIA and HUAC before we act in a radical fashion. We must make our position clear to the students, faculty, and the surrounding community.

In addition to its role in the political economy, it is important to deal with the university as the backbone of what Mills called "the cultural apparatus."* He defined this as all those organizations and *milieux* in which artistic, scientific and intellectual work goes on, as well as the means by which that work is made available to others. Within this apparatus, the various vehicles of communication—language, the mass arts, public arts, and design arts—stand between a man's consciousness and his material existence. At present, the bulk of the apparatus is centralized and controlled by the corporate rulers of America. As a result, their use of the official communications has the effect of limiting our experience and, furthermore, expropriates much of that potential experience that we might have called our own. What we need to understand is that the cultural apparatus, properly used, has the ability both to transform power into authority and transform authority into mere overt coercion.

---

*   Ernest "Ché" Guevara, *Guerrilla Warfare.*

*   C. Wright Mills, *Power, Politics and People,* p. 386.

At present, the university's role in acculturation and socialization is the promulgation of the utter mystification of "corporate consciousness." Society is presented to us as a kind of caste system in which we are to see ourselves as a "privileged elite"—a bureaucratic man channelled into the proper bureaucratic niche. In addition to strengthening the forms of social control off the campus, the administration uses the apparatus on campus to legitimize its own power over us.

On the campus, the student press, underground newspapers, campus radio and television, literature tables, posters and leaflets, artist and lecture series, theaters, films, and the local press make up a good part of the non-academic cultural media. Most of it is both actively and passively being used against us. Any student power movement should (1) try to gain control of as much of the *establishment* campus cultural apparatus as possible, (2) if control is not possible, we should try to influence and/or resist it when necessary and (3) organize and develop a new counter-apparatus of our own. In short, we need our people on the staff of the school newspapers, and radio stations. We need our own local magazines. We need sympathetic contacts on local off-campus new media. Finally, we all could use some training in graphic and communicative arts.

What this all adds up to is strengthening our ability to wage an effective "de-sanctification" program against the authoritarian institutions controlling us. The purpose of de-sanctification is to strip institutions of their legitimizing authority, to have them reveal themselves to the people under them for what they are—raw coercive power. This is the purpose of singing the Mickey Mouse Club jingle at student government meetings, of ridiculing and harrassing student disciplinary hearings and tribunals, of burning the Dean of Men and/or Women in effigy. People will not move *against* institutions of power until the legitimizing authority has been stripped away. On many campuses this has already happened; but for those remaining, the task remains. And we should be forewarned: it is a tricky job and often can backfire, de-legitimizing us.

While student governments vary in form in the United States, the objective reasons for their existence are the containment, or pacification and manipulation of the student body. Very few of our student governments are autonomously incorporated or have any powers or rights apart from those sanctioned by the regents or trustees of the university. Furthermore, most administrations hold a veto power over anything done by the student governments. Perhaps the worst aspect of this kind of manipulation and repression is that the administration uses students to control other students. Most student government politicos are lackeys of the worst sort. That is, they have internalized and embraced all the repressive mechanisms the administration has designed for use *against* them and their fellow students.

With this in mind, it would seem that we should ignore student governments and/or abolish them. While this is certainly true in the final analysis, it is important to relate to student governments differently during the earlier stages of on-campus political struggles. The question we are left with is how do we render student governments ineffective in terms of what they are designed to do, while at the same time, using them effectively in building the movement?

Do we work inside the system? Of course we do. The question is not one of working "inside" or "outside" the system. Rather, the question is do we pay by the established rules? Here, the answer is an emphatic no. The estab-

lished habits of student politics—popularity contest elections, disguising oneself as a moderate, working for "better communications and dialogue" with
administrators, watering down demands before they are made, going through
channels—all of these gambits are stacked against us. If liberal and moderate
student politicians really believe in them, then we should tell *them* to try it
with all they have. But if they continue to make this ploy after they have learned
from their own experience that these methods are dead-ends, then they should
be soundly denounced as opportunists or gutless administration puppets.

We should face the fact that student governments are *powerless* and designed to stay that way. From this perspective, all talk about "getting into
power" is so much nonsense. The only thing that student governments are useful for is their ability to be a *temporary vehicle* in building a grass-roots student
power movement. This means that student elections are useful as an arena for
raising real issues, combatting and exposing administration apologists, and
involving new people, rather than getting elected. If our people do happen to
get elected *as radicals* (this is becoming increasingly possible) then the seats
won should be used as a focal point and sounding board for demonstrating the
impotence of student government *from within*. A seat should be seen as a
soap-box, where our representatives can stand, gaining a kind of visibility and
speaking to the student body as a whole, over the heads of the other student
politicians.

Can anything positive be gained through student government? Apart from
publicity, one thing it can be used for is money. Many student-activities funds
are open for the kinds of things we would like to see on campus: certain
speakers, films, sponsoring conferences. Money, without strings, is always a
help. Also, non-political services, such as non-profit used-book exchanges, are
helpful to many students. But in terms of radical changes, student government
can do nothing apart from a mass, radical student power movement. Even
then, student government tends to be a conservative force within those struggles. In the end, meaningful changes can only come through a radical transformation of both the consciousness of large numbers of students and the
forms of student self-government.

Fighting for reforms and making a revolution should not be seen as
mutually exclusive positions. The question should be: what kind of reforms
move us toward a radical transformation of both the university and the society
in general? First of all, we should avoid the kinds of reforms which leave the
basic *rationale* of the system unchallenged. For instance, a bad reform to
work for would be getting a better grading system, because the underlying
rationale—the need for grades at all—remains unchallenged.

Secondly, we should avoid certain kinds of reform that divide students
from each other. For instance, trying to win certain privileges for upper class-
men but not for freshmen or sophomores. Or trying to establish non-graded
courses for students above a certain grade-point average. In the course of
campus political activity, the administration will try a whole range of "divide
and rule" tactics such as fostering the "Greek-Independent Split," sexual double standards, intellectual *vs.* "jocks," responsible *vs.* irresponsible leaders, red-
baiting and "non-student" *vs.* students. We need to avoid falling into these
traps ahead of time, as well as fighting them when used against us.

Finally, we should avoid all of the "co-management" kinds of reforms.
These usually come in the form of giving certain "responsible" student leaders

a voice or influence in certain decision-making processes, rather than abolishing or winning effective control over those parts of the governing apparatus. One way to counter administration suggestions for setting up "tripartite" committees ($\frac{1}{3}$ student, $\frac{1}{3}$ faculty, $\frac{1}{3}$ administration, each with an equal number of votes) is to say, "OK, but once a month the committee must hold an all-university plenary session—one man, one vote." The thought of being outvoted 1,000 to 1 will cause administrators to scrap that co-optive measure in a hurry.

We have learned the hard way that the reformist path is full of pitfalls. What, then, are the kinds of reformist measures that do make sense? First of all, there are the civil libertarian issues. We must always fight, dramatically and quickly, for free speech and the right to organize, advocate, and mount political action—of all sorts. However, even here, we should avoid getting bogged down in "legalitarianism." We cannot count on this society's legal apparatus to guarantee our civil liberties: and, we should not organize around civil libertarian issues *as if it could*. Rather, when our legal rights are violated, we should move as quickly as possible, without losing our base, to expand the campus libertarian moral indignation into a multi-issues *political* insurgency, exposing the repressive character of the administration and the corporate state in general.

The second kind of partial reform worth fighting for and possibly winning is the abolition of on-campus repressive mechanisms, i.e., student courts, disciplinary tribunals, deans of men and women, campus police, and the use of civil police on campus. While it is true that "abolition" is a negative reform, and while we will be criticized for not offering "constructive" criticisms, we should reply that the only constructive way to deal with an inherently destructive apparatus is to destroy it. We must curtail the ability of administrators to repress our *need to refuse* their way of life—the regimentation and bureaucratization of existence.

When our universities are already major agencies for social change in the direction of *1984,* our initial demands must, almost of necessity, be negative demands. In this sense, the first task of a student power movement will be the organization of a holding action—a resistance. Along these lines, one potentially effective tactic for resisting the university's disciplinary apparatus would be the formation of a Student Defense League. The purpose of the group would be to make its services available to any student who must appear before campus authorities for infractions of repressive (or just plain stupid) rules and regulations. The defense group would then attend the student's hearing *en masse.* However, for some cases, it might be wise to include law students or local radical lawyers in the group for the purpose of making legal counter-attacks. A student defense group would have three major goals: 1) saving as many students as possible from punishment, 2) de-sanctifying and rendering disfunctional the administration's repressive apparatus, and 3) using 1) and 2) as tactics in reaching other students for building a movement to abolish the apparatus as a whole.

When engaging in this kind of activity, it is important to be clear in our rhetoric as to what we are about. We are not trying to *liberalize* the existing order, but trying to win our *liberation* from it. We must refuse the administrations' rhetoric or "responsibility." To their one-dimensional way of thinking, the concept of responsibility has been reduced to its opposite, namely, be nice, don't rock the boat, do things according to *our* criteria of what is permissible. In actuality their whole system is geared toward the inculcation of the values of a planned irresponsibility. We should refuse *their* definitions, *their* terms, and even refuse to engage in *their* semantic hassles. We only need to define for *ourselves and other students* our notions of what it means to be free, constructive, and responsible. Too many campus movements have been co-opted for weeks or even permanently by falling into the administrations' rhetorical bags.

Besides the abolition of repressive disciplinary mechanisms within the university, there are other negative reforms that radicals should work for. Getting the military off the campus, abolishing the grade system, and abolishing universal compulsory courses (i.e., physical education) would fit into this category. However, an important question for the student movement is whether or not *positive* radical reforms can be won within the university short of making a revolution in the society as a whole. Furthermore, would the achievement of these kinds of partial reforms have the cumulative effect of weakening certain aspects of corporate capitalism, and, in their small way, make that broader revolution more likely?

At present, my feeling is that these kinds of anti-capitalist positive reforms are almost as hard to conceive intellectually as they are to win. To be sure, there has been a wealth of positive educational reforms suggested by people like Paul Goodman. But are they anti-capitalist as well? For example, we have been able to organize several good free universities. Many of the brightest and most sensitive students on American campuses, disgusted with the present state of education, left the campus and organized these counter-institutions. Some of their experiments were successful in an immediate internal sense. A few of these organizers were initially convinced that the sheer moral force of their work in these free institutions would cause the existing educational structure to tremble and finally collapse like a house of IBM cards. But what happened? What effect did the free universities have on the established educational order? At best, they had no effect. But it is more likely that they had the effect of strengthening the existing system. How? First of all, the best of our people left the campus, enabling the existing university to function more smoothly, since the "troublemakers" were gone. Secondly, they gave liberal administrators the rhetoric, the analysis, and sometimes the man-power to co-opt their programs and establish elitist forms of "experimental" colleges inside of, although quarantined from, the existing educational system. This is not to say that free universities should not be organized, both on and off the campus. They can be valuable and useful. But they should not be seen as a primary aspect of a strategy for change.

What then is open to us in the area of positive anti-capitalist reforms? For the most part, it will be difficult to determine whether or not a reform has the effect of being anti-capitalist until it has been achieved. Since it is both difficult and undesirable to attempt to predict the future, questions of this sort are often best answered in practice. Nevertheless, it would seem that the kind of reforms we are looking for are most likely to be found within a strategy of what I would call 'encroaching control." There are aspects of the university's administrative, academic, financial-physical, and social apparatus that are potentially, if not actually, useful and productive. While we should try to abolish the repressive mechanisms of the university; our strategy should be to gain *control,* piece by piece, of its positive aspects.

What would that control look like? To begin, all aspects of the non-academic life of the campus should either be completely under the control of the students as individuals or embodied in the institutional forms *they* establish for their collective government. For example, an independent union of students should have the final say on the form and content of *all-university* political, social, and cultural events. Naturally, individual students and student organizations would be completely free in organizing events of their own.

Second, only the students and the teaching faculty, individually and through their organizations, should control the academic affairs of the university. One example of a worthwhile reform in this area would be enabling all history majors and history professors to meet jointly at the beginning of each semester and shape the form, content, and direction of their departmental curriculum. Another partial reform in this area would be enabling an independent union of students to hire additional professors of their choice and establish additional accredited courses of their choice independently of the faculty or administration.

Finally, we should remember that control should be sought *for some specific purpose*. One reason we want this kind of power is to enable us to meet the *self-determined* needs of students and teachers. But another objective that we should see as radicals is to put as much of the university's resources as possible into the hands of the underclass and the working class. We should use the student press to publicize and support local strikes. We should use campus facilities for meeting the educational needs of insurgent organizations of the poor, and of rank and file workers. Or we could mobilize the universities' research facilities for serving projects established and controlled by the poor and worker, rather than projects established and controlled by the government, management, and labor bureaucrats. The conservative nature of American trade unions makes activity of this sort very difficult, although not impossible. But we should always be careful to make a distinction between the American working class itself and the labor bureaucrats.

One question almost always confronts the student movement on the campus. Do we try to win faculty support before we go into action? Or do we lump them together with the administration? What we have learned in the past seems to indicate that both of these responses are wrong. Earlier in this paper, I remarked on the kinds of divisions that exist among the faculty. What is important to see is that this division is not just between good and bad guys. Rather, the faculty is becoming more and more divided in terms of the objective functions of their jobs. To make the hard case on one hand, the function of the lower level of the faculty is to teach—a potentially creative and useful activity; on the other hand, the function of most administrative and research faculty is manipulation, repression, and—for the defense department hirelings—destruction. In general, we should develop our strategies so that our lot falls with the teaching faculty and theirs with ours. As for the research and administrative faculty, we should set both ourselves and the teaching faculty against them. Also, during any student confrontation with the administration, the faculty can do one of four things *as a group*. They can 1) support the administration, 2) remain neutral, 3) split among themselves, and 4) support us. In any situation, we should favor the development of one of the last three alternatives rather than the first. Furthermore, if it seems likely that the faculty will split on an issue, we should try to encourage the division indicated above. While it is important to remain open to the faculty, we should not let their support or non-support become an issue in determining whether or not we begin to mount political action. Finally, we should encourage the potentially radical sectors of the faculty to organize among themselves around their own grievances, hopefully being able to *eventually* form a radical alliance with us.

Probably the most exploited and alienated group of people on any campus *are* the graduate student teaching assistants. The forces of the multiversity hit them from two directions—both as students and as teachers. As students, they have been around long enough to have lost their awe of academia. As faculty, they are given the worst jobs for the lowest pay. For the most part, they have no illusions about their work. Their working conditions, low pay, and the fact that their futures are subject to the whimsical machinations of their department chairmen, make them a group ripe for radical organization. Furthermore, their strategic position within the university structure—makes them potentially powerful as a group if they should decide to organize and strike. If they go out, a large part of the multiversity comes grinding to a halt. The kinds of demands they are most likely to be organized around naturally connect them with a radical student power movement and with the potentially radical sector of the faculty. Furthermore, these considerations make the organization of a radical trade union of TAs a crucial part of any strategy for change. We should see this kind of labor organizing as one of our first priorities in building the campus movement.

Almost all colleges and especially the multiversities have a large number of blue-collar maintainence workers on campus. Within the state-supported institutions in particular, these people are often forbidden to organize unions, have terrible working conditions, and are paid very low wages. Their presence on the campus offers a unique opportunity for many students to become involved in blue-collar labor organizing at the same time that they are in school. Secondly, since these workers usually live in the surrounding community, their friends and relatives will come from other sectors of the local working class. Quite naturally, they will carry their ideas, opinions, and feelings toward the radical student movement home with them. In this sense, they can be an important link connecting us with other workers, and our help in enabling them to organize a local independent and radical trade union would help tremendously. Finally, if we should ever strike as students, they could be an important ally. For instance, after SDS at the University of Missouri played a major role in organizing a militant local of non-academic employees, they learned that, were the union to strike for its own demands in sympathy with student demands, the university as a physical plant would cease to function after four days. It is obviously important to have that kind of power.

One mistake radical students have been making in relating to the worst aspects of the multiversity's academic apparatus has been their avoidance of it. We tend to avoid large classes, lousy courses, and reactionary professors like the plague. At best, we have organized counter-courses outside the classroom and off the campus. My suggestion is that we should do the opposite. Our brightest people should sign up for the large freshman and sophomore sections with the worst profs in *strategic* courses in history, political science, education, and even the ROTC counter-insurgency lectures. From this position they should then begin to take out their frustrations with the work of the course while they are on the job, i.e., inside the classroom. Specifically, they should be constant vocal critics of the form and content of the course, the prof, class size, the educational system, and corporate capitalism in general. Their primary strategy, rather than winning debating points against the prof, should be to reach other students in the class. Hopefully, our on-the-job organizer will begin to develop a radical caucus in the class. This group could then meet outside of the class, continue to collectively develop a further radical critique of the future class-work, to be presented at the succeeding sessions. If all goes well with the prof, and perhaps his department as well, they will have a full-scale academic revolt on their hands by the end of the semester. Finally, if this sort of work were being done in a variety of courses at once, the local radical student movement would have the makings of an underground educational movement that was actively engaged in mounting an effective resistance to the educational *status quo*.

There is little doubt that the hippy movement has made its impact on most American campuses. It is also becoming more clear that the culture of advanced capitalist society is becoming more sterile, dehumanized and one-dimensional. It is directed toward a passive mass, rather than an active public. Its root value is consumption. We obviously need a cultural revolution, along with a revolution in the political economy. But the question remains: where do the hippies fit in? At the present time, their role seems ambivalent. On the one hand, they thoroughly reject the dominant culture and seem to be life-affirming. On the other hand, they seem to be for the most part, passive consumers of culture, rather than active creators of culture. For all their talk of community, the nexus of their relations with each other seems to consist only of drugs and a common jargon. With all their talk of love, one finds little deep-rooted passion. Yet, they are there; and they are a major phenomenon. Their relevance to the campus scene is evidenced by the success of the wave of "Gentle Thursdays" that swept the country. Through this approach, we have been able to reach and break loose a good number of people. Often, during the frivolity of Gentle Thursday, the life-denying aspects of corporate capitalism are brought home to many people with an impact that could never be obtained by the best of all of our anti-war demonstrations.

However, the hippy movement has served to make many of our people withdraw into a personalistic, passive cult of consumption. These aspects need to be criticized and curtailed. We should be clear about one thing: the *individual* liberation of man, the most social of animals, is a dead-end—an impossibility. And even if individual liberation were possible, would it be desirable? The sublimation of reality within the individual consciousness neither destroys nor transforms the objective reality of other men.

Nevertheless, the excitement and imagination of some aspects of hippy-dom can be useful in building critiques of the existing culture. Here, I am referring to the provos and the diggers. Gentle Thursday, when used as a provo (provocative) tactic on campus, can cause the administration to display some of its most repressive characteristics. Even something as blunt as burning a television set in the middle of campus can make a profound statement about the life-styles of many people. However, people engaging in this kind of tactics should 1) not see the action as a substitute for serious revolutionary activity and 2) read up on the Provos and Situationists rather than the Haight-Ashbury scene.

During the development of radical politics on the campus, the student movement will pass through a multitude of organizational forms. I have already mentioned several: Student Defense League, Teaching Assistants' Unions, Non-Academic Employees' Unions, and of course, SDS chapters. Another important development on many campuses has been the formation of Black Student Unions, or Afro-American cultural groups. All of these groups are vital, although some are more important than others at different stages of the struggle. However, for the purpose of keeping a radical and multi-issue focus throughout the growth of the movement, it is important to begin work on a campus by organizing an SDS chapter.

From this starting point, how does SDS see its relation to the rest of the campus? I think we have learned that we should not look upon ourselves as an intellectual and political oasis, hugging each other in a wasteland. Rather, our chapters should see themselves as *organizing committees* for reaching out to the majority of the student population. Furthermore, we are organizing for something—the power to effect change. With this in mind, we should be well aware of the fact that the kind of power and changes we would like to have and achieve are not going to be given to us gracefully. Ultimately, we have access to only one source of power within the knowledge factory. And that power lies in our potential ability to stop the university from functioning, to render the system disfunctional for limited periods of time. Throughout all our on-campus organizing efforts we should keep this one point in mind: that sooner or later we are going to have to strike—or at least successfully threaten to strike. Because of this, our constant strategy should be the preparation of a mass base for supporting and participating in this kind of action.

What are the organizational forms, other than those mentioned above, that are necessary for the development of this kind of radical constituency? The first kind of extra-SDS organization needed is a Hyde Park or Free Speech Forum. An area of the campus, centrally located and heavily travelled, should be selected and equipped with a P.A. system. Then, on a certain afternoon one day a week, the platform would be open to anyone to give speeches on anything they choose. SDS people should attend regularly and speak regularly, although they should encourage variety and debate, and not monopolize the platform. To begin, the forum should be weekly, so that students don't become bored with it. Rather, we should try to give it the aura of a special event. Later on, when political activity intensifies, the forum could be held every day. In the early stages, publicity, the establishment of a mood and climate for radical politics, is of utmost importance. We should make our presence felt everywhere—in the campus news media, leafletting and poster displays, and regular attendance at the meetings of all student political, social, and religious organizations. We should make all aspects of our politics as visible and open as possible.

Once our presence has become known, we can begin to organize on a variety of issues. One arena that it will be important to relate to at this stage will be student government elections. The best organizational form for this activity would be the formation of a Campus Freedom Party for running radical candidates. It is important that the party be clear and open as to its radical consciousness, keeping in mind that our first task is that of building radical consciousness, rather than winning seats. It is also important that the party take positions on off-campus questions as well, as the war in Vietnam. Otherwise, if we only relate to on-campus issues, we run the risk of laying

the counter-revolutionary groundwork for an elitist, conservative and corporatist student movement. As many people as possible should be involved
in the work of the party, with SDS people having the function of keeping it
militant and radical in a non-manipulative and honest fashion. The party
should permeate the campus with speeches, films, and leaflets, as well as a
series of solidly intellectual and radical position papers on a variety of issues.
Furthermore, we should remember that an election campaign should be fun.
Campus Freedom Parties should organize Gentle Thursdays, jug bands, rock
groups, theater groups for political skits, and homemade 8mm. campaign films.
Finally, during non-election periods, the Campus Freedom Party should form
a variety of CFP *ad hoc* committees for relating to student government on
various issues throughout the year.

The next stage of the movement is the most crucial and delicate: the
formation of a Student Strike Coordinating Committee. There are two preconditions necessary for its existence. First, there must be a quasi-radical
base of some size that has been developed from past activity. Secondly, either
a crisis situation provoked by the administration or a climate of active frustration with the administration and/or the ruling class it represents must exist.
The frustration should be centered around a set of specific demands that have
been unresolved through the established channels of liberal action. If this kind
of situation exists, then a strike is both possible and desirable. A temporary
steering committee should be set up, consisting of representatives of radical
groups (SDS, Black Student Union, TA's Union). This group would set the
initial demands and put out the call for a strike within a few weeks time. Within
that time, they would try to bring in as many other groups and individuals
as possible without seriously watering down the demands. This new coalition
would then constitute itself as the Student Strike Coordinating Committee,
with the new groups adding members to the original temporary steering committee. Also, a series of working committees and a negotiating committee
should be established. Finally, the strike committee should attempt to have
as many open mass plenary sessions as possible.

What should come out of a student strike? First, the development of a
radical consciousness among large numbers of students. Secondly, we should
try to include within our demands some issues on which we can win partial
victories. Finally, the organizational form that should grow out of strike or
series of strikes is an independent, radical, and political Free Student Union
that would replace the existing student government. I have already dealt with
the general political life of radical movements. But some points need to be
repeated. First of all, a radical student union *must* be in alliance with the
radical sectors of the underclass and working class. Secondly, the student
movement has the additional task of radicalizing the subsector of the labor
force that some of us in SDS have come to call the new working class.
Thirdly, a radical union of students should have an anti-imperialist critique
of U.S. foreign policy. Finally, local student unions, if they are to grow and
thrive, must become federated on regional, national, and international levels.
However, we should be careful not to form a national union of students lacking
in a grass-roots constituency that actively and democratically participates in
all aspects of the organization's life. One NSA is enough. On the international
level, we should avoid both the CIA- and Soviet Union-sponsored International
Unions. We would be better off to establish informal relations with groups
like the Zengakuren in Japan, the German SDS, the French Situationists, the

Spanish Democratic Student Syndicate, and the third world revolutionary student organizations. Hopefully, in the not too distant future, we may be instrumental in forming a new International Union of Revolutionary Youth. But there is much work to be done between now and then. And even greater tasks remain to be done before we can begin to build the conditions for human liberation.

11.3.   NACLA: Who Rules Columbia?

[The clamorous occupation of Columbia University in New York was based on the struggle against a university directed by a nonacademic administration which represented the connections between research and education, on the one hand, and the military-industrial interests of high finance, on the other. "Who Rules Columbia?" prepared by NACLA, is an analytical documentation on the extra-academic interests which control the university and determine its orientation and programs. Selections from the document are reprinted below. NACLA pamphlet, 1968.]

Introduction

There has been a failure to understand the real issues behind the Columbia uprising. The press has put forth a variety of misleading theories to explain the rebellion: the generational gap, the plotted leftist putsch, the failure of the university to respond to current and changing student needs, breakdown in communication, impatience, a sort of Rite of Spring, general anxiety over the Vietnam war . . . theories which obfuscated the truth.

This pamphlet has been produced to clarify and explain the central issues. It will attempt to show concretely how Columbia University is set up not to service the needs of its own constituency—faculty and students—but rather to service outside interests which, by controlling Columbia finances, effectively control its policy. These outside interests, represented on the Board of Trustees, have organized the university as a "factory" designed to produce the skilled technicians and management personnel which the U.S. industrial and defense apparatus needs. The millions channeled into the university coffers by the agents of these interests are, for them, essentially an investment in people which, like any investment, is expected to yield certain returns.

The concept of the university as an investment determines the nature of grading systems and scholarship mechanisms which provide the rewards and punishments that channel human talents into specified occupations. The examination system does not test learning as such. Creativity and originality are sacrificed; testing is geared to show the ability to perform under pressure and to function in an hierarchy which channels instructions from the top down.

Our analysis focuses upon two sources outside the university from which Columbia trustees and key administrators derive their power: 1) the control of money (we will show how Columbia's dependence on outside sources of income affects its internal policy); and 2) the control of strategic decision-making positions maintained by their corporate, defense and foundation connections (we will examine the organizational associations of the trustees to show that the interests they represent are those which the university curriculum and finances are manipulated to serve).

This control by non-indigenous and non-academic interests is the crucial issue behind the student rebellion. The student contention that the trustees represent illegitimate power is based on a concept fundamental to democracy: that the authority of the rulers is legitimate only insofar as it represents the ruled. By seizing the university buildings, the students sought to dramatize the illegitimacy of the authority of the trustees and to effect, if only briefly, a redistribution of power. The student action shattered two fundamental aspects of control: property was seized, violating one of the most sacred of ideas; and, with the exposure of Kirk's files, the veil of secrecy was torn away (secrecy has always been one of the strongest weapons of control).

However, we have derived our analysis from open sources: *Standard & Poor's Directory, Who's Who in America, The New York Times,* financial magazines and corporation prospectuses. We assumed that major power decisions were made at board meetings and that from an analysis of the interests represented therein, we could predict what would happen in a given situation. The documents liberated from Grayson Kirk's office clearly substantiate our theories. They are in fact the proto-textbook which negates everything the students were being taught at Columbia; the courses were irrelevant or themselves a form of pacification; what they taught was abstract, misleading, calculated to conceal the roles for which students were being trained.

. . . .

International Corporations: Administering the Empire

After World War II heavy surplus profits from consolidated industries and the saturation of home markets created a need for either heavy investments domestically (which would have to be financed through a radical restructuring of the capitalist organization of the economy) or heavy investment expansion abroad. The larger corporations chose to extend their foreign frontiers and today we find such giants as Standard Oil (N.J.), Texaco, Colgate-Palmolive, Singer and National Cash Register deriving over half their profits from foreign sales. Direct investments (outright U.S. holdings in plants and equipment) have skyrocketed from $5 billion to $55 billion between 1945 and the present. Between 1960 and 1965 alone nearly 2,200 companies engaged in about 6,000 separate activities—primarily construction of new plants and the expansion of existing operations.

As the corporations have extended their overseas operations they have required greatly increased numbers of men to manage their investments: men trained in international law, international business management, diplomacy, languages, public relations and social scientists who are experts in foreign cultures. The corporate financial interests turned to the university to fulfill these needs, offering generous amounts of money, privileges for university administrators and high-level access to the prestigious, exciting world of international affairs in return. Columbia's School of International Affairs was created in 1945 to fulfill these needs.

As indicated on the "Top 22" chart, seven of Columbia's rulers have primary ties to either U.S. corporations or non-profit organizations with an international domain. Grayson Kirk was the first director to join Mobil Oil's board from outside its corporate ranks (in 1950). Mobil Oil is heavily dependent on foreign reserves in North Africa and the Near East for its survival. Frederick Kappel is a director of Standard Oil Company which derives over half its profits from foreign sales. William Burden's American Metals Climax has extensive mining interests in Southern Africa.

Several of the "Top 22" occupy prominent positions in the cultural penetration winning converts to the American way which facilitates corporate expansion abroad. Kirk and Lawrence Wien are both trustees of the Institute of International Education which handles all U. S. student exchanges and channels foreign students to meet the needs of U. S. business abroad. Other trustees and administrators play key roles in organizations financing foreign cultural and intellectual programs such as the Asia Foundation, African-American Institute, America-Korea Foundation and the Near East Foundation.

Since the most enlightened elements in the corporate and financial elite (among others) wish to avoid as much as possible the tensions and dislocations caused by war and direct confrontation, they backed the creation of a diplomatic and intelligence apparatus for channeling and manipulating events to make conflict less disruptive. President Kirk's previous contact with the international diplomatic and intelligence community through his academic posts in international affairs and the State Department's security section facilitated Columbia's training of diplomats and intelligence personnel at the School of International Affairs. The role of Columbia administrators and trustees in such foreign policy-making and intelligence organizations as the Council on Foreign Relations, Asia Foundation and CIA are discussed below.

Columbia University also trains specialized technicians and produces some of the new technology needed by these international corporations. For example, the booming offshore oil industry benefits directly from the technology developed at Columbia's Lamont Geological Observatory.

With the recent increase in foreign investments in the Third World and the increased threat (more and more overshadowing the previous "threat" of Soviet communism) of Third World nationalism, U. S. corporate and financial interests have stressed nation-building in the poor countries. By nation-building they mean creating a favorable infrastructure for capital investment. This involves, among other things, penetration and manipulation of those more "primitive" and esoteric societies and coopting indigenous elites, and requires anthropologists, sociologists, linguists, political theorists, journalists and psychologists familiar with these societies. The SIA accommodated these needs by adding institutes in Third World studies.

The School of International Affairs

The School of International Affairs (SIA) has become, in the space of a few years, one of Columbia's largest and most important divisions. When founded in 1946, the School operated on a total budget of $60,000; by 1964 the School's annual budget was well over a million dollars, and the Regional Institutes each accounted for hundreds of thousands of dollars more. In 1967, the School listed a Faculty and staff of over 150 members, which included some of the most prestigious—and powerful—figures in the Columbia community. President Grayson Kirk and Vice-President Truman both hold academic positions on the SIA's Faculty.

Originally composed of the School itself and the Russian Institute, the SIA's empire now encompasses eight Regional Institutes (each representing a major segment of the world), and several dozen research projects and institutes. In 1964, the School launched a $32-million fund-raising campaign to expand its activities further, and to finance a new building for the School. The building, named the Edward John Noble Building after the School's heaviest contributor, is now under construction at 118th Street and Amsterdam Ave., on a site once occupied by apartments.

The purpose of the SIA has never been in doubt: to train experts in international affairs and foreign areas for administrative positions in America's expanding overseas empire. This function is set forth clearly in a description of the School which appears in the Columbia University *Bulletin:* "The School of International Affairs is a professional school which was established in 1946 with the purpose of training, in conjunction with the regional institutes, a select group of students for staff and administrative programs in international fields." That this task is being realized can be shown by statistics on the activities of SIA alumni: in 1967, Dean Andrew Cordier estimated that 40 percent of the School's graduates worked in the international agencies of the U.S. Government, while another large segment worked for corporations, foundations or law firms engaged in international activities.

. . . .

Columbia and the U.S. Intelligence Community

The very nature of the Cold War struggle against Communism and the drive for empire require extensive non-military resources. The U.S. intelligence community, under the direction of the Central Intelligence Agency, is in charge of enlisting the expertise and the cover of non-governmental organizations. Through covert penetration of civilian branches of the government, voluntary groups, corporations, law firms, research centers, cultural projects, foundations and universities, the CIA is able to mobilize and coordinate for government service much of the seemingly a-political work of U.S. civilian society.

The primary tasks of the U.S. intelligence community are gathering and analyzing strategic information for decision-makers and positioning trained personnel in key locations to manipulate the course of events. (For a history and discussion of the CIA see, Wise and Ross, *The Invisible Government.*) Like several large universities, Columbia offers excellent opportunities for achieving these goals. Most of the evidence points to indirect relationships, but because the CIA is closed and secret and because the Columbia Administration refuses to discuss its CIA relations, it is quite possible that CIA-CU ties are far more direct and pervasive than the public data now indicates. In fact, our own information indicates that these ties are so direct as to involve a highly influential group of men in dual positions of leadership—inside Columbia *and* in the CIA itself.

One level of association involves individuals connected with Columbia who are also affiliated with CIA-related organizations. Three types of CIA-relationships are identified in the following table.

CIA-Related Organizations

I. ORGANIZATIONS HEAVILY FUNDED BY CIA:
Asia Foundation
African-American Institute

American Society of African Culture
Committee of Correspondence
Free Europe Committee

II. ORGANIZATIONS WHICH RECEIVED SOME FUNDS FROM THE CIA:
Institute for Int'l Education
John H. Whitney Trust
American Council for Emigrés in the Professions

III. COVERTLY PASSED CIA FUNDS:
Fairfield Foundation
Foundation for Youth and Student Affairs
Cleveland H. Dodge Foundation
Edward John Noble Foundation
David, Josephine and Winfield Baird Foundation, Inc.
William Benton Foundation
Catherwood Foundation
W. Alton Jones Foundation
J. M. Kaplan Fund, Inc.
Lucius N. Littauer Foundation
Aaron E. Norman Fund, Inc.
Rubicon Foundation

. . . .

The Defense-Research Nexus

The military plays two roles during the period of empire expansion and consolidation. Since access to foreign markets through trade and investment is essential, the military maintains the trade routes, first with the Navy and now with the Air Force. Secondly, conspicuous U.S. military presence and periodic demonstrations of force serve to dampen the development of national resistance to U.S. penetration.

There has been a shift in U.S. military strategy from massive retaliation to the use of limited war as the Soviet "threat" has declined and the "threat" of third world nationalism has increased. As nationalists increasingly engage in guerrilla warfare [as in Vietnam and Guatemala] the Defense Department is forced to rely on sophisticated technology to readjust the balance of power. It is the role of the University to provide vital technological weaponry.

Columbia's "Top 22" include good examples of the defense complex. William Burden's Lockheed Aircraft and Moore's General Dynamics together received 10% [$3.6 billion] of all U.S. military contracts. Burden is also Chairman of the Board of the Institute for Defense Analyses which specializes in the evaluation of advanced weaponry and counterinsurgency methods, and serves as the idea factory of the Defense Department. The section below on the Institute for Defense Analyses describes its other close relationships with Columbia. John Dunning, a trustee of Columbia's Riverside Research Institute [RRI], a Defense Department consultant and expert on atomic energy, is a director of three private corporations dependent on military contracts. Dunning's City Investing Corporation, a major subcontractor of Burden's Lockheed Aircraft, manufactures spray defoliant dissemination systems for use in Vietnam. It was General Dwight D. Eisenhower and Grayson Kirk who brought Columbia University's financial support for defense or defense-related projects from less than 1% [in 1945] to about 48% in 1968.

Columbia helped develop the atomic bomb. Its Lamont Geological Observatory under contract maintains a seismograph on the ocean bottom of California for detecting nuclear tests. The military research, secret contracting and defense financing of Lamont and several other Columbia-related research centers are described below.

. . . .

National Corporations:
Administering the Home Country

In a time of turmoil and expansion it is important to maintain a healthy mother country. A well-satisfied domestic population is less likely to question overseas ventures and more willing to take part in their prosecution. Two vital preconditions for a "healthy," smooth-running, industrialized mother country are skilled labor and social stability. The demands of industry are constantly changing and this requires a constantly reeducated population. At the same time some social conflict is inevitable; but the corporate state thinks it has found the means to regulate its direction and intensity.

National corporations' interest and dependency on the university has a long history. The technical-managerial elite that administers private corporations and the government are all products of the universities, particularly their professional schools. To coordinate the complex flow of modern production requires a high degree of professional training. Without engineers and scientists, innovation and adaptation would come to a standstill. Finally, national corporations are most dependent on a consumer-oriented population. Since profit depends on constant expansion it becomes necessary to train more of the population to increasing consumption patterns.

The chart of Columbia's Top 22 reveals primary relationships to leading national corporations (aside from mass media companies) for five of the rulers and several of the others have secondary interests. The Banks which have financial connections with national corporations and hence an interest in their welfare, are also represented on Columbia's Board of Trustees. Because of their business outlook these men have guaranteed the highest priority for the Engineering, Business and Law schools. Consequently, each of these schools has expanded far out of proportion to the other units of Columbia. They spend the most money, maintain the largest plants, and command the most attention from the administration.

. . . .

Corporation executives have become increasingly aware of the need for social controls over potentially disruptive elements, especially those in the ghetto. Since they are not inclined to invest in low-return operations, they have channeled tax-deductable and foundation funds into the creation of pacification teams trained by the University. The School of Social Work turns out personnel whose approach is ostensibly therapeutic. The standard formula is to convince the disadvantaged that their life difficulties stem from inner sickness rather than disruptive social conditions. This approach treats the poor and potentially rebellious as patients. Instead of removing the cause of their discontent—something that would cost a great deal of money now allocated to overseas priorities—they pacify through treatment. The origins of this therapeutic social work is charity; the effect is to rob the individual of his dignity by requiring him to adjust to intolerable conditions.

Mass media is another form of pacification. By reaching a vast number of people through a limited number of sources, it can create an image of the world that is supportive of the system. To distract is to pacify; the mass media transforms reality into symbols that deaden social awareness. The lack of alternatives creates a climate of coercive persuasion.

Columbia has been instrumental in shaping the mass media industry. New York is the industry's capital and Columbia is its favorite university. Eight of the Top 22 are leading figures in major mass communications firms; their influence is mirrored in the size and national status of the Journalism School. The School is well-endowed by the corporations it serves (particularly *The New York Times*, CBS, *Time*, and Cowles publications), and in turn shapes its program to satisfy ther needs.

Another function of the mass media is the training of people to develop artificial hunger for mass consumption. As consumption habits become ingrained, the home markets expand. Every blatant or subliminal technique is used to convert natural tastes into the unnatural. This growth in consumption creates high turnover of goods and customers work harder to feed their habits, draining potential monies from those sectors of the population that are already deprived. One of the side effects is to create contempt for property on the part of the already poor minorities. If property is presented as a function of fad, how valuable can it be?

The interdependence between the University and mass media corporations is best exemplified by *The New York Times'* coverage of the April 27th mass arrests on the Columbia campus. Two leading *Times* editorial writers (Gelb and Rosenthal) were secretly briefed by the police and prepared their story long before the actual arrests. The news stories of other *Times* reporters which revealed police brutality were suppressed and the *Times* published editorials favorable to the administration. This was clearly calculated to project a favorable public image for Columbia. Moreover, in the past, A. M. Rosenthal has offered his services to Kirk when the administration needed to rebuff community leaders that were critical of the proposed gym.

. . . .

Conclusion

The student uprising was the logical and necessary culmination of a long struggle between the propertied and the propertyless, between the powerful and the powerless. Community participation against the university was one of the special features of this struggle. The rebellion mirrored perfectly the growing fight against government policy on a national level.

In order to avoid a clash between property and its function and the community-student opposition, it was necessary to satisfy human needs, but, as the gap between the priorities of the powerful and the powerless widened, as the property needs created inhuman demands and the demands of humanity increased, the only thing that could resolve the issue was, finally, an uprising which seized and redistributed property and, in so doing, redistributed power.

From the pronouncements of the administration, it would seem that these rebellions, at Columbia and other campuses, are unprecedented. Actually, Columbia itself has experienced various kinds of opposition, considered as extreme in their day as the riots appear in our own day. The famous riotous commencement of 1811 resulted in a number of arrests; the Civil War period was wracked by violence over the issue of the draft.

The point of no return for Columbia University in its commitment to the war effort and to profit and property was reached in the coup of 1967 when the academic administrators, Barzun and Chamberlin, were ousted in favor of the managerial manipulators (Truman and Goodell). Now in power are men committed to manipulation, financial and real estate speculation, men on the make.

The generalized fight became hardened and objectified by the surfacing of the IDA and the Morningside Park Gym issues; while they seemed separate, they were ineradically fused, each representing different aspects of property and property drives. The IDA represented commitment to aiding the war effort which, under its anti-communist guise, hunted for new markets in the Communist and third worlds. The gym represented institutional expansion, creation of a service area for empire-building trainees—a frozen negation of domestic, irrelevant populations. Colonialized community and colonialized student needs fused; as an unbearable tension was reached, this new community moved to stop the work on the gym and seized the buildings symbolic of their training and rededicated them to new purposes, seized property and rededicated it to anti-poverty priorities. This action symbolized the need to stop the destructive direction the country was taking.

The students had tried other means before. There had been peaceful demonstrations, pickets, petitions, appeals to debate the issues publicly; there was a questioning of the decision-making rights, appeals to conscience on moral grounds. This earlier stage implied a naïve faith in the democratic process or, rather, that the democratic process worked, went deep and was a part of administration and student body. It was believed that misunderstanding, a basic obtuseness rather than greed and power, motivated the administration; that when the issues were debated fairly and openly some kind of rapprochement could be reached. The liberated documents from Grayson Kirk's files revealed that beneath the surface, there had never been democracy and that profit needs, manipulation, were basic to administration behavior.

What were the results of these demands: They were ignored, they were met with aloofness, professionalism and expertise were interjected (the students were neither trained nor fit to decide these weighty problems of state), arrogance was the order of the day, and when pressures were applied by the student body, suspension was threatened. Implicit in this form of coercion was a death threat: once out of the university, the students were subject to the draft. This process was paralleled in the surrounding community. The University through Morningside Heights, Inc. acted like the lowest slum lord clearing a building to escalate the value, using threats, coercion through law, cutting off heat, involving tenants in long legal struggles, refusing to accept rent and then serving dispossesses. And when protest mounted, symbolic community leaders were chosen from the community who would then negotiate with the administration for concessions that were nothing more than holding actions in an inevitable and total seizure of the community. These leaders had the ground cut out from under them after they had served their purpose . . . and while they dickered for minor victories, their base of power was slowly being eroded. Not content with the Morningside area, the University was moving further and further into Harlem itself, continuing to carve out a huge training enclave to process students to run the empire.

The peculiar feature of Columbia's policy was its hard-line approach, its refusal to deal with legitimate protest at all. In this, other universities have at least been more sophisticated, granting some of the student demands, willing to hold dialogues which, on the surface, seemed meaningful. There has been a smoother interaction, but the struggle has merely been put off, for the other universities will all come to their Columbia uprisings.

Basic to the students' understanding was their understanding of their University position and what the University meant. More and more, defense research defined scholarship. As the needs of international corporate expansion overseas grew for a pool of technicians who shaped material and minds into the proper use-framework, this operation molded curriculum and, in turn, kept the atmosphere proper in a political sense. The schools would be financed if the empire was to be served and if the schools refused to participate, other more pliable schools with officials on the make for money would be found. On the national level domestic markets had to be serviced and people had to be induced more and more to escalate their consumer needs. What this meant on the student level was that, in terms of future expansion needs, the student was a raw commodity that had to be processed into usable forms, had to be made into interchangeable parts on an assembly line basis so that there would be a pool for corporate and defense use. The very creation of this pool insured that there would be intense competition among the trainees and part of this process of preparation for fitting in meant that a preliminary process had to be undertaken, the process of dehumanization, alienation, the creation of a proper subservient mood (subservient in the sense that fierce competition for money and property was permitted, but competition with the system was dangerous and must be considered first neurotic and then subversive. It is no accident that the suicide rates are so high in the universities).

Since priorities were given over to expansion, the community, especially the Blacks and Puerto Ricans, were considered irrelevant; investment in this area was too prohibitive since there was easier money to be made elsewhere; i.e., in defense contracts and in the manufacture of high turnover, easily consumable products, war matériel.

As the tensions mounted, legitimacy (legitimacy of the rulers) became illegitimacy when the conflict between maintaining the old legitimacy and satisfying needs indicated that all efforts would have to go into the turning out of goods and the preservation of the property that turned out these goods.

What other way was there, then, to cut through the illegitimate basis of power than to seize the University? And this seizure of property cut through to the raw nerve of the University. Even this might have been mediated but for the liberated documents in Grayson Kirk's office which exposed once and for all, what a sham the appearance of democracy, or paternalistic expertise was. Here was the truth! Here were the secrets! Here was what really went on. The documents undercut all the needs for secrecy justified in the name of national interest. What it was all about was the scramble for money, the fight for markets to make money; what it was all about was manipulation of markets and stock rigging and money plays on the way to power. That the whole defense establishment in all of its manifestations was tied in with corporate interests, tied in with real estate speculation, tied together by contacts, and that the whole process of market escalation was furthered by a series of men on the make who made the decisions that they clothed in the patriotic rhetoric of national security and sanctification of the cold and hot war fight to free the enslaved world. All this was covered by a sanctified university facade which, to the financial detriment of students and faculty, permitted high level robbing to go on without let or hinderance.

The meaning of this seizure of property and the codes of behavior in property protection and accumulation was perceived all to clearly by the administration, especially the crude hard liners who know their operations were the shadiest; realizing they had the most to lose most immediately, the rhetoric gave way to a club. A struggle for survival was mounted by the students and the community as the administration was aided by the overwhelming and ponderous control of almost all the media; history was rewritten as it happened. And, as we have pointed out, it was no coincidence that trustees included Sulzberger of the *Times* and Paley of CBS.

Beatings and jailings followed. The strike represents the lack of recognition of students and community by the powers who rule the University. Student amnesty is a fundamental precondition to settling the strike; it announces and solidifies that the power has shifted in favor of the students and the community, it justifies their cause and creates the grounds for a more formal surrender of power and even the possibility of reshifting the course of the University. It implies the recognition of community needs and if expansion is needed, it argues that expansion must be begun in a way that services the community, the neglected domestic front, and solicits their participation.

The administration's response to student demand was another evasion: establishment due process. The establishment position was clearly defined in this statement by Herbert A Deane, Vice-Dean of Graduate Faculties (*Spectator*, April 24, 1967). "A university is definitely not a democratic institution. When decisions begin to be made democratically around here, I will not be here any longer." *Spectator* quoted Deane as adding, "Whether students vote 'yes' or 'no' on an issue is like telling me they like strawberries." Appearing to take a softer line, it was the same rulers who appointed the Cox Commission and laid down the ground rules for inquiry—all in an attempt to relegitimize the administrators and the old order. All the members represent the establishment and have establishment hearts. Three are lawyers (Cox, Rifkind, and Amsterdam, a Philadelphia lawyer) committed to due process within the rules established by the rulers: no hidden data, such as liberated documents, can enter into the discussion. One, Lewis, is a sociologist whose position, along with the nature of his discipline, presumes objectivity and the viewing of things as they are without moral bias . . . which is to say, keep things the way they are. The fifth, Dana L. Farnsworth, is the head of Harvard student health services; he has glorified the role of an establishment agent-informer. He has stated, "The psychiatrist and the college police force must often work closely together." For him and for many other psychiatrists, psychiatry in America is a variation of the police function. Whom they cannot adjust they will call mad.

The rebellion has precipitated cleavages among Columbia's rulers. Uris and some of his supporters have insisted on represssion. Rockefeller has come out for student dissent. The very crudeness of Uris' action delegitimized the University and the more sophisticated forces have recognized this result. The

Rockefellers have longer-range institutionalized interests and can afford the wait that new money cannot: their interests still lie with an overseas empire and they are intently committed to the mass production of technicians and pacifiers. Furthermore, they realize that the domestic front has reached an incredible turmoil. To show the fist is to negate the idealistic principles on which this country was founded; suspensions of civil rights would bring people into the fight who, believing that democracy works, wouldn't otherwise join the struggle.

What Columbia meant was that no longer were the weak to be manipulated by the strong, whose revivifying worth was the property they had amassed. They were now open to scrutiny. It became clear that there is a real and legitimate basis for the seizure and redistribution of property to rechannel it into the service of human needs.

11.4.   *TOM HAYDEN:* **Two, Three, Many Columbias**

[The occupation of Columbia suggested the kind of action which students and nonstudents can undertake in the present circumstances in America to obstruct the functioning of certain institutions particularly crucial to the system. Tom Hayden, who witnessed the occupation, indicates in this article some possibilities for direct action. From *Ramparts,* June 15, 1968.]

The goal written on the university walls was "Create two, three, many Columbias"; it meant expand the strike so that the U.S. must either change or send its troops to occupy American campuses.

At this point the goal seems realistic; an explosive mix is present on dozens of campuses where demands for attention to student views are being disregarded by university administrators.

The American student movement has continued to swell for nearly a decade: during the semi-peace of the early '60s as well as during Vietnam; during the the token liberalism of John Kennedy as well as during the bankrupt racism of Lyndon Johnson. Students have responded most directly to the black movement of the '60s: from Mississippi Summer to the Free Speech Movement; from "Black Power" to "Student Power"; from the seizure of Howard University to the seizure of Hamilton Hall. As the racial crisis deepens so will the campus crisis. But the student protest is not just an offshoot of the black protest—it is based on authentic opposition to the middle-class world of manipulation, channeling and careerism. The students are in opposition to the fundamental institutions of society.

The students' protest constantly escalates by building on its achievements and legends. The issues being considered by seventeen-year-old freshmen at Columbia University would not have been within the imagination of most "veteran" student activists five years ago.

Columbia opened a new tactical stage in the resistance movement which began last fall: from the overnight occupation of buildings to permanent occupation; from mill-ins to the creation of revolutionary committees; from symbolic civil disobedience to barricaded resistance. Not only are these tactics already being duplicated on other campuses, but they are sure to be surpassed by even more militant tactics. In the future it is conceivable that students will threaten destruction of buildings as a last deterrent to police attacks. Many of the tactics learned can also be applied in smaller hit-and-run operations between strikes: raids on the offices of professors doing weapons research could win substantial support among students while making the university more blatantly repressive.

In the buildings occupied at Columbia, the students created what they called a "new society" or "liberated area" or "commune," a society in which decent values would be lived out even though university officials might cut short the communes through use of police. The students had fun, they sang and danced and wisecracked, but there was continual tension. There was no question of their constant awareness of the seriousness of their acts. Though there were a few violent arguments about tactics, the discourse was more in the form of endless meetings convened to explore the outside political situation, defense tactics, maintenance and morale problems within the group. Debating and then determining what leaders should do were alternatives to the remote and authoritarian decision-making of Columbia's trustees.

The Columbia strike represented more than a new tactical movement, however. There was a political message as well. The striking students were not holding onto a narrow conception of students as a privileged class asking for inclusion in the university as it now exists. This kind of demand could easily be met by administrators by opening minor opportunities for "student rights" while cracking down on campus radicals. The Columbia students were instead taking an internationalist and revolutionary view of themselves in opposition to the imperialism of the very institutions in which they have been groomed and educated. They did not even want to be included in the decision-making circles of the military-industrial complex that runs Columbia: *they want to be included only if their inclusion is a step toward transforming the university*. They want a new and independent university standing against the mainstream of American society, or they want no university at all. They are, in Fidel Castro's words, "guerrillas in the field of culture."

How many other schools can be considered ripe for such confrontations? The question is hard to answer, but it is clear that the demands of black students for cultural recognition rather than paternalistic tolerance, and radical white students' awareness of the sinister paramilitary activities carried on in secret by the faculty on many campuses, are hardly confined to Columbia. Columbia's problem is the American problem in miniature—the inability to provide answers to widespread social needs and the use of the military to protect the authorities against the people. This process can only lead to greater unity in the movement.

Support from outside the university communities can be counted on in many large cities. A crisis is foreseeable that would be too massive for police to handle. It can happen; whether or not it will be necessary is a question which only time will answer. What is certain is that we are moving toward power—the power to stop the machine if it cannot be made to serve humane ends.

American educators are fond of telling their students that barricades are part of the romantic past, that social change today can only come about through the processes of negotiation. But the students at Columbia discovered that barricades are only the beginning of what they call "bringing the war home."

FURTHER READINGS

Aronowitz, Stanley. "Columbia: Turning Point for Radical Strategy." *Guardian*, June 1, 1968.
Avorn, L. (ed.). *Up Against the Wall Ivy League*. New York: Atheneum, 1968.
"The Campus Goal Is Student Power." *National Guardian*, December 17, 1966.
Center for the Study of Democratic Institutions. *Students and Society*, A Special Occasional Paper. Santa Barbara, California, 1967.
Davidson, Carl. *Toward a Student Syndicalist Movement or University Reform Revisited*. Working paper for the National SDS Convention at Clear Lake, Iowa, August 1966. Reprinted in *Our Generation, New Left Notes* and *Anarchy*.
Columbia Strike Coordinating Committee. "Columbia Liberated." Pamphlet, 1968.
Garson, Marvin. *The Regents*. Independent Socialist Club, February 1967.
Greenstein, M. Robert. "The McNamara Incident at Harvard." *Dissent*, March/April 1967.
Interview with Mark Rudd. *Partisan Review*, Fall 1968.
Lichtman, Richard. "The Ideological Function of the University." *International Socialist Journal*, December 1967.
"New Voices on Campus, A Symposium." *Mademoiselle*, August 1965.
Pope, Richard. *"Democracy and the University."* SDS pamphlet, October 1965.
Potter, Paul. "The Intellectual as an Agent of Social Change." SDS pamphlet, 1963.
_____. "The New Radical Encounters the University." SDS pamphlet.
_____. "The University and the Cold war." SDS pamphlet.
Rudd, Mark. "Activist Answers Columbia Prexy." *Guardian*, May 11, 1968.
"The Siege of Columbia." Editorial, with the collaboration of the Liberation News Service. *Ramparts*, June 15, 1968.
Smith, A. Jack. "SDS Heads Back to the Grassroots." *National Guardian*, September 17, 1966.
Smith, A. Jack. "Multiversity: The Struggle for Student Power." *The National Guardian*, December 10, 1966.
Viet Report. Special, "The University at War," January 1968.
Weissman, Steven, and Tuthill, Doug. "Freedom and the University." SDS pamphlet, April 1966.
Zinn, Howard. "Dow Shall Not Kill." SSDC pamphlet, 1967.

Four:
Problems
and
Perspectives

12

New Morality

12.1. *RAYMOND MUNGO:* **The Road to Liberation (A Letter to What Used to Be His Draft Board)**

[For many new radicals, the connection between private and public life is one of the necessary bases for the construction of a new "life-style." Raymond Mungo, formerly a student at Boston University, is one of the founders of the Liberation News Service and a draft resister. The following letter of March 6, 1968, is his declaration of refusal to comply with military service. From *Resist,* April 1968.]

Local Board #61
301 Essex Street
Lawrence, Massachusetts

Sirs:
    This day, whether or not you know it, is an historic one for America. It is the day on which thousands of young Americans will sever their ties to the

Selective Service System, return their cards, and cease to cooperate with a system which has already sent 8,000 American men and perhaps half a million Vietnamese to their deaths—a system whose entire *raison d'être,* in fact, is the taking of life.

Now, I don't have a draft card to send you as I willfully destroyed the one you issued me on August 9, 1965—the twentieth anniversary of the bombing of Nagasaki. And I can't say you've asked much of me physically, as you've simply issued me II-S deferments annually without so much as a word exchanged between us. In fact, the first I communicated with you at all was on July 20, 1967, when I refused the II-S which you offered me (and to which I was "legally" entitled) as a graduate student at Harvard University.

In fact, I can't say that conditions arising from the war in Vietnam have especially affected me in material terms. While it is true that I remain poor, I did get, while this war was going on, a fine education for which I paid only a fraction of the tuition costs. I was never in worry for food, shelter, or clothing, nor even for luxuries like books, transportation, entertainment, etc. I simply worked when money ran out, and then I edited the campus newspaper—the *Boston University News*—in order to earn tuition funds. On graduation from college last spring, I got job offers, several lucrative fellowships at major universities, requests for articles from large and prestigious publications, even an assortment of credit cards from oil companies convinced that I am now a responsible citizen worthy of enrollment in the computerized depths of their corporate memories.

At 21, I am independent, well read, capable of earning a more than substantial income, white, and already a success in the sheer economic terms of American one-upsmanship (my parents' income never exceeded $5,000 annually in Lawrence mills).

I am everything but free. And it is freedom alone that I cherish and that I must achieve.

I am not free to leave because the government of this country, over whose laws I have had no influence, restricts my travel, or attempts to, and subjects me to harassment when I attempt to return (as at Logan Airport only last month, on my return from a Czechoslovakian meeting with the North Vietnamese and the National Liberation Front, political sponsor of the South Vietnamese Vietcong). I am not free to stay because you will make demands on my integrity—you and the government, the telephone company, the income tax, the rental agents, the publishers, will want me to pay for my "share" in a war I did not start and will not further. I am not free to "drop out" and live alone, because unspeakable atrocities are being commited in my name daily, and I must continue to speak out against them daily. I am not free to marry because, like Bob Dylan, I fear to bring children into this world.

As a necessary first step toward achieving my freedom, then, I should begin, like Thoreau, to sign off all the ugly things I never signed on to. I hereby denounce, abrogate, and sever any relationship I may have had with your board and the government agency it represents. I ask you not to further bother me with unsolicited inquiries, junk mail, and questions so personal as to be obscene. I do not recognize in your board any authority over my actions, public or personal.

When I originally left Lawrence, in 1963, I was 17 years old. I did not then know of the city's historic importance as the site of the 1912 labor strikes which brought A. J. Muste, Dorothy Day, Elizabeth Gurley Flynn and a whole generation of radicals into the fight for something resembling humane policy on the part of the capitalist system.

I went on to college on a large scholarship, convinced that my main objective was to become bourgeois and never have to work in a Lawrence mill again, as I had in the summers preceding. Consequently, I did not chafe at the university's meaningless regulations—making one's bed, taking one's exams, wearing respectable clothing and acting "responsibly."

No left-wing radical or subversive elements or acquaintances changed my mind—merely a growing awareness of reality. Whereas, for example, I considered the reality of a child's not having enough to eat or a place to sleep that was not crowded with other children, their diseases and their unhappiness, most of my classmates had never experienced these things and didn't honestly believe they existed. Whereas I thought the theatre, art, music, the university were devoted to the cultivation of the intellect and spirit, others clearly thought—and controlled them on the principle that—the intellect is valuable only insofar as it can pay for itself. Whereas I felt that human life was probably more valuable than anything else in our spheres of reality, powerful and dignified men obviously believed it was cheap.

So I sat in second-balcony seats that were outrageously overpriced, suffered through lectures preached to 800 students and more via microphones and slides, and registered for the draft.

Then, in 1964, when the president of the university announced his intention to censor the student newspaper of which I was fiercely proud and which had been lobbying for a 10 per cent decrease in prices in the university bookstore, I became an activist. Freedom of the press, in the face of its denial, became more important than my staying in school and remaining ineffective. Freedom to speak, the first time I practiced it, became important enough to suffer the jeers and scorn of the students there who didn't care that their own integrity was being stolen.

As men, naturally, we feel a need to defend everything we are personally involved in and committed to, and I would be the first to admit that anti-social behavior, when it becomes a danger to others, ought to be controlled in some fashion, whatever the personal convictions of the man who commits it. But when behavior which could only be called pro-social—lobbying for students' rights, for civil rights, for an end to war—was being punished by police savagery, prison terms, and social disgrace, I could not help but feel like an innocent man wronged.

I am going to tell you now that this country is on the verge of civil war, and I am glad of it.

There are not merely two or three Americans living side by side but in uneasy coexistence—there are at least five, and their interests cannot possibly coexist much longer. On the one side, there are the bourgeoisie and the ruling classes, the men who own this country and run it, and who are not in the least reluctant to buy their ranch-houses and their dinner-jackets with the blood money of dead Americans and dead foreigners the world across.

These are the new fascists of America. You have seen them. You probably belong to them. They are the men and women who do not rise to cheer their fuehrer when he makes a war speech, when he talks of assembling the greatest concentration of firepower in the history of the world over the tiny nation of Vietnam, but who blandly applaud him from their $100-a-plate seats. You have seen them. They were in Los Angeles, in Boston, in San Antonio only last week. They pay for international murder because the dividends are blue-chip.

(2) There are the working classes and the poor—two distinct groups gathered here together because their political attitude is approximately equal. The former believes it has a democracy and goes forth to the polls every four years to choose a man who could not possibly be better or much worse than the last. The latter do not vote because they have nothing to believe in. Both do nothing toward reclaiming their country.

(3) There are the intellectuals, or some of them, whose acute sensitivity to national issues recognizes the peril we are in and burns toward doing something to alleviate it. But they feel incapable of making change because their very words, their honest thoughts, are twisted and distorted by the men in power to make them seem subversive and disloyal (which they certainly are, in a very healthy sense) and they risk losing their jobs, possibly being unable to feed their children. This risk is too great, for they are only men.

(4) There are the blacks, and they are poor as well. But they know much better than their white brothers why they are poor and they will fight with armed insurrectionary techniques because that is the only way they will succeed. You have seen them. They burned Detroit, Newark, Boston, Plainfield, Hartford, Los Angeles. They will burn Lawrence too, and I am glad of it.

(5) There are the young, and they too have nothing to lose but the hypocrisy and the despair they have know in the world of the fathers. I belong to this group. I want to make love when I am in it, to smoke pot when my mind is not at ease, to meditate when I feel I need it, to rebuild in man's image what has been built and destroyed too many times over in the witness and image of a foolish and irrelevant God. I do not want to kill the Vietcong, among whom I number some friends, or anybody else. I want to retire Lyndon Johnson to a chicken farm somewhere, to give people decent places to live, to give artists the right to create and exercise that virility which is their most precious asset, to let people be when they wish it, and to destroy forever the concept of morality—religious regulations, national allegiances, corporational loyalties—and replace it with humanity. I want to destroy America and find the world.

You have seen these dissident revolutionaries—these intellectuals, these blacks, these youth. They have not been sufficiently oppressed materially to force them underground because the monied interests do not yet see the danger to their hegemony which these people represent. We are affluent revolutionaries, some of us, but many others are quite poor. I have no stocks, no bonds, no savings accounts, no house and car, no wife and children. I have no stake in this country except what it can say for itself as a moral and humane force. It says to me that it is the greatest force for evil, the worst hater of mankind, unscrupulous murderer, alive today. I renounce it.

Johnson may be a Nazi, as many have said, but so are you, so is Romney, so is Kennedy, so is Nixon, so is Rockefeller, so is Dirksen, at least as much as Johnson is—and I don't intend to play Jew for any of you. I will not be a slave to an economy and a government which depends on human suffering for its very existence. There is nothing you can take away from me that you have not already robbed—all I have left that is valuable is my spirit and my personal liberation, and that cannot be placed behind bars. The "final solution" to America's problems may be fought in its streets, or perhaps (some fervently hope) in the determination for reform of its emerging generations. But the problems must be solved. I am here beginning that process by trying to make you at least aware that they *exist*.

The war in Vietnam will end, of course, and with it the agony of my friends and your fellow men in North and South, who will win their freedom decisively and at the same time teach America something of how valuable is love and determination compared to military might. After the U.S. has been defeated there, however, we still have centuries to erase here. Mississippi still exists and is worse now than during the so-called "civil rights movement." Landlords and grocery store magnates still ensure the slow starvation of my brothers and sisters in the ghetto. Policemen still maim and kill people because they have long hair, or dare preach against killing. None of us are safe.

Out of violence only more violence can come. No pistol will make me safe—what could possibly make me think that it would? Cops on street corners don't make me more secure—rather the contrary. Who will be the next to get that old knock on the door? Armies don't make our homes safer— they invade them and rob us of our youth and others of their arms, legs, lives. We who choose to object to America's perversity will all, sooner or later, end up in the can. The thought that the government believes such incarceration will make it "secure" from us then is the final irony.

Because we will win out or else there will be nothing left to win. All your antiballistic shields will not protect you from an atomic holocaust, from the 200 shrapnel wounds you've given to a small Hanoi schoolteacher, from the collapse of your furniture stores and your government. Our increasing numbers will end war or war will end us all.

Chu hoi, gentlemen! Come to the open arms of humanity or resign from it! Have the courage to follow me (or anybody else you choose) to a personal *giai phong* from the whole fucking constipated regime you so willfully and thanklessly serve! If you remember your youths at all, don't send other young men off to die and kill in the most senseless slaughter of your age! Don't wait for the inevitable judgement, the judgement which Bertolt Brecht could fore- see in the 20's in his libretta to *The Three Penny Opera*:

> *You gentlemen can wipe off that laugh from your face—*
> *Every building in town is a flat one!*
> *Your whole stinkin' place will be down to the ground,*
> *Only this cheap hotel standin' up safe and sound.*
> *And you yell, "Why do they spare that one?"*
> *And you say, "Why do they spare that one?"*

> *Sincerely yours*
> *Raymond A. Mungo*

12.2.   Confessions of a Middle-aged Pot Smoker

The first time I ever got high on pot was at a party about a month ago. At my house.

I'd smoked grass before, five or six times. If you go to parties on the east side, young parties, people will be smoking. Sometimes openly, passing around what looks like a home-made cigarette, or maybe a pipe. Sometimes more conspiratorially. If several people go into the bathroom or a bedroom together and lock the door they probably are not having an orgy, but smoking.

Pot is social. Everyone shares a single joint till it's all gone, smoked down to the very end, stuck on a pin or in a roach clip. Or a pipe is passed from hand to hand, mouth to mouth. And you'll be offered a smoke, like you'd be offered a drink. No one gets uptight if you refuse.

But when I smoked I never felt much. Usually I'd been drinking a bit and felt a little high anyway so it was hard to tell what the effects were. I'd keep asking people, "Am I high?" "What am I supposed to feel?" "Are YOU high now?" They told me to look for a glow around the lamps.

Sometimes I could tell the others were high. Some would giggle a lot, or their faces and bodies would fall into a relaxed slump, or they'd stare at something ordinary and say how beautiful it was, or they'd look dreamy and smile. But often they looked and acted "normal."

I smoked joints, pipes and a hookah. The hookah is best because the hot smoke is cooled by being filtered through water or wine. I would drag the smoke deep into my lungs, like you're supposed to, and hold it so long that when I exhaled, almost no smoke would come out. Still nothing.

People told me I was putting up psychological barriers, not letting myself get stoned. "Intellectuals" are supposed to be quite pot-resistant. I read where Kenneth Rexroth said he never could get high, so he gave up. But I'd had the experience of "giving in" to other drugs that doctors had administered as medicines or anesthetics: diet pills, pain killers, cough medicine, sodium pentothal—and I'd liked that, I'd "gone with it."

The first time I got high on grass was at my house. As a party was breaking up someone offered me a joint and I took several deep drags. The smoke was very hot and burned my throat, but I didn't feel any other effect and assumed that as usual nothing would happen.

When I got to bed where I was quiet and at rest and paying attention to myself I began to feel strange. I told my husband, "Wow I feel weird!" My body felt high-strung, tingling and light. It wasn't entirely pleasant. Suddenly a huge wave of anxiety began building. I thought something bad was going to happen, I didn't know what. I felt scared, I began to shiver.

"Hey maybe I'm high," I thought to myself.

I closed my eyes and knew for sure. There were all these crazy pictures in my head. The first one I remember was like a huge watery ocean with millions of tiny nipple-like waves, all different silvery colors. That one went away and I saw a row of hundreds of Greek columns, fading into the distance. Then one picture changed into another so fast I didn't have time to describe them to my husband, who was lying beside me.

Crazy "psychedelic" designs came and I understood all those hippie posters. Lots of symmetry tiny details, naive composition, and it all seemed to mean something. But really rather corny. In fact I didn't like the pictures much at all—they were too childish, too commercial even. I wanted them to stop coming, but they wouldn't.

I knew I was the one who was making them up, and I didn't want to, but I couldn't stop. I resigned myself to watching them, being bored. When I'd open my eyes they'd go away.

I was still shivering, feeling anxious. I began to think someone had dropped acid on me—this was too intense for pot. But who would do that? There was only one guy at the party I didn't know—it had to be him. He looked evil anyway. He was the one who'd given me the joint. Maybe the joint had something else in it? I tried to remember what I'd read. DMT happens very fast. Hash? Heroin? No, that's silly. But still the sinking scared feeling was like what I'd read about acid.

Another part of me knew this was wrong, just part of the paranoia that often accompanies pot, and that I was OK. My husband was worried, wondered if I wanted a tranquilizer or a doctor or anything. I knew I didn't.

My throat had a lump in it from the smoke and it seemed to be getting larger. Maybe it would close off my windpipe and I'd choke to death. I tried to relax and stop shivering. I took deep yoga breaths and that helped a little.

Now my hands and feet were burning too, but pleasantly. And between my legs. I began to feel very turned on erotically.

When we made love I began to relax. The shivering stopped. When I'd close my eyes the pictures were still there but now they were great, and helpful sexually. Geometric designs in gorgeous colors, all sexually symbolic. I remember two: a wide road disappearing over the horizon with two mountains on either side—that was me—the picture and my body were one, somehow. Another was a huge pile-driver kind of thing, all purple and pink and white, in motion—that was him in me.

I could feel him inside me and me around him, more than usual. My whole body felt good—and sensitive. Time was slowed down; when I closed my eyes it seemed that long times had passed, but when I opened them I realized otherwise. I felt that I was going to come very quickly, but I think it was about as usual, I'm rather slow. But it was very fine sex.

Afterwards, I shivered some more but didn't worry about it. I lay awake for a while, watching the pictures, and then fell asleep. I felt great the next day.

The second time I smoked and got high was about a week later, again at an east side house, down in the basement. All middle-aged people this time, all new smokers. Seven people there, on cushions on the floor, but only three of us smoking. Rock music on the phonograph. Three candles in glass bowls on the floor.

We passed one joint around and I felt my heart beat get faster, my palms got cold. I recognized my old friend anxiety again. Not much else, not for the others either. Conversation flowed, the music flowed. We drank some orange tonic to soothe our throats.

We lit another stick. The anxiety, which had calmed, reappeared, my stomach felt queasy. I had to move around, get up off my butt, go upstairs to the bathroom, and my knees were trembling when I did. Alone in the upstairs part of the house, everything was very intense and a little bit scarey, but OK, under control.

Back downstairs I seemed to notice the candles for the first time. How come I hadn't seen how beautiful the colors were before? Pink, green and purple, and they seemed so right together. I looked at them awhile, alternately trying to figure out how it was that they struck me differently now, and then just digging them.

One of the other smokers was talking but paused in the middle of a sentence and said, "Gee, I forgot what I was going to say," and he laughed. "Yeah," I said, "because it doesn't really matter." He was amazed that I knew exactly what he was thinking. We laughed some more, he looked beautiful and happy.

The other smoker was stretched out now, drifting, dreaming. He looked asleep but would sometimes lay a few words on us. Not as witty as he usually was—in fact he was making the kind of stupid jokes he'd ordinarily be embarrassed to tell. I could tell he knew it, but didn't care. It didn't matter.

My anxiety was gone and I felt contented and happy. I was listening to Joan Baez and humming along with her. My voice sounded great.

The Animals were the next record and I was waiting to hear them—thought I might get up and dance. On the other hand, that might be too much trouble, I was pretty comfortable now, lying across the cushions, my head on my husband's lap. (He never smokes.)

The hostess went to the record player and took off the Animals which was just ready to play, and put on Hillel and Aviva singing Arab folk songs. I could almost get annoyed at something like that. But what the hell, it doesn't matter, Hillel and Aviva are kind of nice anyway. Yeah, I really DIG Hillel and Aviva, come to think of it.

The dreamy smoker was stretched out on his stomach, on the floor beside the couch. I walked over and lay down on the couch and stared at his back. His shirt was pulled up and I stared at his bare skin. I wanted to touch him, just touch the skin of his back. Partly because I got the idea he was sad and needed comforting, but mostly just for the touch. But I didn't. Too many possible hassles with husbands and wives. I thought about it for what seemed like a long time (time was messed up again) but didn't. It really didn't matter.

I had the burning between my legs again too—I wanted sex almost just for physiological relief of the burning—not because I felt particularly sexy.

A hall light was slanting over the tile floor. As I lay on the couch I could see the fake pebbles in the tile and the shadows were great. I looked at the floor, not getting bored but not thinking it was particularly beautiful or interesting or anything. I just kept on looking at it, for a long time.

Our highs began to wear off, we all woke up a little and ate some pepperoni, it tasted great, spicier than usual. Pretty soon we said goodbye and drove home. The next day things looked clearer than usual and I kept thinking about the sweet nutty smell of burning grass. I'll smoke again, I'm sure.

12.3.   *NAOMI JAFFE and BERNARDINE DOHRN:* **The Look Is You**

[Among the movements of the New Left which are trying to link individual psychological liberation with the political struggles against the repressive character of the society, the Women's Liberation Movement (WLM) is fast developing in many cities. The authors of the article are active in the WLM, and Bernardine Dohrn is interorganizational secretary of SDS. *New Left Notes,* March 18, 1968.]

Two tits and no head—as the representation, in glossy color, of the Women's Liberation Movement—is an apt example of *Ramparts'* success in making a commodity out of politics.

Over the past few months, small groups have been coming together in various cities to meet around the realization that as women radicals we are not radical women—that we are unfree within the Movement and in personal relationships, as in the society at large. We realize that women are organized into the Movement by men and continue to relate to it through men. We find that the difficulty women have in taking initiative and in acting and speaking in a political context is the consequence of internalizing the view that men define reality and women are defined in terms of men. We are coming together not in a defensive posture to rage at our exploited status vis a vis men, but rather in the process of developing our own autonomy, to expose the nature of American society in which all people are reified (manipulated as objects). We insist on a recognition of the organic connection of the unfreedom of all groups in society.

The consciousness that our underdeveloped abilities are not just personal failings but are deeply rooted in this society is an exhilarating and expressive breakthrough. There is the terror of giving up the roles through which we know how to obtain a certain measure of power and security. But again and again there is the rejoicing in the unexplored possibilities of becoming vital potent human beings.

By refusing to be kept separate from other women by feelings of dislike, jealousy, and competitiveness, we have begun to discuss and research ourselves in our context—to demystify the myth of women by analyzing the forces which have shaped us.

Women suffer only a particular form of the general social oppression, so our struggles to understand and break through society's repressive definitions of us are struggles which have to attack the foundations of that society—its power to define people according to the needs of an economy based on domination.

The dynamic of that economy is a changing technology, which creates an ever-greater scale of production. Lack of social control over this increasing production (the planned use of the productive forces for and by the people of the society) means that the goal of productivity is profit, and profit can only be sustained if markets can be found (or created) to absorb an increasing volume of goods.

This is the dynamic of imperialism—the relentless search for new markets which drains the resources of the Third World and cripples its independent economic development. It is also the dynamic of the domestic imperialism of consumption: the creation of internal markets through a process which defines persons as consumers and cripples their development as free human beings.

Women are the consummate products of that process. We are at the same time the beneficiaries and the victims of the productivity made possible by advanced technology. The innovations that offer us immediate freedom also force us into the service of an overall system of domination and repression. The more we realize ourselves through consumption the greater the power of commodities to define and delimit us. "Women must be liberated to desire new products." (market research executive)

The same new things that allow us to express our new sense of freedom and naturalness and movement—swingy, body-revealing clothing, fun-gimmicky accessories—are also used to force us to be the consumers of the endless flow of products necessary for the perpetuation of a repressive society. Miniskirts and costume-clothes and high boots and transparent makeup are fun and expressive and pretty; at the same time they are self-expression through things—through acquiring rather than becoming—and it is the expression of all human needs through commodities which sustains an economy that has to produce and sell more and more goods in order to survive.

"But the real point about that swinging 16-to-24 group is not their spending power, but the fact that they have become market leaders. They have created a climate that has enabled fashion to catch on as a new force in the market, driving apparel expenditures higher and higher." (*Fortune,* October 1967)

The same rise in productivity that requires more consumption of more goods also creates more leisure time—so leisure time becomes consumption time, and consumption becomes increasingly a major sphere of life activity. A culture of consumption is created through the mass media, supported by the $16-billion-a-year advertising industry, to channel all potential human development into commodity form.

Deeply set in human nature is the need to have a meaningful place in a group that strives for meaningful social goals. Whenever this is lacking, the individual becomes restless. Which explains why, as we talk to people across the nation, over and over again, we hear questions like these: 'What does it all mean?' 'Where am I going?' 'Why don't things seem more worthwhile when we all work so hard and have so darn many things to play with?' The question is: Can your product fill this gap?" (from an advertising agency report)

The increased economic importance of consumption is reflected most deeply in the role of women, who are said to make 75% of all family consumption decisions and at whom 75% of all advertising is directed. This consumption culture shapes us as women and as people into an essentially passive mode of being, which in turn enables us to be exploited in the productive sphere in meaningless, low-paying clerical jobs. Women are culturally manipulated to see our work roles as being of secondary importance (since we are defined primarily by our sexual roles); we therefore serve as a reserve army of labor for the lowest-status white-collar jobs, drawn into the labor force when needed, and told to find fulfillment at home when employment is slack.

Or, as in the case of professional and semi-professional women, our very status as "independent women" is the source of our exploitation, forcing us into work and leisure roles which reinforce an illusory image of freedom and creativity. The work-role demands of status and travel open new areas for the creation of commodity "needs," and professional women as consumers are used to create styles and tastes for the larger population.

So our passive roles as producers and consumers reinforce each other, and in turn are reinforced by and perpetuate our passive social-sexual roles. These roles are based on receptivity—being through acquiring objects, rather than becoming through projecting oneself onto the world to change it (active mastery of the world). Real control over one's life is not the same as the illusion deliberately created by commodity culture through a choice of commodities. "Choosing oneself" in commodity form is a choice pre-defined by a repressive system.

The passive-receptive woman role, a product of the structure and development of American society, increasingly defines the culture of that society. Men, too, do not control their environment or project themselves onto it to change it (potency). Although active mastery is still considered a male mode, it is increasingly irrelevant to a society based on the compulsive consumption of commodities. "What is self but a permanent mode of selection?" (advertising executive)

The relationships of a market economy are reflected and reinforced in the dynamic and the forms of human relationships. The real needs of people are translated into a currency of possession, exclusivity, and investment—a language of commodities in which people are the goods. Both men and women are manipulated into functioning within these categories; it is the uniquely visible condition of women as primarily sexual creatures—as decorative, tempting (passive-aggressive), pleasure-giving objects—which exposes the broader framework of social coercion.

Psychology, as a social institution, works in the service of this pacification of human needs and desires. Its categories begin with a historically-bound notion of the restrictive implications of female biology. ("Anatomy is destiny."— Freud) Concepts of women as mutilated men, penis envy, and the electra complex (a mechanical inversion of the oedipal situation) exemplify a society which produces people who are taught to experience themselves as objects. These definitions allow only the possibilities of a passive mode—at best, the liberalism of a "creative" resignation to fulfillment through realizing our femininity (feminine equals intuitive—unobtrusive—servile—non-castrating —warm—sensitive—cuddly—supportive—rhythmic—good-smelling—sensuous—satisfying—creative, and so forth).

In our social-sexual roles, again, the innovations that offer us immediate freedom also force us into the service of an overall system of domination and repression. Technological emancipation from enslavement to our bodies (for example, The Pill as the Great Liberator) is offered to women as the realization of freedom now. ". . . Almost every aspect of the New Girl's personality reflects her final freedom from the sexual status that was the fate of women in the past." (*Playboy,* January 1968)

But this greatly expanded area of permissive erotic gratification and personal control occurs inside the context of greater social control and dehumanization. The desublimation is repressive. The liberating potential of expressed sexuality is channeled into mutually exploitative relationships in which people are objects, and into the market economy in which sexuality is a cornerstone. Liberalized sex begins to define the shape and texture of leisure time—in a commodity framework. Again we are beneficiaries and victims. Thus, a more sexually active role for women actually reinforces a broader passive mode of consumption.

If women are made into objects, the object-relationships between men and women make human communication and community impossible for both; if women are defined by their sexual roles, they are only a paradigm case of the reified role structures that stifle the creative spontaneity of men and women alike.

A strategy for the liberation of women, then, does not demand equal jobs (exploitation), but meaningful creative activity for all; not a larger share of power but the abolition of commodity tyranny; not equally reified sexual roles but an end to sexual objectification and exploitation; not equal aggressive leadership in the Movement, but the initiation of a new style of non-dominating leadership.

Our strategy will focus on the unique quality of our exploitation as women, primarily in our vanguard economic role as consumers. Women Power is the power to destroy a destructive system by refusing to play the part(s) assigned to us by it—by refusing to accept its definition of us as passive consumers, and by actively subverting the institutions which create and enforce that definition.

12.4.   **Free Church of Berkeley: Liberation Litanies**

[Radical ferments are developing within different groups and institutions. In the church, too, they are present as is shown in these invocations of the "Free Church of Berkeley," in which there is an attempt to propose a "new morality" for religion.]

The Free Church Affirmation

God is not dead.
God is bread.
The bread is rising.
Bread means revolution.
God means revolution.
Murder is no revolution.
Revolution is love.
Win with love.
The radical Jesus is winning.
The world is coming to a beginning.
Organize for a new world.
Wash off your brother's blood.
Join the freedom meal.
Plant the peace garden.
The asphalt church is marching.
The submarine church is surfacing.
The war is over.
The war is over.
The war is over.
The liberated zone is at hand.

Invocation of the Saints

Bridegroom of poverty, our brother Francis of Assisi, follower of Jesus and dropout, friend of the creation: *Stand here beside us.*
Confessors in flames, Norman Morrison, Roger LaPorte and all their companions, immolated for the sake of peace:
Confessor in Russia, Boris Pasternak, poet of reconciliation:
Confessor in Denmark, Søren Kierkegaard, diver in the sea of his own soul:
Confessor in America, Henry David Thoreau, hermit and resister:
Good Pope John, friend of the poor, who longed for the unity of mankind:
Apostle of nonviolence, Gandhi the Mahatma, reproach to the churches:
Mask of the Christ, Gautama the Buddha, fountain of compassion:
Peacemaker in America, A. J. Muste, father of activists:
Peacemaker in the world, Dag Hammarskjöld, denier of himself:
Priest and panhandler, Benedict Joseph Labre, fool for Christ:
Madman in America, Johnny Appleseed, planter of Eden:
Witness in England, John Wesley, street minister:
Faithful harlot Mary Magdalen, first witness of new life:
Inductee of Africa, Simon of Cyrene, who carried the cross of your liberator:
Visionary and poet, William Blake, on trip by power of imagination:
Visionary and preacher, George Fox, who founded a society of friends:

((Visionary and apostle, John the Evangelist, resister to the power of the
Beast:
Visionary of Italy, Catherine of Siena, social worker:
Doctor and evangelist, Luke the beloved:
Patron of nurses, Florence Nightingale:
Priest and scientist, Pierre Teilhard de Chardin, voyager in the past and in
the future:
Those who speak the soul's language, Bach, Mozart, Beethoven and their
brothers:
Monk and pacifist, Martin of Tours:
Peter Maurin, Catholic worker:
Amos of Tekoa, leader of protest:
Martin Luther, reformer and leader of protest:
Martyrs of Africa: Perpetua, mother; Felicity, slave; and your com-
panions:
Martyrs and confessors, Polycarp, Ignatius and Justin, who refused the
incense to Caesar:
Martyr in Prague, Jan Hus, reformer:))

Holy Innocents of Birmingham, in your undeserved deaths:
Victims of lynching, known and unknown, brothers of Stephen the martyr:
Victims of Hiroshima and Nagasaki, pierced by needles of flame:
Victims of Coventry, Dresden and Tokyo, caught up in a storm of fire:
Victims of Auschwitz and all concentration camps, in your despair and death:
Children of Viet Nam, mutilated to preserve a way of life:
Martyrs in the streets of Selma; Jonathan Daniels, seminarian; James Reeb,
minister; and all your companions:
Martyr in Bolivia, Camillo Torres, priest and revolutionary:
Martyr in Germany, Dietrich von Bonhoeffer, confessor and revolutionary:
Martyr in Athens, Socrates, philosopher and hippy, Christian before Christ:
Martyr in Austria, Franz Jägerstätter, draft-resister:
Martyr in America, Martin Luther King, organizer for peace and justice:
Unwed mother, blessed Mary, wellspring of our liberation:
Our hero and leader, Jesus the manual laborer, root of our dignity:
Our hero and leader, Jesus the prophet, who resisted the establishment:
Our hero and leader, Jesus the Liberator, a king because first a servant:
Our hero and leader, Jesus the poet, who laid down a new form of speech:
Our hero and leader, Jesus the son of God, bright cornerstone of our unity in a
new Spirit: *Stand here beside us.*

FURTHER READINGS

Allen, Pamela. "What Strategy for Movement Women?" *Guardian,* October
5, 1968.
Culver, Elsie Thomas, "The 'Free' Church of Berkeley's Hippies." *The
Christian Century,* April 10, 1968.

Goldfield, Evelyn, with Sue Munaker and Heather Booth. "Women in the Radical Movement." *Radicals in the Professions Newsletter,* March 1968.

Jones, Beverly, and Brown, Judith. *Toward a Female Liberation Movement.* Mimeograph, Florida, 1968.

New York Radical Women. *Notes from the First Year.* Mimeograph, collection of articles. June 1968.

13
Cultural Revolt

13.1. *BERKELEY BARB:* From the Haight

[The hippie nonmovement has always swung between a position of complete individual disengagement and a "cultural revolution" with social implications for American society. This is an opinion which appeared in the *Berkeley Barb,* October 26, 1967, just after the decline of the hip wave of Summer 1967.]

I can speak for myself, as anybody in all honesty can, but I am here like many others for some of the same obscure reasons. H[aight]-A[shbury] seemed like the last hope; an outpost of humanity in a land of deodorized plastic mannequins engaged in one way or another in the computerized annihilation of the Vietnam people and the destruction of human emotion here in America.

Almost everybody here was at one time or another engaged in some form of political activity whether it be civil rights, anti-war or both. Yet long before it happened, it seemed to most of us that white middle-class America was charging down a blind alley that ended at the Army's bayonets and club swinging Oakland police defending America's military establishment against the people for whom it was created to protect. The white man had put his hope in the black man to make his revolution, and the black man answered, "Make your own, whitey, I'm through working for you."

White political activists, unable to create a base in their own communities, were tossed out of the ghettos, ignored, and abused. Peaceful demonstrations, civil disobedience, electoral politics: the tools of the brainwashed middle class that the authorities permitted them to use could change the course of the Vietnam war about as much as Senator Fulbright's speeches to a deaf Senate. But most of white America, inculcated with years and years of propaganda in their schools, were too numb and scared to admit the facts of reality.

Pacifists chained themselves to a drafted brother in a vain attempt to arouse the conscience of those who had none. The great society had whitewashed the mind and soul of the American people. They were bought off, bludgeoned, coerced, and forced to obey. Psychologically America was sick. Their minds had turned into mechanical obedience machines incapable of doing anything they were not allowed to do. Those who disobeyed and rebelled were sent to the psychiatrist to be reconditioned into a state of stoic obedience.

Almost anyone over thirty-five, as Dr. Dylan said, couldn't be trusted. You knew only too well the concessions, the lies, the crimes they had committed in order to be where they were. How many times had they looked the other way, salved their conscience with a new car, or cheated and abused the ones they were supposed to love in order to alleviate their agony and escape reality? Yes, they could not be trusted, and that goes for the millions of black men whose minds are white and can be bought off with a shiny new Cadillac.

So we left, dropped out, lit up our pipes and popped our acid. There was nothing left to do. So few seemed to understand, so many were afraid of losing that airconditioned life of luxury without feeling in the wasteland of America called the suburbs.

People's minds, it seemed, had been destroyed by too many words, their values too distorted, their fears too great. We were waiting, trying to live out the time until it was all over. Until we could just forget and somehow live in a world too horrible to endure any longer. Yet we pumped the nation full of acid, pot and what have you. We created a new perspective, new forms, a new culture; a clear cut tribute to the decadence and horror of the America we refused to take part in.

We told the nation, its youth, that they were not alone in their feelings, their dissatisfaction, their agonized torment. Something was really wrong with America that could not be cured by a new anti-poverty program, a peace offensive, or wage increases.

America had become a nation of scared individuals believing that they alone were insane with desires and feelings that must be suppressed in order to conform. Conform, conform, in your heart of hearts and obey. What other choice was there? The question created us and we created a choice.

There would probably be no H-A without the war and perhaps the anti-war movement would not have reached the cold brutal turning point from disobedience and submission to rebellion and violence had there been no "hippies"; the pre-hippies, hippies, and past hippies who marched, got arrested, sang, screamed and cried; who philosophized, ignored the law and were pushing all the time.

Hippies are more than just people who walk down Haight Street with beads, bells, long hair, stoned on drugs. They are a concept, an act of rejection, a militant vanguard, a hope for the future.

You might say that some of us were waiting, waiting, to see if what has happened could ever take place. The law for most of us is the law of the men who control, dominate, and rule. It is broken every day without a thought. The only fear is that of being caught and ending up in jail.

The law is made by the rulers, for the rulers, and in their interest alone. They violate it at will in a country where the people are allowed to dissent but never actually to act to bring about real change. White middle-class America is allowed to protest the war in Vietnam, to fortify their ego, but never once will they legally be permitted to do anything that will actually alter its conduct or bring it to a halt. It seemed as if the youth of America just could not disobey their parents, their teachers, the "elected" masters; but we did, openly and defiantly, and we were the first!

To stop this war, this carnage, we must do what we are not permitted to do. We must break the law. The law we never made, but was made by people who told us they were our servants and had become our masters; our masters ruling us for their own designs and destroying our lives for their own purpose.

We have been exploited by our government and our social and economic system into working and dying for a crime that benefits only our leaders. We on Haight Street had openly refused to be used anymore to be manipulated, coerced, and destroyed as human beings. And we told the whole nation.

Yes, we are political; yes, we are revolutionaries; yes, we represent by the way we live a complete break with the American way of life. Yes, we stand for a new culture based on cooperation, love, and peace rather than competition, hate, and violence. Yes, we are certainly helping to end the wars here in America between man and man and the war there between two ways of life. Yes, there is a revolution going on in the world and a fight to the death between two social orders, two ways of living and thinking.

We have gone AWOL from the great American Army that is our society, renouncing the easy plush future that could have been ours, yes we have deserted. We had come to the conclusion that our society was corrupt, vile, and heinous, and that to obey any of its dictates, any of its concepts was to doom us eventually to a living death killing others as we died.

Yes, we are committed, dedicated people choosing between two ways of life, two social orders, two concepts. We have renounced the meaningless morals and promises of an evil society. We have abandoned it, physically, intellectually, emotionally, and economically.

But now the age of peaceful, lawful protest and dissent is over. With smashed skulls and blood white America has come to the conclusion it had sought to avoid at all cost. That we are living under a tyrannical, violent system of oppression that will stop at nothing to achieve its aims, and that if we desire to end the destruction of human life here and abroad there is no alternative but illegal and violent measures.

This is the truth our government has sought to hide and conceal. This is the truth that many of us have always known but were afraid to admit. This is the reality of America today which we must change and alter our lives accordingly or else acquiesce, bow our heads silently in submission and take our place in the great American Army set on death and destruction. And it is just this that is becoming more and more impossible for increasing numbers of Americans, and one of the many reasons is the long-haired hippies.

13.2.   **Yippie!**

[The Youth International party (*Yippies*) is a nonparty that tried to engage the hippies in "psychological guerrilla warfare" against the establishment. The following manifesto is a call for demonstrating on election day 1968.]

Come into the streets on Nov. 5, election day. Vote with your feet. Rise up and abandon the creeping meatball! Demand the bars be open. Make music and dance at every red light. A festival of life in the streets and parks throughout the world. The American election represents death, and we are alive.

Come all you rebels, youth spirits, rock minstrels, bomb throwers, bank robbers, peacock freaks, toe worshippers, poets, street folk, liberated women, professors and body snatchers: it is election day and we are eveywhere.

Don't vote in a jackass-elephant-cracker circus. Let's vote for ourselves. Me for President. We are the revolution. We will strike and boycott the election and create our own reality.

Can you dig it: in every metropolis and hamlet of America boycotts, strikes, sit-ins, pickets, lie-ins, pray-ins, feel-ins, piss-ins at the polling places.

Nobody goes to work. Nobody goes to school. Nobody votes. Everyone becomes a life actor of the street doing his thing, making the revolution by freeing himself and fucking up the system.

Ministers dragged away from polling places. Free chicken and ice cream in the streets. Thousands of kazoos, drums, tambourines, triangles, pots and pans, trumpets, street fairs, firecrackers—a symphony of life on a day of death. LSD in the drinking water.

Let's parade in the thousands to the places where the votes are counted and let murderous racists feel our power.

Force the National Guard to protect every polling place in the country. Brush your teeth in the streets. Organize a sack race. Join the rifle club of your choice. Freak out the pigs with exhibitions of snake dancing and karate at the nearest pig pen.

Release a Black Panther in the Justice Department. Hold motorcycle races a hundred yards from the polling places. Fly an American flag out of every house so confused voters can't find the polling places. Wear costumes. Take a burning draft card to Spiro Agnew.

Stall for hours in the polling places trying to decide between Nixon and Humphrey and Wallace. Take your clothes off. Put wall posters up all over the city. Hold block parties. Release hundreds of greased pigs in pig uniforms downtown.

Check it out in Europe and throughout the world thousands of students will march on the USA embassies demanding to vote in the election cause Uncle Pig controls the world. No domination without representation.

Let's make 2-300 Chicago's on election day.

On election day let's pay tribute to rioters, anarchists, Commies, runaways, draft dodgers, acid freaks, snipers, beatniks, deserters, Chinese spies. Let's exorcise all politicians, generals, publishers, businessmen, Popes, American Legion, AMA, FBI, narcos, informers.

And then on Inauguration Day Jan. 20 we will bring our revolutionary theater to Washington to inaugurate Pigasus, our pig, the only honest candidate, and turn the White House into a crash pad. They will have to put Nixon's hand on the bible in a glass cage.

Begin now: resist oppression as you feel it. Organize and begin the word of mouth communication that is the basis of all conspiracies. Coordinate information and ideas by writing to Youth International Party, % Eldridge Cleaver, *Ramparts* magazine, 495 Beach St., San Francisco, California, 94133.

Every man a revolution! Every small group a revolutionary center! We will be together on election day. Yippie!!!   **Stew Albert, Abbie Hoffman,**
Jerry Rubin

13.3.   *GARY SNYDER:* **Buddhism and the**
Coming Revolution

[Oriental spiritualisms and mysticisms are among the ingredients of the "cultural evolution" of the hippies and other sectors of the new generation. Gary Snyder is a poet, expert on Buddhism, who lives in San Francisco.]

Buddhism holds that the universe and all creatures in it are intrinsically in a state of complete wisdom, love, and compassion; acting in natural response and mutual interdependence. The personal realization of this from-the-beginning state cannot be had for and by one "self" because it is not fully realized unless one has given the self up, and away.

In the Buddhist view, what obstructs the effortless manifestation of this state is ignorance, which projects into fear and needless craving. Historically, Buddhist philosophers have failed to analyze out the degree to which ignorance and suffering are caused by social factors, considering fear and desire to be given facts of the human condition. Consequently the major concern of Buddhist philosophy is epistemology and "psychology" with no attention paid to historical or sociological problems. Although Mahayana Buddhism has a grand vision of universal salvation, the ACTUAL achievement of Buddhism has been the development of practical systems of meditation toward the end of liberating a few dedicated individuals from psychological hangups and cultural conditionings. Institutional Buddhism has been the development of practical systems of meditation toward the end of liberating a few dedicated individuals from psychological hangups and cultural conditionings. Institutional Buddhism has been conspicuously tyrannies of whatever political system it found itself under. This can be death to Buddhism, because it is death to any meaningful function of compassion. Wisdom without compassion feels no pain.

No one today can afford to be innocent, or indulge himself in ignorance of the nature of contemporary governments, politics, and social orders. The national politics of the modern world maintain their existence by deliberately fostered craving and fear: monstrous protection rackets. The free world has become economically dependent on a fantastic system of stimulation of greed which cannot be fulfilled, sexual desires which cannot be satiated, and hatred which has no outlet except against oneself, the persons one is supposed to love, or the revolutionary aspirations of pitiful poverty-stricken marginal societies like Cuba or Vietnam. The conditions of the cold war have turned all modern societies—Communists included—into vicious distorters of man's true potential. They create populations of "preta" hungry ghosts with giant appetites and throats no bigger than needles. The soil, the forests, and all animal life are being consumed by these cancerous collectivities, the air and water of the planet is being fouled by them.

There is nothing in human nature or the requirements of human social organization which intrinsically requires that a culture be contradictory, repressive and productive of violent and frustrated personalities. Recent findings in anthropology and psychology make this more and more evident. One can prove it for himself by taking a good look at his own nature through meditation. Once a person has this much faith and insight, he must be led to a deep concern with the need for radical social change through a variety of hopefully non-violent means.

The joyous and voluntary poverty of Buddhism becomes a positive force. The traditional harmlessness and refusal to take life in any form has nation-shaking implications. The practice of meditation, for which one needs "only the ground beneath one's feet" wipes out mountains of junk being pumped into the mind by the mass media and universities. The belief in a serene and generous fulfillment of natural loving desires destroys ideologies which blind, maim, and repress and points the way to a kind of community which would amaze "moralists" and eliminate armies of men who are fighters because they cannot be lovers.

Avatamsaka (Kegon) Buddhist philosophy sees the world as a vast interrelated network in which all objects and creatures are necessary and illuminated. From one standpoint, governments, wars, or all that we consider evil are uncompromisingly contained in this totalistic realm. The hawk, the swoop, and the hare are one. From the "human" standpoint we cannot live in those terms unless all beings see with the same enlightened eye. The Bodhisattva lives by the sufferer's standard, and he must be effective in aiding those who suffer.

The mercy of the West has been social revolution; the mercy of the East has been individual insight into the basic self/void. We need both. They are both contained in the traditional three aspects of the Dharma: wisdom (prajna), meditation (dhyana), and morality (sila). Wisdom is intuitive knowledge of the mind of love and charity that lies beneath one's ego-driven anxieties and aggressions. Meditation is going into the mind to see this for yourself—over and over again, until it becomes the mind you live in. Morality is bringing it back out in the way you live, through personal example and responsible action, ultimately toward the true community (sangha) of "all beings." This last aspect means, for me, supporting any cultural and economic revolution that moves clearly toward a free, international, classless world. It means using such means as civil disobedience, outspoken criticism, protest, pacifism, voluntary poverty, and even gentle violence if it comes to a matter of restraining some impetuous redneck. It means affirming the widest possible spectrum of non-harmful individual behavior defending the right of individuals to smoke hemp, eat peyote, be polygamous, polyandrous, or homosexual. Worlds of behavior and custom long banned by the Judaeo-Capitalist-Christian, Marxist West. It means respecting intelligence and learning, but not as greed or means to personal power. Working on one's own responsibility, but willing to work with a group. "Forming the new society within the shell of the old"—the IWW slogan of fifty years ago.

The traditional cultures are in any case, doomed and rather than cling to their good aspects hopelessly it should be remembered that whatever is or was in any other culture can be reconstructured from the unconscious, through meditation. In fact, it is my own view that the coming revolution will close the circle and link us in many ways with the most creative aspects of our archaic past. If we are lucky we may eventually arrive at a totally integrated world culture with matrilineal descent, free-form marriage, natural-credit communist economy, less industry, far less population and lots more national parks.

13.4. *DIANE Di PRIMA:* **Revolutionary Letters**

[Diane Di Prima is a poet who passed through the beat experience of the 1950s. She began in April 1968 to write her "revolutionary letters" in which she calls for a "total revolution with the abolition of history and civilization.]

#8

Everytime you pick the spot for a be-in
a demonstration, a march, a rally, you are choosing the ground
for a potential battle.
You are still calling these shots.
Pick your terrain with that in mind.
Remember the old gang rules:
stick to your neighborhood, don't let them lure you
to Central Park, everytime, I would hate
to stumble bloody out of that park to find help:
Central Park West, or Fifth Avenue, which would you choose?

go to love-ins
with incense, flowers, food, and a plastic bag

with a damp cloth in it, for tear gas, wear no jewelry
wear clothes you can move in easily, wear no glasses
contact lenses
earrings for pierced ears are especially hazardous

try to be clear
in front, what you will do if it comes
to trouble
if you're going to try to split stay out of the center
don't stampede or panic others
don't waver between active and passive resistance
know your limitations, bear contempt
neither for yourself, nor any of your brothers
NO ONE WAY WORKS, it will take all of us
shoving at the thing from all sides
to bring it down.

#14

are you prepared
to hide someone in your home indefinitely
say, two to six weeks, you going out
for food, etc., so he never
hits the street, to keep your friends away
coolly, so they ask no questions, to nurse
him, or her, as necessary, to know
"first aid" and healing (not to freak out
at the sight of torn or half-cooked flesh
to pass him on at the right time to the next
station, to cross the canadian border, with a child
so that the three of you
look like one family, no questions asked,
or fewer, to stash letters, guns, or bombs
forget about them
till they are called for, to KEEP YOUR MOUTH SHUT
not to "trust"
even your truelove, that is,
lay no more knowledge on him than he needs
to do his part of it, a kindness
we all must extend to each other in this game

#15

When you seize Columbia, when you
seize Paris, take
the media, tell the people what you're doing
what you're up to and why and how you mean
to do it, how they can help, keep the news
coming, steady, you have 70 years
of media conditioning to combat, it is a wall
you must get through, somehow, to reach

for instinctive man, who is struggling like a plant
for light, for air

When you seize a town, a campus, get hold of the power
stations, the water, the transportation,
forget to negotiate, forget how
to negotiate, don't wait for De Gaulle or Kirk
to abdicate, they won't, you are not
"demonstrating" you are fighting
a war, fight to win, don't wait for Johnson or
Humphrey or Rockefeller, to agree to your terms
take what you need, "it's free
because it's yours"

#19
(for The Poor People's Campaign)

if what you want is jobs
for everyone, you are still the enemy,
you have not thought thru, clearly
what that means

if what you want is housing
industry
            (G.E. on the Navaho
            reservation
a car for everyone, garage, refrigerator,
TV, more plumbing, scientific
freeways, you are still
the enemy, you have chosen
to sacrifice the planet for a few years of some
science fiction utopia, if what you want

still is, or can be, schools
where all our kids are pushed into one shape, are taught
it's better to be "American" than black
or Indian, or Jap, or PR, where Dick
and Jane become and are the dream, do
look like Dick's father, don't you think your kid
secretly wishes you did

if what you want
is clinics where the AMA
can feed you pills to keep you weak, or sterile
shoot germs into your kids, while Mercke & Co.
grows richer

if you want
free psychiatric help for everyone
so that the shrinks,
pimps for this decadence, can make

it flower for us, if you want
if you still want a piece
a small piece of suburbia, green lawn
laid down by the square foot
color TV, whose radiant energy
kills brain cells, whose subliminal ads
brainwash your children, have taken over
your dreams
degrees from universities which are nothing
more than slum landlords, festering sinks
of lies, so you too can go forth
and lie to others on some greeny campus

THEN YOU ARE STILL
THE ENEMY, you are selling
yourself short, remember
you can have what you ask for   ask for
everything

13.5.   **International Werewolf Conspiracy: A
                                             Little Treatise on Dying—Fight Foul,
                                             Life is Real**

[The following leaflet was distributed at University of California, Berkeley, November 1968, on the occasion of the fight to obtain credit for a course given by black militant leader Eldrige Cleaver. The content is inspired by the position of such groups as the "Up Against the Wall, Motherfuckers" of Lower East Side, New York.]

The student is shit. He is the privileged person in an underprivileged world of suffering, but only because he does not recognize his own boredom as a form of imprisonment, of torture. He is not only deadened to reality, he is also deprived of the consciousness of his own suffering. He accepts himself as "normal," but it is only the normality of his repression that makes him like the rest of society.

The students movement is blind to itself: it does not understand the forces that push it into action, it cannot connect its struggle with its own life. (The issue is clearly not credit for Cleaver's course, or racist hiring practices—*the issue is not the issue,* and Cleaver for janitor is no solution.) The student movement seeks "demands" everywhere, but because students cannot see the absurdity of their own lives and their own imprisonment, they cannot begin to imagine what the struggle is for.

Students in France, in Japan and especially in Mexico, are struggling and dying in the streets in the real fight for *their* liberation . . . and revealing the poverty of our own movement and the terrible artificiality of our "struggles."

The real struggle will be easy to recognize because it will cut thru all the bullshit in which we are trapped. It knows its objectives. Its tactics are clear. It moves with confidence. It is struggling to WIN.

We begin by killing the enemy within us, within the hearts and minds of those with whom we would share our bodies and our lives. We come together in small bands with those who we have learned to trust, preparing for the long struggle with the enormous power of the institutions that repress us.

AN ACT OF DESTRUCTION IS AN ACT OF LIBERATION.

The function of the student movement is not to make demands on the university, but to destroy the existence of the "student" as a social role and as a character structure. YOU MUST DESTROY THE STUDENT WITHIN YOU. For only then can the struggle begin against the institutions and masters which have trained us for the submission and slavery in which we now participate. Our goal is not to win concessions, but to kill our masters and create a life which is worth living . . . and IN AMERICA LIFE IS THE ONE DEMAND THAT CAN'T BE FILLED.

13.6.   *ALLEN GINSBERG:* **How to Make a March/Spectacle**

> [In the 1950s, the beat generation introduced an imaginative and creative mood into the revolt against the "American Way of Life." Allen Ginsberg, the most representative poet of that generation, wrote this piece on the occasion of the Vietnam Days of Protest which took place in Berkeley in the fall of 1965. *Liberation,* January 1966.]

If imaginative, pragmatic, fun, gay, happy, *secure* Propaganda is issued to mass media in advance (and pragmatic leaflets handed out days in advance giving marchers instructions)

The parade can be made into an exemplary spectacle on how to handle situations of anxiety and fear/threat

(such as Spectre of Hells Angels or Spectre of Communism)

To manifest by concrete example, namely the parade itself, how to change war psychology and surpass, go over, the habit-image-reaction of fear/violence.

That is, the parade can embody an example of peaceable health which is the reverse of fighting back blindly.

Announce in advance it is a safe march, bring your grandmother and babies, bring your family and friends. Open declarations, "We aren't coming out to fight and we simply will not fight."

We have to use our *imagination.* A spectacle can be made, an unmistakable statement OUTSIDE the war psychology which is leading nowhere. Such statement would be heard around the world with relief.

The following suggestions manifest or embody what I believe to be the conscious psychology of latent understanding of the majority of the youth and many elders who come out to march.

And once clearly enunciated by the leaders of the march will be clearly understood and acted upon by them. Necessary to TRUST the communal sanity of the marchers who already demonstrated that community when they first SAT DOWN.

Needed: an example of health which will paralyze the Angels and also manifest itself thru mass media reportage.

N.B. A negative psychology, of becoming scared by threats, adrenalin running in neck, uprush of blood to head, blind resentment, self-righteousness,

fear, anger and active return of violence is exactly what the Angels "power structure" press and fuzz THRIVE ON
what the young people who come march don't want and are dragged by what will decrease the number who come and discourage the great many on the fence who wd come to a good scene.

THE FOLLOWING are specific suggestions for organizing march and turning marchers on to their roles in the Demonstration.

• 1. Masses of flowers—a visual spectacle—especially concentrated in the front lines. Can be used to set up barricades, to present to Hells Angels, Police, politicians, and press and spectators whenever needed or at parade's end. Masses of marchers can be asked to bring their own flowers. Front lines shd be organized and provided with flowers in advance.
• 2. Front lines should be the psychologically less vulnerable groups. The Women for Peace or any other respectable organization, perhaps a line of poets and artists, mothers, families, professors. This shd also be announced (publicized in advance).
• 3. Marchers should bring CROSSES, to be held up in front in case of violence; like in the movies dealing with Dracula. (This for those who use crosses or Jewish Stars.)
• 4. Marchers who use American Flags should bring those: at least one front row of Marican flags and myriads in the spectacle.
• 5. Marchers should bring Harmonicas, flutes, recorders, guitars, banjos and violins (Those who don't use crosses or flags.) Bongoes and tambourines.
• 6. Marchers should bring certain children's Toys (not firecrackers or balloons whch cause noise hysteria) which can be used for distracting attackers: such as sparklers, toy rubber swords, especially the little whirling carbon wheels which make red-white-blue sparklers. Toy soldiers.
• 7. In case of heavy anxiety, confusion or struggle in isolated spots marchers could be led in
Sit Down
Mass Calisthenics
• 8. In case of threat of attack marchers could intone en masse the following mantras
The Lord's Prayer
Three Blind Mice (*sung*)
OM (AUM) *long breath in unison*
Star Spangled Banner
Mary Had a Little Lamb (*spoken in unison*)
• 9. More interesting Zen/Spectacle SIGNS
As in Oakland So in Vietnam
Everybody's Made of Meat
Nobody Wants to Get Hurt—Us or Them
Everybody's Wrong Including U.S.
Hells Angels   Vietcong   Birch Society
DONT FLIP
We Love You Too
• 10. Candy bars carried by marchers to offer Hells Angels and Police.

• 11. Marchers encouraged to carry copies of the Constitution if they have them; or can buy them.

• 12. Little paper halos to offer angels, police and spectators and patriots. patriots.

• 13. A row of Marchers with white flags, and many white flags in mass.

• 14. Those who have movie cameras bring them and take pictures of spectacle or any action. (To combine for documentary film which could be used in court in case of legal hassels later, and also to circulate for propaganda and profits.) Monitors who can shd have cameras.

OTHER MORE GRANDIOSE POSSIBILITIES.

• 15. Corps of student newsmen to interview newsmen, propagandize and soften and charm TV crews etc.

• 16. Small floats or replicas in front:

Christ with sacred heart and cross (*invite church groups to prepare*)

Buddha in Meditation (*invite Zen people to come march and meditate on floats*)

Geo Washington, Lincoln, Whitman etc. (*float or living masquerade*)

Thoreau Behind Bars (*float*)

Hell's Angels Float—With Halos, happy, praying (*no ugly provocative caricature*)

Birch Society Float (*Old ladies in tennis sneakers*)

Dixieland Band Float dressed as Hitler Stalin Mussolini Napoleon and Caesar (*See Universal Soldier song*)

• 17. At first sign of Disturbance, P.A. Systems swing into vast sound *I Wanna Hold Your Hand* and marchers instructed to dance (if not doing calisthenics or Lord's Prayer). (These could be schematized as strategy 1, 2, 3, etc for diverting crowd and angels from Violence.)

• 18. The Mime Troupe in costume a block down the march, walking doing pantomime.

• 19. Sound trucks with Bay Area Rock and Roll Bands every two blocks, Jefferson Airplane, Charlatans, etc. (These bands have their own sound systems.) This scheme to pick up on the universal Youth rockroll protest of Dylan, Eve of Destruction, Universal Soldier, etc. and concretize all that consciousness in the parade.

• 20. Front (or toward front)—Toy army costume, Civil War or Rev War or WW I uniforms and signs

NO MORE
LEAVE ME ALONE

13.7.   *KEITH LAMPE:* **From Dissent to Parody**

[The following article was written after the Pentagon demonstrations of October 1967. It marks the beginning of a period in which the different components of the protest (political, individual, psychedelic) came together in a common front of dissent and resistance. Keith Lampe is an ex-journalist and ex-college teacher who dropped out to work full time in the Movement. He was a non-founder of the Youth International party (Yippie).]

They busted me (but not my skull) shortly after midnight Saturday: manly mop-up of maybe twenty of us as last pocket of resistance on right side of Pentagon upper level. I was placed into a van with 35 others—so crowded not all of us could sit—and kept there locked up stationary for one hour and 25 minutes. Total darkness except for two of us who could see through a few tiny peepholes. It cooked up to about 140 Fahrenheit, I'd say, and we decided not to talk and to breathe shallowly. I was amazed by the silent cool and pride of my colleagues. I thought if it weren't for the peepholes as my lucky reality-crutch, I would quickly have condensed downward into a puddle of paranoia.

Finally I started yelling through the peepholes about an injured man inside—and the doors were opened. Next we were approached one at a time by slick smiling Justice Dept. lawyer who said, "Now you can get on the bus and get a free ride to Union Station—or else you can continue to be processed." I said, "Sounds like Mississippi justice: boy, you better be out of town by sundown." He said, "Not at all—you can return to the Pentagon tomorrow and demonstrate and be arrested." He incredibly smiling all this time and with complete command of the various Middle Atlantic States politeness patterns. I thought, Hey, they're panicky about soaring arrest statistics freaking out their public relations—so I decided to remain and be a statistic.

That weekend is probably the best thing in American history since the Boston Tea Party and marks the public beginning (the old folks just now picking up on it) of the Second American Revolution. Most of the kids I met in jail are so strong inside themselves they can groove behind bars—and thus the regime's control system, based on incarceration, may become ineffectual. The regime is nervous about this: did you have an opportunity to watch Huntley and Brinkley twitch and fart for a week afterwards?

What's happening Mr. Jones, is that a whole generation is starting to say to its parents. "You can no longer get us to kill and be killed for your uptight archaic beliefs." To its parents. One of the people busted for blocking the entrance to the Selective Service headquarters in Washington October 24 was the daughter of the number two or three man inside.

We've always been moderately smarter than the overground journalists covering our demonstrations. Now, though, we've moved so fast we've lapped them—and so their attempts to smear us often will play right into our hands. Example: Remember the beautiful photo in *Time* of the free man poking flowers in the soldiers' rifle barrels? It looked like *Time's* single sympathetic concession to us. Well, I later learned they regard the picture as an example of the soldiers' saintly forbearance: look, folks, they didn't even smash that guy's face in.

Now in November the overground press is vastly less relevant and the underground press vastly more relevant. The Underground Press Syndicate and the Liberation News Service have a combined readership of two and a half million and it's growing much more quickly than its overground counterpart.

Just two weeks ago we were talking about "hippies" or "the psychedelic movement" on the one hand, and "straight peace activists" or "resisters" as something quite distinct. Now the two are tightly communal aspects of the same thing—and who can hang a name on it? It's like wind, or water. Superbly leaderless. The bull horns at the Pentagon were passed around almost as freely as the joints and sandwiches and water jugs. (From now on, any peace organization must, to be representative, include a call for legalization of marijuana in its language.)

Things to do next? First, work hard on the next draft-card turn-in scheduled by The Resistance. Get parents and chicks to sign Anti-Draft Cards: A Family That Disobeys Together Stays Together. Organize Merry Prankster freakout guerrilla squads to continue zapping the regime in local ways. Turn the regime into a dirty joke. Hit them in their dignity syndrome, which is emphatically their Achilles tendon.

About two weeks ago I spoke transatlantically with Allen Ginsberg who was worried about possibilities of violence October 21–22. He suggested best way to cool the scene would be mass nudism. Well, there wasn't time for that—and it was too cold—but what about next May (if we haven't yet won) 100,000 beautifully naked people advancing on the Pentagon carrying posies and chanting *Hare Krishna?* Lissome chicks slowly undressing the MP's as weapons fall from their hands . . . and probably they won't smash our skulls because beating on naked bodies makes them too conscious of *latent* sado-masochism. Eh?

Because the regime now is forced to take us seriously, it may choose conspiracy indictments as the best way to spook us and break our will. Conspiracy indictments have recently been used with great success to emasculate the labor movement even further—and with some success against southern rednecks.

It's important to zap the courtrooms whenever one of us is forced to appear on a conspiracy charge. Turn the whole pseudo-legal scene to parody— that's what it really is anyway. Hundreds howling through the courts and adjacent corridors "hysterical naked" or costumed as baseball players, longshoremen, doctors, investment brokers, little old ladies in tennis shoes, fraternity boys, especially clowns. A pageant. Feel good. A final passing-in-review of the whole national style which must be swiftly transcended to avoid intercontinental nuclear war.

FURTHER READINGS

Davidson, Carl. "Has SDS Gone to Pot?" *New Left Notes,* February 1967.
Garson, Barbara. *McBird.* New York: Grove Press, 1967.
Kornbluth, Jesse (ed.). *Notes from the New Underground.* New York: Viking Press, 1968.
Roszak, Theodore. "The Counter Culture: Youth and the Great Refusal." *The Nation,* March/April 1968.
Silber, Irwin. "Playing the System's Game." *Guardian,* August 17, 1968.

14

New Society

[Many groups of the Movement are trying to implement Utopia "here and now" in the present society. The Diggers were in San Francisco during 1967, spreading the message of the free city. *The Realist,* August 1968.]

Our state of awareness demands that we uplift our efforts from competitive game playing in the underground to the comparative roles *of free families* in *free cities.*

We must pool our resources and interact our energies to provide the freedom for our individual activities.

In each city of the world there is a loose competitive underground composed of groups whose aims overlap, conflict, and generally enervate the desired goal of autonomy. By now we all have guns, know how to use them, know our enemy, and are ready to defend. We know that we ain't gonna take no more shit. So it's about time we carried ourselves a little heavier and got down to the business of creating free cities within the urban environments of the western world.

Free Cities are composed of Free Families (e.g., in San Francisco: Diggers, Black Panthers, Provos, Mission Rebels and various revolutionist gangs and communes) who establish and maintain services that provide a base of freedom for autonomous groups to carry out their programs without having to hassle for food, printing facilities, transportation, mechanics, money, housing, working space, clothes, machinery, trucks, etc.

At this point in our revolution it is demanded that the families, communes, black organizations and gangs of every city in America co-ordinate and develop Free Cities where everything that is necessary can be obtained for free by those involved in the various activities of the individual clans.

Every brother should have what he needs to do his thing.

Free City

An outline . . . a beginning.

Each service should be performed by a tight
gang of brothers whose commitment should enable
them to handle an overload of work with ability
and enthusiasm. "Tripsters" soon get bored, hopefully
before they cause an economic strain.

Free City Switchboard/Information Center

should coordinate all services, activities, and aid and direct assistance where it is most needed. Also provide a reference point for legal aid, housing, machinery, etc.; act as a mailing address for dislocated groups or individuals and guide random energies where they are most needed. (The work load usually prevents or should prevent the handling of messages from parents to their runaway children . . . that should be left up to the churches of the community.)

Free Food Storage and Distribution Center

should hit every available source of free food—produce markets, farmers markets, meat packing plants, farms, dairies, sheep and cattle ranches, agricultural colleges, and giant institutions (for the uneaten vats of food)—and fill up their trucks with the surplus by begging, borrowing, stealing, forming liaisons and communications with delivery drivers for the left-overs from their routes . . . best method is to work in two shifts: morning group picks up the foodstuffs and the afternoon shift delivers it to the list of Free Families and the poor peoples of the ghettoes. everyday. hard work.

This gang should help people pool their welfare food stamps and get their old ladies or a group to open a free restaurant for people on the move and those who live on the streets. Giant scores should be stored in a garage-type warehouse equipped with freezers and its whereabouts known only to the Free Food Gang. This group should also set up and provide help for canning, preserving, bread baking, and feasts and anything and everything else that has to do with food.

Free City Garage and Mechanics

to repair and maintain all vehicles used in the various services. the responsibility for the necessary tools and parts needed in their work is entirely theirs and usually available by maintaining friendly relations with junkyards, giant automotive schools, and generally scrounging around those areas where auto equipment is easily obtained. The garage should be large enough and free of tripsters who only create more work for the earnest mechanics.

Free City Bank and Treasury

this group should be responsible for raising money, making free money, paying rents, for gasoline, and any other necessary expenses of the Free City Families. They should also organize and create small rackets (cookie sales, etc.) for the poor kids of the ghettoes and aid in the repair and maintenence of the machinery required in the performance of the various services.

Free City Legal Assistance

high style, hard nosed, top class lawyers who are willing to defend the rights of the Free City and its services . . . no honky, liberal bleeding heart, guilt-ridden advocates of justice, but first class case-winners . . . turn on the best lawyers who can set up air-tight receivership for free money and property, and beat down the police harassment and brutality of your areas.

Free City Housing and Work Space

rent or work deals with the urban gov't to take over spaces that have been abandoned for use as carpentry shops, garages, theatres, etc., rent whole houses, but don't let them turn into crash pads. Set up hotels for new arrivals or transients by working out deals with small hotel owners for free rooms in exchange for light house-work, porter duties, etc. Big warehouses can be worked on by environmental artists and turned into giant free dance-fiesta-feast palaces.

A strong trio of serious business-oriented cats should develop this liberation of space within the cities and be able to work with the lawyers to make deals and outmaneuver urban bureaucracies and slum landlords . . . one of the main targets for space are the churches who are the holders of most real-estate and they should be approached with no-bullshit hard-line.

Free City Stores and Workshops

nothing in these stores should be throwaway items . . . space should be available for chicks to sew dresses, make pants to order, re-cut garments to fit, etc.

The management should all be life-actors capable of turning bullshitters into mud. Important that these places are first class environments with no trace of salvation army/st.vinnie de paul charity rot. Everything groovy. Everything with style . . . must be first class. *It's all free because it's yours!*

Free Medical Thing

should be established in all poverty areas and run by private physicians and free from any bureacratic support. The Free City Bank should try to cover the expenses, and pharmaceutical houses should be hit for medical supplies, etc. Important that the doctors are *brothers* and do not ask to be salaried or are not out to make careers for themselves (witness Dr. David Smith of the Hippie Free Clinic in San Francisco who is far from a brother. . . very far).

Free City Hospital

should be a house converted into bed space and preferably with a garden and used for convalescence and people whose funds have been blown or who have just been released from a state institution and who need the comfort and solace of their people rather than the cold alienated walls of an urban institution.

Free City Environmental and Design Gang

gangs of artists from universities and art institutes should be turned on and helped in attacking the dank squalor of the slums and most of the Free City Family dwellings . . . paint landscapes on the sides of tenements . . . fiberglass stairwells . . . make crazy. Tight groups of good painters, sculptors, designers who comfortably construct environments for the community. Materials and equipment can be hustled from university projects and manufacturers, etc.

Free City Schools

schools designed and run by different groups according to the consciousness of their Free Families (e.g., Black Man's Free School, Anarchist's Creative Arts School, etc.). The schools should utilize the space liberated for them by the Free City Space Gang.

Free City News and Communication Company

providers of a daily newspaper, monthly magazine, free Gestetner and printing of notices for other groups and any special bulletins and propaganda for the various families of the Free City. The machinery should be kept in top condition and supplied by any of the various services. Paper can be scavenged at large mills and cut down to proper working size.

Free City Events . . . Festival Planning Committees

usually involves several Families interacting to sponsor tours for the kids . . . Balls, Happenings, Theatre, Dance, and spontaneous experiments in joy . . . Park Events usually are best set up by hiring a 20-foot flat-bed truck for the rock band to use as a stage and to transport their equipment; people should be advised by leaflets to bring food to exchange with their neighbors; banners, props, balloons, kites, etc. should be handled by a committee; an electrician should be around to run the generator and make sure that the P.A. systems work; hard work made easy by giving responsible people the tough jobs.

Co-operative Farms and Campsites

the farms should be run by experienced hands and the Free Land settled on by cottage industrial people who will send their wares into the Free City. The farms must produce vital food for the families . . . some free land that is no good for farming should be used as campsites and/or cabin areas for citizens who are in need of country leisure, as well as kids who could use a summer in the woods.

Scavenger Corps and Transport Gang

is responsible for garbage collection and the picking up and delivery of items to the various services, as well as liberating anything they think useful for one project or another. They are to be responsible for the truck fleet and especially aware of the economic strain if trucks are mis-used by tripsters.

Free City Tinkers and Gunsmiths, Etc.

will repair and keep things going in the houses . . . experienced repair men of all sorts, electricians, and carpenters. They should maintain a warehouse or working space for their outfit.

Free City Radio, TV and Computer Stations

demand Free time on radio and TV stations; demand a Free City frequency to set up your own stations; rent computers to call the punches for the revolution or use them in any constructive way possible.

Free City Music

Free Music
Where is the place that your music comes from
do you know
What determines the rest between phrases
The Interval that grows from the cluster
of sounds around it
Hanging behind the beat
Clipping the front of it
That's the gift
The thing that blows through a body responds to spirit and a mind that
doesn't lock itself
It's that thing
We're all made of, forget about, and then try to grab again
That thing that's all there and all free
The fretless infinite string banjo has invented new means of music which it
must buy from itself to sing

$ * $ * $

fat man owns the carnival and all the booths play business. he double hypes the want glands, lets *you* buy in and then displays what's available to the crowd. all of a sudden you got something to lose. he spreads the news and pays for it by telling kids they're ugly blemished smelly unimaginative and dull . . . then sells them cures, says to you, "here kid, change the name, change the games, do anything you want, but don't give it away." that game's called vested interest and it can apply to anything.

fat man runs a crumby joint, but it's the only joint right? *He'll be there until we free the goodies*

Art forms and life forms interact
look at fat mans *Life*
look at fat mans *Time*
look at fat mans forms
The record industry, dance-hall promotion rackets and the artist-star-celebrity-hero roles they support and promote are fat man forms and are cramping the number
the dance-light show package hasn't changed since its form crystallized and it became business. it reached the end of its evolution. kids don't dance they watch, because the bands are pro now and you don't play *with* a pro. when you pay to go to a dance the medium is business . . . the problem is to free the form and the carnival.

Some Ideas for Liberating the Ferris Wheel:

A) *Contracts could demand free cuts on all albums*
a name group might take one side of an album and divide the other into sets of two tracks each of which they would give away. give a brother a piggy-back over the business-shit to the ears of our people. two truths don't compete

B) *A certain number of records be released in plain white folders.*
saving all art and printing costs and leaving free space for local artists to use. Ready mades would cost more.

C) *Scrap liner notes and "photos-of-the-band"*
print charts of the tunes, diagrams of cheap amps and pick-ups so local wizards can plug in more kids, good poems, clothes patterns, recipes.

D) *Add 1% to all royalties to be used for free forms*
equipment for free rehearsal rooms
sound systems for free concerts
musical communes for non-working cats.

E) *Send other bands on your publicity junkets*
after all its not just *your* sound is it its *the* sound you're all part of. make that clear to people. free fat man's star trip by giving away your names. how many times can you go to Des Moines?

14.2.   *MARVIN GARSON:* **The Movement:**
It's Theory Time

[Marvin Garson, a longtime activist of the New Left and now editor of the *San Francisco Express Times,* with these articles speaks for the recent anarchic tendencies within the Movement. *San Francisco Express Times,* June 26, July 3, and July 17, 1968.]

What's wrong with the New Left? What happened to all the magic in phrases like "participatory democracy" and "let the people decide"? Why have they degenerated into pure demagogy? And what did they mean in the first place?

The slogans suggested that what we basically needed was real democracy in place of the present sham democracy, substantive democracy in place of formal democracy. We needed new institutions through which people would really be able to "participate in making the decisions that affect their lives."

The idea was right there in the name of the most prominent New Left organization: Students for a Democratic Society.

The model of the New Society was supposed to be the New Left organizations themselves. The agonizing problem has been that these organizations, while impeccably democratic, have been a stone drag.

There has been plenty of bitching about bureaucracy inside the New Left, but most of it has been ill-founded, For every leader who has tried to tyrannize over the rank and file, there have been a hundred who have earnestly done their best to involve the rank and file in decision-making. Where the typical labor leader tries to keep his followers away from meetings whenever something important is up for decision, the typical New Left organizer drags as many people as he possibly can to meetings, and tries to get opposing points of view set forth as fairly as possible. The heartbreaker has been that for some reason people don't WANT to go to meetings, don't WANT to participate.

The implications are ominous. After the Power Structure has been overthrown, will people still have to be dragged to meetings? How can you run a society democratically if people don't WANT to "participate in making the decisions that affect their lives"? Won't power eventually fall into the hands first of revolutionary leaders and then—as the excitement fades away—of a new generation of bureaucratic hacks? It's an old argument—Michels made it 60 years ago (his "iron law of oligarchy")—but no Marxist has ever been able to refute it.

Let's start off with a different principle of organization, and next week we'll see where it leads.

Suppose, instead of getting together with people you agree with in the abstract, or people whose economic interests are the same as yours, suppose you get together with people whose company you find congenial, people who are really into the same things you are, people who work and play well together. In other words, instead of forming political parties or unions or protest groups, suppose you form gangs or families or communes. (You don't all have to live under the same roof, just as long as you live in the same city—or better, the same neighborhood.)

The main difference between a revolutionary gang and a revolutionary party is that a party, by definition, seeks state power. It puts forth a program which it takes very seriously, and expects the public to take seriously; for it is on the basis of that program that the party intends to re-order society once it gains the power of government.

A revolutionary party says: If you want "structural reform," or "peace, bread and land," or "true democracy," or "social ownership of the means of production," then put us in power. Vote for us, or (depending on the circumstances) pick up a gun and join our army.

Conservative parties also ask you to put them in power, by ballot or bullet. Is there no difference, then? Certainly there is—program. And that is why revolutionary parties quarrel and split so much about the "correct program," because in the final analysis, that's all they have. The program can't be too sectarian, too far beyond the masses; it can't be opportunist, sacrificing its revolutionary content; it has to be just right.

A revolutionary gang (or family or commune) is more modest. It carries out projects which seem productive and are fun to do; but it understands that there are plenty of other gangs around with their own projects, just as worthwhile.

Since it is not a candidate for power, it does not need to present to the public a formal program for the reorganization of society. Since its members respect and trust each other from the start—they joined the group because it was congenial, not because it was "correct"—they can dispense with the parliamentary formalities. (Roberts Rules of Order is an important defensive weapon that can save your life in a political jungle, but it's usually unnecessary among friends.)

In a gang/family/commune, communication isn't limited to a weekly two-hour meeting. People are always running into each other, so bright ideas can be converted into action quickly and efficiently.

The rules are simple and natural. If your bright idea needs five people to carry it out, then you have to get four other people excited enough to do it with you.

The projects may be offensive or defensive, legal or clandestine, constructive or destructive, depending entirely upon the temperament of the people involved. Maybe you like children, and want to set up a cooperative nursery or school in your neighborhood. Maybe you like redwoods, and want to dynamite the bulldozers that are logging them off. Maybe you like guerrilla theater, and want to stage a little show at a Board of Supervisors meeting. Anything goes.

You are not pushing the name of your group, but word gets around among other gangs/families/communes in the city. You make contacts, get to know each other, share services, collaborate on certain projects. Gradually you develop a strong sense of solidarity. Taken together, you are now a significant creative and disruptive force, sometimes amusing, sometimes threatening, always active.

But what does this have to do with revolution, with the creation of a Free City?

Revolution is such an overused word that I'll have to start by clarifying it, clearing away all the ideological garbage littering the ground. Sorry, it's not MY fault.

The most common idea—and the most childish—is that revolution is the armed seizure of power by revolutionaries. A revolutionary, in this image, is someone who is young, bearded, wears a fatigue jacket and beret, clenches his fist, and carries a sidearm—in short Fidel Castro or a reasonable facsimile thereof. (Some schools of thought hold that the revolutionary should also smoke pot and say fuck on television; others consider this frivolous nonsense. It is a minor difference which can be settled after the revolution, most likely at gunpoint.)

If you imagine yourself one of the revolutionaries, it's a very noble prospect plus you get a lot of pussy. But the real test must be how it looks from down below. And from below, it looks a great deal like dictatorship.

Fatigue-jacket revolutionaries will reply: dictatorship in FORM, perhaps, but democracy in CONTENT—the opposite of what we have now. A revolutionary government would give land to the peasants—whoops, wrong country —would, uh, end racism-and-exploitation by ending the corporate system that perpetuates it.

That discussion won't get much further unless we switch now to the more sophisticated revolutionaries who all this time have been smirking along with me at the romantic Maoist-Fidelistas. They are a little older, more historically minded: they've read Marx and Lenin and Trotsky, and also people you never heard of—from Rosa Luxemburg ("Red Rosa," martyred in the German revolution of 1919) to Kuron and Modzelewski, now serving long prison terms in Poland for trying to organize a revolutionary socialist party in opposition to the Gomulka regime.

They believe it is not enough to expropriate industry from private owners; it must be kept from falling into the hands of a new, "socialist" ruling class of bureaucrats administering property which belongs to the people only in legal theory, not in fact. Very good. And how do you insure democratic control of industry? Why, by setting up workers' councils in each industry which operate with full respect for all the normal democratic procedures—especially the right to establish caucuses and factions, and the right to strike. The economy, in short, will be run the way a government is SUPPOSED to be run; it will be like a gigantic New Left convention—impeccably democratic and a stone drag, as I said last week.

Some people call democratic voting a "means of expression." It is that, but it is the poorest means of expression that I can think of. Isn't it more satisfying an expression to sing, or tinker with your car, or have a fistfight, or write on a wall, than to pull a lever? No, voting is a defensive weapon, not a creative instrument; it is something you use to make sure you don't get entirely fucked over by would-be dictators of any variety, but not something you build your life around.

The democratic process is in fact painful and boring for all but the few who are so skilled in the game itself that they find it exhilarating regardless of its content; everyone else looks for excuses to stay away. This means, of course, that power falls into the hands either of faceless bureaucrats or of "groovy" revolutionaries who govern by decree "in the true interests of the people." Once again: how can you run a society democratically if people don't WANT to "participate in making the decisions that affect their lives"?

The only way out is a revolution which is consciously determined to go BEYOND democracy. "Beyond democracy"—that will stick in many throats. Let me over-explain it, just to make sure.

When I say democracy, I mean majority rule. When I speak of going beyond majority rule I don't mean minority rule; I mean no rule at all.

A storm of protest: Anarchy! Madness! Our society is too complex to run without laws, discipline, control. True—but don't be smug about it; start to change it. Start right now, and let your revolution be a dramatic speeding-up of the process.

Our technology is such that it can only be administed by an elite. That's true too—after all, it was an elite that set down the design criteria for the engineers to follow. Did you think they ordered their own functions to be designed away? Do you think they told the engineers to be sure to remember that free men would be working in those factories and offices?

Perhaps it's impossible to run a steel mill or an electric power plant in a free and creative way. In that case, run it automatically. If computers can fly a supersonic jet plane at a constant altitude of 100 feet over rough terrain while making it take evasive action and launch bombs on target and screw up enemy radar (the plane flew two miles in the time it took you to read that half-sentence), then certainly computers can run a steel mill.

Will there be any work left for people to do? Certainly. We'll have the time to build our own houses, for instance, with our own hands, with master workmen around to supervise and instruct. How's that for a start? Better than rent subsidies?

Sorry I didn't get around to explaining how the revolutionary gangs /families/communes fit into the revolution, but first things first.

The first objection is always: what about the masses? Revolution is supposed to be nothing less than "the entry of the masses into history," and how can that happen if mass organizations are replaced by little groups of friends running around planting bombs?

The point, though, is not to help the masses enter history but to help the masses exit from it. A mass is like a giant blob of dough; it gets kneaded by one elite or another, but cannot do anything for itself. Revolution, in 1968, does not mean grabbing hold of the mass and throwing it onto the left-hand pan of the scales; revolution means breaking up that sticky, shapeless mass once and for all so that no person, clique, party or ruling class will ever again be able to pound those 200 million Americans into shape. We will be ready for revolution only when so many people have carved out spaces to breathe in and work in that society looks more like a honeycomb than a blob of dough.

It comes in two stages. First, large numbers of people have to drop out psychologically—that is, learn how to think for themselves and be willing to accept the status of mental outlaw. Millions of people, especially the young, have done that over the last ten years.

The second stage—barely begun as yet—comes when they begin to actually implement their ideas in their working lives.

For example: it is important that so many people perceive how empty and stupid elementary education is. But it is not enough if people vote for (or abstractly "support" in any other way) a solution to the problem, however clever that solution may be. Teachers themselves have to be willing to put their ideas into practice and ignore the Board of Education; parents have to be willing to organize their own schools if necessary; otherwise it's still all talk.

Every industry has its own inchoate underground of people who take pride in doing good work, who aren't in it just for the money, who get angry when their employers make them sacrifice quality for the sake of profit. Let that underground get together and suddenly a real alternative to corporate capitalism will exist. Some will call it anarchism, or communism, or a petty bourgeois deviation, but for once the name won't matter.

In these times revolutionary politics consists fundamentally of precipitating active, functional groups out of the homogeneous mass, finally on such a scale that virtually the whole population comes alive. It can only be done by example, never by preaching. That means the revolutionaries have to be themselves organized in functional WORKING groups—gangs, families, communes, affinity groups, whatever you wish to call them.

However technical the work such revolutionary groups perform, they remain basically political whether engaged in running a free bus line or blowing up draft boards, they calculate every project primarily for its effect upon the public consciousness. It starts out with revolutionary intellectuals. It ends up with revolutionary carpenters, teachers, doctors, mechanics, machinists, programmers—what once were "the masses."

FURTHER READINGS

"The Digger Papers." *The Realist.* August 1968.
Goodman, Paul. "The Diggers in 1984." *Ramparts,* September 1967.
Lynd, Staughton. "A Good Society." *Guardian,* April 20, May 18, and July 13, 1968.   .

15
Alternative
Structures

15.1. *RAYMOND MUNGO:* **The Movement and Its Media**

[Ray Mungo was one of the initiators in 1967 of the Liberation News Service, the press agency of the Underground and Movement papers, today operating through two different branches. *Radicals in the Professions,* January 1968.]

That the history of radical journalism in this country is so brief and so pathetic is perhaps the greatest testimony to the clear failure of the organized left to significantly influence the course of the nation's actions, as it is writing and speaking, rather than acting, which the left has done best and most consistently in the last hundred years. Pamphlets, leaflets, flyers, newsletters, poop-sheets of various kinds, magazines, underground mimeographed documents, weekly and even daily newspapers—all have seen the light of day and died unnoticed shortly thereafter. No radical paper has managed to be self-sufficient (*The Daily Worker* went weekly some years ago, and will now return to daily only through a munificent inheritance; *The National Guardian,* too has always depended on large contributions from isolated richies, who of late have been less numerous), and none has managed to attract a readership large enough to be legitimately called "mass." *Ramparts,* which despite some justified antagonism from the left must still be considered a radical magazine, has achieved a phenomenal circulation of 250,000, largely through spectacular headlines in the established media following major exposés in its pages.

So, the radical press is foredoomed by its ancestors (who, fortunately, may still be proven wrong) to remain uneven in quality and unstable in general. Yet, and ironically, we have to admit that it exists and is growing now at a faster rate than it ever has in most of our lifetime. The older papers have remained, and new ones are born literally every week, many of them underground efforts devoted at least in part to a positive statement on a new lifestyle and morality as well as serious criticism of the old established ones. Iowa City has a militant, politically active underground paper, *Middle Earth;* Dallas has been shaken by the impolite presence of *Notes from the Underground,* and Austin/Houston by *The Rag,* both very maturely anti-war; Syracuse and Bloomington, Seattle and Spokane, Lawrence, Kans. and Northampton, Mass., all have popular and reasonably well-established biweekly undergrounds. And in the places where the underground papers are manifestly uninterested in political action, more "political" papers are filling the gap: in New York, Jeff Shero's *The Rat* v. *East Village Other;* in Boston, Rowland Koefud's *Le Chronic* v. *Avatar;* in Berkeley, Marvin Gerson's *Express-Times* v. *The Barb.*

What we are witnessing, then, is a tremendous renaissance of the beautiful and careful art of serious, honest and mature little-magazining, integrally a part of the expansion of the new (largely student-oriented) left and in reaction to injustices for blacks at home and conscious murder in Vietnam and countless other places abroad. The 150 newspapers who joined Liberation News Service when it was founded in September have somehow become 300. And most of them are supporting, if meagerly, talented radicals who otherwise would be forced to drop out or prostitute themselves to the corporate will of an established press which is in incestuous league with the complex of scoundrels who run our government and own our purses. LNS alone supports ten people.

There is a class of people in this country, emerging fresh from high schools and colleges or perhaps dropped-out of them, who have both the skill and the maturity to be of immeasurable worth to the movement in radical publishing; but there has always been a problem in putting this natural resource to its best ends. What, after all, is a young man or woman who wants to edit, write, design, or photograph to do if he or she is unwilling to prostitute very deep political and moral principles to a dishonest and socially harmful established media? What meaningful work is there? Increasingly, the answer is no longer *The National Guardian, Liberation* magazine, or the several other well-established and smoothly-functioning radical publications who are always in need of money but seldom of more full-time staff; nor is it in immature student publications or those underground sheets devoted largely to prurient interests and unsubtle senses of humor. Because there is a war in Vietnam, because there is a Stokeley Carmichael, because there is an active Resistance, there is also a new audience for independent publications, counter-institutions which can be started anywhere by anyone of high competence and serious commitment, and which will support (albeit meagerly) at least a small group of dedicated people, give them leave to devote themselves full-time to this exciting new project. At last, we are at a point where it is no longer necessary to get one's training doing summer rewrites for *The Washington Post.* At last our radical press, disparate and spread-out as it may be, is standing on its own.

Liberation News Service enters as a national office coordinating news, photos, teletype communications and good karma for those papers which want it and need it (and they are many) and giving them both a national perspective which would otherwise be impractical and a sense of fraternity with a developing and growing movement of individuals. From its roots, LNS had no capital or prestige; but it did have two essential factors which have made it work to date—a handful of people eager to try the idea and convinced that the time was right, and an operational procedure which offered a good deal of hope for self-sufficiency. Because LNS is a service rather than a newspaper or magazine available to the general public, it did not have the costs of typesetters, the worries of advertising, the need to hawk itself on the streets, etc. Its most pressing physical needs were large sums of money to handle immense telephone bills, teletype bills, and postage necessary to speak and listen to other people around the entire country and world—to know everything that was going on and to get it to newspapers for redistribution to the people of America. It is still, of course, a long way from our vision of maximum efficiency and stability, but already shows objectively hopeful signs of becoming an essential service to the movement—a channeling center through which important news and good writing can reach our constituency wherever it is at the minimum cost and duplication of effort. (And it should be noted that 100 college newspapers presently receive, and liberally use, LNS's material.)

LNS, with its three-times-weekly distribution (via first class mail) of news and its chain of Western Union TELEX contacts around the country, all for the benefit of newspapers, made itself a subdivision of something called The New Media Project, which at the moment is simply a working name but which is intended to include new media of all kinds—ghetto "underground" radio stations, high school newsletters, professional radio outlets with some social conscience (like WBAI-FM in New York), community television, etc., all part of a concerted effort to revolutionize the consciousness of the country, while leaving each member free to develop the creative potential necessary to make his paper or radio or TV unique and outstanding. The New Media Project, in short, intends to make it no longer necessary for Americans to rely on UPI or *The New York Times*, with their chronic dishonesty, for "facts" about any occurrence anywhere, and to "open up" to Americans news of people and places they are denied in the established press—news of Havana, Hanoi, Peking, South Africa, university insurgency, sexual freedom, serious psychedelic research.

In a sense, then, we have already reached the position where a young man or woman, looking for decent and intelligent uses for his love and mind, knows where to go for a job—in Detroit to *The Fifth Estate*, in Chicago to *The Bridge* or *The Seed* or *New Left Notes*, etc. But we are still in that virgin/ exploratory phase in which, lacking suitable answers in the newly established radical press, he can and should go somewhere where the need is evident and do his own thing, add another voice and organize another community around another newspaper which differs radically from the bourgeois concept of press. It will inevitably be a struggle, and probably will remain so for years after he starts, but our movement is a progressive one, a comprehensive one, that requires that kind of pioneer spirit (if you can pardon the outrageous metaphor). Police harassment, a struggle with keeping high standards, and financial instability will all threaten the new media, but the people do, honestly, want to know and it is from them—not ads or Chase Manhattan's millions—that support will be forthcoming to keep the new project alive.

In short, it is important to write and edit and speak, and we must continue doing it, without fear for our security, and be ready for, and help to shape, the action of the future.

15.2.   **Some Newsreel Documents**

[Newsreel is a group of Movement film makers who have made political and journalistic documentaries.]

INITIAL STATEMENT OF THE NEWSREEL

Where Do We Start From? (Dec., 1967)

We are (1) involved in a process of liberation from many of the assumptions of American society, as well as a struggle to change its systems of organization and control; (2) our solidarity is with those who are attempting to make this liberation and this change tangible in America and in other countries, and we intend to make films that are relevant to these people and to their work; (3) our understanding of news is defined by *our* experience of American society, by what affects us and is important to us, an experience that is close to that of people working for change.

Who Are We?

that we consider news: demonstrations, acts of resistance, countless inequities
As individual film-makers we have been covering many of the events

and abuses, people whom we value, situations and ways of seeing that seem either indicative or productive. Sometimes these films were made and sometimes not. Most often they were made too late and did not go to the people who could use them best. Now we have come together.

We come from many different areas of film-making, and for most of us film-making has been inseparable from social activity of one form or another. Therefore, we are film-makers who are trying—through the formation of an organization that can make different kinds of films rapidly and get them out to groups who can use them well—to make ourselves and our work relevant to others involved in the struggle for change here and abroad.

What films should we make? Let us talk provisionally about three kinds of films: news, educational, tactical. . . .

Organizers in different areas of work, university students, ghetto groups, anti-war groups, hippie organizations, all those who can use these films as tools in their work. . . .

These films will be available to anyone. We hope that their relevance will attract audiences who are not usually reached. But they will reach such audiences only if they are brought to them by people who understand what it is to organize, and how to use such films to increase and activate social and political awareness.

We want to emphasize that we are initially directing our work toward those in the society who have already begun their redefinition.

At the start we will use existing networks like SDS, the Underground Press Service, anti-war groups, the Resistance, community projects . . . to find various groups around the country (and abroad) who can use the films effectively, can show them frequently, and who have sufficient contacts in their cities to get the films out to other different groups, like churches, film clubs, anti-poverty groups, neighborhood organizations. . . .

In principle we want to provide prints of the films free of cost to all groups who can use them. Decisions concerning this will depend on our success in raising a substantial sum of money to finance the whole project.

It should be clear that we are trying to do two things at once: (1) create and maintain a permanent newsreel group in New York City, capable of producing at least two films a month . . . and getting 12 to 14 prints of each out to groups across the country; (2) to increase the activity of this group, while enlarging the distribution network, and sparking the creation of similar news-films groups in other major cities of the U.S.

It is not practical for a group in New York to make a film about the Oakland demonstrations . . . or the Detroit rebellion. Each city should not be sending footage to us. They must make their own short films aimed at fulfilling the same needs as ours. Therefore, one of our highest priorities is to aid in the formation of such news-film groups around the country: by sending experienced people, by sharing technical information, by creating a reliable and flexible distribution apparatus.

Memo: A Note on Distribution (Jan., 1968)

Our principle concern is the creation of what we call the community distribution network. This network is based on individuals and activist groups throughout the country, functioning as distributors at the grass-roots level. The model for the operation of the community distribution network depends on an understanding of how such groups or individuals, whether they are in-volved in anti-war work or domestic movement-building or radical political organization, penetrate the communities that they work in.

We have begun by drawing on our contacts with key people and groups across the country. Arrangements are made with them to receive THE NEWS-REEL films regularly, as they are completed. Each group we choose has many different kinds of contacts in the community where they work. The contacts range from alliances with groups doing similar work, to the wide spread of more neutral organizations who are always on the fringe of radical activity, like church groups, liberal groups, leagues of voters, elements from the local high school and university, and many others. What we assume is that or-ganizers from the contact-group will carry THE NEWSREEL films outward into the community in the course of their work. Where they have to speak on a subject, and there is a relevant film, they will bring the film; where another group could use a film, they will get it to them. The contact-group is not really a true "film distributor." The films become tools that they use in the course of their work, and like any other tools, they help the group in its organizing work, and serve to bring the group into contact with more people. It is reasonable to assume, for example, that if THE NEWSREEL films maintain sufficient quality, local community screenings will be set up on a regular basis, thereby creating another forum for the contact-group and others. In addition, the films should create their own demand. Our experience has been that when a group has films that are wanted, they are often given opportunities to speak to and work with groups that they might never otherwise be in touch with.

Some Ideas About Where THE NEWSREEL Is After Two Months (Feb., 1968)

(1) We've completed four films. Another four are close to completion. At least eight others are in various stages of production.

(The question of what kind of film THE NEWSREEL wants to make is not defined, and it isn't clear that it can or should be. Each new film produced or accepted by THE NEWSREEL sharpens that definition. What has to be kept in mind is something I think we're agreed on: that we're making films for people to use to broaden activity in many different areas, to increase and deepen the base of what we call the movement in the United States. Our pri-mary concern is making films that can be profitably used within the community distribution network that we're creating. We disagree among ourselves what kind of films are best for this very broad purpose: that's because we don't know [to an extent it's an empirical question], and because no one else has con-sistently made this attempt; part of THE NEWSREEL's important business is to explore this whole question.)

(2) We have begun setting up the community distribution network. Twelve points across the country have been established initially. (Within a week these contact-groups will have received NEWSREEL films 1, 3, 4.) We have been obliged to limit the community distribution network because we don't have the money to make enough prints. We could expand to 50 contact-groups easily. More than this will require additional work. At this point the only additions to the network are those groups who can afford to pay print-costs on each film.

(3) We have some indication that theatre rental of our films will be pos-

sible. The run of Newsreel #1 at the New Yorker was unexpectedly successful. We will get other theatres in NYC and across the country if we do the
work to contact them.

(One of the problems that this raises: theatrical distribution is very attractive to film-makers, obviously. We could easily get siphoned off into making films for a steadily growing theatrical demand, losing the focus of the
community distribution network, which is far harder to develop.)

Speech to a Communications Forum (March, 1968) (Excerpts)

THE NEWSREEL is the beginning in the development of national centers
of film communication. As independent film-makers we believe film to be a
major element in any communication network. (As independent film-makers
we are also part of the revolution which has taken place in the film industry;
in fact many of us are responsible for those changes which have taken place
over the last few years. The very fact that these changes have taken place
relates directly to the very existence of THE NEWSREEL.)

Film distinguishes itself from other media by its ability to relate or convey
the visual/audio emotional quality of a situation or event.

The applications of film as a medium are many. We see film in terms of
the normal single screen projection which we are all used to; but multiscreen
media-mix presentations are extremely valuable in dealing with visual/time
relationships, in turning people on, in expanding consciousness, or in dis-
orienting the unconscious; there are also the so-called "guerrilla" applications
of film whereby film and/or slides are projected from a truck onto walls,
screens, buildings, etc., in this way reaching people in a completely different
context. All three of these applications are being developed by the Newsreel.
The importance of each cannot be underestimated or ignored.

THE NEWSREEL is composed not of specialists (like the networks) but
disciplined generalists with varying degrees of skill in the different areas of film-
making. This means two things: that members are basically interchangeable
in terms of work and responsibility; . . . that by pooling our equipment and
technical knowledge we are capable of operating with little if no initial
funding.

The purpose of THE NEWSREEL is two-fold: *a.* to act as a primary
means of communication between existing communities or movements thereby
solidifying new and developing social identities, and at the same time providing a viable instrument for formulating these new identities. *b.* to act as a
tool for organizers and groups for reaching the uncommitted or uninformed
thereby expanding movements of change.

Some Unfinished Business (April, 1968)

. . . When THE NEWSREEL was in its initial stages we were working
from two different yet related bases. The first was our own personal attitude in
and about film, our ideas about it as a medium of expression, and in a vague
way where most of us were at or had come to as film-makers. The second
flowed from a release of energy which seemed to focus around things social
and/or political. Regardless of what our origins were we have managed to
create and maintain a reasonably stable and useful cooperative of sorts.
We've been able to initiate 14 films, 9 of which have been completed, all in a
reasonably short amount of time. So far so good. But . . .

. . . Our major failing is that in our work we have in no way attempted any sort of redefinition in the subjects that we choose to film, in our identity as a group, or in the very "film" that we make. For the most part we have relied on coverage and presentation as our basic format. In extending ourselves we have gone into those areas dominated by the "media"; our imaginations have failed to probe what would be considered new ground; this applies to our film technique as well as our politics (whatever the fuck that is). . . . In trying to present this viewpoint and that viewpoint we have failed to investigate our own. We have failed to realize that though we as film-makers may be often removed from an event or action or subject, . . . whatever it is that we are filming involves us also. The tendency for us has been to involve ourselves peripherally, mainly because that is the most comfortable place for us to be. It is no great accomplishment to be able to cover a peace march or a demonstration; . . . we might only be imitating the coverage of the networks which is exactly what we don't want.

When we first started we deluded ourselves into thinking that . . . across this country there exists a monolithic movement called . . . the "new Left" with hundreds of dedicated organizers . . . starving to death because they don't have films to organize with. Not only doesn't this group of organizers exist but the movement is hardly monolithic; its existence is vague and its direction is almost invisible. Given the fact that the "political" reality of the so-called movement is ambivalent, that it's top-heavy with leadership (most of which is uninspired), we should no longer be working under the impression that we are servicing any one group or organization.

The fact is that we have little to relate to outside our own political and social realities (at this point anyway), and we have failed to do even that. Instead we have tended to work from some abstract base of understanding what is going on out there.

. . . We must begin to spell out exactly what our objectives are, not in written terms but in the films which we make.

More Unfinished Business (Oct., 1968)

Now that we've got 16 films made, with 6 more in the works . . .

15.3.   Radio Free People

[Radio Free People is a Movement group devoted to producing and distributing broadcast tapes and other related activities.]

The First Amendment of the United States Constitution denies to Congress (and by implication and legal precedent to all other branches of government) the power to interfere with the freedom of the public media. It thus affirms the absolute need for the free exchange of ideas in a perpetually self-renewing democracy. Those who would claim, then, that freedom of speech is a functioning reality in America need simply invoke the First Amendment as proof. But nowhere does our Constitution forbid the exercise of private economic control over public awareness.

In American commercial broadcasting the advertiser has ultimate control over program content. He is privileged to withhold the money necessary to support the operation of the inherently expensive electronic media. Such control is all the more difficult to challenge now that not only the advertisers but the media themselves are coming rapidly into the hands of a few worldwide supercorporations. Thus, American radio and television mold public consciousness with a heavy, unrelenting, and increasingly invisible hand, and serve their owners almost to the complete exclusion of genuine public interest.

Not only the commercial advertisements, but the programming itself tends (often subliminally) to reinforce the prevailing "consumption ethic" at the expense of nearly all else. This is the ethic which defines and values a person in terms of the commodities he acquires and in which people themselves become commodities with an assigned marketplace value.

Distraction may be an especial necessity in our high-pressure world. But the level of cultural fare in the mass media has fallen past mediocrity into carefully engineered blandness, helping to perpetuate the crudest, most simpleminded and obedient elements in our culture. Such escape entertainment acts to dull the senses and neutralizes any faint impulse to question the meaning of one's existence, to reconcile the obvious contradictions in our society, or to act upon any healthy convictions which may involve nonconformity.

News management and blackout are everyday occurrences. Selected events are reported, but seldom their content or implications. There are historical and geographic areas from which almost no news or analysis ever reaches us. Such blackouts breed suspicion, rumor and fear, and are understandable only if the intent of the media is to help turn the American public into ignorant, acquiescent soldiers in a Holy War.

"Mass appeal" (catering to the "average" public taste without regard to how it got that way, how it might be deepened and expanded, or even to how it was sampled) is the primary criterion of American broadcasting. This ethic denies a meaningful public voice not only to powerless minority groups, but even to the majority of U.S. citizens, who are unable to articulate—much less form—a politics or a culture other than that which they are fed via the mass media. The faceless "average American" of the TV ratings begins as a statistical abstraction and becomes a literal reality, whose tastes, motivations and politics are exactly those he is conditioned to have.

The small amount of "educational" broadcasting unhappily must justify itself to the various institutional interests which foot most of the bill, and consequently abdicates its responsibility to get to the root of serious public issues.

Meaningful audience feedback, and public dialogue with the media, are minimal.

It has been said that the public media are like the nerves of the organism we call society, and that when the nerves cease to transmit pain the organism lives in imminent danger of a swift and bewildering death. Social malaise pervades America today, as it has for many years, and yet the Federal Communications Commission, under considerable commercial and political pressure, goes no further than to acknowledge a few of the symptoms. It aggravates the causes by tending to rigidify philosophical diversity into only two "sides" (equal time for both) guaranteeing not dialogue or mutual enlightenment, but merely the charade of contest. "Public service" requirements established by the FCC are satisfied in the most perfunctory ways, largely because such programming brings no revenue.

Opinions are predigested, debates rehearsed, program safely prerecorded, and real live spontaneity snuffed out, all under the watchful eye of the commercial or institutional sponsor, and the inscrutable face of the studio clock. Time is money.

Today in America, thought control is a reality.

Radio Free People exists as a functioning alternative to thought control. Our primary goal is to eliminate all restrictions on the freedom of the public media to convey unpopular points of view; a freedom which can be preserved only by its own exercise. Our philosophical perspective is fundamentally radical, which dictates absolute respect for the rights of those who disagree with us to form associations offering information and opinion without employing economic or political coercion in any form whatever.

We hope to achieve our goal by introducing honest, outspoken radio programs, and by helping communities to establish independent local audio and radio outlets and production units. We are also working towards the creation of an international audio network.

Stimulating Independent Production

RFP is compiling a handbook dealing with all essential aspects of creative audio production, geared to intelligent newcomers to the field, who may employ relatively inexpensive, easily obtained equipment. It is very much against our philosophy of decentralism to have all production originate in New York or other large cities. We will emphasize in our catalogs programs of high quality produced on individual initiative or by local groups. We will stress high technical standards, but content always gets priority.

Inaugurating "Community Listening Groups"

It is unrealistic to forget that in many parts of the United States the free expression of unpopular points of view may be—perhaps quite literally— suicidal. In these areas, where obtaining air time on local stations or establishing CCR outlets may be impossible, we will encourage people to create private Community Listening Groups. These would meet, prehaps weekly, in schoolrooms, churches, public halls or private homes. They would have the further advantage of encouraging direct communication among listeners, resulting hopefully in the formation of groups devoted to eradicating basic social ills. A nominal admission fee or contribution could completely defray the cost of ordering RFP tapes. Any surplus could be applied to the financing of action groups. The Community Listening Group amounts to a new medium of communication whose potential is presently unexplored. We think it is limited only by the involvement and imagination of the participants.

RFP also has some further objectives. Among these are:

1. To establish a center for the intensive study of the ways in which thought control is currently being practiced. Special emphasis will be placed upon the conscientious gathering, organization and dissemination of hard evidence.

2. To serve as a nucleus for research into the unique electronic needs of an enlightened radical movement, and to gather engineers and technicians who would in turn train others in the communications arts and technology. Examples of such needs are: low-power radio stations, low-cost recording facilities, a nationwide net or ham-radio and other shortwave communications and news distribution, low-cost hi-fi and sound-reinforcement systems for active people and organizations.

3. To offer a viable, stimulating alternative outlet for the skills and talents of people already active in broadcasting and allied fields, and to assist them in examining the social consequences of what they do.

4. To establish an economically self-sustaining business which would act as a clearing-house for electronic and communications ideas, services, and hardware. Like the many successful Movement printshops and publications, this would help set the movement for social change on its own feet.

15.4.   **Meta Information Applications: Technology in a Radical Context (or The Beginnings of a Radical Technology)**

The computer industry had its origin in the Manhattan Project, which developed the first atomic weapons, and since then virtually all research and development in the computer field has occurred within the military sector of the American economy. This is in no sense accidental; the very structure of American Capitalism requires that the extensive resources necessary for the development of a new technology come from the military. As a result most technical people—scientists, engineers, mathematicians, systems analysts, programmers . . .—are oppressed: they have no control over the content of their work or the use to which it is put. In fact, whether they work for private companies or for universities, the first applications of their work are apt to be for military purposes; and the more interesting the work is technically, the more certain it is that this will be the case.

Scientists who are opposed to the maintenance of the American empire abroad through armed or covert oppression are apt to adopt an ostrich attitude toward the consequences of their work.

They are apt to say that during work hours they develop and implement their own purely technical ideas, and that the uses to which that work is put once it is out of their hands neither is nor can be any concern of theirs. They are the craftsman of knowledge and technique, and cannot know who will use the tools they fashion. As a matter of fact, everyone knows who pays for the research—the Department of Defense—and he who pays the piper calls the tune.

Of course, there may be an occasional surprise for the ostrich, as when an intelligence system for identifying NLF leaders in Vietnamese villages is applied to locating and identifying militants in the ghettoes of Detroit or Cleveland. These surprises can make it more difficult for the scientist to preserve his artificial innocence.

People who write contract proposals know that the way to get money to pay for research is either to do work which the Department of Defense needs, or to appear to do so. Much basic research goes forward under the wretched guise of being useful to the military. But then most of it eventually is.

Scientists tend to be a fairly liberal group. The ideology of the university departments which train them still relies heavily on the myth of the scientist as a lonely (often persecuted) seeker after truth. The work reality is that of someone producing a product according to the requirements of a military machine, with no control over what happens to that product, and often no access to it after it is finished.

Consequently, there is an opportunity for organizing a large group of oppressed workers in critical areas of the American economy. This opportunity has been ignored by the new left—largely because of a tendency to equate technology with the institutions and individuals who control it (in this society).

In any work situation an individual can be radicalized if he can be brought to a recognition not only of the oppressive way in which his work *is* used, but further of how it *could* and *ought* to be used, based on radical political assumptions about how society ought to be constituted.

People in the computer field can be radicalized when they begin to understand what *could* be made of their work, as well as what is presently made of it. A new left computer software company called Meta Information Applications, has been formed to begin the task of radical organizing in the computer field.

M.I.A. is structured as follows. There will be two basic categories of work: (1) Good work—work that the people in the company judge to be worthwhile for radical political and technological purposes. In a good society this is the sort of science directed toward satisfying human needs and oriented toward human values; work that the scientist would be rewarded for pursuing, by the society. In our profit-oriented militaristic empire, we do not assume that good work will be paid for by anyone. (2) Bad work which will be as limited and as harmless as possible—work done simply in order to support the individuals who constitute M.I.A. and to provide whatever resources M.I.A. requires.

American society traps people in a consumption cycle in which the only aim of work is the accumulation of money for the aimless consumption of goods. As they are caught up in this system, people lose sight of their original work goals. M.I.A. confronts this situation directly by creating for people a genuine opportunity to decide that the primary purpose of their work should have radical political and technological ends. The continual choice between the two types of work will provide the participants in M.I.A. with a real chance to break the consumption cycle, thus deepening the process of their own radicalization.

More specifically, M.I.A. proposes the following kinds of work:

Radical Political and Technological Work

a) Theoretical or practical technical work that can contribute to an advancement of the field and raise the level of technical sophistication of the people in the company; for example, the development of better computer techniques to help rationalize economic organizations, or basic theoretical research.

b) Production of educational material on the nature and purpose of the computer industry and affiliated fields; the ultimate aim of such work would be political organizing.

c) Studies of potenital theoretical and political uses of technology, for example, in proposing a radical alternative to contemporary urban life.

d) Use of information technology for movement groups engaged in research and analysis like NACLA (North American Congress on Latin America) or research projects of Students for a Democratic Society or Movement For a Democratic Society, the off-campus branch of SDS.

e) The construction of a technical system that replaces the notion of value based on profit with the notion of value based on human potential.

f) Simplification of bureaucratic work of movement organizations like the Guardian or REP (Radical Education Project).

g) And many more.

Money Work

a) Commercial programming and consulting work for relatively harmless institutions like museums and hospitals (remembering, however, that all sources of money are elements of the capitalist structure).

b) The development and leasing of proprietary programs such as small-scale information retrieval systems.

c) Consulting and research projects for bad customers where the nature of the work permits the incorporation of self-limiting features which void the potential (bad) uses by the customer.

Meta Information Applications needs people who identify strongly with the movement or need a way to do so, and who are computer people, especially programmers and software types. If you are interested in computers because they represent an easy way to make money, forget M.I.A.: it's not for you. M.I.A. will be staffed by people who express their creativity working with computers, but do not want to be creative at the expense of their brothers, in the service of the corporations and corporate armies.

M.I.A. is incorporated in the state of New York. It is capitalized in such a way that putting in money or buying stock gives *no* control over the company. After a probationary period, every person who works for M.I.A. becomes part of the decision-making apparatus: one man, one vote. People will hassle out with each other what work to do and what to get paid.

The military and corporate giants have had a monopoly on technology long enough. Now is the time for us to develop and utilize technology for the people. Now is the time to humanize computer technology. Join the Struggle!!!

15.5.   *RONNIE G. DAVIS:* **Guerrilla Theater: A Way of Life**

[Ronnie G. Davis is the director of the San Francisco Mime Troup, a theatre group which is engaged in agit-prop activities for a cultural alternative. The article was written in November 1967 and published in various papers.]

If the eye be jaundiced, pluk it out.
If the society is rotten, rid theyself of it.
If the world be immoral, change it.

The social assumptions which one accepts will determine the type of theater one creates; street theater, park theater, worker's theater or warmed-over bathroom theater. Theatrical discussions must include the socio-political attitudes of the performers in order to comprehend why some believe theater a tool of change and others "love the theaaaater."

It is of course entertaining to read quasi-revolutionary statements and scurrilous attacks on the theater and society for a readership that is outside the mainstream of action; however, we shall continue in hopes that words on paper may communicate thoughts that will lead to action.

My own theoretical premise:
Western society is rotten in general, capitalist society in the main and U.S. society in the particular.

The basis of the disease is private property; it puts the value on all things in terms of money and possession and splits man's personality into fragmented specialties, thus making him useless on the dance floor yet well-equipped to run an IBM 1324. The idea of community so necessary to a healthy individual is hemmed in by the picket fences surrounding each patch of wealth and the concept of total man has been sutured by idiotic efficient specialization. (This is a simplification of the condition; for further information read: Marx, Freud, Norman O. Brown, H. Marcuse, Regis Debray, C. Guevara, Sun Tzu, Mao Tse-tung, Thorsten Veblen, Carl Oglesby, Gary Snyder, etc.)

For the theater that wishes to change the above and to present alternatives, the problem is in many parts: personnel, program, place, public.

The personnel (actors, directors, tech, etc.) must come from the class they want to change. If you are middle-class dropouts, workers for the working class, Mexican-Americans for Mexican-Americans, etc. Social work theater is out; play for your own kind—you understand them, and they identify with you.

The program depends upon the ingenuity of the group. It may be rock-and-roll music or street puppets, but whatever the style of theater, the content has to be a result of the experience of the personnel. To make this more clear: We asked ourselves in the Mime Troupe how we could stop the war—we then did a satire on our own antiwar pacifism (*L'Amant Militaire* by John Holden and others).

The place you do it in indicates your style/your feelings/your attitudes ... Regis Debray: "The revolutionary in the mountains is different than the talking revolutionary in the city."

Or McLuhan: "Media is part of the message. ... Location is the platform or the sponge for your program."

The public is made up of all those who think they see you in them and all those whom you know; friends, aficionados, tourists and sometimes peers.

It's all very simple on paper, but the making and the proper use of materials depends upon your own anlysis of the needs and possibilities in your own location. To present commedia dell'arte in the middle of Canada may only be a historical exploration. But whatever the presentation, it must engage the common issues, it must become essential to the very existence of the community (i.e., it feeds off and feeds into the community) and it must become a significant moral force.

Success in terms of money, commercial fame, fancy magazine spreads and foundation grants from state, federal or local sources is usually out unless you live in the advanced neosocialist countries where criticism of prevailing conditions is in order. Viz: Jean-Louis Barrault with *The Screens* (National Assembly almost stopped it) or Kenneth Tynan and Laurence Olivier with *Churchill* by R. Hochuth (censored by the Public Censor). In those less than advanced government-subsidized countries, the theater as moral force will, as does the single artist, have to live by its wits. To live by your wits is not to imitate the hustler who is a low-class capitalist, but rather the Latin-American guerrilla who is a low-class socialist.

The object is to work at a presentation that talks to a community of people and that expresses what you (as a community) all know but what no one is saying: thoughts, images, observation and discoveries that are not printed in newspapers nor made into movies: truth that may be shocking and honesty that is vulgar to the aesthete.

—Prepare to go out of business at any moment.

—Prepare to give up your house, your theater or your troupe, and even you ideas if something more essential comes along.

—Travel light and keep in shape.

—Ideas like property cannot be private.

—Nothing is sacred—only sometimes tenderness.

That is the prescription for a theater company that is meaningful. Like a life that is valuable, you must begin by dropping out, getting away, leaving behind, dumping, junking the waste of dishonorable middle-class institutions, groups, ideas and debris of years of decay. (They are cynical, bored and depressed anyway.)

The first step may be dramatic; to walk away or drop out from middle-class America (middle-class America is all over the world). Yet the act of creating a life style that replaces most, if not all, middle-class capitalistic assumptions with a life style that won't quit, is a full-time job of a full-time guerrilla.

Which of course is the only way to live.

15.6.   **The Children's Community**

[The Children's Community of Ann Arbor, Michigan, is an alternative structure to both public and private schools, initiated by a group of parents in Summer 1965. The school, accredited by the state through second grade, is attended by 24 children and has a full-time staff of 6 people.]

Kids in schools today, public and private, are over-taught. Teachers are eager to interpret, point out relationships, generalize, conclude; subjects are neatly divided and organized, sequenced, fit into units. Learning in this situation is memorization. "Discovery learning," much discussed by educators, becomes meaningless when the "discovery" is preplanned, with proper steps, sequence, and predetermined answer. And when there is added to this the created motivation to "get the answer," to gain the teacher's approval, and conform to standards and judgments, learning is no longer self-stimulating and self-rewarding. In The Children's Community, learning is considered a process, in which kids in their desire to make sense of the world are allowed to explore, to perceive relationships, to construct their own principles, make their own discoveries and conclusions. Teaching in this situation, where kids supply their own current, changes its role. Adults, who know the potentialities of materials and activities, are present to make suggestions and ask questions. The Primary Schools in Britain are rapidly changing their structure as it becomes clear that kids can pace themselves, that they know what they are ready to learn, and what their interests are.

In order for this kind of learning to be possible, there must be many different kinds of manipulative and open-ended kinds of materials available, as well as the opportunity for many different activities to go on simultaneously. The relationships between adults and children must be of mutual trust and respect, without force, punishment, grades, or rewards. And it is very important that there be an atmosphere of freedom and acceptance. Kids choose what they want to learn, so that learning is a building onto their interests and experience; it is an integral part of growth. When they ask a question, it is because they want and need to know the answer. Because there are no value judgments made about the importance of one thing over another, or outside standards to strive for, children maintain and strengthen their confidence in their own abilities. They learn whatever is important and relevant to them. Anxiety, to please or to conform, only hampers learning and creates children who are answer-centered, fearful, interested not in learning but in escaping negative judgment. Children in a free situation are allowed to grow, not just in knowledge, but in confidence, curiosity, independence, self-respect.

Another important aspect of The Children's Community is a different approach to integration. Half the children in the school are black, and half are white. But the school is not a melting pot; there is no attempt to assimilate one culture into another. No value judgments are made about background, interests, or language; each child brings something of his own to an accepting environment where there is real exchange. When one culture is considered superior to another in any sense, some children are made to deny themselves and their background to "remake" themselves in another image; the children of the "accepted" culture learn that they are somehow better than other children.

The Children's Community is a community school. Community people and parents assist in the classroom, bringing their own talents and interests, and participate with the staff in making the major policy decisions. We use the community through frequent trips as our extended classroom. This gives kids a sense of the community and how it works, and the opportunity to learn through direct experience.

And, finally, the school exists as a model for this approach to education, which is being more and more widely discussed.

15.7.   **The Radical Education Project: An Introduction and an Invitation.**

[The Radical Education Project, set up in 1966 as a branch of SDS, is today an independent organization.]

REP is an effort by activists and intellectuals to develop a research, education, and publication center designed to strengthen the movement toward a new left in America.

REP invites the participation of all people who identify with the forces of radical democracy in America and abroad. We seek everyone who can make a contribution to the intellectual and educational work of research, speculation, writing, and speaking which is a necessary precondition to effective politics.

REP sees three central needs, and from them it defines three objectives:

1) The need for competent research on the issues of left program and theory. It is no recent revelation that the theoretical framework of the left needs development in terms of the contemporary character of imperialism, capitalism, mass culture, technology, abundance, and in terms of the experience of socialist revolutions and American reforms. Nor is it a new discovery that the left is starved for the hard data, documentation and concrete proposals necessary for effective political action. REP seeks fact and theory and program.

2) The need to educate the student activists who are now drawn toward the radical movement on "single issues" such as Vietnam or poverty, or on "gut reaction" against the whole of American society. Unless action is supported by education youthful recruits are soon lost. A chief job of the student movement is to provide activists with the intellectual equipment and tools of society analysis necessary to sustain radical value commitment once away from the campus. REP seeks to develop needed educational resources.

3) The need to extend the movement beyond students and the most dispossessed. While we can lament the obvious fact that a politically significant left does not exist in America, it is clear that to build such requires striking roots in the professions, among university faculties, in the arts and in many of the "mass organizations" like churches, unions, etc. Not only must the radical sympathies that lie in these diverse social locations be mobilized, but these people must be included and engaged in developing a radical program for the transformation of the particular conditions of their own life and work. REP will try to broaden the scope of the movement.

The narrowness of the movement prevents it from describing tasks which can define for a teacher radical work, as a teacher, for a researcher or a doctor or lawyer, or artist or writer, radical work that draws on his particular talents and affects his particular part of society. The consequence is that most people support occasional protests and otherwise withdraw into cynicism.

We believe that radicals must make their politics manifest in their daily life and work. There is no politically neutral activity. The use of one's talents, the direction of one's energies has effect. The greatest moral and political challenge facing leftists is how both to live in America, to work in the institutions which provide income and status—and yet to change America. We don't have simple answers. And we approach this problem humbly, as one which affects and torments all of us.

REP seeks to create a framework in which people can create for themselves radical vocations which both affirm their individual talents and training and infuse their work with a moral and political purpose.

Our Politics:

REP does not start with a political line. It recognizes that ideology, theory, is essential for a political movement. But ideology is not an intellectual overlay. It must develop organically out of the interaction between political experience and continual analysis. REP hopes to contribute to this process by encouraging analysis, by checking old theory against current fact and experience, and by distilling from experience new theory and new implications for action. We seek clarity of values, precision in social criticism, concreteness in projecting both utopian alternatives and immediate reforms. We seek, by using all the tools of intellect and intuition, a view of the dynamics of history and social change which points to the forms of human intervention which can transform the present into a future fit for man.

While we do not start with a prepackaged ideology, we do begin with political convictions. Formulations are tentative, if only to avoid retreat to the slogans and clichés that have too long dominated the left and impeded self-analysis. Yet, the need for continual refinement of analysis does not imply permanent agnosticism, the postponement of assertion or the retreat from action.

We identify with a community and vision of democratic radicalism, humanistic, committed to individual freedom and the general welfare. There are beliefs shared by this community:

—that the great promise of American abundance is perverted and thwarted by the functioning of contemporary capitalism.

—that privilege, exploitation, inequality as components of class division of labor are no longer necessary, if they ever were, as conditions for abundance.

—that the possibility of still greater wealth for some Americans cannot justify a political economy based on the exploitation of other countries and the continued poverty and oppression of their populations.

—that the forms of democracy cannot be judged in the abstract apart from the actual freedom and humanness which they allow and the actual accountability of the holders of power to those affected by the decisions of power.

—that in America, where formal democracy is highly developed, the important decisions governing the course of social development and the quality of individual life and opportunity are not democratically made or accountable.

—that America is held in political and moral stalemate not only by sheer economic and political force, but also by a deadening ideology of national chauvinism, celebrating the American Way of Life, the American Dream, the American Century.

—that anti-communism is a central element in this ideological manipulation of belief, of what is true, what is good, what is possible, what is necessary. It provides the cover to "rationalize" the most brutal applications of military and economic power.

—that violent revolution is to be recognized and deplored for its high human cost; but that where the oppressed lack political power violent overthrow may be the necessary, though not sufficient, precondition to economic and political freedom.

—that issues such as the war in Vietnam or the oppression of the American underclass cry out for action. The work for long-term research, education, organization, theory, does not relieve the obligation for immediate, passionate protest.

These statements are certainly no catechism. They do begin to define a political perspective. If your disagreements are marginal—questions of qualifiers, semantics, ommissions, implications, emphases—then we consider you a colleague and associate. We invite your participation in REP and in the collective work of clarifying belief and infusing action with analysis. If your disagreements are central and substantive, then we consider you audience and antagonist. We invite your participation in political debate.

REP is non-exclusionist. We reject the rhetoric of anti-communism and the myth of human affairs as a morality play between the forces of good and evil, capitalist freedom and communist slavery. We are open to all those who would feel comfortable in our company. Our criteria of judgment in matters of politics and belief will be facts, argument and values.

The Scope of REP:

The REP staff has prepared a prospectus for the project which describes in detail the range of subject matter which we see as relevant and for which we are recruiting competance. If you are interested in the project, we will send you this prospectus. Here we want simply to indicate the scope of our concern.

I. *Values and Utopias:* The foundation of a movement is its moral position, its aspiration, its assertion of the possible and the desirable. The value issues of democracy, individual freedom, and general welfare in industrial society and in revolutionary ferment are complex, but that does not make them less important. Political judgments are ultimately value judgments. But more than clarity about values in the abstract, we need to develop concrete models of the structure of institutions and social relations that would embody our shared ideals—the nature of work and income, the control of production, the political institutions necessary for participatory democracy, education, family life, etc.

II. *Analysis of Myths and Realities:* The major part of REP work, and the major intellectual and educational need of the movement, is the analysis of what exists, of the myths through which people understand or misunderstand reality, and of the contradictions between myth and reality which provide leverage for change. Special studies will be organized on:

—the American Ideology (pluralism, corporatism, anti-communism, etc.)

—the world reality: international political economy, western Europe, the third world, global conditions and issues.

—problems and structures of the national political economy.

—cultural institutions in tension.

—mass media and the arts.

III. *Strategies for Change:* The movement must analyze not only the targets of change and the forces of motion in society, but also how to orient and develop its own resources in terms of those forces. REP projects five types of studies in this area:

—an analysis of social movements and revolution, both in America and elsewhere, in terms of their relevance to the contemporary situation.

—articulation and debate between various theoretical conceptions of political strategy.

—analysis of the movement itself and identifications of current strategic issues.

—an analysis of agents to reform and potential agents of change in America.

Finally we will try to identify the current issues of struggle in America and make *concrete proposals* relevant to the immediate aspirations of those in struggle, but which would expose the institutional blocks to significant change. Such issues requiring specific analysis and proposals include (besides the War and poverty): university education, urban planning and renewal, automation and employment, income, welfare, collective bargaining, economic development, etc.

We are seeking people who have interests and competance in these areas to work with REP.

. . . .

15.8.   *BOB GOTTLIEB and MARGE PIERCY:* **Movement for a Democratic Society, Beginning to Begin to Begin**

[This article was a working paper for the Vocations for Radicals conference in Boston in March 1968. Bob Gottlieb is working on the Movement for a Democratic Society in New York City. *Radicals in the Professions Newletter,* March 1968.]

The structure and sanctions of this society are not such as to feed contented tired radicals. The system is actively hateful and oppressive even to those who reap moderately high rewards for making it grind on. Perhaps the Norman Rockwell images of the golden age of small-town American life reflect a period when the bourgeoisie did live tranquilly and had a sense of control over their own lives, as well as the lives of their servants and the poor. But the middle class compulsively consumes now to support the system, with a gnawing sense of being cheated and betrayed by the objects which are supposed to define them as knowing, as having arrived. The middle class controls very little that matters—not the conditions or purposes of their work, the myths that pour into their living room every night, the environment they live in. The sense of being manipulated and harassed, the sense of failure is a quiet, daily, muffled thing.

Once you have developed a radical analysis of the society it is hard to forget how to see and hear through the Daily Smog-Smear. Once you have learned to express the contradictions in the society, it is harder than ever to suffer them like the weather. If we do not aim to have the movement geared to producing neurotic 25-year-olds who feel their politics have only disabled them—made it harder for them to make friends, to communicate with others, to raise their children, to live with their consciences, to endure—then we have to make a Movement that provides people with radical work, with radical life style, with radical activities and groups and communities and politics that function off the campus.

We have learned to decode the rules of the university in this society: as manpower channeling device training us for our slots in the corporate machine, as pool of research and devolpment talent for the government and the corporation, as means of penetrating underdeveloped countries through the apparently neutral sector of technological assistance. There are few other institutions for which we have developed as clear an understanding, because what other institutions have we taken on in the same way? We have fought administrations all over the country, done research on university contracting and boards of trustees and real estate holdings. We have developed counter-institutions—free universities and counter-courses—and have attempted to take over pieces of schools to introduce changes that would give students more control. We must take on other major institutions in the same way in order to preserve ourselves alive and to build a Left that will change more than the slogans on buttons people wear.

The MDS (Movement for a Democratic Society) chapters we are beginning to begin to begin have two immediate constituencies. The first is Movement graduates—old SDS people who have drifted away, or who feel the Movement has stayed on the campus and thus shoved them out. Our second constituency is all the discontented, alienated, radical, or potentially radical people who can be brought into the Movement. Some have been through radicalizing experiences in the past. Perhaps they took part in the civil rights movement in the early '60s. Some arrive at opposition to the system through opposition to the war or the draft. Others are fed up because they are sickened by what it means to try to be a good teacher in a coercive school in a rotten city, or a good case worker monitoring the sex lives of poor black women on ADC dole.

Local Chapters—Structure

The campus provides a ready-made definition of a chapter. People who belong to a chapter are joined by the common school environment, common occupation (student), common enemy (represented on campus by the administration), and common prospects (flunk out/drop out/get drafted/stay in/get channeled).

An MDS chapter is not so easy to define. We can form chapters around a profession where people identify strongly with their jobs (e.g., doctor or teacher). If a person has a job he hates or that he works at only to make it from day to day, it would be difficult to imagine he would feel drawn to a roomful of people with similarly lousy jobs, as a basis for starting to talk about their lives or to act politically. An artist or doctor may feel that the most important thing about him is what he does in his field, but someone who proofreads or types or sells or codes is going to reject such an initial definition.

We can create chapters with a loose neighborhood focus—e.g., Upper West Side MDS or Brooklyn-Park Slope MDS. A neighborhood MDS would appear reasonable mainly if a group really wants to organize in their neighborhood or to deal with local problems. However, in some cities women might be reluctant to cross the city at night by themselves but willing to travel to a meeting in their own area. Similarly, in cities with lousy public transportation, a neighborhood MDS might be convenient.

Chapters can be made up of people who already know each other. We might as well take advantage of patterns of association in trying to build stronger patterns. The temptation for such a group is to act out personal tensions in their politics, or to soften into Local Friday Night Socialist Coffee and Cake and Gossip Wing-Ding. If an effort to get people moving on projects is consciously made, then the ready-made community of friends can weld itself into a solid, viable political unit.

Chapters can coalesce around a common attitude. The Lower East Side UPAGAINSTTHEWALLMOTHERFUCKERS are united by a desire for direct action and small street demonstrations, and by a common tough free-wheeling style. In like manner, chapters can form around a common concern such as urban problems (e.g., air pollution, transit system, welfare) or research into the power structure.

In any city, chapters can coexist of all types: built around a common profession, a common neighborhood, a common interest or lifestyle, a common acquaintance with each other, or the desire to work together on some project. The common denominator could be a randomly selected bunch of people who share only the expressed desire to start an MDS or relate to the Movement in some undefined way. A common denominator could be young women with children who are stuck home and want to help each other get into the Movement. An MDS chapter could consist of a group that performs guerrilla theater together or a commune which shares a house or a pad and wants to put out an underground paper or organize in their area.

Above all we need to stay loose in imagining what forms MDS chapters will take. A person might belong to more than one, and groups should be communicating all the time at least on the level of "we are doing this action or this piece of research or talking about this problem." People should circulate among groups where there is something going on they want to deal with.

What we *can* begin to define for MDS chapters are functions they must perform if they are to form an emerging powerful Left in America and help their members to survive and grow as radicals. Some tasks are aimed at survival and some at service to the Movement and some more at making the Movement grow—which is the only way we all may survive. Different chapters will put emphasis on different functions, and during its history any chapter will vary its emphasis according to the needs and experiences of its body and the political situation it swims in.

Local Chapters—Functions

1. *To help the people in it to relate to the Movement.*

In New York, for example, there are already a number of going Movement projects which young adults can work on: *CAW,* the radical arts magazine; the *Rat,* the radical underground paper; the Newsreel Project for making documentary films; the projected *Underground Underground,* a newspaper to be passed out on the subway to give a radical slant to the sort of slice of life and scandal and horror stories that the *Daily News* fattens on; the SDS weekly 15-minute program on WBAI-FM; draft counselling; drop-out counselling; planning and taking part in demonstrations such as the garbage demonstration at Lincoln Center (initiated by an MDS chapter) or the coming *Times* demonstration. One of the regular tasks of an MDS apparatus in any city has to be to acquaint members with what's happening.

However, working on a project is for many not a sufficient means of relating to the Movement or surviving as a radical, and simply being plugged into an existing project is no replacement for being part of an MDS group.

It is equally important for MDS people to take political roles in shaping the Movement, to argue their opinions at workshops, at councils, to introduce resolutions, write for New Left Notes and the regional newsletters, visit SDS chapters and talk to chapter people. Older radicals can talk to college chapter people about what it will be like in the real world in whatever they are training for. Many chapters would find it useful to have a radical doctor, a radical lawyer or engineer visist them as a kind of counter-placement service.

Finally, chapters can initiate and carry out projects of their own. For instance, teachers and city planners could unite to produce a radical critique of the Bundy report on New York schools. Artists and Writers MDS in New York is coordinating an Anti-State Fair, an anti-imperialist exposition for the first weekend of the Ten Day Spring Offensive of SDS. It aims at exposing the imperialist nature of the United States, how the power elite channels and manipulates and colonizes you; and presenting ways to get out of the system and fight it—not just a horror show but alternatives. It will also be used to recruit people into the Movement and into the demonstrations and other activities of the Ten Days.

2. *To provide a two-way flow of radical analysis and information.*

The Movement can help MDS members fight the way society impinges on them, from reading the morning paper as a form of research to interpreting the form of co-optation such as the McCarthy campaign. The Movement must speak to the oppression of its people after they have passed through the manpower channeling devices of the university factory and have been assimilated into the production/consumption apparatus of domestic imperialism. It is people who have worked in the corporations, taught in the schools, practiced medicine in the clinics and done research under the massive umbrella of the Department of Defense contracting, who have the most to say about the subtle forms of middle class oppression, the pressure for consumption, the powerlessness and alienation of the physically comfortable. MDS members can contribute a critical attack of the institutions they have come against, either in the form of suggestions for organizing with these institutions or in the form of defining what a radical version of those institutions would be, or the ways in which they actually function as opposed to the rhetoric of their mask.

An artists' group is gathering material for a pamphlet exposing the Museum of Modern Art. If when they have written such a pamphlet, they then organize a demonstration, perhaps to go in and change the name of "Guernica" to "Vietnam" during one of the regular museum talks in front of that painting, we will be linking functions one and two in a politically useful way.

Further, because MDS people have jobs and contacts in various professions and institutions, we are in a position to provide information and intelligence that full-time organizers and full-time Movement research people may need but cannot get access to.

3. *Working inside institutions.*

In order to develop a serious political movement, the New Left has to begin to create radical programs and strategies within the institutions of America. We have begun to do this within the university. Outside the university, serious radical organizing has been minimal. As students graduate they enter, broadly speaking, two sets of institutions—both key to the functioning of America Capitalism. One set, work-place institutions, contain a variety of roles for which one is trained by the university. These range from service of client-oriented work (health, social work, city planning, law) to roles within the productive or technological sphere (engineers, technicians) to cultural, educational, informational work (artists, college teachers, research scientists).

The other set, leisure-time and consumer institutions, equally shapes roles in which middle class participation and acceptance are crucial for the system to expand and reap profits.

The specifics of that institutional strategy are far from well-formulated. In fact, a task of MDS chapters is to begin to specify such strategies. For one, our radical values tell us that the content and purpose of work and consumption *must* be based on human rather than profit needs. That assumption will cause us to create projected radical alternatives to what exists today. In effect, an organizing strategy. Secondly, we see the need for popular control over the institutions of work and consumption. As in the student movement, we have to begin to see who specifically controls the institutions we inhabit, and to start to raise consciousness so that people can say not simply that we must control the decisions that affect our lives, but that we must control the institutions we participate in. In effect, a strategy for power.

4. Creating counter-institutions.

About four years ago, a number of people within the New Left worked out a notion of parallel institutions and/or counter-communities. They felt that, especially within ghetto life, the construction of viable alternative institutions would serve as a radical focus. People would drop out of existing structures and bring closer the point of revolution (i.e. total disregard of existing institutions and the growth of counter-communities turned into the real communities of social life). This thinking culminated in the Assembly or Unrepresented People, which symbolized an alternate political structure of "American democracy." However, the nature of these parallel institutions was symbolic and at best they were politically useful insofar as they raised people's consciousness. Most of these attempts were seen in a deceptive manner (say, the community of love) in that their ostensible purpose (a real alternative) had little to do with their actual nature (a symbolic protest).

In the last year or two, another kind of parallel or counter-institution has developed within the New Left. These institutions, however, have concrete political objectives. They have come not *uniquely* out of the need of political and social opposition to current institutions, but as well out of the *needs* of the Movement. The Movement needs a political paper to provide information and analysis of what concerns it, material that cannot be found in existing media. The Movement has people who can write, gather information, have general technical skills (or can learn them) concerning the mechanics of a newspaper. Thus, the underground paper. The political critique of the existing media is inherent in the nature of the underground paper. For it to become a viable political instrument it has to be seen in an organizing context. People who read it and who are not tied to the Movement can be turned on by such a paper. It can be an organizing tool as well to those trained media technicians (journalists, for example) who see the quality and value of an underground paper.

The Newsreel Project is another example of a media counter-institution. Radical documentary filmmakers do their films as they wish, controlling the process, setting their own professional standards, and using the products as direct and exciting Movement propaganda. When Newsreel Project people film a demonstration, they do so from the inside as participants. They do not change the nature of meetings by introducing the alien or hostile eye of uninvolved observers. They participate and record and share. The excellence of the film is in itself a criticism of establishment efforts to report the same events, when they are reported at all. They distribute their films in part through existing institutions, a way of criticizing the system's products from within. Further, when the Newsreel Project workers show their films at colleges, often they make a political presentation. They can also politicize filmmakers alienated from the dominant media. The film showings are thus an organizing tool.

The counter-institution also has a service function. For the MDS constituency—people out of school and into jobs, maybe with a profession to which we are emotionally committed, maybe with dependents or habits of comfort or interest to support—we *must* work out alternative jobs, alternative ways of living in the society, alternative ways of bringing up and educating children. We need counter-forms of recreation and enjoyment and communication to replace the cultural manipulations, the addiction to consumption, the passivity of packaged entertainment, the subtle conditioning and gross lies of the media.

We must take into account the degrees to which a person identifies with his work. His satisfaction in it must be differentiated from the effect of the institution in which the work is done (e.g. the good kindergarten teacher in the concentration camp school). No matter what we do, the system makes it distasteful. If creation feels good, marketing is full of anxiety, compromise and competitiveness. You and your work become commodities on a par with Kleenex and hair conditioner. The systems analyst finds his beautiful new programming language used to control riots in the ghettoes next summer.

People in service professions, the arts and sciences often do strongly identify with their work. What are you? I am a physicist. I am a doctor. I am a sculptor in welded steel. People who cannot abandon their profession without feeling mutilated have the most immediate need for work-place counter-institutions. These new work-places must enable a man to sort out what is truly creative in his field, the real meat of it, from the part that is merely professional obfuscation.

For a doctor, this sorting out might mean setting up a truly radical health service, a clinic in the ghetto to provide not only medical services but to teach the skills people can perform for each other. We must separate out the truly skilled and creative part of being a doctor and eliminate those activities created by the profit-oriented health industry (you too can make $100,000 a year by prescribing our diet pills), and those parts which are obfuscation and professionalese invented and protected by the desire for prestige and for private property purchased by years of peonage in medical school and internship.

Counter-institutions by their existence liberate the imaginations of people within the system. Every counter-institution answers those questions so often posed to the Movement: But what do you want? What else is there? Thus counter-institutions have political as well as service and survival functions. Unlike the parallel institutions, counter-institutions have real substantive purpose, filling both political and service needs of the movement.

5. *The Movement employment agency.*

This service would guide people to "minimal" jobs in any field they are willing to work in—jobs that pay enough to live on and involve the least hassle of those available inside the system. One Movement poet has a part-time job selling tickets. He works from five to nine—it is a relaxed period in his day—he uses the phone and makes a living. When such a job falls vacant, we should move another person into it. Somebody else works as research assistant to a sympathetic professor, doing her own Movement power structure research. Someone else has a job in a loose interracial private school where teachers are allowed to follow some of their own ideas. The idea is to free the person to spend his energies on Movement projects and support himself without feeling compromised or ground under.

6. *Your politics is your life: a sense of community.*

The Movement is one of the only places where people can and actually do try to deal with each other as human beings, after college. However, if the only alternative we can offer adults is to join the Movement and live like the younger organizers, or stay put and give money, we have little to offer. The basically religious stipulation to leave all and cleave only unto us will produce a hard core devoted cadre of the pure, but will not organize enough people to change one stop sign. And it will not speak, except on the level of daydream, to the man who has kids to support. We must develop a radical community of young adults both working in the Movement and working in the establishment institutions. We must do this in spite of obvious conflicts of economic levels and life styles between MDS people and the younger, full-time Movement people.

This conflict of life styles will probably be strongest with the MDS people who are working within establishment institutions, organizing there and pushing for structural changes. That is a role with inherent tension anyhow, and if tension is added coming from life style—the organizer at IBM in his grey flannels and attaché case *vs.* the "real" SDS organizer in workshirt and bare feet—we might as well give up functioning there altogether, because we will punish the people who try to carry it out.

Some of the difficulty of SDS people in accepting older folks as real radicals stems from the feeling that poor whites and blacks, the working class are the real oppressed and thus the only ones worth identifying with. Since Movement people have to survive and often survive well on less than welfare clients, the more affluent life-style of MDS people and potential MDS people makes their noses crinkle with mistrust. But we have to understand, to believe, to act out, that oppression in this society does not consist *only* of low income, poor housing and racism. If that were the case, the millenium would come with a guaranteed annual income and the War on Poverty would be the revolution.

We can develop our sense of middle class oppression by remembering how we passionately do not want to be like our parents, what we revolted from. We need to define middle class lives of desperation. We must articulate how the oppression that we experience is real and politically valid, and that the quality of our lives is a potent political issue. It is infinitely easier for us to feel anger about the direct brutal exploitation of Bolivian tin miners or Vietnamese peasants than the soft, genteel exploitation of suburban housewives—because the first is naked, murderous oppression—but we cannot build a Left in America simply on identification with peasants and guerrillas in the Third World.

Furthermore, the roles that university-trained people fulfill are crucial to the functioning of the economy. University-trained workers are instrumental in maintaining an economic system that relies more and more on advanced technological processes and the distribution and use of information. Stockpiling is essential to a contemporary industrial plant, and stockpiling processes are in the hands of technically skilled workers.

Further, leisure-time and consumption, essential components of the American system of domination and control, rely heavily on middle-class acceptance and passivity. Who buys the automobiles, television sets, and most of the consumer durable goods? Read any issue of *Fortune,* and one doesn't have to guess that the steady and increasing consumption of durable goods is necessary to keep American Capitalism thriving. And Capitalism has developed the social and political manipulative techniques—such as advertising, planned obsolescence, and style changes—that damn well force consumption down our throats. That is real and political oppression. The development of a movement community is a real response to oppression and as it stands today is perhaps the most substantive opposition to the key forms of oppression in the society. Perhaps even a vanguard opposition.

7. We are all organizers.

The people who should organize among the university-trained working class are members of the university-trained working class. Every MDS person is an organizer if he can speak and write to his friends and associates. We need on all levels to move from middle class self-hatred, from a feeling of personal failure or personal frustration, to a sense of middle class oppression as a political issue which we can answer in our own lives politically together and use to reach others and join them with us in the Movement.

8. We must find ways to give financial support without feeling used.

Every MDS group should support its own functioning: the newsletters, mailings, phone bills, mimeographing that go into maintaining such groups and communicating between them. If there are Movement people who have left their jobs and are spending time on MDS organizing or projects, then the MDS groups should support them. If a particular group contains an organizer, it would be reasonable for the group to take care of him.

In addition, we can use our jobs. Some of us could hire Movement people as research assistants or part-time secretaries. We can provide occasional use of offices, machines, typewriters, darkrooms, cameras, tape recorders, perhaps a big room for a meeting. We may have access to a xerox or mimeograph machine. We may be able to get office supplies—paper, ribbons, pens, stencils. Perhaps we have a professional discount on books or other useful objects.

We can help each other by sharing skills. A dentist can fix teeth. We can share objects such as a car or a washing machine. We can use our skills in ways useful to the Movement, like taking photographs of a demonstration for use in an underground paper.

This list of functions and of ways in which an MDS can emerge is not intended to be a closed system but only suggestions which can open discussion and provoke experimentation. It is imperative that a real MDS be created within the next year for SDS and the Movement to survive. The building of a city-wide MDS will take time, hard work and patience. This is the first step.

FURTHER READINGS

Boyd, Malcolm (ed.). *The Underground Church*. London: Sheed and Ward, 1967.

Estrin, Ellen Elizabeth, and Folson, Michael B. "Radical Theater . . . Who Does It Speak To?" *The Movement,* May 1967.

Gitlin, Todd. "Guerrillas Hit New York." *San Francisco Express Times,* July 31, 1968.

Guardian. "The Movement and the Message." November 1968.

Haber, Barbara and Al. "Getting by with a Little Help From Our Friends." Radical Education Project, July 1967.

Harrell, William. "Antitotalism and Counter Society." *Liberation,* May/June 1966.

James, Melody. "Theater That Does Something." *The Movement,* April 1967.

Junker, Howard. "The Free University: Academy for Mavericks." *The Nation,* August 16, 1965.

Pepper, Thomas. "Growing Rich on the Hippie." *The Nation,* April 29, 1968.

Radical Education Project. "Radicals in Professions," selected papers, October 1967.

Valdez, Luis Miguel. "El Teatro Campesino." *Ramparts,* July 1966.

16

In Search of a
Class Analysis

16.1. *GREGORY CALVERT:* **In White America: Radical Consciousness and Social Change**

[The following speech, given by Gregory Calvert, national secretary of SDS, at the Princeton Conference of February 1967, marks a new approach of the student movement *vis à vis* radical activity inside the university. Calvert is now working on a book on *The New Left and the New Capitalism. The National Guardian,* March 25, 1967.]

Let me begin by telling you a story which I recently heard. It is a story about the guerrilla forces in Guatemala and about how they work. I do not know what image you might have in your head about the mode of operation of Guatemalan guerrillas—I am not even certain about the accuracy of this story. But, in any case, it makes sense to me and it speaks to me about who we are—the new radicals.

It is said that when the Guatemalan guerrillas enter a new village, they do not talk about the "anti-imperialist struggle" nor do they give lessons on dialectical materialism—neither do they distribute copies of the "Communist Manifesto" or of Chairman Mao's *On Contradiction.* What they do is gather together the people of the village in the center of the village and then, one by one, the guerrillas rise and talk to the villagers about their own lives: about how they see themselves and how they came to be who they are, about their deepest longings and the things they've striven for and hoped for, about the way in which their deepest longings were frustrated by the society in which they lived.

Then the guerrillas encourage the villagers to talk about their lives. And then a marvelous thing begins to happen. People who thought that their deepest problems and frustrations were their individual problems discover that their problems and longings are all the same—that no one man is any different than the others. That, in Sartre's phrase, "In each man there is all of man." And, finally, that out of the discovery of their common humanity comes the decision that men must unite together in the struggle to destroy the conditions of their common oppression.

That, it seems to me, is what we are about.

The movement for radical social change in America is going through an important period of self-reexamination which is reflected in a myriad of ways: the often compulsive concern with ideology, the desperate attachment to militant tactics, the frustration, pessimism and despair in the life of full-time activists. This crisis has its roots in a very important failure—the failure of the Southern-based movement in the black community to mobilize a sufficiently powerful mass of people to alter the American system in any significant way. As a friend of mine, long-time SNCC staff member, put it: "We thought we could move enough people to move America, but America turned out to be incredibly more rigid than we had ever expected. We were on the move, but America just wouldn't budge. I look back now and wonder what sort of simple ideas we must have had in our heads to have ever believed in that possibility."

If we face up to this crisis honestly, if we look American reality hard in the face, two things emerge. First, we have to admit that—like it or not—

we live in urban industrial capitalist America, in white America and not in the rural South. We owe SNCC a deep debt of gratitude for having slapped us brutally in the face with the slogan of black power, a slogan which said to white radicals: "Go home and organize in white America which is *your* reality and which only you are equipped to change." Secondly, we are thus forced to ask ourselves whether in white America there exists the possibility for organizing a truly radical, an authentically revolutionary movement for change. Finally, we must face the fact that unless such a potential exists, then the basic arguments of the Progressive Labor Party or other Third-World oriented groupings bear serious reading. If a mass movement cannot be built in white America, then individuals with revolutionary hopes and perspectives must orient themselves toward Third-World revolutions and develop those methods of activity which will maximize the impact of peasant-based revolutions on the structure of the American imperialist monster. The problem is a search for a constituency, for an agent of social tranformation, for "the revolutionary class." If no such constituency can be developed, then our only hope lies with external agencies, with revolutionary developments in the Third World.

Let me say that I am not overflowing with optimism regarding the possibility of building such a movement. There are two things which go through my mind: 1) American corporate capitalism is an incredibly brutal and dehumanizing system, whether at home or abroad, but, 2) it is also fantastically adept at masking its reality at home. Some have called it "benevolent fascism," and there lies a key to its operation: it operates domestically by intimidation, regimentation, and conditioning, and prefers not to use overt repressive force. Why? because to do so is to reveal itself for what it is, and to open the possibility of rebellion.

The importance of American aggressive imperialism for the development of a domestic movement, the importance of Vietnam and the Vietnams to come, is that it reveals America to America, that the liberal facade is shattered and the American expansionist system reveals its brutality and aggressiveness and its dehumanizing horror in all its nakedness.

I am going to speak today about the problem of consciousness in American society and about the possibility of developing radical or revolutionary consciousness. I approach the problem of organizing from this viewpoint because 1) the objective conditions of oppression in America seem to be manifest and 2) because those objective conditions are not perceived, and 3) because the major problem to which organizers must address themselves in this period is the problem of false consciousness.

Let me posit a first principle: All authentically revolutionary movements are struggles for human freedom.

Contrary to what was suggested here last evening, revolutionary mass movements are not built out of a drive for the acquisition of more material goods. That is a perversion and vulgarization of revolutionary thought and a misreading of history. Revolutionary movements are freedom struggles born out of the perception of the contradictions between human potentiality and oppressive actuality. Revolutionary consciousness interprets those social economic and political structures which maintain the existing gap between potentiality and actuality as the objective conditions of oppression which must be transformed. Revolutionary consciousness sees the transformation of those oppressive conditions as the act of liberation and sees the realization of the previously frustrated human potentiality as the achievement of freedom. The bonds of oppression are broken and the new reality is constructed.

What is fundamental to this process is the mass perception of the contradiction between potentiality and actuality. In a given hitsorical situation that contradiction may take the concrete form of economic deprivation in the face of the possibility of material abundance and the struggle for liberation may take the form of a drive to eliminate the conditions which prevent the achievement of that abundance. In a situation of economic abundance, the drive for freedom will rest on different perceptions and will set different goals. But the struggle in either case is a struggle for freedom, the form of which depends on the given stage of historical development—that is, on the level of development of human potentiality.

There is only one impulse, one dynamic which can create and sustain an authentic revolutionary movement. The revolutionary struggle is always and always must be a struggle for freedom. No individual, no group, no class is genuinely engaged in a revolutionary movement unless their struggle is a struggle for their own liberation.

The point which is important to understand is clearly illustrated by the difference between radical or revolutionary consciousness and "liberal" consciousness. The profound gap which separates a liberal reform movement from a revolutionary freedom movement is revealed in the dynamics of the participants.

Liberal reformists (including revisionist social democrats inside and outside the CP) react out of guilt motivation, that is, the contradiction to which they address themselves is the contradiction between what they have (comfort, goods, security) and who they are (which they posit as the universally human), on the one hand, and what others (the poor) do not have (the poverty and lack of opportunity of the poor) and what others are (the immediacy of satisfactions in underclass life perceived as uncivilized behavior). Their conscience reveals to them the injustice of their unearned position and their own self-image, as universally valid for humanity, is challenged by the life-style of the underclass. Their response is to close the gap, to resolve the contradictions and the accompanying psychological tensions by means of activity to "raise" the underprivileged to their own social-economic level and to draw them into the same nexus of relationships in order to impose on them their own image of humanity.

The liberal reformist is always engaged in "fighting someone else's battles." His struggle is involved in relieving the tension produced by the contradictions between his own existence and life-style, his self-image, and the conditions of existence and life-style of those who do not share his privileged, unearned status.

The liberal reformist accepts and defends his own self-image, his own vision and experience of humanity, and generalizes it to all men. He wants everyone to be "white, happy, and middle class." Should those toward whom his good works are directed (e.g., SNCC with its statement of Black Power) ever challenge his view of the human-universal, he reacts by rejecting them, however subtly or brutally.

The liberal does not speak comfortably of "freedom" or "liberation," but rather of justice and social amelioration. He does not sense himself to be unfree. He does not face the contradictions between his own human potential, his humanity, and the oppressive society in which he participates. To deal with the reality of his own unfreedom would require a shattering re-evaluation of his subjective life-experience.

Liberal consciousness is conscience translated into action for others. It may or may not include alienation or a sense of the meaningless of one's experience. When these latter elements are present, they are interpreted in a personalistic fashion (as personal guilt) and the solutions envisioned are privitized (e.g., a trip or a trip to the psychiatrist). Liberal consciousness is rarely consciousness of personal oppression, and, therefore, interprets oppression in the society as based on "misunderstanding" or "irrationality." Individual therapy or cultural liberalization and education are seen as the means of correction.

Radical or revolutionary consciousness perceives contradiction in a totally different fashion. The gap is not between oneself, what one is, and the under-privileged but is the gap between "what one could be" and the existing conditions for self-realization. It is the perception of oneself as unfree, as oppressed —and finally it is the discovery of oneself as *one of the oppressed* who must unite to transform the objective conditions of their existence in order to resolve the contradiction between potentiality and actuality. Revolutionary consciousness leads to the struggle for one's own freedom in unity with others who share the burden of oppression. It is, to speak in the classical vocabulary, class consciousness because it no longer sees the problem as someone else's, because it breaks through individualization and privitization, because the recognition of one's own unfreedom unites one in the struggle of the oppressed, because it posits a more universally human potentiality for all men in a liberated society.

The problem in white America is the failure to admit or recognize un-freedom. It is a problem of false consciousness, that is, the failure to perceive one's situation in terms of oppressive (class) relationships. Only when white America comes to terms with its own unfreedom can it participate in the creation of a revolutionary movement.

When we have talked about the "new radicalism," about the "freedom movement," with a passionate conviction, we have been talking about a movement which involves us, you and me, in a gut-level encounter with, disengagement from, and struggle against the America which keeps us in bondage. It may have begun in a very personalistic fashion, out of a private sense of our individual alienation from the U.S. corporate-liberal capitalist monster and from "the bomb" which was its logical but unthinkable con-clusion. But, it has and must move beyond the level of our own bewilderment, confusion, and despair about America. It moves to the final realization of our common oppression.

We should realize that Marx was quite correct when he said the true revolutionary consciousness was class consciousness. What he meant by that was that in order to change society people must realize that they are united in common struggle for their own liberation from objective conditions of oppression. Like the Guatemalan guerrillas of whom I spoke, he was saying to people that their struggle was the struggle of unfree men—not for individual salvation—but a struggle for collective liberation of all unfree, oppressed men.

What has held the new radicalism together, what has given it its life and vitality, has been the conviction that the gut-level alienation from America-the-Obscene-and-the-Dehumanized was a sincere and realistic basis for challenging America. What has often left the new radicals impotent and romantic is their failure to understand the dynamics of the society which produced their gut-level alienation, that is their failure to understand that what seemed humanly and emotionally real could be understood in terms of a fundamental and critical analysis of American corporate-liberal capitalism. There was a crying out of their own being against America, but a failure to understand why that revolt was authentically related to the necessity and the possibility of revolutionizing America.

That situation has begun to change. The new radicals are beginning to produce an analysis of America which enables them to understand themselves and the greater reality of American society in a way which authenticates their own revolt as a realistic basis for understanding the way in which we can be freed. It begins to relate the anarchist demand, "I want freedom," to the revolutionary socialist analysis which points the way to collective liberation.

If the analysis is correct and if false consciousness is the major obstacle to organizing a revolutionary movement, then it would seem to follow that our primary task at this stage of development is the encouragement or building of revolutionary consciousness, of consciousness of the conditions of unfreedom. A question immediately arises however—"To what extent is consciousness of unfreedom subject to the influence of variables which are independent of the question of economic remuneration or consumption level?" That is to say, since the society can buy people off with goods, are there other sufficiently potent radicalizing experiences apart from economic deprivation which radicals can work with?

This is an important and complex question. It is perhaps the failure of the old left to arrive at a satisfactory answer to that question which was responsible for its fervent attachment to the concept of the inevitability of the collapse of capitalism—the catastrophic event which would reveal both the objective contradictions of the system and create the proper subjective response on the part of the exploited.

Without necessarily ruling out the possibility of such an economic cataclysm in the capitalist world, the new left is hardly notable for its faith in the inevitability of the event. Thus deprived of the *deus ex machina* which the old left was certain existed in the wings, we new leftists have been driven by a special urgency which gives rise to a variety of inventive activities designed to reveal to people their unfreedom and to offer them alternatives and hope. Certainly the organizing of the new radicals has been one of their most characteristic features.

In the end, however, our ability to organize and to radicalize in an effective manner depends on more than our sensitivity to individual human beings. It requires the kind of careful analysis and conceptualizing which has produced the so-called Port Authority Statement (I hope you realize that the intent of the title was humorous!). The whole notion of the "new working class" provides a powerful tool for understanding the present structure of advanced industrial capitalism.

First, it breaks through the "myth of the great American middle class." Not only are millions of Americans held captive by that notion, but it has also been a major psychological obstacle for most radicals. If white America is mostly middle class, and if being middle class means not being oppressed, then there is no possibility for finding the resources upon which a radical movement can be built in white America. What we have come to understand is that the great American middle class is not middle class at all. None of the 19th Century definitions of the bourgeoisie apply; not the upper bourgeoisie—the owners of capital; not the petty bourgeoisie—the owners of small property; not, finally, even the professional bourgeoisie, which in the 19th Century meant those favored few whose education gave them independence within the economic system. The vast majority of those whom we called the middle class must properly be understood as members of the "new working class": that is, as those workers who fill the jobs created by a new level of technological development within the same exploitive system.

Secondly, it enables us to understand the special role of students in relation to the present structure of industrial capitalism. Students are the "trainees" for the new working class and the factory-like multiversities are the institutions which prepare them for their slots in the bureaucratic machinery of corporate capitalism. We must stop apologizing for being students or for organizing students. Students are in fact a key group in the creation of the productive forces of this super-technological capitalism. We have organized them out of their own alienation from the multiversity and have raised the demand for "student control." That is important: because that is precisely the demand that the new working class must raise when it is functioning as the new working class in the economic system. It is that demand which the system cannot fulfill and survive as it is. That is why it is potentially a real revolutionary demand in a way that demands for higher wages can never be.

Thirdly, we can see that it was a mistake to assume that the only radical role which students could play would be as organizers of other classes. It is still important, vitally important that student organizers continue to involve themselves in ghetto organizing, in the organizing of the underclass. That work is a vital part of the movement and it is first from ghetto community organizing that the demand for control was clearly articulated. But it is now important to realize that we must organize the great majority of students as the trainees of the new working class. We must speak to them of the way in which the new working class is created—of the meaningless training which is passed off as education and of the special coercive devices like the Selective Service System with its student deferments designed to channel them into the multiversity.

Finally, we must be sensitive to those places in the social strata where false consciousness is being broken down, where the middle-class myth is crumbling, where groups are beginning to struggle for their own freedom. In terms of the concept of the new working class, certain groups have begun to respond: social workers, teachers, the medical profession. All of these are service groups, it is true, and, interestingly, there is in all these areas a characteristic contradiction between a high level of articulated aspiration and increasingly oppressive conditions. We need radicals in all those areas in order to articulate more clearly the political ramifications of the demands for control and meaningful work.

Though there has as yet been no mass organizing on the part of engineers, it is encouraging to note that an engineering student at Iowa State University (the cow college of the corn belt) was just elected student body president on a platform calling for student control which brought nearly 10,000 students to the ballot boxes.

We must be sensitive to the fact that a mass movement in America will take time to develop and that it requires the involvement of a broad range of social strata, old and new working class, students and underclass. What counts is that America is beginning to break up, that the myth of the great American middle class is crumbling, that white Americans as well as black Americans are beginning to recognize their common oppression and are raising their demands for freedom which can be the basis of a movement which could revolutionize America.

16.2.   *JOHN and MARGARET ROWN-*
                                                TREE: **Youth as a Class**

[The following is an abridged version of an article which appeared in the February 1968 issue of the *International Socialist Journal:* a rewritten version has also been published on *Our Generation,* summer 1968. John Rowntree teaches economics at York University and Margaret Rowntree teaches political science at the University of Toronto.]

The essential exploited class for the perpetuation of the existing economic system is now the young. The young occupy the critical work-places: They man the war machine and the idea factories. They absorb by their own sacrifice the surplus that the irrational economic system cannot dispose of.

But, one may ask, how long can this process continue? How long can young people be kept out of the labor force? How large can the army and the graduate schools become? It is our thesis that the exploitation of the young is reaching its outer limits, and that, for the stability of the administrative imperialist system, it has already gone too far.

As happens when a class is exploited, young people are beginning to become aware of their exploitation. Many have taken the essential first step to consciousness, the rejection of the present system, and are available to develop a consciousness of themselves as a class.

A significant number have gone even farther and are coming to see a relation between what is wrong with their position in American society and what is wrong with that society as a whole.

Alienation and Class Formation

If the young have become a class of soldiers and students, then, like all exploited classes, they are subjected to alienation of their labor. Not only, however, is the young worker's product taken from him but the dilemmas of monopoly capitalism make his work increasingly unproductive and therefore subjectively repugnant.

Yet the labor of youth is so essential to the perpetuation of the administrative imperialist system that rejecting this alienated labor meets strenuous attempts at repression, which fosters still greater group identity. In addition, the young are alienated not only from their labor, but also from their own potential.

By denying that young people are adults for longer and longer periods after biological maturity is reached, the system denies young people the "traditional" integrated personalities of manhood or womanhood.

Alienated labor and the alienation of one's own future lead to the many subjective expressions of discontent that psychologists and sociologists discuss as the "problems of youth." Although some of these analysts offer valuable insights, they do not see that the young are wretched for systemic rather than moral-aesthetic reasons.

But how can we talk about the oppression of youth in the Great Society where so much is promised? Young people do grow up, after all. Would not a little patience on the part of the young, a little attention to their studies and their patriotic obligations, guarantee them the benefits of the two-car, three-car garage Great Society of Tomorrow?

Our answer is no. Although the young may grow older, youth *as a class* cannot be satisfied with a promise of benefits of monopoly capitalism today. "Youth" comprises a constantly increasing number of years. In the interim, youth are promised prosperity only to be unemployed, under-employed, or unproductively employed; they are promised security only to be denied even the dignity of having their maturity recognized.

Let us look first at the objective alienation of youth, the appropriation of the product of their labor for the ends of others. Marx views man's capacity for labor as his distinguishingly human characteristic, and the appropriation of human labor in the capitalist production process as the essence of its dehumanization. When a man's product is taken, the relation of the worker to his world is irremediably deformed by the inhuman quality of his work situation.

In advanced capitalist society, not only is the worker's product alienated from him, but increasingly the labor itself does not even produce a meaningful product to be taken away. Baran and Sweezy make clear that unproductive work is an important way of absorbing the surplus that threatens to suffocate advanced capitalist society. And the young not only are subjected to classic alienation of their labor but also are almost wholly employed in unproductive work.

If the soldier does his work badly, he bears the double burden of alienation and poor craftsmanship. But if he does his work well, his double burden is alienation and collaboration with the morally reprehensible regime that is exploiting him. His labor is coerced (either through literal conscription or through the denial of significant alternatives).

However, the authorities are eager to prevent the soldier from becoming conscious of his alienation. Soldiers develop certain skills, such as killing, that governors are reluctant to see used for personal ends. This is why citizen armies are preferred. It is hoped that thorough patriotic indoctrination can cause them to refrain from using their newly learned skills for ends contrary to the governors'.

Rulers do not count on positive incentives alone; they punish dissent swiftly and severely, since it is imperative to prevent cracks in the monolith of loyalty. Obviously the army does not face the immediate prospect of successful internal rebellion. Nonetheless, the patriotic ideology of the armed forces is essentially fragile. Morale could be threatened by the mildest deviance, by the perception of their alienation by even a few of the young men in the army.

It is easier to see the unpleasantness of the soldier's position than that of the student's. Yet studying has lost any trace of the self-propelled activity that it may once have been, and has become a *form of labor;* the student's problem is the same as the soldier's—alienation. His mental labor power, which is very productive in his young years, is taken from him as objectively as the muscular labor power of the soldier is taken from him. To make him sufficiently mystified so he will submit to this, the student is told he is investing in himself (in the same way the soldier is indoctrinated with loyalty). Yet if he asks himself why he is in school, the student must honestly respond with answers that have little or nothing to do with his personal development and growth. Instead he must admit that he is in school because he cannot get a job (recall the unemployment figures above). If he is over 18, he may be drafted if he leaves school; but if he stays in school he continues to train for an occupation that is likely to be unproductive.

Student labor is thus alienated, in the sense that the product is for the future employer rather than for the student himself. Furthermore, the whole education industry has been adapted to the production of technology for the administrative imperialist state, so that education is a critical socialized industry, and developments within that industry are crucial for the system as a whole.

The interest of the Central Intelligence Agency in the National Student Association is an indicator of the recognition of student potential. The increasing use of universities for government research, classified and open, strengthens the ties between the academy and the battlefield. Universities are the research and development centers for government. (Recall that 75% of university research budgets are Federal Government financed.)

Therefore, as in the case of the armed forces, when students begin to become aware of their alienation, they pose a real threat to the status quo. The university is not a monolith, like the army, and wide ranges of verbal deviance are tolerated; however, the repression of students by university officials on the University of California and other restive college and high school campuses when overt resistance is attempted can be seen to be motivated by the same fears that lead courts-martial to be particularly punitive to political offenders in the armed forces.

We should expect to see overt repression grow as the number of students and their awareness of their own alienated situation increase. (Recall that 37.4% of civilian young men (18–24) and 20.2% of young women (18–24) were in schools in 1965.)

The two largest sources of youth labor, then, are alienated labor. We must now confront an even more pervasive form of exploitation, the denial of adulthood to youth. Since the discussion of youth became fashionable, one frequently hears that almost half the population is under 25.

But since when is 25 the dividing line between child and adult? Biological maturation can hardly be later than 14. Yet the societal recognition of that maturity has been delayed for about ten years, and the delay is constantly growing. How long can "maturity" be delayed before the quality of the maturity changes?

We argue that extending "childhood" so long beyond its natural limits leads at first to adolescent psychological "growing pains," but then, dialectically, to the construction of youth societies in which the young mature according to their own standards.

When this happens, the class formation is complete; to become an "adult" involves changing classes and joining the class enemy—"going straight." Increasing numbers of young people are finding the class change too difficult and are getting older without becoming "adult." Others take on "adult" roles, but not adult psychology; they remain sympathizers of the proletarian youth class.

The relatively recent innovation of adolescence embodies contradictory aspects: the adolescent is biologically and mentally mature, but declared still too young to marry or work. Instead he is exhorted to enjoy his ever lengthening years of "freedom" and to have a good time.

But how? if the young are not free to marry and have a family, their awakened sexuality is denied socially acceptable outlets. If they are not allowed to work, their maturing minds are essentially idle. The system wastes the best years of young lives, offering freedom from drudgery but not freedom to do anything worthwhile. The idleness of the young is the essence of bourgeois freedom—the absence of restraint—and its cruelest mockery.

Although the delay of maturation distorts the lives of all young people, it works perhaps the greatest hardships where it reinforces other discriminatory handicaps, and is thus particularly severe for black youth and for young women.

Blacks experience the worst job discrimination; as a whole, nonwhite unemployment rates are twice the unemployment rates of the white labor force. This ratio persists among the young; thus, in 1965, while whites between 16 and 19 years had a 13.4% unemployment rate, nonwhites between 16 and 19 years had a 26.2% unemployment rate. In 1964, the median income of nonwhite families was only 56% of the median income of white families. In the face of such discrimination, it is not surprising to find a large number of blacks in the professional military—the major U.S. institution that really gives "equal pay for equal work."

This equality of exploitation wages and this inhuman work reveals equality in the U.S. today for what it is and has surely fostered the rise of black power politics led by the young blacks who bear the brunt of the administrative imperialist system.

Young women also experience multiple discrimination. First, because they are women and second because they are young. Young women in the present period are in transition between roles, often finding satisfaction in neither. If they seek to leave the traditional role, they enter a job market where they face severe discrimination (the median income of women is about one-third that of men, largely because so many are forced to work part-time) and no consideration for the ways in which they differ from men. Yet they cannot decide to withdraw from the unfair competition and stay at home because this traditional role no longer exists due to the exploitation of the young men whom they marry.

Women married to young men see them excluded from adulthood. An increasing portion of young marriages take place while the husband is in the armed forces or in school. The couple's parents or the young wife provide the support. Exploitation of the young has in this way closed off the traditional escape of women into the home. Increasingly, therefore, we should expect to see young women playing an important role in the formation of youth class consciousness.

James S. Coleman in *The Adolescent Society* (1961) recognizes that young people have built sub-societies as a remedy for their alienation from the dominant society. He sees that young people are maturing by their own standards rather than those of the adult society, and that this is an important challenge:

> Now the levers [by which children are motivated] are other children themselves, acting as a a small society and adults must come to know either

how to shape the directions this society takes, or else how to break down the adolescent society, thus re-establishing control by the old levers.

I suspect that this latter solution would be exceedingly difficult, for it flies in the face of large-scale social changes, and would seem to require a re-organization of work and community which is hardly in the offing. The major thesis of this book is that it is possible to take the other tack, to learn how to control the adolescent community as a community and to use it to further the ends of education.

Coleman sees clearly the process of class formation in the young, the threat that they pose to the older society, and the totalitarian measures that will be necessary if the threat is to be controlled so that adolescents can continue to be manipulated by the adult-designed educational structures. Such well-intentioned advocacy of repression suggests that the "conflict of generations" is reaching the proportions of a true class war.

Class Consciousness

We have argued that young people form a class in the advanced capitalist economy of the United States. Because the "growth industries" in the United States today are defense and education and because the majority of young people labor in these socialized industries, youth is the class whose exploitation is essential to the perpetuation of the system; if the young should refuse to submit to their exploitation in the army and the schools, if they should refuse to accept their lengthened childhood and demand to be treated as the mature persons that they are, the system would face a mortal threat.

Youth culture and politics have developed in the last decade from individualist passivity to collectivist activism; instead of stressing the distance remaining on the road to class action, let us see how far youth has come.

Viewed one way, "youth culture" is an invention of merchandisers and a vehicle of false consciousness. However, it can also be the crucial support for alienated youth, making it possible to translate disaffection into open revolt.

The flood of popular journalism about the young, although of little analytical value, shows that youth culture is causing discomfort to the dominant society. Most of this reportage concentrates on the consumption rather than the production aspects of youth culture, focusing on trivia—dress, music and drugs.

Dress has always offered a means of identifying classes and cultures, and the particular garb worn by the contemporary youth *for identification* seems in no way to be novel. Similarly, drug use, although it promotes a certain kind of group identification because it is illegal and because of the exaggerated adult reaction to drug use by youth, is a secondary rather than a primary concern. If drug use were to end (or to be legalized), the structure of youth culture would only be modified in detail.

Music cannot be quite so easily dismissed, since it is produced as well as consumed within youth culture. We shall consider it below as a means of communication.

Here we stress that it is not consumption patterns but, instead, their relations to the system of production that bind people together. It is the ties forged by the class role of young people in the defense and education production industries that lead them to adopt similar consumption patterns, attitudes, and modes of behavior.

The armed forces should therefore be a locus of emerging attitudes and behavior for a large group of young people. Unfortunately, the kind of data that would help us assess the formation of draftee subcultures is not readily available.

We can, however, look at the behavior of students and the unemployed young. Since black youth have developed a level of consciousness of their oppression far exceeding that of white youth, it is not necessary to ferret out developments in black political consciousness from cultural phenomena.

In the discussion of youth culture we will concentrate on white youth. White youth culture can be seen as becoming increasingly collective and activist in the last decade: autonomous communities are larger and more numerous; forms of collective activity are more frequent and more comprehensive; and, most important, modes of communication have become much more intensive and sophisticated.

The youth communities—Haight-Ashbury, the East Village, etc.—are important mainly because they define a quasi-political boundary between the young and the others. Therefore, like black ghettos, school grounds, and campuses, villages provide a base from which youth can organize and a setting in which political learning can take place.

This learning is usually offered in abundance by the harassment of government authorities (especially police) representing the irate public of olders who feel threatened by the young.

The political potential of the villages is reinforced by the communalism of contemporary culture. Communal modes of living and eating are an integral part of the youth communities; the operational definition of the ubiquitous exhortation to "love" seems to be to share.

"Be-ins" and "love-ins" are large-scale collective events that parallel the style for which the young strive in their personal relations. Contrast this style with the nihilistic, individualistic, painfully withdrawn Beat of the 1950's. While the Beat sought to lose his ego in Zen, the hippies seem to seek merely to escape their bourgeois individuality in groups.

These cultural traits are overshadowed in importance by the sophisticated musical and literary communication which the young have developed.

The music and literature of the 1950's were concerned with the inner state of the creator—introspective jazz and poetry. These forms were the treasures of a tiny group who correctly viewed themselves as in constant danger of being demolished by the tyrannical mediocrity of the Eisenhower years.

Contrast this introspection with the open, public, self-confident quality of today's music and journalism, which confronts the dominant society head-on. This confrontation is quite clear to the young, although the language in which it is couched may confuse the olders. (Bob Dylan says: "You know something is happening here, but you don't know what it is, do you, Mr. Jones?")

This confusion is intentional; the young "put on" the dominant society by talking at many levels, most of which the olders cannot understand. This means that their ideological content is much clearer to the young than to their half-listening olders. *Double entendre* is the stock in trade of resistance literature, and the lyrics of youth songs are like the poems that were used for communication in Nazi-occupied Europe.

In addition to the language, youth puts on the dominant society with the high volume and electronic violence of rock groups. The Beats whispered. Youth today shouts.

The shouting goes on not only from the stage but from the pages of youth newspapers as well. The underground press is a literary revival of participant journalism—by, for, and of the young. Few underground papers are more than three years old; the recent formation of the Liberation News Service with several hundred affiliates throughout North America signifies the birth of a continental system of communication in the youth culture.

The underground press has been largely ignored by the popular analysts, perhaps because the style and format of the underground press makes them uncomfortable. The put-on perferred by most underground editors is the gratuitous use of nudity and four-letter words.

Even a casual examination of these periodicals belies the common allegation that the youth culture is apolitical. On the contrary, the youth papers are well-informed, full of insight into the decay of North American society, quick to report police and government harassment of their own or other minority groups (racial-ethnic minorities and "outlaw" groups such as motorcycle clubs), and imbued with a strong sense of solidarity with revolutionaries such as Ché Guevara and Mao Tse-tung.

And perhaps even more significant, the underground press serves as a means of communication and mobilization within the villages and between them, as well as with youth groups outside the villages.

The political trends are as hard to interpret with certainty as the cultural, but they point in the same direction. The young have outgrown the nonviolent civil rights movement, South and North; the New Left is foundering; "black power" and "student power" are increasingly common slogans; class consciousness is growing.

The development from the Beats to the hippies was a development from individualist to collectivist cultural forms; parallel political developments can be seen, from individualist tactics (passive nonviolent resistance) to collectivist communitarian tactics (participatory democracy) to rudimentary class action (black power, student power, draft resistance, etc.).

At the same time the content of youth politics has matured, from issue politics in the liberal tradition to the "grass roots" politics of the archetypal New Left and further to the contemporary power politics in the ghettos and the schools.

. . . .

Let us return, in conclusion, to a historical, developmental view. Youth politics is not yet consistently revolutionary, but the changes in a decade are breathtaking. From an apolitical beginning, young people have taken up, used, and discarded issue politics and nonviolence. They have also tried and discarded "grass roots" politics and communitarian utopianism.

Black youth are rapidly moving to a clear-cut revolutionary position. White youth have been catching up and are increasingly coming to understand their crucial class role in overthrowing the administrative core of imperialism.

Unrest will get worse in the ghettos and in the schools and will develop in the military unless the conditions that make for unrest are changed. And since those conditions are embedded in the economic system itself, we may expect growing confrontations between youth and the administrative imperialist system.

We have argued an essentially optimistic thesis, denying that history in the United States stopped after World War II. We have found that internal production has changed to meet the needs of what we call the administrative imperialist system. Its distinguishing characteristic is the dominant dynamic role in employment creation and surplus absorption played by the defense and education industries, industries whose labor is provided in large measure by youth.

This shift in the mode of production led to a shift in the internal exploitation of the system, from the working class in general to the young in particular. As soldiers and students, the young experience moral and material alienation of their labor; rejection by the dominant society hastens both sociologically and psychologically the process of class formation among the young.

This class has begun to express itself in its own ways, both culturally and politically; class action by youth as a class can be seen on every hand. The "problems of youth" will be not only better understood but also sooner solved when we see through the "conflict of generations" to the contradictions of capitalism underneath.

Any attempt to "organize" young people in traditional ways will probably fail. Instead, young people must be addressed via action; their understandable skepticism about the value of political action can be overcome by offering to them modes of action that are demonstrably effective. This means that the young can be recruited only for confrontation with the system, not for negotiations with it. Increasingly, however, we argue that the young will be invited to lend a hand if they can.

16.3.   *DAVE GILBERT, BOB GOTTLIEB and SUSAN SUTHEIM:* **Consumption: Domestic Capitalism.**

[This paper was developed in discussion with the Wisconsin Draft Resistance Union. This version was written with Bob Gottlieb, Dave Gilbert and Susan Sutheim. MDS pamphlet No. 1, 1968.]

Human history is a record of groups of men struggling to control their environment, in order to meet human needs—needs which are developed and defined in the context of that struggle, and which constantly change. Human needs change quantitatively: as population increases, a greater scale of production is required to sustain it. And they change qualitatively: the introduction of new technology creates a need for new kinds of tools, skills, services. The pressure of new needs creates a demand for new technology: new technology creates new needs.

Human activity is socially organized. The social organization of labor and the technical apparatus that men use to manipulate their environment comprise the notion of *production*. The *means of production* is the human labor and technical apparatus that men have at their disposal in the struggle to control their environment. The means of production changes historically; new tools and machines are introduced and human labor is consequently reorganized. Changes in the means of production lead to new social needs, to new forms of social organization and production, and to new forms of social stratification.

As feudalism develops into capitalism and the country/agricultural productive base develops into an urban/industrial base, the structure of society accordingly changes: a new class structure develops. For *class* most simply refers to who controls (and who does not control) the means of production in any historical situation. Class includes also the whole spectrum of differentiated social roles and differential access to power, both of which ultimately flow from control of means of production and concomitant division of labor (cf. Marx and Engels, *The German Ideology*).

Modern American capitalism fits this general historical model. But in one important area—the interaction of new technology and new needs—the historical process has been distorted. Instead of human needs providing the impetus for the development of new technology, the needs emerging from new technology are consciously manipulated to serve the survival needs of the capitalist system. This distortion is the result of a qualitative change in the means of production—the introduction of cybernated technology—which provides the basis for new forms of exploitation, and which also creates historically new potentials for human liberation.

The Economic Dynamic of Modern Capitalism

In modern American capitalism, the control of most industries is in the hands of a few large corporations. This economic form of control is called *oligopoly*. Oligopolistic firms tend to eliminate price competition. Although historically price competition was largely responsible for the introduction of new technology, other incentives for technological development still remain. One: Intra-industry competition—technology is introduced to enhance profits and the size of the market share, within a given industry with a given price structure, by lowering costs through higher productivity. Two: Inter-industry competition—technology is introduced in order to expand into new markets through new products and processes produced at lower costs. Three: International competition—technology is introduced to compete for markets with other capitalist countries through higher productivity and innovation. Four: The cold war—technology is used to compete with rising productivity in the socialist countries and at the same time, to secure the continuing loyalty of the domestic population by offering them a higher standard of living.

All these incentives allow for the *partial* development of technology. The long term trend of modern capitalism is towards automation and cybernation (cybernation is the automated control of automation). The *rate* of introduction of new technology under modern capitalism is far slower than, in terms of human needs, it ought to be and in terms of what is *technologically* possible, far slower than it need be. But full cybernation is not possible under the social form of capitalism.

For the nature of capitalist society inhibits the trend towards automation and cybernation. Introduction of new technology means greater productive capacity. When this increase in production is not met with a simultaneous increase in consumption, capitalism faces the threat of an *underconsumption* crisis. Because there is no social control over production and consumption, the corporations will retard the growth of productivity in order to avoid underconsumption. The tension between the need to introduce new technology (inter- and intra-industry competition, etc.) and the restrictions that the threat of underconsumption place on that need is a central contradiction of modern capitalism.

The Sources of Underconsumption

The cost structure of production of modern capitalism is highly vulnerable to the threat of underconsumption. A corporation employs new technology in order to increase productivity—lower costs per unit produced. Costs *per unit* decline as a function of total volume produced. If consumer demand slackens, machines cannot be laid off (as workers can be): machines are fixed, as opposed to flexible, costs. The more dependent production is on technology, as it tends to be, the greater the proportion of fixed to flexible costs. A firm must cover basic fixed costs of production before it can start to realize profits; the breakeven point rises as a function of the introduction of new technology.

Harvard Business Review (Sept.-Oct. 1967, page 8) puts it this way: "One of its [technology's] 'side effects' will be on costs. Costs inevitably become stickier and breakeven chart curves flatten out when capital is substituted for labor. As a result, business will have an even greater incentive to maintain continuously higher levels of output. . . ." What this clearly implies is that business has a great incentive to maintain continuously higher levels of *consumption,* for if output produced is not bought, profits evaporate.

But there is, under modern capitalism, an apparently irresolvable impediment to domestic consumption: *maldistribution of wealth,* which is a structural feature of modern capitalism for several reasons. One, the accumulation of capital for investment is done privately. Two, control over the means of production is based partially on private ownership (i.e., wealth). Three, social privileges are partially realized through relative wealth.

The maldistribution of wealth affects the economic structure of modern capitalism in two ways: one, a disproportionate relationship of investment funds to consumption funds; and two, inability to fully utilize consumption funds. The first problem results in what are called *underconsumption cycles;* the second in *discretionary income.*

Underconsumption Cycles

The goal of modern capitalism is profit. Profit, by and large, is made available for reinvestment, in order to achieve and maintain a competitive market position necessary to continue realizing profit (see the earlier discussion on the economic dynamic of capitalism). The high proportion of the value of a product taken as profit is not available for workers' wages which, by and large, are devoted to consumption. The social structure and values of capitalism, then, result in a disproportionate income devoted to investment funds as opposed to consumption funds. Investment (purchase of machinery, new processes, research, etc.) is used to increase the production of consumer goods. Hence profitable utilization of investment funds is dependent on the level of consumption. But consumption, as stated above, is constricted by the high proportion of profit to wages. Hence a cycle of underconsumption tends to emerge. The inability to use investment funds leads to laying off workers in the production of machinery (producer goods). This in turn leads to a further slack in demand for consumer goods, which in turn leads to underutilization of investment funds, which leads to laying off workers. . . . and so the cycles goes.

Discretionary Income

Secondly, under modern capitalism, the problem of maintaining and increasing sufficient consumer demand is aggravated by maldistribution of wealth within the consumer sphere. Maldistribution of wealth means that, on one end of the spectrum, there is a group of people with very low (or no) income; while on the other end, there is a group of people with very high income. The group with high income has great consumer buying power; the group with low income, least consumer buying power. But the low income group is under much more pressure to spend its *full* income—it must, simply to meet survival needs. The high income group is under no necessary pressure to spend its full income: after survival needs have been met, it can choose to spend or to save. Over and above the survival level, it enjoys *discretionary income*. If people with dicretionary income choose not to buy as many consumer goods as they potentially could, there is, at least short term, underconsumption.

Furthermore, discretionary income is rising. *Fortune*'s (Dec. 1967) figures on discretionary income—defined as the sum of all family income above $7,500—indicates that it now constitutes about one third of all personal income. *Fortune* estimates that it will grow to about 37% by 1975. (Since definition of discretionary income is somewhat arbitrary, these figures provide only general orders of magnitude and growth.)

Correlated with the growth of discretionary income is the increased proportion of durable goods—cars, household appliances, sports equipment— and luxuries on the consumer market. With these goods, a consumer has a good deal of leeway to defer consumption decisions by repairs, disregarding style changes, choosing to do without. The growth of discretionary income and the growth in the proportion of durable goods and luxuries to other consumer goods have served to make consumption very flexible.

Thus the general tendency is for production costs to become more and more rigid, while consumption becomes more flexible. As this tendency continues, the potential for economic crisis is clear: under particular political-social circumstances, demand can contract violently (people can choose not to spend their discretionary income), while producers have very little leeway to respond, since they are committed to a structure of high fixed costs.

How Modern Capitalism Deals with Underconsumption

An interesting aspect of a potential underconsumption crisis is that Keynesian techniques are largely irrelevant. Measures to increase income (welfare, negative income tax, guaranteed minimum income) do not raise consumption and investment in a situation where an already significant proportion of consumers already have sufficient income but neither need nor want to spend it. Economic reforms are still available. The government can and does create demand *directly* (although most of the important "multiplier effect" would be lost in this situation) and can attempt limited redistribution of wealth. But as the potential magnitude of this sort of crisis grows, there are definite limits to what can be done within a capitalist structure: relative maldistribution of wealth and the exploitation of labor is systemic to capitalism; it is necessary to maintain class privileges. Further, the type of social situation likely to precipitate such a crisis (e.g., widespread urban rioting) might well limit the government's flexibility.

In addition to limited redistribution of wealth and demand creation, modern capitalism deals with the problems of underconsumption through its policy of imperialism, both foreign and domestic. Foreign imperialism is becoming more and more a policy of extending markets: securing the investment and consumer potential in other countries. This policy holds true especially in Western Europe; the resultant political and social tensions give rise, e.g., to the nationalistic politics of Gaullism. Even more impressive is American foreign policy of the 60s, which encourages internal economic growth in the Third World both in order to improve market possibilities, and to create a native bourgeoisie that serves as a bulwark against socialist revolution (i.e., stabilizes the investment and consumer markets, to use State Department jargon). In fact, securing markets and encouraging a certain kind of economic growth, while preventing revolution, is the essence of corporate liberal foreign policy. The meaning of Vietnam is underscored by the fact that the danger of underconsumption is heightened every time a successful socialist revolution cuts off another area from U.S. economic domination.

The other form of imperialism has to do with the ways capitalism deals with the problem of insufficient consumption domestically. First, capitalism has to make sure that a certain proportion of investment funds are used in ways other than increasing true productivity. Simply put, these funds are used to create new industries whose specific purpose is to create the desire to consume more. These industries include communications media that extend corporate influence and control to every sector of the population, and advertising that not only distorts and manipulates real needs, but also creates the desire for a quantitative increase in consumption. Similarly, funds invested in new technology are used to create waste and obsolescence: style changes, planned breakdown, gimmick products.

Paralleling the deflection of technological innovation into nonproductive channels of the various industries that contribute to the management of demand. The way to insure that demand does not fall below a certain level is to manipulate and distort people's needs, to make them consume more and more and more. Market research and advertising are the key demand—management industries, but others contribute. —It is not an entire accident that maxiskirts finally made it into the consumer market the month after *Bonnie and Clyde* hit the movie houses. (The fashion industry has been pushing maxiskirts unsuccessfully for two years.)

But modern capitalism and its policy of imperialism has aroused political responses which have the potential to destroy it. The response to America's attempts to secure markets abroad is, increasingly, the emergence of national liberation movements. Similarly, waste production and the management of demand (domestic imperialism) seems to be leading to the development of a large-scale domestic movement (a new left) reacting against meaningless jobs and manipulative consumption. In fact, the development of some of the industries key to the survival of modern capitalism (e.g., mass media, mass education) themselves contain the roots of its potential destruction. For people—especially the young and the blacks—are becoming more and more aware of the gap between potential social wealth and the reality of their own lives, whether in the ghetto, in the classroom, or on the job.

Commodities and Men

In capitalist society, wealth is measured in terms of the accumulation of commodities (products), with money serving as the universal commodity, the medium of exchange. In earlier periods of history, products were directly consumed by the producers and their overlords. Commodities are distinguished from non-commodities by the fact that commodities have a market (or exchange) value, in terms of which they can be traded for other commodities or for money. In a capitalist system, commodities include the majority of *men*, since the majority of men must sell their labor power on the market in order to live.

The more commodities men produce, the greater is men's control over nature and the greater is the potential for human liberation. But at the same time, every extension of commodities is a negation of human freedom. The key to this contradiction is the position of the majority of men as commodities. Men who sell their labor power do not conceive, create and consume their own products for their own purposes. Rather, they produce according to the needs of the capitalists who hire them for the purpose of making profits. Thus, a worker confronts his own product not as an extension of himself and his control over his environment, but as an alien object outside himself. The more man produces, the greater the power of these alien objects. Moreover, capitalism constantly creates (*must* create) new needs and new products, thus extending this alien power over him. (Marx: *The Economic and Philosophical Manuscripts of 1884; Capital,* Vol. 1, Chap. 1.)

Under modern capitalism, the process of creating—or more accurately, the channeling into commodity form—of basic human needs has reached a qualitatively new phase. Of course the natural process of the extension of human needs with the overall development of society has continued. But the high productivity now possible with the introduction of automated technology, and the correspondingly lesser necessary labor time, has made cultural activity and other social needs—*non-commodity needs*—important, and increasingly important in proportion to purely material needs.

Simultaneously, the economic dynamic of modern capitalism, as discussed earlier, demands a constant rise in consumer (commodity) sales. Thus those who control production must consciously develop needs for specific commodities, in order to increase consumption. They must even create life styles defined by consumption, to assure that higher income levels don't permit sudden, capricious drops in demand. Leisure time becomes consumption time. Sports and culture are not extensions of human social activity, but are commodities for which we buy a $2 ticket, or enjoy at home via television (consumer durable good) while watching beer commercials and drinking beer.

The basis for creating and manipulating consumer needs in using and redirecting real human needs, associating them with a given commodity. Thus the needs for sex, love, personal identity and creativity, etc., are used to sell products with which they have no necessary connection. Thus, not only do man's products become an alien power outside himself; at the same time, his own (socially formed) inner needs are turned against him, to make him desire those same alien products.

The logical extension of this process is man defined and delimited by the commodities outside himself. Man becomes defined by what he has, rather than what he is and does. A magazine ad announces: "Your clothes *are* you." Masculinity is a red convertible with a stick shift. Security is a house in the suburbs. Love is a warm blanket.

Exploitation

Exploitation, traditionally, has been defined as the difference between what a worker produces and what he receives. The difference goes to the person who bought the labor of the worker, in the form of profits, rents, etc. The quantitative aspect of a commodity's social value is derived from the amount of human labor that went into it. The costs of producing a given commodity, other than the direct application of human labor—things such as raw materials and machinery—are themselves products of labor. This notion of exploitation fitted the context of early industrial capitalism, where the direct material wealth associated with human labor could be fairly easily measured and thus the exploitation of the working class fairly accurately asssessed.

Before attempting to reformulate exploitation in terms of modern conditions, it will be useful to distinguish carefully between *oppression* and exploitation—terms that have often been confused for each other. Exploitation refers to a *class* situation—the degree to which a man's labor is appropriated—under a given productive system. Oppression refers to the situation of a social domination in the context of the total environment, not simply to men's labor. How a man is oppressed can be seen by the difference in the conditions of his life relative to the conditions of the most privileged group in the society—the oppressors. The conditions of life include material wealth, physical environment, culture, etc. In a given society, the exploited and the oppressed are not identical, although they certainly overlap. Thus, in modern America, a technically skilled worker might be the most exploited (given his relative labor value), and a ghetto dweller the most oppressed (given the relative misery of the total conditions of his life). This distinction is important for any critique of society (e.g., this one) which attempts to include class conditions as well as environmental conditions within its scope.

The traditional approach to exploitation made sense when most of the commodities consumed by the working class went to the physical sustenance of the worker and his family according to minimal social conditions. The worker consumed in order that he continue to work. This was defined as the social reproduction of labor. But the pattern of working class consumption has changed significantly under modern capitalism. On one level, the growth and complexity of capitalist society has resulted in a rise in the cost of the social reproduction of labor (higher standard of living). Secondly, qualitatively new processes involving such things as a $16 billion advertising industry, planned obsolescence, and frequent style changes (to all of which a worker is of course subject) have assumed importance with respect to the notion of exploitation. These new processes, discussed earlier in connection with the management of demand, can be defined in relation to exploitation as *waste production*.

As decribed earlier, management of demand is crucial to the survival of modern capitalism. Waste production concomitant with the management of demand amplifies the notion of exploitation as appropriation of labor, and extends the notion of exploitation into the sphere of consumption. Here is how it works: Part of a worker's labor goes into the production of waste. For example, a worker produces a light bulb. Some of his labor is utilized to make sure that the light bulb will burn out sooner than it should (planned obsolescence). Not only is that amount of his labor wasted; the worker will have to buy two, three, many light bulbs (instead of one that would last and last), thus helping to fulfill the capitalist system's need for people to consume, consume, consume.

The amount of time the worker expends on waste production is part of the social costs of production: the social costs of maintaining the irrational capitalist system which entails the necessity of constantly increasing consumption. Early industrial societies also had their share of the social costs of production (for example, expenditures for the state and defense). But these costs have been increased so drastically by modern capitalism that the quantitatives change verges on a qualitative change: exploitation extends to the consumer sphere. Thus the notion of exploitation proper to modern capitalism must include not only the difference between what one produces and what one receives, but also the difference between what one ought to be able to produce (were it not for waste production) and what one ought to receive (enough, but not an addictively increasing enough). In short, exploitation under modern capitalism is the difference between potential social productivity and overall quality of life (including both work and consumption). This new and total form of exploitation is important in the way it has affected class structure, consciousness, and the potential for creating a new society in contemporary America.

Class, Constituency, and Consciousness

The class structure of a society is based on men's relations to the means of production in a given historical period. The key aspects of these social relations are: one, the control or non-control of the means of production; and two, the expropriation of value (men's labor)—the dynamic of profits and exploitation. The means of production and the concomitant forms of exploitation are constantly changing, and with them, the class structure of society changes. Therefore, during the last half of the 19th century, with the emergence of factory labor and the early crude industrial plants, the industrial working class became potentially the most revolutionary class, because of its essential relation to production coupled with its being the most *exploited* group in the society. Yet the industrial working class always constituted a minority of the population.

For a class to develop revolutionary action, it must achieve a certain degree of class consciousness. Consciousness develops out of experience, life activity, which for the working class was primarily *direct* activity in production (directly productive work). And it was *shared* experience, based on a common relationship to the means of production. With the perception of common interests, political organization and revolutionary activity can follow.

In modern American capitalism, certain quantitative and qualitative changes have occurred within the class structure. These changes can be traced to the way technological change has affected the economic structure and the form of exploitation. Fundamentally, these changes have led to an alteration in the productive system itself. Production has become increasingly *socialized.* This means two things: one, the extension of commodities into all spheres of human activity besides those directly connected with material needs (everything ranging from cultural and educational industries to defense); and two, a restructuring of work because of the tremendous growth of jobs that no longer relate directly to material production (more and more jobs have to do with the machines that turn out products rather than with products directly; there has been a huge increase in jobs that deal with the social aspects of production—e.g., accounting, advertising, social services).

The restructuring of work has produced a series of new contradictions in capitalism. First, there is the tendency to increasing job specialization and fragmentation that technology is responsible for and which capitalism desires. But the technological trend towards cybernation creates the *potential* for jobs being integrated, and for each person's work being more and more involved with the overall development and benefit of society. Secondly, the waste production allowed by the social irresponsibility of capitalism stands in contradiction to its technologically possible elimination, and to the creative and meaningful work that we are taught (both in school and through corporate advertising) to seek.

Any examination of the American class structure must integrate these new contradictions. Because of the increasing socialization of production, the American ruling class is defined not only by those who control the means of production and directly profit from the labor of others, but also includes the people who control such nonproductive sectors as education and communications. The changes in class structure in the working class and underclass—those who do not control the means of production or the nonproductive sectors which contribute to the maintainence of the capitalist system—have been more complicated.

The socialization of production which has led to a restructuring of the work force differentiates various strata within the American working class. The oldest and most recognizable of these strata is the *traditional working class,* which is still a crucial force in production and constitutes about 30% of the work force. This group works directly on production. Because the technological trend is toward automation and cybernation, the traditional working class will possibly diminish. But because of the internal contradictions of capitalism, automation is introduced at an uneven rate, allowing the traditional working class to survive and to play an important role.

The traditional working class, as well as other strata of the working class, has been affected by the rise in the domestic standard of living. They, as well as everyone else, feel the brunt of new forms of exploitation in their role as *consumers.* It is this fact more than anything else that can potentially link the traditional working class with other groups.

Since the other strata of the working class are more directly affected by the changes in the nature of *work,* they can be defined, for lack of a better term, as the *new working class.* This group can be subdivided into three kinds of work: technical work, human service work, and white-collar (middle sector) work.

Technical work: With the growth of technology and automation, more and more laborers work directly on machines, which in turn produce a product. Such jobs include inventing, designing, building, programming, repairing and supervising machines—jobs generally for technicians and engineers. Although workers of this type existed in the early stages of capitalism, they have by now become a special strata because of their tremendous growth in numbers and their importance in the new technology. Although still a small percentage of the work force, it is the fastest growing sector.

There are several aspects of technical workers' experience that relate to political consciousness. Their high pay, relatively privileged positions, and possible promotion into management all militate against radical political consciousness. These factors, however, tend to diminish as technical workers come to constitute a larger percentage of the work force. On the other hand, their relatively great rate of exploitation (stemming from high labor value plus exploitation through waste consumption) enables them to perceive first hand the nature of waste production and could lead to radical consciousness. This radical consciousness is based on the perception of the gap between potential and reality: the central contradiction of capitalist production. The potential of modern technology in the service of creative and rational control of production includes the elimination of waste production and the possibility of integrated, creative work responsible for the development of the whole society. The reality of capitalist production is meaningless (if not destructive) and boring work, and the manipulated consumption of waste.

Human service work: With socialized capitalist production, more and more jobs are created that deal with people (including their physical environment and culture) as commodities. These jobs include teaching, social work, city planning, medicine, law, architecture, communications, and entertainment (which used to be called culture). Generally classified under the general rubric of professional work, the essential contradiction in these jobs has to do with the quality of life in America, with its manipulated passivity and misery. "Professionals" are turned against their clients; to the extent that this is effective, service workers do not develop radical consciousness. The development of radical consciousness comes when a "professional" realizes that the system of which he is an instrument, and through which he victimizes his clients, is in fact victimizing him. A teacher, for example, realizes that his role in the educational system is the socialization—brutalization and channeling—of children into the "American way of life." The teacher wants to be a creative educator; he is in fact a cop in the classroom. The recognition of this contradiction can turn him against the system itself.

White collar and middle sector work: These jobs fall in the area of the social costs of production. They include workers in sales, advertising, accounting and clerical work. This group is the largest sector of the work force, constituting more than a third of the total.

The question of consciousness here is blurred by ambiguous class positions (class being based on relation to the means of production). These workers sell their labor power on the market, yet do not directly create value. Essentially, their function is to help the capitalists appropriate surplus value (realize profits). Their wages, however, do not come from direct expropriation of other workers: they are not capitalists. Rather, the middle sector is paid according to the prevailing market and social standards to perform labor necessary to the capitalists for realizing profits. The middle sector is essentially a special sector of the working class (cf. Marx's discussion of the "mercantile wage worker" in *Capital*, Vol. III, pp. 289–300). Further, the middle sector workers are highly exploited in terms of our new definition of exploitation, in that they realize little value compared to their expenditure of time and energy.

Historically, this sector has shown both socialist and fascist potential. The revolutionary potential of middle sector workers today is dependent on their ability to perceive their exploitation as *consumers*, relying on leadership exerted by other strata of the working class.

Strategy for the New Left

As has already been clearly indicated, changes (and coming changes) in the work force imply new strategic directions. Unlike the 30s, strategy can no longer be based on material demands alone (wage demands in reaction to economic crisis). Rather, it must be based on a more encompassing projection of the social and economic alternatives to the status quo. Briefly, we propose a strategy that posits, on the one hand, a critique of the reality of meaningless jobs, manipulated consumption and growing maldistribution of wealth, and on the other hand, a vision of the liberating potential of a fully automated, fully communist society.

Two vanguard groups have emerged in America: youth and the underclass, specifically blacks. The underclass includes the chronically poor and unemployed. They are the most oppressed. Further, they have been treated more and more as commodities within the service sector of production. And as they are socialized by the service sector, they are brutalized—to which systematic racism contributes. The most radical demands they can raise— which go beyond the demand to be included in the system—can force the whole society to confront itself. They have the potential of developing a nonmarketable culture, nonmarketable because it could include elements antipathetic to the system as a whole. But if black people are forced to develop in isolation from the rest of society (cut off by racism when they can't be bought off by liberalism), their potential power will be limited because of their non-relation to production.

Youth, and particularly students, can also reject the system as a whole. As trainees in a system of exploitation, their rejection of the role of trainee is a rejection not simply of the specific task they are being trained for, but a rejection of the process as a whole. This includes a rejection of consumer culture and manipulative consumption as well as the rejection of meaningless work they refuse to participate in (viz., the hippies). It can extend—has begun to extend—to a global critique of American capitalism's role both at home and abroad.

Youth, as the object of intense socialization of education, are best able to perceive the potential that socialized production contains. Yet they are being trained for individual roles as workers and consumers that are boring, uncreative, wasteful. The perception of this fundamental gap between potential and reality leads youth to radical consciousness. And we have already begun to develop alternatives to the existing system. In the liberated buildings of Columbia, in the dropout communities of New York, San Francisco, and dozens of other cities, we are beginning to build our own commonwealth, our own culture.

This class analysis is more static than the current situation in fact is. With the growth of technology, production comes to be based more on the general productivity and technical level of society as a whole than on any particular group of workers. In other words, while technology has tended to fragment job structure, it has also socialized production as a whole, creating the basis for the perception of a unity of interests among all sectors of the working class and the underclass. Exploitation through consumption provides a further basis for socialization and unity of interests. While there are different styles of consumption among different classes, the mass culture developing out of advertising and mass media provides a partial basis for common experience within the working class.

In the short run, job fragmentation will necessitate constituency politics as a prelude to a full class politics. Potential constituencies might include the sectors and subsectors of the working class already discussed, as well as groups such as students, women and consumers, which constitute overlapping constituencies. To avoid reformism, and even fascism, such constituency politics must be based on relating the concerns of each constituency to the central contradictions of capitalism and imperialism. Through the experience of common struggle against exploitation and oppression, the constituencies can develop into a full class movement, a movement to abolish class.

Technology, Repression, and Liberation

The opening paragraphs of this paper pointed out the distortion of the historical relationship between needs and production under modern capitalism. Production is held back because of the threat of underconsumption which in turn stems ultimately from the maldistribution of wealth. And yet, were it not for the irrational and anti-human organization of production necessitated by modern capitalism, modern technology provides the real potential for a post-scarcity economy* for the first time in history. Further, cybernation points to a mode of production that can abolish the necessity of externally imposed labor. Only through the elimination of material scarcity and division of labor can the basis of social domination be abolished. Then, man's activity becomes defined by its own, consciously determined needs, not by external necessity. This potential, embodied in the increasingly socialized means of production, creates the basis for communist revolution and a new quality of human relationships. Marx described this potential a century before full automation made it an imminent reality:

> As large-scale industry advances, the creation of real wealth depends less on the labor time and the quantity of labor expended than on the power of the instrumentalities set in motion during the labor time. These instrumentalities, and their powerful effectiveness, are in no proportion to the immediate labor time which their production requires: their effectiveness rather depends on the attained level of science and technological progress; in other words, on the application of this science to production. . . . Human labor then no longer appears as enclosed in the process of production—rather man relates himself to the process of production a supervisor and regulator. . . . He stands outside of the process of production instead of being the principal agent in the process of production. . . . In this transformation, the great pillar of production is no longer the immediate labor performed by man himself, nor his labor time, but the appropriation of his own universal productivity, i.e., his knowledge and his mastery of nature through his social existence—in one word; the development of the social individual. *The theft of another man's labor time, on which the wealth still*

---

* For an excellent discussion of the economics of "fully automated full communism," see E. J. Nell's article "Automation and the Abolition of the Market" in *New Left Notes*, Aug. 1967.

rests today, then appears, as a miserable basis compared with the new basis which large scale industry itself has created. As soon as human labor, in its immediate form, has ceased to be the great source of wealth, labor time will cease, and must of necessity cease to be the measure of wealth, and the exchange value must of necessity cease to be the measure of use value. *The surplus labor of the mass* has thus ceased to be the condition for the development of the universal faculties of man. The mode of production which rests on the exchange value thus collapses. . . . [*Grundrisse der Kritik der politischen Oekonomie*, pp. 592–596 *passim,* translated by Herbert Marcuse in *One-Dimensional Man*, pp. 35–6.]

FURTHER READINGS

Cole, Lewis, Gilbert, Dave and Gonzales, Juan. "Fascism, American Style." *Guardian,* November 2 and 9, 1968.

Calvert, Gregory, and Neiman, Carol. "Socialist Consciousness and the New Left." *Guardian,* August 24 and 31, September 7, 1968.

_____. *The New Left and the New Capitalism.* New York: Random House, 1968.

Deutscher, Isaac. "The 'New Left' and the 'End of Ideology.'" *Intercontinental Press,* July 7, 1968.

Domhoff, William. *Who Rules America?* Englewood Cliffs, New Jersey: Prentice-Hall, 1967.

Gilbert, David and Lond, David. "US Imperialism." SDS pamphlet, 1968.

Gottlieb, Robert, Tenney, Gerry, and Gilbert, David. "Toward a Theory of Social Change in America." *New Left Notes,* Vol. 2: No. 20, (May 22, 1967).

Greeman, Richard. "A Critical Re-examination of Herbert Marcuse." *New Politics,* August 1968.

Horowitz, David. "One-Dimensional Society?" *International Socialist Journal,* December 1967.

Ignatin, Noel. "Learn the Lessons of U.S. History." *The Movement,* February 1968.

_____. "Organizing Workers: Lessons for Radicals." *Guardian,* July 6, 1968.

Interview with Herbert Marcuse. *Guardian,* November 9 and 16 and 23, 1968.

Nell, Edward J. "Automation and the Abolition of the Market." MDS pamphlet No. 2, February 1967.

Schwartz, Robert, Bayne, Ted, and Israel, Jared. "US Capitalism—Prosperity or Crisis?" *New Left Notes,* Vol. 20: No. 21 (May 22, 1969).

Steege, Ted, *et al.* "Radicals and the Professions." *Our Generation,* V: 2 (1967).

17

New Politics

17.1 *ROBERT SCHEER:* **Scheer Speaks for Himself**

[Robert Scheer ran a radical campaign in the Democratic primary election in California's seventh congressional district. Even if defeated, his 45% of the vote was considered a success for the left. The following dialogue is excerpted from *Serge Lang: The Scheer Campaign, 1967.* Scheer is editor-in-chief of *Ramparts.*]

SL—*Why did you want to run for Congress?*

SCHEER—The war in Vietnam. Things had gotten to a point where I felt I had to change the course of my life and do something more significant against the war than just occasionally speaking. I felt Cohelan was a very important target, because he typified the whole style of politics that I held accountable for the war.

SL—*What is that style?*

SCHEER—Well, he had these private feelings, he had reservations, he understood the complexities, but his public posture was support for the President. He typified what American Liberalism had come to be in the Cold War.

SL—*Can you summarize the reason for your attack on this liberalism?*

SCHEER—The thing that's disturbing most of all about Cohelan is the great futility about his politics. The sense of exasperation, that nothing could be done, that wars are inevitable and one has to learn to live with them, that the problems of West Oakland are unfortunate but we were slowly doing something about them. There is a great weariness about his whole position. That's the way life is and that's all one can expect from it. And I made the campaign to show that a different style is possible. I refused to accept war in any form, be it hot or cold, as a permanent condition of our life. I refused to accept it as reasonable that we can spend 60 billion dollars a year on armaments, but that we can't find 60 billion to rebuild cities like Oakland, or to help out the minority groups. I guess the basic difference is that I'm young enough to feel outraged, and the campaign was an expression of it.

SL—*How did you feel when you faced people?*

SCHEER—The basic decision I had to make was: Do I scrounge for votes and try to make myself acceptable to them, or do I tell them what I have in my mind? The great problem in campaigning is, you get tired. You start to repeat yourself. You get tired of provoking people. You lose a certain freshness that you have when you say something for the 50th time. What I had to do before every time I spoke, be it to 5 people in a living room, or to 500 people, I had to prime myself. I thought of the people who were going to be at this meeting, I challenged my right to speak to them. What did I have to say to them? Why should they be interested? What were my real motives? I tried—and of course I didn't always succeed—I tried in each talk to have some kind of new insight, some kind of new approach, because I found that unless I had a new idea in each speech, which excited me, I could not pull it off. I would be bored with the speech, and the people would know it. This was really the most difficult thing about the campaign, for me personally, because every meeting was an encounter. I was as frightened speaking at the end of the campaign as I was at the beginning. You see, I didn't have any of the usual things going for me that a politician has.

SL—*Like what?*

438

SCHEER—For one thing, my campaign was not based on my personal ties with the community, my wife, children. The ordinary campaign speech deals with this sort of thing, it stresses the years of service to the community, the friends you have, the number of organizations you belong to. The candidate emphasizes how closely related he is to his audience and how much good he will do for them, good in the most superficial sense, upon being elected.

The stance of the other candidates with whom I appeared at candidates' night was very similar, be they John Birchers or Liberal Democrats. They all wanted to cut taxes, improve protection, improve schools. They disagreed on whether they were better Democrats or better Republicans than the other guy.

My stance at such a meeting was one of almost deliberate alienation, deliberate because I was interested in provoking thought. Most people at meetings for candidates are half asleep. So, for example, when I went up in front of a Negro audience, I said: "You shouldn't trust any politician, especially a white politician that comes in front of you. They lie continuously."

SL—*Did that apply to yourself?*

SCHEER—Yes. I said there is no reason for you to think I am an exception.

SL—*What was the reaction to that?*

SCHEER—People would sit up. I'd say: "I have some ideas—my point of view. See if they ring true to you, what do you think about it." I always said I don't want people to be neutral about my campaign. I wanted to be judged by the enemies I was making in the community. I felt that every time *The Oakland Tribune* attacked me, it was a victory. It proved to the people in the community whom I wanted to appeal to, that I was on the right track.

When I went before white middle-class audiences, I'd begin with the thing that would most disturb them, like the troop-train demonstrations. But I'd try to treat them in an extremely reasoned and low-keyed manner.

It worked. I spoke to a lot of community groups. Rotary, Lions, Chamber of Commerce. I can't think of a single one when there wasn't an exchange between me and the audience. Most of these people were hearing talk like this for the first time of their lives.

SL—*Did they tell you this?*

SCHEER—Oh absolutely. They'd come up to me afterwards. . . . There was a man who came up to me once, he had three sons in the Army, two in Vietnam, and he believed in the war in Vietnam, and he was all shaken up.

SL—*But he wasn't hostile to you?*

SCHEER—No, no. He asked me where he could find the information I'd just been talking about. I can't think of one single person in the district who treated me rudely, who threatened me in any way. A lot of them were critical. The typical remark that I got from people, say from the white middle-class community, or the working-class community: "You are the first one of those Berkeley types that made sense." Then I'd say: "Have you ever heard one?" and they said, no, but they'd seen them on TV. So I was the first live person whom they had met who said these things.

In that sense, I'd say the tactics of the VDC, like troop-train demonstrations, the march through Oakland, they provided a basis for the campaign, because they forced the issue on Vietnam. They made the dissent about the war public and visible. The average person in the community, you know, would watch these people protesting on television. All right, but at the same time, they couldn't understand what these were all about. They saw that something was going on, that these people cared a lot, but what they were doing was so alien to their normal style that they turned against it with great hatred. I can't think of anything so hated in this community as the VDC or the FSM, for that matter. But at least people knew that they existed.

What we did is, we capitalized on this interest. We came without the picket signs. I personally always dressed as conservatively as possible, and we came with the rational arguments. We never denied our connection with the people who had protested. I always defended the troop-train demonstrations. I never denied I was in the VDC, but I did not threaten these people stylistically myself. I always very carefully marshalled my evidence, layed out my logic, and always ended my pitch by saying: "If you don't agree with me, I'll stay all night. I'll discuss it with you." And above all, the campaign was doing something very traditional—I was a candidate.

SL—*What about your relations with the students at the University? I think you spoke three times on Sproul Hall steps. Do you remember what you said there?*

SCHEER—In a sense I told them that Sproul Hall steps was an indulgence. That these rallies on Sproul Hall steps could easily degenerate into being mere gossip sessions in the town square. Because if all they did was come to talk about these problems, then it was not significant. I also argued against one-shot political activity. You go out to picket for Civil Rights and for Peace, but there's no attempt to have a lasting impact on the community. The campaign was a challenge to them because it meant going out into the community. It meant doing precinct work, which on a radical issue was a lot harder than carrying a picket sign. It meant talking to the uncommitted. I talked about some of the issues that were important to the community. How very few people on campus even knew there were such issues, and yet, to people in the community, these were a lot more important than an abstract call for civil rights.

There's a more basic point, though, that I made speaking at the University. Most of the campus radicals embodied a real contradiction. They were quite willing to put their bodies occasionally on the line, but not their minds. The radical ferment at Berkeley had produced very little in the way of scholarship, new ideas, theories, and I tried to suggest that the reason for that was that these young intellectuals were in fact beholden to the establishment. The same people who got arrested once a year, would the rest of the time grind out hack work in sociology or political science, which in no way contributed to the betterment of society, but rather deliberately fogged the issues. In fact, some of the old radicals I had known at Cal were involved in vicious projects for the Defense Department. I think we had a very strange relationship on the campus. I think we had a better response from the nonpolitical section of the campus than any other activity that had taken place on campus, except the FSM.

For instance, I got better response when I spoke at the dormitories, student clubs, or the Student Coop than I did from radical activists. Particularly the nonstudents that Feuer makes so much of —we had very few of that special category, you know the professional nonstudents who are either drugged on LSD or on Marxist Theory, and they couldn't overcome this.

SL—*So this group played almost no role in your campaign?*

SCHEER—That's right, this campaign was hard work, it means coming in every day, pouring over precinct maps, walking the district, arranging meetings with groups in the community, doing library and field research, writing material, and many of those kids would come around, stick for a few days, and that was it. The description of Berkeley as a haven of professional non-students is just bull—you know—grossly inaccurate. The average student is a damned hard working person. We were continuously having the problem of graduate students who had their exams, couldn't spend much time on the campaign. Kids with $A-$ averages, top of their class. Most of the people who worked in the campaign were people who had jobs, housewives, people who had children.

SL—*Could you tell me something about the tensions of the campaign?*

SCHEER—The tension was obvious. The youngest people who had come out of the radical movements were continuously suspicious of electoral politics, and suspicious of people with previous political experience. Among them there was great fear of the CDCer: This was supposed to be a type. On the other hand, the older people were very much concerned about the "non-seriousness" of the younger people, what they thought was the irresponsibility. I think in both instances it was an obvious irrationality, growing out of the age differences. At the beginning, it was very tense, but things evolved. At the end, everything came together. A major achievement of the campaign was that there people were able to come together.

SL—*So you think this was one of the major achievements?*

SCHEER—Of course. I used to go nuts with this stuff. I used to get calls at one o'clock in the morning about someone saying the CDCers were taking over the campaign, and at other times, someone was saying the VDCers were taking over the campaign. These were euphemisms for young and old. The last month of the campaign, this tension had pretty much gone out of it. In fact, these arguments were finally treated as a joke.

SL—*What's another achievement of the campaign?*

SCHEER—It was a radical campaign that was terribly serious and had an impact on the community. The radical electoral campaigns in the past, nobody ever knew they took place. These previous liberal campaigns had very limited objectives, like School Bonds. This was a campaign that had very disturbing things to say, and yet was treated seriously by the people in this district. For example, we challenged the traditional Negro leadership. We wouldn't support Byron Rumford, because he was too conservative. He was very bad on the University, FSM, hadn't supported the militant civil rights movement, seemed to be for the war in Vietnam. He was the sponsor of the Fair Housing Act, and had been in office for 17 years. We bucked that leadership, and yet we carried even the middle-class Negroes.

Listen, we took on a man with a 95% ADA rating, in a Democratic district, and 45% of the Democrats said it wasn't good enough.

Another achievement of the campaign is that we ran an issues campaign. People said it wasn't possible to run an issues campaign.

SL—*What's the significance of your campaign, even though you lost?*

SCHEER—We didn't lose, because our first concern was to raise the issues in the community. That was our first intent, and nobody can deny that we raised the issues. The majority of the community knew that I was right, and had to make up their mind on the issues. For the first time, they had to take a stand on the war in Vietnam, and live with the implications of that stand, which I spelled out very closely. We succeeded in putting the voter on the spot. That was our prime objective. In that sense, we won.

Another objective we had was to embolden people who usually are so frightened of the American public, who worked for candidates they didn't believe in, that didn't inspire them in any sense, and we taught them that they didn't have to settle for that. It was a lesson for such people throughout the state. In particular for people in California, where you have the CDC, a grass roots organization that never delivered on what they cared about. In that sense, I would say that the elimination of Casady by Brown was the single most important boost to our campaign. The grass roots liberals throughout California became enraged, and many people worked in our campaign who would not otherwise have done it.

So the campaign set a whole new style of politics, showing that one can be honest and effective at the same time. I think we are going to see it grow in California, if not the country.

Another achievement of the campaign was that it was the first post-Cold War campaign. We simply freed ourselves of the whole baggage of the Cold War, of the charge of Communist influence. It bemused us more than it terrified us. We talked about a world of peace and completely denied the need for this huge military establishment. Our whole domestic program was geared towards taking Defense expenditures and applying them towards improving American cities—which challenged the whole idea of the International Communist Conspiracy. See, we took this Sino-Soviet dispute to be a fact which completely confounded the assumptions of American foreign policy, and this was something the average voter could understand.

[There were a few moments of silence, and then Scheer said:]

I think the main achievement of the campaign was that it was bold. Left liberal politics during the Cold War was characterized by fear, and our stance was arrogant. That's it.

17.2   **California Peace and Freedom Movement Program**

[The following is the first part of the program of California Peace and Freedom Movement, adopted at the founding convention held in Richmond in March 1968.]

General Principles

The basis of human dignity is the ability of people to make the decisions that affect their lives—to order their private lives as they choose, and to decide collectively with their peers on matters of collective concern.

The fundamental decisions which affect people's lives are economic decisions. The people have power over their economy only when they can make it work to fulfill their needs. But today in America the public institutions of government, by which the people might exercise such power, are the willing servants of an industrial state which, operating through millions of functionaries who are "only doing their jobs," manages the economy and thereby the lives of the ordinary people in the interests of expanding profit and continued national and world-wide domination.

Individual wage-earners are defined as inferior to the employers who manage them. Collectively, through unions, they are still subordinate to the people who buy their labor.

Black people as individuals are at the mercy of brutally racist police and subtly racist employers. Black communities are invariably governed by white power structures "downtown." The same holds true of other oppressed minorities.

Individual soldiers must follow even the most arbitrary orders of superior officers under penalty of court-martial. They are not allowed at all to organize themselves for redress of grievances, let alone to demand justifications for a war in which they risk their lives.

Students, youths, welfare clients, and many other kinds of people find themselves in the same position. And *all* Americans are subject to government interference in their private lives.

The Democratic and Republican parties are the public expression of those who hold a disproportionate share of power in private life. The Peace and Freedom Party supports the efforts of the powerless to gain dignity by exercising some real control over their own lives: black people trying to organize their own communities, wage-earners who strike for their rights against their employers or in wildcat action against undemocratic unions, soldiers who refuse to commit acts that violate the dictates of conscience—all the people who stand up and resist.

The main task of the Peace and Freedom Movement is to organize people to begin to gain real and concrete power over the institutions which control their everyday lives. One important way to accomplish this is to project into the electoral arena the voices of people fighting for human dignity, to make it clear that the demand for human dignity is at root a demand for power—and that the people will have this power only when we all can democratically assure that our economy works to fulfill human needs rather than to increase the power and profit of a small minority. The function of Peace and Freedom candidates is to act as the tribunes of Americans who have begun to fight back.

Foreign Policy

The Peace and Freedom Party stands for the right of all peoples to determine their own destiny. It opposes the U.S. foreign policy of economic, political and military domination over the affairs of other nations. We are dedicated to the reversal of America's systematic economic, military and political exploitation of the peoples of the world. This domination establishes the U.S. as the major obstacle to the attempts of other peoples to overcome their misery and oppression and to establish for themselves an existence rooted in self-determination and dignity. The war in Vietnam is not an accident; it is the logical consequence of an American economic imperialism which requires the subordination of foreign resources, markets, and political structures to the needs of corporate property and profit. Under the pretence of protecting the world from Communism, America supports reactionary regimes throughout the world, thereby thwarting the aspirations of its peoples and maintaining them in a condition of bondage.

We oppose the same conduct on the part of any other nation, without exception. Although our major concern as Americans is with the imperialistic foreign policies and wars of our own country, we also oppose the imperialistic interventions of any other nation, capitalist or Communist.

The Peace and Freedom Party supports the struggle for human liberation and freedom wherever that struggle takes place. We defend the right of all exploited people to the control of their own economic resources and political systems in a world of just, stable pride and the continuing diminution of military threat and power. We understand that no such radical change in American policy is possible under the present American military-industrial complex, the source of that American imperialism which so brutalizes the nations of the third world. The power of monopoly capitalism must be broken and replaced by a mass movement whose concern is the democratization of all aspects of American life.

This fundamental restructuring is neither easy nor imminent, but it can be accomplished through our persistent and dedicated effort. The façade of American life masks a system of domestic and foreign exploitation which the repressed people of the U.S. and of the world are coming militantly to oppose. To articulate this struggle and to join its ranks is the effort worthy of our labor and sacrifice, the hope of men throughout the world, and the unique human challenge of our times.

Ban all aggresssive wars; immediate withdrawal from Vietnam!

Minority Liberation

We of the Peace and freedom Movement, recognizing the white racism which pervades this society, and recognizing further the oppression existing in this country, stand for an immediate end to racism, and for self-determination for all minorities. We support the right for all oppressed minority communities to police themselves and maintain economic and political control over their own lives. We also recognize that law and order cannot be separated from justice and that these must arise from the community itself.

It is the responsibility of the majority community to make available to minority communities sufficient resources to make possible fully adequate education, housing and income for all of the people.

We are pledged to building a political movement which will ultimately permit the masses of whites, blacks and other oppressed minorities to ally in a common struggle for their common interests.

We endorse the Black Panther Party for Self-Defense ten-point program.

. . . .

17.3.

JULIAN BOND: **The Future of the Democratic Party**

[Julian Bond, former SNCC leader, is a member of the legislature of Georgia, in which he was not seated twice in 1966 for his opposition to the war in Vietnam. At the 1968 Democratic Convention, he led an independent Geogia delegation which supported the nomination of Senator McCarthy. *New York Free Press,* October 31, 1968.]

I don't have the slightest idea about what the future . . . if any . . . of the Democratic Party in the United States might be.

I do know that in this section of the country, there are no "Democratic parties" as you might know of them in New York State. Instead, we have

Governor's parties, headed and directed by whatever man who calls himself a Democrat happens to be in power at the time.

The Southern task, therefore, is building a party of some kind, calling it either "Democratic" or "Freedom Democrats" or whatever.

In Georgia, a first step toward that goal has been taken. There is a state-wide organization here called the Democratic Forum. It was this group that called the convention that elected the challenge delegation that went to the Chicago Convention.

My hope is that this group can become a party, or more correctly, an organized group of Georgians who place high priority on electoral politics a great deal to the left of the organized electoral politics so common to this region.

That process, if it is to be successful, will take nearly eight or ten years, I believe, and a lot of hard work and a lot of money.

Black people in Georgia are a state-wide minority, although we are a majority in some counties and will be a majority in Atlanta within five years. In these areas I would favor all-black (or at worst, majority black) political organizations that could effectively, democratically, direct the political thrust of a group of people for whom politics means both street improvements and civilizing the police, as well as a chance to influence and direct policy-making on a city, county and state level.

For this election, in November, what strikes me as the biggest difference between Southern and Northern outlooks is that most Kennedy-McCarthy supporters I know in this region are hoping for, if not working for, the election of Vice-President Humphrey because of their fear of the Strom Thurmond influence in a Nixon government, while their Northern counterparts are mostly not participating in the November election on a presidential level.

Those of us here, of course, are subjected to much abuse by those persons unfortunate enough not to have to live here. We are called "shills" and "prostitutes" by our Northern brothers and sisters, which is an indication, I believe, that now that the sit-in demonstrations and Freedom Rides have paled, and voter registration efforts lost their excitement, that there isn't much interest up yonder in us folks down here. But that's life.

17.4.   *CARL OGLESBY:* **An Open Letter to McCarthy Supporters**

[The 1968 presidential campaign of Senator Eugene McCarthy had an attraction for a section of young people and of the movement against the war. Carl Oglesby, university teacher, was SDS president in 1965 and is author of *Containment and Change.*]

. . . .

Is McCarthy the pay-off of those years of protest? Does he represent the partial fruition of our efforts to build a movement for changing America?

Or is he only another attempt to emasculate that protest?

Is he what the Movement has been working for? Or against?

How in fact are we to define McCarthy so that we can at least be sure that we're talking about the same thing?

Perhaps by his record? Surely you're tired by now of listening to the dreary list of his illiberal votes: his assent to the witch-hunt politics of the '50s (as late as 1959 he voted for the Student Loyalty Oath Bill), his vacillation on civil rights (in 1961 he voted against withholding Federal aid from segregated schools), his occasional anti-Labor stands (against extension of minimum-wage coverage in 1960 and against the rail workers in 1963), and maybe most galling of all, the tardiness of his opposition to the War (he voted for every war appropriation bill, for the Tonkin Gulf resolution, and against the 1966 amendment which would have exempted non-volunteering draftees from service in Vietnam). He has consistently opposed the admission of China to the UN, and clings to the view that there is nothing structurally wrong with our foreign policy: "We still have the fleet," he said last November, "we still have Japan, we still have a position in South Korea, we have built up a strong base in Thailand. . . ." And in April, asked if we needed to take a new approach to international affairs, he answered "No. We do in Vietnam, in Southeast Asia. But not in Korea, not in Japan, not in India, not the North Atlantic Treaty Organization."

But you have heard this.

You are doubtless a little worried about the suggestion of hypocrisy in his dissent. He sought to provide an alternative, he said when he announced his candidacy last November, to those who "become cynical and make threats of support for third parties or fourth parties or other irregular political movements." As if so explicit a subordination of content to form were anything but the essence of cynicism.

You have often been informed, moreover, that his chances of victory are galactically remote. You knew this, after all, from the start.

So add it up.

His record: to be charitable, call it ambiguous.

His present policies: to give the benefit of the doubt, say that they do not quite hit the nail on the head.

His real power: to be optimistic, assume that it is still in the process of formation.

What is the sum?

McCarthy-in-Practice

A definition of McCarthy-in-practice: the probably unproductive compromise of policies which are ambiguous, if not dubious, to begin with.

Which is merely one way of putting what most of you already claim to know.

Then why do you continue to support him?

We think there are reasons. One has to do with an illusion. Another with a reality. And another with a failure of nerve.

You visualize McCarthy as a man in the process of change. You imply that he should no more be judged by what he used to be than, for example, SDS itself.

In a time like this, that is no ground for fantasy. Above all we need clarity now, not subtle evocations of mood. And in the measure that McCarthy has been clear, his case against the War remains explicitly a traditional case for anti-Communist containment.

It was only his dedication to the containment policy which led him to challenge the Administration in the first place. He saw the truth to which political vanity had blinded Johnson, namely that it was not possible to impose upon the Vietnamese a government of French colonial officers, and that the desperate attempt to do so was creating the gravest crisis of the Cold War period: it was cracking the Atlantic Alliance. Not alone in his awareness, he was also not the first to voice it. We do not say that his decision to oppose Johnson openly was easy. Within its own framework, it was perhaps even courageous. But this courage is that of the timid among the craven, the diffident among the abject, the whisperer among the silent. There are other standards of courage in a world which remembers Ché Guevara, meets again every day the ordinary Vietnam peasant, and knows Fanny Lou Hamer. Compared to what we need, in any case, his distinction is a small excursion from an abysmal norm.

We think you project onto the future McCarthy the virtues which you know he must come to possess. The current moral and physical turmoil certainly seems to beg for heroes. McCarthy is honest. He has candor and integrity and intelligence enough to distinguish victory from defeat. With a desperation which we can easily understand, you treat him as if he were already the man he has not yet even promised to become. This is illusionment.

The Reality: It is just that Left politics in America is hard. There is not much room for movement in that direction. Not much is possible. Play to secure the marginal victory and avoid the central defeat.

So it comes down to the famous bird in hand.

If it does nothing else, the McCarthy campaign represents itself implicitly as the Leftmost ideological position at which political realism still endures. Above all, you have told us, this is no time for utopia, romance, or extremist provocations. The very power of the case the New Left made for stopping the War, in fact, is a conclusive argument for an expedient politics. So McCarthy won't join the Vietcong. At least he'll bring off the capitulation without totally freaking everybody out.

Don't demand the final salvation of the whole world tomorrow.

Demand, instead, the end of the War today.

Don't demand socialism tomorrow.

Demand, instead, that capitalism, starting today, begin creating for itself a more human heart.

Don't demand for tomorrow that real democracy establish itself in our society.

Demand, instead, that the old elites at once start behaving better.

Very tempting, this realism of ideals, and we ourselves will cheerfully confess a preference for effectiveness over usefulness.

But this practicality—with respect to exactly what policies does it commend itself to us? How desirable in themselves are these policies? And how exclusively are they the property of McCarthy?

McCarthy has already persuaded us that his overriding objective is the defense of the same American Empire which we find flatly unsupportable. That he should see the cessation of large-scale military action against Vietnam as the pre-condition of revamped containment/imperialism—we find this not at all hard to understand. This is also why the big corporations have turned against the War. They, too, want to find new security for those key positions in Europe and Latin America which the Vietnam "diversion" has left exposed. They, too, are passionately concerned about the international equilibrium of the dollar, and they understand that a sharp de-escalation of the War is a basic current requirement for the health of the North Atlantic economic system.

McCarthy (and Rockefeller), among all the candidates, possibly understood this best, maybe even first. That may be commendable. The point, however, is that in one way or another the futility of the War has become clear even to Nixon. Any President must contrive to abandon the War. The Vietnamese have so decreed.

McCarthy's campaign is important. It is one manifestation of the breakdown of the political coalitions put together in the 1930s. At least indirectly, it expresses the emergence of a newly politicized and activist "grass roots" constituency—that of the post-war generations. It imperfectly embodies the new spirit of participant democracy.

But practicality? Realism? Granted the sincerity of his occasional New Left-sounding flourishes, McCarthy's "practicality" amounts in the end to the adulteration of the necessary critique of the War, the obscuring of its sources in the system of American expansionism. It amounts to a moderating of already timid proposals which therefore lose whatever character they might have had: better negotiations, maybe, inviting the NLF into a coalition whose other elements are precisely the forces which the NLF has been struggling to expel and which have precious-little constituency other than the US State Department, and on all other problems of foreign policy the retention and even reinforcing of the Truman-to-Johnson containment line.

No question: Such a policy is "practical," "possible," and "realistic." We've had it for years.

And we haven't even raised yet the most obvious question: Since so many of you argue that we New Leftists should have compromised a bit for the sake of this "realistic alternative" we wonder why so few of you have argued that McCarthy can win?

The Failure of Nerve: Almost every young supporter of McCarthy we talk with is well to the Left of his champion. Many express the same dissatisfactions with his policies that we have expressed. Almost nobody thinks there is more than a hundred-to-one chance of his winning. The bird in the hand which was supposed to justify all sorts of tactical compromises turns out on inspection to be only a possible bird in the hand.

Then why all the excitement about "really making a difference"?

We have to say this bluntly:

We think you are afraid of your own politics, and that you are employing the McCarthy campaign as a means of making your dissent look respectable and "legitimate."

Fear of honest thought and its political imperatives; of effecting a clean break with the powerful institutions which have squandered so many lives; of abandoning the security of the system whose outrages you attack; of becoming your own "base of legitimacy": Is McCarthy a reprieve?

So What Do We Want You To Do?

Above all, to understand your own importance.

Not to borrow others' causes for fear of the difficulty of your own.

To grasp the fact that the authenticity which you find in McCarthy is there only because you have put it there; that his special virtues are merely small versions of your common possibilities.

Honesty? Yes. You are more honest.

Rebelliousness? Yes. Your rebellion is better, even if it has not yet dis-covered its proper gait and idiom. You dance better. You write better poems.

The only really interesting practicality of his campaign, in fact, is that it has your support. He needs you. The institutions which have mis-educated, mis-employed, mis-ruled your lives need you.

You don't need them.

This battle, after all, is one that we have begun: the young ones began it, not the old ones. Only the young ones will be loyal to it. The old ones remember too many defeats and erroneous victories. It is our generation's fight. For obvious reasons, its imagery condenses around Vietnam, America's ghettos, the inflicted povery of the Third World. But its underlying content goes beyond them.

We think that the present stakes are immense. What we think is happen-ing, in all this confusing and frightening disorder, is the unfolding of a new stage of human history, the writing by a new generation of a new human agenda—old in its essential hopes, new in the possibility of their realization.

A birth is trying to take place. Certain high-class killers in league with certain clowns are trying to hold the baby back, while a few political priests suggest politely that the birth of a little finger might be permissible. In behalf of everything old, used up, and dying—in other words, in behalf of their own privilege—they fight against everything new. So many undertakers in the delivery room.

The point is not to make deals with them there, but to get them out.

"That cannot happen."

Perhaps that is true. But since it must happen, it will, and whether it can or not makes no difference.

Like most of us, you are mostly of the middle and upper-middle classes. We have not been hungry, cold, or afraid. We have grown up with the Cold War, which made anxiety an ordinary state, and the Machine, a presence in our lives at once abstract and immediate, and which made habit of miracle.

Our task is first to clarify the main issues of the world we must live in.

Revolutionary communism? That is the primary form taken on by the struggles of the forcibly dispossessed to re-possess themselves of their identity and destiny. American power has no business opposing those struggles. Americans indeed must learn to rejoice in the human bravery that brings them into being. For when those who are now oppressed are not oppressed, then the masters will also be liberated from their permanently desperate vigils.

The militant nationalism of American blacks? Far from being a threat to us, this anger enriches us and we welcome it. There is no man, no law, no government that can substitute for this creative movement of the people.

The defense of property rights? Americans have already been de-prop-ertied by the very system whose demand for property worship is most feverish. Our task is not to lament this event, but to move forward through it. We do not deny that once upon a time property rights constituted the base of the de-velopment of social wealth. Men paid a high price in suffering for the political guarantee of these rights to a privileged elite. There is no longer the remotest need for either that suffering, that guarantee, or that elite. Current and future wealth is wholly socialized in every respect but that of ownership. The com-pletion of its socialization is the only way to avoid the on-coming international war of race and class and to restore the chance of national sanity.

Our parallel task is to create the political means by which we can pursue our objectives.

This requires, above all, that we face a simple fact: Political institutions designed to perpetuate a system of power will never become instruments for the transformation of that system.

If you want to stop not only the Vietnam War but the system that begot it, if you want not merely to blur the edges of racism but to change the system that needed slaves in the first place and could "emancipate" them only into ghettos in the second, if you want not merely to make deals with irrationality but to liberate reason for the conquest of joy, then you will have to go outside the system for the preparation of your means. You will have to go inside yourself first to rediscover the feeling of your own possible freedom, and from there to the feeling of the possible freedom of others.

Pride and communion.

That's what the Movement is about. That's what we think you should be about.

FURTHER READINGS

Booth, Paul. "Electoral Politics." In *Beyond Dissent: Papers from the New Left*. Garden City, N.Y.: Doubleday, 1967.

Committee for Independent Political Action, Position. Document undated. Mimeograph.

Davis, Rennie, and Lynd, Staughton. "New Politics Versus a Movement in Revolt and New Politics and The Movement." *National Guardian*, August 26 and September 2.

"A Fourth Party." Editorial, *The New Republic*, July 6, 1968.

Friedman, Mike, and Lyons, Kit. "McCarthy and the Democratic Party: The Two-Party System in Crisis." *Independent Socialist*, August 1968.

Garson, Marvin. "The Whites: A Clown Show." *Los Angeles Free Press*, September 22–28, 1967.

_____. "PFP Candidate Concedes as Polls Open." *San Francisco Express Times*, November 1968.

Kopkind, Andrew. "They'd Rather Be Left." *New York Review*, September 28, 1967.

Lasch, Christopher. "The New Politics 1968 and After." *New York Review*, July 11, 1968.

Lens, Sidney. "Confusion and Promise." *New Politics*, Winter 1967.

Oglesby, Carl. "Yankees vs. Cowboys." *Guardian*, April 13, 20 and 27, 1968.

Stein, Buddy, and Wellman, David. "The Scheer Campaign." Reprinted by Radical Education Project, originally published in *Studies on the Left*, January/February 1967.

Symposium on New Politics (Chicago's Black Caucus). *Ramparts*, November 1967.

Symposium on New Politics. *Studies on the Left*, IV: 3, Summer 1964.

18
What Is To Be Done

18.1. *WILLIAM DOMHOFF:* **How To Commit Revolution**

[The following text is the second part of a speech delivered at a strike meeting held by students at the University of California at Santa Cruz in April, 1968, and published in the *Midpeninsula Observer* of July 15 and 19, 1968. William Domoff is a professor at Santa Cruz and author of *Who Rules America?*. The author's intention was to raise critical questions for the New Left, not to state a final position or a solution to the dilemmas which radicals are presently facing.]

. . . .

Now to a program for taking the reins of government from the power elite in order to carry out the plan developed by revolutionary visionaries. It is on this point that we are likely to find the most disagreement, the most confusion, the most uncertainty, and the most fear.

But I think you do have something very important to go on—the ideas and experiences and successes of the Civil Rights and New Left and Hippie movements of the past several years. If they have not given you an analysis of corporate capitalism or a set of blueprints, which is their weakness, they have given you the incredibly precious gift of new forms of struggle and new methods of reaching people; and these gifts must be generalized, articulated, and more fully developed.

I have a general term, borrowed from a radical hippie, that I like to use because it so beautifully encompasses what these movements have given to you—psychic guerrilla warfare—the "psychic" part appealing to my psychologist instincts and summarizing all the hard-hitting nonviolent methods, the "guerrilla warfare" part hopefully giving to those who want to take to the hills some satisfaction, so that they will stick around and participate in the only type of guerrilla warfare likely to work in corporate America.

For make no mistake about it, psychic guerrilla warfare is a powerful weapon in a well-educated, sedate, highly industrialized country that has a tradition of liberal values and democratic political processes.

And it is the kind of guerrilla warfare that America's great new acting-out girls can indulge in on an equal basis with any male anywhere. It is the confrontation politics of the New Left—teach-ins, marches, mill-ins, sit-ins, push-ins, love-ins, folk rocks, be-ins. It is the nonviolent, religiously-based, democratically-inspired confrontation morality of Martin Luther King, and it is the unfailing good humor, psychological analysis, and flower power of the Hippie. Together they are dynamite.

Before I suggest how and where to lay this psychological dynamite, I know I must force myself to say a few words concerning what you are wondering about most, the role of violence. The words aren't easy for me to say, a look at history makes the ground shaky under me, and many will secretly or openly assume that this is cowardly rationalization by an academic.

Despite all this, I reject the lesson of history by claiming that the situation is different in this overindustrialized, sedate country: I don't think violence will work in corporate America, 1968. I don't believe in non-violence as a way of life as some people do, so I don't argue from any philosophic base. I have never been adverse to violence or denied its necessity in past revolutions.

No, I'm just afraid violence is not a winning strategy in corporate America, and a winning strategy is the primary concern of the revolutionary consultant.

This doubt about the usefulness of violence in corporate America was also the opinion of one of the greatest violent revolutionists of all time, certainly a man who stands as tall in my gallery of revolutionary heroes as any man.

I refer to Ché. Indeed, it is almost a tragedy that those who love and admire Ché, and at the same time dream of physical guerrilla warfare in the U.S.A., should overlook his very first premise for it—people take to physical guerrilla warfare only when they have lost all hope of nonviolent solutions. Ché is said to have laughed long and hard when asked about the possibility of guerrilla warfare in this country. He too apparently believed that what works in the maldeveloped, exploited hinterland does not necessarily apply to the overdeveloped, affluent capitalist center.

Americans have not lost their hope. Furthermore, they are not likely to lose it by any of the means currently being used to escalate physical confrontations, for such confrontations do not "expose" the most fundamental aspects of the political system.

The only way people would lose their faith in the political system, if they are capable of losing it at all, is in a full and open and honest test of its promise.

And if you argue that people won't listen, that they haven't listened in the past few years, then I say it's because you haven't yet brought to them an analysis that rings true enough, that you haven't yet hit them with a program that is exciting enough, and that you haven't yet provided them with a plan of attack that is believable enough to be worth trying.

I say you really haven't turned on with all your intellectual and libidinal resources, that you haven't given them your best shot. What you have done so far is great, but it is only a prelude. You've got to escalate your incredibleness, your audacity, your cleverness, and your playfulness, not your physical encounters, if you are to break through the American malaise.

Enough of such moralizing and breast-beating. Back to psychic guerrilla warfare. How do you direct this dynamite to its task of destroying the ideological cover of the corporate rich?

First, you start a new political party, a wide-open, locally-based political party dedicated to the development of blueprints for a post-industrial America and to the implementation of them through psychic guerrilla warfare. It should be a party open to anyone prepared to abandon all other political affiliations and beliefs—in other words, it would not be an Anti-This-Or-That coalition of liberal Democrats, Communists, Trotskyists, and Maoists.

In fact, ignore those groups. The best members will drop out and join yours. For the rest, they have no constituencies and would soon fall to fighting the Old Fights among themselves anyway—Communist and Anti-Communist, Pro-Soviet and Anti-Soviet, and On and On ad tedium.

No, you don't need that—it would destroy you like it destroyed them. Indeed, they need you, for if you got something going the party would be big enough for all of them to work in without seeing each other or having to defend the Old Faiths.

Before I go on, let me pause to make some things clear. Lenin was great. So was Trotsky. So were Eugene Debs and Thomas Paine, and so are Mao and

Fidel, but they have nothing to teach you except guts and perseverence because your situation is different. Honor them for their courage and their example, but most of all, for their ability to let go of sacred texts and do what was necessary in their given society even when it contradicted received doctrine (as it always did).

If they could forget the sacred texts of their masters, why can't you go beyond theirs? You need your own Lenins, not theirs, your own Chés, not theirs, and I suspect they will be as different as the first is from the second.

So what does your party do besides present a constant withering critique of corporation capitalism and build blueprints of a post-industrial America? It practices all forms of psychic guerrilla warfare whenever and wherever there is a possible convert. Eventually, and on the right occasions, it even enters elections, not to win votes at first, but to win converts. In making its pitch, it doesn't ask men and women to quit their jobs or take to the hills, but rather it asks them to commit their allegiances to new socioeconomic arrangements, to help develop new social and intellectual institutions, to financially support the growth of the party, to read party-oriented newspapers, to convert and neutralize friends and neighbors, and even to stand firm if the corporate rich try something funny.

But what about the military, you ask? Everyone knows that any serious revolution must not only isolate the ruling social class and eliminate its economic base, but it must do away with the army that is its ultimate instrument. How is that possible in America? By keeping it a civilian, draftee army and by infiltrating its officer ranks. As long as the American army is not a standing, professional army, as long as it is made up mostly of civilian recruits serving short terms, then you have control of that army to the degree that you have the loyalty of the majority of citizens.

However, to ensure leadership, at a certain point it would become necessary for party members to sacrifice themselves, not by avoiding the draft, but by joining the ranks of military officers. If that sounds like a very great sacrifice, I agree, but perhaps it will appeal to those among you who like undercover games.

Let me be sure I am being clear. Now is not the time to begin infiltrating the army, but at some point along the line that would become a prime task. The only task of such infiltrators would be to make sure that the corporate rich could never turn military fire-power on the nonviolent revolution.

They would do this by advocating one thing and one thing only—the subservience of the military to civilian government, the refusal to take sides in an internal political controversy. In so doing they would be indistinguishable from non-party members within the military who truly accepted this tradition. It may be that there are many of those but that should not be counted on.

Now who does this party address itself to as its agitators and organizers drive around in open-air trucks, complete with folk rock bands, shouting out their message and distributing their handbills in every town, county fair, ghetto, and shopping center in the country? What is its potential constituency?

The answer is first of all a very general one, but this very generality frees American revolutionaries from trying to duplicate the past or fit into theoretical molds.

You should direct yourself to anyone disgusted with the present system and assume that your potential constituency is everyone not wrapped up in the power elite.

This even includes sons and daughters of the corporate rich who have seen enough and want out—and they've always been there in small numbers on the American Left and Right anyhow, so why pretend differently?

I suggest as follows: the initial base is, as C. Wright Mills said, radical intellectuals and students. The intellectuals have got to start talking like Gene Debs and Malcolm X. They have got to blast out of the classroom and clinic like Mills and Benjamin Spock, carrying their revolutionary consultation services to every group in the country that will send them an airplane fare or bus ticket.

What with the protection of tenure and the right of academic freedom, and with lots of universities opening up in Canada, Australia, and New Zealand, professors are the least vulnerable group in American society. They ought to be ashamed of themselves for not raising a hundred times more ruckus than they are now.

These professors and their students also have to continue work on the analysis, and began involving people in their local community to work on the blueprints. They should form small study-action groups in every university, college, and junior college town in the country.

These small study-action groups have to prepare themselves for a psychic blitz of their most important constituency. That constituency is simply called youth—blue collar, white collar, white skin, black skin, who cares? They are pouring out of schools like crazy, affluence has made them somewhat independent and hang-loose, many of them don't communicate with their parents, and they're going to be a majority in a very few years.

Catch them in those years when they are sociologically part of a unique subculture and psychologically looking for something moral and true and meaningful for their lives, and sock it to them with analyses and programs that will make them as wise to the slick McCarthys, Kennedys, and Rockefellers as they are to the Rusks, Johnsons, and Nixons.

If you don't get them the first time around, at least they have something to chew over when they get out there in the boredom of being a clerk-typist, or probation officer, or real estate salesman. I know that right now an amazing number of the young are enamored of the integrity and professorial cool of Eugene McCarthy, but that's all he's got. With no program but a little more of the same, wedded to corporation capitalism, and committed to a party with a reactionary Southern wing and a fistful of New York investment bankers, his time is going to run out if he can't produce.

Young people react to the put-on, they hate to be fooled or talked down to or pandered to, and some day they will have had enough—they will remember Humphrey's sell-out, if you are there to remind them; they will remember Johnson's campaign fibs about his plans for Vietnam, if you never let them forget it; and they will start looking around again.

After youth, the early appeals of the party must be to the disaffected teachers, librarians, nurses, and bureaucrats of the white collar class. They are the ones hit by inflation and hurt by the limitations on government spending, not the unionizing blue-collar workers with their built-in cost-of-living raises. And besides, you've got something immediate for them—thanks to the Hippies, you can teach them how to be happy. Happy? Yes happy.

Get your Hippie friends out of the woods, put a light trim on their beards and hairdos, and start them to work on the poor, wasted paper pushers and people manipulators. I'm serious. They can be had. They're going nowhere, they're restless, and their rage shows how jealous they really are. Their kids— using flower power and psychic guerrilla warfare—can cajole them over the line.

After all, these people raised the turned-on kids. Their emptiness and searching is reflected in their children, who have to resort to modern-day ambrosias and Eastern mystical religions to overcome their boredom. If the kids can be had, the parents can be had, if you handle them with psychological bribery and good-humored taunts rather than threats and insults.

As I've implied throughout, an effort has to be made toward those on the Right. I'm under no illusions about the difficulties of this, but I insist that it is necessary to dismiss talk about racism and fascism on the Right: all white Americans are racists, and parts of the blue collar world are probably worse than the Right. As to fascism, if we get a European-style dictatorship in this country, it will probably be more like France anyway, and it will be instituted by the corporate rich presently in power in order to get around their difficulties with Congress and local governments.

So forget all this talk about fascism, which has scared American revolutionaries into the laps of the liberals almost as well as the cry of Communism has scared the Right into the arms of the corporate rich. Old Left and liberal talk about fascism amounts to their fear of angering the corporate masters to the point where they call on their supposed Right-wing shock troops.

See if you can make contact with those people on the New Right, who really have no place to go because there is no turning back now that the huge corporations have destroyed individual capitalism. Of course they don't share your program, but they do share your view of the power structure and your desire for more individuality and local autonomy.

In dealing with the New Right, it is essential to respect individuality and personality. Neither Left nor Right really does this despite their rhetoric. A revolution must transcend personality and respect individuality if it is to get to its task of reaching large masses of people. In fact, personal diversity will be an asset in getting the attention of all types of people. Different religions, different styles and different hair arrangements must be de-emphasized (not changed) and consciously subordinated by self-analysis and devotion to common goals through the mechanism of the blueprints.

The enemy is corporation capitalism, not religion, personality structure, or type of oral indulgent—pot on the Left, alcohol on the Right—used to lessen anxiety and dispel depression.

Why haven't I mentioned black people till now? Aren't they important? Am I just another Whitey who doesn't care about the black man? Not at all. I suggest that you do what the black man has told you to: let him do his own thing and you get to work building a party that can unite with him some day far off down the road after you've overcome your racism and he's made up his mind about where he's going and with whom. For now the black man is right—you've got nothing to tell him, and he's got to go it on his own in order to win his manhood. Nobody has ever been given anything worth having. Finally some black men are learning that freeing fact.

Of course black people should be welcome in your party, as should anyone who shares your beliefs, but I suspect it will be a while before many will be along.

One group is going to go a separate and/or violent route. They have had enough and they will have to see some fine action from a revolutionary party before they are going to buy any dreams and hopes again. I don't blame them. I for one will never get uppity or moralistic if some blacks decide to bring the whole mess to the ground. I understand their rage, I feel their rage.

But despite my sympathy I don't mistake the catharsis of wrecking the system for changing it. Revolutionary movements grow more slowly and have positive goals. I hope you can show these black radicals something so they'll work with you, because the ones I've watched have the juice to turn the masses on like nothing I've ever seen. Malcolm X was the finest American agitator since Eugene Debs, and a revolutionary party would need a hundred more like him.

Then there's another group of blacks who are committed to non-violence but who think John F. Kennedy freed them! Imagine. Like the Socialists of the Old Left, their hangup is a faith in the Democratic Party that knows no bounds, through thick and thin, Raw Deal and Screw Deal. Pictures of JFK abound in their homes. The tragic thing about this group is that they don't know they freed themselves—they pushed that smooth-talking young conservative to the wall before he would make a move.

These people don't know their own power. Nor do they understand the limitations of the present socioeconomic system; they are still hoping it will assimilate them economically. Apparently their faith in God and American democracy even includes corporation capitalism. Many even refuse to talk about the Vietnam war, hoping that their white masters will give them a little more if they keep their traps shut about the repression of other colored peoples.

What about blue collar workers? First, create a party they have to react to. And don't waste time trying to control or shape labor unions, which are conservative bureaucratic institutions these days, rightfully looking out for the working man in day-to-day battles with the corporate leaders. Confront these people at home, at school, and at play, and get them involved in the party and its activities. In short, don't get caught in Old Left fixations.

Now I know there are many thousands of dedicated and far-seeing blue collar workers who would be with you from the start, heart and soul, sweat and tears. But don't get the idea that any great percentage of organized labor will be willing to risk leaving the Democratic Party. Right now they have it relatively good—as long as they are working, or are insulated against automation, or have cost-of-living raises built into their contracts as checks against inflation. But no matter how nicely some of the corporate rich treat blue collar workers in wartime, don't worry, because there is no question about where the blue collar masses would be in a showdown if you have done your homework carefully.

Let's assume that the party is not snuffed out in its early stages and that it grows. Then the power elite is in a bind; they will have to compete with it, which means a move towards the Welfare State, or, failing that, they would have to repress it, which would be the great watersheld for American liberals, liberalism, and democracy.

If you are nonviolent, open, of all religions, and not tied to a foreign power, they would be destroying America to move on you. Liberals would have no course but to join the fight on your side or admit that socioeconomic privileges are more basic than political institutions and values; some might even be annoyed enough to join you in air-conditioned, music-equipped prison cells that the corporate rich are likely to provide. More generally, at that point the masses of people in America would have to draw their own conclusions about what is to be done.

Your job is to force them to make that choice between democracy and corporation feudalism by taking the system on its promise and testing it to its limits. Either way, you win—a democratic, non-violent takeover or proof to all that when it gets down to the nitty-gritty, even in America, the only way to power is through the barrel of the gun.

To conclude, let me outline what you should do today and tomorrow if you are revolutionaries (if you are in California, wait until after the November elections so as not to undercut your many friends who are working hard in the Peace and Freedom Party). First, start a chapter of a future revolutionary party. Call it, say, the American Revolutionary Party so as to make your intention clear from the start.

Then, to set the sort of tone you want for the thing, print up a membership card, something like, "I, the undersigned, am a card-carrying member of the American Revolutionary Party, dedicated to replacing corporation capitalism with a post-industrial America through psychic guerrilla warfare."

Then start a chapter newsletter in which you invite people to discuss and develop blueprints for your local area—for running its schools, its beaches, its universities, its utilities, and its factories. Send particularly good ideas and articles, especially those relevant to the national level or other cities, to the editorial staff of the nationwide party journal.

At the same time, begin to hold classes in which you teach about the nature of corporation capitalism and discuss blueprints for a post-industrial America. Such educational efforts are a must, one of the best lessons to be learned from the Old Left, and they are the start of the parallel educational structure that each local chapter should strive to develop.

As soon as you have enough people in the chapter who are dedicated and know what it's all about, then you look for opportunities to reach larger numbers of people through confrontation politics—marches, rallies, sit-ins, whatever, but always including explicit mention of the party and its goals.

If there is a local bond issue asking for higher property taxes to support the schools, then that's the time to show in detail how the corporate rich distort the tax structure and force the burden on the middle levels, even to the point of bribing the tax assessors in some cities. Agree with the New Right that taxes are killing them and tell them why, agree with the liberals on the need for better schools and show them how they would be in a post-industrial America.

If the issue is an increase in the gasoline tax, then maybe that's the time to shock conservatives about the price manipulations and tax dodges by the pious oil companies who help finance the New Right.

In short, armed with a real understanding of the present system and the beginnings of plans for a better one, you use every occasion possible to get people's attention and gain converts.

If you bother to go on campus for other than speeches to interested student groups, use picketing not to stop recruiters or Dow Chemical agents but to educate and convert more students and professors. Aside from exposing the complicity of leading universities and research institutes in the machinations of the corporate rich (which ranges from CIA involvement at MIT and

Michigan State to overseas economic front men at Stanford Research Institute), your main concern is elsewhere.

The university is not the key structure in the system, and just exposing its uglier aspects is enough to get you a careful hearing from most students, and even some professors.

This advice about dealing with the universities is part of a larger strategy: ignore the corporate rich and their tag-alongs. You have no criticisms or suggestions to offer them. There is nothing they can do to satisfy you, short of joining your party. Don't try to change them and their policies. Leave that for liberals.

Talk to people, don't debate with the power structure.

Now, once the party exists and has distinct identity, you can of course support just causes. You are for anything that makes people's lives better. The important thing is to show that you are for these causes without getting so caught up in them that you can't see the forest for the trees. Don't get sidetracked.

Once you have a good-sized local chapter, then add "politics" to your other activities. This consists of developing parallel governments and councils (like shadow cabinets) ready to step in if and when, and of running for legislative offices in the hopes of winning and thus gaining a better platform from which to reach people.

But action would not take place only on the local level. All the while, the many locals would be in contact through social (not, ugh, business) meetings at regional and national levels. Then too, they would contribute representatives and ideas and money to a loose national party structure which would consist mostly, at the outset, of the editorial staff of the nationwide journal and the organizers, agitators, and revolutionary consultants who would travel around the country helping to organize and strengthen locals.

Every chapter would contribute a few members to this national-level effort each year, thus ensuring that a great many members from all over the country get national experiences and perspective. This not only cross-fertilizes the locals and helps maintain an overall outlook, but it provides some basis for the selection of candidates for national offices.

During the summer the national organization would also coordinate the Student Organizing Teams who would in groups of 20–30 spend several weeks in every hamlet in the country carrying the message of the party to the hinterlands. The groups would be made up of those with an empathy for and knowledge of rural America, including return-to-the-land type of Hippies.

Their goal would be to develop a chapter, however small, in any settlement or town where people would listen. And listen they might, for the descendants of those people who became Populists in the 1890's and took potshots at local bankers and judges in the 1930's are being had once again by the corporate oligarchy.

What do you do next? What do you do if the infiltration of the army is not very far along and the corporate rich attempt to suppress your fast-growing movement? Well, you can't expect to anticipate everything.

If your analysis is sound, if your blueprints are appealing, and if your psychic guerrilla warfare has blown the minds and ideological cover of the power elite, then you are part of the most exciting, inspiring, and creative thing in human history: an unstoppable mass movement that can take care of itself. Masses in action, armed with ideas and moral fervor, cannot be beaten.

The real problem for you, then, is not how to end. The real problem is how to begin. And good luck.

18.2.   *JOHN* and *BARBARA EHREN-REICH:* **From Resistance to Revolution**

[The authors are graduate students in biology who have been active in the antiwar and community-organizing movements in New York. They are also authors of a book on the international student movement of spring 1968. From *Monthly Review,* April 1968.]

For at least five years young people in this country have struggled against "the system." That "system"—first no more than the links between red-neck cops and corrupt courts—has grown in our eyes to include the universities and firms we work for, what we see in the streets, how we have been trained to see ourselves. The cost of the struggle has already been great. We have seen friends beaten, jailed, exiled, and even killed. We who continue the struggle do so at the cost of our careers, maybe our lives. But, except for isolated moments of community, the *worth* of the struggle remains vague. We see more and more sharply what is wrong, how the wrongs are related. We have even come to call the system—"capitalism." But the confrontations which have trained our eyes for evil have, by their daily urgency, dimmed our vision of the future good, the "what-for." What follows is less an essay than a credo. We know what we are fighting against. We have this small glimpse of what we are fighting for.

We say it now, not just because to dream together is comfortable. The movement has been a ditch-to-ditch defense of ordinary, decent liberal values. It has been at times heroic, but it has always been a defense. To take the offensive, to fight to win, we must have some notion now of what it means to win. So thoroughly have we been taught to equate "vision" with "hallucination," that even we on the Left sometimes forget that without a vision there can be no strategy; and without strategy our tactics can only be isolated acts of despair.

Our Vision of Society

Under capitalism, the individual and social needs of men are subordinated to the imperatives of capital. At work, the social relations of men cooperating to produce socially required goods or services are hidden by the isolated relations of each man to the things he is producing. Relations between men are transformed into relations between things. And what a man produces, how he produces it, his relation to the other workers, are all determined by the needs of the company, not by the needs of the men. Management may try to convince workers to identify with the company, but managerial decision-making is never offered to workers. They are, finally, commodities too, just like the raw materials and machinery for production.

At home we are similarly limited. It is not only that our choices of opportunities for recreation or of things to buy are limited to those choices that are profitable for someone else. It is not only that our environment is increasingly fouled with noise, with toxic gases and filth, vulgarized with ugly bill-boards and buildings. It is not only that the services we all know we need—good schools, health care, transportation—are inadequately provided because they profit no one. It is that we ourselves are crippled as people. How far into ourselves the personal implications of capitalism reach, no one—writing now and in this society—can say. Our relationships to those closet to us are defined by possessive contracts. All the conditions of our work and leisure turn us into isolated, suspicious individuals, dealing with each other and with ourselves as things, as means to certain ends.

It should be stressed that these phenomena are not simply the result of "manipulation." It is not a few evil men that separate us from each other. It is not the mass media and advertising that have twisted our personalities into weird parodies of the bourgeois ideal type. No doubt such manipulation does play a role in shaping us, but it is, in a way, incidental. What we have become suits our real condition. We have made the adaptation our society demands. The priority of capital is not just something that is hammered into us by text-books and television. It is the condition of our lives, ingrained in every decision: from where to live and work to how to love or mourn.

We counter this with the vision of a society in which human needs take priority over the imperatives of capital. In the light of the above discussion, these needs are almost self-evident. First, the minimum biological conditions for human life must be met: adequate food and shelter, clean air, free and easily accessible medical care, freedom from the threat of an arbitrary death in war. Just above the bare minimum for human survival are the needs for recreation, leisure, basic possessions and enough education to guarantee employment. But there are other sorts of needs, felt faintly or acutely, depending on the pressures of biological needs: we need friendship, affection, love. We need work—not jobs but work, work which is both personally satisfying and socially meaningful. Finally—and if this is not felt as a need, we dare to say that it is because the need itself has been distorted to fit a capitalist "ethic"—we must have freedom. Freedom for a man to work out what he has to do, and to do it.

It takes no deep studies of anthropology, philosophy, or psychology to state these needs. It takes no special moral sensitivity or political orientation to know that they are urgent. But the first conclusion that we draw after recognizing these needs is not so obvious: we insist that these needs be met for *all* people. We reject a society which provides health and comfort for any fraction of its members and not for all. We reject societies which provide physical security for all but reserve creative expression for a tiny elite. We reject sub-societies, e.g., utopian communities which try to satisfy internal, individual needs in isolation from the larger society. We reject a society in which anyone is denied the means for his full development as a human being. This is not to say that men are or should be intellectually, artistically, etc., equal. But in a society which on the one hand breeds a race of janitors and a class of typist-clerks, and on the other hand nurtures a special stock of the professional elite—in such a society we have no idea of the real possibilities for human variability or "inequality."

We believe that for the first time in history the demand for universal satisfaction of these basic needs can be met without a drastic, authoritarian reorganization of society. Technology, which so far has served largely to magnify the differences between rich and poor, between rich and poor countries, can be "unleashed" in the service of all men. We can see the technological resources of the defense and space industries, for instance, being applied to ever cheaper production and faster distribution of necessary goods and services, to freeing men from tedious jobs, and to solving everyday problems of transportation and housing. In fact, not only have technological advances made the demands realizable, but they have aggravated the needs themselves: people who cannot afford a dentist can read about $100,000 heart transplant operations; people who travel only by Greyhound can read about supersonic airliners. Surely the technology which produced nuclear submarines and ICBM's can design a fully automatic subway train which costs a nickel a ride.

It is clear that a society which can meet these needs for the greatest number of people must be organized differently from our present society. The shift from capitalist priorities to human priorities entails much more than the creation of new "super-agencies," the "humanization" of corporations, or the allotment of more money for the same old poverty and health programs. We believe that the shift requires a basic reorganization of all our present institutions, the abandonment of many, and the creation of some new ones.

In the case of meeting biological needs, this is completely clear. Technology can develop without reference to human needs; public agencies can come to serve narrow bureaucratic interests—they will not spontaneously turn to solving human problems. But with a rational distribution of our technical resources, there is no doubt that the biological needs of all our people could be met.

In the case of the more specifically human needs—for friendship, purpose, and freedom—many will ask whether *any* social organization can possibly meet them. Aren't many anxieties and discontents just part of the "human condition," and inaccessible to social solutions? Now, it is never easy to distinguish between the "human condition" and the "condition of humans in our society." For instance, no one could pretend to know to what extent a painful sense of individual alienation is inherently human and to what extent it is inherent in the majority of human societies. In the absence of such knowledge, we simply state our belief: that the conditions for man's fullest freedom and creativity are social conditions. It goes without saying that satisfaction of material needs comes before satisfaction of creative energies. However, we not only depend on each other materially, but our very ideas of what is "meaningful" about a task, "beautiful" in art, or "good" about an action, are almost always derived from, or at least shared with, others in our society. Even our sense of what it is to be an individual is socially defined. Right now we see only dimly how society might begin to reorganize itself for the greatest individual fulfilment of the greatest number of people. We do not *know* whether *any* social organization could approach satisfaction of these psychological needs. We know only that none has really tried.

The society we strive for is one in which human goals—individual and social, material and psychological—take priority. Production, education, politics—all must be validated solely by the contribution they make to human welfare, not by whether they yield economic growth, balance the budget, or protect the rights of American investors abroad. In such a society men can become truly human, can exercise all their talents and skills, can relate to other people in a free and open manner. And it is this truly human existence, made possible by directing all our society's resources to human needs, that is our ultimate vision and our ultimate goal. The question we must ask is then—what institutions enable us to build such a society?

Prerequisite Institutions

One institutional change is inescapable. We have seen that the evils of our society derive from a system in which the economic well-being of a relatively small group of corporations takes priority over the needs of the great majority of the people. "Taking priority" means simply this: a small group of people, due to their institutional positions, have economic and social aims that conflict with the needs of the great majority. That small group has the power to insure that it is in their interests, not in those of the majority, that decisions are made. We work for a system where the needs of the great majority of Americans will come first and where the decisions of the great majority of Americans will prevail. It is clear that we must take the source of this power from those who now misuse it, and give it to the people. Now the source of that power is ownership of factories, of utilities, of banks. The uses of power are determined by the economic and political organization of society. Power used by private owners is power used in the interest of private owners. To them, profits and corporate expansion are the primary goals, not what is produced and why. The prerequisite for a human society is: control of the factories, the banks, the utilities, the networks of transportation and distribution, in the hands of the people.

We must be very clear about what we mean by "placing power in the hands of the people." Many forms of nominal public control and ownership are irrelevant or even antithetical to socialism as we conceive of it. For instance, suppose the American people theoretically owned everything and elected Lyndon Johnson (or any one man) to administer it. What could be worse? We reject styles of "socialism" in which power is nominally public but decisions are made by a bureaucracy, far removed from the people. Nor would we want popular control to mean that public needs would be ascertained by sociological and psychological studies rather than by direct popular participation in decision-making. Finally, by "public ownership" we do not mean a system in which personal possessions such as homes, cars, hi-fi sets, could be confiscated in the name of economic "justice." In fact, it is easier to state what we do *not* mean by public control than what we do mean. All we can say is that institutions must be developed through which the great majority of the people actively, self-consciously and in a fully informed way, control *all* political, civil, and economic institutions in the interests of all the people.

The hard problem is to determine what institutions can insure true public control and what strategies will create these institutions. What can democracy mean in a nation of 200 million, in a city of 500,000? Conversely, what can power mean to a town of 5,000 or a family of four? But there are even harder problems, problems which only *begin* with the end of private ownership and elite domination of the means of production and distribution. To be sure, capitalism has created these problems, but that does not mean the ending of capitalism will solve them. Public ownership of the means of production is only a *technical condition* for solving the problems of our society. But it is only with public ownership that it is possible to begin to build a human society. Only to begin.

The Initial Tasks

We start with some fairly straightforward tasks that, almost everyone will agree, are essential. We want clean cities with adequate housing, safe streets, and efficient public transportation. For those who prefer it, we want spacious suburbs, from which the jobs and culture of the city are easily accessible. We want the places we live to be not too far from the places we work and from the places we might go to play. In school, we want our children to learn the things we think are important for them as people, not just skills for making a living. We want medical care aimed at keeping us well, not just at salvaging us when we are sick. And when we do get sick we want good care without worrying about the cost. Since we want people to be free to choose their own life style, we need nurseries where mothers who want to work can leave their children, and special school or job arrangements for mothers who want to be with their children most of the time. We want to feel that our children's well-being and opportunities do not depend on our own efforts alone, but are insured by a community of concern. We want to grow our own way, without financial worry, without being coerced by institutions such as the draft. Finally, we want to grow old in a society in which old age is not a disease, but a part of life and a part of life of the community.

These we agree on as goals, whatever the diversity of mechanisms we propose for achieving them. Our experience and our analysis tell us that capitalism cannot adequately meet all of these needs; that in fact, it constantly recreates these needs or other new needs. But all of these goals must be considered transitional goals. Their satisfaction does not comprise socialism. These goals state the minimal conditions for life that every human being should be assured of. They are the goals we see from our present, imperfect society: the restructuring of everyday life in order to make possible a fully human existence.

Even in achieving these limited, transitional goals there is a problem of "human nature." Can an advertising man bend his talents to creating new media for a new kind of humanistic education? Can a production worker who has spent his life putting wheel lugs on Chevrolets reorganize production procedures to make them less alienating? Can children who were taught to be suspicious grow up to teach other children to love? We have all been dehumanized. We are strangers to the joys of working together, without personal profit, for difficult goals. Our social instincts have been constrained to the services of the narrow economic interests of the family or of the corporate team. Our imaginations have been repressed to fit a limited vision of career, family, and fun. We try to reassert our creativity, our imagination, our social nature in hobbies, in popular music and games, in getting "culture." But our every effort is distorted by the mass media and manipulated into nothing more than new consumption desires. There is no greater example of the atrophy of our humanity and imagination than the question, all too frequent even among those who consider themselves socialists: "But what will we do when hunger and poverty are conquered? What challenge will be left?" The jaded spirits who ask this will not spontaneously take up the struggle for a new society and a new man. We can only hope that if they do join the struggle, their sense of human possibilities will grow and their vision will expand beyond the transitional goals of material security.

And yet, we must do more than hope. Ultimately we want not only material well-being for all, we want the possibility of a new kind of man. But even to achieve the transitional goals requires some of the changes in people which are part of the ultimate goal. We see then that humanism—socialist humanism—is not just a value which we have fancifully imposed on society. It grows directly out of the present society. Capitalism generates needs—material and psychological—that cannot be solved by capitalism. It creates problems that cannot be solved within capitalism. But those very needs are nothing more than the appearance in objective, material form of the humanistic needs we have been discussing. The humanistic ethic we speak of is not some abstract and idealistic philosophical construction. It is the condition of the solution of the very real and material problems which we face now.

Eternal Revolution

What will it be like after the transitional goals of material comfort are achieved? What will men turn their minds and energy to when they are free to use their minds and energy? We believe—and this is at the core of our belief as socialists—that only then can people begin to work on the most profound human problems. Only then can we begin to face our biological limitations. So far, art and technology have served the narrow interests of capital. What will it be like when they serve the interests of our deepest concerns? Men may work to end disease. They may even question whether death is necessary. Or, they may seek social adaptations to the fact of death. They may demand to know whatever can be known about the physical world. Or they may seek to feel, through art, what cannot be known. We struggle now in the world of men so that someday men will struggle, as men, in the world.

But ultimately, how can we discuss, except in the vaguest terms, what the truly socialist society will be like? All of us living now are blinded by our present to the possibilities of the future. What we know, we know as words like "truly human" and "common goals," not as experience. At heart, the fundamental human assumptions are alien to our experience. Our very notions of "individuals" and "society" are fraught with the tensions of individuals in an inhuman society. What it would be to be an individual in a socialist community of individuals united by common goals we can barely imagine. When we talk of "socialist man" we speak of someone almost unimaginably different from ourselves.

On the other hand, we *can* talk about the institutions which would actually enable people to make decisions about their lives. We can talk about factories that are run by the workers who man them, consistent with the needs of a national plan but otherwise with full autonomy. We can talk about changing the nature of production within such a factory so that it satisfies the humanity of the people who work in it rather than the demands of absolute maximal economic efficiency. We can talk about the use of techniques to minimize the amount of time that any individual has to spend at boring or heavy work. We can talk about new methods of teaching, new curricula, new integrations of parents into the educational process. We can talk about political mechanisms to truly democratize government, to change it from a distant, repressive agency into an immediate expression of the decisions of the great masses of Americans about anything which affects them jointly. All such discussions are discussions of people not very different from people now, with all the hang-ups we have accumulated.

We live in times which, with respect to socialism, are prehistoric. The critical problem is this: how can we now take the first steps to what will be, finally, a qualitative change in man? Saying that the change will take generations and may, in fact, never end, does not answer the question. Boot-strapping must start somewhere. It must start here. We, with our narrow vanities, must become teachers whose studies will surpass us as teachers. In spite of the lids on our own imaginations, we must still be able to imagine how men's imaginations can be freed. We, with our past of prejudice, of repression, must work from within our own limitations, through institutions of our own making, to create unlimited men, unlimited institutions.

Now, it should be clear that each generation that follows us will, to the extent that we now succeed, ask the same questions. The problem, in short, is eternalizing the revolution. How do we institutionalize revolution, so that we always proceed from our present imperfection toward a perfection which we never reach and never fully comprehend? It is not that upheaval for its own sake is desirable, but that at any given time we must make use of our historically limited perceptions to move toward a less limited existence. Our only assumptions are that human nature has virtually unbounded potentialities. The biological limitations of our natures are negligible in comparison with our biological flexibility. But we have had limited historical possibilities of exploring human nature. It is only in the socialist future that we can systematically begin to unfold ourselves, to test our real potentialities. This would be true freedom. Institutionalizing this search for freedom is the problem of creating the institutions of socialism.

Conclusion

Let us recapitulate. The goal of socialism is a truly human society. By this we mean a set of material restructurings of our society so that human needs are met, so that human needs take priority over all others. In a deeper sense we mean vast changes in human nature, changes in the way we relate to each other, to our work, and to society. But the achievement of even the more limited, material goals requires beginning to change people. We cannot create any set of institutions which people as they are now can just step into and proceed promptly toward the restructuring of society. Revolutionary élan may last for a while, but eventually we must seek institutional means of eternalizing revolution. The struggle to change material conditions, even in the most immediate sense, requires the struggle to change people, just as the struggle to change people depends on the ability to change the conditions under which men grow up and live and work. The processes are simultaneous, not sequential. The condition of freeing ourselves from the bonds capitalist society has created—material, cultural and psychological—is "socialism," which is in fact the very changes in human personality, relations, and daily life that we have talked about. The concrete goals and the human goals are separable only on paper. In practice they are the same. But none of this can occur spontaneously. It requires institutions which have their own evolution or even their own dissolution built into them. The task of building a socialist movement and the task of socialism after the revolution are in this sense the same—to undertake reforms the struggle for which and the achievement of which change people into better revolutionaries, better socialists, better people.

18.3.   **Guardian: The Forces Exist to Make a Beginning**

[The radical newsweekly *Guardian* has become more and more the spokesman of a large sector of the New Left. The viewpoint that follows marks an important step in the development of the New Left. *Guardian*, November 23, 1968.]

In recent weeks and months the Guardian has addressed itself in Viewpoints and news articles to critical evaluations of the U.S. radical left.

If we have concentrated overmuch on tactics, it was due to the difficulty of evaluating a strategy which does not exist. Some organizations on the left, of course, posit very specific strategies. But the radical movement in general— which by far overwhelms the collectivity of radical parties—is without a strategic conception of what its next step should be, much less how it goes about taking power in America.

Viewing the radical movement today, we find it to be disorganized and lacking in direction, a relatively shapeless collage of weakness and occasional strength projected to center-stage in U.S. history by an objective domestic crisis.

The black movement is still the cutting edge of our movement, though its knife appears to be sheathed at this moment. The student movement, especially Students for a Democratic Society, is the consistently growing element. The peace movement ebbs and flows largely in reaction to the single issue of Vietnam. It has failed to become an anti-imperialist force of relevance, although it has exerted enough influence to damage the Democratic party. The workers' and poor peoples' movements have yet to develop into popular forces.

Regardless of where any of these sectors happen to be at a given moment, one overriding fact is apparent: none has evolved a broad perspective of social change in America: none has a strategy for beyond the next confrontation or beyond the next election. Very few look beyond the immediate concerns of their specific section of the broader movement.

To view our movement in this light is not defeatism. The converse is true. Were we to see the movement as defensive, as in the latter 1950s, concerned in the main with protecting itself from the onslaughts of a marauding and inevitably triumphant enemy, then perhaps talking plainly about ourselves would lead to disaffection and pessimism. Today's movement, however, is aggressive: the enemy cannot triumph, though we ourselves might perish.

As an aggressive movement we cannot afford the luxury of illusion. Mistakes and wasted energy can be fatal. The mistakes and confusions of the radical left today must be honestly examined if we are to fulfill the revolutionary potential that is ours.

Today's radical movement did not spontaneously generate from the bottom of the box of Cracker Jacks, although it may look that way at times.

First, the left in the U.S. has a tradition from whence we have extracted a vast array of experience, much of it bad, some quite useful. This we tend to forget.

Second, there are literally hundreds of reasons why there is a vital radical left today as opposed to the dying remnant of a left just 10 years ago. Without going into detail, the left today is a result of growing racial and political consciousness in the black community; the brutal, imperialist—and losing—war in Vietnam; a revulsion against repressive moral and cultural mores; the incipient breakdown of conventional institutions of ruling-class domination, brought about by technological and population changes compounded by our economic system's inability to respond to ought but the buck or the bomb.

Each of these manifestations, of course, has a cause: the contradictions inherent in the political-economic system of capitalism. As these contradictions sharpened, our movement gained. With a new Republican administration, perhaps impeding the liberals in implementing schemes intended to rationalize the contradictions (what else are liberals for?); the impending loss of Vietnam; a new understanding that America is not such an affluent society after all; the increasing disaffection of youth; the gnawing distrust of the two old political parties; the racial, educational and urban crisis—all these factors and many more will assure that capitalism's contradictions worsen in the next years.

To this developing crisis there is only one radical answer: hasten it. We must provide the system with its death knell, not its medication.

Today's crisis in America is a fantastic opportunity for our movement, but only if we fully and without illusion understand both the crisis and our relationship to it as a revolutionary force. This latter implies that we must begin to evaluate ourselves very critically and, if necessary, begin anew in a different direction.

The reevaluation process has already begun, though mainly on the question of tactics, which is unfortunate. To confront or not to confront appears to be the question for the antiwar and student movements. Indeed, many confrontations seem to be masochistic affairs. At the correct time and place, however, with sufficient numbers and favorable terrain, confrontation is enormously useful in building the movement. The problem is that confrontation is increasingly a tactic of frustration, resorted to in virtual despair by those who are driven to disregard whether or not they can win a confrontation and, winning possible, what such a victory means in terms of long-run objectives.

Of greater import than the outcome of this debate is the fact that it is not at all clear whether those engaged in discussing tactics for the radical left understand that tactical confusion is a direct derivative of strategic confusion.

Our movement wastes a great deal of tactical energy because our tactics are not guided by strategic considerations—strategy in this sense meaning a particular terminal goal and a rational means of achievement.

What is our goal? How do we achieve that goal? What is the tactic of the day consistent with the long-range achievement of that specific goal?

Not too many years ago it would have been fruitless for our movement to entertain these questions. The movement in general was simply not prepared to think in such terms, existing as a moral spasm reacting from liberal concern about particular issues without benefit of an anti-capitalist critique, hardly willing to deal with questions of violence, revolution and the like.

Recognizing that the level of political consciousness in the movements for social change remains all too low, we believe the radical left in general has gained enough experience and understanding in the last few years to begin thinking in terms of long-run strategic methods and goals.

At one time, again, it did not particularly matter whether the tiny (non-party) left understood revolutionary theory or developed a relevant analysis of America and a class analysis of society. To remain indifferent today, however, with our movement in a period of growth and America in crisis, connotes a serious lack of purpose and commitment. (We trust this will not be construed a paean to armchair radicals who have spent their entire adult lives theorizing without contributing more than a token damn to the struggles for social change in this country. We wouldn't trade one "apolitical" kid street-fighter for the bunch of them.)

A tremendous amount of work remains, naturally, before we are able to devise a strategy for social change in our country. We must begin to understand not only capitalism as an economic system, but how it insinuates itself into every aspect of American life. We must understand the institutions of domination and repression in our society—even though these institutions are known by such euphemisms as as "the university," "the corporation," "the welfare department," "the public school," "the mass media," "the entertainment industry," "the philanthropic foundation," and, too often, "the union," among many others. (The fact that confrontation tactics concentrate particularly on one overt force of domination, "the police," is the political flaw of the "streetfighting man": the cop beats your head; the more subtle institutions beat your essence.)

We do not believe anyone has fully analyzed the nature of American capitalist society or has developed a completely rational strategy for taking power from the ruling class. No textbooks will provide us with the answers, but they provide us with critically relevant tools for finding these answers. We must absorb revolutionary theory and we must engage in revolutionary practice: both are essential. The American revolution—as all revolutions— will be a variation of a theme of liberation and violent upheaval, peculiar in many respects to the nation in which it takes place. It will be a revolution which could only take place in America, as the Cuban revolution could only have taken place in Cuba, the Russian in Russia, the Chinese in China.

The American revolution will be an extraordinarily long and difficult process. Since neither patience nor courage is our signal virtue, life patterns may have to change to accommodate the reality of our task.

We think conditions are ripe for beginning. Clearly the missing ingredient is a broad, radical organization which would include many thousands of individuals and some organizations of the left who are isolated or so fractured as to have no impact. The organization we have in mind would provide independent radicals with a base to work from, a grouping within which to find revolutionary relevance. Since we are far from the answers which must be attained before being in a position to say, "we have the theory, the practice, the strategy, the tactic," we do not envision a revolutionary party at this point. But we can envision an anti-imperialist, anti-capitalist organization, at first containing many already existing elements on the left, broadening to include a diversity of Americans—workers, students, blacks, minorities, the poor.

The forces exist to make a beginning. Our movement today is split into dozens of small groups and into organizations defined by particular issues and causes, lacking coherent tactics, much less strategy. Although it is hardly likely all independent radicals would fit comfortably into a multi-issue movement, we are convinced a great many could do so with ease—and profit for the movement for revolutionary change.

18.4.   *HERBERT MARCUSE:* **On The New Left**

[The following is the complete text of a talk given the 4th of December 1968 by Herbert Marcuse at the twentieth anniversary program of The

Guardian, as taped by Radio Free People and transcribed by Liberation News Service. Marcuse was introduced by Bernadine Dohrn, inter-organizational Secretary of SDS, who called him, "a writer, philosopher, a man who The New York Times called 'the ideological leader of the New Left.'"]

I'm not responsible for what the New York Times calls me. I never claimed to be the ideological leader of the left and I don't think the left needs an ideological leader. And there is one thing the left does not need, and that's another father image, another daddy. And I certainly don't want to be one.

There's one thing, I would like to resume what Carl (Oglesby) just said. We cannot wait and we shall not wait. I certainly cannot wait. And not only because of my age. I don't think we have to wait. And even I, I don't have any choice. Because I literally couldn't stand it any longer if nothing would change. Even I am suffocating.

I want to give you today as realistic a picture of the situation of the left as I can think of. This will require some theoretical reflection for which I do not really apologize, because if the left gets allergic against theoretical consideration, there's something wrong with the left. (Applause.)

Let me start by pointing out the two contradictions with which our movement—and I say our—is faced. On the one hand, we all feel, we experience, we have it in our bones, that this society is getting increasingly repressive, destructive, of the human and natural capabilities to be free, to determine one's own life, to shape one's own life without exploiting others.

And we—let us not only mean we here in this room, it means all those who are repressed, who are enslaved by their jobs, by the unnecessary and still so necessary performances that are required from them, by the morality that is required from them, all those who are exploited by the internal and external colonization policy of this country—this large WE, in bad need of change, but, on the other hand, I think we have to admit that in large part if not the majority of this population does not really feel, is not aware, is not politically conscious of this need for change. This presents, as I can see it, the first great problem of our strategy.

The second great problem for our strategy—we are constantly faced with the demands, "What is the alternative? What can you offer us that is better than what we have?" I do not believe that we can simply brush aside this question by saying, "What is necessary is to destory; afterwards we will see what comes." We cannot for one very simple reason. Because our goals, our values, our own and new morality, our OWN morality, must be visible already in our actions. The new human beings who we want to help to create—we must already strive to be these human beings right here and now. (Applause.)

And that is why we cannot simply brush this question aside. We must be able to show, even in a very small way, the models of what may one day be a human being. But the alternative, precisely in these terms, I still believe the alternative is *socialism*. But socialism neither of the Stalinist brand nor of the post-Stalinist brand, but that *libertarian* socialism which has always been the integral concept of socialism, but only too easily repressed and suppressed.

Now, if this is the alternative, how do we transmit it, because people will look around and will say, "Show us, where is this kind of socialism?" We will say, it is perhaps, it is probably going to be built up in Cuba. It is perhaps being built up in China. It is certainly fighting in Vietnam (against) the super-monster. But they will look around and say, "No, this isn't socialism. Socialism, as we see it, socialism is what we have in the Soviet Union. Socialism is the invasion of Czechoslovakia." Socialism, in other words, is a crime.

And how can we meet this contradiction? The two contradictions which I just outlined, I think, can be telescoped into one. Radical change without a mass base seems to be unimaginable. But the obtaining of a mass base—at least in this country—and in the forseeable future—seems to be equally unimaginable. What are we going to do with this contradiction?

The answer seems to be very easy. We have to try to get this support. We have to try to get this mass base. But here we meet the limits of democratic persuasion with which we are confronted today. Why the limits? Because a large, perhaps a decisive, part of the majority, namely the working class, is to a great extent integrated into the system; and on a rather solid material basis, and not only superficially. It is certainly not integrated for ever.

Nothing is forever in history.

And the contradictions of corporate capitalism are more serious than ever before. But this does not and cannot and should not foster the illusion that such an integration, temporary integration, has indeed taken place, that can be loosened only if the contradictions within the system become more aggravated. They do, we have seen it during the last years and it is out task— since such a disintegration will never happen automatically—it is our task to work on it.

The second item—why we are here faced with the limits of democratic persuasion—is the mere fact that the left has no adequate access to the media of mass communication.

Today, public opinion is made by the media of mass communication. If you cannot buy the equal and adequate time, if you cannot buy the equal and adequate space, how are you supposed to change public opinion, a public opinion made in this monopolistic way.

The consequence; we are, in this pseudo-democracy, faced with a majority which seems to be self-perpetuating, which seems to reproduce itself as a conservative majority immune against radical change. But the same circumstances that militate against democratic persuasion also militate against the development of a revolutionary centralized mass party, according to the traditional model. You cannot have such a party today, not only because there are no revolutionary masses to be centralized, but also because the apparatus of suppression is infinitely more effective and powerful than it ever was before, but even more and perhaps most so, because centralization today does not seem to be the adequate way of working for change and obtaining change. I will come back to it in a few moments.

Here I want to add one more thing. I said that the contradictions of corporate capitalism today are as serious as ever before, but we have immediately to add that today that the resources of corporate capitalism are equally strong and they are daily strengthened by the cooperation, or shall I say, the collusion, between the United States and the Soviet Union. What we are faced with, and I think this is one of the old-fashioned terms we should save and recapture, is a temporary stabilization of the capitalist system, a temporary stabilization, the task of the left is a task of enlightenment, a task of education, the task of developing a political consciousness.

I would like to discuss under three headings very briefly the target of the strategy of the New Left, the methods and finally, the organization of the New Left. First, as to the target: we are faced with a novelty in history, namely with the prospect or with the need for radical change, revolution in and against a highly developed technically advanced industrial society, which is at the same time a well-functioning and cohesive society. This historical novelty demands a re-examination of one of our most cherished concepts. I can here of course only give you a kind of catalog of such re-examination.

First, the notion of the seizure of power. Here, the old model wouldn't do any more. That for example, in a country like the United States, under the leadership of a centralized and authoritarian party, large masses concentrate on Washington, occupy the Pentagon and set up a new government, seems to be a slightly too unrealistic and utopian picture. (Laughter.)

We will see that what we have to envisage is some kind of diffuse and dispersed disintegration of the system, in which interest, emphasis and activity is shifted to local and regional area.

The second concept that should be re-examined is the role of the working class. And here I would like to say a few words to one of the most defamed notions today, namely the concept of the new working class. I know what can be said against it, and what has been said against it. It seems to me that the concept of the new working class simply comprehends and anticipates tendencies that are going on before our own eyes in the material process of production in capitalism, namely that more and more highly qualified salaried employees, technicians, specialists, and so on, occupy a decisive position in the material process of production. And even in orthodox Marxian terms, just in this way become members of the industrial working class. What we see, I submit to you, is an extension of the potential mass base over and beyond the traditional industrial working class to the new working classes that extend the rage of the exploited.

Now this extension, which indicates a large but very diffuse and dispersed mass base, changes the relationship between what we may call leading minorities or cadres of the left, politically militant, and the masses. What we can envisage is not, as I said, this large centralized and coordinated movement, but local and regional political action against specific grievances—riots, ghetto rebellions and so on, that is to say, certainly mass movements which in large part are lacking political consciousness and which will depend more than before on political guidance and direction by militant leading minorities.

A few words on the strategy of the New Left. To the degree to which the pseudo-democratic process, with the semi-monopoly of the conservative mass media, creates and constantly reproduces the same society and a largely immune majority, to that degree must political education and preparation go beyond the traditional liberalistic forms. Political activity and political education must go beyond discussion and writing. The Left must find the adequate means of breaking the conformist and corrupted universe of political language and political behavior. The Left must try to arouse the consciousness and conscience of the others, and breaking out of the language and behavior pattern of the corrupt political universe, a pattern which is imposed on all political activity, is an almost super-human task and requires an almost super-human imagination, namely the effort to find a language and to organize actions which are not part and parcel of the familiar political behavior, and which can perhaps communicate that what is here at work are human beings with different needs and different goals which are not yet and I hope never will be co-opted.

In terms of the establishment and in terms of the rationality of the establishment, such behavior would and must appear as foolish, childish and irrational, but that may very well be the token that here is the attempt, and the at least temporarily successful attempt, to go beyond, to break out of the respressive universe of the established political behavior.

Now, last, to the organization of the New Left. I already mentioned the obsolesence of traditional forms of organization, for example, a parliamentary party. No party whatsoever I can envisage today which would not within a very short time fall victim to the general and totalitarian political corruption which characterizes the political universe. No political party, but also no revolutionary centralism and no underground—because both are all to easy victims to the intensified and stream-lined apparatus of repression.

As against these forms, what seems to be shaping up is an entirely overt organization, diffused, concentrated in small groups and around local activities, small groups which are highly flexible and autonomous.

I want to add one thing here that may almost appear as heretic—no primitive unification of strategy. The left is split! The Left has always been split! Only the right, which has no ideas to fight for, is united! (Much laughter.)

Now the strength of the New Left may well reside in precisely these small contesting and competing groups, active at many points at the same time, a kind of political guerrilla force in peace or so-called peace, but, and this is, I think, the most important point, small groups, concentrated on the level of local activities, thereby foreshadowing what may in all likelihood be the basic organization of libertarian socialism, namely councils of manual and intellectual workers, soviets, if one can still use the term and does not think of what actually happened to the soviets, some kind of what I would like to call, and I mean it seriously, organized spontaneity.

Let me say a few words on the alliance which I think should be discussed in the New Left. I would suggest not an alliance even with the Devil, as Lenin said, because the Devil today has become much too strong. He will eat us up. No alliance with liberals, who have taken over the job of the un-American committee. (Applause.) Who have taken over the job of the un-American committee in denouncing the left, doing the job the committee has not yet done, and I think I don't have to mention names, you know perfectly well. But instead, alliance with all those, whether bourgeois or not, who know that the enemy is on the right, and who have demonstrated this knowledge.

Let me come to the summary of the perspectives for the New Left. I believe, and this is not a confession of faith, I think this is at least to a great extent based on what you may call an analysis of the facts. I believe that the New Left today is the only hope we have. Its task—to prepare itself and the others, not to wait or to prepare today, yesterday and tomorrow, in thought and in action, morally and politically, for the time when the aggravating conflicts of corporate capitalism dissolve its repressive cohesion and open a space where the real work for libertarian socialism can begin. The prospects for the next year, the prospects for the New Left are good if the New Left can only sustain its present activity. There are always periods of regression. No movement can progress at the same pace; sustaining our activity would already be a success.

And, a word on a friend or enemy on the left. Those who denounce especially the young of the New Left who fight for the great refusal, and who do not conform to the fetishism and the fetishist concepts of the Old Left and the Old Liberals—those who denounce them as infantile radicals, snobbish intellectuals, and who in denouncing them, invoke Lenin's famous pamphlet; I suggest to you that this is a historical forgery. Lenin struck out against radicals who confronted a strong revolutionary mass party. Such a revolutionary mass party does not exist today. The Communist Party has become and is becoming a party of order; as it itself called itself. In other words the shoe is today on the other foot. In the absence of a revolutionary party, these alleged infantile radicals are, I believe, the weak and confused but true historical heirs of the great socialist tradition.

You all know that their ranks are permeated with agents, with fools, with irresponsibles. But they also contain the human beings, men and women, black and white, who are sufficiently free from the aggressive and repressive inhuman needs and aspirations of the exploitative society, sufficiently free from them, in order to be free for the work of preparing a society without exploitation. I would like to continue working together with them as long as I can.

FURTHER READINGS

Aranowitz, Stanley. "Task for New Left: Get Yourselves Together." *Guardian,* November 23, 1968.

Deming, Barbara. "On Revolution and Equilibrium." *Liberation,* February 1968.

Ehrenreich, John and Barbara. "From Resistance to Revolution." *Monthly Review,* April 1968.

Guardian. "The Election Will Come and Go—Will We?" October 26, 1968.

Lens, Sidney. "The Road to Power and Beyond." *Liberation,* November 1968.

Lynd, Staughton. "The Future of Radicalism" and Christopher Lasch's reply. *The New York Review,* September 12, 1968.

Mann, Eric. "Appraisal and Perspectives." *New Left Notes.* March 4 and 18, 1968.

Oglesby, Carl. "Revolution: Violence or Nonviolence." *Liberation,* July and August 1968.

Rotsein, Rich, *et al.* "The New Movement and Its Organizational Theory: Responses to 'Wasteland Culture.' " *Our Generation,* Vol. 5: No. 4 (1968).

THIRD PART

Chronology, Glossary, and Bibliography

ONE:
Chronology of Events

1954 *May:* The Supreme Court decision to desegregate the public-school system was implemented only in the Southern border states, encountering massive resistance in the Deep South.

1956 The Montgomery, Alabama, boycott of segregated buses lasted 381 consecutive days. The action, inspired and led by Martin Luther King, marked the growing prestige of the black leader and of the method of nonviolent civil disobedience which he practiced.

1957 Federal troops intervened in Little Rock, Arkansas, to force the enactment of school integration, opposed by Governor Orval Faubus.

1958 *April:* At the University of California, Berkeley, a group of progressive students—SLATE—placed themselves on the ballot of candidates for seats in the student government. Subsequently other progressive candidates presented themselves at different universities: POLIT at Chicago, SCOPE at Oberlin, VOICE at Michigan, and ACTION at Columbia.

1959 During the academic year 1958–1959, students from Northern and Southern high schools took part in two marches in Washington organized by Bayard Rustin for the integration of the public school system.
January: The dictatorial regime of Fulgencio Batista in Cuba was overthrown by guerrillas under the leadership of Fidel Castro.
Summer: The Student Peace Union was organized in Chicago, the majority of them young socialists belonging to the Young People's Socialist League (YPSL).
October: Fred Moore, an eighteen-year-old student, engaged in a one-man protest against obligatory military training at the University of California, Berkeley. Mass demonstrations followed in December.

1960 *February:* The first sit-in of black students took place in Greensboro, North Carolina. Many more sit-ins, marches and demonstrations in favor of integration occurred during the following months throughout the South.
February: A march was held in San Francisco in protest of Caryl Chessman's death sentence. Chessman received his sentence in spite of the widespread humanitarian movement in his favor.
April: The Fair Play for Cuba Committee was formed in the San Francisco Bay Area.
April: In Raleigh, North Carolina, the Student Nonviolent Coordinating Committee (SNCC) was organized as a coordinating body for young people and students who had taken part in the sit-ins and other direct actions in the South.
April: In England, a pacifist march from Aldermanston to London was organized by the Campaign for Nuclear Disarmament (CND).
May: 68 students were arrested in the protest demonstration organized against the House Un-American Activities Committee (HUAC), which was meeting in San Francisco to investigate presumed subversive activity.

Spring: Student demonstrations were held in South Korea and Turkey against their dictatorial regimes, which were subsequently overthrown.

June: The leading group in the formation of Students for a Democratic Society (SDS) was formed with the support of the League for Industrial Democracy (LID), oriented toward social-democracy and Fabian socialism.

Summer: Thousands of students visited Fidel Castro's Cuba.

Summer and autumn: Operation Abolition, a film inspired by McCarthyism in which J. Edgar Hoover, the director of the FBI, explained the plans of the communist conspiracy, became the object of debate on many campuses, creating a climate which was ultimately favorable to the defense of civil liberties for the opposition.

September: The Bay Area Student Committee for the Abolition of HUAC was formed.

November: John F. Kennedy was elected President of the United States.

Autumn: C. Wright Mills published *Listen, Yankee,* an attack on American policy toward Cuba.

1961 *January:* The United States broke off diplomatic relations with Cuba. Campus demonstrations followed.

February: Demonstrations were carried on at the United Nations against the assassination of Patrice Lumumba.

March: The Peace Corps was organized under the initiative of President John F. Kennedy.

April: An attempt was made, supported by the CIA, to invade Cuba from the Bay of Pigs. Campus demonstrations followed.

May: The first integrated bus took CORE and SNCC activists on a Freedom Ride from Washington to New Orleans. During the trip, violent attacks were made on the black and white integrationists.

Summer: Protests using acts of civil disobedience were organized by various peace movements and pacifist groups against the bomb-shelter construction program.

August: SNCC began its voter-registration campaign in Mississippi, with McComb at the center.

September: Robert Williams, president of a local NAACP chapter, urged the blacks to arm themselves in self-defense. Accused of kidnapping, he left the United States and was granted exile in Cuba, where he began to broadcast over Radio Free Dixie.

September: The black voter-registration worker, Herbert Lee, was assassinated during his activity in Mississippi.

November: Vigils were organized, by students inspired by the peace movement, against the resumption of nuclear testing.

1962 *February:* The student wing of SANE broke off from the parent organization, rejecting its practice of ideological discrimination among the members.

February: Peace demonstrations against the resumption of nuclear testing were organized in Washington by the Student Action for a Turn Toward Peace and by the Student Peace Union.

May: A boat manned by pacifists in the Committee for Nonviolent Action (CNVA) attempted to sail to the Christmas Islands, where nuclear tests were being carried out.

June: After several months of preparation, the manifesto of the SDS, the Port Huron Statement, was approved at a meeting of that organization.

October: For the first time, a black man—James Meredith—was admitted to the University of Mississippi. White racists responded with violence.

October: The Cuban Missile Crisis exploded.

November: Several peace candidates ran for election outside the two traditional parties. Among the candidates was Professor H. Stuart Hughes of Massachussetts. Young Movement activists became involved in the electoral campaign.

1963 *Winter: The Other America,* by Michael Harrington, was published. The book revealed to the general public, for the first time, the facts about poverty in the United States.

March: The voter registration campaign in the Deep South was intensified. It was coordinated by the Council of Federated Organizations (SNCC, CORE, NAACP, SCLC) and conducted mainly by SNCC activists.

April: Dr. Timothy Leary and Professor Richard Alpert were dismissed from Harvard University for performing experiments with hallucinogens on students.

August: 200,000 people took part in the march in Washington for civil rights. John Lewis of SNCC gave a speech opposing the Kennedy administration.

November: The Freedom Ballot—free elections for choosing a black governor of Mississippi—was organized by SNCC activists and students from Yale. More than 80,000 people voted, four times the number of blacks registered to vote in the state.

November: President John F. Kennedy was assassinated in Dallas. The man thought to be the assassin, Lee H. Oswald, was also killed, shortly thereafter.

December: The SDS became involved in local community organizing, developing the original plan which had been based solely on research. The Education Research Action Project (ERAP) coordinated 12 projects in neighborhoods of Northern cities where poor whites and blacks lived.

1964 *March:* Malcolm X broke with the Black Muslims and proposed a plan for an all-black nationalist party.

April: The Progressive Labor party (PLP), whose position was openly pro-Chinese, emerged from a split on the Communist party.

May: The May Second Movement was organized. Within the scope of the movement against the war in Vietnam, it took an anti-imperialist line and a position of solidarity with the Vietcong.

Spring: In Haverford, Yale and New York City, groups of young men belonging to the May Second Movement declared their refusal to present themselves for military service.

Summer: A large mobilization project for civil rights developed in the South, with the participation of more than 800 young volunteers. The goal of the project was the registration of black voters, opening of freedom schools, organization of local communities; it led to the formation of the Mississippi Freedom Democratic party. Bob Moses coordinated the voter-registration campaign and Staughton Lynd, the freedom schools. Both blacks and whites were killed during the summer.

Summer: Riots broke out in Harlem.

August: The Democratic party convention was held in Atlantic City. The delegation from the Mississippi Freedom Democratic party, which demanded to be accredited as the Democratic delegation from that state, was offered instead a humiliating compromise, which the delegation refused.

September: Political activity was prohibited on the campus of the University of California at Berkeley.

October: The Free Speech Movement (FSM) arose at Berkeley; it consisted both of political clubs and of students not associated with any particular group.

November: Lyndon B. Johnson was elected President of the United States.

December: The University of California at Berkeley was completely paralyzed as a result of occupation by students. Following a series of mass arrests, the FSM won the right to engage in political activity on campus.

1965 *January:* The MFDP challenge of the racist representatives from Mississippi to the Congress was rejected twice.

February: Malcolm X was assassinated during a public speech.

February: The systematic American bombardment of North Vietnam began.

March: Martin Luther King led a march from Selma to Montgomery, Alabama, as a means of applying pressure for the new civil-rights law. There was violence, and Viola Liuzzo, a white activist, was killed.

March: The first teach-in on the war in Vietnam was held at the University of Michigan. Within two months, hundreds of teach-ins took place at universities, and in May a national teach-in was held in Washington.

March: American troops invaded the Dominican Republic in order to "prevent a Communist take-over."

April: An antiwar march organized by SDS was held in Washington with about 70,000 people participating. The reputation of SDS grew on a national level, and within three months, the number of local chapters grew from 35 to more than 100.

May: 12,000 people participated in a teach-in at Berkeley organized by the Vietnam Day Committee. The speakers included Norman Thomas, A. J. Muste, and Norman Mailer.

June: Julian Bond, one of the leaders of SNCC, was elected to the Georgia state legislature. The election was invalidated because of Bond's opposition to the war in Vietnam.

August: With the signing of a new civil-rights law, the phase of legal struggle in the South came to an end.

Summer: The first all-black party, the Lowndes County Freedom Organization, was formed in Alabama.

Summer: Riots occurred in the black ghetto of Watts in Los Angeles. More than 30 blacks were killed; Martin Luther King declared that the civil-rights movement was insufficient to deal with the problems of black people.

Summer: A Free University—the largest project of this kind—was organized in New York.

Summer: The Assembly of Unrepresented People, promoted by Staughton Lynd, Robert Parris and Dave Dellinger, met in Washington, where 350 demonstrators were arrested.

Summer: Following the first burning of draft cards by students and young non-students, Congress approved a law making such acts punishable as crimes.

October: Nationwide antiwar demonstrations were organized by the National Co-ordinating Committee To End the War in Vietnam. The International Days of Protest culminated in a march in Washington.

November: Norman Morrison, a Quaker pacifist, immolated himself in front of the Pentagon as an act of solidarity with the Vietnamese people.

November: 40,000 people participated in a Washington march organized by the National Committee for a Sane Nuclear Policy (SANE) and by SDS, whose president, Carl Oglesby, spoke at the rally.

1966 *January:* The SNCC conference in Atlanta approved a resolution calling for de-nunciation of the Vietnam war and encouraging resistance against military service.

April: Stokely Carmichael was elected president of SNCC.

May: Sit-ins protesting the Vietnam war and the connections between universities and local draft boards were held at Wisconsin, Chicago, and other universities.

June: James Meredith began a march across Mississippi and was shot on the second day. Other black leaders, including Stokely Carmichael and Martin Luther King, continued the march. The slogan "Black Power" was used for the first time.

Spring and summer: Robert Scheer, an editor of *Ramparts* magazine, organized an electoral campaign for the Democratic party nomination to Congress in the San Francisco Bay Area. He won 45 percent of the votes on a radical platform firmly opposing the war. Other radical campaigns were led by the candidate to the Massachussetts Senate, Thomas Boyleston Adams, and by James Weinstein of the Committee for Independent Political Action (CIPA) in New York City. Riots took place in Chicago and Cleveland.

August: SDS held its annual convention at Clear Lake, Iowa, where the main tendency which emerged was toward a return to political work on the university campuses. The strategy of student power was formulated.

Summer: Three soldiers at Fort Hood, Texas, refused to obey orders regarding the war in Vietnam.

September: The *New York Review of Books* published Stokely Carmichael's article "What We Want," in which the president of SNCC explained the meaning of Black Power.

Autumn: The first pledges to refuse military service were taken by students at Yale and other campuses. The slogan "We Won't Go" became the symbol of draft resistance.

December: The national council of SDS approved a resolution condemning the Vietnam war, attacking military conscription as coercive and antidemocratic, and pledging to work for the building of antidraft unions.

1967 *Winter and spring:* Demonstrations were held at Berkeley against the recruitment of Marines on campus, the CIA, and the Dow Chemical Company, manufacturer of napalm. Strikes and arrests followed.

April: The Resistance was formed in California. Within the antidraft movement as a whole, this group emphasized the aspect of noncooperation. A parallel movement developed in Massachussetts.

April: Many antiwar demonstrations were organized by the Spring Mobilization Against the War. The demonstrations culminated in the marches held in New York (with 200,000 participants) and San Francisco (65,000 participants). A group of several hundred young men burned their draft cards in New York's Central Park.

Summer: Riots occurred in Newark, Detroit, and other Northern cities. The police and National Guard opened fire, and in all, over 80 people, almost all blacks, were reported killed.

Summer: About 30,000 student volunteers participated in the Vietnam Summer project in more than 700 cities.

September: The national Black Power conference was held in Newark.

September: The National Conference for New Politics—the largest meeting of liberals and radicals, both black and white, held up to that time—took place in Chicago. The conference did not reach an agreement on the strategy to be followed by the various groups during the 1968 election year.

October: A series of activities and demonstrations against the war developed throughout the country, culminating in a march of 75,000 demonstrators against the Pentagon. Many intellectuals, including Norman Mailer, Noam Chomsky, Robert Lowell, Sydney Lens, and Dwight MacDonald, also participated.

October: 1,500 draft cards were collected and sent to the office of the Selective Service System during the first national day of resistance to the draft. In Oakland, California, confrontations between police and demonstrators occurred in the course of Stop the Draft Week.

November: A registration drive began in California for a new party, the Peace and Freedom party, organized particularly through the efforts of the Independent Socialist Club. The PFP was able to place itself on the ballot for the primary elections in January by registering more than the 67,000 people required by state law.

December: Senator Eugene McCarthy entered the race for the Democratic presidential nomination on a Vietnam peace platform.

1968 *February:* After Senator McCarthy's initial victories in the primaries, Senator Robert Kennedy entered the race for the Democratic presidential nomination.

March: The Peace and Freedom party held its founding convention in California. During the spring and summer, PFP groups were organized in other states. Candidates of the Peace and Freedom–Black Panther party coalition were placed on the ballot in the California primary elections.

March: Lyndon B. Johnson announced his decision not to run in the November presidential elections. Vice-President Humphrey then entered the race for the Democratic nomination.

April: Martin Luther King was assassinated in Memphis, where he had gone to lend his support to striking black sanitation workers.

April: Following King's assassination, riots occurred in many black ghettoes in Northern and Southern cities, including Washington. In Oakland, young black militant Bobby Hutton was killed in an encounter with the police.

April–May: Columbia University in New York was occupied by black and white students. The causes of the demonstrations and occupations were the University's policy with respect to the black community of Harlem, the close connections between University research institutes and the CIA, and the University administration's policy of close cooperation with interests of the country's large corporations. The students were joined by groups of faculty members.

May: Students revolts broke out in Germany, Italy, and France. The movement began by the students in France threatened the institutions themselves and ultimately the government.

June: Presidential candidate Robert Kennedy was assassinated in Los Angeles immediately following his victory in the California Democratic primary.

June–July: Following a Berkeley demonstration expressing solidarity with the French students, confrontations between the police and demonstrators took place repeatedly over a four-day period. In August, after the Chicago Democratic convention, confrontations occurred again in Berkeley, where a state of "civic disaster" was declared.

July: Cleveland was the scene of four days of violent confrontations between police and blacks. Eight blacks and three policemen were killed.

August: Eldridge Cleaver, black leader, was chosen as presidential candidate by the Peace and Freedom–Black Panther party coalition.

August: Troops from the Soviet Union and other allied countries of the Warsaw Pact invaded Czechoslovakia.

August: In Chicago, under a state of siege and controlled by the police and national guard, Hubert Humphrey won the presidential nomination at the Democratic convention. Thousands of demonstrators were brutalized by the police, wounded, and arrested. The Chicago demonstrations were organized by the National Mobilization Committee to End the War, the "Yippies" of the Youth International party and other organizations of the New Left and black liberation movement.

September: Huey Newton, leader of the California Black Panther party, was sentenced to 15 years in prison, convicted of having killed a policeman.

September: In New York and Oakland, California, episodes of violence occurred on the part of the police against militants and the headquarters of black power organizations.

October: Ex-GIs and GIs held a peace march in San Francisco.

November: In the week before the presidential election, a "GI Week" was organized. It took the form of a series of actions planned to call soldiers' attention to questions of peace.

November: Richard M. Nixon was elected President of the United States.

TWO:
Organizations

The New Left is composed of many movements, associations, groups, and committees; some organizations are structured and permanent; others are essentially temporary and/or dedicated to single issues. All of them, at any rate, are organized along decentralized lines. There are no official organizations of the New Left, because, by this term, we mean a political position resulting from a variety of movements, rather than an organized political force. Without claiming to provide a complete list, we have included here many organizations which in some way can be considered part of the Movement, or which, more generally, are of some interest to the Left. For the sake of clarity, the organizations are grouped according to the following categories:

1. National organizations of the Movement
2. Other national organizations of interest to the left
3. Organizations concentrating mainly on specific issues, temporary movements, and *ad hoc* committees:
   A. Civil rights
   B. Peace, pacifism, antiwar, antidraft, antimilitary
   C. Community organization
   D. Civil liberties
   E. Black Power
   F. Nonwhite minority groups
   G. Anti-imperialism
   H. New morality
   I. Professionals
   J. Parallel structures
4. "New Politics" organizations
5. Traditional left

Also included in the list are organizations which were no longer active in 1968, but which were influential during the period from 1960 to 1968. We have placed an asterisk (*) next to those organizations which, in our judgment, are particularly important in the Movement today or which have played an important historical role in the development of New Left politics.

1. National Organizations of the Movement

Movement for a Democratic Society (MDS)
New York, N.Y.
Formed in 1968 as a movement for radicals who are no longer students, the MDS has the following objectives: (1) to maintain a political relationship between young adults and the Movement; (2) to provide radical analyses and information; (3) to organize workers, particularly technicians, within existing institutions; (4) to create counter-institutions; (5) to function as an employment agency for Movement people; (6) to develop a new life-style among adult radicals; (7) to organize the middle-class, i.e., the new, university-educated, working class.

Northern Student Movement (NSM)
New York, N.Y.
    Movement which developed in the North as a counterpart of SNCC in the South during the early years of the civil-rights campaign. Dedicated mainly to organizing at the local level.

Southern Student Organizing Committee (SSOC)
Nashville, Tenn.
    White radical student movement active in the South since 1964, mainly in the realm of civil rights.

*Students for a Democratic Society (SDS)
Chicago, Ill.
    Founded in 1960, having evolved out of the Student League for Industrial Democracy, it spread nationally after the publication in June 1962 of the Port Huron Statement, a manifesto of the values and policy of the new young radical movement. It took part in the peace movement and supported the campaign for civil rights in the North; in 1963 the national conference approved the document *America and New Era,* which attacked the liberal positions of Kennedy's New Frontier and pointed out the potentially revolutionary groups in American society. From 1963 to 1965 it became involved in community organization of the poor through the Education Research Action Project (ERAP), after 1965 placed itself in the forefront of the movement against the war in Vietnam and, since 1967, has taken the lead in formulating the strategy for political action within the universities known as Student Power.
    SDS is a national organization with branches on more than 400 campuses. There are over 7,000 paying members affiliated with the national office, but the number of sympathizers who support and participate in the activities of the local chapters has been estimated to be at least five times this number.
    The members' political positions vary according to the local situations. The organization does not practice ideological discrimination, and therefore SDS contains the entire spectrum of the left, from sympathizers with liberal positions to the Maoists of the Progressive Labor party, from libertarians to anarchists. However, the central nucleus of the association is composed of students with a cultural and political background that is original, with respect to traditional politico-ideological categories: this group certainly forms the widest segment of political cadres in the New Left.
    The SDS has a decentralized organization. The national office, whose headquarters are in Chicago, is run by a staff of three people dedicated to coordination, education, and interorganizational contacts. Following the 1968 national convention, regional offices were created with headquarters in New York City, New England, Ithaca, New York; Philadelphia, Southern California, Texas, and Washington; these offices serve as centers for regional coordination.

2. Other National Organizations of Interest to the Left

*American Civil Liberties Union (ACLU)
New York, N.Y.
    National association with many local chapters. Promotes legal action and offers political support of civil liberties.

Center for the Study of Democratic Institutions
Santa Barbara, Calif.
    Liberal center for study and research.

Emergency Civil Liberties Committee (ECLC)
New York, N.Y.
    Committee which offers free legal assistance in exemplary cases, in the field of civil rights and civil liberties.

Institute for Policy Studies (IPS)
Washington, D.C.
    Leftist institute for study and research.

*National Lawyers Guild (NLG)
New York, N.Y.
    A left-wing organization of lawyers which provides information particularly in the areas of civil rights, civil liberties, welfare, and the draft.

University Christian Movement (UCM)
New York, N.Y.
　　Left-wing, Christian-inspired movement working within the universities.

3. Organizations with a Special Area of Interest, Temporary Movements, *AD HOC* Committees

A. Civil Rights
Congress on Racial Equality (CORE)
New York, N.Y.
　　Civil-rights organization with its base in the North. In recent years it has attempted to combine black rhetoric and militancy with programs of action aimed toward integraton of black and white communities.

Council of Federated Organizations (COFO)
　　Coordinating body for the various civil-rights organizations (SNCC, SCLC, CORE and NAACP), created in 1963 to help coordinate the campaigns in the South.

National Association for the Advancement of Colored People (NAACP)
New York, N.Y.
　　With 1,500 chapters and almost 5,000 members, the NAACP is the largest and most traditional civil-rights organization, working through legal pressure and supported by a middle-class black and white base.

National Urban League (NUL)
New York, N.Y.
　　An association not involved in "direct action." It works mainly in conjunction with capitalist groups and emphasizes cooperation with the white society.

Scholarship, Education and Defense Fund for Racial Equality (SEDFRE)
New York, N.Y.
　　Educational and legal program developed by CORE.

*Southern Christian Leadership Conference (SCLC)
Atlanta, Ga.
　　Civil-rights organization which developed around Martin Luther King. It follows methods of direct action and nonviolent civil disobedience. Working almost exclusively in the South, it has extended its domain of interests from the struggle for integration to education, housing and jobs.

Southern Conference Educational Fund (SCEF)
Louisville, Ky.
　　Old progressive integrationist organization working in the South and dedicated to combating discrimination.

Southern Regional Council
　　Moderate organization working in the South.

*Poor People's Campaign
Washington, D.C.
　　Campaign organized by the Southern Christian Leadership Conference (SCLC) in spring 1968, to obtain jobs, housing, food, and public assistance for poor people. The campaign ended with the construction of a poor people's encampment, Resurrection City, in Washington, D.C.

Student Nonviolent Coordinating Committee (SNCC)
　　See the section on Black Power.

B. Peace, Pacifism, Antiwar, Antidraft, Antimilitary
American Friends Service Committee (AFSC)
Philadelphia, Pa.
　　Committee of Quakers, it provides aid for conscientious objectors and promotes pacifist and nonviolent direct action.

*Central Committee for Conscientious Objectors (CCCO)
Philadelphia, Pa.
　　Provides specialized assistance and material for conscientious objectors.

Clergy Concerned About Vietnam
New York, N.Y.
>Group of clergymen of various faiths opposed to the war in Vietnam.

**Committee for Nonviolent Action* (CNVA)
New York, N.Y.
>Promotes nonviolent direct action of a radical nature.

Fellowship of Reconciliation (FOR)
Nyack, N.Y.
>Includes different religious groups and promotes education for peace, especially among clergymen and young people.

National Black Antiwar Antidraft Union (NBAWADU)
New York, N.Y.
>Formed in 1968 to organize antidraft and antiwar resistance in the black communities.

**National Committee for a Sane Nuclear Policy* (SANE)
New York, N.Y.
>The largest peace organization at the beginning of the 1960s, with emphasis on the fight against the bomb. Its youth wing, Student SANE, broke off from the parent organization in 1960 because it refused to practice ideological discrimination among its own members.

**National Coordinating Coommittee to End the War in Vietnam* (NCCEWV)
Madison, Wis.
>Committee organized to coordinate the various antiwar projects, it played a leading role in the 1967 and 1968 demonstrations.

National Service Board for Religious Objectors (NSBRO)
Washington, D.C.
>Provides draft counseling assistance, recommends lawyers, and gives advice on alternative service.

Peacemakers
Cincinnati, Ohio
>Libertarian and pacifist group.

Quaker Action Group
Philadelphia, Pa.
>Quaker pacifist organization.

**Resistance*
Berkeley, Calif.; Boston, Mass.; New York, N.Y.
>Groups of draft resisters, formed in spring 1967; emphasizes noncooperation, open confrontation with military authorities, and mutual solidarity among draft resisters.

**Student Peace Union* (SPU)
New York, N.Y.
>The largest student political organization from 1959–1962, took a "third camp" position, and worked in the area of peace. It declined during 1963 and subsequently dissolved, except for a small office in New York.

Veterans for Peace in Vietnam
New York, N.Y.
>Group of veterans opposed to the war.

Veterans and Reservists to End the War in Vietnam
New York, N.Y.
>A direct action group.

**Vietnam Day Committee* (VDC)
Berkeley, Calif.
Temporary committee active at the University of California, Berkeley, in 1965.

War Resister's League (WRL)
New York, N.Y.
   Affiliated with War Resisters International (WRI), it represents a nonreligious pacifist point of view.

C. Community Organization
Arkansas Southern Student Organizing Committee
Malvern, Arkansas

Buckman Project
Portland, Oregon

Council of the Southern Mountains Volunteers
Oak Ridge, Tenn.

Economic Research Action Project (ERAP)
Chicago, Ill.
   National office for coordination of the different community organizing projects, formed by SDS in 1963 and dissolved in 1965.
   The projects affiliated with ERAP were operating in Cleveland, Ohio; New Haven, Conn.; Appalachia; Baltimore, Md.; Oakland, Calif.; Boston, Mass.; Cairo, Ill.; Hazard, Ky.; Newark, N.J. (Newark Community Union Project, N-CUP); and Chicago, Ill. (Jobs or Income Now—JOIN).

Federation of Southern Cooperatives
Atlanta, Ga.

Minneapolis Community Union Project
Minneapolis, Minn.

National Community Union (NCU)
   Organization which coordinates various local projects.

Poverty/Rights Action Center (P/RAC)
Washington, D.C.

South Side Improvement Organization
Syracuse, N.Y.

Southern Cooperative Development Program
Lafayette, La.

United Farm Workers' Organizing Committee
   At the time of this writing, the UFWOC is in its fourth year of a strike and boycott against California grape growers.

D. Civil Liberties

American Civil Liberties Union (ACLU)
   See section 2.

Emergency Civil Liberties Committee (ECLC)
   See section 2.

Free Speech Movement (FSM)
Berkeley, Calif.
   Formed at the University of California, Berkeley, in autumn 1964 to demand freedom for political activity on campus. It was composed of representatives from all Berkeley political groups and students not affiliated with specific clubs.

National Committee to Abolish HUAC
Los Angeles, Calif.
   Formed in response to HUAC's investigating activities at the beginning of the 1960s.

National Lawyer's Guild (NLG)
   See section 2.

E. Black Power
Black Panther Party (BPP)
Oakland, Calif.

    The BPP was formed in October 1966 in Oakland, California, through the efforts of revolutionary black nationalists inspired by the teaching of Malcolm X. In 1968 the BPP fielded candidates in the California state elections and national elections in coalition with the Peace and Freedom party, the first alliance between a "Black Power" group and a group of white radicals. Eldridge Cleaver of the BPP was the coalition's presidential candidate. (See Introduction.)

Student Nonviolent Coordinating Committee (SNCC)

    Formed in April 1960 as a coordinating committee for the groups involved in direct action for integration in the South, it adopted the principle and method of nonviolence. The SNCC activists were at the center of most of the projects and actions for civil rights over the five-year period from 1960 to 1965; in 1961 they participated in the freedom rides of integrated buses, in 1962 organized poor black communities in Mississippi and other states of the Deep South, in 1963 went on to mass voter registration, organizing the Freedom Ballot to choose a black governor of Mississippi, in 1964 occupied the center of the huge summer mobilization which led to the creation of the Mississippi Freedom Democratic party, and in 1965 took part, along with other organizations, in the Selma-Montgomery march in Alabama. With the election of Stokely Carmichael as president in spring 1966, SNCC abandoned the principle of nonviolence and during 1966 and 1967 became the center for black militants espousing Black Power. By 1968, SNCC had lost much of its organizational power, although it still remains a point of reference for black revolutionary politics. (See introduction.)

Lowndes County Freedom Organization (LCFO)
Lowndes County, Ala.

    Formed in 1965 through the initiative of SNCC activists, it was the first party composed solely of blacks. It competed in elections, and also was the first organization attempting to implement Malcolm X's teachings on the need for an autonomous organization of black people.

F. Nonwhite Minorities
Alianza Federal de Pueblos Libres
New Mexico

    Organization of Mexican-Americans.

American Indian Youth Congress

G. Anti-Imperialism
Avoid Vietnam in Latin America (AVILA)
Washington, D.C.

    Anti-imperalist group composed mainly of clergymen or Catholic ex-clergymen involved in supporting revolutions in Latin America.

Fair Play for Cuba Committee
San Francisco, Calif.

    Temporary committee working from 1960 to 1962 to promote a policy of friendship with Castro's Cuba.

May Second Movement (M-2-M)
New York, N.Y.

    An anti-imperialist group in solidarity with revolutions in the Third World, influenced by the Progressive Labor party. It was the first organized group to focus on the imperialist nature of the war in Vietnam, denounce the connections between the university and the military apparatus, and demand immediate withdrawal of troops from Vietnam. It dissolved at the end of 1965.

North American Congress on Latin America (NACLA)
New York, N.Y.

    Informal organization for research and education against the Vietnam war and imperialism, and in favor of the liberation movements in Latin America.

H. New Morality
American League to Abolish Capital Punishment
Massachussetts

    Organization opposing capital punishment.

Association for the Study of Abortion
New York, N.Y.
> In favor of liberalizing abortion laws.

Legalize Abortion
Los Angeles, Calif.
> In favor of liberalizing abortion laws.

*Sexual Freedom League (SFL)
Berkeley, Calif.
> Active in the realms of politics, education and law, it encourages individual sexual expression and promotes the revision of existing laws regarding sexual activity, abortion, censorship, divorce, etc.

Society for Individual Rights
San Francisco, Calif.
> Association for the defense of rights of homosexuals.

*Women's Liberation Movement
New York, N.Y.
> Promotes political and educational activity against the exploitation and inferior status of women in American society, with emphasis on the New Left itself.

I. Professionals,
Center for Emergency Support
Washington, D.C.

Community of Legal Defense Fund
Chicago, Ill.

Conference of Socialist Scholars
> Annual conference of scholars dedicated to problems of socialism.

Demopax
Washington, D.C.
> Group which organizes radicals in the scientific community and distributes educational material concerning the responsibility of technicians and professionals in their professions.

Medical Committee for Human Rights
New York, N.Y.
> Association of doctors promoting the professional practice of medicine in accordance with the principles of human rights.

New University Conference (NUC)
Chicago, Ill.
> Formed in March 1968 as a coordinating body for radically oriented professors and students in the universities.

*Radical Education Project (REP)
Ann Arbor, Mich.
> Program for independent education, research and publication, initiated by SDS and dedicated to the cause of democratic radicalism as well as to the creation of a New Left in America.

Southern Rural Research Project
Selma, Ala.

The Teachers Incorporated
New York, N.Y.

United Farmworkers Association
Delano, Calif.
> Union of migratory agricultural workers and a successful community organizing project focused around the Delano and other grape strikes in California and Texas.

Urban Planning Aid
Cambridge, Mass.

J. Parallel Structures
American Documentary Films
San Francisco, Calif.
   Films for the Movement.

The American Playground
Washington, D.C.
   Movement theater group.

Bread and Puppet Theater
New York, N.Y.
   Movement theater group

Child Development Group of Mississippi (CDGM)
Mississippi
   Independent program in the children/poverty area, promoted by people close to SNCC in 1965.

The Children's Community
Ann Arbor, Mich.

*El Teatro Campesino
California
   Movement theater group organized by and for Spanish-speaking Mexican-Americans.

*Free Universities
   Alternative free universities contrasting with the academic programs and bureaucratic organization of official universities, both public and private. Among the most important free universities are those of Berkeley, Calif., New York, N.Y., and Stanford, Calif.

Gut Theater
New York, N.Y.
   Movement theater group.

Meta Information Applications
New York, N.Y.
   Technology in a radical context.

*Newsreel
New York, N.Y.
   Group of film-makers which was formed in 1968 to produce political, educational, and journalistic documentary material at the service of the Movement.

Pageant Players
New York, N.Y.
   Movement theater group.

Radio Free People
Brooklyn, N.Y.
   Produces and distributes tape-recorded programs, researching carrier current, stimulating independent production, and inaugurating "community listening groups."

*San Francisco Mime Troupe
San Francisco, Calif.
   Movement theater group.

4. Organizations for a New Politics

American Independent Movement
New Haven, Conn.

Committee for Independent Political Action (CIPA)
New York, N.Y.; Chicago, Ill.

Freedom and Peace Party (FPP)
New York, N.Y.
    Formed in 1968, with its base in New York City.

*Mississippi Freedom Democratic Party (MFDP)
Mississippi
    Organized in 1964, mainly through the work of SNCC activists, as an alternative to
the racist-dominated Democratic party of Mississippi. At the 1964 Democratic Convention it was not accredited, and the MFDP challenge of the Democrats elected to Congress
in 1965 also failed to succeed.

*National Conference for New Politics (NCNP)
    A national convention of heterogeneous groups of radicals and liberals, whites and
blacks, which met in Chicago in September 1967. It did not come to any decisions on the
problem of the campaign for a "new politics" in 1968.

National Democratic Party of Alabama
Birmingham, Ala.
    Political organization for poor whites.

New Party
    Formed in 1968, with its base in Michigan. Left-liberal orientation.

*Peace and Freedom Party (PFP)
    Organized in autumn 1967, in California, through the initiative of activists of the
Independent Socialist Club, members of "new politics" groups and other independent
radicals. It was placed on the ballot for the California state and national elections and,
subsequently, for the presidential elections in about ten other states. In coalition with
the Black Panther party, it nominated Eldridge Cleaver as presidential candidate in the
1968 elections.

5. Traditional Left

Communist Party-USA (CP-USA)
    Formed in 1919, it passed through its major crisis during the period 1945–1956, when
it almost totally dissolved. It now numbers about 10,000 members, mainly in New York
and Los Angeles.

Dubois Clubs of America
San Francisco, Calif.
    Marxist youth group formed in 1964.

Independent Socialist Clubs of America (ISCA)
    The ISCA occupies a "third camp" revolutionary socialist position. Formed in 1962,
it has about ten local clubs and several hundred members. Many of its members,
especially in Berkeley, also belong to New Left organizations such as the Peace and
Freedom party.

League for Industrial Democracy (LID)
New York, N.Y.
    Founded in 1905, the LID serves as an educational center for the "Democratic left,"
fulfilling the functions of a sort of Fabian Society. Social-democratic orientation.

Socialist Party (SP)
    Founded in 1901, it is the heir of a long tradition. Its most important leaders have
been Eugene Debs and Norman Thomas; today it is almost totally inactive.

Progressive Labor Party (PLP)
    A Marxist-Leninist organization with a pro-Peking orientation. Founded in 1962,
the PLP has less than 1,000 members. Many of its young members also belong to local
chapters of SDS.

Progressive Youth Organizing Committee (PYOC)
    Youth front-organization, precursor of the DuBois Club.

Socialist Workers Party (SWP)
    Trotskyist-oriented socialist party founded in 1938. Has several hundred members.

Spartacist
Revolutionary Marxist group which developed out of a split among the Trotskyists.

Young People's Socialist League (YPSL)
Youth organization of the Socialist party with a few hundred members.

Young Socialist Alliance (YSA)
Youth organization of the socialist Workers party with a few hundred members. Its members are also active in other committees, anti-imperialist and antiwar movements.

Youth Against War and Fascism (YAWF)
Marxist-oriented group of about 300 members, with its base in New York.

THREE:
Press

Due to its flexible and decentralized character, the New Left has no official press, and therefore most of the periodical publications in this area reflect the opinions, politics, and attitudes of particular Movement groups. We have listed here those publications which are related to the New Left or which often contain information about it, classified for convenience according to the following categories:
1. Nationally circulated publications related to the New Left
2. Publications of the Movement
3. Underground Press
4. Nationally distributed periodicals of interest to the left
5. Political magazines of interest to the left
6. Movement periodicals or bulletins dedicated mainly to one sector of activity:
   A. Civil rights
   B. Peace, pacifism, antiwar, draft resistance, antimilitary
   C. Community organizing
   D. Black Power
   E. Nonwhite minorities
   F. Anti-imperialism
   G. New morality
   H. Professionals
   I. New Politics
7. Periodicals of traditional left organizations

This list includes publications no longer appearing in 1968, but which were operating during the period 1960–1968. We have indicated with an asterisk (*) those publications which in our opinion are particularly important in the Movement today and have had a historic importance in the development of New Left politics.

1. Nationally Circulated Publications Related to the New Left

*Guardian
New York, N.Y.
Weekly, national and international news and forum for political debate. Formerly *The National Guardian*, progressive weekly which began as supporter of third candidate Henry Wallace's campaign in 1948, and subsequently, of traditional-left positions. Its style, political content, and editorial staff were "overhauled" and during 1967–1968 it took on more and more the features of the national weekly closest to the New Left.

*Liberation
New York, N.Y.
Monthly, informational services and political debate. Prevalently pacifist, radical and libertarian in tone. Edited mainly by a group of adult radicals, it carries opinions of New Left spokesmen and provides accounts of Movement activities.

Mayday
Washington, D.C.
    Two-page weekly published beginning in autumn 1968. Brief news items and political comment.

Ramparts
San Francisco, Calif.
    Illustrated bimonthly, informational services, comments and opinions. Progressive Catholic monthly until 1966. Reached a circulation of 250,000 in 1968. Reflects the opinions, political interests, and style of the New Left.

2. Movement Publications

The Activist
Oberlin, Ohio
    Political-student biannual.

Anarchos
New York, N.Y.
    Anarchism, ecology, and libertarian technology.

The Campaigner
New York, N.Y.
    Bimonthly of the SDS Labor Committee of New York and Philadelphia.

Caw
New York, N.Y.
    Bimonthly published by the regional office of the New York SDS, dedicated mainly to radical culture.

Freedom North
New York, N.Y.
    Eight issues per year, published from 1962 to 1965 by the Northern Student Movement.

Movement for a Democratic Society Newsletter
New Orleans, La.
    Southern radical bulletin.

The Movement
San Francisco, Calif.
    Monthly carrying news, opinions, and comments. Formerly affiliated with SDS and SNCC, it calls itself "the voice of the people in the struggle for power."

New Left Notes
Chicago, Ill.
    Official weekly of the national SDS office. News, comments, and opinions mainly of SDS political cadres.

New South Student
Nashville, Tenn.
    Monthly published by the Southern Student Organizing Committee. Analyses of history and radical politics in the South.

Our Generation
Montreal, Canada
    Radical and pacifist publication appearing every four months, widely circulated in North America.

Paper Tiger
Boston, Mass.
    Radical monthly of the adult New Left in New England.

Radical America
Madison, Wis.
    Bimonthly containing mainly historical articles on radicalism in the United States.

3. Underground Press

As the left does not have widely circulated daily or weekly newspapers, the Underground Press or Free Press, which has grown enormously in the years 1967–1968, represents the real channel of information, formation, and mass mobilization for the Movement. It is necessary to divide the Free or Underground Press into different categories, which can give an approximate idea of the prevalent tone of this new type of mass communications medium. The three categories we have adopted here for classification are: (1) mainly political in orientation (P); (2) mainly service for all cultural and political aspects of the Movement (S); (3) exclusively mystical-psychedelic in tone (M). While it is difficult to establish the exact number of underground newspapers in circulation in the United States in 1968 because of the continual publication of new papers and the termination of older ones, we can say that the total number certainly exceeds a hundred and that the number of readers is estimated to be at least 333,000 (*The Wall Street Journal*) and at most 4.6 million (Marshall Bloom of Liberation News Service). Two organizations serve and connect the different papers: the Liberation News Service (LNS—now split into two branches, New York and Massachussetts) which sells articles to subscribers and serves about 400 papers, and the Underground Press Syndicate (UPS), a sort of co-operative which allows about 60 papers to reprint articles with the simple heading "UPS." The following list contains some of the major underground newspapers (in 1968); the definitions and circulation figures are taken from the *Underground Press Guide*.

Avatar
Cambridge, Mass.
(M) Biweekly. "*Avatar* is the symbol of community revival."

Berkeley Barb
Berkeley, Calif.
(S) Weekly, circulation 60,000. "The Berkeley Barb represents news and feature coverage of any movement, tendency or issue in action."

The East Village Other
New York, N.Y.
(M) Weekly, circulation 60,000. "The editors of the paper, who are all artists, poets, and active writers, wanted to expand the role of the artist as creator-communicator in the sphere of journalism."

Los Angeles Free Press
Los Angeles, Calif.
(S) (P) Weekly begun in 1964, circulation 90,000. "Provides information to link together the various sections of our far-flung liberal population."

Midpeninsula Observer
Palo Alto, Calif.
(P) Biweekly, "The kind of news and type of analysis the people cannot get from any Midpeninsula newspaper. We emphasize clarity, conciseness, accuracy and professional standards of journalism for unprofessional purposes." Radical orientation.

Open City
Los Angeles, Calif.
(S) (P) Weekly, circulation 20,000. "We are especially interested in covering those areas of conflict which the sell-out daily press so nervously ignores, those areas where angry and determined minorities continue to challenge the worst contemporary madness and injustice."

The Oracle
San Francisco, Calif.
(M) Irregularly bimonthly, circulation 90,000. It is "a visionary journal that relates social repression and reaction to the ecstatic intelligence of man . . . a rainbow report from the inner eye."

The Rag
Austin, Texas
(P) Radical weekly directed primarily to the academic community. "We believe a radical newspaper must be actively involved against imperialism and the immobility of the establishment."

The Rat
New York, N.Y.
　　(P) Radical and libertarian weekly.

The Realist
New York, N.Y.
　　(M) (P) Published monthly but not on schedule. Iconoclast paper published since the second half of the 1950s, involved in the creation of a libertarian society.

San Francisco Express Times
San Francisco, Calif.
　　(P) Weekly, circulation 15,000. Radical and libertarian oriented, for the creation of a revolutionary movement without authoritarian structures.

The Seed
Chicago, Ill.
　　(P) (S) Every three weeks, circulation 12,000. "The need for an organized opposition to the Establishment is bigger than we are. . . . We say that the *Seed* is the voice of the Chicago undeground."

The Village Voice
New York, N.Y.
　　(S) (P) Weekly widely circulated in New York. It was the first underground paper, appearing in 1957, and has gradually become an expression of the "respectable" underground on liberal-radical positions.

Washington Free Press
Washington, D.C.
　　(P) Weekly, circulation 12,000. "The WP is faced with the nearly impossible task of making the capital of the Free World come true. Its editorial staff is openly New Left; its goals are explicitly revolutionary."

4. Nationally Distributed Periodicals of Interest to the Left

Commonweal
New York, N.Y.
　　Weekly liberal Catholic orientation.

I. F. Stone Weekly
Washington, D.C.
　　Biweekly, formerly weekly. Four small-format pages of acute political analysis and comment edited entirely by the independent radical journalist I. F. Stone.

The Nation
New York, N.Y.
　　Liberal weekly of analysis and comment.

National Catholic Reporter
Kansas City, Kan.
　　Radical activist Catholic weekly, newspaper format, national coverage, analysis.

New Republic
Washington, D.C.
　　Liberal weekly of analysis and comment.

The New York Review of Books
New York, N.Y.
　　Biweekly, long book reviews, opinions and cultural and political essays of liberal and radical orientation.

5. Political Magazines of Interest to the Left

Dissent
New York, N.Y.
　　Bimonthly, edited from 1956 in collaboration with the League for Industrial Democracy. Its tendency is "Democratic left," social-democratic and Fabian.

Monthly Review
New York, N.Y.
    Monthly independent journal dedicated to analysis of domestic and international politics from a socialist and Marxist point of view.

New Politics
New York, N.Y.
    Quarterly of analysis and comment. Forum of debate for different positions in the socialist spectrum.

News and Letters
Detroit, Mich.
    Marxist-humanist periodical.

New University Thought
Detroit, Mich.
    Periodical begun in 1959. Comments and opinions prevalently of left-wing liberal orientation.

Partisan Review
New York, N.Y.
    Political and literary quarterly, forum of debate for various left-wing positions.

Studies on the Left
New York, N.Y.
    Published every four months (1959–1965), bimonthly (1965–1967). It was the theoretical journal of debate and information closest to the New Left.

6. Movement Periodicals or Bulletins Dedicated Mainly to One Sector of Activity

A. Civil Rights
Southern Courier
Montgomery, Ala.
    Ceased publication in 1968.

The Southern Patriot
Louisville, Ky.
    Monthly published by the Southern Conference Educational Fund.

The New South Student
Nashville, Tenn.
    Monthly published by the Southern Student Organizing Committee (SSOC).

B. Peace, Pacifism, Antiwar, Antidraft, Antimilitarism
The Ally
Berkeley, Calif.
    Free publication for the armed forces.

The Bay Guardian
San Francisco, Calif.
    Pacifist-inspired monthly.

The Bond
Berkeley, Calif.
    Antiwar paper dedicated to servicemen.

The Catholic Worker
New York, N.Y.
    Christian pacifist periodical of varied information and comment, with wide coverage of war-resistance activity.

Peacemaker
Yellow Springs, Ohio
    Published every three weeks; libertarian and pacifist, with emphasis on noncooperation with war and war taxes.

Resist
Palo Alto, Calif.
    Periodical dedicated to draft resistance.

The Resistance
Boston, Mass.
    Periodical dedicated to draft resistance.

Sanity
Canada
    Antimilitary, pacifist monthly.

Student Mobilizer
New York, N.Y.
    Publication of the Student Mobilization Committee to End the War in Vietnam.

Task Force
San Francisco, Calif.
    Antimilitary periodical dedicated to servicemen.

Vietnam G.I.
    Antimilitary periodical distributed free to servicemen.

Win
New York, N.Y.
    Biweekly with news of pacifist and peace activity, published by the War Resisters' League and the New York Workshop on Nonviolent Action.

C. Community Organization
Common Sense
Cleveland, Ohio

El Malcriado
Delano, Calif.

Firing Lines
Chicago, Ill.

M-Cup News
Minneapolis, Minn.

West Side Torch
Chicago, Ill.

D. Black Power
The Black Panther
Oakland, Calif.

The Inner City Voice
Detroit, Mich.

E. Nonwhite Minorities
El Malcriado
McAllen, Texas
    Publication of the Chicago Press Association for the Mexican-American minority.

El Grido
Berkeley, Calif.
    Published every four months, journal of contemporary Mexican-American thought.

El Papel
Albuquerque, N.M.
    Publication of the Chicago Press Association for the Mexican-American minority.

La Raza
Los Angeles, Calif.
    Publication of the Chicago Press Association for the Mexican-American minority.

F. Anti-Imperialism
AVILA Newsletter
New York, N.Y.
   Anti-imperialist bulletin concentrating on problems of Latin America.

NACLA Newsletter
New York, N.Y.
   Informational bulletin of the North American Council for Latin America.

*Viet Report
New York, N.Y.
   Anti-imperialist monthly of analysis, information, and comment, published during the period 1965–1968.

G. New Morality
Women
Chicago, Ill.
   Bulletin of the Women Liberation Movement of Chicago.

H. Professionals
NUC Newsletter
Chicago, Ill.
   Bulletin of the New University Conference, an organization of radical students and professors.

Radicals in the Professions Newsletter
Ann Arbor, Mich.
   Bulletin published by the Radical Education Project.

I. New Politics
19
New York, N.Y.
   Biweekly published during the 1966 electoral campaign of James Weinstein with the CIPA in New York City.

Peace and Freedom News
Berkeley, Calif.
   Bulletin of the California Peace and Freedom party, during 1968.

7. Periodicals of Traditional Left Organizations

Challenge
New York, N.Y.
   Monthly of the Maoist Progressive Labor party, published in English and Spanish.

Daily World
New York, N.Y.
   Official daily of the Communist Party-USA, formerly published as a weekly under the title *The Worker*.

Independent Socialist
Berkeley, Calif.
   Periodical of the Independent Socialist Club, of interest for the New Left.

International Socialist Review
New York, N.Y.
   Bimonthly of Trotskyist orientation.

The Militant
New York, N.Y.
   Weekly, official organ of the Trotskyist-oriented Socialist Workers party.

New America
New York, N.Y.
   Monthly of the Socialist party, of social-democratic tone.

The Partisan
New York, N.Y.
> Periodical of Youth Against War and Fascism.

People's World
San Francisco, Calif.
> Weekly inspired by the West Coast Communist party.

Progressive Labor
New York, N.Y.
> Review published by the Maoist Progressive Labor party.

World Revolution
New York, N.Y.
> Review published every four months by the Maoist Progressive Labor party, dedicated to Marxist-Leninist struggle throughout the world.

Young Socialist
New York, N.Y.
> Monthly of the Trotskyist-oriented Young Socialist Alliance.

Selected Bibliography

Besides the readings that follow each section of the documents, bibliographical material of general interest is listed here in two groups: A. *Inspirers* and B. *On the New Left.*

A. Inspirers

Baron, P. A., and P. M. Sweezy. *Monopoly Capital.* New York: Monthly Review Press, 1966.

Camus, Albert. "Neither Victims nor Executioners." Originally published in *Combat,* 1946 and reprinted by *Liberation,* March 1960.

Chomsky, Noam. "The Responsibility of Intellectuals." *New York Review,* 1967.

Fromm, Eric. *Socialist Humanism.* Garden City, N.Y.: Doubleday, 1966.

Ginsberg, Allen. "Howl." San Francisco: City Lights, 1955.

Goodman, Paul. *Growing Up Absurd.* New York: Vintage, 1960.

————. *People or Personnel* and *Like A Conquered Province.* New York: Vintage, 1968.

————. The Black Flag of Anarchism. *The New York Times Magazine,* July 19, 1968.

Gorz, André. *Strategy for Labor.* Boston: Beacon Press, 1967.

Lynd, Staughton (ed.). *Non-Violence in America.* Indianapolis: Bobbs-Merrill, 1967.

Mailer, Norman. Hipsters and Beats (p. 343) and The White Negro (2. 311). In Mailer, Norman, *Advertisements for Myself.* Berkeley Medallion Book, New York: G. P. Putnam's, 1959.

Marcuse, Herbert. *Reason and Revolution.* Boston: Beacon Press, 1960.

————. *Eros and Civilization.* New York: Random House, 1961.

————. *One-Dimensional Man.* Boston: Beacon Press, 1964.

————. "Repressive Tolerance." In *A Critique of Pure Tolerance,* Boston: Beacon Press, 1965.

————. "Marcuse Defines His New Left Line." *The New York Times Magazine,* October 27, 1968.

Mills, C. Wright. *White Collar: The American Middle Classes.* New York: Oxford University Press, 1951.

————. *The Power Elite.* New York: Oxford University Press, 1965.

————. *The Causes of World War Three.* New York: Simon and Schuster, 1958.

————. *Listen, Yankee: The Revolution in Cuba.* New York: McCraw-Hill Book Company, 1960.

————. "On the New Left." *Studies on the Left,* 1961.

————. *Power, Politics and People.* New York: Ballantine, 1965.

B. On The New Left

Altbach, Philip, D. Hale and S. Kelman. "The New Left." *New Politics,* Spring 1965.

Aronson, Ronald, and John C. Cowley. "The New Left in the United States." In *the Socialist Register,* edited by Ralph Milliband and John Saville. London: The Merlin Press, 1967.

Baxandall, Lee. "Issues and Constituency of the New Left." *Liberation,* April 1966.
Birnbaum, Norman. "Staggering Colossus." *The Nation,* September 2, 1968.
Bottomore, T. B. "Blacks and Students: Critics of Society." *The Nation,* November 25, 1968.
Davidson, Carl. "On SDS." *Guardian,* November 16, 1968.
Draper, Hall. "In Defense of 'New Radicals.' " *New Politics,* Summer 1965.
Flacks, Richard E. "The Liberated Generation: An Exploration of the Roots of Student Protest." *Journal of Social Issues,* XXIII (1967).
Gans, Herbert. "A Rational Approach to Radicalism." *Studies on the Left,* VI: 1 (January/February 1966).
Genovese, G. "The American Left—Old and New." *National Guardian,* February 19, 1966.
Horowitz, Irving Louis. "Radicalism and Contemporary American Society." *Liberation,* May 1965.
Howe, Irving. "New Styles in 'Leftism.' " *Dissent,* Summer 1965.
Jacobs, James. "SDS: Between Reform and Revolution." *The Nation,* June 10, 1968.
Jacobs, Paul, and Saul Landau. *The New Radicals: A Report with Documents.* New York: Vintage Books, 1966.
Kahn, Tom. "The Problem of the New Left." *Commentary,* July 1966.
Kelman, Steve. "The Feud Among the Radicals." *Harper's,* June 1966.
Kenistan, Kenneth, *Young Radicals: Notes on Committed Youth.* New York: Harcourt, Brace and World, 1968.
Kolakowski, Leszek. What Is the Left Today? Replies. *Evergreen,* June 1967.
Kolko, Gabriel. *The Decline of American Radicalism in the Twentieth Century.* Ann Arbor, Michigan: Radical Education Project, 1967.
Kopkind, Andrew. "Are We in the Middle of a Revolution?" *The New York Times Magazine,* November 10, 1968.
Lasch, Christopher. *The New Radicalism in America 1889–1963. The Intellectual as a Social Type.* New York: Vintage Books, 1967.
Munk, Michael. "The New Left." *The National Guardian,* pamphlet, 1965.
The New Student Left. An Anthology, edited by Mitchell Cohen and Dennis Hale. Boston: Beacon Press, 1967.
Newfield, Jack. *A Prophetic Minority.* New York: Signet Books, 1966.
_____. "The Student Left: Idealism and Action." *The Nation,* November 8, 1965.
_____. "The Student Left: Revolt Without Dogma." *The Nation,* May 10, 1965.
"New Radicalism." *Partisan Review,* Spring, Summer, and Fall 1965, and Winter 1966.
O'Brien, James. "The New Left 1960–65" and "The New Left 1965–67" and "The New Left 1967–68." *Radical America,* May/June 1968 and September/October 1968 and November/December 1968.
Oglesby, Carl. Speech at the National Guardian Annual Dinner, November 1965. *The National Guardian,* November 1962.
Petras, Jim. "The New Left in the United States." *International Socialist Journal,* September/October 1965.
Radosh, Ronald. "American Left, Liberal or Radical?" *Monthly Review,* Summer 1963.
Rossman, Michael. "A New Left Memoir." *Commentary,* July 1967.
Roussopoulos, Dimitros. "What Is the New Radicalism?" *Our Generation,* Vol. 6: Nos. 1 and 2 (Summer 1968).
Thoughts of the Young Radicals and Four Critical Comments on their Views on America. Harrison-Blaine of New Jersey, Inc., and The New Republic, 1966.
Waskow, I. Arthur. "The New Student." *Our Generation.* Reprint.
Weinstein and Sklar. "Socialism and the New Left." *Studies on the Left,* VI: 2 (March/April 1966).
Zinn, Howard. "The Old Left and the New: Emancipation from Dogma." *The Nation,* April 4, 1966.